strategic
internet
marketing

strategic
internet
marketing

SUSAN DANN

B.A., M.Pub.Admin., Ph.D., F.A.M.I., C.P.M.
QUEENSLAND UNIVERSITY OF TECHNOLOGY

STEPHEN DANN

B.A., B.Com.(Hons), Ph.D., A.A.M.I.
GRIFFITH UNIVERSITY

John Wiley & Sons Australia, Ltd

First published 2001 by
John Wiley & Sons Australia, Ltd
33 Park Road, Milton, Qld 4064

Offices also in Sydney and Melbourne

Typeset in 10.5/12 pt New Baskerville

National Library of Australia
Cataloguing-in-Publication data

Dann, Stephen, 1973–.
Strategic internet marketing.

   Bibliography.
   Includes index.
   ISBN 0 471 34300 5.

   1. Internet marketing. I. Dann, Susan J. II. Title

658.8/4

Cover photograph and internal design:
© 2000 Digital Vision and © 2000 Photodisc, Inc.

Illustrated by the John Wiley art department

Printed in Singapore by
Kyodo Printing Co Pte Ltd

10 9 8 7 6 5 4 3 2 1

To our family, our friends and everyone
who helped make this book a reality.
SJD & SMD

To 404: Not Found — the hardest working page on the Internet
S. Dann & S. Dann

Contents

PREFACE XIV

ACKNOWLEDGEMENTS XVIII

HOW TO USE THIS BOOK XX

Part 1
DEFINITION AND DOMAIN 1

CHAPTER 1
The technological revolution 2

Introduction 3
What is the Internet? 3
    A brief history of the Internet 4
    The pieces of the puzzle 5
The new landscape for marketing 9
A detailed overview of this
    textbook 10
    Part 1: Definition and domain 10
    *Part 2: New marketing strategies for
      the new media* 10
    *Part 3: Marketing fundamentals in
      the interactive age* 11
    *Part 4: Strategic marketing
      applications for the Internet* 12
    Part 5: The future 13
Summary 13
DISCUSSION QUESTIONS 13
REFERENCES 14
WEB SITES 14
FTP SITE 14

CHAPTER 2
Concepts and terminology 15

Introduction 16
Definition and domain of the
    book 16
    *Defining elements: What makes the
      Internet click?* 17

Defining the parameters 1:
    Operationalising the Internet 18
    Conceptualising cyberspace 19
    Mapping cyberspace 20
    *The value of conceptual geography
      in cyberspace* 25
Defining the parameters 2: Marketing
    theory, marketing philosophy and
    the choice of the marketing
    mix 26
    In defence of the marketing mix 26
    Three levels of marketing 27
    *Alternative readings of marketing
      and the Internet* 29
Defining the parameters 3: Focusing
    on consumer behaviour ahead of
    business to business
    marketing 32
Defining the parameters 4:
    Internationalisation, global
    marketing and international
    marketing online 33
Defining the parameters 5:
    Post-modern consumption 34
Cultural considerations 36
    The Internet culture 36
Summary 38
DISCUSSION QUESTIONS 38
REFERENCES 39
WEB SITES 39

Part 2
NEW MARKETING STRATEGIES FOR THE NEW MEDIA 41

CHAPTER 3
Unique features of Internet-based marketing 42

Introduction 43

The (r)evolution of online
marketing   43
   Evolution of online marketing   44
Unique features of the Internet
compared to other media   49
   Interactivity   49
   Variety and customisation   52
   Global access   54
   Time independence   54
   Interest driven   55
Why adapt to the online world?   56
   Going online: Factors to
     consider   56
   Going online: Reasons why other
     businesses are there already   57
   Drivers and attractors: Get me to the
     Web on time   57
   Inhibitors: Reasons not to be
     digital   60
The adaptation of the offline to the
online   61
   Retailing   61
   Information search   63
   Entertainment online   63
   Utility functions   64
The consumer (r)evolution   64
   Advantages of Internet-based
     marketing for the consumer   65
   Changing consumer
     expectations   65
Summary   66
DISCUSSION QUESTIONS   *67*
REFERENCES   *68*
WEB SITES   *68*
NEWSGROUPS   *69*

CHAPTER 4

Consumer behaviour   70

Introduction   71
Innovation adoption and the
Internet   71
   Innovation adoption and the really
     new product   71
   Innovation adoption: Curves,
     contagions and cultural
     differences   73
   Diffusion of innovations: The need,
     want, use and show-off approach
     to adoption   77
   Diffusion of innovations: Rogers'
     five features of innovations   78

   Diffusion of innovations:
     Personality, predisposition and
     psychographics   80
Adoption profile of Internet
users   81
   Innovation adoption overview   81
   Implications of the current Internet
     adopters   85
Internet user categories   87
Internet use behaviours   89
   Why people use the Internet   90
   Internet specific behaviours: Don't
     try this offline   92
Restrictions and constrictions:
Factors preventing full use of the
Internet   96
   1. Cost: Time and money   96
   2. Internet literacy   97
   3. Fear   97
   4. Lack of desire: No benefit, no
     consequence, and no value   98
   5. Expectation gap: Promised the
     Earth, delivered a bucket of
     soil   99
Implications for marketing   99
   Lower the barriers   99
   Lower the expectations: Promise the
     achievable, and deliver more than
     promised   100
   Securing the Internet   100
   Accept rejection as a legitimate
     choice   101
Summary   101
DISCUSSION QUESTIONS   *102*
REFERENCES   *103*
WEB SITES   *103*

CHAPTER 5

Creating cyber-communities   104

Introduction   105
Cybercommunity foundation:
Dichotomous structures   105
Cybercommunity foundation:
Theoretical foundations and
communications models   106
   Communications models   106
   Definitions of community   112
   Construction of identity in the
     cybercommunity   116

Value of cybercommunity to
  business   118
  Cybercommunities as reflections of
    reality: The social Petri
    dish   122
Community creation: Roll your own
  society   122
  Setting up a community   124
  What helps a community
    succeed?   126
  Cyberspace as a place: Destination
    marketing for
    cybercommunities   127
Summary   129
DISCUSSION QUESTIONS   130
REFERENCES   131
WEB SITES   131
NEWSGROUPS   131

CHAPTER 6

*Applications for business and
non-business*   132
Introduction   133
Applications of the Internet: Macro-
  level strategic decisions   133
  Guiding the online development:
    Strategic questions for strategic
    direction   134
Applications and implemented
  solutions: Using the Web for
  success   137
  Wholesale/retail: Selling
    online   138
  Retailing online: Issues, advantages
    and limitations   138
  Retailing online: Conceptual model
    of the process of going
    online   141
  Export industries: Selling beyond the
    borderless   143
  Recreational services   147
Summary   154
DISCUSSION QUESTIONS   155
REFERENCES   156
WEB SITES   156

CHAPTER 7

*Internet in marketing
strategy*   157
Introduction   158

Objectives — what are we trying to
  achieve by going online?   159
  Setting specific online marketing
    objectives   162
  Internet marketing and strategic
    growth options   164
  Porter's generic competitive
    strategies   165
  Strategic growth options   168
Segmentation and positioning   171
  Segmentation   171
  Positioning   173
Integration   175
Implementation   177
  Blueprinting   177
  Budgeting   178
  Ten strategic keys to unlocking the
    potential of the Internet   178
Summary   181
DISCUSSION QUESTIONS   182
REFERENCES   183
WEB SITES   183
NEWSGROUP   184

Part 3

MARKETING FUNDAMENTALS IN
THE INTERACTIVE AGE   185

CHAPTER 8

*The role of product in Internet
marketing*   186
Introduction   187
What is the product?   188
  Multilevel product concept   189
  The online product   190
Successful Internet products   193
  Physical products: Traditional
    delivery in the new world   194
  Services and digitised
    products   197
  Internet-specific product
    opportunities   202
New product development   203
  New product strategy   205
  Exploration   206
  Screening   209
  Business analysis   210
  Development   211
  Test marketing   211
  Commercialisation   212

Online new product
development 212
Summary 214
DISCUSSION QUESTIONS 215
REFERENCES 215
WEB SITES 217

CHAPTER 9

**Promotion 1: Internet in
promotional mix** 218
Introduction 219
Promotion and the Internet:
Something new, something
borrowed and something
not-so-new 219
Attracting users to the online world:
Promoting the web site 219
Philosophy of promotion 221
Foundations of promotion 223
Six tenets of promotion 223
Integrated marketing
communications: This goes with
this and this goes with that 225
Communicating the URL: Home
(page) on the range 226
Elements of the promotional
mix 228
Three dimensions of promotion:
Message, format and
context 230
Reviving the dead pointer: Mixing it
up in the promotion of the
URL 232
Creating awareness: Image is
nothing, context is
everything 232
Promotional mix online 101: Using
the promotional tool kit
online 241
Banner advertising: Click here to
receive more promotional
materials 241
Promotional mix online 102: The
distinct differences 243
Summary 244
DISCUSSION QUESTIONS 245
REFERENCES 245
WEB SITES 246

CHAPTER 10

**Promotion 2: The Internet as a
promotional medium** 247
Introduction 248
Value and role of internet in
promotion: Marketing on the
Web 249
The Internet: A recap of the good, the
bad and the interactive 250
Metatheory of web site design 251
Post-modern consumption and the
Internet 252
Metatheory 101: Styles of web site
structures 253
Metatheory 102: Strategic frameworks
for web site design 255
Design philosophy: The art of the
Web 259
The three design schools 260
Strategic integration: Putting the site
together 264
Attractors on the Web: Types of web
sites 264
Categories of design: Types of home
pages 267
The 6M of web site design 268
Summary 269
DISCUSSION QUESTIONS 270
REFERENCES 270
WEB SITES 271

CHAPTER 11

Pricing strategies 272
Introduction 273
Total price concept 273
Total price concept: A consumer
perspective 274
Total price concept in electronic
markets 276
Pressures on Internet pricing 278
Lower costs to the seller 278
Environmental turbulence 279
Taxation issues 280
Investment philosophy 281
Cyberculture 281
Universal pricing knowledge 283
Setting pricing objectives 284
Financial objectives 284
Market-based objectives 285
Psychological objectives 288

Pricing strategies   289
Issues in pricing for online
    activities   290
    Nature of the product   291
    Total cost to the consumer   293
    *International currency transactions
        and the impact of different
        payment systems   293*
Summary   295
DISCUSSION QUESTIONS   *296*
REFERENCES   *297*
WEB SITES   *298*

CHAPTER   12

Distribution   299

Introduction   300
The Internet and distribution: You
    can get there from here   300
    *Determining the right
        distribution   301*
    *Saying it in delivery: IMC and
        distribution mechanisms   302*
The worldwide place: Distribution
    over the wire   303
    *Marketspace: The place of electronic
        distribution   306*
    *Value in the marketspace: Virtual
        channels and chains   307*
The big issues in Internet
    distribution   309
    Channel conflicts   309
    *Non-store distribution
        mechanism   310*
Making it so: Technical implications
    of Internet distributions   311
    *Technical considerations 101:
        Keeping it real   312*
    *Technical considerations 102:
        People make the process   314*
Putting the pieces together:
    Distributing the mix   315
    Distribution and product   315
    Distribution and price   316
    Distribution and promotion   316
Summary   318
DISCUSSION QUESTIONS   *319*
REFERENCES   *319*
WEB SITES   *320*
NEWSGROUP   *320*

Part 4

STRATEGIC MARKETING APPLICATIONS FOR THE INTERNET   *321*

CHAPTER   13

Services marketing online   *322*

Introduction 323
The service product   323
    *Traditional points of
        differentiation   325*
    *Impact of online delivery for
        traditional service concepts   330*
Defining the service product   334
    *Classifications of service
        products   334*
    Customer support   336
Consumer behaviour and the online
    service product   338
    *Search behaviours and service
        type   338*
    Risk reduction strategies   340
Training the customer to be a
    co-producer   340
Technology as the means not the
    end   341
Summary   343
DISCUSSION QUESTIONS   *343*
REFERENCES   *344*
WEB SITES   *345*

CHAPTER   14

Relationship marketing in a 'one-to-many-to-one' environment   346

Introduction   347
Domain of relationship
    marketing   347
    *Core concepts of relationship
        marketing   348*
    *Suitability for relationship
        marketing   349*
    *Philosophical principles of
        relationship marketing   350*
Relationship marketing online   354
    *Three levels of relationship
        marketing   354*

Value of relationship building in new
media   355
   Creating relationships online   356
   Limitations, distractions and
     problems: Barrier to online
     relationship marketing   359
   Value of cybercommunities for
     building relationships   361
Role of trust in e-commerce   363
   Operational conditions: Where does
     trust need to occur?   363
   Barriers to trust   363
   Improving trust online   364
Business to business   365
   Business to business marketing
     online   365
   New roles and new opportunities:
     Market makers   366
Summary   366
DISCUSSION QUESTIONS   367
REFERENCES   367
WEB SITES   368

CHAPTER 15

International marketing   369
Introduction   370
Is all Internet marketing,
   international marketing?   371
   Globalisation vs localisation   372
   Entry mode — is it still an
     issue?   378
Export industries   379
   Types of exporting   379
   Impact of the Internet on barriers to
     export   380
   Conceptual framework for exporting
     and the Internet   382
   Differences between traditional and
     online exporters   384
SMEs, internationalisation and the
   Internet   384
Analysing potential markets   387
Implementing the international web
   presence   389
   Overcome personal
     boundaries   389
   Convert atoms into bytes   389
   Do not compete, be unique   389
   Be a specialist not a generalist   390
   Serve a specialised market   390

   Operate in advanced digital
     markets   390
   Develop indigenous digital
     partnerships   390
   Use technology to foster global
     relationships   391
Summary   392
DISCUSSION QUESTIONS   393
REFERENCES   393
WEB SITES   394

CHAPTER 16

Marketing research   395
Introduction   396
Foundations of market research: How
   and why of finding out who and
   what   396
   The online advantage   396
   The other side of the coin:
     Disadvantages of the
     Internet   397
   Review of the market research
     process   397
Types of market research   401
   Objective of collection   401
   Method of collection   403
New paradigm or new routines?
   Internet-based market
   research   405
   Changing environments   405
   Information storehouse   407
Scanning the environments in
   Internet market research   408
Market intelligence through Internet-
   based market research   408
   Consumer intelligence   409
   Competitive intelligence   410
Conducting online market research:
   New paradigm or new
   routines?   410
   Online focus groups   411
   Online surveys   412
   Ethnography   413
   New routines   413
Issues concerning online
   research   417
   Anonymity   417
   Privacy   417
Limitations of online research   418
   Information overload   418

Information quality   419
Speed   419
Security   419
Skewed demography   419
Ease of access   419
Putting the pieces together: Online
    market segmentation   419
        iVALS, and Internet user
            types   420
        Segmentation method   420
Summary   425
DISCUSSION QUESTIONS   425
REFERENCES   426
WEB SITES   426
NEWSGROUP   426

Part 5

THE FUTURE   427

CHAPTER   17

Future directions   428
Introduction   429
What will the Internet be?   429
The role of marketing in the
    future   430
        Scenario one: Getting it right   431

Scenario two: Getting it
    wrong   433
Scenario three: Just not getting
    it   434
Ethical considerations of strategic
    Internet marketing   434
        Online privacy   435
        Internet security   435
        Marketing by intrusion and
            observation   436
        Putting up with the
            neighbours   438
Future proofing a strategic internet
    marketing text   443
        Surviving the future   443
        Predicting (and adjusting to) the
            future   443
Summary   446
DISCUSSION QUESTIONS   447
REFERENCES   447
WEB SITES   448

ACADEMIC REFERENCES   449

APPENDIX: USEFUL WEB SITES   463

GLOSSARY   481

INDEX   491

Preface

Reason for writing the text

There are a range of reasons to write a textbook, and some of those reasons are altruistic, pragmatic or ambitious. For the most part, the authors found that the majority of textbooks in the area of Internet marketing had a consistent set of 'features' that they felt were limiting the development of Internet marketing, such as:

- most texts in the field were too busy emphasising what is different about the Internet, and not what can be adapted from past and present marketing knowledge
- too much focus on the 'how to' aspects of building web sites and not the 'why have one'
- lack of books which integrate the lessons of alternative and traditional aspects of marketing
- lack of strategic thinking in e-commerce and Internet marketing as a whole.

As a result of these general feelings, the authors set out to design a book that integrated all relevant aspects of marketing with Internet and e-commerce practice rather than treating each as a separate item to be catalogued, shelved and kept away from each other. Marketing is a holistic, whole of organisation approach, and this textbook attempts to encompass a holistic view of marketing in the age of electronic commerce.

Why us?

Strangely enough the authors assume if you happen to be reading the preface then chances are you own the book. If not, then the short sales pitch for why this strategic internet marketing text should be your book of choice is twofold.

First, we acknowledge that the Internet is not for everyone, nor is it universally applicable and certainly it can never be the panacea for everything. A sense of perspective and limitation on the Internet brings the book into focus on the areas where the Internet can be used, should be used and is quite useful. Many of the contemporary writers in the field of the Internet, and e-commerce, have taken an evangelical approach to spreading 'the good word of the Internet'. This of course means that the message should be taken with the appropriate grains of salt (we prefer to think of this book as having been pre-salted).

Second, this particular text has a blend of practical experience, theoretical models, contemporary culture and marketing philosophy that sets it apart from the majority of the texts in the field. Having made reference to nearly 200 refereed journal articles, textbooks and research papers, along with

400 different web sites, has given the book a solid grounding in the theory, practice and reality of the Internet. As authors, we have been prepared to acknowledge when and where the application of a theory or technology is uncertain, and where changes can (or should) occur. The text has been designed around integrating the wider domain of marketing theory into applications suited for use on the Internet, or to explain the Internet. The technology of the global network of networks may be new, but the people on the keyboards are the same people with the television remote controls or supermarket trolleys that we've come to love and research in marketing.

Thanks/acknowledgements

Susan would like to thank everyone who has offered support, assistance and advice over her career that led to this point. Particular thanks are due to those people who have given me a chance by employing me over the years and shaping my attitude and approach to the whole publication process through incidental comments that they probably don't even remember. In particular two stand out — Professor Geoff Kiel (University of Queensland) who said, 'if you don't write it, it can't be published' and Professor Paul Wilson (Bond University) whose comment, 'there's no point in doing research if you're not going tell people about it', made a big difference. Special thanks are also due to Associate Professor Janet McColl-Kennedy who assisted me enormously during the early phases of my academic career by giving me the experience and opportunities to publish well beyond anything that I could have reasonably expected at the time.

One of the dangers of working in the university sector is that over time it is easy to become inwardly focused and lose touch with the 'real world' — even if your university prides itself on being part of it. During the course of writing this book there have been a number of people and organisations that have made sure that this doesn't happen. The informal input of members of the Australian Marketing Institute, the Queensland State Council and National Board has been invaluable in ensuring that the book remains focused and useful to industry. In addition, AFLQ unconsciously put themselves forward as a live case study of innovation adoption, the AFL gave a sense of perspective for how the other side of the industry works, and why academia isn't as bad as it looks on the inside. Two major players who have to be thanked for their influence, advice and example along the way are Ken Livingstone (Mayor of London and former title holder of 'Most Odious Man in Britain' award) and Ross Palmer (CEO Palmer Group) — two men from opposite ends of the political spectrum keeping things in perspective. It's hard to get frustrated about a paragraph in a book in comparison to the daily grind of running London or managing a chain of highly successful international organisations.

Susan would also like to thank her students over time for asking the sort of questions that made her think of the answers which contributed significantly to the final book. It helped when it came to explaining the concepts that, to the authors were self explanatory, largely because we'd explained the idea in detail to ourselves. A special thank you goes to the Griffith University Contemporary Issues in Marketing Class of 1994 who thought, 'this new fangled email thing would never work and would never catch on'. If only they were correct, we could all get out of the house more. Thanks also go to several of the survivors of that class who later admitted that the Internet made no sense to them in 1994, but had the decency to send their apologies by email.

Stephen would like to thank a wide range of people, influences and supporters. However, he's already spent his excess baggage word limit somewhere in chapter 4, and will restrict himself to a few dedications here. Thanks go to the extended digital families that are the #atxf and #atbuffy chat groups, with special mention to everyone who told him to go away and finish writing that book. Special and direct thanks go to Annette Fraser (advice and web site suggestions), Melanie King (web site suggestions, and chatboard advice), Robert Whyte (knowing the answers, or knowing a guy who knew the answer), the people who Rob knew who answered the really tough questions, Robin Harrison (for actually working in the IT sector and answering questions about his day job) and to Joanne Jacobs who knew the right answers, but also knew the right questions to ask as well. Joanne also was frequently on the receiving end of the prototypical ideas, which seemed to always start with, 'Does this make sense to you?'. Thanks go to her for her editing input, knowledge of things technical and trivial, and her support during the process.

Without the support and collective hive mind of the cast and crew of the ATXF and ATBuffy cybercommunities, much of my practical experience in this book would have never have happened (I can't tell if this is a good or a bad thing). To everyone I know who had a major impact in shaping this book, thanks for setting up the opportunities, obstacles, clear paths and blocked passages that led me to being where I was at the time Darren said, 'Would you like to write a book for Wiley?'. The chaos maths behind it couldn't have happened without your random input. Finally, a big vote of thanks to my colleagues at Griffith University for their support, advice, and unfailing ability to keep me in my day job. Even if they didn't see me for most of the year when I was writing the book, the pay cheques kept coming and nobody asked me for my ID when I went to use the printer.

Susan and Stephen would like to thank Darren Taylor for getting us into this and getting us out of it in record time with the lowest possible body count. Special thanks also go to Pam Hollander, John Millman and the cast and crew at Wiley Publishers in Milton. An extra set of appreciative thanks go to Caroline Hunter who was on the first receiving end of the manuscript, and had the task of seeing if we were making sense. Thanks go to the reviewer team of Denise Jarratt, Colin Jevons, Elaine Leong, Sharon Purchase and Jamie Murphy.

Both authors would like to acknowledge the invaluable role played by Jean Shepley, as our research assistant and production manager. As a research assistant she found materials that made a significant difference to the quality of the final outcome, and as a production manager, she made us make it to that final outcome.

Finally, a collective set of thanks go from the writing team to the support team of Jean and Michael Dann — our parents, editors, and the people who never considered that having two S. Danns in the family would cause this much confusion.

A special thank you in advance to DETYA for recognising that dual authored books by Dann S. and Dann S. are in fact dual authored. We cannot tell who wrote what, and to the best of our knowledge (and we were there at the time), no author contributed more than 50 per cent to the total of the book.

Finally, thanks go out to the people who assisted in the process, from the editors to the layout artists at Wiley, and to the buyers who are currently holding this text in their hands and wondering if this sentence is referring to them.

Acknowledgements

The authors and publisher wish to thank the following copyright holders, organisations and individuals for their assistance and permission to reproduce images and text in this book:

Figures

Figures 5.1, 5.2, 5.3, 5.4, 5.5: reprinted with permission from the *Journal of Marketing*, published by the American Marketing Association, D. Hoffman & T. Novak, vol. 60, no. 3, July 1996. Figure 6.4: courtesy of Artisan Entertainment. Figures 2.4, 2.5: screenshots reproduced courtesy of AT&T. Figure 2.1: diagram from 'Information Management: A Proposal', by Tim Berners-Lee, www.w3.org/History/1989/proposal.html; reproduced by permission. Figures 9.5, 9.6, 9.7, 9.8, 9.9, 9.10: © S. Dann. Figure 3.1: reprinted from *Decision Support Systems* by O'Connor & O'Keefe, © 1997, vol. 21, no. 3, with permission from Elsevier Science. Figure 14.1: © 1999 Epinions, Inc. Figure 4.5: © ICQ. Figure 16.6: screenshot reproduced with permission of Inventix Software. Figure 13.1: reproduced with permission of the Association of Marketing Theory and Practice; reproduction without permission prohibited. Figure 6.5: screenshot © Musée du Louvre. Figures 4.1, 4.2: reproduced from M. Parthasarathy, S. Jun & R. Mittelstaedt, 'Multiple diffusion and multi-cultural aggregate social systems', in *International Marketing Review*, vol. 14, no. 4, 1997; figure 6.1, from R. O'Keefe, G. O'Connor & H. J. King, 'Early adopters of the Web as a retail medium: small company winners and losers', in *European Journal of Marketing*, vol. 32, no. 7/8, 1998; figures 6.2, 15.3, from S. Saimee, 'Exporting and the Internet: A conceptual perspective', in *International Marketing Review*, vol. 15, no. 5, 1998; figure 7.3, from R. Simeon, 'Evaluating domestic and international web-site strategies', in *Internet Research: Electronic Networking Applications and Policy*, vol. 9, no. 4, 1999; figure 10.1, from H. A. Wan & C. Chung, 'Web page design and network analysis', in *Internet Research: Electronic Networking Applications and Policy*, vol. 8, no. 2, 1998; figure 10.3: diagram from M. Lu & W. Yeung, 'A framework for effective commercial Web application development', in *Internet Research: Electronic Networking Application and Policy*, vol. 8, no. 2 1998; figure 12.3, from R. Weiber & T. Kollman, 'Competitive advantages in virtual markets: Perspectives of information-based marketing in Cyberspace', in *European Journal of Marketing*, vol. 32, no. 7/8; figures 16.7, 16.8, 16.9, 16.10, from F. Sarabia, 'Model for markets segments, evaluation and selection', in European Journal of Marketing, vol. 30, no. 4, 1996; © MCB University Press. Figures 16.4, 16.5: samples © 2001, Media House Software, Inc. All rights reserved; reprinted with permission. Figure 15.1: screenshot courtesy of Mick's Whips. Figure 4.4: screenshots reproduced courtesy of MTVi Group L.P. All rights reserved. Figure 2.2: reproduced by permission of Tamara Munzner. Figure 2.3: Contribution of the National Institute of Standards and Technology; not subject to copyright. Figure 9.11: reproduced with permission of the Palmer Group. Figure 7.1: reproduced from J. Viljoen & S. Dann, *Strategic Management*, third edn, © Pearson Education Australia, 2000, p. 377. Figure 13.3: screenshot reproduced by permission of phpwebhosting.com. Figure 3.2: reproduction of screenshot by permission of Porsche AG. Figure 15.2: © R. M. Williams; reproduced with permission. Figure 9.6: reproduced with permission of Sanity. Figure 16.2: reproduced with permission of Site Statz. Figures 5.6, 5.8: screenshots reproduced by permission of Sluggy.com. Figures 6.3, 6.4: screenshots reproduced by permission of the Smithsonian Institute. Figure 5.7: screenshot © User Friendly Media, Inc. Reproduced with permission. Figure 5.9: Vtown screenshot reproduced with permission of Virtual Communities. Figure 9.2: Whiskas® label reproduced courtesy of Uncle Ben's of Australia.

Text
Table 15.3: adapted from S. Poon & C. Jevons (1997), 'Internet-enabled international marketing: A small business network approach', *Journal of Marketing Management* 13, www.journalofmarketingmanagement.com, © Westburn Publishers Ltd. Table 7.1: reproduced from R. Simeon, 'Evaluating domestic and international web site strategies, in *Internet Research: Electronic Networking Applications and Policy*, vol. 9, no. 4, 1999; table 8.1, adapted from I. Phau & S. M. Poon, 'Factors influencing the types of products and services purchased over the Internet', in *Internet Research: Electronic Networking Applications and Policy*, vol. 10, no. 2, 2000; table 8.2, adapted from J. Durgee, G. C. O'Connor & R. Veryzer, 'Using mini-concepts to identify opportunities for really new product function', in *Journal of Consumer Marketing*, vol. 15, no. 6, 1998; tables 11.1, 11.2: adapted from T. Strader & M. Shaw, 'Consumer cost differences for traditional and Internet markets', in *Internet Research: Electronic Networking Applications and Policy*, vol. 9, no. 2, 1999; © MCB University Press.

Every effort has been made to trace the ownership of copyright material. Information that will enable the publisher to rectify an error or omission in subsequent editions will be welcome. If copyright holders in such instances contact the publisher's Permissions Department, the publisher will arrange to pay the usual permissions fee.

How to use this book

Strategic Internet Marketing has been designed with you — the student — in mind. The design is our attempt to provide you with a book that both communicates the subject matter and facilitates learning. We have tried to accomplish these goals through the following elements.

The chapter opening page outlines the learning objectives of the chapter and offers a topical quote relevant to the material presented in the chapter.

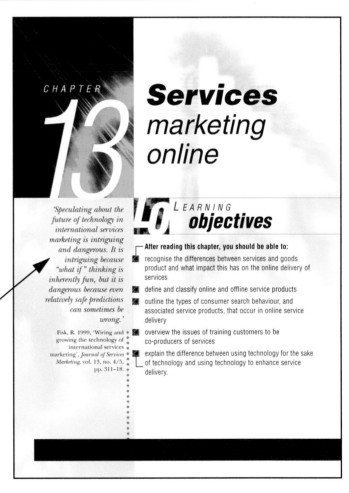

CHAPTER

13

Services marketing online

'Speculating about the future of technology in international services marketing is intriguing and dangerous. It is intriguing because "what if" thinking is inherently fun, but it is dangerous because even relatively safe predictions can sometimes be wrong.'

Fisk, R. 1999, 'Wiring and growing the technology of international services marketing', *Journal of Services Marketing*, vol. 13, no. 4/5, pp. 311–18.

LEARNING objectives

After reading this chapter, you should be able to:

- recognise the differences between services and goods product and what impact this has on the online delivery of services
- define and classify online and offline service products
- outline the types of consumer search behaviour, and associated service products, that occur in online service delivery
- overview the issues of training customers to be co-producers of services
- explain the difference between using technology for the sake of technology and using technology to enhance service delivery.

Internet marketing insights are found in each chapter. They present a range of issues, developments and experiences in Internet marketing. This feature links the chapter content to industry.

Internet marketing INSIGHT
Delivering services across the Internet

One of the major areas of service provision on the Internet is the delivery of Internet services such as web hosting, domain registration or email server hosting. The provision of services for the new medium in the new medium poses some interesting applications for service marketing. In the early days of the Internet, the service provision of Internet hosting tended to be a local industry as the host was usually the same provider for the company's Internet access and web site. Commercial ISPs provide a varying range of server space with their monthly accounts (usually 5 to 10 meg.). Gradually, as the Internet user base expanded, more companies offered dedicated web site hosting as a core service, instead of a supplementary service to their Internet access provision.

Phpwebhosting.com is a US-based company which provides a unique approach to online service delivery of web site hosting by offering a no-frills, flat-rate service to anyone in the world, thus removing the initial issue of separability. What makes the Phpwebhosting strategy interesting is the fact that they have used the Internet to negate the need for either service provider or consumer to be near to point of production. The client base of the company, which operates out of Indianapolis, has grown tremendously, and now covers every continent with the exception of Antarctica — all accessing the **server farm** which is located in Fort Lauderdale, Florida.

■ **Figure 13.3** phpwebhosting.com
Source: www.phpwebhosting.com

(continued)

In addition, service products can also be categorised by their capacity to be translated into international services, which is examined in the Focus on Strategy vignette.

FOCUS ON
Strategy

International services: Wiring and exporting services

The globalisation of the Internet has led to many services becoming international exporters of services without initially intending to reach a global market. Clark and Rajaratnam (1999) classified international services as one of four possible types:

■ *contact-based* — services where people cross borders to perform services, such as consultancy, teaching or other skills-based delivery of service

■ *vehicle-based* — services relayed across a communications channel such as television, radio, or the Internet

■ *asset-based* — services which require establishing a head office and/or production facility in a new country

■ *object-based* — services that can be impregnated onto a physical object (CD, video cassette), or where the service is applied to an object (repairs to machinery).

For Internet-based services, vehicle-based and object-based exporting is the most common form of international trade that these organisations can, and will, conduct by being online. The majority of Internet-based services are engaged in delivering their core service product using the Internet, with the emphasis on delivering within the confines of the PC. Clark and Rajaratnam (1999) observed four factors which impact on the delivery of vehicle-based services:

■ the medium must have the capacity to carry the service — for example, MP3.com streaming audio is viable only on modem speeds of 56k or higher

■ access limitations such as licences, contracts, exclusivity arrangements with offline providers and territorial limitations that can apply to restrict Internet-based international services. Many of the competition web sites (particularly ones requiring you to punch a monkey in banner adverts to enter) are limited to being able to provide prizes only to US residents. As yet, there are no international laws to prohibit the punching of monkeys in banner adverts, so these sites continue to offer rewards to people who are not eligible to receive them.

■ the need for specialised equipment or software — restricts access to the delivery vehicle. Consumers need to have an Internet connection, plus the relevant software to access the service delivery on the site. Constant upgrading and development of display software such as Macromedia Flash (www.flash.com) or Shockwave (www.shockwave.com) often require users to upgrade their viewing software before the service can be accessed. Of greater concern (and frustration) has been the propensity of technologies such as DVD to become regionalised. Regional codes for software products limit the ability to export vehicle- and object-based services which are dependent on these technologies.

(continued)

Focus on strategy highlights the need for sound strategy and strategic planning in Internet marketing. This feature is found throughout the book and presents diverse, international Internet marketing experiences that reinforce the role of strategic planning and management in this field.

The summary outlines and reiterates the core issues explored in the chapter.

To ensure that the move to delivering Internet-based services is smooth and effective the following steps are recommended (Fisk et al. 2000):

- provide marketer input into the technology of customer interface design
- stay customer focused, not machine focused
- make services technology invisible to the customer — customers are interested only in the service outcomes, not how they got there, what they did on the way, or how fundamentally clever the programmer was for developing the process
- insist on a design that delivers service flexibility that adequately meets the needs of the consumer without excessive complexity.

 ## Summary

The Internet opens up a whole new world of opportunities for services marketers, not only to create new, online service products, but to enhance their current service product mixes. As in all areas of marketing, however, the key to successful service product development and delivery is to fully understand the complexity of the product involved and then listen to the needs of the consumer before responding with a specific service offering. The flexibility of the Internet, and the relatively low marginal costs involved in new service product development online, provide a range of temptations for services marketers to become technologically rather than consumer driven. Successful services firms, however, are those that recognise the technology as being the means to the end (customer satisfaction) rather than the end in itself.

This chapter has examined the nature of the service product in detail, both as it exists traditionally and as it is being adapted in the online environment. In doing so, it has shown how some of the traditional difficulties facing services marketing, such as the normal lack of service consistency, are easier to overcome via Internet delivery. It also examined classifications of service products, the nature of the online service product and its relationship to the total service offering of the organisation. Finally, the chapter concludes with a reminder of the importance of staying customer, rather than technology focused, in the design and delivery of online services.

Discussion *questions*

13.1 Outline the traditional points of differentiation between goods and services. Which of these differences has the greatest impact for online service delivery?

13.2 How has online delivery altered offline service delivery? Give examples of how web-based services can impact on offline services.

13.3 Do online services have to have an offline presence? Can a service exist purely in the online medium or does it still require some offline capacities? Discuss with examples.

13.4 Outline the classifications of service product. Find online examples of each type of service product.

(continued)

Discussion questions help to develop and refine understanding of the issues presented in the chapter.

Glossary

24–7 (24 hour 7 day a week) access: the accessibility of the I[...] or day of the week

3D cyberspace: a graphical representation of the Intern[...] person perspective

actual product: the tangible product including style and ac[...]

advocates: a member of a cybercommunity who leads by e[...] nity, and often is a most prolific member of the group

affective commitment: a form of relationship commitment[...] committed to the relationship, the less desire that indivi[...] or to seek alternative arrangements

affective event: a commitment based on liking, emotic[...] bonding with the other party

alpha geek: the most technically accomplished or skilful p[...]

Archie and Veronica: Archie and Veronica are historical e[...] the name given to the Internet FTP search server, and[...] Oriented Netwide Index to Computerized Archives) wa[...] mechanism for searching **gopher systems**. Both were[...] Archie comics series.

asynchronously: the method by which communications can be conducted in **delayed time**, or without the need for both parties to be present at the exchange

attraction: the level above awareness that conveys a sense of attraction to recipients so that they will want to visit a web site and will take active steps to meet this desire

attractor: a type of web site that is specifically intended to have the most potential to interact with the greatest number of visitors in a select target market

attributes and benefits: the salient attributes considered important to a consumer, and believed to be the basis for making a purchase decision

augmented product: the additional benefits or services attached to the purchase of the actual product such as social prestige or service warranty

avatar: a representation of the user, normally found in social interaction mediums like MUDs, IRC, USENET and email

awareness: the knowledge of the existence of a product, web site or idea

bandwidth: the volume of information per unit time that a computer, person, or transmission medium can handle

bargain hunter: a type of online web user who seeks the free, the trial samples and the giveaways that are available on the Web

bleeding edge/cutting edge: cutting edge is defined as the most recent version of any technology, product or idea. The bleeding edge is the next version of the cutting edge, long before it is sufficiently stable to be released into the marketplace. Bleeding edge is commonly used to refer to new technologies with small, but dedicated, user bases who are willing to put up with flaws, glitches and unfinished goods in order to test the new systems.

blueprint: (also blueprinting): the tool that helps bring together the organisation's requirements for online and offline marketing activities and integrating the two into the overall strategic direction of the company

bureaucratic index: an assessment score based on level and number of regulations and procedures which must be navigated by the exporter/international marketer in entering that country's market

A comprehensive glossary provides definitions of all the key terms in the text. With many new terms in the field of internet marketing, this glossary is an invaluable resource.

www.jwiley.com.au/tertiary/strategicinternet/dann/wiley.com.au

Definition and domain

■ **1**...*The technological revolution*   ■ **2**...*Concepts and terminology*

The first section of the book outlines the definition and domain of marketing, the Internet and how the two can be successfully integrated. **Chapter 1** explores the background and historical development of the Internet, and the involvement of marketing and commercial interests in shaping the future of the medium. **Chapter 2** looks in depth at the conceptual domain of marketing, strategy and the Internet in order to prepare the reader for the following parts. Emphasis is placed on exploring the conceptual domains of many of the key areas of philosophy and theory that underpin the book, including the notion of cyberspace together with a brief overview of post-modern marketing.

part **1**

CHAPTER

1

The technological revolution

'... *buckle your seatbelt,*
Dorothy, because Kansas
is going bye-bye.'

Cypher, 'The Matrix' (motion
picture) 1999.

LEARNING
objectives

After reading this chapter, you should be able to:

- provide a definition of the Internet
- appreciate the historical development of the Internet
- identify the different elements of the Internet
- recognise the advantages and disadvantages of the different elements of the Internet for marketing.

Introduction

Strategic Internet marketing is the combination of a knowledge of the Internet, application of strategy and an understanding of how marketing can be used effectively and appropriately in any given environment. This chapter lays the groundwork for this textbook by defining the Internet and several of its components such as the World Wide Web and email. The purpose of the chapter is to provide an overview of this textbook and the Internet and to briefly demonstrate how the Internet melded with the online commercial aspirations of the 1990s to develop the contemporary Internet.

What is the Internet?

To answer the question, 'What is the Internet?', you have three options. You can borrow from the popular culture film 'The Matrix' and farm off responsibility for explaining the Internet in favour of experiencing it. Alternatively, you can talk about global networks, protocols, programming languages, FTP servers, web browsers and a range of technical issues. The third option is to present the Internet as a giant social network of information and personal interaction and lift a description from William Gibson's 1984 book *Neuromancer*. At the heart of the problem of answering the question is the fact that nobody who has seen it for themselves can explain the Internet to someone else with any real degree of satisfaction. This is partly because of the complexity of the system and largely because the interest-driven nature of the Internet means that the most important aspect of the Internet that could form the focus of an explanation will differ from person to person. For the purpose of this textbook, the definition of the Internet established by the Federal Networking Council (FNC) (www.fnc.gov) in 1995 will be used. It states that:

the 'Internet' refers to the global information system that:
(i) is logically linked together by a globally unique address space based on the Internet Protocol (IP) or its subsequent extensions/follow-ons;
(ii) is able to support communications using the **transmission control protocol/ Internet protocol (TCP/IP)** suite or its subsequent extensions/follow-ons, and/ or other IP-compatible protocols; and
(iii) provides, uses or makes accessible, either publicly or privately, high level services layered on the communications and related infrastructure described herein.

Source: Federal Networking Council 1995, *Resolution: Definition of 'Internet'*, www.fnc.gov/Internet_res.html

Within the global information system of the Internet, there are four distinct, structured layers:
- **hardware infrastructure**. This includes the computers, cables, power lines and power supplies that provide the actual backbone through which the Internet is housed and accessed.

- **software infrastructure**. This is the domain of the **three-letter acronym (TLA)** where the **TCP/IP protocols**, **IP addresses**, **packet routing**, **HTTP**, **FTP** and **SMTP** all conduct their business, mostly without human intervention, and enable the computers of the Internet to exchange information.
- **intellectual infrastructure**. This is the content on the Internet created by the users of the Internet. This is the first level at which human-to-human information exists in a context accessible to the general public. The intellectual infrastructure may include program software, images and text materials. While this area is generally associated with the Web, it can also take place in FTP servers, USENET and email.
- **social infrastructure**. This is the level of the human-to-human relationships conducted across the medium of the Internet. This is the level where the **cybercommunity** (see chapter 4) can be found as it represents a level of exchange that moves beyond pure data exchange and into the development and maintenance of relationships between people (Dann & Dann 1999).

The focus of this textbook is on the intellectual and social infrastructure of the Internet because these are the domains in which e-commerce, marketing, business and personal transactions take place. Hardware and software infrastructure issues are best examined either through the Internet using groups such as the Internet Society (www.isoc.org) or through LivingInternet.com (www.livinginternet.com), who maintain a comprehensive historical, cultural and technical database that attempts to explain the how and why of the Internet.

A brief history of the Internet

According to a consensus of opinion across a range of Internet history web sites, it appears that the launch of *Sputnik* in 1957 was largely responsible (or to blame) for the development of the Internet. The launch of *Sputnik* created the US–USSR arms and technology race, which in turn was responsible for the creation of DARPA (Defence Advanced Research Project Agency). Following a series of developments in computers, information technology, communications systems and university science labs, the Internet 1.0 emerged as a recognisable form in 1969 as the ARPANET. From there it linked universities, government and military agencies and was restricted to these organisations. Between 1969 and 1990, there were many significant milestones to the IT/Internet community in the development of Internet technology. The details of these milestones can be read on the Internet Society's history pages (www.isoc.org/internet/history/).

The next significant milestone for marketing and online commerce occurred in 1990 as the Internet changed from a private network between academia, government, military and select industry groups to becoming accessible to mainstream society. The World Wide Web made its debut in 1990 courtesy of Tim Berners-Lee and his web server software. What came next was a complicated explosion of web-related software and popularity with Mosaic (www.ncsa.uiuc.edu/SDG/Software/Win/Mosaic/), then Netscape (www.netscape.com), Internet Explorer (www.microsoft.com) and Lynx (lynx.browser.org) providing easier access to the Internet. The first major wave of commercial Internet access arrived in 1995 when a significant spike of Internet and web users appeared from outside university and government access. From there, the rapid expansion of the Internet has seen an unheralded march of technology, people and ideas using the Internet for commercial and non-commercial purposes.

Internet marketing INSIGHT
The early lessons for marketing online

When the floodgates opened on the Internet, the cultural clash between USENET and mass marketing should have shaped the course of marketing's involvement in the Internet and should have brought spam to a standstill. The conflict was based around the mass unsolicited posting of commercial advertising by two lawyers, Laurence Canter and Martha Siegel, to over 6000 newsgroups at once. The response from the USENET community was sharp and devastating, with the lawyers receiving 200 megabytes of data of protest mail in less than two days. The story of the Canter and Siegel Green Card incident is legendary in the Internet community and should have stood as a clear and present 'instruction set' to online marketers.

The message was simple — respect the environment of the Internet. Less polite messages were also suggested, though these were tempered with the instructions to stay within the accepted limits of the commercialisation of the Internet. The lesson to be learnt from the event was not that the Internet was rejecting commerce but rather that it was enforcing the in-house self-regulation that had kept it operating as a functional system. The issue with **spam** has never been the content, but always the method of message delivery given that **spamming** creates unnecessary Internet 'waste' and impacts on the operations of legitimate messages. It was the medium, not the message, that was the problem. For marketers, it meant that they had to conform to the rules of the Internet, rather than believing that the Internet was just like television, only bigger.

It also demonstrated that the self-regulation mechanisms of the Internet were more than willing to take on commercial interests that were in violation of the online codes of conduct. Unfortunately, the **noise-to-signal ratio** of spam to content in certain newsgroups and several web-based mail providers is approaching a level that is crippling the legitimate operation of these services. Rampant destruction of Internet locations such as Usenet and floods of unsolicited email is leading to a point where legislation and legal action will be considered the only practical method of defending the viability of these environments.

The pieces of the puzzle

The Internet is a global network that hosts a series of services, such as email, that exist as independent elements. The elements listed here are not intended to be a comprehensive list of everything that can be found or used on the Internet. That job is left to Yahoo!. Rather, this is a list of some of the common Internet elements of value to online marketers.

The World Wide Web

The World Wide Web is the graphical user-friendly end of the Internet that came into prominence in the mid-1990s following the success of a series of web browser programs. It has remained the most accessible element of the Internet for self-publication because web sites can be created, published and accessed without reference to a centralised broadcast authority.

The Web is based primarily on the hypertext markup language protocol (HTML) and a series of programming languages such as Java, Perl and common gateway interface (CGI). (For a comprehensive list of the web technologies, see the World Wide Web Consortium web site (www.w3.org).) Away from the alphabet soup of programming, file types and the *.htm, *.asp, *.php and *.shtml file extensions, the most significant aspect of the Web is the hyperlink. One small step for code, one giant link for web browsing. The hypertext system allows the user to navigate to, from and through web sites, providing an almost seamless journey through the more graphical front-end of the Internet.

For marketing, the Web is the place to be conducting business, hawking the company wares and developing an effective customer interface. Even in the early days of the commercialisation of the Internet, the Web was seen as the 'official' venue for electronic commerce, and it is conceded by even the non-business Internet purists as a place to allow commercial endeavours. The ease of access for publishing web sites, the speed of updating and near ubiquity of the 'Web as Internet' mindset in the general public makes the World Wide Web a viable venue for conducting business.

Email

Electronic mail was the first point at which the Internet was officially declared open for non-business users. Email has a range of ways, means and options, from the web-based email accounts of Hotmail (www.hotmail.com) through to email applications such as Eudora (www.eudora.com) and the traditional Unix-based email systems of Pine (www.washington.edu/pine/).

The commercial value of email lies in the ability to strengthen relationships with staff and customers after the initial contact is made, either online or offline. Email can be a very potent supporting mechanism for an online organisation as the real-time/delayed-time communications can be used to defeat the time and geographic constraints associated with telephone and conventional mail. The fundamental flaw in using email for e-commerce is that the user bears the end cost of receiving the mail and, consequently, many unscrupulous individuals have attempted to take advantage of this cost-cutting measure with unsolicited email. The end result has been to create an environment where spam is rampant and unsolicited email is unwelcome. Even solicited email and opt-in lists are finding that the negative opinion of email-based marketing and the heavy flow of unsolicited email to web-based accounts such as Hotmail are reducing the overall value of the medium.

Real-time communications

Real-time communications are those person-to-person Internet communications that are transmitted and received instantly or with a lag of only a few seconds.

Lag is the time period between sending the message and the message being received by the computer or user. Heavy levels of Internet traffic, particularly on popular Internet relay chat servers can create lag times of up to several minutes. Real-time conversations are usually the domain of the following systems on the Internet:

- **Internet relay chat (IRC)**. IRC was written in 1988 and is a system of real-time text communication that is divided into 'channels' (digital equivalents of rooms) to enable users to chat in groups or privately. The commercial application of the IRC channel has been in the creation of cyber-communities (see chapter 5) or as a medium for online focus groups (see chapter 16). Popular interface software for accessing IRC channels include mIRC (www.mirc.co.uk) and IRCLE (www.ircle.com).

- **web chat systems**. These systems, working on a similar mechanism to the IRC, are used for real-time communication based on a web site or integrated into a web page. They can be written to be integrated into an IRC server (for example, www.jpilot.com) or as stand-alone systems that operate from the web site (for example, chatcity.com.au). Web chats differ from bulletin boards by the emphasis on real-time exchange, whereas bulletin boards are designed for delayed-time interaction.

- **multi-user dungeons (MUDs)**. MUDs and other structured artificial worlds make use of real-time communication systems to create virtual worlds for communications and interaction. These areas are predominantly the domain of cybercommunity structures designed and developed to host artificial game worlds (for example, www.mudconnector.com), although they can be used for conferencing and as virtual tourist locations (see chapter 5 for details).

The priority behind the real-time communications systems is to create environments where the Internet can be used to facilitate one-to-one or one-to-many communications in real time and usually in a text-dominated environment. Even videoconferencing systems such as Netmeeting (www.microsoft.com) offer real-time text and file exchange as an integrated part of the package.

Delayed and mixed time

Delayed-time communications are systems designed to allow for messages to be left in a public forum to be accessed at a later date without needing the original poster of the message to be present. These systems take advantage of the one-to-one and one-to-many-to-one nature of the Internet as a medium where text messages can be stored and archived as easily as they can be accessed in real time. Mixed-time systems allow users to make use of either immediate messaging or delayed delivery. Common systems using these features are:

- **paging services**. These are messaging software systems that can send short text messages across the Internet. Common systems include ICQ (www.icq.com) or iChat (www.ichat.com), which include contact lists, real-time chat and the capacity to directly exchange files.

- **USENET**. This consists of a worldwide hierarchy of newsgroups clustered around seven major topic areas. Users post messages to the newsgroups and the newsgroup messages are broadcast across the news servers around the Internet. USENET.org (www.usenet.org) offers a fairly comprehensive overview and introduction to the USENET culture and the technical issues of how newsgroups and news servers work. Marketing and business has a particularly poor reputation within the USENET environment due to early errors of judgement and several deliberate breaches of the cultural norms as illustrated in the Internet marketing insight on page 5. For the marketer, the best value of these groups comes from unobtrusive observation (see chapter 16) or their role as cybercommunities (see chapter 5). There are specific newsgroups available for the discussion of commercial trading activities; however, commercial interests may be best suited to withdraw from the Usenet environment and focus on the web-based activities.

- **bulletin boards**. These are the non-USENET messaging boards, either contained within web sites (for example, www.stormwrestling.com/comments) or as independent boards on a collective site (for example, www.insidetheweb.com).

The basic value of the communication elements of the Internet is found in the people who use them and the information and communities that can be found in these locations. By careful observation and involvement in the communities that are formed around the communication systems, low-level **permission marketing** may become acceptable within the context of the group in which the marketer is involved. However, none of these communication systems are viable promotional media as promotional messages are unwanted and will result only in creating hostility towards the online marketer and their brand. Promotion is best left to the Web and left out of the messaging systems.

Data exchanging: The rest of the Internet

Data exchanging is the catch-all category that defines the miscellaneous categories of the Internet. While technically all of the above categories are involved in the exchange of data, this category is primarily focused on the movement of software, data units or specific file types. The most common data-exchange method is **file transfer protocol (FTP)**.

File transfer protocol is the software systems that are used for the transferring of files to or from one computer to another, usually a server, across the Internet. Common FTP programs such as Bulletproof FTP (www.bpftp.com) offer functions that enable the software to be used to send and receive files from a specific site. Unlike ICQ, where the transferring of files is from person to person, FTP uses an intermediary server system that can be used as the digital equivalent of a 'take one free' distribution outlet more commonly associated with newspapers and pamphlet stands. FTP sites are often integrated into web sites to cater for downloadable files, such as those held by Tucows (www.tucows.com). The most common application of FTP servers in marketing is in the distribution of demonstration software, patches or updates (for example, ftp://mirror.aarnet.edu.au).

There are other functions available for peer-to-peer file sharing, such as Napster (www.napster.com) or Gnutella (www.gnutelliums.com); however, these are not yet at the point at which they can be fully recognised or recommended as marketing tools.

The new landscape for marketing

The Internet, television and radio all share one point in common: no matter how radical and new the technology that created it was or how different it was from the medium before it, the same people who read newspapers, watch TV and listen to the radio will also use the Internet.

The medium is new and the messages need to be tailored for the new environment, but the receivers of the Internet are still the same people who have televisions, radios and newspapers. Marketers need to recognise that while the landscape may be different and the complexities of the delivery of marketing, products and promotion across the Internet need to be addressed, the familiar landmarks of the listening, viewing and reading audience remain. People still want the same basic functionality of education, entertainment and information from the Internet.

However, the Internet is not television with words, just as the television was not radio with pictures. The implications and developments of ubiquitous access to a global network of communications have yet to be fully realised. One recognised impact of the Internet in the short history of the medium has been to open up the online world to globalisation and internationalisation, where information crosses borders with greater ease than people or goods ever can.

FOCUS ON
Strategy ◉

The changing and evolving world of online marketing

If one truism of the Internet can be guaranteed along with death and taxes, it has to be the unstoppable march of the progression of the Internet. Since this textbook was commissioned, one of the landmarks of the early days of the Internet, Infoseek, ceased to exist, only to be replaced by the Go.com portal (www.go.com); Microsoft released a new operating system, new web browser version and upgrade pack for the operating system; Linux and Macintosh rolled out new versions of their operating systems; and many thousands of web pages have come and gone. The Internet is still a very young medium and the rapid rate of development from the first release of Mosaic to the contemporary version of Netscape and Internet Explorer has shown no sign of slowing down.

This means that marketers cannot rest on previous successes and must continue to evolve and develop new means and mechanisms to take advantage of the benefits of these developments and avoid the pitfalls. This textbook sets out to provide both a snapshot in time and a set of fundamental principles to build upon for future upgrades to marketing knowledge.

A detailed overview of this textbook

The textbook is divided into five sections, each of which can stand alone as a module or can be used in a linear sequence. While a textbook is not a hypertext environment, cross-referencing has been used to link related sections and to emphasise the need for integrated approaches to marketing on the Internet.

Part 1: Definition and domain

The first element of this textbook establishes the characters and the main motivations of the Internet, as well as the what and why of concepts and terms associated with marketing and the Internet

Chapter 1: The technological revolution

Chapter 1 gave a brief history and outline of how recent technological advances have revolutionised the way in which marketers do business. The content was fairly self-explanatory and included a brief history of the Internet and a few of the key terms of the Internet.

Chapter 2: Concepts and terminology

Chapter 2 overviews many of the key concepts and terms associated with the Internet and lays down the conceptual groundwork for later chapters. This chapter provides an overview of some of the philosophical issues that are associated with the pragmatics of marketing in the virtual environments of the Internet.

Part 2: New marketing strategies for the new media

The second section of this textbook explores the new features of the Internet that set it apart from the traditional avenues of radio, television and print media.

Chapter 3: Unique features of Internet-based marketing

This chapter will highlight the unique attributes of the Internet and how these attributes can be used in marketing campaigns. In particular, it outlines the value of adapting marketing techniques to maximise the inherent advantages of the Internet. Emphasis is placed on explaining how factors such as time independence and 24-hour access can be incorporated into marketing strategy.

Chapter 4: Consumer behaviour

The fourth chapter in this textbook focuses on examining the unique aspects of the current Internet population, including the adoption profile of Internet users, the factors that influence how and why people use the Internet, and the fears, such as security issues, that prevent consumers from using the Internet to its full potential.

Chapter 5: Creating cybercommunities

Community creation addresses the creation, establishment and facilitation of cybercommunity structures. The fifth chapter examines the issues associated with establishing an artificial cybercommunity structure and the factors necessary to maintain and strengthen existing structures. The section on establishing a community structure addresses the range of technical structures available in the context of their appropriateness for certain types of campaign. The emphasis in the chapter is on understanding how to apply these features of the Internet to marketing and not on the technical programming details required to implement them. Community structure and support is addressed in terms of the resources, both technical and human, required to maintain an existing or newly developed cybercommunity.

Chapter 6: Applications for business and non-business

Applications for business and non-business groups concentrate on demonstrating how the Internet can be used for small, medium or large businesses; non-profit organisations; government departments; and other organisations. The emphasis of the chapter is on highlighting the potential benefits of the Internet while outlining a set of realistic expectations for both monetary and non-monetary returns from having an active Internet presence.

Chapter 7: Internet in marketing strategy

Following on from the applications chapter, this chapter focuses on how to integrate an Internet presence into an organisation's marketing strategies. It concentrates on demonstrating how the Internet can be a part, rather than an adjunct, of conventional marketing strategies. The emphasis in this chapter is on the value of an integrated approach to marketing strategy, and leads into the following marketing mix chapters.

Part 3: Marketing fundamentals in the interactive age

The third section of the book moves from the discussion of the Internet and its applications into the use of the marketing mix in the online world. This section takes a practical look at how the unique features of the Internet can be used within the marketing mix.

Chapter 8: The role of product in Internet marketing

The chapter on product examines the type and nature of products suited to being part of an Internet marketing campaign. It reviews three distinct product areas — services, ideas and tangible goods — and how the Internet can be used to enhance the marketing of these products. In addition, the chapter outlines the role of the Internet in new product development, both for online and offline products.

Chapter 9: Promotion 1: Internet in promotional mix

Chapter 9 is the first of two chapters governing the role of the Internet in the promotional mix. This chapter looks at how promotional activities involving the Internet can be integrated into the traditional promotional mix. This chapter leads into chapter 10, which discusses the role of the Internet as a promotional forum.

Chapter 10: Promotion 2: The Internet as a promotional medium

This chapter builds on the previous chapter's application of the Internet as an element of the promotional mix. Using a 'how-to' approach, this chapter deals with the fundamental philosophical issues of web site design and management in light of the use of web sites as promotional tools. It incorporates the basics of web page design, web site management and the importance of design consistency in conjunction with appropriate models of information distribution (layered, vertical and horizontal site structures) without going into detail of HTML coding. Web page design addresses critical issues of readability, graphical content and interactivity.

Chapter 11: Pricing strategies

This chapter overviews the role of pricing, both at the monetary and non-monetary level, involved in the marketing of ideas, products and services on the Internet. It explores how non-monetary costs such as time and effort can be as much of a barrier to success online as high financial costs are barriers to success offline.

Chapter 12: Distribution

The final chapter of this section addresses the issues of distribution and channel management with regards to the Internet as both a local and international marketplace. Emphasis is placed on addressing issues of distribution by product type, with reference given to issues raised throughout part 3.

Part 4: Strategic marketing applications for the Internet

The fourth part of the book reviews specific applications of marketing on the Internet to explore how issues such as service delivery or market research can be conducted in the new media.

Chapter 13: Services marketing online

This chapter addresses the opportunities and challenges that the Internet poses to service marketing. Services marketing has been in the unique position of having experienced many of the issues associated with Internet marketing, such as intangibility, on a regular basis. The chapter addresses how the key characteristics of services, in particular intangibility and inseparability, can be applied in the online marketing environment.

Chapter 14: Relationship marketing in a one-to-many-to-one environment

This chapter examines the value of the Internet for relationship marketing by using the interactive capabilities of the Internet. Issues of customised web sites, email and the development of customer cybercommunities are addressed in terms of their applicability to marketing, rather than the technical issues concerned with developing and implementing these systems.

Chapter 15: International marketing

The Internet has helped to break down the traditional barriers to entry into international markets. In particular, it has opened up possibilities for small business and service-based organisations to compete in the global marketplace through the minimisation of problems associated with time and place dependency. This chapter highlights the potential for global marketing activity for organisations of all types through the use of the Internet.

Chapter 16: Marketing research

Online marketing research represents more than just simply placing a survey on a web site. New tools and techniques designed to take advantage of the unique characteristics of the Internet are overviewed, along with discussions as to how existing marketing research tools can be adapted for use in the new medium. The chapter also explores the principles of market segmentation in the online environment.

Part 5: The future

The fifth and final part of this textbook looks at the future directions for Internet marketing and the issues and implications arising from new technologies in marketing.

Chapter 17: Future directions

The final chapter outlines the implications that may arise from marketing's involvement in the Internet. It overviews the potential for the future of online marketing as well as summarising marketing's current position in relation to the Internet. This section also explores the ethical issues associated with the development and use of new marketing tools in the media, with an emphasis on preserving privacy and security on the Internet.

Summary

The history of the Internet can be traced through its development from being the domain of scientists and academics through to becoming a mass market medium. The multi-level concept describes the Internet as consisting of four distinct, structured layers — hardware infrastructure, software infrastructure, intellectual infrastructure and social infrastructure — where the hardware and software infrastructures support the human activities on the Internet. The following chapter explores the intellectual and social infrastructure in greater detail and explores the integration of commercial interests into these two layers.

Discussion questions

1.1   What is the Internet? Outline the FNC definition of the Internet. Which level/s of the Internet does this definition most accurately describe?

1.2   Outline the benefits and disadvantages of the different elements of the Internet for marketing.

1.3   How can marketing repair its reputation in the online world? Are there sections of the Internet that should be off-limits to commercial activities?

References

Dann, S. & Dann, S. 1999, 'Cybercommuning: Global village halls', *Advances in Consumer Research*, vol. 70, no. 25, pp. 379–84.

Federal Networking Council 1995, *Resolution: Definition of 'Internet'*, www.fnc.gov/Internet_res.html

Gibson, W. 1984, *Neuromancer*, Ace Books, New York.

Web sites

http://chatcity.com.au
http://lynx.browser.org
www.bpftp.com
www.eudora.com
www.fnc.gov
www.fnc.gov/Internet_res.html
www.gnutelliums.com
www.go.com
www.hotmail.com
www.ichat.com
www.icq.com
www.insidetheweb.com
www.ircle.com
www.isoc.org
www.isoc.org/internet/history/
www.jpilot.com
www.livinginternet.com
www.microsoft.com
www.mirc.co.uk
www.mudconnector.com
www.napster.com
www.ncsa.uiuc.edu/SDG/Software/Mosaic/
www.netscape.com
www.stormwrestling.com/comments/
www.tucows.com
www.usenet.org
www.w3.org
www.washington.edu/pine/

FTP site

ftp://mirror.aarnet.edu.au

Concepts and terminology

'It is man who is the content of the message of the media, which are extensions of himself.'

McLuhan, M. 1972, in Varey, R. J. 1999, 'Marketing, media and McLuhan: Rereading the prophet at century's end', *Journal of Marketing*, vol. 63, no. 3, pp. 148–54.

LEARNING *objectives*

After reading this chapter, you should be able to:

- understand the definition and domain of the Internet, cyberspace and marketing

- recognise key definitions of Internet terminology

- outline the various conceptualisations of cyberspace

- identify the uses of mapping in cyberspace

- overview the role of conceptual geography for Internet marketing

- outline the value of the marketing mix, and the three levels of marketing, for exploring Internet marketing

- recognise the value of focusing on online consumer behaviour ahead of business to business marketing

- appreciate the differences between international and global marketing on the Internet

- understand how and why people can re-create themselves online using post-modern consumption

- identify cultural considerations involved with marketing in the Internet culture.

Introduction

This chapter explains several of the key areas, assumptions and definitions that impact on the examination of strategic Internet marketing. Establishing the definition and domain of the Internet creates a point of reference for the ideas and examples in the rest of the text. In particular, this chapter examines the operating parameters of this text in regards to the Internet, cyberspace, marketing theory, consumer behaviour, international marketing and post-modern consumption. It also provides a brief overview of Internet culture and the major elements that impact on online marketing. In addition, this chapter explains how the text is structured.

This text was constructed to be used in both a linear and non-linear fashion. Each chapter can be used as a self-contained modular unit (cross-referenced to relevant sections of related chapters), or as a structure that builds on previous chapters. In order to accomplish this task, key concepts are referenced and defined in the chapters where they are discussed. Where themes, definitions and concepts appear repeatedly throughout the book, they have also been gathered in this chapter as a summary. The level of repetition of a concept indicates the significance and relevance of that concept to the domain of strategic Internet marketing.

Definition and domain of the book

A linear-based text trying to describe the multimedia, interactive, non-linear landscape of the Internet is always going to face a few problems with its selection of definitions, conceptualisations and authority sources. Any form of predictive statement will be most likely to have been proved, disproved or implemented by the time the book reaches print. A book cannot hope to replicate the dynamic nature of the Internet, since a book is a snapshot that represents understanding framed at the time of writing. This, in the development of the field of Internet marketing, is the competitive advantage of the book — it is not a bug, it is a feature. The strength of the book is that it is a constant. It acts as a reference marker and anchor for the development and mapping of the interaction of marketing and the Internet.

Consequently, some of the decisions made concerning definitions, selection of theory and example, are grounded by the need to establish a link between the present, the past and potential developments of the future. This text sets out to use marketing theory as the basis to discuss the relationship between marketing practice and the Internet. In order to achieve this end, several key parameters need to be defined. What is presented in this chapter is not the definitive statement of how the worlds of strategy, marketing and the Internet should be defined. Rather, it represents the operational vocabulary of the book and represents the working definitions used throughout the remainder of the text.

Defining elements: What makes the Internet click?

There are several recurring themes in the discussion of the elements and features of the Internet. These are presented here as an introduction and overview of the common definitions that shape understanding of the Internet. The most common ideas governing, describing and influencing the Internet are:

- **computer-mediated communication (CMC)** is the use of computers and computer networks as communication tools by people who are collaborating to achieve a shared goal. CMC does not require the physical presence or co-location of participants. It provides a forum for continuous communication, free of time constraints (Kaye 1991).
- **remote hosting** is the process by which a user in one geographic location hosts their web site, files or other information on a computer in another geographic location.
- **one-to-many-to-one communications** are those computer-mediated communications that are published by an individual to a public sphere, such as a newsgroup. They are read and responded to either directly to the individual, or indirectly to the newsgroup by other readers (Hoffman & Novak 1996).
- **real time** is where person-to-person Internet communication is transmitted and received instantly or with a lag of only a few seconds.
- **delayed time** is where messages or similar content can be left in a public forum to be accessed at a later date, without the need for the original poster of the message to be present.
- **marketspace** operates as a parallel to the physical world of the marketplace as the conjunction between ideas and exchange, where goods, services, ideas and money can be exchanged as items of value (Weiber & Kollman 1998). The marketspace–marketplace continuum demonstrates that value chains of product services, procurement, distribution and production can be found and solved in both on- and offline environments.
- **cybercommunities** arise where a group of individuals engaged in computer-mediated communication moves beyond the basic exchange of information into the formation of a community structure that is based on the exchange of shared goods of value (Dann & Dann 1998).
- **flow** is the state of mind where interaction with the Internet becomes a unified movement from one site or event to the next. The individual has little or no awareness of distraction, outside influences, or irrelevant thoughts (Hoffman & Novak 1996).
- **telepresence** is the perception of physicality inside a cyberspace environment (Steuer 1992; Shih 1998; Novak, Hoffman & Yung 1998).
- **lean media** are communications media that tend to strip away non-verbal cues and information that are present in a face-to-face environment (Montoya-Weiss et al. 1998).
- **24–7 (24 hour, seven days a week) access** is the accessibility of the Internet irrespective of the time of day or the day of the week. The implication behind 24–7 access is the creation of a site and system that is operational, available and fully functional for 24 hours, all year.

Defining the parameters 1: Operationalising the Internet

The first parameter that needs to be established is the Internet, which is a task first undertaken in chapter 1 and continued throughout the entire book. The Internet is both the machinery and machinations of technology, software and systems interacting with each other as much as it is the interaction between the human members of the community. For the purpose of this text, the emphasis of the marketing strategies is placed squarely on human interactions. Predictions of intelligent shopping agents who scour the Internet for the best bargains, deals and prices are being made, but these agents will still report back to human masters. Only when computers are capable of applying for their own credit cards and earning their own incomes will marketing need to focus on the computer-to-computer transactions that are currently the domain of engineers.

The classical view of the Internet as the interconnected series of networked networks focuses on only the physical nature of the medium and ignores the social aspects used by marketing. However, no discussion of the Internet can ignore the hardware and software infrastructure levels, as these shape and limit the social interactions possible through the Internet (see chapter 1 for details of the four infrastructure levels).

F O C U S O N
Strategy 👁

Marketing within hardware and software infrastructures

Marketing's involvement with the Internet should be left at the intellectual and social structural level, where the roles it plays as an arbiter and creator of society are useful to the Internet, and society. At the lower levels, the demands of technology and capacity should drive decisions about standards, software and infrastructure requirements. A well-waged public relations and marketing campaign that sees a poor solution implemented at the expense of a technically superior option will ultimately break down the structure of the Internet. The strength of the development of the Internet has been the emphasis on the best solutions being implemented irrespective of any branding, marketing or promotional campaigns. If the technology can do the job in the best fashion, it should be selected on that basis alone. Similarly, the success of the network of networks rests in the lack of a controlling body, dominant market owner or a monopoly on key software. It is doubtful that a proprietary TCP/IP protocol, with a nifty brand name and a catchy slogan, would have led the Internet to the phenomenal growth rate it experienced, if each step of the way was marred by licensing fees, royalties and heavily negotiated distribution deals.

Similarly, the **open source** software community is demonstrating that a comprehensive model of open standards — non-proprietary systems that are selected on an evolutionary 'best fit' approach to problem solving — can result in success without the need for expensive, brand dominated marketing campaigns. The open source movement shows that the market concept can still exist without recourse to the traditional accoutrements of advertising and branding. Many of the products and services actively traded in these markets are delivered with an emphasis on solution-based products that best meet a market need, at the lowest tolerable cost and distributed as widely as possible, either by word of mouth promotion or bundling with similar solutions. In contrast, many of the product failures of the Internet (at all levels, but predominantly the software infrastructure) have occurred where the organisation decided to deliver a proprietary vision of what it believes the market should need, rather than what best solved the problem.

In the open, global competition of the Internet, best-fit solutions are more easily accessible, thereby reducing the power of individual organisations or groups to implement poorer quality but better promoted standards. Marketing practitioners involved in these levels of the Internet need to focus on satisfying market needs ahead of creating strong brands and complex product bundles.

Conceptualising cyberspace

One of the key conceptual issues of the Internet is the debate about the 'physicality' of cyberspace. Much of the written work that attempts to define the Internet gives it an inherent physical environment. Gibson's (1984) definition of 'cyberspace' assumes a physicality, created by shared understanding and defined by graphical representation. Gibson (p. 51) wrote:

> Cyberspace. A consensual hallucination experienced daily by billions of legitimate operators, in every nation, by children being taught mathematical concepts... A graphical representation of data abstracted from the banks of every computer in the human system. Unthinkable complexity. Lines of light ranged in the non-space of the mind, clusters and constellations of data. Like city lights, receding...

Gibson's cyberspace defined a set of parameters for the future development and explanation of the Internet even though Gibson probably thought of the definition as a really good place to put a storyline. The impact is most clearly observed in the descriptions and conceptualisation of the Internet as a 'place' where the descriptions of activity (surfing, browsing) and location (site, home page, home.html) are drawn from physical events in the real world. Of course, this has to be balanced against the information/library lexicon of the Internet (index.html, linking, directory), the mechanical aspects (search engines) and the propensity for in-jokes (spiders, web crawlers, **Archie and Veronica**). The joy of working with, on and in the Internet is the meeting and merging of so many different influences, drawn from the pragmatism of engineering and science, the newer influences of marketing and commerce, and the historical tendency of the computing genre to make strange in-jokes.

Of all aspects that define the Internet, the geographic metaphors dominate the market with their ability to make the intangible nature of the Internet into something that at least looks real, even if it is just a model of reality. Cyber-geography, the art of digital mapping, is best viewed as an aid to under-standing how (or why) the Internet exists, rather than to create a comprehensive mapping system.

Mapping cyberspace

Whenever maps have been created to describe known areas, the small problem of describing the unknown emerges. The easiest solution was to simply label the uncharted section 'Here there be monsters'. Admittedly, although a map of cyberspace that contained Heretherebemonsters.com would sell quite well, it would not describe the unknown of the Internet quite so well. (However, mapping the Web in this manner could be a more practical solution than some of the alternative web directory structures that have been put into place.)

The earliest map of the World Wide Web was developed by Tim Berners-Lee (1990), who graphically described the proposal for the development of hypertext (figure 2.1).

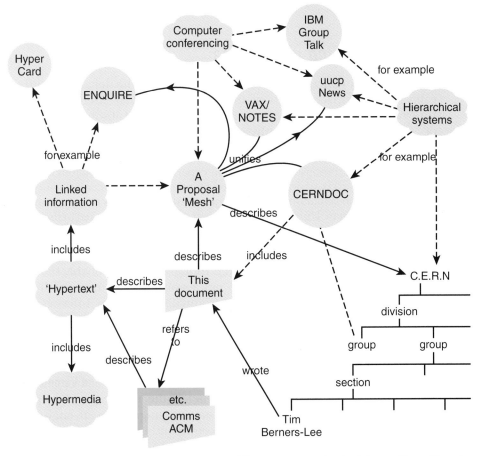

Figure 2.1 A back of the napkin guide to hypertext

Source: Berners-Lee, T. 1990, Information Management: A Proposal, www.w3.org/History/1989/proposal.html

The fact that the World Wide Web emerged from this tangled flow chart is more indicative of the way the Web works than any other milestone in the development of the Internet. Berners-Lee's proposal contained one of the more interesting conceptualisations of the value of hypertext-based systems. His initial design recognised the ability of his (then) small system to be able to describe complex systems as 'a large three-dimensional model, with people represented by little spheres, and strings between people who have something in common at work'.

The person who can ultimately take the credit (or blame) for starting the world on the path to the dotcom revolution conceived of cyberspace as a three-dimensional structure that linked people (by string) to other people with shared interests. From the Web-as-a-ball-of-string approach came a series of three-dimensional maps of the interrelationships within a web site (see figure 2.2).

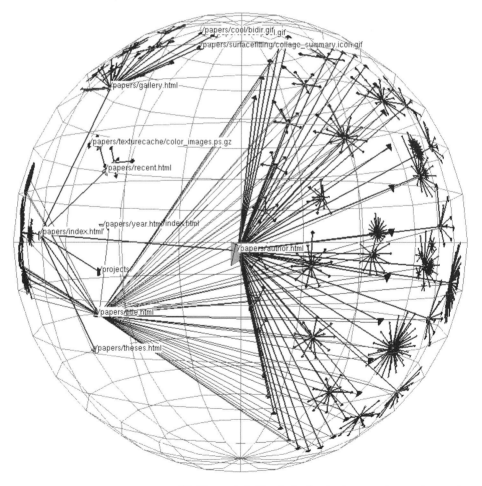

Figure 2.2 The 'ball of string' approach to web mapping

Source: Munzer, T. 1997, 'H3: Laying Out Large Directed Graphs in 3D Hyperbolic Space', 1997 IEEE Symposium on Information Visualisation, October 20–21, Phoenix, AZ, pp. 2–10 (http://www-graphics.stanford.edu/papers/h3/)

Conceptualising web sites as spherical shapes for mapping page to page interaction has proven to be a more viable method of creating a sense of physicality for a web site than using a two-dimensional path map (see figure 2.3).

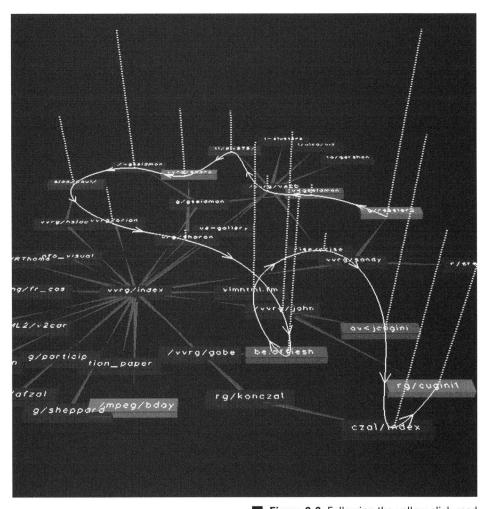

Figure 2.3 Following the yellow click road

Source: Visualization and Virtual Reality Group, National Institute of Standards & Technology, www.itl.nist.gov/iaui/vvrg/index.html

The value of conceptualising web sites as physical spaces, either through three-dimensional, navigable spheres such as figure 2.2 or through click-paths such as figure 2.3, extend far beyond their use as site design tools. One of the major issues facing the Internet is the intangibility of a system that exists only within computer networks and the user's understanding of the Internet. Cospace (cospace.research.att.com) attempted to create a graphical layer that resided over the top of the Web as a navigable network of rooms and portals (figure 2.4). The aim of the layer was to aid community interaction around popular web sites.

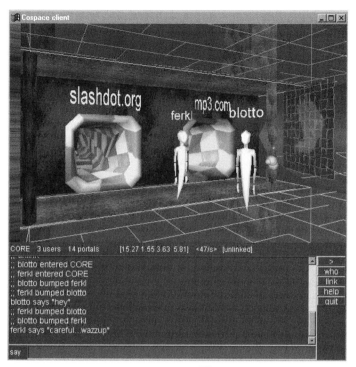

CORE 3 users 14 portals   [15.27 1.55 3.63 5.81] <47/s> [unlinked]
```
;; blotto entered CORE                                          >
;; ferkl entered CORE                                          who
;; blotto bumped ferkl                                         link
;; ferkl bumped blotto                                         help
blotto says "hey"                                              quit
;; ferkl bumped blotto
;; blotto bumped ferkl
ferkl says "careful...wazzup"

say
```

■ **Figure 2.4** Tunnelling through the Web

Source: cospace.research.att.com

Despite the inherent attractiveness of the physicality of cyberspace and the software representations of the Web as a real world, these systems have proved remarkably unsuccessful in gaining popular support and long-term success. The Internet marketing insight below outlines the rise, and temporary pause, in the development of publicly accessible three-dimensional representations of cyberspace.

Internet marketing INSIGHT
The rise and stall of three-dimensional cyberspace

In the early years following the mass outbreak of the Internet, a range of three-dimensional environments sprung up to attempt to realise the Gibsonesque descriptions of cyberspace. The popularity of the text-based World Wide Web and the success of fixed environment online games such as MUDs and constrained first person three-dimensional games such as *Wolfenstein*, *Doom* and the later *Quake* trilogy (www.idsoftware.com), all contributed to a desire to construct a threedimensional graphic 'Internet'. (In this context, the three-dimensional worlds sought to replicate chat, email, web-style navigation, MUD-style interaction and a range of text, audio and visual content. No one element of the Web, USENET, or other Internet system was dominant.) Several attempts were launched with varying degrees of cost and success.

(continued)

Cospace (cospace.research.att.com) was developed as an attempt to link web navigation with three-dimensional environments where users could freely interact with each other while visiting the web site. The system was independent of the site, as it ran in conjunction with the user's activities rather than on a site-by-site basis, although 'Cospace aware' sites could modify their appearances in the environment. From the marketing point of view, it was an almost ideal scenario of being able to augment a web site with an attached three-dimensional interactive room of product samples, advertising and displays.

Figure 2.5 Cospace
Source: cospace.research.att.com

In addition, as with most **avatar**-based systems, users were able to take on their own images and shapes and engage in many of the activities of post-modern consumption available through **cybercommunity** involvements (see chapter 5).

One of the major problems experienced by the pioneering three-dimensional systems can be attributed to the disparity between the technology needs of the system and the available systems for the end user. **Bandwidth** requirements for downloading graphically intensive environments usually slowed the web surfing experience, created lag times between interactions and placed high traffic level stresses on participating servers. In addition, the gap between the perceived ideal of the **three-dimensional cyberspace** experience created by movies, television and video games and the slow, stop-motion experience of reality created a disproportionately high level of dissatisfaction.

However, there have been some three-dimensional successes, such as the long-running The Palace, which is a graphically-intensive virtual community environment (www.thepalace.com/help/). The Palace began in 1997 as a commercial operation, charging for admission and user software. More recently, it has provided both the client and server software in a range of no-cost/low-cost solutions to encourage more users to join and create Palace servers. One of the critical criteria for the success of a text-only cybercommunity is the need for members to want to interact with other members. Once graphics are added to the mix, the criteria expand to include the desire of the members to interact with each other and their environment.

The Palace's decision to freely distribute Palace server software allows for the individual user to create their own space on the three-dimensional network. This also allows for individuals to stake a claim on cyberspace and exercise control over the content of their areas, which ultimately gives them a sense of ownership of their Palace 'room'. In contrast, Cospace existed at a web site without the input of the web site owner and this lessened the sense of ownership. Although site owners could influence Cospace, it lacked a sense of proprietary 'ownership' experienced by developing sites for The Palace. In a sense, Cospace became the roads and freeways of the Internet, whereas The Palace focused on providing houses and homes. The Palace was able to heighten the feelings of **telepresence** and ownership (either as owner of a room or sense of a physical self through the ownership of an avatar), which has aided its longer term success. Feelings of belonging, ownership and sense of control are all essential elements for the longevity of a cybercommunity-oriented structure (see chapter 5).

The value of conceptual geography in cyberspace

The value of the Internet as a physical place is examined in several places in this text, but most dominantly in the cybercommunity (chapter 5) and distribution (chapter 12) chapters. Cybercommunities rely on the creation of a sense of place, often aided by feelings of telepresence, or virtual structures such as defined rooms and environments. In addition, the assumption of locality and physicality in cyberspace is that it is a conceptual environment where the individual user perceives varying degrees of physical location based on their particular involvement with the Internet. This impacts on marketing's role within cyberspace to the extent in which the sense of physicality creates a set of 'real world' conditions similar to those that are used in retailing, services or distribution. If the three-dimensional worlds of Cospace or The Palace come to dominate the interactions of the online world, giving it a more visual than literary environment, then marketing can slide easily into providing virtual advertising billboards, branded three-dimensional goods and logo-equipped avatars in this graphical environment.

Even without the development of the graphical environments, the perception of the Internet as a 'place' and the feelings of physicality and movement in using the Web have allowed marketers to take physical world marketing knowledge across to the Internet. Web site design theory can be influenced by the same design considerations needed in servicescape (colour, mood, navigation), advertising copy testing (recall, readability) and product distribution (chapter 12). Even in the very heady early days of the Internet, marketing was able to adapt offline skills and knowledge for use in the online environment.

Defining the parameters 2: Marketing theory, marketing philosophy and the choice of the marketing mix

The second parameter to be set is the selection of the appropriate marketing framework for use in the text. One constant in the evolution of marketing theory has been the desire to create and construct a new framework to cover every new application of the core principles to a new arena. The premise of this book is that the Internet is not so radically removed from contemporary understanding of the world that a new philosophy and ideological construct needs to be developed. However, the Internet is still an environment that requires marketing theory to go through the process of adoption and adaptation that allows the core principles to be integrated to best suit the new conditions. Adaptation and evolution are a feature of life on the Internet, (with a touch of creationism thrown in for confusion) whereby knowledge from non-Internet sources, with varying degrees of modifications, can be used online.

The problem with the constant drive towards the development of new theory to describe new environments is the perceived pressure to discard existing tools, or at the very least rename them. The first and most basic tool ever used was a rock. Whether thrown at a moving target, stacked together to establish a territory, used as a tool for cutting, for hunting, or being struck together to form a spark, the basic nature of the rock remained the same. A rock, irrespective of application, is still a rock. Calling it an arrowhead, fence, firestarter, or hand axe or 'ugh' (which was probably the first brand in history) was never going to replace the fact that the core product was a rock. Similarly, the philosophy of marketing remains the same, whether the application of the theory is in electronic commerce, business to business marketing, or if it is being thrown at a competitor. Adaptation of the marketing rock may shape it into a variety of forms that can be best used for specific tasks, such as services marketing or relationship marketing, but it essentially retains the same core philosophical and fundamental principles. Consequently, in this text, we retain the tried and tested (although admittedly not perfect) framework of marketing most commonly known as the four Ps.

In defence of the marketing mix

The following section is both a disclaimer and justification for siding with the established framework of the four Ps of marketing, rather than attempting to define a new mnemonic based on alliteration and a 'new' conceptualisation of online marketing. The basis of this text is that marketing has an established core set of theoretical tools, known colloquially as the four Ps — price, product, promotion and distribution (place). Not every reader will agree with the decision to side with the oft-criticised four Ps ahead of adopting relationship marketing, permission marketing, or any other multisyllable form of marketing. Relationship marketing is discussed in the latter half of the book and is the subject of several other books. Similarly, although many of the commercial applications of the Internet are in the fields of services marketing, services forms only a single dedicated chapter in this text (and appears when and where necessary elsewhere).

At the core of the text is the detailed analysis of the Internet's interaction in the fields of price, product, promotion and place. The purpose of these sections is to demonstrate the issues associated with a single element of the mix and how the Internet can influence the perceptions and realities in these areas. For example, chapter 11 discusses the perception of cost reduction associated with Internet-based retailing, which is a considerable issue for price setting, whether the four Ps or relationship marketing is your dominant marketing theme. Similarly, understanding the impact of digital delivery for idea-based services through an analysis of distribution issues will form a significant element of any services, relationship or permission marketer's investigation into the commercial viability of distributing the service online.

Above all, the marketing mix has also had the advantage of being old hat, unfashionable and considerably better established than the majority of the contemporary strands of marketing. Tinkering with the mix by setting a price, or modifying a product offering, or altering a promotional message or redirecting a distribution channel has been doing the practitioner and academic rounds for many years. For those recently introduced to marketing, the four Ps hold a conceptual validity that may be worn down by the passing of time (and adherence to newer interpretations of marketing). However, the basic understanding that a product needs to be available to a consumer (product) at a price that can be afforded by consumer and producer (price) in a channel that both can access (distribution) after a message from the producer to the consumer alerts them to the existence of the product (promotion) provides a good conceptual basis upon which to examine e-commerce.

Three levels of marketing

There are three levels at which marketing drives business activities:
1. as a philosophy or way of doing business
2. as a strategy or framework for driving business decisions
3. as a series of specific tools and tactics to implement business decisions.

Philosophy
Adopting marketing as business philosophy simply means putting a consideration of your customer's needs at the centre of all decision-making activities. In other words, whenever people in the organisation interact with others,

whether they are direct clients, suppliers or even other members of the same company, they will take both sides' needs into consideration while negotiating a transaction. Marketing as a philosophy is not confined to any specific department or division. Instead, it provides a framework for doing business in all areas and at all levels, from the design, development and delivery of an e-commerce system through to customer contact staff. It even includes the behind-the-scenes systems engineers.

Simple client-focused changes, such as making invoices simpler to read and understand, or redesigning a web site to suit client needs, can have a measurable impact on the way that clients perceive the company's effectiveness. Improved perceptions and attitudes towards the company, in turn, translate into increased loyalty, more sales and greater profits.

While being *client centred* in decision-making is intuitively appealing and makes good commonsense, the danger for many new marketers is that they adopt the concept with such enthusiasm that they end up being *client dominated*. The most important consideration in addressing the needs of a client is to determine whether these needs are in conflict with organisational goals. Not every potential customer is a client that the organisation would want, or whose needs it should attempt to address.

One of the hardest parts of marketing is achieving an effective balance between the needs of the clients and the needs of the organisation. Ultimately, firms exist only, and can survive only, if they consistently make a profit. Customising all products and services to be 'perfect' for each customer is time-consuming, expensive and, in most cases, unprofitable. It is clearly not in the firm's interests to go out of business, nor is it in the interests of your clients. Similarly, just because the world is available to the organisation once it goes online, it does not mean that it is under any moral or other obligation to deliver to the world. A company that uses the Internet to deliver a specific product to a select target market should not feel any obligation to abandon their segmentation strategies just because their site can be accessed by people from outside the target market.

The key to successfully implementing the marketing philosophy within your organisation is to ask, 'how well can we satisfy this customer's unique needs within the limitations and boundaries of our organisation and its products?' It is essential to consider this when engaged in Internet-based marketing, as the customer is far more likely to seek out the company and make demands (or polite requests) of the organisation because of the interest-driven nature of the Internet.

Strategy

Taking a marketing-oriented approach to business development helps firms to create and maintain a competitive advantage over their rivals, both on and offline. By understanding and constantly monitoring changes in the market, firms are better able to design, modify and deliver the right products and services to the right people, for the right price, at the right time. This does not mean ad-hoc or incremental unplanned changes that can lead to problems with **feature creep** and **rampant ad hocery** (see chapter 10). At the strategic level, marketing activities involve the development of information gathering and data-base systems, monitoring of the competitive environment and making decisions regarding not only what products to develop, but how to present and position these relative to other firms. Strategic marketing management involves implementing quality systems to help put the marketing philosophy into practice and provide a framework for the development of specific marketing tactics.

Tactics

Implementing marketing strategy requires the use of specific marketing-focused tactics. These tactics include:

- marketing research tools, such as surveys and focus groups (chapter 16)
- communications activities, such as advertising (chapter 9)
- promotional activities like competitions, publicity generation, public relations and sponsorships (chapter 9)
- building relationships with both consumers and suppliers (chapter 14)
- pricing events, such as discounts or cash backs (chapter 11).

It is this external and applied area of marketing that is most familiar to consumers and nonmarketers. Tactics involve all the final activities of getting the right product or service to the right customers, for the right price, at the right time. Any basic management book will introduce the idea of the four Ps, but it is designing the mixes within the mix where the talent for innovation and creativity is best realised.

Alternative readings of marketing and the Internet

Traditionally the marketing mix has been considered to be the four Ps and that is the dominant model that underpins this book. However, as marketing has expanded its applications, additional elements have been added to account for differences in new activities and environments. For example, up to three new Ps have been added to help define the operations of services marketing, so that people, processes and physical evidence are considered of equal significance to product and pricing. It is not surprising, then, that various attempts have been made to develop a modified marketing mix for specific application to the new online environment. This section explores two alternative classifications of online marketing — Rowley's (1996) five elements of online marketing and Spalter's (1996) seven Is. This is not an exhaustive list of alternative online schema, nor is it presented as the definitive list. These two schema are examined to demonstrate how the traditional concepts of marketing can be adapted (and rebadged) to describe Internet marketing and where these 'new' concepts are discussed within the traditional marketing mix framework.

Five elements of online marketing

Rowley develops the following five elements as an alternative to the traditional marketing mix for the online environment.

- *Promotion* includes advertising and any activities designed to create product awareness (chapter 9). The Internet allows for wider distribution of more complex materials than traditional media. It also allows for tailored product catalogues of varying depth of information.

- *One-to-one contact* is the asynchronous interaction with customers via email and company-developed **opt-in mailing lists** (chapter 7). This should not be mistaken for spam, which has no place in online marketing.
- *Closing* involves setting the price (chapter 11) and closing the deal. It is similar to the use of offline brochure ordering or online catalogue ordering systems.
- *Transaction* is the payment for goods, typically made by digital means such as via online credit card transactions or direct debit.
- *Fulfilment* involves the delivery of goods, either via digital means where feasible, or through more traditional systems (chapter 12).

The alternative five elements suggested by Rowley primarily focus on the use of the Internet as a transaction medium, at the expense of considering issues of product development (chapter 8) and the complexity of online pricing (chapter 11). This alternative also overlooks nontransaction-based Internet marketing for either relationship marketing (chapter 14) or the development of cybercommunities (chapter 5). The value of the five steps is to demonstrate the need to address each step in the online exchange process, from the creation of initial awareness to the delivery of actual performance.

Seven Is for seven Internet brothers: The transition from offline to online delivery

Another view of marketing in the online environment is given by Spalter (1996). Although Spalter is not attempting to replace the traditional marketing mix, his framework of the seven Is gives an alternative view of marketing activity and can be used to assist in the transition from traditional to online delivery of goods and services. The seven Is are:

- *interconnection.* This refers to the development of new distribution channels for goods, services and information represented by the various digital media now available (chapter 12). The ability for numerous, spatially dispersed individuals to interconnect in real time, or **asynchronously**, is central to the shift in the marketing viewpoint needed when moving into the online environment (see the discussion about one-to-many-to-one communications in chapter 5). No longer is the customer bound to obey the trading hours and locations set by the retailer as the Internet offers 24–7, near global access to online retailers. This requires a new mind-set of strategic thinking that can adapt to the demands of the consumer, instead of imposing a set of terms and conditions of operating hours and availability on the customer.
- *interface.* It is important to have a user-friendly, intuitive interface between the marketing organisation and the consumer (chapter 10). The interface is the first point of contact between the marketer and customer and should be both functional and inviting if the transaction is to progress beyond a simple visit. As the Internet becomes a truly global phenomenon it is also important to ensure that sites can be accessed and are appropriately designed so that they cross cultural and linguistic barriers.
- *interactivity.* This is the ability of the consumer to engage in a dialogue with members of the firm that is independent of time and place (chapter 3). Interactivity, both automated through computerised responses or between

individual members of a discussion group, chat list or cybercommunity, forms one of the core features of the Internet that differentiates it from the one-way communications of the television and print media.

■ *involvement.* Involvement requires that the marketer crafts an online atmosphere that is conducive to extended and repeat visits from consumers (chapters 9 and 10). There are a number of ways of generating this involvement, including the design of an inviting interface, linking to popular related sites, leveraging brand equity, integrating the online presence into the offline environment and maximising interactivity. Providing content of benefit to the user, either through information, education, entertainment or repeat purchase, is the key to keeping customer involvement.

■ *information.* The widespread availability of product information is leading to a reversal of database marketing practice in that customers are experiencing **database consuming**. This is where consumers use database technology to target products in the same way as marketers use it to target customers. Understanding the shift in the power relationship between customers and marketers that has occurred as a result of the availability of information is essential for the development of appropriate communications between the parties of exchange.

■ *individualism.* This is the ability and willingness of the marketer to provide the means for a customised product or experience (chapter 8). It also depends on a combination of technology, effective market research and the characteristics of the product (see chapters 8, 12 and 16).

■ *integrity.* Privacy, security and confidentiality of online marketing activities must be ensured. The integrity of the web site will impact on the organisation's success and reputation both on and offline and is fundamental to developing trust on the part of the consumer (chapter 14).

The following table highlights the relative impact of the seven Is on the four Ps.

Table 2.1 Interaction between the seven Is and the four Ps

	Product	Promotion	Price	Distribution
Interconnection	★ ★	★	★	★ ★ ★
Interface	★ ★	★ ★ ★		★
Interactivity	★ ★ ★	★		★
Involvement		★ ★ ★		★ ★
Information	★ ★	★ ★	★	
Individualism	★ ★ ★		★ ★	★ ★
Integrity		★ ★	★ ★	

While no system of classification will adequately fit and describe all marketing activities it is clear that some modification either of the marketing mix, or the way in which it is used and interpreted in the online environment, is needed for long-term success.

Defining the parameters 3: Focusing on consumer behaviour ahead of business to business marketing

The third parameter concerns the choice between focusing on consumer behaviour or business to business marketing on the Internet. This book contains a very obvious and intentional consumer behaviour bias in its analysis of the Internet and marketing's role in harnessing the Internet for e-commerce. Business to business (B2B) has a valued and significant role to play in the Internet, both in developing transaction and delivery systems and as a user of the **marketspace/marketplace** dichotomy. B2B transactions focus on the supply of goods, services and information from one business to another. The Internet has a valued and valuable role for the development of B2B relationships between a range of organisations that may not have otherwise have been able to be part of existing **electronic data interchange (EDI)** networks, or which specialised in low volume, niche components aimed at a global market. Low barriers to entry into the Internet environment, combined with relatively low search costs, have created a marketspace suited to B2B transactions.

However, this book has chosen to take a view of the Internet that focuses on consumer behaviour and business to consumer transactions. There are two major reasons why this approach has taken precedence.

- *Pedagogical.* This book focuses on consumer behaviour-oriented marketing courses that focus on Internet marketing and e-commerce. Throughout this text, the examples, cited web sites and models have a tendency to lean towards consumer behaviour. Where appropriate (and possible) B2B services are mentioned or referenced and B2B features heavily in the chapter on relationship marketing (chapter 14). However, the dominant trend of the book is towards consumer behaviour and business to consumer activities online.

- *Ideological.* At this point of its development, the Internet is still the playground of the people and not industry. With an extraordinarily wide **share of voice**, the Internet has proven to be a marketspace capable of hosting both business and consumer transactions (Watson, Akselsen & Pitt 1998). Share of voice refers to the ability of all users in the Internet arena to be able to promote themselves and speak freely without one or more players being able to buy up the 'voice' of the medium. While the commercialisation of the Internet as a transaction, relational marketing and B2B medium is ever-present, the bulk of Internet traffic and content is based around interpersonal, non-commercial exchange. As long as the medium remains open to the general public to be used for content publishing, content acquisition and interpersonal communications, it will remain a predominantly consumer behaviour-influenced environment.

Ultimately, the individual, acting on behalf of a company or on their own behalf, will make a decision concerning the purchase, acquisition, sale or trade of goods, services and information over the Internet. Consequently, the emphasis in this text is to remain on examining the motivations, activities and influencing factors on the individual's behaviours when online.

Defining the parameters 4: Internationalisation, global marketing and international marketing online

The fourth parameter relates to the Internet as an export medium and a mechanism for global competition and expansion. One of the joys of using the Internet is the global reach that can be achieved from the safety of the user's keyboard. As a virtual country without borders, the Internet is a demonstration model of Adam Smith's frictionless economy theory — until somebody attempts shipping, distribution or any other movement of physical property. Following the logistics nightmare are the financial considerations incurred in buying in a non-native currency (and hoping the exchange rates are relatively stable during longer-term or multi-transaction relationships).

In the context of this book, the terms international and global are defined in the following ways.

- *International* focuses on delivering a product (good, service or idea) primarily to internal markets, but also to a limited range of purchasers who reside outside of the home country of the producer. For example, an electronics boutique that delivers within America may include Canada, but not the UK, Europe or South-east Asia as international shipping destinations. The use of this definition of international is not exclusive to the shared border theory of international delivery so fondly espoused by numerous American e-commerce sites, but based on the notion that the company does ship outside its native borders. It occasionally just does not ship very far outside of the borders and tends to be favoured by sporadic exporters (chapters 6 and 12).

- *Global* focuses on intentionally creating an export orientation to deliver products (goods, services, ideas) to purchasers anywhere within the target market, within the Internet connected world. In contrast to international shipping, global shipping is intended to reach markets where they exist in the world (and not just the lucky Canadian ones). Having a global focus to an e-commerce site tends to orientate the business towards an export focus (chapters 6 and 15).

Internationalisation in this context is related to the fact that the consumer has the opportunity to become a sporadic (or long-term) importer of foreign goods by virtue of e-commerce. While bulk trafficking of goods into and out of a country tends to attract the attention of governments, taxation departments and customs officials, sporadic importers create global competition in markets that were previously believed to be local. MP3.com provides an odd example of a globally focused service that creates both global distribution while simultaneously creating global competition in local markets by making music from any nation available to every nation. Digitisation of services is also leading to further increases in global competition in seemingly local markets, such as programming (www.software-that-works.co.uk), graphic design (www.petersharpe.com) and professional groups such as the HTML Writers Guild (www.hwg.org). All of these high involvement, formerly high contact, services can be offered globally over the Internet. Ultimately, projects are being completed on the basis of their ability to access multiple service providers spread across the time zones. This allows for a constant work flow on a labour intensive digital product, such as a movie (www.starwars.com) or open source programming project (www.mozilla.org).

Defining the parameters 5: Post-modern consumption

It is with some degree of reluctance that post-modernism made it into this book, and featured quite so heavily in the discussion of cybercommunities (chapter 5) and web site design (chapter 10). The reluctance is based largely on the knowledge that any use of post-modernism leads inexorably to the moment where it has to be defined in writing, despite the fact post-modernism seems inherently designed to avoid being comprehensively labelled and defined. It seems remarkably modernist to attempt to scientifically measure post-modernism, and (at the risk of an inherent paradox), post-modernism will not be defined in isolation. This is not a case of passing the buck, but using post-modernism where it is useful for understanding an Internet marketing (and sociological) phenomenon referred to as **post-modern consumption**. Post-modern consumption, in the online world, works on the idea that the individual can create and define themselves through their use, purchase, consumption and even creation of goods and services in the online environment. In the online world, identity has to be manually constructed, either through the use of an avatar or by some other representation (chapter 4). Avatars can range from basic graphical representations in a cybercommunity (www.thepalace.com), through to complex, graphically rich characters in a multi-player gaming environment (www.heat.net), or as a text-based description within a multi-user environment (www.mudconnector.com).

In the marketing context, post-modern consumption takes the power of image creation from the marketer and returns it to the users for an extended period. Consumers can create and define themselves through the consumption of key icons such as Nike shirts (www.nike.com), while wearing Airwalk shoes (www.airwalk.com) and listening to their high technology MP3 player wristwatches (www.casio.com/audio) as they order an Italian dinner (www.pizzahut.com.au) from home and work on a global product (www.mozilla.org). This is nothing new to the marketing world, nor is it new to post-modernism. Mixing and matching the culture, serving your own blend and having it your way is not just limited to good coffee shops (www.gloria jeans.com) and Hungry Jacks outlets (www.hungryjacks.com.au). Much of contemporary marketing theory alternates between bemoaning the death of segmentation, the overabundance of market fragmentation and celebrating the existence of niche marketing. The fundamental shifts in marketing in recent times have seen an explosion of post-modern theories and explanations that more than adequately address the basic issues of the fragmentation of the marketplace.

What makes post-modern consumption on the Internet somewhat more difficult to address is that the consumer, in the digital world, can become the producer of their own identity. Even at the most basic level, the selection of the log-in name for their first Internet account can be used as a point to construct a new identity. The decision to choose 'firstname_surname@serviceprovider .co.uk' or 'warbeast@serviceprovider.co.nz' provides the consumer with ample opportunity to construct a new online persona for themselves.

The beauty of the Internet is the speed and ease with which an individual can re-create themselves to be someone, something or somebody other than themselves. Below is an example of how to create an online persona that can be used as an avatar. Some of the steps may require more advanced skills, others seem relatively commonsense and basic, but all aim to ultimately create a new persona.

Step 1: Choose your objective. There are numerous methods of self-creation online, all of which have a specific outcome, such as role play (MUDs) or anonymous chatting (www.chatcity.com). In this case, the objective is to create a multipurpose persona for chat, web site and email.

Step 2: Establish a base camp. The first port of call in the reconstruction is to pick up a new email account, either through Hotmail (www.hotmail.com), Mail.com, or similar web-based mail providers. The purpose of this account is to provide a central point to construct your identity. (Anyone found spamming from their constructed identity will be asked to leave.) Create this account, using a newly created user name for your new persona. Those struggling with creativity are advised to visit a random name generator for helpful suggestions.

Step 3: Pick your point of origin. Most of the major web portals, such as Yahoo!, offer internationalised services (uk.yahoo.com), which can be used to attain region-specific email. Signing up to a regional account can allow the new persona to acquire an instant set of regional characteristics (English/German/Spanish) depending on the selected account. Using Yahoo.co.nz and selecting 'personalise' results in being offered a Yahoo! ID.

Step 4: Create a new you. Sign into the Yahoo! account, filling out the requisite details and stating your new user name. This is the final point of construction for the avatar to be used in post-modern consumption. We now have two fully operational email accounts, a user identity and a passport into a new world of post-modern consumption.

Step 5: Re-create the new you. Following the creation of identity, engage in post-modern consumption by customising the product offering presented by My Yahoo's approximately 50 different customisation options. Once the customisation process commences, you are now defining who your avatar is on the basis of their preferences.

Step 6: Add features. The advantage to using Yahoo! as a mechanism for post-modern consumption is their wide, integrated base of services, which include web pages through Geocities (geocities.yahoo.com), address books, auctions, calendars, classifieds, clubs, finance and shopping. Just about the only thing your avatar should not be able to do is apply for credit. At this point, the services you choose to use can be used to define your avatar. Will they make use of the online finance services and the customisable stock reports to stay ahead of the market? Has the avatar been developed for chat and social exchange? If this is the case, customise the services to use online address books, messenger systems and personal alerts to warn of new mail.

(continued)

This is a basic, six-step method to create a new Internet persona. However, this only scratches the surface of the possibilities for developing avatars. Post-modern consumption in the online world of avatars also requires the user to give back to the digital landscape. To fully flesh out the avatar, some developmental work on their web site would be needed, if only to provide a set of frequented links to demonstrate their interests in the Web.

Constructing a persona, creating avatars and post-modern consumption are not limited to the Internet. However, the Internet is a fertile ground for exploring and accessing the materials needed for post-modern consumption, given that all users start out anonymously and inherently equal until they can establish a reputation, either by their actions, words or consumption. Post-modern consumption takes the power of defining the consumer away from market segmentation and presents it back to the consumer. In this context, post-modernism on the Internet remains as incomprehensible as it is off-line. However, it has application to consumer behaviour, which is explored further in chapters 5 and 10.

 # Cultural considerations

Cyberspace is not an alien culture, although it does like to sell books about itself with that pitch. When the Internet first met the general public, there was a concern that the Internet was skewed towards white, middle class, educated, American males and that the Internet was simply American culture on a computer monitor. Some of these fears and assumptions were true and others required further examination. The Internet began with a distinct culture that was steeped heavily in ritual, tradition, myth and slightly inexplicable behaviour (at least it was inexplicable to outsiders). The culture of the Internet has survived the arrival of the great unplugged masses, put up with America On-line (AOL) and even accepted Microsoft (not willingly or without holding some grudges). The only major threat facing this culture is the lack of willingness shown by many aspects of commerce to respect its existence.

The Internet culture

If describing post-modernism is difficult, describing the Internet culture makes it look easy. The Internet supports a common culture much in the same way Europe supports a common culture of being 'European'. Within the Internet, there are many tribal cultures that are as rich and diverse as any good cultural cross sample that can be extracted from any country. Snippets and insights into aspects of the Internet culture have been provided when and where needed throughout the text. However, the following section attempts to give an overview of the more common elements of the culture.

- *The gift economy.* This represents those members of the community who build their reputation by what they can give to the community. Respect in these environments is earned by the skills, prowess, abilities and 'gifts' that are freely distributed to the community by their developer (Raymond 1999). The impact of the gift economy aspect of the Internet is examined in greater detail in chapter 11.

- *No central authority.* Whether the Internet was designed to withstand a nuclear strike or not, it was designed with the goal of creating workable chaos by removing the need for a central controlling authority structure. As far as a defensive mechanism goes, this is just about perfect and fool-proof, as the Internet had no single vulnerable point. Instead, it had so many vulnerable points people could never decide which one to attack. The open, unregulated and anarchy-by-consensus nature of the early Internet also established a cultural dislike for centralised authority and controlling mechanisms that sought to limit and restrain the Internet.

- *Authority figures welcome.* Of course, the added confusion of the Internet culture has led to a widespread deference to authority figures. These figures derive their authority from superior knowledge, such as the **alpha geek**, or by having a generally accepted position in Internet society as a leader. Like decentralised networks, nobody truly owns the Internet (although parentage was blamed on several key figures, most of whom sought reliable alibis). The annoyance for late arrivals to the Internet who were used to being offline authority figures was that this new culture frequently failed to notice that they were supposed to be in awe or fear of the newcomer. Anarchism with authority figures (every revolution needs a Bob Dylan or two) has permeated the Internet to the extent that it is starting to impact on the offline world, with revised business models attempting to create (and replicate) these effects in mainstream society.

- *Digital taboo.* One of the most misunderstood elements of the Internet is the idea that it is a wild, lawless frontier where anything goes (and everything did). The Internet is full of protocols, taboos and social values which were developed to preserve and protect the Internet from internal attack. Some of these social values were originally derived from technical considerations, whereas others developed from the need to keep the peace in an environment with no centralised authority. Self-regulation and social pressure (with the occasional vigilante activity) has managed to keep the Internet from needing massive external regulation.

- *The IT culture.* If you create a distributed network of computers, you will need a distributed network of computer engineers, programmers and computer literate people to use, maintain and service the system. The intellectual infrastructure that makes the Internet exist was spawned from an environment dominated by scientists, engineers, academics, programmers, government employees and military personnel. With this in mind, it should not come as a surprise to find a hardcore culture of acronyms, incomprehensible jokes and best, worst and most common grounds between all of the involved cultures. The only thing less comprehensible would have been an Internet developed by scholars, philosophers, art and library studies critics with an underpinning culture equally as baffling, but slightly more readable to outsiders.

■ *Creation of value as a cultural norm.* The final influential aspect of Internet culture is the need for activity to create a form of value for an end user. Much of the criticism of early e-commerce and a large portion of the dislike of spam comes from the lack of value associated with unsolicited commercial activity. Most Internet users have to bear any costs of advertising they encounter, either by added time taken for the download or added traffic. Consequently, the onus of demonstrating value falls onto the marketer to demonstrate that their promotional message creates value to the user, not just the marketer. Nobody has yet demonstrated that an unsolicited email for an unwanted product can actually create value (financial, psychic or otherwise) for an annoyed email user.

The major consideration to keep in mind when dealing with the Internet is to take the same precautions as would be taken when entering any new market which has an established culture, society and a population in the many millions.

Summary

The definition and domain of the Internet are broad and complex areas better suited to a book on that topic alone. The materials presented here are the establishing shots and character development phases of such a book, and are provided to give context to the main body of marketing theory and application. Overviews of key concepts which have first been aired in this section will occur when and where necessary in later chapters to reinforce their importance to the reader. In addition, issues such as the impact of marketing's role in Internet culture will be addressed throughout the text as it becomes necessary (and visible).

Discussion questions

2.1 Does the need to learn a new language of terms, concepts and ideas hinder or enhance marketing's transition to the online world?

2.2 Does marketing have a role to play in the development of the infrastructure of the Internet? Discuss, using an example.

2.3 How valid is the notion of cyberspace as a place? What impact does the assumption of physicality in cyberspace have for marketing?

2.4 Which is more important — the philosophy, strategy or tactics of marketing?

2.5 What are the key differences between international and global marketing on the Internet? Find examples of sites that engage in global, international and local marketing.

2.6 How can marketers take advantage of the ease of creating an identity on the Internet? Does post-modern consumption and the ease of creating a new identity undermine the value of market segmentation?

2.7 Outline the key cultural considerations involved with marketing in the Internet culture. How different is Internet culture from your own culture? What adjustments to your marketing would you need to make to adapt to the new cultural environment?

References

Berners-Lee, T. 1990, 'Information Management: A Proposal', www.w3.org/History/1989/proposal.html

Dann, S. & Dann, S. 1998, 'Cybercommuning: Global village halls', *Advances in Consumer Research*, vol. 70.

Gibson, W. 1984, *Neuromancer*, Ace Books, New York.

Hoffman, D. L. & Novak, T. P. 1996, 'Marketing in hypermedia computer-mediated environments: Conceptual foundations', *Journal of Marketing*, vol. 60, no. 3, July, pp. 50–68.

Kaye, A. 1991, 'Learning together apart'. In A. Kaye (Ed.), *Collaborative Learning Through Computer Conferencing: The Najaden Papers* (pp. 1–24), Springer-Verlag, Berlin.

Montoya-Weiss, M., Massey, A. & Clapper, D. 1998, 'Online focus groups: Conceptual issues and a research tool', *European Journal of Marketing*, vol. 32, no. 7/8, pp. 713–23.

Munzer, T. 1997, 'H3: Laying out large directed graphs in 3D hyperbolic space', 1997 IEEE Symposium on Information Visualisation, October 20–21, Phoenix, AZ, pp. 2–10 (http://www-graphics.stanford.edu/papers/h3/)

Novak, T., Hoffman, D. & Yung, Y. F. 1998, 'Measuring the flow construct in online environments: A structural modelling approach', http://www2000.ogsm.vanderbilt.edu/papers/flow_construct/measuring_flow_construct.html

Raymond, E. S. 1999, *The Cathedral and the Bazaar*, O'Reilly, Sebastopol.

Rowley, J. 1996, 'Retailing and shopping on the Internet', *Internet Research: Electronic Networking Applications and Policy*, vol. 6, no. 1, pp. 81–91.

Shih, C.-f. 1998, 'Conceptualising consumer experience in cyberspace', *European Journal of Marketing*, vol. 32, no. 7/8, pp. 655–63.

Spalter, M. 1996, 'Maintaining a customer focus in an interactive age?'. In E. Forrest & R. Mizerski (Eds), *Interactive Marketing: The Future Present*, NTC Business Books, Lincolnwood, IL.

Steuer, J. 1992, 'Defining virtual reality: Dimensions determining telepresence', *Journal of Communication*, vol. 42, no. 4, pp. 73–93.

Varey, R. J. 1999, 'Marketing, media and McLuhan: Rereading the prophet at century's end', *Journal of Marketing*, vol. 63, no. 3, pp. 148–54.

Watson, R. T., Akselsen, S. & Pitt, L. F. 1998, 'Attractors: Building mountains in the flat landscape of the Internet', *California Management Review*, vol. 40, no. 2, pp. 36–56.

Weiber & Kollman 1998, 'Competitive advantages in virtual markets — perspectives of "information-based marketing" in cyberspace', *European Journal of Marketing*, vol. 32, no. 7/8, pp. 603–15.

Web sites

cospace.research.att.com
geocities.yahoo.com
www.airwalk.com
www.casio.com/audio
www.chatcity.com
www.cybergeography.com
www.gloriajeans.com
www.heat.net
www.heretherebemonsters.com
www.hotmail.com
www.hungryjacks.com.au
www.hwg.org
www.idsoftware.com
www.itl.nist.gov/iaui/vvrg/index.html
www.mozilla.org
www.mudconnector.com
www.nike.com
www.petersharpe.com
www.pizzahut.com.au
www.software-that-works.co.uk
www.starwars.com
www.thepalace.com
www.thepalace.com/help/
www.w3.org/History/1989/proposal.html
nz.yahoo.com
uk.yahoo.com

part 2

New marketing strategies for the new media

■ **3**...*Unique features of Internet-based marketing* ■ **4**...*Consumer behaviour* ■ **5**...*Creating cybercommunities* ■ **6**...*Applications for business and non-business* ■ **7**...*Internet in marketing strategy*

The second section of the book examines the involvement of marketing in this new medium and the new environments of the Internet. The five chapters take a holistic approach of overviewing the integration and application of marketing through the Internet. These chapters integrate the philosophical level of marketing theory, with an emphasis on understanding and meeting customer needs, and integrating the marketing orientation with the involvement in the Internet. **Chapter 3** overviews the unique features of the Internet in comparison to existing marketing media, and looks at reasons for being (or not being) part of the digital marketplace. **Chapter 4** examines the human aspect of the Internet in outlining the consumer behaviour aspects of the Internet. This section of the text examines the motivations for use of the Internet, specific behaviours associated with the use of the medium and reasons individuals do not adopt the new technologies. **Chapter 5** examines the social clanning aspects of the Internet by reviewing the cybercommunity concept, both from a social and marketing perspective. This section explores the nature of communications online, and how marketing can facilitate the creation and evolution of cybercommunities. **Chapter 6** outlines how the Internet can be used for business and government purposes. **Chapter 7** gives an overview of the process of setting objectives and the issues of implementing marketing strategies on the Internet.

3

Unique
features of
Internet-
based
marketing

'The Internet provides
the opportunity to offer
product or service
features that cannot be
done in the "real"
world.'

Breitenbach, C. S. and van
Doren, D. C. 1998, 'Value
added marketing in the digital
domain: Enhancing the utility
of the Internet', *Journal of
Consumer Marketing*, vol. 15,
no. 6, pp. 558–75.

LEARNING *objectives*

After reading this chapter, you should be able to:

- identify how the unique features of Internet marketing differ from traditional marketing

- recognise the different types of marketing web sites that can be implemented for an online marketing presence

- explain how the distinct characteristics of the Internet can be used for marketing purposes

- understand the attractors and inhibitors to use of the Internet by business

- recognise the changes which have taken place in consumer responses to marketing since the advent of the Internet

- recognise opportunities for business marketers in the computer-mediated environment of the Internet

- outline the types of offline services that have successfully adapted to the online environment.

Introduction

One of the most common complaints about the Internet is that it is not television, the newspaper and radio combined into a convenient media buyer-ready package for advertisers, marketers and market researchers to use. The Internet developed in a haphazard manner. Technology was implemented along the criteria of whether it was new, did something different or had technical merit. In summary, the Internet was not designed for commerce.

E-commerce is developing using a similar process of incremental ad hocery, with emphasis being placed on doing what looks new, rather than what might work best for the environment. Thus far, it has been a case of click and miss as marketers struggle to adapt offline promotional techniques, pricing policies, logistics chains, and research tools to the online world. For many marketers, going onto the Internet has been approached without taking the usual precautionary steps for entering a new market. The Internet is new, the environment is unique. Quite a few of the early online commerce attempts had the Internet equivalent of a house dropped on them for breaches of Internet custom, usually for offences related to spamming.

However, the news is not all bad. The rapid commercialisation of the Web, and the benefits associated with careful use of the unique features of the Internet can deliver substantial rewards. The major differentiating factor between success and failure in the new environment is the degree to which the marketer takes advantage of the features of the Internet which differentiate it from 'traditional' media. The purpose of this chapter is to outline five of the most important new features of Internet-based marketing, and how these can be used to the advantage of the marketer. The section also overviews the historical development of marketing online, how it has progressed, and what impact online marketing has had on the consumer.

The (r)evolution of online marketing

Evolution and revolution are words most commonly applied to the new face of commerce online. Evolution represents a gradual change and adaptation to a new environment, where the ideas, practices and models best suited to the new world survive, grow stronger and propagate. Revolution either means we are going around in circles, or a period of dramatic upheaval, where change seems to be the only constant feature. All three definitions seem equally applicable to marketing's approach to electronic commerce.

Marketing has tended to view cyberspace as an unlimited marketspace for commercial use, with the consumers being fair game in the pursuit of profit (Venkatesh 1998). Not surprisingly, the consumer does not always share this view of being a profit waiting to be harvested. Cyberspace, being a consensual hallucination between millions of users, exists as a multitude of environments, both commercial and aesthetic, as well as being public, private and community space (Gibson 1984; Venkatesh 1998). In a world of multiple environments, marketing has evolved through several phases to get to where it is today.

Evolution of online marketing

Online marketing is still a phenomenon which is adapting and evolving in an attempt to effectively take advantage of the unique features of the online environment. These are the features which differentiate online from traditional marketing activity. This text takes the view that evolutionary marketing practice is that which continues to develop through strengths and advantages while learning more about the environment in which it operates. Terms such as evolution are seen as the best metaphors to describe the adoption of new, effective ideas and techniques to address the online consumer's behaviour, needs and wants.

Since the first commercial web sites appeared in the early 1990s usually they have been developed in one of three distinct styles — information publishing, transaction sites or mass customised web experiences. **Information publishing** represents a web site at its most basic, where the content is the experience, and the emphasis is on the provision of information. **Transactional sites** exist for the purpose of facilitating an exchange of any form, usually buying, but more recently for selling as well. **Mass customisation** is where the content and experience of the web site is tailored to the individual user, based on their established usage histories, demographics and other provided information.

The evolution of these styles can be traced to two things — the development of web technology and the development of marketing understanding. When the Web was first popularised, the closest thing to interactive content was the <blink> tags and the occasional animated graphic over slow modem connections. With subsequent developments in interactive technologies, and bandwidth connections, the Web slowly shifted towards a more interactive focus with transactional and customised sites. At the same time the technology was developing, marketing's understanding of what made a decent, let alone good, web site was rapidly evolving to the point of being able to find useful marketing implementations for the new technologies.

1. Information publishing (content provision/interactive brochure)

The first style of online marketing sites is where the organisation uses web pages as pure information sources. In most cases companies still begin their web presence in this way. The responsibility for web development is left in the hands of the IT technicians with little if any input from the marketing division. One of the common trends noted in the development of web sites was illustrated by Murphy (1998) who observed that companies which had a significant offline presence began their web presence using informational web sites. Such sites tended to be linear and very text heavy. Communication is one way and in effect, all such sites serve to provide is an online brochure. While information dissemination will always play a role in online marketing activity it is rarely sufficient for an organisation to rely on a purely informational approach.

Many companies relied on simply migrating existing public relations materials, such as annual reports, company mission statements and press releases, onto the web site. Of course, companies not paying close attention to the nature of the web page found themselves directing their 'readers' to page numbers rather than hyperlinks. In addition, at certain points in the development of corporate web sites, it was easier to see the CEO's vision statement than it was to buy the product for which the company was having such a glorious vision. Questions of corporate confidentiality did eventually emerge, with some corporations flatly denying having ever published confidential corporate mission statements online, even when the aforementioned mission statement, complete with URL, was read back to a company spokesperson.

In contemporary web design, information-based sites still have a purpose and place in web marketing. Although the sites are becoming rarer, they can be valuable for providing specific-purpose, static, instructional materials, such as download or installation instructions which have little, if any, room for customisation. As stand-alone sites, these are less common, although information-based pages frequently make up the core of the more sophisticated transaction and customisation web sites.

2. Transactional sites

Once a web presence has been established, the next step for many companies is to conduct transactions online. Unlike information-based web pages which, due to advances in software design, are relatively easy to design in house, transaction-based systems require complex programming skills. It is neither the intention nor the purpose of this book to describe the programming required to develop a good e-commerce transaction solution. The basic requirement for a successful transaction-based system is a secure interface between the external web page and a back-end computer system designed to validate transactions and manage inventories. Transaction systems can either be housed locally by the company, through a service provider, for example, www.webcentral.com.au or through a virtual merchant system such as Yahoo! Store (www.siteyahoo.com/site/).

For marketing, transactional web sites assume the operation of Bagozzi's (1975) exchange theory, where value is exchanged for value. This may be as obvious as cash for goods from the virtual store, or the exchange of goods for service or services for goods in a bartering network. Less obvious is the exchange of market research registration data for entry into a cybercommunity. The user exchanges his or her demographic details for the benefits of membership and involvement in the cybercommunity, or access to a customised interactive service. Transactional sites are also less dependent on content as the content tends to be self-generating (for the successful sites) in conditions such as online auction houses such as E-bay (www.ebay.com).

The fundamental difference between a content orientation and a transactional site is the requirements on the organisation running the site. Content sites require a constant rate of newly generated content to remain fresh, and attractive to returning customers. However, unlike transaction sites, content sites are not required to operate consistently at real-time speeds. In the case of auction houses, or other e-commerce trading, the expectation of immediate real-time transactions increases the demand on the server equipment and support staff. Offering a real-time auction system on a **24–7 (24 hour 7 day a week)** rotation requires that the site be operational, available and fully functional for the entire 24–7 time period. Content sites can shut down for several hours to perform major service overhauls. This is not recommended for real-time transaction sites.

Content versus transaction has also been a point for cataloguing individual web sites into 'genres'. O'Connor and O'Keefe (1997) identified six genres of web sites based on their content or transactional orientation. These are illustrated in figure 3.1.

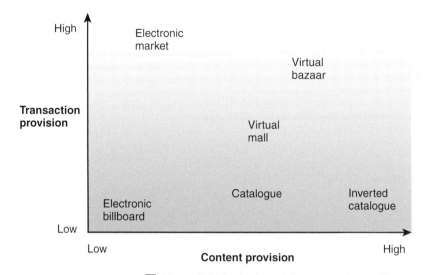

Figure 3.1 Content provision versus transaction provision
Source: O'Connor, G. C. and O'Keefe, B. 1997, 'Viewing the Web as a marketplace: The case of small companies', *Decision Support Systems*, vol. 21, no. 3, p. 178.

- *Electronic billboards* are the basic entry level web sites which consist mostly of static content describing who the company is and what it sells for a living. Some of the more sophisticated sites, particularly those dealing with real world products in the virtual world, offer downloadable accessories such as screensavers, desktop themes and images (for example, www.coke.com).

- *Catalogues* offer the additional facility to order products directly from the web site without needing to access an intermediary or local dealership. Virtual catalogues offer the advantage of being able to link in real time to inventory systems so users can see the number of items available to them, and can tell if a product is out of stock before they choose to order (for example, www.computerstore.com.au).

- *Inverted catalogue* is the virtual catalogue in reverse, so to speak, as it offers a range of free information on a given subject, then has the materials available for sale at the end of the product information. In contrast to the virtual catalogue which is upfront and blatant about being a sales tool, the inverted catalogue gives free information out as a lure to bring the customer to the point of purchase link at the bottom of the page. Many music review sites offer reviews, band information, and then the opportunity to purchase from either the site or an affiliated music distribution site.

- *Virtual malls* are defined as web stores hosted on a dedicated e-commerce server, with a dedicated linking marketplace web site, joining the diverse store systems together. Yahoo!Store (store.yahoo.com) offers dedicated e-commerce servers with or without the cybermall functionality — mostly, however, it is up to the individual owners to make their web presence felt. In contrast, the aptly named Cybermall (www.cybermall.com) offers the opportunity to have the e-commerce web sites linked together in a more traditional mall style arrangement, clustered by primary sales markets (children, maternity) or primary products (toys, clothing). The virtual malls are consumer focused, in contrast to the business to business orientation of the virtual bazaar.

- **Virtual bazaars** are regarded as business to business focal points where businesses can gather to exchange information, services, and buy and sell goods, either through cash, barter or trade arrangements (for example, www.b2b.com).
- **Electronic markets/auctions** represent the ultimate Internet paradox — a web site which has the function of being the sort of intermediary that the Internet was theoretically supposed to wipe out. Electronic markets are also the pinnacle of interaction–transaction web sites as the site host provides only the forums for exchange. The content is generated by the users interacting with each other through the host's virtual environment. In effect, the reason for using an electronic market is to access other users, rather than the market itself. The market merely plays host to the interactions between people rather than being the primary point of attraction. E-markets can range from cybercommunities and information exchanges (for example, www.InsideTheWeb.com) through to virtual auctions (for example, www.ebay.com).

All six web site types represent one or more of the first two styles of Internet marketing web sites. These tend to be represented by the distinctive design issues related to the purpose and intent of the site. Informational sites can be easily identified by their text-focused, brochure-like design, and the distinct impression that this site exists as a paper document somewhere in the company's reception area. Transactional sites, on the other hand, give the impression of interactivity, to the extent that buying from a range of products represents a meaningful interaction. The third type of site also has a distinctive web site design in addition to which it incorporates the first attempt to modify marketing to the Internet.

3. Mass customisation

Mass customisation takes full advantage of the capabilities of Internet technology to store information and create systems which are able to personalise messages and services for individual consumers. Such customisation may be implemented either automatically or manually. Automatic customisation allows tailored content to be delivered to the user on the basis of their past surfing behaviours at the site. Manual customisation requires that users specify in advance what content they wish to view through the use of presets and filters. While automatic customisation has many benefits of convenience for the consumer, its use is somewhat controversial in terms of privacy issues.

One of the major discoveries concerning privacy and mass customisation was the need for open disclosure by the web site that details were being recorded for customisation purposes. Ovans (1999) reports on a study which found that individuals are more likely to buy products which display a level of customisation, if they have voluntarily given the information used for the customisation. In contrast, users were actively hostile towards the same information being used if they themselves had not directly entered the data. The study in question noted also that people are quite happy to give the same information to a computer that they would to a stranger (the test administrator in this case). Information control is a necessary part of extending the user's feelings of power in a computer-mediated transaction. It is one thing to be remembered at a web site where you have been before — it is a totally alienating experience to be greeted by first name as a long-lost friend at a site you have never visited before.

Mass customisation exists also in the deployment of information and services. Microsoft's Window's Update service offers users the opportunity to nominate which areas of software update are of interest to them, and will show only the updates from these selected areas. Portals such as Excite (www.excite.com.au), Yahoo! (www.yahoo.com) and Go.com (www.go.com) offer the opportunity to selectively modify the portal front page, from personal greetings and horoscopes to saved searches and customised news feeds. All of this is done on the basis of user-supplied information that represents a time investment for the user (inputting) and a marketing opportunity for value-added service for the business. However, simply saying hello does not necessarily guarantee success, or a purchase. The customisation must add something of value to the user's experience of the web site, either through reduction of the information overload and clutter, or by remembering preferences and regular orders.

While the types of sites outlined above are presented as sequential, it is not necessary for an organisation to pass through all steps. Similarly, there are many companies on the Web who, for various reasons, have chosen to remain with an information publishing focus. The style of a web site and its features should reflect the nature of the product and company sponsoring the site, and be designed to achieve the specific objectives set for the web-based component of the marketing strategy. Leong, Huang and Stanners (1998) pointed out that the Internet is primarily a rational medium, where information is more effective than emotion in that more information can be displayed based on the user's interests and needs. It is relatively easy to establish a structure of information from casual interest through to deep geek technical knowledge. It is slightly more complex to have 'casual emotional attachment' through to 'deep affection' settings for a web site.

It must be remembered that web sites are complementary media in that they are most valuable when supporting a marketing campaign rather than driving it. A supporting site to a multiple media television, radio and print campaign can be developed to provide detailed product information, downloadable samples of the advertising and strong brand image reinforcement through site design and imagery. Hollywood discovered this approach to movie promotion through information sites to support blockbusters such as 'The Matrix' (www.whatisthematrix.com) where detailed information concerning actors, directors, scripting and other materials are housed, along with downloadable promotional materials such as screensavers, and movie trailers.

Unique features of the Internet compared to other media

One of the early mistakes online marketers made was to not fully appreciate, or take advantage of, the unique characteristics of the Internet which make it such a powerful tool. As outlined in the evolution of Internet marketing, many organisations use their web pages simply as an alternative form of publication with nothing to distinguish them from the printed copy except for a reduction in certain costs.

Effective web-based marketing requires organisations to fully explore the following benefits of the Internet and incorporate these features as appropriate into their marketing strategies. Five unique areas of Internet benefits have emerged across time from a variety of authors:

- **interactivity**, which is the degree to which the user can interact with the web site in a meaningful manner beyond following internal hyperlinks.
- **variety and customisation** are the levels of change, interaction and customised content that can occur on a web site.
- **global access**, which recognises the international nature of the medium, and how local web sites have a global presence.
- **time independence** is the ability of many features of the Internet to be accessed around the clock, seven days a week without the need for a physical or personal presence staffing the web site.
- **interest driven**, which is the extent to which the Internet is a pull medium where online experiences are based on the active seeking out of the items of interest rather than the passive acceptance of whatever push media delivers to the screen.

Interactivity

The greatest advantage Internet-based marketing offers is its potential for interactivity. Promotional activities on the Internet combine the advantages of the single message, mass communication technique of advertising with the potential for individualised service akin to personal selling offline. At the discretion of the potential customer, web sites can move between being passive to active information sources.

Interactivity is defined as the ability to address an individual, gather and receive a response, remember that response, and tailor the next response on the basis of the received information (Ghose & Dou 1998). The greater the interaction between the consumer and the web site, the higher the level of involvement which in turn increases brand loyalty and likelihood of purchase. Being able to interact with the web site does not require a complex AI system. Interactive systems can be as basic as recognising a customer's mailing address if they have previously purchased from the company, through to the complexity of **collaborative filtering systems (CFS)**. CFS have been implemented in several genre-based sales sites like Amazon.com. The secret of the CFS approach is that the interactivity is derived from the consumers completing the database for the organisation. The customer feels they gain value from the recommendations that they pay for by providing the market research data that fuels the system.

When it comes to web site customisation, everybody likes to think that they are unique creatures with individual tastes and habits. Given that we all think alike in this most fundamental belief about individuality, it is not surprising to know that we share common tastes, and collective opinions are rampant among people of similar personality. In the early 1990s, the Helpful Online Musical Recommendation system set out to take advantage of musical tastes over demographic profiles. Using collaborative filtering software, HOMR could recommend albums to the user based on the match between their tastes and other users' tastes. HOMR evolved into the Firefly Network which expanded the range of options available through the collaborative software into books, films, community, web sites and eventually, to other members of the community. In 1997, Firefly was sold to the Microsoft Corporation where they integrated the technology into the Microsoft Passport system.

However, Firefly is not alone in the marketplace. Amazon.com, using Grouplens software, promotes its services of 'if you like that, you'll love this' recommendation system. Customers are given suggestions as to other authors, topics and books that may be of interest, based on the purchasing patterns of previous Amazon.com customers.

Macromedia is offering an off-the-shelf collaborative filtering software system called Likeminds. What began life as a complex proprietary software system has become an off-the-shelf plug and play solution to creating interactive, user driven web sites that recommend more than just themselves to the user. Likeminds also integrates web commerce solutions with recommendation systems in that it can track the processes, clickstream and browsing choices of the user prior to their purchase. When a similar set of processes is identified, the site can offer a solution, based on prior purchasers, to the current user. The Firefly-Likeminds systems add a level of interactivity to the web site that goes beyond recognising the user's name and previous choices into creating value added anticipation systems. If the customer likes that, chances are they will like the site.

················■ Based on www.andromedia.com/products/likeminds/index.html
www.cs.umn/Research/GroupLens/

Holloway, M. 1997 'Pattie'. *Wired* 5.12 December
www.wired.com/wired/archives/5.12/maes pr.html

There are three phases in the development of web-based interactivity in the marketing process:

- *one-way communication*: using the traditional advertising models of one-to-many communications
- *partial interactivity*: using limited direct mail-style feedback systems such as 1-800 numbers and email feedback systems
- *full interactivity*: with bells, whistles and full interaction between consumer, the web site, and the organisation.

Phase 1: One-way communication

Linked in with the first phase of web site design, the interaction with the consumer is simply an extension of the mass communication approach typical of advertising. Information is static and one way with a single message to all consumers. It is in the domain of the electronic billboard, or where the organisation feels that it really ought to be online because everyone else is, but do not have any idea what to do with the site. One common tell-tale sign of a one-way web site is any site that says 'Call our toll free number' in place of offering an email address. In an age of dial-up modems, the user's phone line is already busy — they are not about to disconnect to ring you up to find out about your company. They are more likely to try a different web site. The absolute basic level of interactivity that must appear on a web site is an email address that leads to a staff member of the organisation — if for no other reason than to maintain a semblance of interactive credibility.

Phase 2: Partial interactivity

Under partial interactivity the potential exists for one-on-one communications to develop between the marketer and the consumer. This is usually achieved through the use of email and is the online equivalent of making a phone query. It is a surprisingly effective method of generating goodwill and leading to a sale. Email has a strong tie into word of mouth and personal selling in its effectiveness with regards to reducing prepurchase perceptions of risk and complexity. In particular, sites selling high-risk, complex or subjective products, such as artworks, have found that having just a basic level of email contact has led to additional sales. Many users found that being able to talk to the artists, ask questions and get a range of short responses over a period of time helped reduce the perceived risk of online buying. The presence of an email address, and email interaction also brought a human element into an otherwise impersonal sales event.

Phase 3: Full interactivity

More advanced web sites now offer consumers the potential to be fully engaged in an interactive, virtual community of like-minded individuals. Under full interactivity **one-to-many-to-one communications** are possible, not only with the marketer responsible for the web site, but also with other users through discussion groups. While the marketer may monitor, and to a certain extent direct, the flow and content of communications, the fully interactive site offers the greatest potential for client involvement with the overall marketing process. Ideas suggested in conversation can be used as a trigger for market research, new product development and so on. Interactive sites can offer value-added events for the consumer after the point of purchase, including after sales support, and new product use ideas resulting from the shared experiences of other users.

There is a range of ways in which opportunities for interactivity can be incorporated into the web site. Ghose and Dou (1998) outlined over 20 different options in five categories:

- online feedback systems that include site surveys, product surveys, suggestion boxes, message board systems and email addresses. Any point at which the user is given an opportunity to submit a message to the company through their web site constitutes a feedback mechanism (www.coke.com/cgi-bin/survey/survey.cgi).

- self-service functions whereby the user selects the feature they want to access from the site. This can be used for software downloads, upgrades and repairs, database-driven advice systems, and automated online sales (support.microsoft.com). Adding searchable, frequently asked question lists also reduces the demand on online technical support staff as users are given the opportunity to see if they have encountered a common problem that is easily fixed.
- eye candy, which relates to the visually stimulating interactive content such as multimedia displays, VR presentations, push or streaming media, and online games (www.shockwave.com).
- discounts, prizes and coupons relate to any interaction whereby the user has the potential outcome of gaining something for nothing, a discount or a cost reduction from purchasing at the web site, either directly (www.cdnow.com) or through a third party (for example, www.incredibledvd.com/coupons.html). These are covered in detail in chapter 8.
- user groups relate to the web site-based cybercommunities. This can take forms as basic as email subscription lists for regular product updates and sales notices to anything as complex as a virtual support community consisting of other users of the products. Web sites run by video games companies have produced some of the most impressive user group-based interactive web sites by hosting add-ons and user-created supplements to the commercial product through their web sites (www.homeworld.org). Adding end user-based discussion forums also increases user involvement with the product, even at the point of prepurchase, as they can see an available forum for help and advice in the event of difficulties with the product.

Variety and customisation

Layering of information and pages within the web site provides the visitor with the opportunity of varying and customising each experience with the organisation. Depending on the user's familiarity with the company, its products, and the design of its web site, visits may be directed immediately to a specific purpose, such as ordering an item, or may involve more extensive investigation for information gathering and product comparison purposes.

Variety

Updating and changing elements of the site on a regular basis maintains the interest of regular visitors and encourages them to return. Static web sites which do not change over time and which are linear in terms of their presentation of data tend not to attract repeat visitors. In particular, nothing is more frustrating to a web surfer than repeat visits to a site that promises to be available 'next week', for anything up to a period of six months. On the other hand, while site updates should have a high frequency, site restructures should be minimised, or held over for major events (such as new year, new product launches or new business ventures). While variety is a much needed element of a web site, consistency is a critical element in web site navigation. It is frustrating to return to a site and to have to relearn how to find commonly used features on the site as it has just been 'updated' into a new format. It is like opening the newspaper to find sport on the front page, finance on the back and news in the comics lift-out. It causes unnecessary user anxiety and should be minimised in favour of regular content updates rather than layout changes.

Customisation

The power to direct the flow of information and receive only valued content is a major attraction for consumers. Consumer empowerment in terms of determining what information is required and how it will be accessed, combined with the freedom to choose when it will be enacted upon, gives a new dimension to the buyer behaviour process. Customisation of information helps users gain a sense of control and ownership over their web site experience, especially if customised web sites offer additional value, such as storing transaction histories, or remembering shipping addresses (Arunkundram & Sundararajan 1998). Most information portals offer customisation (mypage.go.com) which includes news filtering, and other custom services.

Customisation of a web site is not limited to interaction with the web pages. Several streaming audio sites offer the opportunity to program their own virtual radio stations (www.live365.com), and make live requests to online radio (www.discjockey.com). Other organisations such as RealNetworks (www.real.com) have integrated customised streaming media channels into their RealPlayer software. Even Microsoft offers the option of a highly customisable streaming content system through the Windows 98 desktop and Internet Explorer. Mass customisation has become more viable as **narrowcasting**, which is the ability to stream specialised content or custom content, has a marginal cost per user lower than that of the revenue per new user.

In particular, the move from the classic broadcasting models to narrowcasting has been made possible by the development of streaming technologies which enable the home user of the Internet to receive reasonable quality audio and video across a telephone line. The major benefit for the marketer is the fact that by offering customisable products from a large product base, the user is bearing the time cost of creating their own product, tailored to their needs.

The marketer has the opportunity for tightly targeted narrowcasting advertising for specific niche interests, for instance, followers of a specific sports channel online can be targeted with sport specific advertising, while the home gardening channel can receive gardening specific advertising content. Most narrowcasters require registration, which normally includes basic demographic information which can be combined to increase the targeting of the narrowcast market. The greatest benefit of the narrowcast is the fact that in conjunction with global access, narrowcasting can target lucrative international market niches that may be too small to warrant targeting through domestic broadcasting.

Global access

By virtue of being on the Internet, web-based marketers can reach potential customers on a worldwide basis. More than ever before barriers to global commerce are being lowered with the result that small local businesses are able to access customers and markets which were inaccessible less than five years ago.

From a consumer perspective this is both empowering and frustrating. Through the use of international direct orders consumers are able to bypass restrictive import policies and purchase individual items online. The advantage for the marketer is that the consumer takes on the risks, taxes and regulatory obligations associated with the product (Paul 1996). However, although web sites have a global presence, many online marketers fail to take the needs of the potential international consumer into consideration when it comes to basic distribution and pricing policies. While some retailers exclude overseas clients by delivering only locally, others use unrealistic and very expensive delivery mechanisms such as international couriers which eliminate any cost leadership that the company might otherwise have enjoyed. In addition, many web sites offer misleading promises of 'shipping internationally' which means either from America to Canada, or within Europe.

Strategic Internet marketing requires organisations to take the full marketing mix into consideration when developing their programs not only on a national but also on an international basis. The poor image many potentially multinational organisations inadvertently project to the international market can have a long-term detrimental effect if and when that company decides to go global. 'International' has become a more nebulous term since the advent of the Internet, and companies that promise global delivery need to have global delivery mechanisms. It is one thing to log onto PizzaHut.com and order a pizza, it is another thing to have a pizza delivery network in every country from which the pizza could have been ordered. Global opportunities exist in the market, but they need to be supported with global logistics systems, which will be examined in chapter 12, Distribution, and chapter 15, International marketing.

Time independence

Access to the Internet is time independent which means that, in theory at least, web-based organisations have no opening or closing hours. In reality most web-based businesses do conform to standard opening hours with many small businesses having erratic access and service standards. Venkatesh (1998) quoted a sign on the front page of a web site explaining the temporary closure of the site was forced by the human operators being down for servicing instead of the computers being offline.

Successful online marketers need to manage the expectations of consumers so that their expectations of service delivery are realistic and in line with the capacity of the organisation. Immediate responses to requests can be automated through email systems where appropriate, although a delayed personal response may generate more goodwill than an immediately received formula response. In a well-resourced organisation, web pages can be directly linked into back-end systems which manage the ordering process. Ultimately the most important issue here is to remember that while web site access is place and time independent, the reality is that instantaneous service delivery is not always possible, nor should it always be promised. While one-click ordering may streamline the process of moving data from the buyer to the seller, when the seller is dealing with tangible goods, the items still need shipping from their warehouse to the buyer. It is the physical movement of goods that still creates the greatest barriers for e-commerce, as distribution and shipping costs may eat away at any pricing advantage, and the shipping times versus shipping cost equations may make online products less attractive to the targeted international niche markets. The greatest frustration of e-commerce is the knowledge that the book you instantly bought online is two to three days away, whereas the book you bought from the store you have in your hands at the point of sale.

Interest driven

'I may not have gone where I intended to go, but I think I have ended up where I intended to be.'

Douglas Adams

The final area of Internet benefit is the fact that web-based behaviour is interest driven. Unlike offline mass communications, such as advertising, which are intrusive and impact upon the subconscious of the potential consumer, access to specific sites requires the consumer to make an effort. The nature of the Internet, in conjunction with it being interest driven, allows for the removal of many of the standard market barriers of time zones, geography and lack of access to remote services. By being able to search by points of interest, and to gather into communities of interest, the Internet has created an environment that most closely represents Adam Smith's perfect market scenario where ubiquitous access to information is shared by all members of the market (Ranchhod 1998). Of course, the limitation of the Internet as the perfect market argument is that not all members of the market have equal access to the available information, either through differences in skills, languages or through restricted access, such as censorship or filtering.

One of the distinctive aspects of the interest-driven nature of the Internet is the degree to which this has been deliberately encouraged as part of the cyber-communing process by a number of corporations. Yahoo!Geocities actively encourages communities of common interest through the neighbourhood structure of its web hosting facilities. Under the Geocities model, web sites are grouped together by linked themes, for example, 'hometown values' (geocities .yahoo.com/Heartland), and within each neighbourhood, members are encouraged to participate in virtual community events and discussions. The generation of communities of interest is based on two factors — the ease of publication on the Internet, and the interest-driven nature of the medium. As users have to actively seek information, it becomes easier for them to find points of common interest, such as those housed by Geocities and similar sites, where they can form communities of common interest. This is explored in further detail in chapter 5, Creating cybercommunities.

In consumer behaviour terms, the problem-recognition stage of the buyer decision-making process is usually already complete prior to the consumer going online. Needs have been identified as a result of other external pressures; the Web simply provides ease and convenience in information searching and evaluation of alternatives. To better direct traffic to a particular site, organisations can use online techniques such as linking with associated pages. Overall, however, given the relative novelty of e-commerce in the broader community, the best way of directing traffic to a site remains with effective offline communications.

Why adapt to the online world?

Having established that the Internet is not the same as the real world, why should people have a business presence online? Inherent advantages such as time independence are meaningless if your organisation is a time-dependent service such as hairdressing. Having 24–7 global access to a hairdresser's web site does not enable you to download a haircut. In the same vein, having global access to the local coke machine may be interesting, but the cola is still going to have to be picked up locally (www.csh.rit.edu/projects/drink.shtml).

So, why bother with the brave new world? There are many reasons for going online; some have more logic to them than others. A common rationale for joining the online gold rush was that if you did not, your competitor would, and you would lose out to your digitally superior opposition. This makes sense only if you or your digitally superior competitor sell products and services suited to the Internet marketplace. For local area house painters to go online, it takes more than a suspicion that other house painters are online to justify the time and money required to set a web site up and running.

Going online: Factors to consider

There are three questions to answer before deciding to go online and bring your web presence to the world. These are:

1. *Is your product Web ready?* Do you have a product that is suited for sale or promotion over the Internet? Software, music and information are products practically tailor-made for digital distribution online. Even traditional tangible goods can be distributed and sold online with relative ease if your organisation has a logistics and support mechanism to back national and international sales. Even intangible services such as hairdressing can be tailored for online success. While hairdressers cannot upload haircuts for digital distribution they can put up portfolios of design styles, prize-winning hairstyles and details of appointment diaries and consultation times (Winzar 1999). Being able to book into a hairdresser electronically, and receive a confirmation email, and a subsequent reminder email may provide a value-added service to the consumer that justifies the online presence. However, if your clientele are not online, and are unlikely to be online anytime soon, there is not much value in the digital booking system.

2. *Are your customers, current and potential, online or moving online?* If your clientele is online, get online to join up with them and to offer them an additional point of purchase or promotion opportunity. Web sites can be used as support for current and new customers of your products and services.

3. *Is the world simply a web site and international mail stamp away?* Products which can be shipped internationally relatively easily, or which are targeted towards niche markets are well suited to having an online presence. Specialist products often have global markets that are viable to access over the Internet that would otherwise be prohibitively expensive if each market needed a physical point of presence.

Going online: Reasons why other businesses are there already

O'Connor and O'Keefe (1997) looked at the drivers, attractors and inhibitors for establishing a web presence. The motivations for moving into the online world are also related to the innovativeness of the company planning their online move. As will be examined in chapter 4 on consumer behaviour, the reasons an innovator chooses for adopting a new behaviour differ from those of the early adopter and early majority. Consequently, as e-commerce becomes more established, the rationale for going online moves away from the 'hey, wow, this looks cool', through the 'this is the fashionable way to do business', and into the more pragmatic 'what benefit will I gain from being online?' approach. All three adoption decisions have relative advantages and disadvantages in deciding to move online; some companies in waiting for a clear benefit may miss their opportunity to gain any benefit, while others, who set up because everyone else was getting a web site, may also find themselves having missed the point. Eventually, it boils down to examining to what extent is having a web presence conducive to business success, consistent with the organisational goals, and can be fitted into the way the company does business. The following list of drivers, attractors and inhibitors is designed to give an overview of possible reasons, drawn from the experience of other organisations.

Drivers and attractors: Get me to the Web on time

Four of the most common attractors to the Internet appear to be relatively universal in application.

1. The financial justification: Cost cutting

Many organisations have seen the Internet as a method of cost reduction, for lowering printing and promotional costs, and for reducing the cost of expansion into new markets. Mass customisation of web sites by user selection powered by automated database systems is seen as a substantial reduction in costs per new customer compared with developing thousands of alternatives in-house, and risking the fact that nobody wants to adopt one of these alternatives.

2. The efficiency argument: Getting better at doing it better

Efficiency has been cited as a reason for moving online and, while there are anecdotal stories concerning productivity rises, the efficiency argument is still subject to debate. Arguably, access to massive knowledge databases, and the ease of searching for information online has improved the effectiveness of information acquisition. It probably has not done anything to speed up getting the information, but it has given easier access to a wider range of sources.

3. The open access argument: This little piggy goes to the world wide market

The Internet has altered the market dynamics in that there is now less need to rely on complex distribution channels to get products to market. This is a dual edged sword though — smaller businesses may become more independent in their distribution, but larger businesses have found that their reliance on intermediaries and distributors has increased. Pepsi and Coke are two of the best known brands in the world, and yet you still cannot order a can of cola from their web sites. Their size, global position, and complex established distribution chains have limited the extent to which they can direct sell from their web site.

The Internet has opened up the world to the small, medium and large business. While much of e-commerce focuses on retailer/wholesaler to consumer interactions, one of the overlooked avenues for business marketing is in business to business distribution. A global Internet presence such as that experienced by a small candy manufacturer (www.peppermints.com) can be augmented by retailer web sites (www.thinkgeek.com) and offline distribution of the products by conventional retailers (Andronicos, a San Francisco grocery store with a web site www.andronicos.com). Small and medium businesses, or intermediary businesses can order specialist goods online to resell into conventional local region distribution channels every bit as easily as the customer can order directly from the wholesaler.

Global logistics are also becoming more readily available with international mail and courier services operating at cost effective rates for small and medium businesses who need to ship non-perishable items. The perishable market is still harder. Mailing a chocolate bar from Asia to Africa does not work as well as mailing a box of computer chips from Silicon Valley to London.

4. The promotional argument: The global digital showcase

The Web offers an unprecedented opportunity to showcase organisational promotions, histories, product details and information that is not feasible in traditional offline media. Rich corporate histories, outlining the development of a company, its philanthropic activities and anecdotes of interest can add personality and spice to a corporate image. The ability of the Web to offer multimedia web sites which can give the most basic 'click to buy' and in-depth corporate history and product detail from the same address gives marketers much greater promotional freedom than they have experienced in the offline world. In particular, using the Internet as a support medium also allows for mixed media promotion where interest is generated in offline advertising, and details are provided online.

The digital showroom — Porsche.com virtually offers a real car experience

'If you really want to understand our customers, you have to understand the phrase, "If I were going to be a car, I'd be a Porsche".'

Peter Shutz, CEO of Porsche AG, *Harvard Business Review*, March/April, 1986, in Ehrlich 1998, *Wiley Book of Business Quotations.*

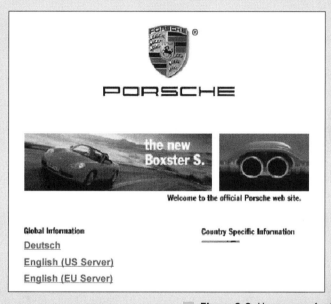

Figure 3.2 Home page for Porsche.com

A Porsche is a Porsche, of course (of course). So what does one of the leading status symbols in the world need with a web site? Porsche understands that their customers want more than just information — a Porsche is a symbol and an experience as well as being a car. So their web site is tailored to meet these needs by delivering an insight into one of the much coveted status symbols of the world, and by providing an insight into what it is to own and drive Porsche. But they have not forgotten the most important basic of a commercial web site — you can still find details on how and where to buy the car itself.

Porsche know that their web site has a target audience that extends beyond the purchasers of luxury vehicles into the aspirant markets. There are those who come to buy, and those who come to dream of owning a Porsche and the site is tailored to make both parties welcome. Using globalisation, mass customisation, interactivity and even a cybercommunity, the Porsche web site addresses the psychic needs of both Porsche owners and would-be owners.

(continued)

Operating on both a global and regional basis, Porsche.com offers regional focus web sites within the main site, giving support to local dealerships at the same time as maintaining a global presence. Interactivity on the site is available through the 'build your own Porsche' interactive sequence that allows users of the site to tailor their own vehicle to their personal specifications — and order it, should their finances match their tastes. Even for the virtual window-shopper, being able to change the colour, styling and custom features gives the opportunity for greater product involvement than simply viewing a static picture of the luxury vehicle. Regular site visitors will be able to avail themselves of the frequently updated news and events details, while the cyber-community structure begins at the front page where it offers links to Porsche owners' clubs.

With the integration of customisation, not only at the Porsche production level but also at the web site, combined with the benefits of 24–7 access, multiple target markets from current owners, would-be buyers and aspirant admirers, Porsche.com has gone beyond being just a global car yard into a luxury car experience.

Inhibitors: Reasons not to be digital

The inhibitors to going online represent not the views of the laggards and the Luddites, but quite often the views of the pragmatic and those with a good understanding of contemporary technology. The greatest inhibitor to online marketing was the most important factor — was there any point in it? A locally focused company with a clientele that was not online is hardly in dire need of a web presence. Possibly an email address and a web account to use to watch the waters of the Internet for competition, innovation and opportunity, but certainly not a need to have a web presence.

The second most common inhibitor to going online was the perception or belief that the company and its products or services were not suited to the Web, or promotion over the Web. Economies of scale for distribution of products, allocation of time and financial resources and the need to find a dedicated company member to coordinate the Internet presence often worked against the smaller organisations which found this price of access to be too steep.

In addition, some organisations have not abandoned their interest in the Internet — just simply postponed it. By viewing the Web with a longer term focus, some companies can afford to wait to move online until the company is capable of being online effectively. There is sound logic in having a good web absence if the alternative is a poor web presence. Companies with plans to expand in the global market may decide to hold off showing their products online until they are fully ready to commit to a 24–7 globally competitive market.

Finally, one of the reasons cited in O'Connor and O'Keefe (1997) was that the technology was not able to support the corporate vision of what they wanted their web presence to look like and the level they wanted it to function at. The promise and potential of the Internet is to have integrated catalogues which link to just-in-time manufacturing which links to just-in-time shipping. The reality of the Internet is not quite as linked and just-in-time ready as the hype often promises. A serious complaint in the e-commerce sector is that the bandwidth available to the consumer is too restricted. The consumer's lack of access to high speed technology, fast connections and widespread Internet use is preventing e-commerce from reaching its full potential. Strangely enough, while sounding more like an excuse than a reason, many organisations are waiting for the Web to develop to the point of high speed home access — fast, efficient and easily accessible — everything the Web promises. At current Internet speeds, many providers of digital content fear that poor performance now will permanently damage future longer term prospects for streaming audio, video and push media content. The airline industry had to wait until the Wright brothers had released more than a few upgrades to their original design before it could start offering high speed passenger transit.

The adaptation of the offline to the online

Despite some of the limitations of the current Internet in terms of bandwidth, diffusion and technological issues, many offline transactions are being replicated online quite successfully. This is a comprehensive, yet not fully exhaustive, list of possible offline user behaviours that have been adapted across to the Internet. The value of examining a list of dual platform behaviours is that it recognises that the Internet can affect certain aspects of marketing behaviour through its unique features, both positively and negatively.

Retailing

Retailing online can range from exotic goods through to the mundane weekly groceries. There are a number of online shopping options, from familiar offline institutions like shopping malls, through to small businesses and online catalogues.

Cybermalls
Online shopping conglomerates exist in the form of cybermalls, coalitions of related goods and services which band together to provide an online shopping environment similar to that of the offline shopping centres. At the top of the food chain in this industry is the mall metaindex such as Cybermall.com (www.cybermall.com) which categorises and reviews various online shopping precincts.

Shopping portals
Shopping portals, such as the 131Shop (www.131shop.com.au) operate as brokers of goods and services where the customer searches the broker site for a product or service and the site returns a list of potential suppliers. The site does not actually sell anything, rather it acts as an intermediary between

supplier and purchaser. Incidentally, the advent of the Internet was supposed to herald the end of the middleperson; instead, the massive amount of information generated by the Internet has provided even greater opportunities for organisations to act as channel managers.

Online department stores

Many of the existing major retail chains in the world have opened up digital branch offices in the attempt to prevent loss of sales to online rivals. These stores range from internationals such as Toys-R-Us (www.toysrus.com), through to national food chains Woolworths (www.woolworths.com.au/) and internationally recognised status symbol stores such as Harrods (www.harrods .co.uk/).

Auction houses

Online auction houses offer Internet users the opportunity to buy and sell secondhand goods on an international mass-market. Sites such as eBay (www.ebay.com) and Sold.com.au (www.sold.com.au/) act as intermediary auction houses between non-commercial sellers. In addition, several search engine portal sites such as Yahoo! (auctions.yahoo.com/) and Infoseek (auction.go.com/) offer auction functions in addition to their core services.

Virtual catalogue sites

Catalogue sites are online specific stores such as Amazon.com (www.amazon.com) which were established to retail a specific category of products through a complex interactive catalogue system. Amazon exists solely as a digital operation, having no affiliated physical premises, which differentiates it from catalogue-orientated retail store sites such as Dymocks (www.dymocks.com/). In addition to Amazon, there are numerous virtual music stores that sell products ranging from physical goods such as CDs from Cdnow (www.cdnow.com) through to purely virtual such as MP3 files from MP3.com (www.mp3.com). The primary focus of the catalogue sites is to offer products through the virtual catalogue without investing in physical real estate.

Digital corner stores: Niche marketing

Digital corner stores occupy the multitude of niche markets that exist to service the specific needs and wants of Internet sub-populations. Other digital stores use the global nature of the Internet to set up a shopfront to sell products to a small, but lucrative, international niche market. Digital stores can range in product depth from single product stores through to Internet niche markets such as the LinuxMall (www.linuxmall.com) which sells products relating solely to the Linux operating system. The global nature of the Internet allows niching on a much greater basis than previously possible with catalogues, direct mail or physical store fronts.

Online factory direct

Online shoppers are able to take advantage of wholesaler direct sales. Most common are the computing industry outlets such as Dell Computers (www.dell.com) or Compaq Computing (www.compaq.com). These sites differ from retailer sites in that they represent manufacturers seeking to sell directly to the end consumer rather than relying on traditional multilevel distribution channels.

Information search

The Internet is primarily an interest-driven medium in which people seek information, ranging from pre-purchase product information, through to post-purchase technical support, and advice. Information search in this context is not limited to the use of search engines; rather, it represents the pursuit of new knowledge through the Internet, and can span all aspects of the Internet, including email, IRC and USENET. In particular, USENET represents a strong source of information on a wide range of topics, from caffeine (news:alt.drugs.caffeine) through to health advice and support (news:alt.support.cancer) and film reviews (news:aus.films).

In addition to information search, there are numerous national and international news services available online, from recognised international media broadcasters such as CNN (www.cnn.com), BBC (www.bbc.co.uk) through to regional television stations such as Canada's CityTV (www.citytv.com) or one of Australia's national radio broadcasters TripleJ (www.triplej.com.au).

Finally, in among the range of informational web sites that are maintained by private individuals on a wide range of subjects, from sport, music, politics and religion, there are numerous commercially focused knowledge sites such as the Encyclopedia Britannica Online (www.eb.com/). Given the origin of the Internet as a primarily text-based medium, and the Web's development from being a method of referencing in a science paper, information is the dominant content of the Internet. Recent developments which have increased the bandwidth capacity of the Internet have seen more entertainment-orientated web sites appearing with sound, video and greater levels of graphics intensity.

Entertainment online

Online entertainment is a progressively expanding market as people move towards virtual entertainment which is free from the traditional venue orientation of most offline leisure activities. While there are obvious restrictions as to what offline leisure activities can be replicated online, new functions such as multiplayer Internet games, ranging from bridge, scrabble and traditional board games through to complex 3D games are increasingly more accessible (www.wireplay.co.uk). Online gambling is also increasing, from the use of online betting agencies (www.centrebet.com.au) through to online casino gaming (www.orientalcasino.com).

The Internet itself is also a source of pleasure — web surfing has been associated with hedonism, pleasure seeking and arousal seeking behaviours (Hoffman & Novak 1996; Raman & Leckenby 1998). While the Internet is still focused towards information exchange, membership of cybercommunities, involvement in online relationships, and online activities are also sources of enjoyment, recreation and pleasure.

Utility functions

As well as recreational, there are practical purposes associated with the Internet, despite what productivity reports are tending to indicate. Merlyn and Välikangas (1998) outline the productivity paradox of information technology — despite much-heralded advances in technology, nobody can actually point to productivity increases directly caused by these advances. However, three core utility functions have arisen from the Internet. These are access to mediated information services, access to personal management services and access to knowledge.

Information access (mediated services)

In terms of the Internet, one of the major advances for business to business operation has been the movement of information and intellectual property online. Searchable archives have both increased the amount of available information while reducing the amount of effort required to access this information. Online patent searches are available through various national intellectual property offices such as Intellectual Property Australia (www.ipaustralia.gov.au/) and the State Intellectual Property Office of the People's Republic of China (www.cpo.cn.net/). Libraries have moved online allowing access to larger digital collections, either directly from the publisher (www.emerald-library.com) or through universities (www.library.uq.edu.au) or through major national libraries such as the American Library of Congress (lcweb.loc.gov/).

Personal management services

Personal management systems related to the online services involve banking (www.anz.com), bill paying and other personal financial management including credit cards (www.dinersclub.com) and share trading (www.barclays-stockbrokers.co.uk). While these systems are not new in comparison to telephone banking services, they do offer the advantage of being able to be performed more easily than phone banking, for the cost of a single Internet connection.

The consumer (r)evolution

The consumers are revolting. The expectations of the market have changed dramatically as a result of access to global markets. There is a wide range of new products, services and ideas and global competition arriving to challenge long-established local monopolies and oligarchies. The use of the Internet is changing the power structure of the market in favour of the consumer and allowing consumers to turn the tables on the marketers. No longer content with accepting push media-orientation advertising and Henry Ford-style 'any product you like, as long as it is a product we are prepared to give you' attitudes — the consumers have gained a series of advantages from the Internet.

Advantages of Internet-based marketing for the consumer

Speed is one advantage that the Internet has to offer consumers. While consumer behaviour as it relates to Internet marketing is discussed in detail in chapter 4, the following points highlight the key benefits of online marketing for the consumer.

The main stages where Internet-aware marketers can influence the buying decision-making process are in the information search and evaluation of alternatives. Accessing a wide range of pre-purchase product information, both nationally and internationally is far more viable online than it has been offline. In particular, potential adopters can talk to current adopters and discuss relative advantages and disadvantages with other users, rather than salespeople.

The Internet provides rapid access to product-related information from a variety of sources. This is of particular value during the information search phase of buyer decision making as it allows for quick, easy and cheap comparisons of goods from multiple manufacturers and providers. Instead of having to physically check prices and styles, consumers are able to make comparisons at their leisure, in their own homes. Whether or not they make the actual purchase online is irrelevant; the fact remains that information search is a key element of consumer buying behaviour and that web-oriented marketers can assist the potential customer by streamlining this phase of the process.

Another benefit for the consumer of the online shopping experience, particularly for high-involvement goods, is that it frees the potential customer from the feeling of pressure often exerted by salespeople. For many consumers this is an added attraction of the online experience although, from the marketer's point of view, there are dangers in becoming too remote and having insufficient opportunity for interactivity.

Post-purchase evaluation procedures aimed at reducing cognitive dissonance and developing ongoing relationships are facilitated by the ease of non-obtrusive, two-way communication online. Help sites, email notification of new products and services and feedback sections on web sites all assist in identifying and correcting possible sources of post-purchase dissatisfaction.

Where the major revolution of the Internet has hit hardest has been in the change in expectations for the offline world, which has now to compete not only with the Internet, but also to contend with the expectations of speed, immediacy, customisation and global accessibility created by the demands of the consumer.

Changing consumer expectations

There are three key drivers behind changing consumer expectations as they relate to all marketers and marketing activities. These are:
- increasing time pressures
- mass customisation
- consumer demands.

Increasing time pressures

Time pressures are a key factor in driving interest in, and demand for, online services. The main advantages that Internet marketing companies are seen to possess relate to the fact that Internet-based services can be accessed quickly, efficiently and at a time convenient to the consumer. This is particularly important for those who have multiple pressures on their time and cannot access traditional services with ease.

Increasingly effective computerised ordering, logistics and delivery systems have contributed to a changing perception of what is considered 'acceptable' in terms of the timing of service delivery. Whereas the standard 28-day turn-around from time of order to time of delivery was considered adequate until recently, most web-based organisations promise immediate, or at the most 48-hour processing times.

Mass customisation

There is an increasing expectation that marketers and manufacturers will take individual differences into account when developing their products and offer a wide variety of products and services suited to any occasion. Thirty years ago mass marketing was common and accepted as adequate, if not good, service. Refining target segments down to niche markets and beyond this, to a market of one, each with its own unique marketing mix, has led to new customer expectations in relation to what organisations should provide.

Consumer demand

Due to a range of social and educational trends, consumers are more demanding now than in the past. Access to information about competitor offerings combined with legislation protecting the consumer has empowered clients who are no longer prepared to accept everything the company says. Consumer empowerment has taken many forms from the increased incidence of complaint behaviours through to demands for openness and accountability on the part of organisations at all stages of the marketing process. Advertising standards ensure that misleading promotional material is subject to controls while consumer protection laws ensure that customers have a form of legal redress if marketers over-promise and under-deliver.

While these trends are not confined to online marketing activities, the capabilities of the new technology mean that increasingly marketers are able to respond effectively to these demands.

Summary

The online marketing environment is fundamentally different to that which exists offline. Those marketers who wish to succeed in this new and evolving world must not only understand, but also fully develop the unique features of the Internet as a means of reaching and serving the customer. In particular, marketers need to take note of the time and space independence of the new environment, its potential for interactivity and the level of customisation of experience that it offers the consumer.

As technology develops and marketing in the online environment evolves, the level of sophistication of various web sites has become correspondingly more complex. Fundamental to successful marketing, however, remains an understanding of what the consumer wants and needs. Increasingly, marketers, rather than technicians, are becoming responsible for overall web site structure and design. The question of what customers need and want, and how they are reacting to online marketing exchanges is explored in detail in the next chapter.

Discussion questions

3.1 What are the five unique characteristics of the Internet? Give examples of how an Internet marketer can take advantage of each.

3.2 Global access offers global opportunities, but does it mean that being online makes it compulsory to have a global focus? Give examples of where a local focus can be of greater benefit for an online company.

3.3 In terms of web site design, do the three distinct styles of web sites represent an evolutionary design process or do they represent distinct marketing objectives?

3.4 Is it more important to be interactive or have variety in a web site? In regard to content of the web site, should it be the domain of the end user to provide the fresh new content through interactive forums or the web site owner through regular updates? Discuss.

3.5 Is time independence and 24-hour access a major issue for local marketers competing against online companies? How can online companies use this to their advantage? How can offline companies address this issue?

3.6 Porsche.com represents the luxury end of the online new car market. Are the features of their web site applicable to lower end consumer vehicles, and to trade vehicles? Examine several online car manufacturer web sites to see if the Porsche.com model is universally applicable.

3.7 In what ways have the unique features of the Internet changed the consumer's offline expectations of marketing? How should marketers respond to these changing expectations?

3.8 Do automated systems such as collaborative filtering software represent an invasion of the user's privacy or a value-adding function to a web site? What are the ethical implications of constructing a mix and match database that matches people by tracking their interests in music, television and web sites?

3.9 Outline two online services that cannot be replicated in the offline environment. Do these Internet-only services represent a new form of marketing, or can existing marketing be used or adapted to meet the new needs?

References

Arunkundram, R. & Sundararajan, A. 1998, 'An economic analysis of electronic secondary markets: Installed base, technology, durability and firm profitability', *Decision Support Systems*, vol. 24, pp. 3–16.

Bagozzi, R. 1975, 'Marketing as exchange', *Journal of Marketing*, vol. 39, October, pp. 32–9.

Breitenbach, C. S. & van Doren, D. C. 1998, 'Value-added marketing in the digital domain: Enhancing the utility of the Internet', *Journal of Consumer Marketing*, vol. 15, no. 6, pp. 558–75.

Ghose, S. & Dou, W. 1998, 'Interactive functions and their impacts on the appeal of Internet presence sites', *Journal of Advertising Research*, March, p. 28.

Gibson, W. 1984, *Neuromancer*, Ace Books, New York.

Hoffman, D. L. & Novak, T. P. 1996, 'Marketing in hypermedia computer-mediated environments: Conceptual foundations', *Journal of Marketing*, vol. 60, no. 3, July, pp. 50–68.

Holloway, M. 1997, 'Pattie', *Wired*, 5, 12 December.

Leong, E. K. F., Huang, X. & Stanners, P. J. 1998, 'Comparing the effectiveness of the web site with traditional media', *Journal of Advertising Research*, vol. 38, no. 5, pp. 44–57.

Merlyn, P. R. & Välikangas, L. 1998, 'From information technology to knowledge technology: Taking the user into consideration' *Journal of Knowledge Management*, vol. 2, no. 2, December, pp. 28–35.

Murphy, R. 1998, 'Case study: Schuh — Clothing for feet on the Web', *International Journal of Retail and Distribution Management*, vol. 26, no. 8, pp. 336–9.

O'Connor, G. C. & O'Keefe, B. 1997, 'Viewing the Web as a marketplace: The case of small companies, *Decision Support Systems*, vol. 21, no. 3, pp. 171–83.

Ovans, A. 1999, 'Is your web site socially savvy?', *Harvard Business Review*, May–June, pp. 20–1.

Paul, P. 1996, 'Marketing on the Internet', *Journal of Consumer Marketing*, vol. 13, no. 4, pp. 27–39.

Raman, N. V. & Leckenby, J. D. 1998, 'Factors affecting consumers' "Webad" visits', *European Journal of Marketing*, vol. 32, no. 7/8, pp. 737–48.

Ranchhod, A. 1998, 'Advertising into the next millennium', *International Journal of Advertising*, November, pp. 427–38.

Venkatesh, A. 1998, 'Cybermarketscapes and consumer freedoms and identities', *European Journal of Marketing*, vol. 32, no. 7/8, pp. 664–76.

www.wired.com/wired/archive/5.12/maes_pr.html

Winzar, H. 1999, 'Internet Editorial', *Journal of Marketing Practice: Applied Marketing Science*, vol. 5, no. 3, pp. 1–3.

Web sites

auction.go.com
auctions.yahoo.com
www.b2b.com
www.ednow.com
www.excite.com.au
www.geocities.yahoo.com/Heartland
www.go.com
lcweb.loc.gov
mypage.go.com
store.yahoo.com
support.microsoft.com
www.131shop.com.au
www.amazon.com
www.andromedia.com/products/likeminds/
    index.html
www.andronicos.com
www.anz.com
www.barclays-stockbrokers.co.uk
www.bbc.co.uk
www.cdnow.com
www.centrebet.com.au
www.citytv.com
www.cnn.com
www.coke.com
www.coke.com/cgi-bin/survey/survey.cgi
www.compaq.com

www.computerstore.com.au
www.cpo.cn.net
www.cs.umn.edu/Research/GroupLens
www.csh.rit.edu/projects/drink.shtml
www.cybermall.com
www.dell.com
www.dinersclub.com
www.discjockey.com
www.dymocks.com
www.eb.com
www.ebay.com
www.emerald-library.com
www.harrods.co.uk
www.homeworld.org
www.incredibledvd.com/coupons.html
www.InsideTheWeb.com
www.ipaustralia.gov.au
www.library.uq.edu.au
www.linuxmall.com
www.live365.com
www.mp3.com

www.orientalcasino.com
www.peppermints.com
www.pizzahut.com
www.porsche.com
www.real.com
www.shockwave.com
www.siteyahoo.com/site
www.sold.com.au
www.thinkgeek.com
www.toysrus.com
www.triplej.com.au
www.webcentral.com.au
www.whatisthematrix.com
www.wireplay.co.uk
www.woolworths.com.au

Newsgroups
news:alt.support.cancer
news:alt.drugs.caffeine
news:aus.films

CHAPTER

4

Consumer
behaviour

*'This is not like TV, only
better. This is life.'*

Lenny Nero (Ralph Fiennes),
'Strange Days', Lightstorm
Entertainment, 1995.

LEARNING
objectives

After reading this chapter, you should be able to:

- recognise the different influences on the diffusion of the Internet throughout society

- appreciate the differences in motivations for use, adoption, rejection and non-use of the Internet among different members of society

- identify the different motivations for using the Internet, and the different types of Internet users

- recognise behaviours unique to the computer-mediated environment of the Internet

- understand the barriers to adoption and use of the Internet

- apply marketing theory and practice to address issues raised by barriers to Internet adoption

- understand how and why people choose not to use the Internet.

Introduction

Understanding the motivations, desires and behaviour of consumers is the key to successful contemporary marketing. Adoption of innovations rests at the core of understanding the consumer — what is it that motivates the individual to change from a regular product, try a new product or try a modified version of an existing favourite? The Internet represents a major innovation adoption decision for the average user — use of it requires the adoption of a range of new behaviours, new products and new services. Once online, the consumer is at the bottom of a steep learning curve of innovation adoption of e-commerce, online banking, email and web surfing. Even the pursuit of new web sites represents the micro-level adoption of an innovation (a new web page) over the continuing use of an updated existing web page (continuous adoption) or the return to an unchanged web site (non adoption).

This chapter takes a broad overview of consumer behaviour in the context of the adoption and use of the Internet. It overviews the diffusion of innovation and innovation adoption literature to examine how and why people move online, and what factors influence this adoption decision. It also overviews the reasons people adopt or do not adopt, and why individuals may choose to reject the use of the Internet. The second major area of the chapter examines what happens to users once they get online, through examining potential Internet user categorisations, the types of online behaviours specific to the Internet, and those shared with the offline world.

Innovation adoption and the Internet

Innovation adoption research is not a new field. While the current rate of new patents and innovations reaching the market is unparalleled in corporate history, the basic process of innovation remains unchanged. Various descriptions of the process of innovation development and adoption have one consistent factor — the diffusion and acceptance of ultra new technologies is by far the most difficult to achieve. Ultra new technologies are also referred to as discontinuous innovations or, more recently, as 'really new products'. They are the sorts of inventions that revolutionise an industry or product category, or are so far removed from previous experience that they require an entirely new learning experience.

Innovation adoption and the really new product

The **really new product (RNP)** is not a new concept. Aggarwal, Cha and Wilemon (1998) used the term to describe innovation that is ground shaking, revolutionary and extremely likely to fail to be adopted. They outlined a series of factors for identifying RNPs:

- The RNP defines a new product category as no existing product category adequately describes the innovation. The Internet represents a new product category, with no immediately recognisable matching prior invention.

Within the Internet itself, the World Wide Web was a relatively easy addition to the range of available Internet functions as it was within the existing product categories of distributed information (web pages) accessed through client software (browsers) that was sufficiently comparable to gopher clients used to access FTP archives. (For the more recent arrivals to the Internet, gopher software was the browser software of file directories and text archives. They have, for the most part, been superseded by the web browser.)

- RNPs represent the development of a new technology which usually is incompatible with existing behaviours, products or knowledge. To use a RNP requires a degree of risk taking as the RNP may or may not become the dominant innovation. The first major competitor to rival the Internet was the Microsoft Services Network (MSN), a proprietary subscriber-based Internet equivalent. It was promoted by Microsoft as a family friendly alternative to the Internet, and against the open free market nature of the Internet. It lasted for approximately six months. MSN shut down as a pay-per-use service, and released the previously subscription-based content on the Internet for free. Early adopters of MSN found themselves in possession of a failed new technology, having risked considerable time, effort and money in getting involved in the service.

- The RNP has a propensity to set the standards. The advantage is that the first RNP to reach the market is by default the best of its kind — it is the only one of its kind. This makes product comparisons difficult, and often quite obtuse, as potential purchasers struggle to find something to compare with the RNP. This is further hampered by the fact that the RNP usually sets the standards and benchmarks by which future generations of the product will be measured, and by which new market structures will evolve to support a successful RNP. The Internet set the standard for information content and service delivery not only within the distributed network category, but also in other areas of service delivery. As noted in chapter 3, instant access to information online has led to a reduction in the perception of acceptable wait-time for service delivery. Whereas 28 days delivery was previously accepted as fast service, expectations are now focused on overnight deliveries, courtesy of the instant information gratification experience of the Internet.

- The RNP is never an easy prospect for consumers to adopt, as they are usually dealing with a new technology that brings with it added complexity and a steep learning curve. All innovation requires some degree of change in the consumer's behaviour, ranging from the mild adjustments associated with continuous innovations, through to the complete revision of contemporary thinking associated with dramatic changes such as electricity, or internationally distributed communications networks. New behaviours require new learning, which in turn develops a subsequent need for training or education in new behaviour. One of the major problems of innovations which require radically new behaviours is that these behaviours are often highly visible, and make the adopter stand out from the crowd. Quite often this will delay the adoption of an innovation as most people have a tendency towards avoiding non-conformist behaviours.

Innovation adoption: Curves, contagions and cultural differences

Numerous models of innovation adoption have been proposed, ranging from cumulative diffusion models first brought to prominence by Bass (1969) through to the multiple diffusion curve theories of Parthasarathy, Jun and Mittelstaedt (1997). Most diffusion curve theories are based on the notion that once an innovation has been experienced in adoption, it becomes a permanent part of the user's purchase repertoire. In contrast to this general theory is Bass' Contagion-like Diffusion Model, which recognises that adoptions can be adopted and rejected at a later point. There are other diffusion curves available, with Mahajan and Peterson (1985) having outlined over 150 different diffusion curve models which were commonly available at the time of its publication. However, this chapter will focus on three models — the classic S curve, the multiple S-curve model, and the contagion-like diffusion model (Bass 1969; Parthasarathy, Jun & Mittelstaedt 1997).

Classic S-curve theory — continual diffusion and constant adoption

The S-curve theory of innovation diffusion assumes that a small group of innovators will try any new product for the sake of the novelty of the experience. They will then be followed by other members of society, and the shape of the S curve represents the speed at which the innovation is adopted. The steeper the curve, the faster the rate of adoption. The S curve is also a cumulative total, assuming that having once adopted the innovation, the user continues with the adoption for the life of the product. Figure 4.1 displays the classic mathematical S-curve model.

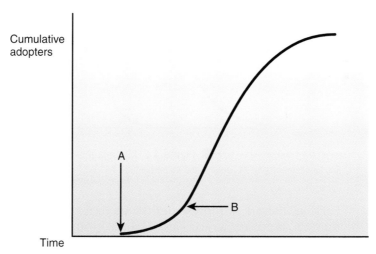

Figure 4.1 Cumulative diffusion curve

Source: Parthasarathy, M., Jun, S. and Mittelstaedt, R. A. 1997, 'Multiple diffusion and multicultural aggregate social systems', *International Marketing Review*, vol. 14, no. 4, pp. 233–47.

Point A represents the point of adoption by innovators. Following adoption of the innovation, it moves slowly through society until adopted by the early adopters. Upon the successful diffusion of the innovation to this social group, the innovation reaches the take off point (Point B) at which time the early majority and late majority of adopters have both adopted the product. Details of these adopter categories are outlined later in this chapter.

S-curve models are used as the foundation for numerous innovation adoption models, including the Rogers (1983) adopter typology. The value of such models is that they offer a predictive function to indicate the rate of time for an innovation to have been experienced, at least once, by the majority of members of a social system.

Multiple sub-populations, multiple S curves and the influence of subcultures

Parthasarathy et al. (1997) proposed that four types of pressure are exerted on innovation adoption decisions — social, individual, product and subcultural influence. Subcultural influence is where social group characteristics such as individualism or collectivism orientation have an impact on the diffusion of an innovation. Unlike the single S curve which aggregates adoption across the total population, Parthasarathy et al. (1997) used multiple S-curve models to examine the progression of an innovation across several social groups. This is illustrated in figure 4.2.

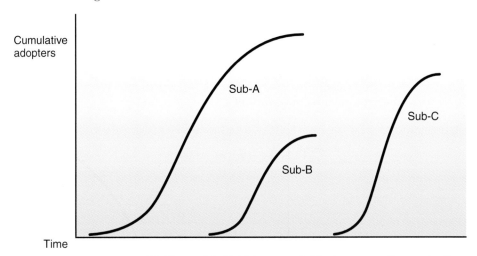

•••••••••••••••••••••••••••••■ **Figure 4.2** Multiple rates of diffusion across three subcultures
Source: Parthasarathy, M., Jun, S. and Mittelstaedt, R. A. 1997, 'Multiple diffusion and multicultural aggregate social systems', *International Marketing Review*, vol. 14, no. 4, pp. 233–47.

Each subculture is represented by its own diffusion curve, where the subculture can represent a race, class or social grouping. The S-curve model implicitly recognises that innovation adoption is also a function of innovation availability. The start and end of each curve varies to the extent that the innovators in Sub-B are adopting at a time early adopters in Sub-A have already adopted, and the innovators, or Sub-C, are adopting at the time innovation has reached the laggard populations of Sub-A and Sub-B. For example, the multiple sub-population model applies to the diffusion of the Internet in that Sub-A can represent the adoption rates of government and military users. Sub-B can be used to represent the education users. It was only when the Internet was made available to the Sub-C, which represents the general public, that commercial users gained the opportunity to adopt the product. So while Sub-C appears to have laggard tendencies, the rate and speed of adoption indicated by the shape of the curve demonstrates a faster take-up rate than Sub-A or Sub-B.

Parthasarathy et al. (1997) explained the difference in take up rates by examining the impact of collectivism versus individualism and the notion of contextuality as pressures exerted on innovation adoption by subculture populations. The collectivism–individualism continuum has a mixed effect on diffusion. In individualist-orientated groups, adoption occurs earlier than in collectivist groups. However, collectivists will adopt en masse once the innovation receives the social support of community leaders. The collectivist nature of the group means that once the innovation is given approval, it has a faster take-off and higher rate of overall adoption than in the individualistic groups.

Contextuality, which is the extent to which products are used to convey meaning, also has an impact on innovation adoption. Where an innovation has a high level of meaning, and the use of contextuality is high, the innovation will be adopted quickly. In contrast, low contextuality groups adopt products based primarily on the utility value of the product — if it is not useful, then it will not be adopted. High contextuality products with little or no utility function will diffuse at a much slower rate in low contextuality communities.

Contagion curves — socially transmitted innovations

The third diffusion curve model is Bass' (1969) Contagion-like diffusion which is the most pragmatic of the models. Bass (1969) acknowledged that innovation adoption is not a permanent state and that, for a variety of reasons, a previously adopted innovation could be rejected after a period of time. Innovations can peak in popularity, and then have declining rates of adoption as people abandon the innovation for a newer, better or different experience. This is illustrated in figure 4.3.

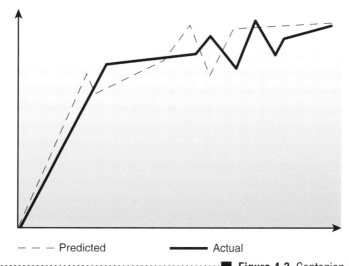

− − − Predicted   ———— Actual

Figure 4.3 Contagion-like diffusion

Source: Bass, F. M. 1969, 'A new product growth model for consumer durables', *Management Science*, vol. 15, pp. 215–27.

Bass' model reasoned that people could adopt an innovation for a short period of time, perhaps to be in fashion, but subsequently reject the innovation for having no value to their lives once the fashion changed. Pokemon, Tamagotchi and Furbies have contagion-like diffusion curves which initially show a slow take-up rate, then an early peak (usually as supplies run out). Following the early peak is a brief decline, usually brought about by a lack of product on the market as a second manufacturing run is commenced to meet demand. The second production wave usually produces the major peak, as everybody acquires the fashionable item. The subsequent decline represents the movement of the innovators and fashion leaders onto the next 'must have' innovation.

The adoption of the Internet is also subject to the contagion model, as many people using the Internet through free access do not continue their adoption of the Internet once the free access is removed (Kingsley & Anderson 1998). When freely available, the relative value of the Internet to the costs incurred remains positive, and the users continue their adoption. Once the safety net of free access is removed, and the user is forced to pay for access, adoption rates decline rapidly as people do not convert from the extended trial period into permanent adoption.

The pragmatic nature of the contagion model is best demonstrated in conjunction with the theory of diffusion of memes. **Memes** are defined as social units of imitation, indicating that they are ideas that can be transmitted by adoption or replication of the meme behaviour (Marsden 1998). Memetic theory argues that strong memes evolve in a way similar to Darwin's survival of the fittest. The strongest meme (innovation) survives and replicates, with a brief period of disadoption (culling), until it peaks, saturates the market, and has no further room to grow. At this point, the innovation meme dies back to a sustainable level in a manner not dissimilar to that of a live species population. In contagion diffusion, and memetic theory, the influence of social trends has a multiplier effect. The decision of social leaders to abandon an innovation is conveyed through society in exactly the same way as the decision to adopt moved through the society.

The meme of socially desirable Internet adoption is currently dominating the market. Two further offspring of this meme are becoming increasingly dominant — the Internet functionality meme and the 'laggard fear' meme. The Internet functionality meme propagates the idea that without the Internet, the business or end users cannot be getting the most out of their lives, and that by using the Internet productivity or education or personal development will be maximised. This meme is gaining popular exposure in the parental markets, particularly among parents of high school children. The unsupported assumption of the meme is that there is an intrinsic functional value in being connected to the Internet. Numerous productivity studies have failed to find any significant benefit to industry by having employees connected to the Internet. In certain circumstances there is sufficient anecdotal evidence to suggest that productivity has declined as a result of unfettered Internet access. However, the productivity meme has continued to propagate, and gain popular acceptance as a reason for being online. Exactly how much more productive does the average household expect to become now it has access to an unlimited supply of distractions?

The productivity meme is also coupled with the 'laggard fear' which promotes the negative side of non-adoption. One of the darker undercurrents of the push towards online commerce, online banking and online government is the implied assumption that failure to be online will mean a lack of access to key services. Laggard fear is also propagated by much of the innovation research, including the assumption that having experienced the innovation once, the user will never want to give up the experience. There is an intrinsic threat implied in the laggard fear meme that somehow the individual is missing out on something really special, and that other people think less of a person for not being online. The simple reality of the situation is that those people who are not online do not have access to the Internet. Whether this is good or bad depends on an individual's needs and wants, and opinion of the Internet. If someone has no particular need to have access to ten thousand Star Trek fan pages, how much is he or she missing out on by not being online? Individual adoption and use of the Internet will ultimately come down to a person's motivations for adoption, and the value that he or she may or may not find in the features of the Internet. No amount of promises of an intellectual nirvana or threats of digital impoverishment promoted by various memes will convince people to adopt a product they do not need or want.

Diffusion of innovations: The need, want, use and show-off approach to adoption

In addition to the factors outlined in the diffusion curve theory, one of the major determinants of whether a product goes from the shelf to the house is whether it meets any of four innovation fascinations outlined by Alpert (1994). **Innovation fascinations** represent an immediate reaction to an innovation experience by the consumer, felt in one of four ways — emotionally, intellectually, social acceptance and practicality. These fascinations are not mutually exclusive and may occur in combination, although one tends to dominate the innovation reactions. Emotional reactions are based on the often groundless desire to 'must have' an innovation for no readily explainable reason beyond 'I want it' or 'because it is there'. Intellectual reactions are based on curiosity and the novelty factor of trying to explore how it works, why it works, and what it actually does. Even then, the intellectual component relates more to the exploratory cognitive nature of the behaviour, which is the pursuit of satisfying a need for novelty or variety. Social acceptability reactions are derived from feelings that the ownership of the innovation will make the user seem trendy, fashionable and socially desirable. It has a strong element of fantasy associated with the adoption of the innovation, and the belief that the innovation is very visible to others, irrespective of whether it actually is or is not. Utilitarian reactions are based on the user sensing an opportunity to use the innovation to meet a currently held need.

For the first encounter with the Internet, many people found satisfaction through the intellectual pursuit of seeing how much information was available, and how much new knowledge could be gained. The novelty value of the Internet was twofold: the Internet as a medium was new, and it provided an apparently limitless range of novel experiences.

Others experienced an emotional response to the Internet in terms of wanting to be involved with it at a level they could not consciously explain, beyond simple statements of desire. As the Internet has become progressively more mainstream, many users are reacting with the social acceptance fascination of adopting the Internet because everyone else appears to be online. The social acceptance adopters are the most likely group to abandon the Internet as soon as it either decreases in popularity among key social commentators, or ceases to be a fashion statement and becomes too widely adopted. It is highly likely that a fashion-based wave of Internet rejection will occur as people declare themselves too sophisticated or 'too cool' to be on the Internet.

The fourth response has been the utility factor of seeing the commercial, practical or useful application of the Internet in the consumer's daily life. Utility adoption has driven much of the commerce-based adoption of the Internet as individual and corporate users seek to use the Internet to enhance their business opportunities. Overall, the initial reaction to the Internet remains a function of personal needs (e.g. need for novelty) and a recognition of the features of the Internet that meet that need (apparent unlimited novelty). These product features of the Internet can be categorised using Rogers' (1983) innovation characteristics profile.

Diffusion of innovations: Rogers' five features of innovations

Rogers (1983) outlined five innovation characteristics he believed had the greatest impact on innovation adoption. Gregor and Jones (1999) used these five factors in examining the diffusion of Internet service in rural and country areas. The value to reviewing the five characteristics in the context of actual adoption is to see how Rogers' (1983) theoretical model is translated into action by ordinary adopters. The five innovation characteristics are:

■ *relative advantage*: the Internet's inherent superiority, which was initially difficult to establish given the lack of comparable products associated with the RNP. The relative advantage was derived from cross comparisons with related communications products like faxes, mobile phones and other telecommunications equipment. The major advantage the Internet demonstrated over other communications technologies was the time-independent nature of email communication. Rural adopters of the Internet also found the information access, and flexibility of delivery to be a value, given their isolation from larger city services.

■ *compatibility*: the degree to which the Internet relates to the adopters' experience. In the case of Gregor and Jones' (1999) rural adopters, they had a high level of communications technology uptake ranging from CB radio through to faxes, satellite phones and other mobile communications technology. The addition of another communications and information avenue was a continuation of their use of a wide range of related, although not identical, technologies. The compatibility of the Internet related largely to the degree to which members of the public had exposure to distributed information systems, networked communications or similar online services. For the vast majority of average home adopters, this exposure was limited, and consequently the Internet was not seen as readily compatible with existing lifestyles. In addition, Internet access often required the adoption of new technology, ranging from the acquisition of a modem through to an entirely new computer system. Further, Internet use behaviours, such as web surfing, email or online chat remain unnatural learned behaviours that are not compatible with the usual experiences of the average home adopter.

- *complexity*: the relative difficulty of using and understanding the innovation. The Internet has a high complexity level, even among rural adopters with extensive experience of other communications technologies. Many studies of Internet users, from academics to farmers, have noted that the complexity and the large number of new skills required for using the Internet are a major barrier to adoption (Applebee, Clayton & Pascoe 1997). Numerous efforts to simplify the Internet and access to the Internet are being made, including offering TV-based Internet access. However, the product still remains a highly complex adoption for many users. This has also been one of the selling points and reasons for adoption by users seeking intellectual stimulation, such as those who experienced Alpert's (1994) intellectual innovation fascination.

- *trialability*: the degree to which an innovation can be experienced separately from total adoption. Due to the fact that the Internet itself is a series of related experiences, such as the Web, chat, email and other online functions, it is possible to adopt the Internet in various stages. In addition, numerous limited-use Internet access products have been developed such as prepaid Internet cards, or limited-hour accounts that can be prepurchased without a need for a complete commitment to an Internet service provider.

- *observability*: the level of visibility of the product to other members of the adopter's social group. Gregor and Jones (1999) found that the Internet was generally regarded as a low-visibility product, which hampered initial attempts to demonstrate the relative advantage and value of its adoption. Low-visibility products, particularly intangible products like software or Internet access, rely on word-of-mouth communications for their visibility. Kingsley and Anderson (1998) commented on the tendency of Internet adopters to mention their Internet usage as a method of raising their social profile, and making their adoption decision more visible to the general community.

In addition to the Rogers (1983) typology, there are other features of innovations which determine their overall success or failure to be adopted. The symbolism associated with the use of a product impacts on the degree to which it is likely to be adopted, particularly in the high contextuality social groups outlined by Parthasarathy et al. (1997). Cost of innovations is also a major factor in determining successful adoption, and the associated issues of cost and pricing of the Internet will be discussed in depth in chapter 8.

The most common reason for the success or failure of an innovation is the degree to which the product characteristics meet the needs or wants of the potential adopter. The Internet, with its complexity, incompatibility, difficulty to operate, master and learn, and relatively high adoption costs meets perfectly the needs of certain members of society seeking a complex challenge that differentiates them from their peers. As access to the Internet became easier, more common and the information on the Internet appealed to a wider audience, the relative advantage of the Internet increased to the point where access to the Internet met the informational, recreational or professional needs of new waves of adopters. As the innovation matures and develops, the product characteristics evolve, adjust and meet the needs of a new wave of adopters, and the specific psychological needs of those adopters.

Diffusion of innovations: Personality, predisposition and psychographics

The influence of personal character traits is the most contentious area of innovation adoption theory. There are numerous models which demonstrate the interaction of various personality traits such as innovativeness, sensation seeking, attention to peer pressure and less well-known characteristics such as dogmatism (Reisenwitz & Cutler 1998). One consistent finding from the innovation adoption literature is that each product category, product class and innovation has an impact on the adopter in a different manner, with certain characteristics having a greater, yet not absolute, influence. Innovativeness, with respect to speed of adoption upon encountering the new product, has the largest impact on adoption, followed by the degree to which the individual waits to seek peer approval for his or her decision. Societal pressures, such as collectivist social groups, or groups with high regard for fashion, reinforce the tendency in the individual to delay adoption if the individual has a high regard for membership of that group.

Other common characteristics include a higher level of education than the average in the social grouping, particularly in the case of complex RNP innovations. Wealth and disposable incomes are also valuable indicators of propensity to actually adopt a product. Many people may have innovative desires, but few have sufficient financial resources to consistently purchase high cost innovations.

Finally, the least-agreed influences on innovation adoption are the demographics of age, gender and ethnicity. Several studies attempt to seek a clean demographic break along gender lines to demonstrate that males and masculinity are a determinant of innovativeness. However, there is no conclusive demonstration of gender determining intention to adopt new ideas.

Social conditioning may produce a greater propensity towards risk-taking endeavours in young males in certain societies; however, social conditioning also generates traditional or conservative young males with an opposition to innovation adoption. Masculinity and femininity also prove to be poor predictors of innovation adoption for no matter how innovative the new lipstick and eyeliner may be, it's unlikely to feature on the 'must have' list of a highly masculine adopter. Product characteristics appear more relevant.

Age is often spuriously associated with innovation adoption, given that higher cost innovations tend to be adopted by older consumers. Closer examination of this phenomenon revealed that the level of disposable income was a greater influence than age. It simply was the case that a 25-year-old innovator with a steady job, no mortgage and good credit was more likely to be able to afford the high-cost innovation than an 18-year-old innovator with no job, no credit and low income.

The base condition for adopting an innovation is the degree to which it meets the needs of the individual. These needs are based on the complex interaction between psychographic variables, the characteristics of the innovation and the extent to which the innovation adoption outcome matches the psychological needs (novelty) and wants (peer acceptance) of the end user. No one profile can generate a comprehensive fit for every innovation. However, a consistent series of factors has emerged from the innovation adoption literature that characterise typical adopters, based on their position in the adoption cycle.

 # Adoption profile of Internet users

'It's been done before.'
George Harrison, in the Simpsons' episode, 'The B-Sharps'.

Innovation adoption overview

While the Internet is still a new environment for many people, consumers using the Internet are less new, and their behaviours towards the adoption of the Internet are far from unique. Despite the inherent novelty of the Internet and user behaviours, adoption of innovations has been a standard part of consumer behaviour research for more than 50 years, and innovation adoption has been a part of daily life for much longer. The same principles and processes that brought fire from being in the domain of the caveman innovator to being in the possession of the laggard caveman are still in application with the adoption of the Internet.

Innovation adoption has been described by a variety of authors and with a series of diagrams and models, some of which have been explained in detail at the start of this chapter. All of these models and explanations have a single common theme — innovations are adopted by a small group of **innovators** who then encourage a second group, the **early adopters**, to try the innovation. Once the early adopters have adopted the innovation, it moves to the **early majority**, through to the **late majority** and off to the end group of **laggards**. At this point, the Internet is moving from innovator groups and early adopter groups in most nations with widely available Internet access. The implication of Internet adoption still remaining in the domain of the innovator–early adopter categories is best explored by examining the characteristics of these groups. Rogers (1995) outlined a five category model of innovation adopters, using a standard bell curve and the S-curve mode of innovation. The five categories of innovators, and their dominant characteristic are outlined in table 4.1.

Rogers' (1983) model is based on a theoretical classification system using the S-curve model of diffusion in conjunction with a bell-curve population distribution.

Table 4.1 Rogers' five categories of innovators

Name	Characteristic	Percentage
Innovators	venturesome	2.5
Early adopters	respectable	13.5
Early majority	deliberate	34.0
Late majority	sceptical	34.0
Laggards	traditional	16.0
		100.0

Source: Rogers, M. R. 1983, *Diffusion of Innovations* 3rd edn, Macmillan, London.

Innovators: Venturesome (try anything once)

The innovators are those people in society who are first to try an innovation. They usually can be identified by four attributes: venturesomeness; substantial financial resources; willingness to suffer setbacks; and an ability to understand and apply complex technological knowledge. 'Venturesomeness' is an almost obsessional desire for the hazardous, risky and avant garde (Rogers 1995). These are the risk takers who need new challenges, new adventures and new experiences. They are also reasonably wealthy, with a higher than average level of disposable income and a willingness to suffer losses and setbacks in the pursuit of something new. Given the consistently high price of innovations and the high failure rate, the innovators in society need to be able to absorb substantial financial losses that come from adopting risky expensive technology. The fourth factor for innovators is the ability to be able to comprehend and use complex technology. Knowing that the likelihood of the technology coming to the market in a user-friendly, plug and play format, straight out of the box is low, innovators need to be able to take the innovation and apply it without relying on comprehensive instructions from the manufacturer or producer.

When it came to adopting Internet access, the innovators could afford to purchase the initial 300 band modem, then progressively upgrade through 1200, 2400, 9600, 14.4, 28.8 through to the 56K modems. The innovator was likely also to already possess the standard of computer required for Internet access, and was more willing to pay the initially high subscription costs. In addition, the innovators also influenced the development of the Internet in that their higher than average abilities to deal with unfamiliar complex technologies meant that the need to reduce the complexity of Internet access was not recognised. It was only when the first wave of early adopters began adopting the Internet that the need to simplify access to the Internet became recognised, and addressed by the market. At this point in the innovation adoption curve, the Internet consisted largely of technologically literate novelty seekers who had a propensity to use highly complex systems, in part for the complexity, but mostly for the newness factor. Consequently the Internet was not the most user-friendly environment for people outside of the innovator group. It is also important to note that the innovator adoption of the Internet had been occurring since its inception in 1968 as a non-commercial network linking government, military and university institutions (Breitenbach & van Doren 1998). It was only the development of the graphical user interface systems associated with the Web that opened the Internet from the innovator group to further adoption by early adopters.

Early adopters: Respectable (The Net is hip. Adopt now to be a social leader.)

Early adopters are the stately and refined members of the adoption cycle compared to the rebellious, devil-may-care risk takers of the innovator category. The fascinating paradox of the early adopter category is that while they are seen as the respectable opinion-formers of society, they take their lead from the successes of the wild child innovators. They share many of the traits of the innovator group, the most significant of which are above-average intelligence, education and understanding of complex innovations. Unlike the innovators, the early adopter is a figure of respectability, and seeks to maintain this reputation and social position through careful selection of the innovations chosen for trial. By the time the innovation reaches the early adopter it has begun to gain mainstream credibility. After having been used by this group for an extended period, it becomes part of the accepted mainstream as it moves into the early majority phases.

Adoption by social leaders has been the most important event in the diffusion of the Internet through society. In the early stages of the 1990s, when public access to the Internet first became available, it was seen as the domain of the 'outsiders', those who ignored or paid little attention to the social norms. The media of the day portrayed the Internet as a dangerous place, full of deviants, pornography and instructions for bomb making. As the Internet diffusion continued through the innovator category into the early adopters, it gained a social acceptance to the point that even the most vocal critics of the Internet had their own Internet presence.

By adopting the Internet, the early adopters brought social respectability to the medium. The movement also brought many applications on the Internet away from the technical for the sake of technicality focus of the innovators towards a more user-friendly interface. Ease of use and social popularity have become more prized than technical difficulty in the diffusion of the technology. As the end of the early adopter and the start of the early majority is reached, more emphasis is being placed on the user-friendly, plug in and play focus which demonstrates advantages, rather than fashion status of being online.

Early majority: Deliberate (needs and wants)

By the time an innovation meets the early majority market most market researchers have lost interest in the product. The early majority is the leading edge of the maturity of the market. Competition multiplies, and a range of almost identical innovations can be adopted to colour coordinate with the other early majority innovations. By the time the early majority were taking their first steps towards home computing, the computer was being offered in more colours than the default shade of business beige. Early majority adopters are consistently categorised as being 'deliberate' in their approach to innovation adoption. These are the people who weigh up the pros and cons of adoption, in contrast to the innovator who adopts for the novelty and the early adopter who takes up the innovation for the fashion leadership.

Adoption based on conscious and calculated decisions that have been subjected to extensive consideration also alters the nature of the marketplace. While the Internet is still primarily the domain of the innovator and early adopter, signs are in place that the early majority are on the way to adoption. Media copy about the benefits of being online, supported by advertising for Internet-based banking and government and commercial services demonstrate the practical benefits of being online.

The movement of the early majority online will also change the social dynamics of the Internet through the sheer weight of numbers of the group. Access and functions will become tailored for ease of use rather than technical complexity. Optional customisation functions will be moved from the front of the software to the ubiquitous 'advanced features' heading, as has been the case with the Microsoft Internet Explorer software.

The progression of Internet diffusion can be seen to parallel the development of web browser software. As the systems have become more powerful, more of the customisable features are being moved towards lesser accessed areas of the options menu, giving a user-friendly 'plug and play' veneer to a complex system. Promotion of the Internet will focus on benefits to be gained, cost reductions to be made and appeal to the rational logical decision maker. Economies of scale and the viability of mass market segmentation also see the early adopters faced with a range of product choices that develop at this point in the product lifecycle.

Late majority: Sceptical (ends up needing, not always wanting)

The latter half of the diffusion curve is often treated unkindly by diffusion researchers who have a bias towards innovation and innovators. However, this group represents over one third of any given market, and it is adoption by this late majority that ensures a universal access potential for a given innovation. The most dominant characteristics of the group are scepticism and resentment towards the technology. Quite frequently these adoptions are made on a begrudging concession to the necessity for the technology, without a desire to actively use it. Many later adopters of electronic banking services such as ATMs or phone banking feel forced into the adoption of the technology as other functions, such as teller services, were withdrawn.

For the Internet, the movement of the late majority represents the Internet's movement from an exclusive tool of university and government sectors to an almost universal system similar to television and telephone. It represents also a dangerous point in the development of the Internet. With the bulk of the market apparently having converted to the technology, albeit with varying degrees of enthusiasm, the potential for the withdrawal of non-Internet service will be very high. The laggard group, and later adopters, may be disadvantaged by the market assuming that everyone is now active online.

The much talked about digital gap between the online-haves and the offline-have-nots will be most pronounced at the time services which had been available on and offline switch to online delivery only. The authors predict that it will be at this point that a government body will propose universal access to the Internet, or impose legislation that forces essential services to remain available offline. As far-fetched as the digital divide may sound, a recent Australian Government proposal for unemployment involved job seekers logging into the employment agencies. It was pointed out that the people who most needed the services were the least likely to be able to afford a computer and the Internet access required to maintain their unemployment benefits. The scheme was abandoned, but it illustrates how assumptions of universal access to popular technology can endanger access to standard services.

Laggards: Traditional (want not, adopt not)

The laggards traditionally are the most neglected and most often criticised group in innovation adoption literature. Characterised, and often stereotyped as traditional conservative Luddites, the laggard group represents the collective category of non-adopters of an innovation deemed to be universal. The important consideration for the Internet marketer is that there are a number of valid reasons why people will choose not to adopt the Internet. These range from cultural and religious reasons, including philosophical objections to networked technologies, through to costs and lack of perceived benefit. Absence of perceived benefit is a major issue for marketing of the Internet and online services, as this affects more than just the laggard category. While many white-collar urban professionals may not be able to perceive of a life without the dependency on email and the Web, rural communities in the First and Third World may not be able to see the point in email in the first place. Why communicate through a computer to the person sitting at the next desk when you can simply turn and talk to them?

The key thing that the laggard community brings to the development of the Internet is the knowledge that the Internet is not universally attractive, has no inherently unique selling proposition and will not become the 'be all' and 'end all' of everyone's life. Laggards also comprise approximately 16 per cent of any given population which makes them an attractive niche market in themselves (Rogers 1995). They also represent a reality check against the assumption that technology is universal, and that the majority of a market equals the totality of the market. Understanding the reasons why laggards choose not to adopt the Internet rather than simply dismissing the category as reluctant to change will also assist the marketer in continuing to understand what product offers have not yet been developed to address the needs of this group.

Implications of the current Internet adopters

One of the most neglected issues of Internet marketing at the end of the twentieth century was the review of how a market full of innovators and early adopters was affecting online marketing. Venkatesh (1998) argues that cyberculture, and the development of cyberspace, have been the responsibility of the young, the risk takers, and the uninitiated, rather than the established social guardians. Consequently, the innovators, not the socially respected early adopters, were creating the ground rules for the online world.

The fundamental shift in the late 1990s towards the online lifestyle had left the marketing industry grabbing at the first pieces of available data to try to predict the future. The misunderstood factor in Internet marketing research has been that the first 10 years of commercialised Internet created a market of innovators and early adopters. To make matters complex, it gave this group global access to innovations, ranging from new business ventures, new ideas and new behaviours through to the relatively mundane novelty of performing common tasks like banking in a new environment. The main reason that this is not of benefit is that innovators are notoriously poor predictors of the future. If the innovators were better predictors, fewer failed products would make it from the drawing board to the living room of the innovator. As the innovators attached themselves to the Internet, they created a market of innovators. When 2.5 per cent of the world's market for Internet use is online, you have a sustainable economy of innovators who will adopt Internet-based innovations for the sake of their inherent novelty. Functionality, ease of use and practical benefit were secondary to the need for novelty felt by the innovative edge of the innovator category who were patrolling the early Internet in a constant search for the next big idea.

With some aspects of the Internet the pursuit of novelty brought benefits such as the World Wide Web. When a group of researchers at *Centre European Rechercher Nucleaire* (CERN) published a method of footnoting scientific papers so that key data could be pursued into detailed explanations outside of the body of the main text, all they saw was a neat indexing function. Early reports of the Web focused on the novelty of being able to move from idea to idea, with a fascination expressed in the movement and flow of information. One of the earliest descriptions of the World Wide Web focused on the intriguing nature of being able to move from document to document (Browning 1993). The notions of novelty expressed in the journalistic accounts were progressively supplemented with comments concerning the feel and the experience — features of value to the novelty and experience-seeking innovators. More recently, the Internet has become a fashion statement, with the proliferation of web site addresses and email contact details appearing on everything from billboards to cola cans to sports fields. The sheer mass of web addresses in public view has moved the Internet from the field of the innovator to the cusp of the early adopter–early majority.

Part of the fundamental shift now occurring with the Internet is the recognition of user types being based on online behaviours, rather than offline activities. Inherent in the Internet is still the innovation bias, as the innovators still tend to dominate the landscape, and the imagination of Internet researchers. With the increase in the user base of the Internet, market segments are being identified, which are not primarily dominated by the try-anything-once innovators, and Internet-based services are being adapted to meet the functionality orientated needs of the early adopter group.

Internet user categories

'There are two kinds of people in the world: people who divide people up into two kinds of people, and people who don't.'

Anon.

The pursuit of market segmentation strategies that neatly divide the Internet user population into manageable market-sized chunks has been a common academic and business pursuit since the mid-1990s. Numerous typologies have emerged based on a range of segmentation bases — psychographics, demographics, and usage behaviours. Some efforts have been made to develop Internet-specific measures of existing offline measures — iVALS has been developed from the standard offline VALS measurement (future.sri.com/VALS/VALSindex.shtml). One critical limitation of the early measures is that they managed to progressively segment innovators into small categories of extremely innovative users through to innovative users.

The iVALS measure quickly became dated by the progression of technology as several novel and unique behaviours were superseded by newer technology. In addition, the use of email attachments from none to frequently could move a user through a range of iVALS categories. It is difficult to believe that the use or non-use of email attachment files is such a critical issue in determining a market segment.

Despite the limitations of some of the earlier attempts to segment the Internet market, there is an inherent value in identifying Internet user types. The progressive development of a body of literature containing a variety of market segment types allows web site designers to incorporate specific features to meet the needs of certain market segments. It is important to remember that there are no 'one size fits all' market segmentation strategies. While each marketing segmentation strategy can draw from the existing literature and findings, the final strategy will be based on a unique set of variables determined by the product and the organisational goals. The market typology presented here, developed by Lewis and Lewis (1997 in Breitenbach & van Doren 1998), is an illustration of the types of market segments that can be developed to outline broad market needs. Lewis and Lewis (1997) identified five types of web site visitor:

- **directed information seekers**: people who search for timely, relevant and accurate information on a specific topic or set of topics
- **undirected information seekers**: the classic 'web surfer' model of the users who follow a random interest-driven path through the Web, clicking on links of interest and information that looks new, interesting or different. These are the types of users most likely to be seeking to experience Hoffman and Novak's (1996) flow concept.
- **bargain hunters**: much like their offline counterparts, this group seek the free, the trial sample and the giveaways that are available on the Web. In addition to searching for discounts, giveaways and free samples, they are most likely to be the downloaders of shareware or freeware programs.
- **entertainment seekers**: this category seeks out the world of online entertainment, from playing Java and shockwave games at web sites through to

experiencing the worlds of online gaming, streaming audio or downloaded music. This is primarily a hedonistic group, which takes pleasure in the consumption of entertainment and entertaining features of web sites.

■ ***directed buyers***: these are the hard core shoppers of the online world. Their mission when online is to purchase goods, services or information, and they are online to find the product they want to buy, rather than to research it, play with it or take home a sample version of it.

The value of the five-point typology is that it outlines a set of market needs concerning web site visitors, and the use of the World Wide Web. The value for the Internet marketer is that these five categories offer an overview of the types of behaviours that can be expected to occur at the marketer's web site. The commercial application of such a typology is to identify which types of web site visitor behaviours are most common among the clientele for your product.

Internet marketing INSIGHT
Music to the eyes

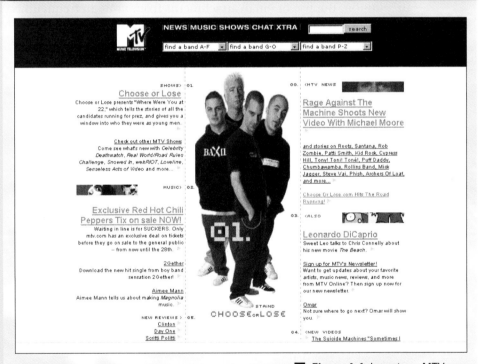

•• ■ **Figure 4.4** I want my MTV.com

MTV represents more than just a television station — the MTV generation has come to signify a group raised on a diet of rock film clips and comfortable access to the television medium. When the Web came along and introduced a new media access point, generations of couch potatoes graduated into mouse potatoes, and MTV.com grew up with them.

MTV recognises that their core business is primarily music and information television, so they did not have their web site competing against their TV shows. Instead, they augmented the MTV experience with a web site that offers a range of features, options, depth, with narrowcasting to reinforce and meet the online needs of their fan base.

The web site has a depth orientation, with a complex index-style front page which outlines dozens of entry points into the site, from a series of three pull-down menus of bands and artists to over a dozen quick links to breaking stories, concert details and rock gossip. Directed or undirected information seekers can find the gossip, tour dates and information they want to know, need to know, or just happen to find interesting. While the core sections remain stable and constant, the gossip headlines update on a regular basis, giving the returning visitor both a sense of familiarity and continually new information tidbits to explore. Direct buyers are focused towards online ticket sales, although these tickets are only useful if you happen to be in the region of the concert (or plan on scalping them through eBay). Entertainment seekers coming to the MTV web site have quick and easy access to a wide range of music and videos, including excerpts from MTV shows, popular bands and new releases. Finally, even the bargain hunters can take home a download or two from the MTV music and promotional screensaver libraries.

MTV's global Internet strategy aims to provide localised country-specific experiences while still providing easy access to MTV's growing network of international sites which currently include the UK, Japan, Latin America, and Korea among others. For instance, the MTV.com site is strongly America-centred, but features an international links hub area on the home page, as well as two MTV UK branded radio stations featured on the Radio MTV.com product.

Source: www.mtv.com

MTV.com's successful integration of the five web visitor sites demonstrates that these market segments are not exclusive categorisations. In fact it is possible to be engaged in two or more of the behaviours simultaneously during a web surfing session — a user seeking specific product information (directed information seeker) may also follow paths of interest (undirected) arising from the sites accessed during the search. In addition, while the Lewis and Lewis (1997) typology describes a set of web site visiting behaviours, it is not a comprehensive overview of online activities and behaviours.

Internet use behaviours

The following section of this chapter looks at the how, why and what of consumer behaviour online. It examines common motivations for using the Internet, specific behaviours that seem to exist predominantly online, and reasons why people may not be getting the most out of the Internet. It examines also reasons for not using the Internet, and reasons for leaving the Internet.

Why people use the Internet

There are nine reasons why people use the Internet. This is not an exclusive list, and people may be engaged in one or more of these use reasons at any one time. The purpose of the list is to explore the motivations associated with online behaviours, to gain a better understanding of how and why people behave as they do online.

1. Anonymity, and the non-corporeal body

Anonymity, and the lack of physical presence, allows a much greater range of consumer freedoms. One of the major differences in consumer behaviour created by anonymity is that it reduces the visibility of the consumer's behaviour to others. While online, and virtually anonymous, it is possible to explore a range of behaviours that would not otherwise be explored due to the visibility, and possible negative social impact, of these behaviours. At the most basic level, one can admit to liking an unfashionable movie (www.badmovies.org/) or at a higher level one can access information concerning potentially embarrassing medical conditions. The advantage of cyberspace is best summed up in the adage, 'on the Internet, nobody knows you're a dog' (*New Yorker* 1993). However, with the advent of cookies, click tracking and other market research techniques, demonstrating a high level of visits to lassie.com, an email address rin_tin_tin@dog-house.fidonet.com, and having a range of bookmarks covering obedience schools and car chasing techniques, will most likely reveal a canine orientation.

2. Communications: Reach out and chat with someone

One of the most common reasons given for use of the Internet was communication, with email heading the list, followed by access to other communications services like USENET, bulletin boards and IRC (Katz & Aspden 1997). Developments in technology are also facilitating low-cost videoconferencing online, and voice-based Internet communications such as Net.phone or Microsoft Netmeeting are allowing consumers to communicate with text, voice and video for the cost of their standard Internet connection.

3. Convenience

Convenience has been cited by many users as one of the major advantages of Internet access. The use of the Internet for practical purposes, such as convenient access to information, is a hallmark of the early majority adopter who seeks a specific benefit from their innovation. In addition, Alpert's (1994) utility innovation fascination is also satisfied by the notion of the Internet providing convenience. This is one of the primary motivations behind the use of online banking and online shopping service by time-starved users with Internet-based lifestyles (Bellman, Lohse & Johnson 1999).

4. Information seeking

The interest-driven nature of the Internet and the Web has created a unique user environment where millions of pages of specialist interest information is available to the average user. Users with a high level of novelty seeking, or who reacted with Alpert's (1994) intellectual innovation fascination, will have found the vast tracts of information available online to be a major reason to use the Internet.

In addition, new services ranging from gossip columns (www.drudgereport. com) through to recognised global news channels (www.cnn.com) are available for 24-hour coverage of events, including fast updates of late-breaking news, and links to in-depth background information. News-orientated users have the opportunity to remain current on a developing issue while also being able to pursue information in greater depth than is possible with a conventional news broadcast.

5. Global access

The global nature of the Internet is an attraction for several categories of web surfers, from novelty seekers wanting to explore the world to utility seekers who gain access to a wide range of international services and products from home. Global access through the Internet also provides a strong sense of community, with families able to keep in contact with members in different countries. Finally, the Internet has opened up a global market to online operators, giving them both a range of customers and products not previously accessible due to high travel costs.

6. Community/sense of belonging/pursuit of common interests and goals

The Internet is an interest-driven medium where consumers seek out information, news or services to meet their needs. One of the major consumer behaviour patterns emerging from the online environment has been the clustering of consumers by shared interest. In particular, the USENET environment with specific topic newsgroups has created a microcosm of dedicated specialist-interest communities. Katz and Aspden (1997) found that one of the significant reasons for going online was to contact people with shared interests — to feel a sense of belonging with similar people. Cybercommuning allows users from a diverse range of backgrounds to gather with a common interest to share information, community and often friendship. **Cybercommunities** are examined in depth in chapter 5.

7. Utility/necessity/fear of being left behind

Utility, necessity and the fear of being left behind are possibly the worst reasons for consumers to become involved with an innovation. Utility-based adoptions, based on using the Internet to meet a need or want, and resulting from either Alpert's (1994) utility fascination or the pragmatic nature of the early to late majority adopter, are common reasons for people moving online. Users experience a pragmatic value from engaging in the use of the Internet, either as part of their work, education or business. However, Katz and Aspden (1997) have already reported indications of laggard fear-based adoptions, common among late majority adopters, where people have adopted the Internet because of a fear of being left out or left behind. These users have not adopted for the potential benefits to be gained, but as insurance against potential losses arising from not adopting. People using the Internet for its utility value are also the most likely to be dissatisfied with current Internet offerings, particularly in regard to expectations gap, and to the speed and quality of services available. For them, the Internet needs to be a functional tool, rather than a pleasurable experience or pleasant community.

8. Recreation, leisure and pleasure

The Internet provides a wide range of entertainment services, including the opportunities to engage in online gaming, gambling, video and movie watching. While the Internet is not television, in terms of the amount of recreational and entertainment content available, large numbers of recreation functions are available. There are networked games, ranging from chess and bridge through to classic board games like Monopoly and Scrabble, and beyond to network computer games like Quake (www.heat.net). **MUDs** (multi-user dungeons) offer recreational as well as cybercommunity and communication functions, as do other chat services (www.mudconnector.com). The **multi-user dungeon** is one of the definitive cybercommunity environments, using a virtual world structure of interlinked rooms and environments for gaming, social and educational functions. The use of the Internet in this context is a hedonistic experience, that differs from inherent merit which values the Internet for the Internet experience, whereas these users are engaged in the Internet for the pleasure it can facilitate.

9. Inherent merit

The final reason for using the Internet lies with the innovators and those with Alpert's emotional innovation fascination. They use the Internet mainly because it is there, because they can, and because they derive pleasure from the experience of the Internet itself, rather than for any specific utility value it may possess (Katz & Aspden 1997). These users are by far the most passionate about the Internet, have the least coherent explanations for their behaviours, and are the most likely to engage in flow-state behaviours.

Following on from these motivations are a range of Internet specific behaviours, facilitated and enhanced by the unique characteristics of the online environment. These behaviours are derived from a combination of the Internet motivations explored above, and the unique behavioural opportunities presented by a computer-mediated environment, free from several key physical-world limitations.

Internet specific behaviours: Don't try this offline

When television became a part of everyday life, certain television watching behaviours emerged, based on the types of satisfaction sought from television. People watched shows from beginning to end, and channel changing decisions were made at the conclusion of a show. The introduction of the remote control generated an entirely new form of behaviour known as zapping, where the viewers moved from channel to channel to avoid commercial breaks. Zapping, as a distinct behaviour, gave rise to a new form of television consumption known as channel surfing, a distinctive television-based pattern of moving from channel to channel, seeking a new stimulus to hold the attention of the channel surfer. Until the rise of the Web, and the adaptation of channel surfing to Web surfing, this behaviour was a television domain-specific action. In a similar manner, the Internet has given rise to domain-specific behaviours that currently reside online. While these behaviours may yet be adapted to a different medium, they are predominantly the unique consumer behaviours of the Internet.

The three major Internet-specific behaviours examined in this chapter represent the combination of the benefits of a computer-mediated environment with specific consumer motivations. One of the greatest advantages of the Internet is the lack of physicality in the computer-mediated environment which allows for a constant expansion process. In particular, the proliferation of web sites and web site hosting has been aided by the fact that they occupy only virtual space. In 1996, privately owned web sites were restricted to approximately one megabyte of space on a standard dial-up account. By 1999, free operations such as Xoom (www.xoom.com) were offering unlimited virtual space on their servers. This increased available virtual space has given rise to new development opportunities without the necessity for physical land. Easy access to virtual space assisted the development of the self-representation behaviours, which in turn led to the enhancement of cybercommunity structures. In conjunction, the limitless, boundless array of web site space, cybercommunities and experiences has also facilitated the engagement of Hoffman and Novak's (1996) flow-state behaviours.

1. Selfrepresentation

Selfrepresentation is explored through two aspects more commonly found in the CME than in other environments. First, the Internet allows for a wider range of self-publishing opportunities than the offline world. Several businesses, such as Yahoo!Geocities (www.geocities.com) and others give away web site server space in exchange for the placement of small advertising banners. Warner Brothers offer theme web server space relating to major Warner Brothers movies and products (www.acmecity.com/thematrix/).

The advent of low cost/no cost online publishing alternatives has led to the development of a self-publishing culture, ranging from web sites that are simply extended CVs or photo galleries of the kids and pets through to complex periodical publications that rival commercial opponents (www.wilsonweb.com/wmt). In addition, the low cost of email has allowed email newsletters and discussion groups to reach thousands of members across the globe at an affordable price. One of the most remarkable of these email newsletters was the *Drudge Report* (www.drudgereport.com), which was an American political email gossip column which first broke the news of the Clinton–Lewinsky affair. As a result of this scoop, the *Drudge Report* rose to fame, and spawned a supporting web site, and a television show on Fox News America. However, not every online self-publishing venture will spawn an international television show, nor will most ventures be looking for this outcome. The self-publishing function of the Internet has allowed small businesses to compete on a 'more' level playing field using the Internet's low cost to develop business projects. Similarly, a lot of musicians, artists and writers are using the self-publishing opportunities to gain exposure to a wider audience than is available to them offline.

The second area of selfrepresentation occurs in the form of the use of **avatars**. An avatar is a representation of the user, normally found in social interaction mediums like MUDs, IRC, USENET and email. To a lesser extent avatars can be used in web sites, though eventually a copyright tag or 'about the author' page gives the identity of the user away. An avatar, in consumer behaviour terms, is a representation of how consumers perceive themselves, and how they wish to be portrayed online. Avatars are discussed in depth in conjunction with cyber-communities in chapter 5. One of the major things that the Internet has allowed, through the anonymity it affords and the use of avatars, is a greater degree of consumer fantasy and role play, normally associated with fashion shopping, to be integrated into communications and online behaviour.

2. Cybercommuning

Cybercommuning, based on computer-mediated environments of shared interests and shared emotional and psychological support, are a feature of the electronic landscape. They predate the Internet, with origins tracing back to telephone party lines, developing through bulletin board systems and finally emerging onto the Internet. The cybercommunity structure allows for clan-ning behaviours based on interests, support needs and identity without the mediator of geography that occurs in offline communities. As with self-publishing, the advent of a virtually limitless array of Internet geographies to host cybercommunity gathering points, from email lists to specific web sites, has reduced many of the entry barriers to the formation of social support groups. Cybercommunities are examined in depth in chapter 5.

3. Flow

The flow concept is most commonly attributed to Hoffman and Novak's (1996) seminal piece on computer-mediated environments. **Flow** was concep-tualised as the state of mind where interaction with the Internet becomes a unified movement from one site or event to the next with little or no aware-ness of distraction, outside influences, or irrelevant thoughts (Hoffman & Novak 1996). Csikzentmihalyi (1975) proposed the concept of flow as a method of characterising human–computer interaction in that it represents a common mode of experience as the user becomes absorbed into the activity. Nel, van Niekerk, Berthon and Davies (1999) identified control, attention focus, curiosity and intrinsic interest in the Internet as elements required for flow. These elements also describe key characteristics of the innovator class, and those adopters who use the Internet for its inherent merit.

One of the most consistent factors reviewed in the flow state research is that the users travel through the Internet from point of interest to point of interest with relatively higher speeds than non-flow state users. Given that each time a new web site is encountered, it will trigger an innovation adop-tion cycle, and one or more of Alpert's innovation fascinations, the flow state susceptibility may be influenced by innovativeness. In order to continue moving through the flow state, new stimulus is required on a constant basis, which feeds the novelty and sensation-seeking elements of the user's persona. Flow will also influence perception of the product characteristics of the new web site.

Relative advantage occurs where the new site provides a new experience to maintain the flow state. Compatibility is usually derived from the new page having been accessed from an existing page. Complexity of the adoption of a new page is reduced as the user experiences several new web page adoptions and becomes skilled in the movements required by the flow state to move to the next stimulus. Finally, the flow state may produce an extended period of site trial, where the web site is adopted for trial to determine if it will support the flow — if not, the site is rejected and a new site is trialled.

For marketers, the flow state produces conflict in the area of research. On one hand, promoting the flow state should technically make the user more susceptible to advertising, particularly the pursuit of click-though advertising banners, and increase mere exposure to numerous web sites. On the other hand, a flow state user is unlikely to purchase from a web site, as stopping to make a purchase will break the flow state. Flow state research has proven difficult and inconclusive, particularly in producing a natural flow state environment in a laboratory setting. In addition, flow state causes the individual to lose perceptions of time, and to focus almost exclusively on flow maintenance behaviours, with little awareness of external events and little, if any, self-monitoring. Self-reporting of flow state activities, especially flow state duration, are very likely to be inaccurate. At this stage, flow remains a concept of interest for exploration by consumer behaviour researchers, but not one that has been comprehensively defined and categorised.

FOCUS ON
Strategy

ICQ — A pager for the Internet

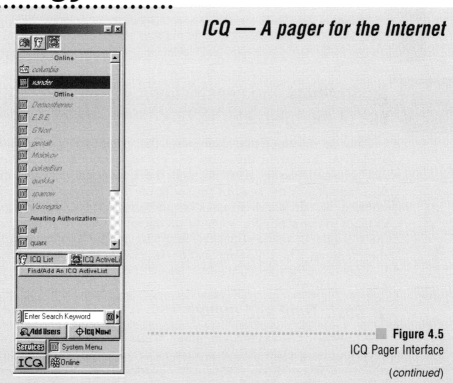

Figure 4.5
ICQ Pager Interface

(*continued*)

What do you get if you combine 24–7 access with global markets, cybercommunities, time-independent and real-time communications and a flower petal logo? ICQ, one of the new wave of Internet communication devices that delivers by capitalising on the unique features of the Internet, has taken the online communications world by storm. Acting as a cross between a pager, an email account and a two-way radio, ICQ offers users the opportunity to send short messages to other users of the ICQ, whether the other user is logged on or not. In addition, users can see whether their friends are online or not through ICQ's notification system. The network offers the value-added services of being able to send greetings cards, voice mail and files.

But there's more to the ICQ network than simply being a facilitated chat system. ICQ was founded to address the market needs created by cybercommunities and self-representation. Offering over 20 themed chat communities, ranging from music discussion to computer self-help, through to car maintenance and beyond, ICQ taps into the interest-driven nature of the Internet, and the potential for cybercommuning. Clanning by interest is aided by the ICQ main web site offering searches by topic, user alias and interest groups. Regular ICQ users are also encouraged to set up ICQ hosted home pages and web sites to further the sense of community among the users.

In addition, selfrepresentation is also supported as users have total control over the degree and nature of information that they provide to the ICQ system. Even the user identification name is left up to the individual, leading to most ICQ user lists looking like a roll call of contemporary cinema and television characters.

The success of ICQ has spawned a range of competitor proprietary networks, including AOL Netscape, Microsoft, iChat and others. Facilitating people-to-people communication is a major business in the Internet, and as more people move online, being able to command the lion's share of the personal communications market is a major objective for any personal Internet pager service.

● ●

Restrictions and constrictions: Factors preventing full use of the Internet

It is not an unreasonable assumption that the processes of self-selection have worked to the extent that most readers of this book are, in varying degrees, pro Internet. Having read through the Internet user types, the innovation fascinations and the reasons for using the Internet, more than a few readers will have recognised themselves in these profiles. From this point of view, it is difficult to conceptualise some of the factors as to why people are not getting the full benefit of the Internet, and why people would voluntarily abandon the medium. The following section overviews five common restrictions and limitations on people's use and enjoyment of the Internet.

1. Cost: Time and money

The Internet is not a cheap medium. While the costs associated with access are declining progressively, and principles of universal access to the Internet are discussed as potential vote-winning platforms for politicians, access to the Internet is still outside the price range of many potential adopters. In addition to the financial costs associated with access, the time costs associated with learning to use the Internet, and the use of the Internet are beyond the time budgets of many people. Even with low cost equipment and easy Internet access, many potential users will not be able to dedicate the time required to gain sufficient Internet literacy to be able to use the Internet to their preferred level.

2. Internet literacy

One of the key selling features of the Internet in the early stage of diffusion was the complexity associated with its use. The Internet began life as an elite medium of scientists, university staff and students, and educated government and military personnel. The core foundation of the World Wide Web remains hypertext, as the text-based medium continues to dominate the Internet functions. This in itself is not inherently bad. It does, however, represent a higher entry level barrier than exists for television or radio. Television does not require literacy, and radio goes one level further in not requiring sight. The Web is a complex, literacy-orientated medium based on the interweaving of ideas, related concepts and textual links to create an ever-expanding network of information. For some people, this is as good a reason as any not to become part of the Internet experience in that the complexity of the medium, the need for literacy skills and the oversupply of variety acts as a deterrent to involvement.

Katz and Aspden (1997) found that one of the early complaints about the Internet was the lack of guides, maps or instruction books to assist new users in navigating through the Internet. While a range of 'Internet for Dummies' style texts have since entered the market, the complaint as to the complexity of the Internet has persisted — the guide books cannot begin to address the sheer size and dynamics of the Internet. Users familiar with the routine nature of television, with published guides announcing the week's viewing in advance find the Internet's constantly evolving and changing medium to be more of a threat than a benefit.

3. Fear

When the Internet first rose to prominence in the conventional media in the early 1990s, it was vilified as a dangerous place full of terrorists, pornography, paedophiles and evildoers. Within the decade, the same Internet is now being touted as a friendly, happy environment where grandparents can play with their grandchildren. The problem facing the expansion of the Internet is that many of the first impressions created by media of it being a dangerous place have remained. First impressions count, and the actions of respected opinion leadership sources such as newspaper editors, current affairs television and talkback radio have tarnished the Internet's reputation. Given that some of the leading critics of the Internet now have web sites, and are actively encouraging their listeners, readers and viewers online, the fact remains the Internet was portrayed as a place to be feared, and that these fears still exist.

The three most commonly cited fears are based on security, privacy, and unwanted content. Security issues constantly dog e-commerce development as horror tales of credit card fraud, hackers and unidentified Internet service charges continue to feature on current affairs programs.

Privacy has also become an issue as user profiles become more easily identifiable through increased market research tracking, and as existing market research databases become available online. Reputable Internet portals such as Infoseek offer services to search various Internet databases for criminal records on business partners, friends and family. Electronic privacy is belatedly becoming an issue in mainstream consumer thinking, despite decades of loyalty programs, market research, and point-of-purchase records which have been building comprehensive offline databases of purchases and interests. The fact remains that privacy will become a major issue for Internet expansion as the perceptions of anonymity give way to perceptions of monitoring by 'Big Brother'.

The third Internet-based fear is the fear of unwanted content. Much of the early anti-Internet media concentrated on the ease with which young children could access pornography, illicit ideas and recipes for bombs, drugs and disaster. Ironically, one major reputable newspaper published sufficient details concerning one of the more notorious e-texts in the hacking field for it to be found within seconds by even the most unsophisticated user.

Unsolicited email for sex sites and other unwanted materials have also increased the perception that the Internet is one long string of unwanted content, and that merely opening a web browser will subject innocents to such imagery. As odd as this seems to a regular user of the Internet, these perceptions give rise to fears concerning the Internet, and how this sort of freely available content will damage the children of the community. Such fears, and anecdotal evidence, led to the rise of the American Communications Decency Act, and similar acts of government across the world.

Another fear associated with the Internet receives less attention in the largely pro-Internet pro-innovation research — the fear of the unknown. Novelty seeking as a motivation for adopting the Internet assumes that a vast field of unknown content, new experiences, and unchartered waters has an inherent benefit. In examining the motivations of laggards and late adopters, a large landscape of unchartered unknown content is a negative factor to be overcome. To them, the unknown is to be avoided rather than explored. The strengths that drew the innovators and early adopters to the Internet are the weaknesses that drive the laggards away. The need for comfort, stability and a reluctance to engage the unknown is seen as a positive when selling nostalgia-based products and services, and yet is roundly condemned and criticised when the same marketers want to sell modern and cutting edge products to the nostalgia market. Some people will never be comfortable in the Internet environment, and should not be expected to be comfortable in an environment that is alien to their needs and desire for security and stability.

4. Lack of desire: No benefit, no consequence, and no value

Not everybody will like the Internet. There are no universal products that appeal to all ages, races, psychographic segments and user profiles. The Internet will be no different in that some people will trial it, use it, and find it says nothing to them about their lives. There will be social groups who will reject the Internet as it offers nothing to them, meets no needs and matches no wants they have. Others will find that the Internet is too slow, too complex, too dull, and not the digital promised land they expected to find, and, with their expectations not met, they will abandon the Internet. Increasingly, the non adopters of the Internet will not be those who have not experienced it, and by mere exposure will come to understand the inherent benefit, but those who have adopted and actively rejected it (Kingsley & Anderson 1998).

5. Expectation gap: Promised the Earth, delivered a bucket of soil

The final reason for Internet rejection will be cognitive dissonance. The Internet is being hyped up out of all proportion to the services it can deliver. Demonstrations of Internet technologies always occur in laboratory-perfect conditions, and never the slow, unstable and unglamorous dial-up connections of the home user. Digital streaming video appears to run smoothly in full screen on the advertising, and when the reality is a jerky, pixilated postage stamp on the screen with low quality audio, the user has a right to feel cheated. The mismatch between expectation and reality will be the greatest cause of abandoning the Internet as users feel conned, cheated or somehow duped that the Internet was not the digital Disneyland promised to them by PC manufacturers and Internet service providers. Already issues of the costs of adoption, lack of standards, the ever-increasing need to upgrade computers to use basic functions, the lack of user friendliness and the overall complexity of being online are taking their toll on the user base. At the present time, the rates of adoption by new users are overtaking the rates of abandonment. However, time is against the Internet as more and more users are experiencing the Internet, and making their adoption and rejection decisions.

 ## Implications for marketing

So, with the cheerful thought that the Internet may not be the answer to everyone's problems, what can marketing do to address the reasons why people are not going online, and are not staying online? Four suggestions are offered as a starting point for further development — lowering the barriers, lowering expectations, securing the Internet and finally, taking no for an answer.

Lower the barriers

The best way to get people online, and keep them online is to lower the barriers to entry. This means more than free computers and free Internet access, or having a government policy of universal access. It represents recognising, legitimising and addressing people's concerns regarding the Internet. Instead of promoting one-click, plug-in and play as being the normal approach to Internet access, recognise the difficulty of access. When the expectation is that you should be able to go online instantly, and the reality is more complex, less confident users feel that they have done something wrong, and this heightens any existing Internet-based anxiety. Legitimising the anxiety by letting the consumer recognise that it is difficult, that other people feel the same way, and that their reactions are normal, lowers the psychic entry barrier.

Second, the Internet offers an opportunity to customise the market to meet the product rather than the product to the market. Having just advocated legitimising customer needs, one of the most important marketing led developments in Internet access could be to increase the average level of information literacy in society. Marketing, through lowering entry costs (price), increasing points of access and demonstration (place), increasing visible instructions and encouragement (promotion) and creating multilayered Internet access based on skill (product) can promote an increase in the general level of information literacy.

Third, value remains the number one priority for Internet-based marketing. If a service, product or good is online, it has to offer a value to the customer that the customer wants or needs. Intrinsic worth, and sheer novelty of being online, will occur by being online. To get beyond the innovator markets, something of value must be exchanged with users who are giving us their time to seek out and access our site. The interest-driven nature of the Internet means that by the time customers come to our web site, we already owe them something in return for the time they have spent seeking us out — meeting this debt will increase the perceived value of the Internet for the end user.

Lower the expectations: Promise the achievable, and deliver more than promised

Services marketing has long been accustomed to having to manage expectations so that what the customer expects is both reasonable and achievable. Unfortunately, the promotion of the Internet as a digital wonderland where services promised are years away from development has created a large negative expectation delivery gap. One of the most simple methods to address this gap is to promise an achievable outcome, and deliver greater benefit than was promised. With the rapid development of Internet technologies, it is better to promise a lower level of service and bet on the technology development improving the delivery than to promise an unattainable level and hope the technology development rises to the occasion. Web-based videoconferencing is one area where the technology is still struggling to match the expectations of the market. In contrast, the online music industry promised downloadable music based on the then current technology. When the **MP3** file format was developed and reduced music file sizes by anything up to a factor of 10, there was a positive service expectation gap in which music, which had been available, became available more easily.

Securing the Internet

Along with recognising that the Internet is a complex medium, marketing has to accept that there will be a long period of slow change concerning perceptions of the Internet. Given the reputation of the Internet, and its relative age compared to television and print media, a long-term view of perception change is necessary. Marketing can assist in the development and improvement of perceptions of the Internet through responsible marketing research online which ensures perceptions of privacy. While the desire to acquire accurate detailed profiles of individuals is strong from a market research and product development point of view, more value is gained by people feeling that their privacy is preserved when they are online. Remember, when people are web surfing from home, they feel secure in the privacy of their home. Taking this feeling of security and privacy away from the user will ultimately do more damage to Internet-based marketing than any benefit that could be gained.

Accept rejection as a legitimate choice

Finally, marketing has to learn to accept the judge's decision. Some people will never adopt your product. They are not fools, idiots or laggards. They do understand the inherent merits associated with your invention. It is just that they have tried it, found they do not like it, and engaged in rational consumer behaviour and rejected the product. Now they are seeking an alternative means of satisfying their needs, just like they did when they sought your product out in the first place. They are sane, logical, rational people who will not use the Internet no matter how hard we try to convince them, or what degree of condescending, abusive or coercive techniques we apply.

Rejection of an innovation is a legitimate part of the innovation adoption cycle, and in any given distribution of a product, approximately 16 per cent of the population will not adopt for a number of reasons (Rogers 1995). Add to that the people engaged in extended trial, who later reject (Kingsley & Anderson 1998), and those who find an innovation which meets their needs more satisfactorily than the Internet currently does, and you'll find a substantial proportion of society will be offline. Accept this as a given factor in your market — your customers may not want to be online, and may resent being forced to go online just because you decided that it would be better for your business for your customers to be online. Let the customers come to you online, but do not force people into a potentially costly and difficult innovation adoption process just to gain access to a product they previously had available to them offline. Remember, even if 84 per cent of the population is eventually online, there will be a 16 per cent offline niche market looking for someone to supply equivalent offline services to them. That is a viable economic niche for an online or offline marketer to pursue.

Summary

For many consumers, the Internet is still a novelty. One of the dangers that marketers becoming involved with online activities face is the assumption that all people are ready and enthusiastic about using the Internet. In reality the market is still relatively narrow, consisting predominantly of consumers who would ordinarily be categorised as innovators or part of the early adopter group. The consequence of this for marketers is that what appeals to this group will not necessarily have broad-based appeal. Similarly, it is important to avoid excluding the main market by concentrating too heavily on the online aspect of the marketing management process.

Innovation diffusion curves can be of great value for marketers in assisting in predicting who will need targeting next based on past patterns of innovation adoptions. By keeping one step ahead of the consumer, marketers can develop a range of targeted strategies which meet the individual needs of their consumer markets. While some authors attempt to categorise users according to various criteria, the rapidly evolving nature of the Internet and the consumer behaviours associated with it mean that any typology based on behaviour is likely to be dated within months. The one key issue of importance for the online marketer is the same as that for any other marketer — find out what the consumer wants, what is preventing them from buying or using the product and develop an appropriate mix to overcome the problem.

Discussion questions

4.1 Does online consumer behaviour differ radically from offline consumer behaviour? Is there a need for new models or do existing models adequately explain the consumers' actions?

4.2 What is the importance of recognising avatars and the use of avatars for online marketing?

4.3 Which of the three innovation adoption models outlined in the chapter best describes the diffusion of the Internet through society? Which one of Rogers' (1985) factors do you believe was the most important for your adoption of the Internet and why?

4.4 Does MTV.com have to address the needs of global web surfers just because it exists in a global medium?

4.5 Collect a series of advertisements for online services. Which of the nine Internet adoption motivations are being promoted through these advertisements?

4.6 Is flow a behaviour that is unique to the Internet or can it occur offline? What are the marketing implications of flow-state behaviours in the online and offline world?

4.7 Does the Internet have a universal appeal? If so, what is that appeal, and how can it be used by marketing to entice laggards and the late majority adopters to go online? If not, how can marketing persuade non-adopters or active rejectors to return to the Internet?

4.8 Which is more important — innovation reaction, product characteristics or personal characteristics in getting an innovation adopted?

4.9 How can a new web site take advantage of innovation reactions and web surfer types in its design and promotion?

References

Aggarwal, P., Cha, T. & Wilemon, D. 1998, 'Barriers to the adoption of really-new products and the role of surrogate buyers', *Journal of Consumer Marketing*, vol. 15, no. 4, pp. 358–71.

Alpert, F. 1994, 'Innovator buying behaviour over time: The innovator buying cycle and the cumulative effects of innovations', *Journal of Product and Brand Management*, vol. 3, no. 2, pp. 50–62.

Applebee, A. C., Clayton, P. & Pascoe, C. 1997, 'Australian academic use of the Internet', *Internet Research: Electronic Networking Applications and Policy*, vol. 7, no. 2, pp. 85–94.

Bass, F. M. 1969, 'A new product growth model for consumer durables', *Management Science*, vol. 15, pp. 215–27.

Bellman, S., Lohse, G. L. & Johnson, E. J. 1999, 'Predictors of online buying behaviour', *Communications of the ACM*, December, vol. 42, issues 12, p. 32.

Breitenbach, C. S. & van Doren, D. C. 1998, 'Value-added marketing in the digital domain: Enhancing the utility of the Internet', *Journal of Consumer Marketing*, vol. 15, no. 6, pp. 558–75.

Browning, J. 1993, 'World Wide Web', *Wired* 1.03, July/August (online at www.wired.com/wired/archive/1.03/eword.html?pg=5).

Csikzentmihalyi, M. 1975, *Beyond Boredom and Anxiety*, Jossey-Bass, San Francisco.

Gregor, S. & Jones, K. 1999, 'Beef producers online: Diffusion theory applied', *Information Technology and People*, vol. 12, no. 1, pp. 71–85.

Hoffman, D. & Novak, T. 1996, 'Marketing in hypermedia computer-mediated environments: Conceptual foundations', *Journal of Marketing*, vol. 60, July, pp. 50–68.

Katz, J. & Aspden, P. 1997, 'Motivations for and barriers to Internet usage: Results of a national public opinion survey', *Internet Research: Electronic Networking Applications and Policy*, vol. 7, no. 3, pp. 170–88.

Kingsley, P. & Anderson, T. 1998, 'Facing life without the Internet', *Internet Research: Electronic Networking Applications and Policy*, vol. 8, no. 4, pp. 303–12.

Mahajan, V. & Peterson, R. A. 1985, *Models for Innovation Diffusion*, Sage Publications, London.

Marsden, P. 1998, 'Memetics: A new paradigm for understanding customer behaviour and influence', *Marketing Intelligence and Planning*, vol. 16, no. 6, pp. 363–68.

Nel, D., van Niekerk, R., Berthon, J. & Davies, T. 1999, 'Going with the flow: Web sites and customer involvement', *Internet Research: Electronic Networking Applications and Policy*, vol. 9, no. 2, pp. 109–16.

New Yorker, 1993, 'On the Internet, nobody knows you're a dog' [Editorial cartoon], *New Yorker*, 5 July 1993.

Parthasarathy, M., Jun, S. & Mittelstaedt, R. A. 1997, 'Multiple diffusion and multicultural aggregate social systems', *International Marketing Review*, vol. 14, no. 4, pp. 233–47.

Reisenwitz, T. H. & Cutler, B. D. 1998, 'Dogmatism and Internet usage by university students: Are dogmatics late adopters?', *Journal of Marketing Theory and Practice*, Summer, pp. 43–50.

Rogers, M. R. 1983, *Diffusion of Innovations*, 3rd edn, Macmillan, London.

Rogers, M. R. 1995, *Diffusion of Innovations*, 4th edn, Macmillan, London.

Venkatesh, A. 1998, 'Cybermarketscapes and consumer freedoms and identities', *European Journal of Marketing*, vol. 32, no. 7/8, pp. 664–76.

Web sites

www.acmecity.com/thematrix/
www.badmovies.org/
www.cnn.com
www.drudgereport.com
www.geocities.com
www.heat.net
www.mtv.com
www.mudconnector.com
www.wilsonweb.com/wmt
www.xoom.com

Creating cyber-communities

LEARNING *objectives*

After reading this chapter, you should be able to:

- outline the theoretical foundations of cybercommunities, and define different types and structures

- give an overview of the communications models and processes that influence the formation of cybercommunity structures

- recognise the formation of identity in cybercommunity, and its impact on consumer behaviour

- identify the value of the cybercommunity for business

- discuss the factors that facilitate the establishment and growth of cybercommunity

- outline factors that assist the success of cybercommunity.

Introduction

Cybercommunities are an area where communications theory, consumer behaviour, personal identity, and technology combine to create an environment that is both enticing and threatening to the online marketer. Communities online are subject to less physical restrictions than their offline counterparts. This gives consumers the opportunity to engage in 'post-modern consumption'. **Post-modern consumption** relates to the creation and negotiation of image, social role and social meaning through the use, purchase, consumption, and now creation of goods and services in the online environment. Image construction and representation is moved from the symbols the user wears to the symbols the user creates and chooses to portray online. In the cybercommunity structures such as the MUD, users define their entire persona, from personal appearance to behaviour, in writing. The community itself can generate environments, social norms and practices far removed from what is possible in the real world. This represents a movement towards self-interest-based niche segmentation, where the user is represented by how they see themselves rather than by how a segmentation strategy believes they should behave, according to their demographic profile.

The relevance of the cybercommunity, and the reconstruction of self-image in the online worlds, is that it represents a new level of market segmentation which goes beyond psychographics. Traditional market segmentation breaks the users into strictly defined categories based on demographics and psychographics. Post-modern consumption creates an environment where individuals act out their self-images, and allows for segmentation at the level of selfrepresentation; that is, how people see themselves, rather than how marketers believe others would see them.

Online marketing has made brave, sometimes misguided and occasionally successful forays into the online community environment. In order to fully understand the benefit of the cybercommunity to marketing, it is first necessary to understand the concept of cybercommunity. This chapter sets out to overview the foundations of cybercommunity and the construction and use of identity in the community environment, before examining the role and value of natural and artificial communities to online marketers.

Cybercommunity foundation: Dichotomous structures

Cybercommunities arise where a group of individuals engaged in computer-mediated communication moves beyond basic exchange of information into the formation of a community structure based on the exchange of shared goods of value (Dann & Dann 1998).

Dichotomies are the foundation of most good typologies, and cybercommunity typologies are no different in this respect. Cybercommunities take one of two basic forms — natural communities and constructed communities. Natural communities arise from human interaction where the exchange of emotional support augments pure information transactions. Constructed communities are created with the purpose of facilitating emotional support transactions. The purpose of the distinction is largely arbitrary — for a community to succeed, it needs the presence of the same factors whether it evolved from people swapping notes on science experiments or from an intention to establish a cancer survivors' support network. Either way, the importance of the dichotomy is to recognise that evolution and construction are two methods of establishing a community.

In addition to the natural–artificial dichotomy is the question of transient–permanent fixtures for the cybercommunity. Transient communities are those cybergroups, the presence of which is only noticeable when the group is active, such as members of an IRC channel or email chat list. Permanent fixtures are those cybercommunities which use dedicated Internet locations, such as multi-user domains (MUDs), newsgroups, permanent IRC channels and web forums. Issues concerning the relative merits of transient versus permanent communities will be examined below. However, as with the artificial–natural dichotomy, there is no inherent merit or negative connotation associated with either format. The decision and selection of the type of fixture for the cybercommunity depends largely on available resources, and which format would best suit the needs of the community.

Cybercommunity foundation: Theoretical foundations and communications models

What distinguishes the cybercommunity from other elements of the Internet is that the cybercommunity combines the elements of content and communication into a value-added function (Barnatt 1998). The Web offers a choice between communications interaction or content, but rarely combines the two elements. Even where the two elements are found in conjunction it is quite often to form the basis of a transaction rather than a community. The cybercommunity offers the opportunity to turn the Internet consumption experience away from a lonely solo existence into a shared experience between geographically diverse people.

In order to explain the cybercommunity phenomenon, it is necessary to examine the three elements that distinguish it from other Internet functions. First, the nature of communications on the Internet needs to be reviewed to demonstrate how it has led to the formation of cybercommunity. Second, the concept and construction of community is overviewed to outline the key characteristics of this value-added process. Finally, the consumption of the cybercommunity experience through the use of avatars and the reconstruction of identity is examined in relation to the notion of community as a value-added experience.

Communications models

There are three levels of model that are of interest in examining communications on the Internet: individual level, group level one-to-many, and group level one-to-many-to-one. Individual-level communications relates to the exchange of information through mediated or unmediated communications between two individuals. One-to-many examines the publishing–broadcast paradigm where a single message is sent to multiple recipients. One-to-many-to-one examines the communication on the Internet where interactivity, publication-broadcast and mediated communication merge to create a new range of communications options.

Individual level-mediated communications

Mediated communication has been occurring since humans determined how to encode messages into a storable format. Figure 5.1 illustrates the basic message communications technology that describes everything from medieval messengers and carrier pigeons to the contemporary telephone.

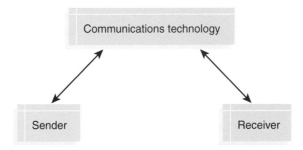

■ Figure 5.1 Mediated communications model

Source: Hoffman, D. L. and Novak, T. P. 1996, 'Marketing in hypermedia computer-mediated environments: Conceptual foundations', *Journal of Marketing*, vol. 60, no. 3, July, pp. 50–68.

The mediated communication model is applicable at any point at which the message communicated is carried by a third party rather than received in direct face-to-face contact between sender and receiver. It is a robust model that demonstrates the encoding–transmission–decoding models familiar to most marketers. The function of such a model is to establish the basic paradigm of mediated communications.

Expanding on this basic paradigm is the concept of computer-mediated communications, which represents a specific method of communications technology. Kaye (1991) defines **computer-mediated communication (CMC)** as the use of computers and computer networks as communication tools by people who are collaborating with each other to achieve a shared goal, which does not require the physical presence or co-location of participants and which can provide a forum for continuous communication free of time constraints. CMC predates the mass popularity of the Web, and was part of the foundation of the Internet in the 1950s, as it was born to facilitate multi-point communications between university, military and government institutions.

Following on from the basic level of computer-mediated communication is the more complex form known as hypermediated communication. **Hypermediated communications (HMC)** are communications transactions that are conducted through the medium of the Web. Where CMC has a greater sophistication than basic-mediated communication, HMC introduces newer elements related to the hypermedia environment. Due to the more complex nature of the hypermedia systems, HMC recognises that it is even possible to exit the environment without actually having completed the communications transaction. Figure 5.2 illustrates the flow chart of hypermediated communications.

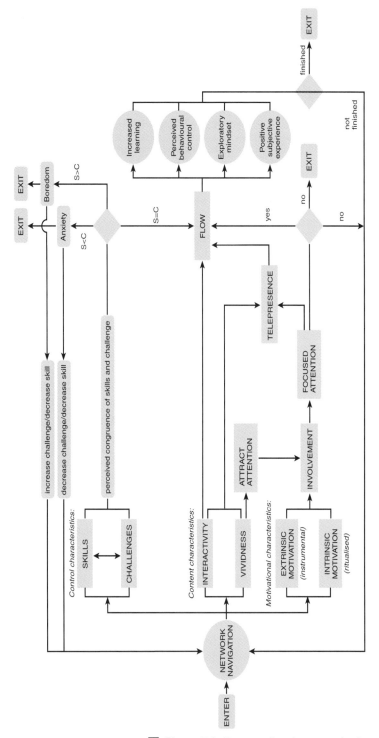

Figure 5.2 Hypermediated communications

Source: Hoffman, D. L. and Novak, T. P. 1996, 'Marketing in hypermedia computer-mediated environments: Conceptual foundations', *Journal of Marketing*, vol. 60, no. 3, July, pp. 50–68.

At the very core of the HMC model is the need for navigation within a hypermedia environment. CMC is reliant on basic front-end software for email, chat or other communications functions which are relatively straight-forward communications devices. In contrast, HMC requires users to first enter the network (Web) and engage in navigation behaviour before they get a chance to start their communications. In effect, first you have to find your way to the phone, through a maze, before you can consider making a call. Consequently, and in part due to the complexity of the environment, many users abandon the navigation before they get to the point of using the com-munications software. For example, in using a web-based chat forum, the user has to go to the site, log into the forum, and then navigate to the front of the message queue to send a new message.

The complexity of hypermediated communications is due to the fact that the three communications models discussed are cumulative, each building on the foundations of the preceding model. In effect, the combined models represent the communications equivalent of Russian nesting dolls. Mediated communication is nested within computer-mediated communication which in turn is nested in hypermediated communication. The full communications benefits of the Internet for marketers are realised through the effective use of a combination of all three models. However, to achieve this, marketers need to recognise that the consumer needs to graduate through the use of each of the models before they can effectively and confidently use hyper-mediated communications. This may mean guiding the consumer through each step rather than standing at the top of the stairs waiting for them to appear. For example, the sequential process of interacting with a company online begins with visiting the web site, moves on to using an email-based forum and, from the email forum, moving into the use of the cybercommu-nity. Each sequential step builds on a set of learned skills from the previous communications innovation adoption. To facilitate the movement, marketers can explicitly encourage the visiting of the web site through advertising. Once at the Web, they can encourage the use of email through signing up for news-letters or feedback links. From the newsletter and the email interaction they can encourage entry into the cybercommunity by providing instructions and technical support.

Group level-mediated communication: Mass media (one-to-many)

The traditional model of communications in the mass media world consists of a message or transmission broadcast from a single point, through a medium, to a range of receivers which decode the message. Figure 5.3 on page 110 illustrates the one-to-many broadcast model.

Where the broadcast model has its greatest strength is in delivering a single message to a mass audience at a relatively low cost. The disadvantage is that this method of communication does not allow for any feedback from the recipient. Consumers and marketers alike are comfortable with this model as it has traditionally been used in advertising and publicity. Due to the lack of interaction between sender and receiver, cybercommunity structures are impossible to develop in this form of mediated environment.

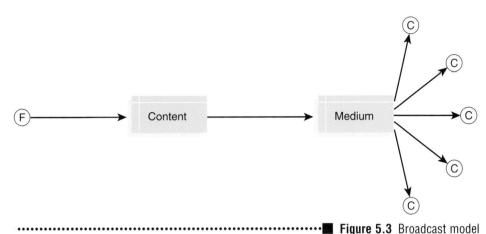

Figure 5.3 Broadcast model

Source: Hoffman, D. L. and Novak, T. P. 1996, 'Marketing in hypermedia computer-mediated environments: Conceptual foundations', *Journal of Marketing*, vol. 60, no. 3, July, pp. 50–68.

 ## Group level-mediated communication: Computer-mediated one-to-one

The major development between broadcast and CMC was the capacity for interaction between sender and recipient. The new mediated environment allows for immediate and/or delayed reaction to the transmitted content. Figure 5.4 illustrates the machinations of CMC.

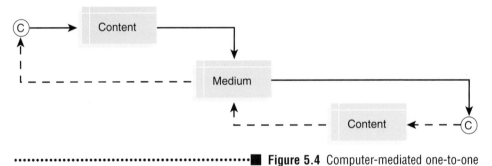

Figure 5.4 Computer-mediated one-to-one

Source: Hoffman, D. L. and Novak, T. P. 1996, 'Marketing in hypermedia computer-mediated environments: Conceptual foundations', *Journal of Marketing*, vol. 60, no. 3, July, pp. 50–68.

The sender–receiver dichotomy becomes a temporary state rather than a permanent state as is the case in broadcast models. Content is generated by the sender–receiver, transmitted through the medium, received and acted upon by the receiver–sender and returned through the medium to the originator. For example, a customer emails a store to ask about the price of a product, the store owner receives the email and replies with the correct price.

This potential for interaction is the basic building block of the cybercommunity as it represents the capacity for interaction and exchange. However, community cannot exist in isolated communications between two individuals. In order to develop a cybercommunity, the third level of mediated group communication needs to be present.

Group level-mediated communication: Computer-mediated one-to-many-to-one

When broadcast was first initiated, it focused on delivering a single communication to as many recipients as there were receiving the message. In contrast, CMC was designed to go in the opposite direction, taking a single message to a single recipient. In the middle of these extremes is the computer-mediated one-to-many-to-one system. This approach merges the CMC time independent personalised message with broadcast's multiple recipients and includes the capacity for direct interaction or indirect broadcasted responses. Figure 5.5 illustrates the operation of the one-to-many-to-one model.

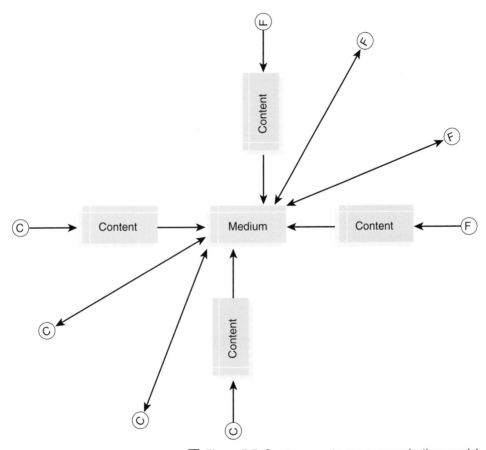

■ Figure 5.5 One-to-many-to-one communications model

Source: Hoffman, D. L. and Novak, T. P. 1996, 'Marketing in hypermedia computer-mediated environments: Conceptual foundations', *Journal of Marketing*, vol. 60, no. 3, July, pp. 50–68.

For example, the manufacturer of a protective case for the Palm Pilot posted information concerning their product to the comp.sys.palmtops.pilot newsgroup. Several people interested in the specifications of the case posted responses to the newsgroup asking for further details, and sparking a discussion between user and manufacturer of the merits of the case. Other readers emailed the manufacturer directly for pricing and other details, or visited the web site without any direct communication with the manufacturer. In this case, the one-to-many-to-one communication was the initial post by the manufacturer. The subsequent transactions in the discussion represent a combination of one-to-many-to-one and one-to-one as individuals either engaged the entire group or other individuals about relative merits of the case.

The medium and the message are both integral parts of the one-to-many-to-one model. Users have four choices as to their role in this environment:

- original broadcaster
- receiver–broadcaster
- receiver–sender
- receiver.

As original broadcasters, they can send messages in a one-to-many style to the medium. Unlike traditional broadcast models, other users of the medium can respond, either directly as receiver–senders or indirectly as receiver–broadcasters. Receiver–senders apply the CMC one-to-one model in that their messages return to the originator, rather than the broadcast medium. Receiver–broadcasters send their messages to the medium as a broadcast style, despite the fact the message may be specifically tailored in response to another member of the medium. This model is best illustrated through USENET news-groups where posts are made as broadcasts to readers of the newsgroup. Responses can be sent either directly to the post originator, or through the newsgroup. Finally, members of the group can simply choose to read the news-group without responding and, in effect, are recipients just as if this were a broadcast medium.

The one-to-many-to-one model allows for the easiest facilitation of the cyber-community structure as the quasi-broadcast of tailored personal responses creates an environment where shared values and communal structures are likely to form. In order to understand how these structures evolve from one-to-many-to-one communications, it is first necessary to examine the nature of community, community formation and the cybercommunity structure.

Definitions of community

There are three forms of community: real community, virtual community and cybercommunity. **Real community** is used to describe communities that are time and geography dependent as they form around a geographic region, feature or social clustering. **Virtual communities** are groups which share a common bond that is not dependent on physical interaction or common geography. Cybercommunities are virtual communities within computer-mediated environments. Virtual communities can exist outside the digital world, for example, the bonds of common interest shared by supporters of a football team can constitute such a community. The virtual community of shared experience and common value (football team support) is not dependent on physical location, but can be aided and encouraged by physical and temporal convergence (football match). Cybercommunities are less prone to requiring physical convergence, although they can be aided by teleconvergence; that is, multiple members of a cybercommunity being online at the same time to exchange information in near real-time transactions.

Concepts of community 1: Shared goods of value

Communities are established when individuals identify with 'collective goods of value' which represent the common points that bind the community together. Collective goods of value was promoted by Rheingold (1993) as the point of identification for a community structure in that a group which had one or more goods of value was far more likely to form a community than a group without these elements. These collective goods include:

- *a common or unifying interest* which is the strongest point of entry for cyber-communities. Due to the Internet being an interest-driven environment, cybercommunities of common interest are easy to identify and to join.

- *shared suffering, experience or belief,* which gives a point of common understanding and experience. This is particularly strong in self-help or support communities where the shared pain is the initial point of bonding. Similarly, shared beliefs such as religion (news:alt.buddhism) or operating systems (news:comp.sys.linux) is also a strong point of bonding.

- *participation and involvement in the community* aids in the development of the community, as the greater the involvement with a group, the more likely it is a member will feel a sense of belonging. Active participation may be either through ordinary membership and use, or by taking on informal roles such as community advocate, instigator or leader (Cothrel & Williams 1999). **Advocates** lead by example in the use of the community, and often are the most prolific members of the group. **Instigators** handle the responsibility of engaging debates, asking questions and starting topics of conversation. **Leaders** are usually the more senior, experienced or knowledgable members of the group who tend to guide the general direction of the group, and handle dispute resolution. The three levels can often act as a hierarchical structure of transition whereby advocates can become instigators who turn into leaders over the passage of time.

- *sense of belonging*, or 'sense of community' is one of the strongest indications of a community. As cybercommunities are extremely nebulous structures at the best of times, a sense of membership and belonging is important for the success and survival of the group. Information exchanges where people simply swap knowledge without feeling any association with the group may meet several of the other community criteria, but lack the critical element of belonging which is necessary to form a community.

- ***social network capital*** is the experience and collective history of the group. Once members of the group begin to develop stronger intra-group ties between one another, the social network capital increases as people invest time and emotion in the group structure. Conflict and resolution are also important aspects of social network capital as the longer a group exists, and the more diverse the membership base becomes, the more likely it is that conflict will occur. This is an essential part of group dynamics as most groups which do not have points of disagreement, conflict and resolution do not tend to last as long as those groups with active 'hot spots' of conflict and debate. This is not to say that conflict must be present, simply that heterogenous groups often develop greater levels of social network capital than homogenous groups.

- *shared knowledge base* is the final component where the group has access to a combined knowledge of the points of interest, the group history and, for groups clustered by interest, of the subject of the group. This is not to say that shared knowledge represents a groupthink mentality. Some of the most fiercely volatile groups in USENET have a well-established shared knowledge base of the points of interest, historical events and structures, but the members rarely agree on any given subject. However, a shared knowledge base may also be held as a result of an information exchange where the collective wisdom is stored and accessed without a sense of ownership of the knowledge

Concepts of community 2: Cybercommunity, digital village living

Cybercommunities are formed on the basis of one-to-many-to-one CMC information exchanges which develop shared goods of value around which a community structure forms, is identified and used as a basis for self-identification and membership. Translated, it means that where people gather together to talk, exchange ideas and information, it is highly likely that friendships will form and that members of the exchange will come to think of themselves as a group, and identify with their exchange as a community.

One of the things about the cybercommunity that also differentiates it from the virtual community is the use of cyberenvironments which create electronic versions of the shared geography of real communities. The cyberenvironment can take one of two forms, a structured artificial world, or an electronic social sphere.

Structured artificial worlds exist as digital representations of the real world, with varying degrees of accuracy. One common environment is the MUD, which is most commonly used for role-playing, game-style environments. The virtual world is structured into a series of rooms and environments where communication is limited to only those within the virtual room. Towell and Towell (1995) overviewed the use of a MUD-style environment, the Multi User Objective Orientated (MOO) as a hosting mechanism for a virtual science conference (bioinfo.weizmann.ac.il/BioMOO/).

At the other end of the scale is the electronic social sphere which exists in IRC or mailing lists when social interaction takes place. The difference between the two is that the MUD exists independently of the human members whereas the social sphere exists only during the interaction between the members. In the middle of the virtual world and the social sphere lies the newsgroup, which is a fixed location, existing with or without members, but which is dependent on humans interacting for it to have substance and meaning. It is the interaction between people that makes the cybercommunity, and this interaction is known collectively as cybercommuning.

Concepts of community 3: Cybercommuning

Cybercommuning is defined as the seamless integration of communications technology with social interaction between members of a cybercommunity (Dann & Dann 1998). It exists as a behaviour where the function of the intra-group communication surpasses pure information exchange to become a social support network. The importance of cybercommuning as a behaviour becomes apparent in the context of similar consumer behaviours such as clanning. Cybercommuning represents a deliberate and conscious behaviour designed to integrate Internet-based activities into a collective structure and to seek membership of a collective structure in the computer-mediate environment.

Concepts of community 4: The nature and structure of the cybercommunity

'Will it be a separate world where people get lost in the surfaces or will we learn to see how the real and the virtual can be made permeable, each having the potential for enriching and expanding the other?'

Turkle, S. 1995, *Life on the Screen: Identity in the Age of the Internet*, Weidenfeld and Nicolson, London, p. 268.

Cybercommunities are constructed worlds designed to meet the needs, wants and communication exchange of their membership. In the development of such an environment, community access is based on the communications ability of the membership, and their access to the tools of communication. Access using communications skills creates a literacy barrier that will inevitably exclude some people from being able to fully access the community. Although some multi-user environments are experimenting with bilingual systems, it would still require users who interact within the bilingual environment to be able to converse in multiple languages to interact with other bilingual speakers.

Despite the language barriers, cybercommunity structures which predominantly depend upon word-based communication also bring about a unique socialisation process where the human body is effectively discarded in the first instance, and members are represented as collections of ideas and written expression. The physical body, and the social cues associated with it are removed and replaced by the perception of the individual as a transmitter of ideas, feelings and communications (Coyne 1998). Part of the effect of the conversion of humanity into the written identity has been the lowering of many cultural and physical barriers resulting from physical cue-based stereotypes.

One popular humorous check list circulating through the email systems of the world outlines one of the tell-tale signs of being online for too long — it is that you could not identify the gender or race of your three closest friends, but you could recognise their ideas in a line-up. The switching of importance from physical identity to verbal portrayal is also part of the nature and construction of identity on the Internet. This is examined further below. Overall, the importance of the switch is that it brings community members together by building social network capital on the basis of exchanges of thoughts and feelings rather than by physical appearances.

Resulting from this social network capital is the fact that a cybercommunity exists through the strength of its members. A cohesive group of shared interest, social support and other goods of collective value is of use only if there are sufficient members of the group to share it. All communities share the economies of increasing returns in that the community needs a critical mass for value to occur. In addition, for the most part the marginal returns improve for all members, as more members join, to a point of critical overflow, where diminishing returns occur as the community becomes too big to manage.

Cybercommunities also take time to establish, grow and strengthen. Much of the Internet has been focused on fast development, high growth rates and quick transition times. In among this chaos, cybercommunities have maintained a longer term orientation and focus, developing in natural cycles of birth, growth, maturity and decline. For commercial operators seeking to engage in the support and the development of cybercommunities, this long-term focus in an apparently short-term environment has led to difficulties. Many operators attempted to take short-term gains, by implementing access fees, subscription rates or other charges in order to make a short-term profit. The result of the short-term profit seeking has been to damage the communities in the long term — most members were able to find low-cost/no-cost alternatives that meet their need for community elsewhere.

The second feature of the cybercommunity is that a community is sold on the basis of selling customers to customers. Using the model of the sports fan, the community sells itself on the value to be derived from other patrons of the community. It is rare to sell a car based on the driving habits of other drivers (except perhaps for safety features) but the attraction of the cybercommunities is the set of behaviours of the other members.

Construction of identity in the cybercommunity

The construction and reconstruction of identity on the Internet has been mentioned in passing in several sections of this book, from the unique features of the Internet through to the new consumer behaviours online. However, the reconstruction of identity is not a new feature to the Internet. Post-modern interpretations of society have argued that identity itself is no longer the easily applied construct of the modernist era, with blurring of boundaries between societies, cultures and social roles. Coyne (1998) argues that identity in the offline world has become harder to define and maintain in accordance with established social roles, and has become a question of negotiation between society and the individual.

In light of the post-modern approach to identity, much of the early writing on the Internet promoted online identities as a new form of freedom to create and renegotiate social structures and personal identity. Most authors in the Internet field have made mention of the relative anonymity of the Internet, the unstructured nature of identity in online communication and communities. Overall, the dominant belief within the field of Internet research is that identity online is negotiable, and that role creation is an achievable and viable consumer behaviour.

However, not all authors agree with the party line of anonymity and identity construction. Whitly (1997) counters the argument of the development of new identity in the online environment by illustrating that identity is formed as part of the self, and that all new identities constructed away from the understanding of self, and self-experience are at best extended mimicry, and at worst, poor forgeries. Credibility of the identity needs to be derived from a reality-based focus, and where an artificial persona is created, inconsistencies often arise between elements of the created persona. In addition, other aspects of socialisation continue to be expressed through the artificial persona, most notably in terms of written style, which can often contain clues about country of origin, age, and even the gender of the writer. Whitly (1997) contends that the mere removal of the body from the communications exchange does not allow for the creation of a new identity without the associated socialisation that would have been experienced by a real version of the new persona.

In between these two extreme positions of disembodied reconstruction of identity, and the socialisation construction, is the middle ground of transient Internet identities. The nature of the Internet and the short period of time the Internet has been available to the mass market has meant that for many users, the exploration of online identity remains a new phenomenon. The long-term effects of the ability to change identity are difficult to predict and, for the most part, most individuals will maintain their personal identity on and offline.

Flores (1998) talks of marketing playing a greater role in the creation of multiple identities to service, manage and identify offers from the marketplace as the role of direct marketing increases. These temporary filtering identities are constructed as an adjunct to the real identity of the individual. Construct 1 may be based on the individual's membership of groups associated with their personal interests and hobbies, Construct 2 may represent their professional interests and memberships and Construct 3 may be used to engage in recreational activities online. All three constructs are aspects of the individual, separated and maintained by multiple aliases to avoid a crossover between work, hobby and recreational identity.

In some online environments, such as networked gaming, identity creation is part of the sports-like atmosphere of the games. Rather than wearing a jersey number, each player becomes known by their alias identity. Identification by alias online in the environment also provides relative anonymity for the players to engage in behaviour and conduct unbecoming of their real life persona, which is both liberating and at times disconcerting. Quasi-anonymity afforded by gaming aliases can offer limited term identity reconstruction within the context of the environment. Lining up against a player known as Angel of Mercy indicates more of the player's online style than facing off against Bob from Accounting. Of course, Bob may also develop a formidable reputation in the environment, but with the lack of visual clues associated with the online environment, names and identities can be used to partially compensate.

It is the use of identity cues that makes the construction of identity vital to the cybercommunity. In environments of trust and support, cybercommunity members become dependent on the strength of the trust placed in the identity of the partner in the communications exchange. Whitly (1997) cites a case of a male psychiatrist who spent an extended period of time impersonating a disabled woman in a series of chat environments. Whitly used this case as an example of how impersonation will be fundamentally flawed due to lack of socialisation. What it also did to the community in which the imposter participated was to divide the group, with those who had engaged the female character in good faith as a female, feeling their trust had been betrayed. Those who felt and expressed the strongest reaction against the impersonation were the people who most closely identified with the character. Given that the environment in which the person existed was a place of support, the charade was treated as a serious social breach. Identity in this context was a less negotiable structure than it would have been in a less support-orientated environment.

The betrayal of the community was also based in part on the social network capital that formed the core of the group. Rheingold (1993) outlined the importance of shared experience as a basis of community formation. Where such experience is based on a subjective offline personal experience, constructions of false identities who allege to have shared such an experience undermine the value of the shared social network capital. Not only does the use of false identity damage the person using it, it calls into question the shared capital, and undermines the core of the group. Where the adopted persona does not have an impact on the shared goods, creation and recreation of identity is accepted and often encouraged as part of the community structure.

A further view on the construction of identity within cybercommunities is based on the influence of the community on the identity. Within a community, an individual can find themselves undertaking leadership or instigator roles that are apart from their usual roles in their offline lives. In groups based on specialist topics, leaders are normally selected on the basis of their skills, expertise and knowledge of the topic. Individuals whose select specialist knowledge of obscure topics of interest may find themselves with greater leadership roles in their online persona than they have received offline. In this manner, the community shapes the persona in that a shy or timid person offline may take a more confident role in their online community as their expertise gives them a position, and persona, of responsibility.

 ## **Value** of cybercommunity to business

Having established that the cybercommunity is a good thing, and that cyber-communities are of inherent value to people, what value can business gain from their existence? There are a range of functions in which a cybercommunity can be used to aid a business including the following:

- *support networks* normally exist outside of the commercial domain, and are usually clustered around aiding the recovery from or coping with an illness. In commercial terms, support communities are primarily about technical rather than emotional support, although creating a network of confidantes can be as useful as purely technical advice.
- *customer to customer communities* can be established to promote discussions between current users, potential users and, occasionally, ex-users of the product. This form of commercial community can be used as a method of word of mouth sales and technical support.
- *customer to company communities*, usually in the form of moderated or hosted communities, can be established to enable users to talk directly to members of the organisation as a feedback mechanism, in addition to the customer to customer communications that can also take place.
- *company to employee communities*, whereby the members of the organisation are given the opportunity to gather together in a cyberenvironment. This is particularly valuable for organisations with geographically diverse offices, or who use a range of contract and permanent staff to be able to have a common ground for staff to meet and interact.
- *loyalty-building communities* are those based around products which have high levels of associate imagery, such as the major cola and sport brands. Pepsi offered a cybercommunity-style web site for its Pepsi Max range to encourage drinkers of the cola to clan together to give referent group support to the decision to drink Pepsi Max.

- *value-added pre- and post-sales communities* are where companies establish the community, and membership of the community, as an adjunct to the sales of a product. Sonic Foundry, publisher of numerous music authoring packages has a cybercommunity structure which can be accessed only by registered users of Sonic Foundry software. The value of the community is in the knowledge that other users in the environment have the guaranteed shared base of knowing about and/or owning the same software.

The cybercommunity structure also gives rise to business opportunities associated with providing middleware to support cybercommunity structures. As communities grow in size, and become a common element of online experiences, the demand for client and host software will increase. One of the major IRC software clients, mIRC, has over 200 000 users on its announcement mailing list.

Commercial community structures also represent markets that have, by self-selection, volunteered to be part of the business's hosted communities. These communities can be used as testing grounds for new product ventures, and can be observed to determine how the product is being used in the field.

Internet marketing INSIGHT

Comic relief — how a cybercommunity structure is building loyalty to online cartoon strips

■ **Figure 5.6** The first episode of Sluggy Freelance (www.sluggy.com)

Source: www.sluggy.com

(continued)

In 1997, two cartoon strips, Sluggy Freelance, and Userfriendly, were first published online in a purely digital distribution. Sluggy Freelance represents an odd journey through the outlandish adventures of the lead characters, whereas Userfriendly, based behind the scenes of an Internet service provider (ISP), runs a socio-political satire of contemporary computing. Both series have struck a chord with the Internet user community. Sluggy Freelance's protagonist characters have Internet-related lives, there are frequent references to cyberculture icons, such as Quake and the series opened with a skewed look at the value of the Internet for society. Userfriendly has seen ongoing debates between the characters over key issues of cyberculture such as Windows 98, Microsoft, Linux and, of course, Quake. Both series make reference to contemporary social events, such as the release of Star Wars Episode I and the media coverage of the Millennium Bug.

USER FRIENDLY
the comic strip　　　　　a userfriendly.org production

Q: What do you get when you put three techs, two salespeople, a designer, two executives and a couple of administrative staff together in an office?

VISITING UF

UF HOME
Daily Static
Cartoon Archive
News Archive
LOTD Archive
Community
The UF Store
F.A.Q.
Contact Us
Advertising Info
Find a Job

UF FRIENDS

BOOK PUBLISHER
O'REILLY
OCTOBER 1999

MONTHLY
linuxjournal

A: Columbia Internet, the friendliest, hardest-working and most neurotic little Internet Service Provider in the world. Throw in a mischievous Artificial Intelligence and a naive but curious Dust Puppy, and you have the makings of USER FRIENDLY, the chronicle of a group of well-meaning but misguided Internet workers.

TAKE ME TO THE CURRENT STRIP!

If you're in the market for a new job, or are looking for geek to fill a job, we encourage you to give the UF-branded career site Geekfinder a try!

Leading-edge company seeks geek
Geek seeks leading-edge career op
USERFRIENDLY.ORG
presents
GEEKFINDER
The seekers leading-edge

KUDOS & KIND WORDS

*"One of the characteristics of healthy cultures is that they can poke fun at themselves. I guess the hacker culture is in good health, because **User Friendly** is hilarious. Its irreverence, sophisticated in-jokes and surrealistic edge are a rocket straight out of the Internet's collective unconscious."*
– Eric S. Raymond, ubergeek

"...the cartoon is so insightful and captures the essence of today's web industry so brilliantly that it's definitely going to be big."
– Nina Furu, columnist, digi.no

Figure 5.7 The Userfriendly homepage
Source: www.userfriendly.org

Part of the success of the cartoon series has been the successful implementation of the marketing mix — a good product, at a well-chosen price (free), delivered through the medium of the Internet and strong use of word of mouth and low-cost/no-cost promotions. In addition to the standard mix, both sites have made strong use of cybercommunity structures. The Sluggy Freelance fans, termed Sluggites, have set up a MUD, several mailing lists, and run teams in two distributed computing competitions. The Userfriendly fan base, known as the UFies, have the 'GeekFinder' job search system housed as part of the Userfriendly community in addition to the usual fan-based structures.

Both sites have taken advantage of four of the five functions of cybercommunities. First, both sites have encouraged their fan bases to form support networks.

Sluggy.com has a Frequently Asked Question (FAQ) list of solutions to common problems of viewing the site from America On Line (AOL) which were provided by AOL users and non-users to help out fellow fans. Customer to customer contact has been the focus of the Userfriendly community, which carries a special feature for organising face to face gatherings of the Userfriendly readership. Customer to company features are a very strong element of both communities. Sluggy has run a series of fan produced retrospective episodes while the lead writers were on leave. Userfriendly turned to the community for advice over programming and technical concerns, and several sections of the Userfriendly site are based on materials donated from the community.

SLUGGY FREELANCE
Community! just keeps
on getting bigger!

SluggyMUX!
"The only MUX in existence with a .poing command"
Info: http://sluggymux.8m.com/
Connect via telnet: telnet://mux.sluggy.com:2025

Sluggy Cards!: **E-mail someone a Sluggy Grouphugs**
Postcard and make their day!
http://www.grouphugs.com

Mailing List Info Here:
http://inigima.8m.com/sluggy.html
http://www.onelist.com/community/Sluggy

Internet Relay Chat Info Here:
http://sluggy.duckpond.org/

Sluggy Newsgoup: alt.comics.sluggy-freelance
Info Here:
http://www.geocities.com/Area51/Orion/8247/newsgroups.html

Sluggy Freelance Teams! Use your computer's spare CPUs under the flag of Sluggy Freelance!
Team Sluggy Freelance (RC5) Join the team and help help crack the RSA's latest computer code challenge.
Info Here:
http://www.charm.net/~ferret/tsf/

Sluggy Freelance (SETI) Join the team and help find real aliens!
Info Here:
http://www.interlog.com/~sunspace/sluggy.html

■ **Figure 5.8** Sluggy Freelance community page
Source: www.sluggy.com

Finally, the communities have a value-adding function to the cartoon — by inspiring loyalty and self-identification with the series (as a Sluggite or UFie), and getting involved in community activities, the two cartoon strips have created a unique brand loyalty. It is not often that people identify as Microsofties or CocaColites, but you'll find Sluggites and UFies across the Web.

Userfriendly (www.userfriendly.org)
Sluggy Freelance (www.sluggy.com)

Finally, cybercommunities based around commercial products also represent the clustering of both pooled experience with the product, and of collective market knowledge. Users of a distinct technology, such as mobile phones, gathered together in a cybercommunity will have a shared knowledge base of brands, pricing, network coverage, features and other industry information such as the profitability of various phone carriers.

Cybercommunities as reflections of reality: The social Petri dish

Cybercommunities are collectives of humans. It may be a computer-mediated environment, but the computers are merely the tools for the humans to express themselves. Consequently, the actions and behaviours of consumers in the cybercommunities are worthy of market research study. In particular, the cybercommunities hosted on commercial product vendor web sites give rise to a self-selected group of strongly brand-loyal individuals, with varying passions for the product.

Not only do cybercommunity members share a common passion for the product or brand in question, they also share a range of common interests and lifestyles. This provides the market researcher with the opportunity to observe and collate opinions on related issues which may impact on the marketing and use of the product.

These are the users most likely to discover product use innovations, give detailed explanations of their personal experiences with the products, and to have encountered the sorts of problems faced by fellow users. They can form self-selecting focus groups, giving out product feature wish lists for free as part of their discussions in their cybercommunities.

In a similar way, USENET product-based newsgroups often produce copious amounts of useful marketing data as part of the discussions and bantering between users. The more generic industry discussion groups often give rise to debate concerning the nature of the industry, and provide usable industry-wide monitoring information.

 Community creation: Roll your own society

This section examines the issues associated with the creation and maintenance, or care and feeding, of a cybercommunity. It is neither the intent nor purpose of this section to explain the programming and technical issues behind running a cybercommunity. Figallo (1998) has an overview of the technical issues of web community design and support. Powers (1997) offers an insight into the programming required to maintain a range of cybercommunity structures. Finally, Horn (1998) outlines the East Coast Hang Out (ECHO) environment which is one of the oldest and most established, if not notorious, cybercommunities. All three books cover various aspects of the technicalities, and social engineering required to establish and support a cybercommunity.

Strategy ◉

Vtown: Virtual city, Virtual community, Virtually home

Vtown is a cybercommunity in its very earliest stages of development and, like any other law-abiding city, once your welcome is completed, the rules and responsibilities of the city, its occupants and visitors are clearly laid out. Right from your earliest introduction it makes clear the policies which operate and that it will abide by. It also clearly sets out its expectations of you as part of the community and what it expects from you as a citizen of this virtual town. The regulations regarding traders who exist within its confines are all available to you before you make your choice to become one of the ever-expanding group of citizens who will be proud to call Vtown home. It even goes so far as to acknowledge that, just like any other town, it will not be able to guarantee the behaviours of those you meet through introductions that will lead you outside its governing body.

Once you have made your decision there is a wealth of information and variety of places to visit to keep the whole family happy. Whether you just want to browse around the shops, catch up on the footy or design your health program it is all there for you to explore, see, and experience. All members of the family, and all tastes are catered for from the kids who can check out their own virtual community through to advice on how to deal with your mother-in-law.

Figure 5.9 The Vtown centre

Source: www.vtown.com.au

(*continued*)

In order to become a member and user of this virtual community and help Vtown to provide the services you desire and require, you need to give specific information about yourself. This information also ensures that your log-in procedure, through your password, remains confidential. The privacy agreement requires honesty from the user and in turn promises confidentiality and integrity from the provider.

Vtown incorporates those web sites that sit beneath www.vtown.com.au and also provides some services to people who access the site — services such as email, bulletin boards and other functions, content and information. The use of cookies is intended to further enhance the ability of the community to respond to the individual needs of its citizens. At this early stage of its development you have plenty of opportunities to assist in the construction of a town that virtually answers all your virtual needs.

The site itself is user-friendly and even in its early stages offers a range of services that will keep most users happy. Its affiliation with both the Catholic Church and union organisations is clear at the registration stage. If, for any reason, you do not want to be involved in a town that has these affiliations you make your choice at this point. The whole town is clear and up front about its aims, its directions and who its friends are. In terms of a cybercity it has all the hallmarks that make for compatibility of users and members. It covers the laws of liability and indemnity operating within the Australian context. All in all if you are looking for a safe, honest community with all the basics in terms of commitment, law and order that you would like from your actual town then this, as it stands, is a good place to be.

Setting up a community

Having determined the value and purpose of the organisation's cybercommunity, there are a range of issues that needs to be considered in setting up the community. The three major issues to be addressed in this chapter are:

- *location*: does the community need a defined structure, transient structure or multiple spaces?
- *community*: what makes a community tick? What people are needed to populate a community? What structures need to be in place?
- *destination marketing for cybercommunities*: how can cybercommunities use tourism marketing techniques to entice users and encourage repeat visits?

Location

The question of permanent cybercommunity structures such as MUDs, web sites or newsgroups should be considered against the flexibility of transient locations such as mailing lists and IRC channels. Does the company want to set up a permanent location to be easily accessed, or can the user find the transient cybervenues easily enough? In summary, the ideal location is determined by whether the community needs or wants a permanent location, semipermanent or transient environment and real time or delayed communications.

The value of the transient community is that it tends to be based in email through the use of mailing lists. Given the almost ubiquitous nature of email in the Internet environment, email-based communities offer the easiest distribution potential. The advantage to the email is also the disadvantage in that lists can become large, and traffic often overwhelms the community member. A Pet Shop Boys fan club mailing list was averaging over three messages a minute during a peak period of debate. Such high volumes threaten to cause more harm than good to a community.

Table 5.1 Matching community location to real-time/delayed-time communications

	Permanent	Semipermanent	Transient
Real time	MUD	IRC	IRC
Delayed	Newsgroup	Web forum	Email list

Transient communities can also be formed in other environments, such as IRC and MUDs. IRC offers a real-time conversation environment without the physicality of the MUD or the delayed time effect of the mailing. IRC environments are good for social interaction, offering immediate gratification to users, but can become unwieldy and difficult to read where large groups are engaged in conversation. The IRC channel is similar to a party in that multiple conversations can coexist in the room, but it takes a skilled user to handle the conversational traffic and follow the separate threads of conversation.

A more permanent real-time environment for a cybercommunity is the MUD. The advantage to the MUD is the presence of a virtual physical world of objects, rooms and location-based interaction. Using virtual space allows users to experience proximity, separability and interact in a more realistic environment. The BioMOO demonstrated the practicality of being able to hold conferences within a cyberspace environment by using multiple seminar rooms all linked to the central environment. Users were able to move from room to room to engage in different forums, or to read different 'speaker's' presentations. Combined with the real-time nature of the MUD, it offers an environment very similar and familiar to the real world. The downside to the MUD is the need for specialist client software, and a familiarity with the nature of real-time MUD environments. Ironically, one of the difficulties faced by the BioMOO was the inability to successfully log the sessions for later use, a problem not usually associated with conference proceedings which focus on the presentation, rather than the audience discussion.

The final environment to consider is the newsgroup or web forum structure which offers the threaded conversational structure of the email mailing list with a physical place of a MUD without the real-time nature. Conversations on a newsgroup may be logged by the server for up to a month, allowing transaction histories to be viewed; that is, newcomers can read a period of the immediate history of the group. This is particularly useful for functions such as FAQs which can be posted periodically so as to be permanently available in the group environment. The newsgroup can also operate in up to real-time speeds depending on the number of active users at any given time.

Community

A cybercommunity needs to have a sense of community before it will be more than a series of well-published good intentions. While the other elements of the Rheingold check list are important, it is essential that the feeling of belonging exists, otherwise a community will not succeed. To create the community environment, the organisation must understand that the community itself is the point of the exercise, and the creation of the community is going to be an investment cost in the long-term future of the organisation.

One of the most important issues in the cybercommunity is that it is a long-term process to create and establish a community. A cyberRomc cannot be installed in a day. The community structures are a process of evolution and development, meaning in blunt terms, long-term costs and investments for long-term gains. Companies need to focus on the big picture of the gains that community can bring, rather than the narrow view of the costs that it incurs. Every aspect of establishing and maintaining a cybercommunity will cost either time or money — usually both.

It also has to be recognised that the community must give benefit to the user, so that the organisation will have to give something before it can expect to receive. To access most communities the user has to give away a range of demographic and psychographic data, so having already incurred the cost, they expect a reciprocal benefit.

What helps a community succeed?

In order to get their cybercommunity to succeed, there are several key areas where the organisations can provide support and assistance.

Many commercial communities are wound up too quickly as part of cost-cutting measures before any return is possible. The problem for the organisation housing the community is that it expected immediate short-term profits rather than the long-term costs associated with communities. Communities which are accessed for free do not preclude the organisation from charging for premium value-added services that extend upon the free service offering. Most communities can be replicated for free, so careful pricing is needed to maintain the critical mass needed for successful community.

The second area to remember is that the community exists for the benefit of members of the community, not the host. The purpose of hosting a community is to provide a service for members. The incidental benefits for the organisation, like the market research and the product information, are just bonuses for the harvesting. This is not a focus group, nor is it a controlled laboratory environment. Communities need to be given free reign to develop and create their own environment, leaders and structures. Companies which give freedom to their community structures, while focusing on providing for some of their needs, have greater success than those who feel a desire to treat the community like a lab experiment.

The natural environment of the cybercommunity is also an important aspect that needs to be carefully observed and maintained by commercial hosts. In any group of people, natural leaders will emerge, and social dynamics will take place to create factions, allegiances and similar psychological groupings within the community. Support should be given to the leaders of the communities, and to those members who are providing value-added services to the community. In many cases, recognition and a note of thanks can be sufficient reward for a community member providing services that would otherwise have been the responsibility of the company hosting the community. The company needs to support or at least passively ignore, any spread of the community beyond the boundaries of the hosted cybercommunity.

One of the key mistakes that can be made with a cybercommunity is to try to force it to stay within a company's allocated domain, so that it can be probed, measured and watched by corporate members. If a community is growing to the point of natural expansion beyond the limits provided by the host organisation, it is a sign of an extremely successful community, and should be encouraged, or at least not actively discouraged. Tacit approval for unofficial sites that support official functions can also lower the costs to an organisation. If a community member sets up a web site to support your commercial cybercommunity, that is a maintenance and development cost that is being provided free in return for the benefit the user has experienced from your community. It is a display of brand and community loyalty that promotes a positive image for the company hosting the cybercommunity.

A major issue in hosting a community is to remember that for a community to survive it needs to be monitored and supported. For the most part a good cybercommunity will be self-supporting and self-generating. However, they are not perpetual motion machines, and as with all human gatherings, there will be peaks and lows and points at which the communities are no longer of value. Cybercommunities which have exceeded their useful lifespan should not be propped up to simply meet a preset budget line expenditure or web site design charter. Similarly, communities that are thriving should not be terminated because their six month time frame has expired. Their value is in that they are living environments which need to be reviewed and monitored over time.

Cyberspace as a place: Destination marketing for cybercommunities

'If you build it they shall come.'

Kinsella, W. P. 1999, *Shoeless Joe*, Mariner Books, Chicago.

There is more to having people clicking down a path to your web site than building a better mouse trap. Cybercommunities are not self-evident benefits to most users, and certainly in the crowded market of the Internet, many users will never get to see more than a fraction of the virtual worlds on offer. If this sounds vaguely familiar, then it is because it is the permanent dilemma of tourism marketing. Tourism marketing deals with how to get people to leave their homes for a brief virtual community stay at a tourist destination. Many of the problems, issues and solutions that tourism marketing has used over the years are applicable to the issues faced by cybercommunities.

In order to apply tourism marketing to the cybercommunity structure, one key assumption must be recognised in that cyberspace must be seen as a place. This philosophical assumption has been variously mentioned explicitly or implicitly throughout both this chapter, and other aspects of this book. The key to treating cyberspace as a location is to recognise the terminology used to describe behaviour within the environment — terms such as 'go online', 'web surfing', 'follow the link', and the subtle implicit messages from the web browser software 'Navigator' and 'Explorer'. People conceptualise cyberspace as a location, due in part to the influence of authors such as Gibson (1984), on the terminology used to describe the Web.

The importance of recognising the assumption of locality and physicality in cyberspace is that it is a conceptual environment. There are no physical boundaries in the Internet, and nothing physical exists within this environment. The user perceives varying degrees of physical location based on their particular involvement in the Internet. Users of MUDs, and fixed environment games (such as Quake) will recognise rooms and arenas as part of cyberspace. Casual web surfers may not even perceive a door or a wall as they follow hyperlink after hyperlink through the Web. So, why then do we adopt the assumption of physicality in a cybercommunity?

There are two reasons. First, cybercommunities can be places within the Internet, recognised as such by their boundaries; for example, MUDs exist only on their home server, or by their location; Vtown exists only at vtown.com.au. Second, people constitute communities, whether they are real, virtual or cybercommunities. Within the cyberspace as a place argument is the Gibson (1984) 'consensual hallucination' clause — it exists as a place because the users have a consensual agreement that it is a place.

The aim of a good cybercommunity structure is to enhance the perception of community as a place with the use of destination marketing. **Destination marketing** is the amalgamation of the tourism products offering an integrated experience to consumers which is consumed under the brand name of the location (Buhalis 2000). **Cyberdestination marketing** takes the amalgamation of the cyberenvironment, the services, community, community members, and experiences which are offered under the banner of the cybercommunity name, location or brand. As part of destination marketing, Buhalis (2000) outlined six key factors for bringing people to a location:

- *attractions* encompasses the reasons for going to a region, be they natural environment, heritage locations, purpose-built venues or special events. Usually the attraction is closely associated with the region, and recognised as the primary drawcard for the area. In the cybercommunity, the attractions can be the people, for example, The WELL (www.well.com) has the attraction of numerous high-profile members, and a range of experts on virtually any subject.

- *accessibility* in the real world depends on the sum of the available transportation system, including roads, rail, air, sea and, with natural environment locations like rainforests, foot, hoof or similar method. Online, it is related to the degree to which the community can be reached by the ordinary user without the need for special software downloads, the availability of the newsgroup on the user's newsserver and the convenience of having the cybercommunity located at an obvious access point. MUDs often have hard-to-remember telnet addresses, and depend on operations such as the Mudconnector (www.mud connector.com) to provide a listing service. Mudconnector acts as a digital tourist bureau for the multi-user environment systems.

- *amenities* for tourism destinations represent the physical facilities of accommodation, catering, retailing and ancillary tourist services. In the virtual worlds of the MUD, these services may be present in a digital form, or could be part of the features of the environment such that players need to retire to an inn, locker room or office before leaving the environment. On transient groups such as IRC, amenities include functional elements like 'ops' which represents a set of key powers to change topic, exclude or remove users, and provide 'ops' to fellow users. Newsgroup amenities can include access to FAQs on various topics, and possibly access to archives through Deja-News.com (www.deja.com).

■ *available packages* in destination marketing tend to be controlled by tour mediators such as travel agents or airlines, offering pre-arranged packages and conditions. Cybercommunities can offer levels of membership, ranging from the basic level of use through to levels associated with control, management and often including capacity to create and modify elements of the environment. Subscriber-based cybercommunities may include free systems with low levels of access, and varying levels of access depending on subscription fees. The WELL offers two access levels, the lower rate providing minimal discussion-level access with the higher fee offering extra services, including the ability to create discussion groups and house web sites.

■ *activities* incorporates all events, activities and related services that will be consumed as part of the tourism experience by a visitor to the destination. Some of these functions are beyond the control of the travel agency and local tourist board, and others are established for the express purpose of attracting tourists, for example, festivals and special events. Cybercommunities also involve various activities, some official, some unofficial, as attractors to the group. Frequently successful cybercommunities have activities that expand beyond the core community structure into other venues, such as face-to-face meetings, or involvement in other group-orientated projects. Some communities will enter teams into online competitions or gaming environments as part of the community group activities. This is particularly prevalent where there is a strong set of shared interests such as online gaming, which forms part of the shared goods of value.

■ *ancillary services* for offline destinations relate to the services used by tourists — services such as banks, post offices and similar services. Cybercommunities often offer second stage services, such as virtual postcards, email address and web hosting (www.geocities.com). Other groups offer internal systems such as post offices within the cybercommunity environment, for example, several MUDs offer mail services for sending letters to other players on the MUD, which can be sent and received only within the MUD environment.

Not all principles of the destination marketing can be applied to each type of cybercommunity structure. Most of the functions outlined are primarily focused towards the more permanent structures, although the use of support web sites can give permanence for transient mailing list-based groups. Overall, these six functions represent additional services that can be implemented by group members, or the host organisation, at minimal additional cost to the host.

Summary

Most online marketers are still failing to take full advantage of the unique features of the Internet. This is most evident in the area of communication where there is a tendency for marketers to stick with traditional broadcast and simple computer-mediated communications models. To fully exploit the potential of the Internet to develop and maintain interest and loyalty among customers, it is important that firms go beyond these relatively simple approaches to communications and move into the hypermediated communications environments.

The application of hypermediated communications, which has the greatest potential benefit for marketers, is in the development and maintenance of cybercommunities. Cybercommunities offer a range of benefits for business. The creation of an associated online community for an organisation not only offers the organisation the opportunity to interact with its clients, it allows those clients and customers to interact with one another, giving support, offering advice and presenting opinions. The organisation is then able to track changes in public perceptions and satisfaction and highlight potential problem areas before they become a major issue. Although cybercommunities are not yet common among commercial marketers, this is one area of online communications that is expected to rapidly expand as the online environment becomes increasingly competitive and firms search for a point of differentiation.

Discussion questions

5.1 Cybercommunity structures can be transient or permanent structures. Outline the advantages and disadvantages of permanent structures. Do the advantages outweigh the disadvantages?

5.2 Give an overview of the communications models and processes that influence the formation of cybercommunity structures.

5.3 Compare and contrast the different types of communities.

5.4 What roles do shared goods of value play in communities? Are these shared goods more or less important for transient cybercommunities compared to permanent cybercommunities?

5.5 Compare the user-derived communities of Sluggy.com with the top-down, community-establishing structures of Vtown. Does Vtown's provision of community construction tools aid or hinder the natural flow of community development?

5.6 What role does identity formation play in the cybercommunity? Do you believe that users should be allowed to use avatars in cybercommunities that discuss sensitive topics? What are some of the ethical considerations of adopting an avatar of a different gender to your own?

5.7 Discuss the value of the cybercommunity for small businesses which are new to the web? Do they need communities or are they the domain of large businesses?

5.8 Cybercommunities grow by the strength of their users rather than by the active intervention of their owners. Discuss in relation to the factors that influence the success of the community. How many of these factors do you believe are within the control of the community owners?

5.9 What are the six A's of destination marketing? Collect examples of cybercommunities that make use of all six of these factors. Which, if any, do you believe are the most important?

References

Barnatt, C. 1998, 'Virtual communities and financial services — online business potential and strategic choice', *International Journal of Bank Marketing*, vol. 16, no. 4, pp. 161–9.

Buhalis, D. 2000, 'Marketing the competitive destination of the future', *Tourism Management*, vol. 21, pp. 97–116.

Cothrel, J. & Williams, R. L.1999, 'Online communities: "Helping them form and grow"', *Journal of Knowledge Management*, vol. 3, no. 1, pp. 54–60.

Coyne, R. 1998, 'Cyberspace and Heidegger's pragmatics', *Information Technology and People*, vol. 11, no. 4, pp. 338–50.

Dann, S. & Dann, S. 1999, 'Cybercommuning: Global village halls', *Advances in Consumer Research*, vol. 70.

Figallo, C. 1998, *Hosting Web Communities: Building relationships, increasing customer loyalty and maintaining a competitive edge*, John Wiley, Brisbane.

Flores, F. 1998, 'Information technology and the institutions of identity: Reflections since "Understanding Computers and Cognition"', *Information Technology and People*, vol. 11, no. 4, pp. 351–72.

Gibson, W. 1984, *Neuromancer*, Ace Books, New York.

Hoffman, D. L. and Novak, T. P. 1996, 'Marketing in hypermedia computer-mediated environments: Conceptual foundations', *Journal of Marketing*, vol. 60, no. 3, July, pp. 50–68.

Horn, S. 1998, *Cyberville: Clicks, Culture, and the Creation of an Online Town*, Warner Books, New York.

Kaye, A. 1991, 'Learning together apart'. In A. Kaye (Ed.), *Collaborative Learning Through Computer Conferencing: The Najaden Papers* (pp. 1–24). Springer-Verlag, Berlin.

Kinsella, W. P. 1999, *Shoeless Joe*, Mariner Books, Chicago.

Powers, M. 1997, *How to program a virtual community*, Ziff-Davis Publishers, Seattle.

Rheingold, H. 1993, *The Virtual Community: Homesteading on the Electronic Frontier*, Harper-Collins, New York, p. 5.

Towell, J. F. & Towell, E. R. 1995, 'Internet conferencing with networked virtual environments', *Internet Research: Electronic Networking Applications and Policy*, vol. 5, no. 3, pp. 15–22.

Turkle, S. 1995, 'Life on the screen: Identity in the age of the Internet', Weidenfeld and Nicolson, London.

Whitly 1997, 'In cyberspace all they see is your words: A review of the relationship between body, behaviour and identity drawn from the sociology of knowledge', *Information Technology and People*, vol. 10, no. 2, pp. 147–63.

Web sites

bioinfo.weizmann.ac.il/BioMOO/
www.deja.com
www.geocities.com
www.mudconnector.com
www.sluggy.com
www.userfriendly.org
www.vtown.com.au
www.well.com

Newsgroups

news:alt.buddhism
news:comp.sys.palmtops.pilot

Applications *for business* *and* *non-business*

'... [H]e told journalists on Wednesday that he still thought the Internet was over-hyped, but businessmen without interest in the Net were regarded as "Luddites".'

Matt Handbury, Executive Chairman, Murdoch Magazines, quoted in *B&T Weekly*, 4 February 2000, vol. 50, no. 2269.

LEARNING objectives

After reading this chapter, you should be able to:

- outline the strategic decisions that need to be made before developing an Internet presence

- identify possible uses of the Internet for business and non-business

- discuss the advantages, limitations and issues associated with e-retailing

- recognise the processes associated with setting up an online retail presence

- give an overview of the issues associated with the online export of goods and services

- define different types of online recreational service provision.

Introduction

In order to succeed in a new environment such as the Internet, it is necessary to have a plan, a sense of purpose and a reason for being online. To boldly go where no-one has gone before really works only in the Star Trek universe. The purpose of this chapter is to outline some of the strategic decisions that need to be considered before committing to an online operation, and some of the applications of the Internet for business and non-business. It is not possible to give a definitive list of the applications for the Internet, as new methods, ideas and applications are being developed on a daily basis. Instead, the chapter will focus on several of the more common areas of Internet application such as online retailing, gambling and the use of the Internet for export industries.

Applications of the Internet: Macro-level strategic decisions

Marketing activity on the Internet, no less than offline, should be approached with a strategic perspective. The best effects for the organisation can only be demonstrated through a full commitment and the integration of online activity with the overall direction of corporate strategy. Many of the early metaphors describing the adoption of Internet marketing chose to make comparisons with the early exploration of America. Terms such as 'Internet gold rush' and 'the electronic frontier' offered romanticised versions of the commercial reality facing early adopters of the Internet. The movement towards the digital horizon is very similar to the exploration of a new land — point in the direction of the unknown, head there and hope to survive long enough to profit from the land. The accuracy of the metaphor is twofold. First, the landscape is untamed and unknown. Second, people were charging out into an electronic wilderness with no plans, no strategies and no clear sense of direction. Consequently, as with the physical world, people got lost, disheartened and spectacular failures dotted the landscape.

The major reason for most of the early failures on the Internet was a combination of a lack of clear strategy for online development, a lack of coordination between the online and offline corporate structures, and a misunderstanding as to the application of the Internet. In particular, many companies misunderstood the strategic environment of the early Internet by applying offline content control mechanisms to online environments, assuming that brand name alone would provide sufficient incentive for the users to pay for content. When subscription-based content failed to sell, as users found alternative sources of information, the Internet was declared to have failed business, and many early movers left the arena after sustaining heavy financial losses.

The common mistake made by these players was that they had not developed a strategic direction for their Internet presence. Instead, they applied offline techniques under the assumption that both the online and offline worlds would react in a similar manner. Further, most saw the Internet as cable television merged with a newspaper, and treated it with no regard to its unique features and potential applications. The strongest survivors from the initial foray into the Internet were the players who realised that the Internet is a new strategic environment and, as such, required new strategic decisions.

Guiding the online development: Strategic questions for strategic direction

The most important element in the development of an online presence, for business and non-business, is to take a strategic approach. Strategy is not restricted to the larger corporate industries, or to the boardrooms of major companies. Individuals, social groups and small business can all take a strategic marketing management approach to their move into the online world. In order to adopt such an approach, the following questions need to be addressed before saddling up and heading into the wilderness of the Web:

- what do we want to achieve by going online?
- what is the main focus of online activity (e.g. promotion, distribution)?
- what additional infrastructure requirements are needed?
- should we patch up existing infrastructure or develop whole new systems?
- how does the new online approach integrate with our existing activities?
- what sort of an electronic marketing blueprint is needed to ensure that the implementation of the program is as smooth as possible in the volatile online marketing environment?

What do we want to achieve by going online?

The first question is the most important question. In order to be able to successfully plan and implement online marketing it is necessary to have a clear reason for going online. The more specific the reason, the more it can be used to establish goals, objectives and be used to tailor the design of the web presence. Possible reasons for going online include:

- *relationship building*, whereby the online organisation can foster closer ties with cooperative organisations where both organisations share a common goal. Building relationships can occur at the mutual support level such as civil liberties as in the case of Electronic Frontiers Australia (www.efa.org.au) and the Electronic Frontier Foundation (www.eff.org).
- *international exposure*, whereby a local producer can take products to the international market without needing to establish branch offices, or form complex distribution channel arrangements in the destination countries.
- *additional service provision*, where a web site can offer products, services, information and updates in addition to the core services purchased offline. The Sonic Foundry Acid Music software uses an online registration system to provide additional software support, including access to updates, a 24–7 technical support system and a cybercommunity (www.sonicfoundry.com).
- *long-term cost reductions in communications activities*, which include a wide range of advertising distribution. These range from internal transmission of advertising copy across the world via email, email itself, and the use of services

such as global press release clearing houses (www.pressreleasenetwork .com). The major advantage to be gained by using online advertising is that it is easy to establish supplemental web sites to support the main promotional campaign. These can provide either additional information or facilitate transactions and online buying.

■ *servicing a community or specialist needs group,* such as a support group for people with Marfan syndrome (www.marfan.org) or common ancestors of the same tribe or clan (www.clangregor.com).

■ *access to new markets,* which can be part of the global opportunity presented by the Internet, or can be as simple as being online to receive orders for takeaway food to be delivered within the local area (www.e-meal.com.au).

All of the suggested reasons are potential starting points; they do not represent an exhaustive list of options. Companies have multiple reasons and purposes for moving online, and their goals and objectives should reflect these reasons. While more does not necessarily guarantee merrier, the wider the range of reasons for being involved in the Internet, the more likely it is that the project will succeed.

One of the points to keep in mind when going online is that the company's vision of where it sees itself going must be balanced with the consumers' desire to go there. As mentioned in chapter 5, the organisation must understand the needs of the customer, including the customer's desire, or lack thereof, to go online for their previously offline transactions. For example, many financial institutions see benefits to the industry in developing online services and providing a 24–7 service interface. The problem is that the changes in consumer behaviour required to move users from the familiar trip to the bank to the new Internet environment can be underestimated.

What is the main focus of online activity?

The second question is dependent in part on the first answer. Once the organisation knows why it needs to be online, it develops a set of clear priorities as to the purpose of the online activity. In specifying these objectives it will guide the focus of online activity in both setting up a web presence, and in guiding online operators as to their roles and purposes.

Honeycutt, Flaherty and Benassi (1998) suggested that there are seven main objectives that can be established as the focus for online activity. They are:

■ *market research* ranging from direct surveys housed on the producer's web sites through to product and concept pre-testing online. The Global Online Episode Survey (www.swd.net.au/geos/) operates one of the largest market research–data-gathering exercises in relation to viewer opinions on science fiction television programs broadcast around the world.

■ *customer service and customer support* orientations are used to provide ancillary service to existing customers (www.dell.com) and to provide dedicated online retailing services (www.weeklyspecials.com.au).

■ *relationship marketing,* which focuses on value adding to the existing buyer–seller relationship through the online presence, which can range from offering repeat orders online (www.discountwine.com) through to technical support services (support.microsoft.com) and reserved sections of web sites for registered customers (mydomain.register.com).

- *product distribution services*, which range from online real-time order tracking such as the UPS courier service (www.ups.com) or software downloads.
- *business to business communications* orientations that allow businesses to establish a range of communications mechanisms, from email systems up to complex automated ordering systems to expedite routine communications tasks.
- *intelligence gathering*, exploiting the capacity of an online presence to track product, customer and market trends (www.iconocast.com), including gaining information on competitors and market movements by observing competitor web sites, and registrations of similar domain names (www.nameprotect.com).
- *communications and promotions* that use the web site for the development, enhancement or maintenance of a brand image (www.jif.com) or corporate image (www.nike.co.jp).

If the purpose is image related, the focus of online activity will concentrate on promotion, whereas if the objective is to provide additional retailing services, the focus will be more on distribution and so on. Focusing on what is needed rather than trying to cover all bases at once will lead to a more effective and efficient use of the Internet in marketing activities.

What additional infrastructure requirements are needed? Should we patch up existing infrastructure or develop whole new systems?

These two questions are closely interrelated. When determining what the organisation wants to achieve, it also needs to work out whether or not it currently has the capacity to achieve its objectives.

One of the common concerns associated with the development of a web presence is the need for ongoing maintenance and updates. Unlike advertising campaigns which can be set to run for an extended period of time without updating or revision, web sites are expected to be live media that are updated frequently. The need for frequent updates gives rise to management concerns as to whether to continue an ongoing service relationship contract with outside web designers, hire or train staff, or to expect that an existing staff member will pick up the responsibility. These are management decisions that need to be based on the skills, revenue and resources of the corporation.

Investment in technological infrastructure is an ongoing process. The extent to which a whole new system is required as opposed to simply adding onto the existing infrastructure will depend on a combination of factors such as anticipated growth rates, and the extent to which the proposed activities are compatible with existing online resources. As mentioned in chapter 5, the decision to host a community on the company's equipment needs to be balanced against the resourcing issues, costs and whether an external provider can provide an equal or greater service for lower cost.

How does the new online approach integrate with our existing activities?

It is not only the online activities that are important in determining the strategic role of web-based marketing activities. The effectiveness of the overall marketing campaign relies on integration of all elements and tools of the marketing mix. The need for integration of message by medium is also important when considering tailoring different messages for different markets through the use of offline and online media. One consideration in the early stages of the diffusion of the Internet was to use a web site to target a different market segment than that targeted with offline advertising. While this is possible, and occasionally viable, the message given by the web site must not conflict with the message given in offline marketing. As there is an increasing level of crossover between offline and online audiences, consumers are likely to encounter both messages. Chapter 7, Internet in marketing strategy, examines the integration of online activities into the existing marketing mix.

 What sort of an electronic marketing blueprint is needed to ensure that the implementation of the program is as smooth as possible in the volatile online marketing environment?

The electronic marketing blueprint is the tool that helps bring together the organisation's requirements for online and offline marketing activities and integrating the two into the overall strategic direction of the company. Effective blueprinting requires leadership and coordination from the top. Creating a blueprint is a dynamic process in which the organisation's list of active projects is constantly updated and revised. New projects are evaluated and, if selected, prioritised. For blueprinting to be successful, it must be perceived as a process, not an outcome, so that it retains its relevance and flexibility at all times. Blueprinting is examined further in chapter 7.

Overall, the fundamental principles of the application of business to the Internet remain the same as the offline world. A successful online organisation needs to have a clear goal, set of objectives and understanding of what they are trying to achieve online. In addition, these goals and understanding of the direction of the company aid the development of an online presence as it can be tailored for specific tasks and purposes rather than trying to be everything to everyone and nothing to anyone in particular.

Applications and implemented solutions: Using the Web for success

Having established that an organisation approaching the Internet for business purposes needs to determine what they want from an online presence, this section outlines some of the many potential applications of the Internet, both for business and non-business. The categorisation and breakdown of types of applications is not exhaustive by any means, and new developments in management, computer and Internet technologies will constantly create new models of online applications.

The applications of the Internet tend to break down to one of five categories:
- *wholesale/retail*, which relates to the transactional sites that exist for the purposes of selling goods and services online
- *export*, which relates to the web sites that are set up for the express purpose of facilitating and transacting export level sales over the Internet. This

differs from online retailing in that export sites are business to business sales whereas the retail sites are primarily focused on customer level sales.

- *recreational services*, which are the entertainment, leisure, pleasure and gaming services that are designed for the online environment
- *promotion*: these sites are the showcase sites of the Internet and one of the Internet-based applications of the promotional mix. Promotional sites are examined in greater depth in chapter 10.
- *Internet-dependent applications* are those functions, services and applications of the unique elements that are dependent on the Internet for their existence, such as the cybercommunities. While the other four types of application have existed in offline forms, these particular applications are specific to either servicing the Internet, or rely on the unique features of the Internet for their existence. Cybercommunities were the subject of chapter 5.

Wholesale/retail: Selling online

Online retailing has attracted the bulk of the e-commerce attention in the media and academic analysis of the applications of the Internet. The main reason for the allure and fascination with the e-retail concept is the movement from the 'bricks and mortar' of traditional store-based retailing to the cross-over world of the 'clicks and mortar' (Bellman, Lohse & Johnson 1999). **'Clicks and mortar'** are the online retailing stores which mirror their offline parent companies in both range of products and market positioning. The third level of retailing to catch the attention of the mass media is the notion of the cyber-mall, the giant electronic shopping centre in cyberspace where the traditional bricks and mortar design of the mall is translated to an electronic arena (www.cybermall.com).

Retailing online: Issues, advantages and limitations

For the business community, e-retailing offers a range of opportunities and added complications above and beyond those normally experienced in the retailing sector. Griffith and Krampf (1998) offered a subdued look at the advantage for the Internet retailer in their three reasons for going online, which are:

- online sales
- communications, promotion and advertising
- customer service.

Griffith and Kampf's rationale for the presence of retailers in the online environment is not very different from the reasons for being online proposed by Honeycutt, Flaherty and Benassi (1998). E-retailing is seen as a simple extension of the process of opening a new chain store in a growing suburb, to opening a digital chain store in the growing virtual suburb of the Internet. The only real difference they saw was the reduction in capital costs involved in setting up the shop.

Even less encouraging is Landry (1998) who simply regards the online retail store as being little more than an order form for repurchasing. Landry (1998) looked at repeat purchasing of shoes believing that the true value of the Internet retailer is in lowering the costs for replacement purchases where the shopper had already expended time and effort in acquiring an original item in the bricks and mortar store. E-retailing in this case emphasised sites that were simply large catalogues where repeat orders could be made directly to the warehouses, without the need for any intermediaries.

However, despite some of the more gloomy predictions for the application of the Internet in the retailing sector, Doherty, Ellis-Chadwick and Hart (1999) outlined a range of potential advantages and disadvantages to online retailing:

- *accessibility*: This point ties into several of the unique characteristics of the Internet in that e-retailers can operate online stores on a 24-7 basis, never having to close the shutters on the web site. They can also be accessed both locally and globally, giving rise to new opportunities for sales, and for brand building in emerging markets. The accessibility to an e-retailer also increases the likelihood of interest-driven shoppers finding niche products sold through electronic stores, either as niche product stores or as a part of wider product lines.

- *new markets*: Access to new market opportunities is frequently seen to be associated with the global orientation of the Internet, and the ability of a web-based store to reach around the world without needing branch offices in each target country. Electronic collectives, such as the Australian group 'Weekly Specials' (www.weeklyspecials.com.au) offer smaller local retailers the opportunity to band together to offer goods and services to a local market through the Internet. In addition to opening their doors to the world, e-retailers can also become accessible to local markets based on product interests and specialist needs, being easier to access through interest-driven searches online. Co-op-based web presences are also easier to establish and maintain than offline collectives, and can create an intra-collective market for exchanging services, such as the Bartercard Network (www.bartercard.com).

- *direct communications, market segmentation and target marketing*: Direct communications in the context of the Doherty et al. (1999) view of the Internet is the ability of the retailer to collate data on market segments and release directly targeted information through the medium using segmentation and adaptive interactive web sites.

- *cost savings*: The fourth and final potential benefit for the use of the Internet is the notion of cost savings that are supposed to occur in the reduction of transaction costs compared to bricks and mortar retailing. This is a possible outcome; however, the Internet is not a cost-free medium, particularly when considering issues such as staffing and constant web site maintenance required for an effective web presence.

Where their work differed from the previous authors is that they argued that the Internet has not reached a point of maturity, and consequently proposed potential applications based in part on future growth, and on the assumption that initial forays into e-retailing would evolve and develop over time. They also recognised that there are several limitations to the advantages of the Internet over the offline world. These are:

- *logistics and supply chains.* A serious issue hampering the development of e-commerce and e-retailing relates to the problem of virtual stores with real products. Distribution chains, supply lines and logistics apply for every good sold online that needs to be delivered offline. One of the most frustrating issues for shoppers online is to be told at the point of purchase, and on some occasions after the purchase, that the e-retailer does not ship to the destination country. Numerous American-based web retailers proudly proclaim that they ship internationally, where international equals Canada. A student of geography will be quick to point out that there are larger areas of the 'international' world than those nations who share a common border with the United States.

   A second problem for the e-retailer is the distribution costs associated with shipping to a global marketplace, both in terms of time costs and financial costs. Many stores can offer instant purchases (and billing) but require four to six weeks for the product to be delivered. The bricks and mortar retailer, for the most part, lets the consumer take the goods with them when leaving the store, or offers to deliver them within the next few working days.

   The final supply chain problem with Internet marketing is guaranteeing supply, even at a local level, for products offered through the web site. Amazon.com operates a traditional bricks and mortar warehousing operation, in conjunction with numerous supply chain agreements with secondhand bookstores for acquiring obscure texts. Given that the role model for e-commerce still relies on a traditional logistics model, traditional distribution channels to supplement even the most advanced e-retailing operations are still a necessity.

- *disintermediation.* Another problem for retailers are the wholesalers who are online and selling direct from the factory to the consumer. **Disintermediation** relates to where the traditional supply chain breaks down as the manufacturer sells directly to the end consumer, and competes against the retailer for the same customer base. Having realised that the supply chain can be circumvented by factory-direct sales, wholesalers are also using factory-direct tactics on the Internet. The concern for retailers is twofold in that they face direct competition from their suppliers for the same customer base, and that suppliers can undercut retailers and gain a greater profit margin on the goods.

- *competition.* In addition to the concerns associated with disintermediation, online retailers face greater immediate competition from other online retailers and virtual merchants. In the online world, switching costs and travel costs associated with moving from one web site to the next are substantially lower than those experienced in travelling between retail outlets. A quite common offline shopping behaviour is to purchase something that only partially meets the shopper's needs or wants at the store they are at rather than continue with their search. With the reduction in time and effort costs in online searching, shoppers are more likely to go to more e-retailing stores than they would in their offline shopping which increases the competitive pressures on the e-retailer.

Retailing online: Conceptual model of the process of going online

One of the outcomes from the constant push by retailing to develop a cyber-shopfront has been the acquisition of a massive pool of trial and error experiences that were investigated by O'Keefe, O'Connor and Kung (1998). Figure 6.1 represents their findings regarding the experiences of the early adopters of the Web as a retail medium.

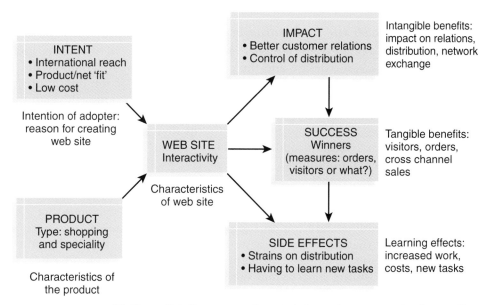

Source: O'Keefe, R. M., O'Connor, G. and King H. J. 1998, 'Early adopters of the Web as a retail medium: Small company winners and losers', *European Journal of Marketing*, vol. 32, no. 7/8, pp. 629–43.

Overall, the six elements can be broken down into three sections:

- ⬛ *precursors*, which cover the factors leading to the decision to move into online retailing, and the pre-existing conditions such as product attributes
- ⬛ *the web site*, which represents the online presence adopted on the basis of the precursors
- ⬛ *the outcomes* which resulted from the online retailing experience.

Precursors

The two main precursors to moving into online retailing are intent and product type. Intent examines the motivations behind the decision to establish an online presence. Three main motivations were outlined by O'Keefe et al. (1998):

- ⬛ *international reach*, which relates to access to the global marketplace
- ⬛ *product/Internet fit*, which looks at the degree to which the company's product or product lines are suited to distribution over the Internet, either through the Internet as a digital product (software) or ordered online as a niche market product

---

- *lower cost*, which relates to the lower entry costs especially where the cyber-shopfront offers global access for less than the cost of buying local real estate.

The second avenue of intention is based on the type of product being retailed. The study found most of the products on offer online were specialty goods or shopping goods. Specialty goods directly address niche markets, and were more likely to be accessed online by interest-driven searches. Shopping goods were categorised as products that were commonly available on the general market, and suited to the Landry (1998) model of e-retailing as a method of reordering quantities of well-known and previously used products.

The web site and online presence

The web site represented the online presence of the store, including such factors as site design and the presence of interactive components. Interactivity is highlighted as a major factor in the success of the online presence in that the more interaction that the consumer is able to enjoy through the site or the web presence, the greater the success of the site. Interactivity is seen in this context as the capacity of the site to deliver product samples, products and two-way communication between customer and retailer and includes the use of cybercommunities.

The outcomes

The final elements of the model are the three outcomes that can occur as a result of establishing and maintaining an e-retailing presence. It should be noted that these are presented in no particular order. Rather, they reflect the categories of impact: the immediate result of the web presence; the question of measuring success; and the side effects of being online.

- *Impact* is the effect of the e-retailing presence on the business. This was found to be a mostly positive outcome with many organisations observing more intangible benefits. These included improved networking and information exchange between customer, retailer and supplier that led to better customer relations and greater control of distribution of the products.
- *Success* was posited more as a question of objectives and measurement of these objectives rather than any specific criteria. The main measures of success uncovered by the research were in terms of number of orders taken online, the number of visitors to the web presence, and any cross channel sales. Cross channel sales are those sales which occur in relation to new clients, customers or markets that are not ordinarily targeted by the organisation. In addition, success can be measured in non-sales terms where the web presence increases intangible benefits such as increased networking or improved relationship marketing opportunities.
- *Side effects* included the more negative impacts of the e-retailing site which were mostly concerned with increased resource demands and strains placed on distribution networks by the new retail opportunities. Many merchants also cited a steep learning curve effect, particularly in increased levels of work required to compensate for the web presence, and the costs associated with learning the new tasks associated with the web presence, such as web site design and maintenance. Costs were also incurred in terms

of time where sites had a high level of email-based interactivity. This required staff members to reallocate time to be able to respond to the increased volume of customer mail.

Online retailing is still a developing area of Internet marketing where many of the issues that are limiting the development and growth of e-retailing, such as physical distribution channels, are the subject of frenzied research and development. It has been a successful application of the Internet, and the many unique features of Internet marketing have been able to be adapted for the benefit of the e-retailer.

Export industries: Selling beyond the borderless

Exporting and the Internet are an ideal partnership in an area of industry which focuses on global markets with a mechanism that creates global market-places. One of the early conceptual problems that occurred in examining exporting and the Internet was in determining where the boundary between regular exporters and sporadic exporters actually lay, and whether the boundary is still a legitimate distinction in the e-commerce environment.

Samiee (1998) outlined a series of axioms, or self-evident principles for exporters using the Internet. The purpose of these axioms is to examine commonly held beliefs, and shared understandings of the experience of exporters, both regular and sporadic, in using the Internet.

- *Sustainable competitive advantage is not solely derived from the Internet.* Samiee (1998) argues that the days of simple reliance on being online as a means of competitive advantage have gone. Export organisations now need an online presence to avoid a competitive disadvantage, or to maintain a level playing field. Exporters still need to make their competitive advantage occur within the context of their offline activities, and to transfer this advantage across to the online dealings, rather than believe that having an export dotcom address is enough.

- *Exporting is an industry that cannot be entered into overnight.* It is not enough to have a web site with a global target market to be an exporter. Long-term involvement in the export industry brings with it an understanding of many of the issues and commercial realities of the export industry that have not been negated by the existence of the Internet. In particular, Samiee (1998) notes that dealing with issues such as international shipping, taxation and differing exchange rates are commonplace to regular exporters, but often not considered by newcomers to the industry. It is possible that the skills and experience of the export industry may be transferred across to the e-retailing sector as more organisations find themselves trying to manage the complexity of trading in multiple nations.

- *Involvement in the Internet is a long-term investment and is not likely to generate revenue in the short term.* Of all of the e-commerce groups using the Internet, only the export industry seems to be prepared to sit back and wait for the costs to be recovered. Most of the other forays online have believed that short-term profits and sales are for the easy taking, needing little more than an order form and a brand name URL for positive results. The export industry approach is to view the Internet as another sales, promotion and communication channel that is a cost to be spent to maintain existing customers who would otherwise have switched to a rival online service. There is no real expectation given by Samiee (1998) that the Internet will provide a constant revenue stream greater than the current offline sales mechanisms. Rather, investment in the Internet is viewed with similar expectations to those held for promotion. This is not to say that Samiee (1998) does not see the Internet as a commercially viable adjunct to the existing export marketing methods. It is the case that the Internet is being used with the expectation of longer term cost recovery and profit, and short-term transitioning of sales from existing offline customers who have moved into online ordering. A future view of the market indicates the potential for the Internet to provide an additional export revenue stream; however, this should not be relied upon to replace existing offline revenue.

■ *Communications security is a major determinant in the use of the Internet for export trading.* Issues such as confidentiality, order security and credit security online are seen as limitations on the application for exporting. Given that exporting relies heavily on relationship marketing, and the development of trust between exporter and importer, both need to have a level of trust in the mediated communications medium. Further developments of cryptography, data security and the stability of Internet communications will eventually lower these barriers. Alternatively, corporate risk assessment of the costs and risks associated with trading online may indicate that the minor risk of data interception, in return for the benefits of online transactions, is an acceptable trade-off.

■ *The Internet has not yet become a ubiquitous medium.* The export industry predates the communications industry by a long time. Early export traders had to rely on packing a shipload of goods and hope for a good market price at the other end of the voyage. Now, with the advent of global telecommunications networks, many of the previously isolated trade ports are accessible. Simply showing up with a boat or plane load of goods, and a degree of optimism regarding local demand is no longer an acceptable business practice. However, not everyone who imports and exports is online, nor will many trading nations come online in the near future. Trade restrictions between nations, either by embargo, war or other reason, will prevent the full spread of the Internet, as will decisions by nations to outlaw computing technologies. Consequently, exporters cannot rely solely on being able to trade online with every possible viable market they may have worldwide. This is where seeing the Internet as an adjunct to the exporting industry's promotional mix and maintaining the competitive advantage in the offline elements is crucial for export success. It is essential to recognise that not everybody is going to be online for the purposes of importing the goods that you are trying to export.

These axioms are regarded as being equally applicable to both classes of exporters, the regular business to business exporter, and the more sporadic business to end user exporter. Figure 6.2 outlines a conceptual model of the processes involved in Internet-mediated exporting for both categories of exporters.

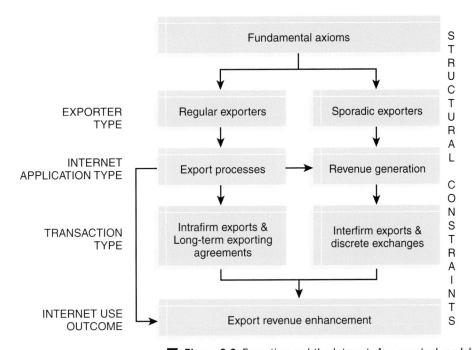

```
                    Fundamental axioms                    S
                                                          T
                                                          R
                                                          U
                                                          C
                                                          T
EXPORTER        Regular exporters      Sporadic exporters U
TYPE                                                      R
                                                          A
                                                          L
INTERNET
APPLICATION TYPE  Export processes  →  Revenue generation C
                                                          O
                                                          N
                  Intrafirm exports &   Interfirm exports & S
TRANSACTION       Long-term exporting   discrete exchanges  T
TYPE              agreements                                R
                                                          A
                                                          I
                                                          N
INTERNET USE                                              T
OUTCOME         Export revenue enhancement               S
```

■ **Figure 6.2** Exporting and the Internet: A conceptual model

Source: Samiee, S. 1998, 'Exporting and the Internet: A conceptual perspective', *International Marketing Review*, vol. 15, no. 5, pp. 413–26.

Exporter type

Business to business exports tend to involve higher quantities of goods, and are negotiated between members of the distribution channel, with all of the usual trappings of industrial marketing being applied. In contrast, sporadic exporters tend to export smaller quantities of their goods directly to individuals who are either the end users, or small speciality businesses. Samiee (1998) has included e-retailers in the sporadic exporter category since they have the potential to export small 'personal use' quantities of goods, but are not in the main business of exporting.

Internet application type

Regular importers can use the Internet for either straight revenue generation or as a mediator for the export processes. In contrast, the sporadic exporter is restricted to the revenue generation function. This is because the purpose of sporadic exports is solely for extra sales to new customers in non-recurring markets. Where a customer base became established in a new market, and the sporadic exporter dedicated part of its business to serving this market, it would be reclassified as a regular exporter. However, if the export activities are mostly irregular purchases made by end users, the revenue generation element is the only part of the model applicable to the sporadic exporter.

Regular exporters can use the Internet either to facilitate trading with existing customers and importers, in which case the model recognises the movement from export processes to export revenue enhancement. Export processes are related to increasing efficiency and data interchange through the use of the Internet to expedite recurring business processes, such as reordering or tracking regular shipments.

Revenue generation refers to the additional sales made by being online, sales that would not otherwise have occurred. For the regular exporter this is a much smaller percentage of business than the sporadic exporter who receives the major portion of export revenue through this approach.

Transaction type

There are four types of transactions mediated through the Internet:

■ *intrafirm exports or imports* are those which occur within the manufacturing of a complex product where multiple components are produced around the world and shipped to an assembly point.

■ *long-term exporting agreements* refer to relationship-based ongoing commitments to supply a fixed level of demand over a long period of time. Both long-term and intrafirm exporting and importing share the common link of having to be tightly coordinated and managed to ensure smooth running, and accurate levels of goods being delivered on time. Consequently, the Internet has had a limited value in providing an alternative data exchange network for the existing electronic data interchange networks and extranets that existed to service these relationships.

■ *interfirm exports* are smaller one-off and non-recurring exchanges between importer and exporter whereby the web site and web presence of the Internet-based exporter are calibrated to act as a sales medium or catalogue.

■ *discrete exchanges* are the exporter to end user sales where the customer buys direct from the web site without recourse to local intermediaries. This forms the basis for the majority of the e-retailer sporadic exports.

Internet use outcome

Ironically, the export industry still regards the primary, if not sole, purpose of Internet use as revenue enhancement. However, the conscious choice of revenue enhancement, rather than online profits, indicates that any use of the Internet that leads to improved revenue is considered to be indicative of a successful investment in the Internet. Unlike the main thrust of e-commerce which regards direct revenue as the sole indicator of success for a web site, Internet-based exporting regards revenue enhancement as the measure of success for the investment and outlay in the web site.

Structural constraints

Inherent in the Samiee (1998) model is the looming presence of structural limitations on the optimism of the potential for revenue enhancement. While these constraints were formulated for reviewing exports, they serve to highlight many of the restrictions on the application of the Internet at a much broader level. These constraints include:

■ *computer literacy*, which is a mandatory part of the use of the Internet and the Web

- *access to the Internet* for importer and exporter. Both parties to the transaction need to be able to be online to conduct business online. In a sense, there is no point being an importer online if the exporters who you want to trade with are not able to access the Internet.
- *ownership of personal computers*, which is related to the first two points in that many businesses are using computers for bookkeeping and transaction recording; however, these are not always used for Internet access for security reasons. In addition, home PC ownership is a major determining factor for sporadic exporters hoping to tap into home shopping e-retailing applications.
- *data flow and related regulations*, which have an impact on the viability of the Internet as a communications medium. Some countries, such as France, Singapore and China, limit the flow of the Internet access through strictly controlled inputs and outputs. Other nations such as the United States place content restrictions on what can be used in the way of data encryption in the interest of national security.
- *language and culture*, which also have a heavy impact on the value of the Internet as a medium for mediating export processes. Web sites need to be multilingual so that the target decision makers are able to use the site in a familiar language. In addition, high-context cultures which place higher value on face-to-face transactions, and the importance of ritual in exchange, may find the automation and impersonal nature of the Internet to be a deterrent to conducting business with the exporter.

The application for the Internet to the export of tangible goods is twofold. It can be a facilitator of transactions and exchange or it can provide access to additional revenue streams outside of the traditional import–export arrangements. The Internet can also be used to export services, as outlined below.

Recreational services

In addition to the Internet itself being a source of recreation for some people, many recreational services have been brought into the online environment to service a global need for entertainment products. As a global marketplace for entertainment emerges through the Internet, many of the issues that have an impact on product exporting will also have an influence on the type and nature of entertainment services provided online.

Entertainment

Entertainment seeking has been a recognised element of consumer behaviour online, including pleasure derived from straight use of the Internet (Hoffman & Novak 1996; Lewis & Lewis 1997, in Breitenbach & van Doren 1998; Raman & Leckenby 1998).

Television online has been a much threatened telecommunications technology that predates the widespread knowledge of the Internet. Early plans for distributed cable networks included video and television on-demand products that would, theoretically, deliver television grade quality in an interactive format. In the interim, while the research and development of on-demand broadcasting continues, the Internet has enabled certain broadcast functions to be distributed across the world without recourse to affiliate networks and licensing agreements.

Music and radio have been the largest benefactor of the growth of the Internet, with the advent of various mechanisms for broadcasting streaming audio (www.real.com), or distributing individual music files (www.mp3.com). The advantage audio has over video is the level of signal compression that can occur without significant loss of usability. In addition, while viewers are used to a constant high quality video presentation on television, radio carries with it an implicit acceptance of variable reception, particularly when used on the move in cars or on portable radios. This has worked to the advantage of broadcasters. They can specify minimum technical limits, such as network speed, as being essential for a quality broadcast, but allow lower speed access so that listeners can use the service at their own risk. As a result, the online listener is more fault tolerant, and willing to accept lower standards of broadcast quality if they feel that it is their equipment, not the broadcast, that is not up to the task. Television, particularly cable television, has established a much higher set of minimum expectations which can act as an entry barrier to online broadcasting.

In an apparent reversal of expectation, cinema promotional web sites have been able to distribute movie trailers for greater success in a much smaller screen size and quality than television commercials. Major blockbuster films such as *Star Wars* (www.starwars.com) and *Blair Witch Project* were able to release advertising materials online in a very reduced quality format that was not only acceptable, but often sought after by the film viewer. Several movie review and preview sites, such as Dark Horizons (www.darkhorizons.com) and Ain't It Cool News (www.aintitcoolnews.com) offer reviews, gossip, news and the downloadable trailers from their sites. These sites are usually operated independently from the major studios, and carry fan-based reviews and industry insider information. However, the majority of the movie-based entertainment sites are there to service one movie, or chain of sequels, rather than provide industry overviews.

F O C U S O N
Strategy ◉

The Hollyweb Hills: Movie promotion on the Internet

When Warner Brothers released the Batman and Robin web site as a teaser to the film release it was the most expensive web production ever developed. In real terms it probably grossly exceeded the appropriate budget for a still developing medium such as the Internet.

What it did for movie promotion was to irrevocably commit the mainstay players of the industry to the Web, and to movie-based, value-added web sites. Every major, and minor, blockbuster movie to come out of the Hollywood production houses in the following years had a Movietitle.com address for sites designed to value add to the movie experience.

Some of the more creative members of the web site portfolios belonged to the major players like *Star Wars* (www.starwars.com), and *The Matrix* (www.whatisthematrix .com). Major production houses, such as Warner Bros (www.movies.warnerbros.com) and Fox Studios (www.foxmovies.com) operate catch-all web sites where their movies of the moment, and previous releases, sit nested under the company brand logo.

Overall, these sites are usually graphics- and media-intensive extravaganzas designed to replicate in part the look and feel of the movie while trying to create as much interest as possible without giving the key plot points away. In short, these are interactive teasers to supplement the movie trailers in the cinema, and to offer merchandise sales, casting information and production details for the dedicated fans.

What the studios probably did not consider when they made their respective decisions to go to the Web for promotion is the rise of the independent cinema releases through the Internet. The most cited of the overnight online successes is *Blair Witch Project* (BWP) (www.BlairWitch.com), which began life as an Internet distributed film originally available for download from the web site. By word of mouse, and copious file transfers, BWP picked up sufficient market interest for the creators to be able to negotiate a major distribution deal for the film. Hollywood had just realised that the most frightening thing in the *Blair Witch Project* story is not the unseen terror in the film, but the unseen terror of the film's promotion.

Having seen the Blair Witch producer create an independent film, release it online, and gain mainstream success, other independent cinema operators are now looking to the Web for their first point of release. Much like the decentralisation of the music industry that arrived with the advent of the mp3, online cinema distribution is only at the beginning of the run. With faster Internet connections, and more and more research being dedicated to producing high quality streaming video, it is only a matter of time before downloadable cinema means independence from mainstream distribution. As it stands, the web site-based DVD sales have brought a new avenue for independent cinema to bring movies to the masses. The question for the big players is whether the curse of the Blair Witch will be the mass acceptance of independent web-distributed cinema, or whether they can turn this new channel to their competitive advantage.

● ●

Gambling

Online gambling faces many of the issues associated with services exporting, not least of which is the fact that it involves the export of an addictive and heavily regulated product. Many of the early players in the Internet believed that the advent of a distributed network technology like the Internet would make restrictive local laws irrelevant when it came to the production and distribution of so-called 'morality goods' such as gambling and adult products. As the Internet has been cited as enabling easier access to sensitive products to minors, more legislation has resulted in an attempt to control and restrict the production, distribution and purchase of these products.

Consequently, the online gambling industry faces similar industry level problems to those experienced in goods exporting, in particular, in the areas of:

- *computer literacy,* Internet access and computer ownership which are required before a gambler can even get near the virtual casinos on the Web

- *security,* both for the player and the casino. Online casinos that rely on electronic automated systems are vulnerable to fraud and fraudulent claims. Added to this is the fact online casinos are reasonably obvious targets for online criminal activity such as hacking or money laundering. Money laundering is also a problem for online casino owners who may find themselves the subject of profits of crime laws in various countries. Data security, and trust in the validity of the online institution is also essential for players to feel comfortable with declaring their credit card details with the casino.

- *gaming regulations,* which differ from state to state even within relatively homogenous countries such as Australia. The state of Queensland has laws in place to legalise and register online gaming, while some other states do not recognise e-casinos as legal entities. Legal ages for gambling differ between various nations, and the legality of types and forms of betting are also subject to regional variation.

- *language and culture,* which also present a major barrier to the casinos. By operating in a global market, online gambling is exposed to the risk of publishing contraband services. Some nations do not approve of gambling, or where betting on sporting events is illegal, despite the legality and morality of such events in the country where the casino's server software is housed.

- *infrastructure requirements* for online casinos cannot be developed overnight, nor can the ancillary support systems for credit verification, age verification, data security and server redundancy. As with exporting physical goods, a range of gambling service issues needs to be addressed and considered before establishing such a venture.

Overall, many major gambling services are adopting the sporadic exporter model of gambling service exporting in that they are setting up secondary services to coexist and support their existing offline gaming venues. Operations such as Centrebet (www.centrebet.com.au) are using the Internet as adjuncts to existing phone-betting services. Customers are normally required to register with the services as phone-betting clients before using the service. In a small touch of irony, most online banking services use a similar system of phone-banking registration before accepting online banking services. The ethics of inducing online banking and betting behaviours through phone services remains to be seen. However, both industries are using similar innovation adoption strategies to move people into their respective online services.

Tourism online

As the Internet began life as an offshoot of educational, government and military facilities, libraries were online long before the advent of the Web.

Once the technology of the Web expanded to include graphics, audio and streaming video at an acceptable level to the public, institutions such as art galleries, museums and other tourist destinations moved online. Many museums and galleries have adopted promotional web sites that allow potential visitors to search through the collections in preparation for their visits. Overall, the majority of these sites act as either pre-visit information systems, with maps provided for planning the tour, or as post-visit, value-added sites where merchandise can be purchased, or more information on a key exhibit can be explored.

Internet marketing INSIGHT
Web site seeing: Tourism goes digital

When the Internet went mainstream, many of the predictions of the social impact of the medium focused on the potential for the world to be seen as a smaller place. No longer subject to the tyranny of distance, and long-distance travel, the Web opened up the world in a manner not seen since the invention of airline travel.

Unlike airline travel, awkward seats and plastic-tasting food were not part of the prerequisites for exploring the world. Instead, the Web provided an avenue of opportunity to museums and galleries to bring their contents to the people, rather than rely on the people coming to them. Historical museums such as The Louvre (www.louvre.fr) and The Smithsonian Institute (www.si.edu) have opened their virtual doors to the digital tourists.

Figure 6.3 The Louvre online
Source: www.louvre.fr

(*continued*)

The Louvre offers a detailed history and overview of the collections in the museum, with an emphasis, albeit in French, on providing greater depth of information that can be searched at the reader's leisure, either as preparation for a visit or afterwards. Opening times, details of travelling exhibitions and special events are also available to assist in planning for visiting the physical location.

The Smithsonian web site operates as a digital clearing house for information concerning the vast array of services, museums, research centres and other functions incorporated under the banner of The Smithsonian Institute. The site offers a dedicated planning service masquerading as a list of frequently asked questions. This information is augmented by clever use of destination marketing to give information concerning accommodation, dining and related services that would be necessary on a trip to Washington to visit the Institute.

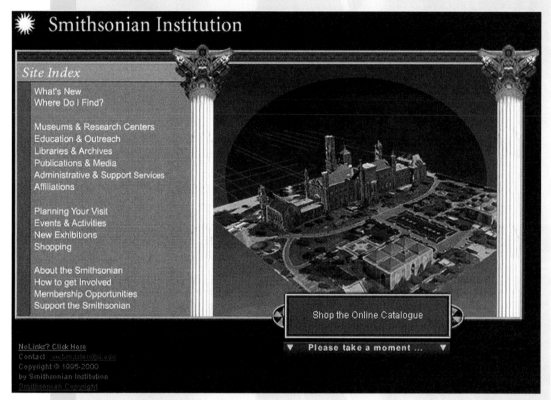

Figure 6.4 The Smithsonian online
Source: www.si.edu

However, the real virtual tourism takes place inside the Virtual Smithsonian (2k.si.edu) where the museum offers a virtual representation of one of their travelling exhibitions. It also makes no apology for designing a site that requires a fast connection beyond that of the standard dial-up modem access which would exclude many users. The designers argue that such a high bandwidth site is necessary to give a full virtual museum experience.

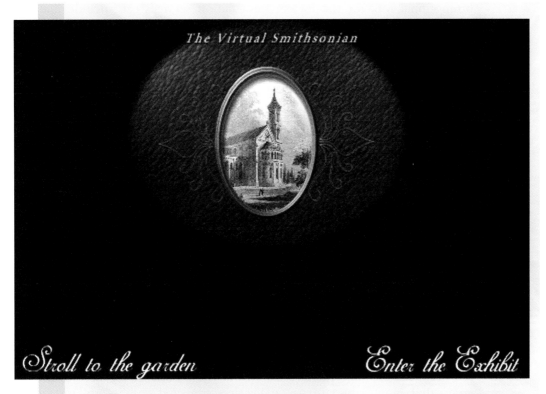

The Virtual Smithsonian

Stroll to the garden   Enter the Exhibit

■ **Figure 6.5** The Virtual Smithsonian
Source: 2k.si.edu

The Virtual Smithsonian site also accurately represents the look and feel of the offline organisation. It sets out to push the boundaries of digital distribution and tele-presence, an ambition in accordance with the organisational objective of increasing and diffusing knowledge and technology.

Cybertourism is not limited to visiting online exhibits and venues for the virtual tourist experience. Destination marketing, discussed as a mechanism for getting visits to cybercommunities in chapter 5, also applies to the use of the Internet for promotion of offline locations. Cano and Prentice (1998) overviewed the use of the Web to promote Scotland as a tourist destination, and concluded that virtual tourism was an under-utilised point of promotion. Several criticisms of the online marketing of Scotland were remarkably similar to the criticisms of information-publishing web sites laid out in chapter 3. Overall, they recognised a need for tourism sites to make greater use of the interactive features of the Internet, from the basic level of providing email contact for potential tourists to the provision of an interactive sample experience of the destination.

Buhalis (2000) also recommended the use of the Internet as an integrated part of destination marketing. Destination marketing web presences can be used to provide information, services and sample experiences as part of the promotional mix for the locale. Information services can include materials about the region, histories, promotional materials and advertising. Service provision may include e-retailing and e-commerce capacities, such as booking accommodation, travel and even pre-purchasing tickets to local attractions. The final element is the use of cybercommunities, webcams and other interactive technologies in an effort to deliver a digital representation of the region.

This would enable potential tourists to engage in **tourism telepresence** through the web site and associated services. Tourism telepresence is the attempt to give a sense of physical location, or being at a destination, through online or virtual means, usually as a trial experience of a tourist destination. For example, many tourist webcams are available ranging from reporting on snow conditions on ski runs (www.cyberski.com.au) through to views from famous historical landmarks (www2.earthcam.com/jfk/) in an effort to create a tourism telepresence.

Summary

Before any organisation goes online it needs to address a few key strategic questions: what do we want to achieve, what are we going to do, how are we going to do it and how does it fit in with our current activities? Surprisingly, few organisations take the time to answer these basic questions with the outcome that many sites are not delivering expected results and instead are simply eating up scarce company resources. Not all companies need to be online and not all industries are equally suited to the new environment. This chapter has given an overview of some of the key applications of marketing in the online environment.

Retailing is the area that has achieved the most recognition in the new environment. By removing the need for a static physical location, it is possible for retailers to reach and service a wider variety of customers than ever before. Depending on the type of product on offer it is possible to exist purely in the online environment, thus making significant savings on traditional logistics and distribution activities — savings which can be passed on to the consumer.

Related to retailing is the expansion of international and export marketing. One mistake many online marketers make is to not recognise that moving into international marketing via the Internet is a major strategic move that can change fundamentally the nature of the firm. In the past such decisions were not taken lightly; however, with the lowered barriers to entry enabled by the new technology, many relatively small firms are moving into the international arena with varying degrees of success.

The third broad category of activities enjoying online success is the recreation industry. In particular, online gambling and tourism have been the focus of significant media attention. National and international inconsistencies in law, and the difficulties associated with enforcing local laws, mean that the implementation of online casinos has been a major issue of contention in the spread of Internet-based services.

Online tourism, however, is much more positively received as it offers the experiential and educational benefits of travel without the expense. The ability for individuals to examine exhibits in museums, view artworks and major tourist attractions online not only provides a service, but helps boost demand for traditional tourism as potential travellers have greater access to information about the destinations that they are considering visiting.

The range of applications that are relevant to Internet exposure is virtually limitless. This chapter has focused on three of the key areas that are currently enjoying success online: retailing, exporting and recreation. Although Internet technology has relevance for all of these online applications, it is in the strategic application of the new technology that the gains are made. The following chapters explore the specifics of how to translate traditional strategic marketing tools and practices into the new environment to maximise the effectiveness of online marketing activities.

Discussion questions

6.1 Which of the six strategic questions is the most important for an Internet start up business to address before setting up on the Internet? Would your answer differ if the business had a long-established offline history?

6.2 Outline the five categories of Internet applications.

6.3 Compare and contrast online retailing and online exporting. How different are the supply chain problems faced by retailers to those faced by exporters?

6.4 What are some of the major advantages associated with online retailing? Do they outweigh the disadvantages? How can marketers address these disadvantages?

6.5 Which precursor to setting up an online retailing store is more important, intent or product? Collect examples of web sites that appear to be 'intent' driven rather than 'product' driven. How do these sites differ?

6.6 Are the export axioms outlined by Samiee (1998) applicable only to online exporting? To what extent could they form the basis of a set of general issues to consider before engaging in online commerce?

6.7 Collect different examples of online recreational service web sites. To what extent do these recreational web sites replicate offline services, and which represent unique applications of the Internet?

6.8 Has the development of audio and video streaming threatened to make television and radio obsolete? Do you believe that web-based broadcasting could replace radio and television, or will it become an adjunct to the existing media?

6.9 How does destination marketing that uses a cybercommunity to promote a location differ from destination marketing used to promote a cybercommunity?

6.10 Is a destination-based web site, such as Cyberski (www.cyberski.com.au) any different in theory and practice to a retailing collective such as Weekly Specials .com (www.weeklyspecials.com.au)?

6.11 Discuss the value of movie promotional web sites. Are they more use before or after the release of the movie?

References

Anon. 2000, 'Matt Handbury defends key home-maker turf', *B&T Weekly*, 4 February 2000, vol. 50, no. 2269, p. 1.

Bellman, S., Lohse, G. L. & Johnson, E. J. 1999, 'Predictors of online buying behaviour', *Communications of the ACM*, December, vol. 42, issues 12, p. 32.

Breitenbach, C. S. & van Doren, D. C. 1998, 'Value-added marketing in the digital domain: Enhancing the utility of the Internet', *Journal of Consumer Marketing*, vol. 15, no. 6, pp. 558–75.

Buhalis, D. 2000, 'Marketing the competitive destination of the future', *Tourism Management*, vol. 21, pp. 97–116.

Cano, V. & Prentice, R. 1998, 'Opportunities for endearment to places through electronic "visiting": WWW home pages and the tourism promotion of Scotland', *Tourism Management*, vol. 19, no. 1, pp. 67–73.

Doherty, N. F., Ellis-Chadwick, F. & Hart, C. A. 1999, 'Cyberretailing in the UK: The potential of the Internet as a retail channel', *International Journal of Retail and Distribution Management*, vol. 27, no. 1, pp. 22–36.

Griffith, D. A. & Krampf, R. F. 1998, 'An examination of the web-based strategies of the top 100 US retailers', *Journal of Marketing Theory and Practice*, Summer, pp. 12–23.

Hoffman, D. & Novak, T. 1996, 'Marketing in hypermedia computer-mediated environments: Conceptual foundations', *Journal of Marketing*, vol. 60, July, pp. 50–68.

Honeycutt, E. D., Flaherty, T. B. & Benassi, K. 1998, 'Marketing Industrial Products on the Internet', *Industrial Marketing Management*, vol. 27, pp. 63–72.

Landry, T. 1998, 'Electronic Commerce: A New Take on Web Shopping', *Harvard Business Review*, July–August, pp. 16–17.

O'Keefe, R. M., O'Connor, G. & Kung H. J. 1998, 'Early adopters of the Web as a retail medium: Small company winners and losers', *European Journal of Marketing*, vol. 32, no. 7/8, pp. 629–43.

Raman, N. V. & Leckenby, J. D. 1998, 'Factors affecting consumers' "Webad" visits', *European Journal of Marketing*, vol. 32, no. 7/8, pp. 737–48.

Samiee, S. 1998, 'Exporting and the Internet: A conceptual perspective', *International Marketing Review*, vol. 15, no. 5, pp. 413–26.

Web sites

2k.si.edu
mydomain.register.com
support.microsoft.com
www.louvre.fr
www.aintitcoolnews.com
www.bartercard.com
www.BlairWitch.com
www.centrebet.com.au
www.clangregor.com
www.cybermall.com
www.cyberski.com.au
www.darkhorizons.com
www.dell.com
www.discountwine.com
www.efa.org.au
www.eff.org
www.e-meal.com.au
www.iconocast.com
www.jif.com
www.marfan.org
www.movies.warnerbros.com
www.mp3.com
www.nameprotect.com
www.nike.co.jp
www.pressreleasenetwork.com
www.real.com
www.sonicfoundry.com
www.starwars.com
www.swd.net.au/geos/
www.towd.com
www.ups.com
www.weeklyspecials.com.au
www.whatisthematrix.com
www2.earthcam.com/jfk/

Internet in marketing strategy

'The World Wide Web can be described as a technology in search of a strategy.'

Gilbert, D. C., Powell-Perry, J. and Widijoso, S. 1999, 'Approaches by hotels to the use of the Internet as a relationship marketing tool', *Journal of Marketing Practice: Applied Marketing Science*, vol. 5, no. 1, pp. 21–38.

LEARNING *objectives*

After reading this chapter, you should be able to:

- determine suitable objectives that can be achieved by the use of the Internet in marketing

- outline different types of strategic growth options

- understand the importance of segmentation and branding in the positioning of the online product

- explain the importance of integrating Internet activities into the organisation's overall marketing strategy

- understand the role of the Internet in integrating the firm's overall marketing mix

- know the role and value of blueprints and budgets in implementing strategic marketing

- overview the 10 generic strategic elements to consider for Internet marketing.

Introduction

Many of the perceived failures of Internet marketing activity can be attributed directly to a failure to understand the role of strategy in incorporating online activities into an organisation's marketing function. This chapter looks at the key strategic issues associated with online marketing before examining each element of the marketing mix in detail in following chapters.

Marketing strategy takes its direction from the overall objectives of an organisation. While the marketing philosophy of client centeredness underpins all activities within a firm, the specific managerial activities associated with the marketing function include:

■ researching the market
■ developing market segmentation strategies
■ targeting key segments
■ creating positioning strategies for the product
■ developing an appropriate marketing mix that appeals to the target segment, and
■ conducting all of the above activities for the purpose of achieving organisational goals.

This chapter is divided into four main sections, each of which addresses a key strategic issue associated with setting objectives: using segmentation and positioning; integrating the mix, strategies and web site operations; and establishing the implementation policy for the strategies.

The first of these sections examines the importance of setting explicit and realistic objectives. Fundamental to all successful strategy is knowing where you want to go and what you want to achieve. Frequently, organisations go online with no clear objectives in mind and with no real understanding as to what the purpose of the site is.

Second, good marketing is based on a thorough understanding of the market. While market research is the subject of a separate chapter (chapter 16), this section discusses why segmentation should be used to identify specific target markets, tailor web site design, and assist positioning strategies. Good positioning is an important element of long-term success for any on or offline organisation.

Third, the success of the online component of any organisation's marketing program will depend on the extent to which it is integrated with the rest of the firm's activities. Hard decisions have to be made when moving online — whether to retain existing branding and positioning strategies, whether to try an appeal to the same markets on and offline and how the online activities of the firm can be used to complement, rather than compete with, existing marketing functions.

Finally, no matter how detailed and complementary the strategy that a firm develops is, it will not succeed without an appropriate implementation plan. Implementing the strategy involves a whole-of-organisation approach to ensure support for cross-functional activities. Without this holistic approach, online marketing activities will be treated as an add on, rather than being a full part of the organisation's operations.

Objectives — what are we trying to achieve by going online?

It is not possible to know if a marketing strategy has succeeded or failed if you do not know what it is you were setting out to achieve. An Internet site that exists for only six weeks may be seen as a failure, unless it was set up with the objective of servicing a short-term event such as the Olympics (www.olympics .com) or World Cup Soccer (www.worldcup.com). Within that short time frame, it may have achieved its objectives more easily than an Amazon.com (www.amazon.com) has over several years.

It cannot be emphasised too strongly that objectives, if they are to be useful in an applied situation, need to be:

- *specific* — the objective needs clearly to specify what the organisation is trying to achieve by designing and implementing a particular strategy. How does the web site integrate into the company? What is the purpose of the web site?

- *measurable* — objectives need to be quantified in some way so that they can be measured, otherwise tracking of success or failure becomes guesswork. Guesswork is better suited to lotteries than strategies, since, without clearly defined measures, no-one can know how successful a web site really is at achieving its specified objectives. It may be that a simple tool such as hit counters could be enough to measure the success of an objective, if the objective was to create a popular web presence to promote awareness of a brand name (www.reebok.com).

- *actionable* — objectives must be action-oriented or, in other words, should be written in such a way as to imply the 'how' as well as the 'what'. Announcing that the corporate objective is to become the fourth best country and western music web site is specific and measurable, but lacks action. Adding the context of 'fourth best country and western web site by providing Napster users with easy access to relevant MP3 servers' presents a specific, measurable and actionable site objective.

- *realistic* — goals must be reasonable and realistic. Many organisations attempt to go from unknown start-up companies to industry superstars overnight. Overly ambitious goals usually lead to failure, as the organisation exceeds its technical, physical and personnel capabilities. Deciding to go from an unknown Internet trade magazine to being a superior choice to *Wired* magazine (www.wired.com) in six months is unrealistic. Similarly, releasing a web browser and expecting to defeat both Netscape and Microsoft overnight is equally highly unlikely. Objectives can be determined only after a realistic assessment of the organisation's resources, capabilities, competition and external environments.

- *timetabled* — time lines are essential if objectives are going to provide real direction to the company. It is important to know not only what the company wants to achieve, but when it wants to achieve it, to be able to determine if it has reached the objective within the time frame. A good indication of the success of a web site can be determined by linking it to a date associated with another part of the company's operations. For example, an online electronics retailer (www.jaycar.com.au) may set an objective of averaging 1000 hits per week, prior to the release date of a new catalogue, and 1500 hits per week in the month following the catalogue. The offline event (release of a catalogue) gives a timetable event to use for the web site objectives.

Unfortunately, despite these clear guidelines, SMART (Specific, Measurable, Actionable, Realistic, Timetabled), objectives are rarely seen in marketing plans or strategies in practice. Most objectives are written in vague, unmeasurable and difficult-to-monitor terms. Many are simply broad expressions of intent or desire. Griffith and Krampf (1998) outlined a range of common Internet strategic objectives, such as:

- enhancing communications
- increasing online sales
- improving customer service
- increasing market share.

None of these objectives provides accurate guidance as to exactly what, how and by when the organisation wants to achieve them. In order to be usable, they need to be reworked into a format that looks less like a New Year's Resolution, and more like a business objective, for example:

- enhancing communications to the target market of subscription-based book readers by introducing an announcement mailing list, and posting weekly updates to the mailing list and web site
- increasing overall book sales by 10 per cent, using the web site to target online book buyers in the next six months
- reducing customer service calls by 10 per cent over six months, by providing online customer cybercommunities for help, assistance and advice during normal North American business hours
- increasing market share from eight to 12 per cent in the northern region by Christmas, by using a locally targeted web site in conjunction with direct mail.

What are appropriate objectives for companies to pursue in relation to their online activities? There is no simple answer to this question as suitable marketing objectives are dependent upon the overall strategic direction of the organisation. The key to effective online marketing is a combination of a thorough understanding of the market, integration of online activities with the rest of the organisation and appreciating and exploiting the strengths of the Internet in helping to achieve these broader-level objectives.

A thorough understanding of the target market is vital, given that after the initial expectations of quick and easy success online, many organisations are counting the costs and believing that they have failed. Many market failures were attributed to one of two factors: first, consumers failed to take part in the predicted rush to become involved in the new online environment simply because they were not interested in shifting to online activities. The costs of moving from traditional retail outlets, giving up high levels of familiarity with existing stores, strong risk aversion, combined with fears over Internet fraud led many consumers to see no value in changing their offline behaviour to an online equivalent.

Second, many organisations set objectives for their Internet presence that were too broad and which proved to be unmeasurable. Strangely enough, many of these organisations found that they could not account for a success or failure of an operation in terms of achievements of goals, or other observable impacts. The only observable set of statistics associated with a web site were the direct costs spent on establishing the web presence. The initial reaction to failure was to cut back on the costs and abandon the web presence, rather than to review the strategic purpose of being online. In order to give a web presence a reasonable chance of success, it is necessary to establish a set of SMART objectives.

Leong, Huang and Stanners (1998) outlined managerial perceptions of the effectiveness of the Internet as a marketing tool, and found a relatively positive set of attitudes. They identified web sites as being:

- valuable for conveying information in a fashion similar to direct mail activities. Web sites could be used in a manner similar to direct mail catalogues for providing product information and indirect sales.
- more cost effective in terms of reaching the target market than traditional methods such as direct mail. The interest-driven nature of the Internet, combined with segmentation and automated customisation of web sites allowed tailored messages to be delivered at a lower cost per reader than direct mail.
- effective in precipitating action on the part of the consumer, although not as effective as point-of-purchase displays or telemarketing
- effective for both long- and short-term promotions, indicating that the Web can be both a fast turnover site and be used for longer term promotional events, allowing for longer time frame goals to be set for measuring effectiveness
- not effective in grabbing attention. The potential customer must seek out a web site and is unlikely to chance across it in the course of their normal Internet use
- less effective in relation to changing or maintaining attitudes than television or outdoor signage. Web sites have less capacity to deliver messages suited to attitude change when compared to television or billboards.

They also acknowledged that the web site is a rational medium, which makes it less likely than television to elicit emotional responses to advertising. It is hard to imagine a collection of web users wiping tears from their eyes as a banner ad loads on their computer screen, yet television advertising content can elicit a significant emotional response (Leong, Huang & Stanners 1998).

The Web has a clear set of perceived strengths relative to other activities, but it is not the most effective medium for all marketing activities. Based on these benefits, specific goal-oriented objectives should be developed to take advantage of the strengths of the Internet. The most efficient use is to adapt existing activities within the firm which fit best the strengths of the Web, and the organisational objectives. While the Web is currently perceived as a complementary medium and marketing channel rather than a competitive one, it does appear to pose a distinct threat to direct mail activities, particularly in areas of catalogue-based sales. Understanding these views helps marketers to start looking to the future in terms of developing effective marketing objectives in relation to their online activities.

Setting specific online marketing objectives

Online marketing objectives should reflect the overall role that management perceives the Internet can play in complementing existing marketing activities. These objectives can be broadly defined under the following categories:

- *cost-oriented objectives*, which focus on using the Web to reduce costs and increase savings for the firm
- *sales-oriented objectives*, where the web site is focused towards increasing sales volume
- *behavioural change objectives*, which revolves around moving customer transactions into the online environment
- *information dissemination objectives*, which use the Web as a channel for distributing product information, ideas or knowledge
- *promotional objectives*: which is where the web site is integrated into the promotional mix as an advertising tool
- *entertainment-oriented objectives*, which turn the web site into a digital theme park designed to entertain, amuse or give a positive emotional experience to the user.

These objectives can occur in parallel in that it is possible to establish an entertainment-oriented site with promotional objectives (www.disneyland.com).

Cost-oriented objectives

An organisation may decide to move some or all of its activities online because there is a genuine saving to the firm to be gained (O'Connor & O'Keefe 1997; see also chapter 11, Pricing strategies, and chapter 12, Distribution). Specific objectives would be worded in terms such as 'reduce the costs involved in the administration of invoices to clients by 10 per cent in the next six months by implementing a system of direct online ordering' or 'reduce expenditure on the printing of brochures by 25 per cent in the next 12 months by updating information online'. Sites such as Amazon.com have used the cost reduction objectives on the Internet by removing their need for physical retail outlets.

Sales-oriented objectives

Some products are particularly suited to being sold on the Internet, either by their nature as digital information products or because of their specialist nature (Chapter 8, The role of product in Internet marketing and chapter 12, Distribution). Organisations selling these products online can reasonably set sales-based objectives to reflect the main purpose of the web site. Such objectives would generally reflect standard sales objectives such as 'to achieve $x value of sales' or 'to sell x units of product' in a given timeframe. Detailed objectives based on sales within geographic areas, or specific target markets can also be set.

Sales-oriented web sites see the Internet primarily as a distribution and retail channel whereby customers may buy direct from the manufacturer rather than relying on traditional retail outlets (O'Connor & O'Keefe 1997). Sales-oriented sites are also common among business to business companies that can use the sales sites for reordering raw materials, and for setting up low-cost electronic data interchanges (b2b.yahoo.com).

Behavioural change objectives

For some organisations, improvements in both effectiveness and efficiency can be achieved by moving key activities to predominantly online delivery. In many cases, this will involve changing the current behaviour of consumers, so that they also move online with the service provider. Online banking has seen the greatest planned shift in consumer behaviour, as financial institutions accelerate the movement to electronic transactions by gradually withdrawing offline alternatives.

In the case of sites with behavioural change objectives, these can be set in terms of numbers of current clients acquiring online banking access, numbers of transactions undertaken online and proportion of online transactions compared to traditional transactions. For example, an objective may be 'to increase the proportion of online transactions to 10 per cent of those conducted in branch offices within 12 months'. The most obvious examples of these sites are the online banks such as Lloyds (www.lloydstsb.co.uk), Chase Manhattan (www.chase.com) or ANZ (www.anz.com). Less obvious shifts have occurred in the delivery of government services such as online tax submission (www.irs.gov) and patents searches (www.ipaustralia.gov.au).

Information dissemination objectives

Information dissemination may be strictly related to products and services, such as catalogue-style sites (www.jaycar.com.au) or may be related to health (www.nutrition.com), lifestyle (www.organic-lifestyle.co.uk), political (www.alp.org.au) or cause-related marketing issues (www.amnesty.org). Given that the aim of such sites is to maximise exposure to ideas and information, success indicators would include traffic statistics, interlinking with other sites and the quantity and quality of participation in cybercommunities. A typical objective of a site based on information dissemination would be 'to increase the number of active participants on the web site's cybercommunity by 20 per cent over the next three months' or 'to double the number of hits to the second level of information pages of the site within 12 months'.

Promotional objectives

Most of the web sites currently in existence are based around promotional or communication objectives (O'Connor & O'Keefe 1997). There is some degree of overlap between information orientation and promotional sites, although the promotion sites tend towards the persuasive rather than the straight out informative (see chapters 9 and 10). The effectiveness of a promotions-based web site should be measured by standard promotional objectives, such as recognition and recall, satisfaction or sales inquiries generated. Sample objectives could include 'to achieve a response rate of 25 per cent within one week of mailing out a new product release to our existing email list' or 'to achieve a recognition rate for the URL of 30 per cent among the target market within six months of launching the site'.

Entertainment-oriented objectives

Entertainment-based sites often operate as an adjunct to offline promotional campaigns and are popular for existing well-known brands and products. The success of the site can be measured in terms of repeat visits, unsolicited publicity, such as reviews (www.netguide.com), mentions in mainstream media (ninemsn.com.au), popularity indexes (www.web21.com), site indices as well as through qualitative feedback on site. Formal objectives may include 'to generate at least one return visit within one week from 75 per cent of visitors' or 'to improve the popularity of the site as indicated by its relative positioning on X ranking (a specific media ranking)'.

Note that only two of these categories of objectives imply a component of financial success. Generation of profits (or loss minimisation) should only be considered a measure of success or failure where the objective's express purpose was to generate sales and/or reduce costs. Success or failure of the web site and the firm's online marketing component is directly tied to the specific objectives set in relation to Internet activities.

In the vast majority of cases there is no explicit profit objective tied to the development and maintenance of the web site. As has been demonstrated by the advertising industry for many years, awareness and liking of a product, while precursors to purchase, do not inevitably lead to purchase. Use of the web site will neither necessarily lead to increased sales online nor, in many cases, should this be the objective of the site.

As a communications medium, web sites play a far greater role in developing and maintaining relationships and disseminating information than they do in generating direct online sales. Some of the objectives listed are investments in long-term gains rather than potential channels for short-term profit, much in the same way advertising and promotion can be an investment in the long term development of a brand identity.

The value of the web site and its perceived success should be determined in light of these broader functions which are likely to lead indirectly to increased sales. Some web sites will serve the purpose of being online versions of window shopping where potential consumers browse online, compare prices, styles and product information and then go to a traditional outlet to actually purchase the product. By doing this consumers believe that they are combining the best of both worlds. Cross subsidisation of online activities from more traditional elements of the organisation is both appropriate and, in many cases, necessary. Evaluation of the web site's success can be undertaken effectively only if it is considered within the context of its role in the overall strategy of the organisation.

Internet marketing and strategic growth options

It should be recognised that the Internet does not exist in isolation, either in the real world, or in the planning phase of an organisation. The integration of the Internet into a firm's strategic marketing activities must be considered at all stages of the strategic planning process to determine what role the Internet can play, and how it can be used to maximise corporate strength and minimise weakness using its unique features. Given the existence and continued widespread expansion of the Internet, it should now be included as an element of analysis within the context of all strategic frameworks, whether the analysis is concerned with the development of a web presence or not.

This chapter will examine Porter's generic competitive strategies and Ansoff's strategic growth options models as a demonstration of how the integration of online marketing can assist in developing strategies. (For further reading on strategy, see Viljoen, J. and Dann, S. 2000, *Strategic Management: Planning and Implementing Successful Corporate Strategies*, Addison-Wesley Longman, Sydney.) Remember, a thorough analysis of the organisation and its environments is necessary before these, or any similar models, can become useful planning tools.

Porter's generic competitive strategies

Porter (1980) outlined the three major options that an organisation can use when competing in any market. These are based on the strategic segment that the firm is targeting combined with the strategic advantage that the firm can offer, and summarised in figure 7.1.

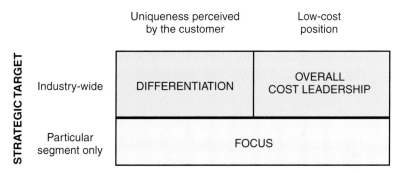

Figure 7.1 Porter's generic competitive strategies

Source: Viljoen, J. and Dann, S. 2000, *Strategic Management: Planning and Implementing Successful Corporate Strategies*, Addison-Wesley Longman, Sydney.

Essentially the organisation has three choices that it can engage in:

- **product differentiation**, which is where the company differentiates its product or service on some specific basis that is valued in the eyes of the consumer
- **cost leadership**: become the cost leader within the industry
- **niche marketing**, which is where it finds a specialist niche in the market and focuses on this segment with the hope of dominating it.

Effective use of the Internet as part of the overall marketing strategy and within specific campaigns can assist in the development of strategies focused on any one of these positions. While the generic strategies provide clear direction as to where the organisation should position itself, explicit incorporation of Internet marketing strategies can assist in the operationalisation of the decision. Strategic planning is more than just declaring the intention to become a cost leader in a niche market in six months time. It requires the company to tailor the generic models and concepts to set specific goals that are relevant to their organisational strengths, abilities, market and products.

Product differentiation: One-of-a-kind productions

One of the strengths of the Internet for existing products and organisations is that it is relatively easy to add value to an existing product or service mix simply by adding complementary online services. The point of differentiation may be objective, for example, software program updates which can be downloaded via the web site and significantly improve productivity (windowsupdate .microsoft.com), or subjective — an image of caring, quality or customisation. To maintain a successful strategy of differentiation, these additions must add up to a product mix that is not easily replicated by competitors and one which is valued by current and potential customers. The Apache web server software provides a range of modular functions that can be downloaded to provide customised web server solutions that form a product bundle that is difficult to replicate (www.apache.org). Replication of functionality can occur in rival web hosting software; however, the differentiation occurs in the combination of functionality with customisation, and access to the open source code.

In order to make the product differentiation approach work in the online environment, planning needs to be conducted to answer the question — how can the organisation use the unique attributes of the Internet to add value, and differentiate this product, from their competitors? Being able to answer the question requires the organisation to understand the nature of the Internet (chapter 3), the nature of the product (chapter 8) and the nature of the business.

Cost leadership: Driving the dollar further

Money has been the major issue for much of the discussion concerning the Internet. Moving online has often been a major cost-cutting measure, resulting in significant savings for an organisation, which in turn creates a potential opportunity for price reductions (chapter 11). This can be used to create a distinct cost advantage, which allows the organisation to position itself as a low-cost, value-for-money player in the online marketplace. Low cost does not have to mean low quality, given the benefits accrued from experience and economies of scale. The nature of the digital product (chapter 8) and digital distribution (chapter 12) has created an environment where an information product can become an inexhaustible supply, which reduces the need for scarcity-based economic pricing (Raymond 1999).

It is also important to note that a low-cost corporate strategy does not always translate into an especially low price in the market due to the psychological barriers to adoption for very low cost goods (see chapter 11).

Some cost leader organisations can succeed in the longer term because they maintain greater profit margins by lower margin over higher volume than their direct competitors (higher margin, lower volume). If the movement of the organisation into online distribution results in cost reduction, a strategic decision is needed as to whether to:

- take the profits
- pass the savings on directly to consumers
- use the additional revenue for longer-term investments in new product technology or cross-subsidisation of other elements of the product and service mix.

Cost leadership is a difficult strategy to visibly determine from examination of a web site, as price setting is determined by a range of factors (chapter 11).

Niche market strategy

'As a rule, we say anything you can sell through conventional venues can find a niche online.'

Honeycutt, E. D., Flaherty, T. B. and Benassi, K. 1998, 'Marketing Industrial Products on the Internet', *Industrial Marketing Management*, vol. 27, pp. 63–72.

Niche marketing has proven to be a popular strategy that allows an organisation to develop a specialised marketing mix, under a specific brand name to appeal to a narrow target market. The nature of the Internet as an interest-driven medium (chapter 4) coupled with the cybercommunities (chapter 5) has allowed marketers to develop micromarkets of common interest, irrespective of geographic barriers. Unlike mail order catalogues (which have to find the consumer), niche marketing online is aided by the consumer seeking out the niche product.

The attraction of niche strategies to online marketers is due largely to improved technologies combined with the geographic reach of the Internet which allows for more precise segmentation of the market. However, the niche market still must be large enough to be sustainable, for example products such as exotic (and expensive) remote control toys. Draganfly Toys (www.rctoys.com) sell a range of remote controlled flying objects, helicopters and accessories direct to the consumer as recreational goods, and business to business as novelty promotional products.

Alternatively, market niches can be serviced through systems such as E-bay (www.ebay.com), where specialist goods can be offered by hosted auction. Traders of specialist goods, such as rare collectibles or memorabilia can make use of these global electronic secondary markets instead of having to establish their own marketplaces (Arunkundram & Sundararajan 1998). Other systems such as specialist interest newsgroups (alt.rec.collecting.stamps.marketplace) and mailing lists provide niche communities of interest that can be accessed readily and easily by online marketers.

Overall, the general trend in choosing a generic marketing strategy is similar for both companies which operate predominantly online and in the traditional environment. Larger, more established firms are more likely to be able to pursue product differentiation and cost leadership. Smaller, newer firms tend to take a niche market approach due to resource restrictions, although strategic use of the Internet for targeted niche marketing can overcome some of these restrictions, such as those faced by iFive Brands.

In May 1997 Adam Smith and Brett Canfield, then employed as programmers at game publisher *Wizards of the Coast*, were delayed on their way to an early morning meeting and consequently missed their usual morning coffee. In an attempt to keep awake they tried extra strong mints in lieu of coffee. From this incident the idea of portable, convenient and tasty caffeine emerged. After a year in development (and the accumulation of a major debt) Penguin Caffeinated Mints hit the market, aided and assisted by their Internet marketing web site (www.peppermints.com), and a targeted application of online psychographic niche marketing.

With a product aimed at 'coders, clubbers, adrenaline junkies and survivors of overlong meetings everywhere', Penguin Mints rapidly attained an almost cult-like status within that particular market, as it accurately described a large portion of the Internet's more experienced users. In addition, by targeting a psychographic niche, and using the Internet as a global distribution mechanism, the iFive brands was able to overcome many of the geographic limitations they would have otherwise faced in launching an offline campaign.

As a niche market product Penguin Mints have limited distribution, with one fifth of their sales coming directly through their web site. In addition, the Peppermints.com site also provides consumers with the opportunity to post testimonials, communicate with the makers and generally give their opinion on the products. (As a result of this feedback, iFive have introduced two new products to their line — Penguin Lights which are a decaffeinated mint and Penguin Reds which is a caffeinated cinnamon flavour.) As well as their own online sales system, hosted through Yahoo! Stores (stores.yahoo.com), iFive retail through several well-known Internet merchants who target similar market niches (www.thinkgeek.com).

Although the subsequent novelty value of Penguin Caffeinated Mints may have helped promote the product to a wider audience through media stories and celebrity usage (the distinctive tins have been spotted at a number of high profile events), the web site, and online marketing targeted at their original market niche has been the key to their success. The use of the Internet as the promotion, sales and data collection medium (unsolicited feedback and suggestions) has allowed iFive to compete in the international market on an almost equal footing to their larger multinational rivals.

Source: www.peppermints.com

Strategic growth options

A second strategic framework of value to Internet-based marketers is Ansoff's strategic growth matrix. The two axes of the matrix focus on the organisation's customer base or markets and the products which it markets (figure 7.2).

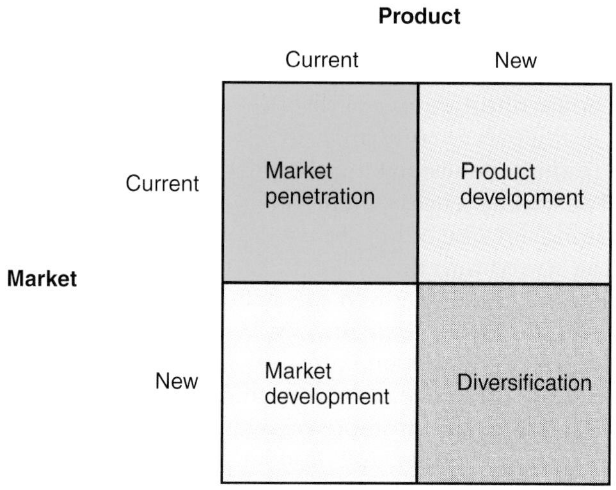

Product

	Current	New
Current	Market penetration	Product development
New	Market development	Diversification

Market

■ **Figure 7.2** Ansoff Matrix

Source: Brassington, F. and Pettitt, S. 1997, *Principles of Marketing*, Pitman Publishing, Melbourne.

This model proposes that organisations can achieve growth based on one of the following four strategies:

- *Market penetration.* This strategy is appropriate when the organisation wishes to minimise risk by selling more of the firm's existing products to its existing customer base. Traditional marketing strategies used to achieve market penetration commonly focus on sales promotion activities such as price discounts and competitions or on heavy spending on reminder advertising. Moving customers and sales functions online with the expectation that existing customers can choose to purchase from store or web site represents a market penetration policy (www.kmart.com.au).
- *Market development.* This strategy is used when a firm wants to move into new market segments and retain its current product mix. This can be achieved by repositioning the product for a new target market, finding alternative uses for the product so that it appeals to a new market segment or moving into a new geographic area. Establishing an online presence to coexist with the offline stores is, by definition, market development as the Internet represents a new region.
- *Product development.* Where the organisation retains its existing customer base and achieves substantial growth by development of new products. These products are either complementary to existing products (www.smh.com.au) or take leverage from the brand name of the firm (www.sonymusic.com) and are created to serve the ongoing needs of the organisation's identified target market. Web sites can either be developed to on-sell these new products, or be the new product or offering that complements the existing product. The online version of the *Sydney Morning Herald* operates as a parallel product to the printed versions, whereas the Sony Music web site provides a new array of information products which leverage off the company's existing brand reputation in the music industry.
- *Diversification.* In some cases an organisation may wish to set up a totally new division which draws on neither its existing customer base nor its

product lines. Diversification is the highest risk of all strategic growth options but may be appropriate where emerging needs in unrelated markets have been identified and are not being met by existing companies. Some of the strangest diversification arrangements can be achieved online, as the parent company can mask its ownership through domain names and trading names making the portfolio difficult to track, and associate.

The online environment offers substantial benefits to organisations implementing any one of the strategies outlined above. Existing target markets can be better served with the overall aim of further penetrating that market through the integrated use of the web site as both a promotional medium and a channel of distribution (www.mp3.com). MP3.com promotes artists, free music and its own range of products while also providing the distribution channel for MP3 files. Coca-Cola uses coke.com to promote the Coke™ brand, sell Coca-Cola-related merchandise, and promote regional Coke sites (www.coke.com.au) as additional information channels for product promotions and competitions. Just about the only thing that the Coke.com sites cannot deliver over the Internet is the cola itself.

Given its global nature, creating a web site automatically exposes the organisation to potential new markets. Online market development as part of the integrated strategic direction of an organisation needs to be carefully managed at all levels to ensure that the right customers are serviced without placing undue strain on the organisation. Minimising market exposure to undesirable markets can be achieved by limiting other elements of the marketing function such as distribution (chapter 12) and payment systems (chapter 11) to specific geographic regions, thus making the site irrelevant to all but the desired market (also known as America).

Market development can occur under the existing organisational structure by explicit targeting of the technologically literate with current services (www.etrade.com.au). Market development in the online environment is dependent primarily upon the successful behavioural segmentation of the market. Online share trading implicitly targets users with high disposal incomes, high levels of confidence in conducting online transactions, and a high level of Internet experience.

Product development is also readily achieved by moving key functions online or by providing additional services or information-based products to existing customers online. Exclusive online products can be developed and promoted to existing customers as a product development growth strategy. These can be complementary to existing products or services, for example, including an online help function (support.microsoft.com) or detailed product information online (www.ferrari.com).

Alternatively, new products that leverage the brand and existing product line can be developed, such as Kodak's digital camera range which has specific software accessories to the main camera product which are available only online (www.kodak.com). The success of an online product development strategy depends upon the extent to which the existing target market is already involved in Internet-based commerce. It would not be an appropriate strategy for organisations where the majority of the target market is not computer literate and does not, or cannot, access the Internet.

Finally, the rapid growth in, and perceived attractiveness of, the 'new economy' has meant that many existing firms have undertaken significant diversification into Internet-related businesses in an attempt to capitalise on this market. Although diversification is the most risky strategy available to organisations, the rapid and continuing development of the online market makes it attractive as demand, in the short term, continues to outpace supply. As the market matures, diversification into Internet-based companies is likely to become less attractive.

Despite the overall attractiveness of the market, however, a lack of understanding of online consumer behaviour has seen many companies lose significant amounts of money. Similarly, a lack of strategic focus for online marketing has meant that the Internet has not delivered the profits that many initially expected. Rampant cost cutting, and below-cost pricing, in the name of acquiring market share, has left companies such as Reel.com (www.reel.com) and Amazon.com (www.amazon.com) posting large losses, and threatened with bankruptcy. Depending on web sites to become profit centres (or even cost-recovery) centres has had an impact on the bottom line of many traditional media products, such as Encyclopaedia Britannica (www.eb.com) which has gone from selling offline at a premium price to giving the product away free online.

The relevance of the Porter and Ansoff strategic models lies in helping marketers to focus and learn from the experiences of other companies in similar situations, both on and offline. Simply being involved on a new playing field such as the Internet does not negate the strategies used successfully in other environments. Each generic strategy has embedded within it a guide for the development of specific objectives and by applying these models, an integrated marketing strategy becomes easier to design.

Segmentation and positioning

'However, although this will enable online retailers to market their goods more variously, they will still need to stick to the same product ranges, merchandising profiles and pricing strategies. They may be able to say different things to different customers, but they cannot be all things to all men.'

Pavitt, D. 1997, 'Retailing and the super high street: The future of the electronic home shopping industry', International Journal of Retail and Distribution Management, vol. 25, no. 1, pp. 38–46.

Fundamental to all successful marketing strategies, and implied by each of the models highlighted, is effective segmentation and positioning. Segmentation is the division of a heterogenous marketplace into small, more homogenous groups that can be the subject of more focused marketing messages, branding and product customisation. Positioning strategies relate to the image of the company and its products compared to the competing brands and companies in the market (Belch & Belch 1997).

Segmentation

Segmentation is a complex issue of strategy, positioning and market research which is covered in depth in chapter 16. As a strategic decision, segmentation plays a major role in shaping the whole of the marketing mix, from the product offering through to the acceptable price and distribution mechanism, and influences the type and nature of the communications message. This section sets out to examine the basic tasks and a four-step analysis model for a segmentation strategy.

Sarabia (1996) outlined the basic functional tasks of segmentation as being the search for and selection of information about customers that is used for the positioning decisions and design of the marketing mix. This is broken down to four basic tasks:

1. *Describing the segment* amounts to determining which sets of information could be used to cluster users into homogeneous groups, identify them again later, and tailor the firm's offerings (marketing and product) to their needs. Sen et al. (1998) outlined web-specific information needed for online segmentation:

   ■ usage patterns, which relate to the online behaviours, duration of stay at the web site or similar web sites, and the number of repeat visits

   ■ Internet experience was the length of time and depth of experience the user had with the Internet, the Web, and related technical systems such as email or IRC

   ■ familiarity was defined as familiarity with the Internet (related to experience) and with the brand, web site or product offered by the company

   ■ usefulness of the site was the extent to which the site was believed to address the needs of the target user (chapter 10) or offered goods or services that addressed a specific need (chapter 8)

   ■ technical characteristics were the demographics and psychographics of the user's computer systems, such as the web browser used (Netscape or Internet Explorer), the operating system, modem speeds and other characteristics of software and hardware used to access the site. The design requirements for a WebTV friendly web site are fairly radically removed from the design necessary to be transmitted to a handheld Internet access device like a mobile phone or Palm Pilot.

   Having determined this range of information, and created uniquely identifiable homogenous segments, the next step is to compare these subsets of the market with the firm's requirements.

2. *Comparing the segment to the firm's requirements* is the process where the firm determines the extent to which it can address the needs of the marketplace while still holding true to the organisational goals and objectives. It is important not to override the goals and objectives of an organisation just to service a need in the marketplace. Winner's curses still exist, even in the online world, where the end result of successfully addressing a market need results in a loss to the company addressing that need. Online marketers need to remember that just because the world audience is available, it does not need to be addressed, and if a subset market segment can better meet the needs of the firm, and have their needs met, there is more profit in a targeted niche market than untargeted global markets. Comparison of the market segment with the firm's requirements, goals and objectives also helps set the positioning strategy by finding the best match between the market and firm.

3. *Selection of the most interesting segment* is the point where the firm decides which segments to address, and which segments to leave alone. The selection of

the most interesting segment is an important decision for the online marketer as it will determine a large portion of the design of the web site (chapter 10) along with influencing the whole of the marketing mix and product positioning decisions.

4. *Making the marketing mix decisions* is the implementation phase where the firm tailors the marketing mix, branding, positioning and web site design and delivery to meet the specified and known needs of the market segment.

Segmentation 102: Four-stage analysis

Sarabia (1996) also specified four stages of analysis to use during the market segmentation process. These are:

- Stage 1: Study the segment. In the first stage, the marketer must determine whether or not the segment holds any interest for the firm. Interest is determined by the degree of fit between the product and the market, the capacity of the firm to deliver the product to the segment and for both parties to gain benefit and value from the exchange.
- Stage 2: Analysis of the firm in relation to the segment. Having decided the segment is interesting and viable, the firm must analyse its own capacity to deliver upon the promises it intends to make to the segment. Many online retailers have skipped Stage 2 in favour of deciding the world is their market place, even if shipping to Outer Mongolia is well beyond their capacities. Other firms have used Stage 2 to determine the limits of their capacity (and willingness) to ship goods (which usually seems to be the US border).
- Stage 3: Analysis of the effects of the firm's decisions about segments. If the segment and the firm seem to have a strong match, the third stage is to run a series of analyses to determine the impact and effects of the decision to address this segment. Addressing an online market niche for digital product delivery may have an impact on the capacity of the IT department to guarantee consistent high speed access to the organisation's web site. Alternatively, entering the global market with an easily copied product innovation may reduce the firm's competitive advantage in its native region, while opening it up to global competition.
- Stage 4. Final evaluation and construction of an evaluation matrix. Finally, having run the first three analyses, the firm needs to construct an evaluation matrix for each segment it is considering entering to determine the highest priority segment to address. (Details of this final step are examined in chapter 16.)

The idea of the four basic tasks and four stages of analysis is to run them in parallel, so that where necessary, outcomes from a task or analysis can be used as information for the other. This should generate the best possible set of information and is used for the segmentation process, which can then be used to assist the positioning and branding decisions.

Positioning

Positioning strategies are determined by aligning the company, and the product offering, within the marketplace in relation to the other competitors and their products. Suffice to say, this is a subjective process informed by objective measures of product perceptions and market research. It is impossible to specify every different type of positioning strategy because each and every one is based on the specific dynamics of the marketplace in which it will exist and evolve. However, like Porter's (1980) generic strategies, several generic positioning types do exist, and these were outlined by Belch and Belch (1997) as:

- **attributes and benefits**, which are the salient attributes considered important to the consumer, and believed to be the basis for making a purchase decision. Web sites can be positioned by speed of access, frequency of update, and relevance of content.
- **price quality** is where the product is positioned by price so that high quality prices attract a high price tag to indicate their value, and low end products use discounting techniques (see chapter 11).
- **use or application** is where the product is positioned specifically to be associated with a specific task or application, so that an online retail store can be associated with the weekly shopping (www.greengrocer.com.au) or a digital product can be associated with an event (www.superbowl.com) or season (www.christmas.com).
- **product class** is where the product is positioned against products and/or services outside of the product category, for example, airlines compete against trains, buses and other airlines for domestic travel. Online versions of offline services, such as radio stations (www.wildfm.com.au) compete against other online music services (www.mp3.com) and alternative forms of on and offline entertainment (TV, radio or live concert).
- **product user** is positioning based on associating a group of users with a product. Slashdot (www.slashdot.org) has the most blatant positioning strategy in the corporate tag line 'Slashdot: news for nerds' which clearly identifies their position among information sites by its relevance to a select Internet psychographic segment.
- **competitor** positioning is done by focusing on a specific competitor and outlining the difference between the product and the competitor. This is rampant among web browsers, operating systems and similar competing programs. Known affectionately as holy wars, the competitor-based positioning in the word-of-mouth marketing online is mostly associated with the eternal Macintosh versus Windows 'debate' conducted across USENET and related venues (Raymond 1996, 2000). For the most part, competitor positioning online only serves to point out another possible source of product satisfaction to the consumer, and should be avoided where possible. Low switching costs and ease of movement through the Web means consumers are prone to engaging in cross comparison investigations to confirm (or disprove) competitor-based claims.
- **cultural symbol** positioning uses images or icons which incorporate cultural images or icons as part of the product positioning strategy. This occurs at the domain name level where the selection of a regional domain (.uk, .au or .nz) or the perceived global nature of the .com can be used as a cultural icon (Schlegelmich & Sinkovics 1998). The Excite.com chain of portals offers both US/global domain access with excite.com and a range of region-specific domain portals such as Germany (www.excite.de), United Kingdom (www.excite.co.uk), or Australia (www.excite.com.au).

The selection of a positioning strategy also influences the company's branding decisions.

Online branding

Branding in the online environment begins with the domain name, and the selection of a regional or global orientation (Schlegelmich & Sinkovics 1998). Companies such as Procter and Gamble (www.pg.com) own a range of brand name-specific domains names for their primary products, such as Vicks (www.vicks.com) and Pringles (www.pringles.com). In addition, they purchased a range of common word domains including some of the less savoury reasons Procter and Gamble products would be required such as Badbreath.com (www.badbreath.com). Brands also play a major role in the reduction of perceived risk associated with shopping online (chapter 12). In addition, branding web pages can be used to create, develop and maintain image associations with known (or soon to be known) brands by careful site design and positioning (chapter 10).

Integration

Integration is the third piece of the strategic puzzle where the marketing mix, segmentation, positioning, and strategic objectives are integrated into a single coherent outcome to be acted upon in the implementation phase. The fundamental principle of strategic marketing is the necessity to integrate the whole of the organisational activities towards producing a single set of outcomes related to the company's core strategic objectives. The role of strategic Internet marketing in this instance is to bring the whole package together in the online arena, so that the marketing mix, the web site and the company's on and offline objectives all integrate smoothly, and for the maximum beneficial outcome. However, turning a set of objectives into a web site takes more than good luck and positive thoughts.

Simeon (1999) developed a model to demonstrate how four strategic functions — attracting, informing, positioning and delivering (AIPD) — could be integrated to deliver the strategic outcomes of profitability or virtual branding (figure 7.3, page 176).

Attracting is the ability of the site to bring the consumer to the information it contains, which is in part a factor of offline advertising (chapter 9), online design and promotion (chapter 10) and general social awareness of the Internet presence. Informing is the delivery of content, information, service or persuasive elements of the web site (chapters 8, 10 and 13). Positioning is the role of the web site in furthering one of the many positioning objectives listed above through the design, appearance and content of the site. Finally, delivering is the capacity of the site to provide information, service or products as required by the user (chapter 12). When these four elements are successfully interlinked they can produce either profit-orientated outcomes (reduced costs, increased sales, other revenues) or can create a sense of virtual branding. **Virtual branding** is where the web site establishes a presence in the mind of the consumers, independently of the product or service it promotes (Simeon 1999). Table 7.1 on page 176 demonstrates a range of strategic options, and key stakeholders, involved in establishing an AIPD-orientated web site.

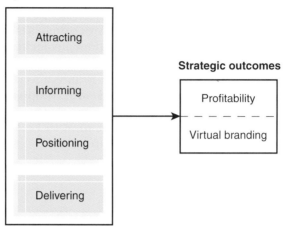

Figure 7.3 Attracting, informing, positioning and delivering: the AIPD model

Source: Simeon, R. 1999, 'Evaluating domestic and international web site strategies', *Internet Research: Electronic Networking Applications and Policy*, vol. 9, no. 4, pp. 297–308.

Table 7.1 Strategic dimension of the AIPD approach

	Attract	**Inform**	**Position**	**Deliver**
Stakeholders and strategic orientation	customers investors advertisers suppliers affiliates community promotion campaign	customers investors advertisers suppliers affiliates community managers	service provision image creation differentiation public relations	Web technology interactivity reliability security speed flexibility supply networks

Strategic action and strategic factors	Internet advertising
	other media
	   advertising
	freeware/gifts
	entertainment
	search engines
	portal sites
	banners, sweepstakes
	link exchanges
		company history
		guiding vision
		products/services
		organisational
		   structure
		financials
		recruitment/HR
		surveys
		executive teams
			market reports
			transaction types
			layouts/design
			simulations
			market targeting
			community related
			   international links
			auctions
				search engines
				databases, forms/
				   reports
				software, chat, email,
				   telephone
				audio, video
				animation, Java
				financial tools

Source: Simeon, R. 1999, 'Evaluating domestic and international web site strategies', *Internet Research: Electronic Networking Applications and Policy*, vol. 9, no. 4, pp. 297–308.

This list of potential stakeholders and strategic actions is not exhaustive. Rather, it gives examples of potential stakeholders, positioning strategies, and possible delivery issues to consider when designing a corporate site. It is designed as an illustration of possibilities to consider, rather than a set of prescriptive measures to follow.

Implementation

After determining the answers to the broad strategies, questions of what the company expects from the Internet and how it is best going to employ this technology to achieve these ends, the next key issue is implementation. Regardless of how well-developed a strategy is, it is nothing if it is not implemented effectively. One tool that is particularly useful in the design of implementation strategies is the blueprint. Just as any successful physical construction requires a detailed design plan and blueprint, online activities require similar techniques. The electronic marketing blueprint is a tool that helps bring together the organisation's requirements for online and offline marketing activities and integrates these into the overall strategic direction of the organisation. Similarly, budgeting is a strategic issue that needs to be determined at the outset of an Internet marketing plan.

Blueprinting

Blueprints allow managers across the functional areas of an organisation to determine the extent and level to which sections will be affected by the decision to adopt an Internet-based marketing strategy. It is important to remember that marketing as a strategic function is cross-disciplinary and its effects are not confined to the marketing section alone. Choosing a marketing strategy that turns the organisation from a regional retailer to global sporadic exporter will have an impact across the whole organisation, and will require a holistic approach from the organisation for it to succeed.

Blueprinting decisions need the support and involvement of management in the development process as the blueprint decisions:

■ *are critical to overall organisational success.* Full management support for the movement to an Internet marketing process is needed as changes to products (chapter 8) for distribution online or from online ordering needs to be addressed by the logistics management (chapter 12).

■ *may cut across several product lines or divisional boundaries.* Developing a web site involves the coordination of IT divisions and marketing divisions (chapter 10). If the site development also requires the redevelopment of the product for digital distribution (chapters 8 and 12), then engineering and the production departments will also need to become involved in the blueprint.

■ *frequently require the resolution of cross-functional conflict.* One of the advantages of blueprinting is that it maps out areas of potential inter-divisional conflict before the production (and conflict) commences. Once products are expected to be shipped, and customer orders have been taken, it is usually too late to decide who really should have been responsible for what function in the online marketing and distribution processes (Kalakota & Robinson 1999).

The success or failure of internal marketing efforts to gain support for external marketing plans involving Internet activities will arise from how effectively the blueprinting process is supported by the management. It requires leadership and coordination from the top as it is a dynamic process in which the organisation's list of active projects is constantly updated and revised, projects are evaluated and, if selected, prioritised, and have impact on budget allocations. For an online marketing blueprint to be successful, it needs the involvement and support of the management from the start to the completion of the process.

Budgeting

Budget allocations for Internet-based marketing activities are often difficult to predict and may be subsumed into the overall marketing budget. A dedicated Internet marketing budget helps managers to evaluate what the total investment in this activity is, and what sort of returns they are getting. There are a number of different methods for determining a budget for online marketing including being based on:

- last year's budget plus an allowance for cost increases and new activities (valid only where the web site existed last year)
- a percentage of company sales (assumes a sales orientation for the web site to continue providing its own revenue stream for survival)
- a percentage of the overall marketing budget (integrated element of the mix)
- a reallocation of existing marketing budget (assuming that the increase in Internet activity will lead to a decrease in more traditional marketing activities)
- competitor budgets and activities (reading the competition's annual reports from their web site to determine their budget allocations)
- needs and creating an effective online presence (investment cost plus running costs)
- a graduated plan linked to results (more success, more money).

Both budgeting and blueprinting need to be perceived as processes not outcomes, so that they retain their relevancy and flexibility at all times. Again, as with most of the content of any decent strategy guide, budgeting and blueprinting need to be adapted to meet the specific needs of an organisation, based on an analysis of the company, the market and the competition.

Ten strategic keys to unlocking the potential of the Internet

When looking at implementation it is critical that both strategic and tactical issues are considered. While there are no hard and fast rules or simple templates to be applied for setting strategic directions, Bayne (2000) identifies 10 key strategy areas which need to be considered before going online. These are:

1. view the Internet as an adjunct
2. use email strategically

3. cross-pollinate
4. provide extra value
5. analyse content and use
6. repurpose material
7. design with online in mind
8. plan frequent revisions
9. manage for the long term
10. set reasonable goals.

View the Internet as an adjunct

For all companies at this point online presence is part of a continuum. Organisations have both an on and offline presence — the degree to which they are predominantly one or the other will dictate how they are perceived.

On and offline marketing activities are synergistic and must be fully integrated for success. Putting up a web site alone is not enough to be an online marketer. A web presence should not be seen as a direct, immediate substitute for existing activities such as direct mail. To be successful, the web site should complement existing activities and be designed to best meet identified customer needs.

Use email strategically

Use customer email addresses judiciously — do not overwhelm the customer with emails just because it is easy to do. Because of its cheapness and ease of use, the potential for email abuse is greater than for other communications media.

If you do not have the email addresses of existing or potential customers, use creative ways to gain them, for example, competitions using business cards as an entry form.

Email-based marketing is best handled through **opt-in functions** where the user chooses to become involved in the mailing list, or to receive the announcements. The value of the opt-in function is that it generates lists of people who already hold high levels of involvement and interest in the product or service being offered. In this manner, opt-in functions can be used for market development. Only ever rely on opt-in mechanisms for generating email lists. Any organisation or company that tells you that unsolicited email is an acceptable method of online advertising is selling mailing lists.

There is an established cultural history that aggressively opposes the sending of unsolicited **spam** email. Spam is the generic term used to describe any commercial email that is perceived to be unsolicited, or which has made use of an untargeted bulk distribution of a message across email lists, newsgroups or IRC channels. The majority of Internet Service Providers' terms and conditions of acceptable use prohibit the transmission of spam, usually with the penalty of being blackballed by the provider. Spam is a serious e-commerce misdemeanour in that it generates unnecessary and undesired mail traffic that reduces the available bandwidth available for legitimate purposes.

Cross-pollinate

The best form of promotion for online activities is offline. People still encounter the majority of their marketing information, promotions and advertising offline via radio, billboards, newspapers, magazines and so on. Incorporate your web or email address on all offline promotional activities to prompt visits by potential and current users. This is covered in depth in chapter 9.

Provide extra value

Create a reason for people to visit you online. While this may sound obvious it is not always done. What benefits does a visit to the web site offer the consumer? Do you offer extra information not available elsewhere, a cheaper distribution alternative, or additional services? Web sites can also be used as a focus for promotional activities such as competitions, to test future offline advertising and provide communities of users with opportunities to interact with each other and the organisation. Value provision and virtual value chains are discussed in chapters 11 and 12.

Analyse content and use

The design of the web site will influence how it is used and the value repeat customers derive from it. Many web sites choose to use a tiered approach to information dissemination and service use. For example, while general information is available to all visitors, detailed information, access to company statistics or access to online buying may require registration on the part of the user (www.thesims.com).

Further, do you want customers to contact you directly? While the interactive personalised component is one of the features of the Internet, the cost of maintaining such activities is high. Analysing the pattern of requests and incrementally adding information to the open access web site, either through interactive help functions or through frequently asked questions (FAQ) lists should reduce repetitive message traffic. Dingoblue (www.dingoblue.net.au) provides a general level FAQ that handles commonly asked questions about the service, and a series of specific FAQs to address the needs of registered users. To access details specific to the use of the Dingoblue software or services, the users must log in with their account user name and password. Within this secured area are also a series of value-added functions such as account management, and the ability to contact a tech support staff member directly through an interactive chat forum.

Repurpose material

Repurposing is a term that means to take content from one medium and re-use it on another. While a purely online brochure approach is to be avoided, much of the information and text already designed for offline purposes can be used online. One of the advantages to a limited amount of repurposing is that it assists in creating consistency of image for the organisation across media platforms (chapter 10).

Design with online in mind

Not all materials from traditional media translate effectively into the online environment. The impact of online advertising and promotion needs to be felt in a single frame whereas offline can use techniques such as double page spreads, consecutive pages, teaser campaigns and so on to create an impact. In addition, online design can include features not available offline such as animations. The key to successful design is in creating a web site or page which has elements consistent with offline activities in terms of tone and style but which, at the same time, takes advantage of the features of the Internet which are examined in chapter 10.

Plan frequent revisions

Customer expectations of immediacy regarding the Internet mean that it is more of an issue when a web site is out of date than when a brochure is. Allowing a web site to be static or become dated gives a negative perception of the organisation from the consumer's perspective even if this is, in reality, unjust. In addition, frequency of revision is also determined by the type and nature of the product — a currency exchange site (www.xe.net/ucc) that offers less than up to the minute currency conversions will be perceived to be out of date faster than a site detailing a past event. The most important factor in site design and frequency of revision is the need to keep the positioning strategy, and corporate image, of the site as the determinant of revision speed. Any web site still promoting an event as current after the due date of the event will permanently damage the company's reputation for speed and efficiency.

Manage for the long term

Online marketing activities will not necessarily return immediate, measurable, financial gains. Given the continuing reluctance of most consumers to purchase online or give out too much personal detail, the online marketer has to be patient. Many consumers use the Internet to browse potential purchases, yet when the time comes to actually make the purchase, they will go to the more familiar environment of the traditional retail outlet.

Set reasonable goals

Related to the whole chapter, and the SMART objectives, some companies can point to quick Internet successes; most achieve more modest goals. This is where the importance of realistic objective setting comes into the strategic equation. The inclusion of the Internet into marketing activities should be as a means to achieve the ends of the organisation, not the end in itself. While the web-based components of the marketing mix have the potential to become as important as the other elements, the adoption and use of this new technology is a gradual, evolutionary process.

Summary

This chapter overviewed the generic models and strategies which need to be considered when planning a move into the Internet. Many of the conventional marketing strategy models from the offline world still apply in principle, given that the decision to expand a market on or offline is still the same decision. By understanding the different types of strategic growth options available, and determining appropriate objectives, organisations can determine whether to use the Internet to attract new customers, increase sales from existing ones, or develop an entirely new niche of users. The importance of the branding and segmentation in this context is that it lends itself to allowing the organisation to understand the needs and wants of the customer base it currently has, and the one it is proposing to address with the new online offerings.

Integrating the Internet activities of the organisation into the overall marketing strategy was highlighted as a key objective. Without the understanding of how the Internet presence can influence and impinge upon the activities of the whole of the organisation, the company cannot successfully implement a strategic, planned online operation. Blueprinting was suggested as one possible method by which the various roles of the organisation could be assessed so that conflicts could be detected (and resolved) before the company went online.

Finally, the chapter outlined 10 generic strategic elements to be considered when planning the movement into the Internet environment.

Discussion questions

7.1 What are the six marketing objectives of a web site? Which objectives are best suited to a cybercommunity web site and which are suited to an e-commerce retail web site? Justify your answer.

7.2 Define the different types of Porter's strategic growth options. Find examples of web sites which use these approaches.

7.3 How can segmentation be used to assist the development of a web site? What are some of the types of data needed for web segmentation?

7.4 Collect a series of web sites and determine which positioning strategy they are using. Can a site have more than one positioning strategy?

7.5 What is the significance of branding for a web site? Does the URL for a corporate site need to be the brand name of the company or the product? Collect examples of branded and unbranded domain names.

7.6 Explain the importance of integrating the activities of the web site and Internet marketing into the organisation's overall marketing strategy and business activities.

7.7 Which method of budgeting should be used for a small information web site, large e-commerce site and a medium sized cybercommunity site? Why? Does your answer differ based on the size of the operation or the nature of the site?

7.8 Outline the 10 generic strategic elements to consider for Internet marketing. Which of the 10 is the most important? Which is the least important?

References

Arunkundram, R. & Sundararajan, A. 1998, 'An economic analysis of electronic secondary markets: Installed base, technology, durability and firm profitability, *Decision Support Systems*, vol. 24, pp. 3–16.

Bayne, K. M. 2000, *The Internet Marketing Plan*, 2nd edn, Wiley, New York.

Belch, G. E. & Belch, M. A. 1997, *Introduction to Advertising and Promotion: An Integrated Marketing Communications Perspective*, 4th edn, Richard D. Irwin Publishers, Sydney.

Brassington, F. & Pettitt, S. 1997, *Principles of Marketing*, Pitman Publishing, Melbourne.

Gilbert, D. C., Powell-Perry, J. & Widijoso, S. 1999, 'Approaches by hotels to the use of the Internet as a relationship marketing tool', *Journal of Marketing Practice: Applied Marketing Science*, vol. 5, no. 1, pp. 21–38.

Griffith, D. A. & Krampf, R. F. 1998, 'An examination of the web-based strategies of the top 100 US retailers', *Journal of Marketing Theory and Practice*, Summer, pp. 12–23.

Honeycutt, E. D., Flaherty, T. B. & Benassi, K. 1998, 'Marketing Industrial Products on the Internet', *Industrial Marketing Management*, vol. 27, pp. 63–72.

Kalakota, R. & Robinson, M. 1999, *e-Business: Roadmap for Success*, Addison-Wesley, Sydney.

Leong, E. K. F., Huang, X. & Stanners, P. J. 1998, 'Comparing the Effectiveness of the Web Site with Traditional Media', *Journal of Advertising Research*, vol. 38, no. 4, pp. 44–57.

O'Connor, G. C. & O'Keefe, B. 1997. 'Viewing the Web as a marketplace: The case of small companies'. *Decision Support Systems*, vol. 21, no. 3, pp. 171–83.

Pavitt, D. 1997, 'Retailing and the super high street: The future of the electronic home shopping industry', *International Journal of Retail and Distribution Management*, vol. 25, no. 1, pp. 38–46.

Porter. M. E. 1980, *Competitive Strategy*, The Free Press, New York.

Raymond, E. S. 1996, *The New Hacker's Dictionary*, 3rd edn, MIT Press, Boston.

Raymond, E. S. 1999, *The Cathedral and the Bazaar*, O'Reilly, Sebastopol.

Raymond, E. S. 2000, 'The Jargon Manual', Version 4.2.0.

http://www.tuxedo.org/~esr/jargon/

Sarabia, F. J. 1996, 'Model for markets segments evaluation and selection', *European Journal of Marketing*, vol. 30, no. 4, pp. 58–74.

Schlegelmich, B. B. & Sinkovics, R. 1998, 'Viewpoint: Marketing in the information age — can we plan for an unpredictable future?' *International Marketing Review*, vol. 15, no. 3, pp 162–70.

Sen, S., Padmanabhan, B, Tuzhilin, A., White N. H. & Stein, R. 1998, The identification and satisfaction of consumer analysis-driven information needs of marketers on the WWW', *European Journal of Marketing*, vol. 32, no. 7/8, pp. 688–702.

Simeon, R. 1999, 'Evaluating Domestic and International Web site strategies', *Internet Research: Electronic Networking Applications and Policy*, vol. 9, no. 4, pp. 297–308.

Viljoen, J. & Dann, S. 2000, *Strategic Management: Planning and Implementing Successful Corporate Strategies*, Addison-Wesley Longman, Sydney.

Web sites

b2b.yahoo.com
ninemsn.com.au
stores.yahoo.com
support.microsoft.com
windowsupdate.microsoft.com
www.alp.org.au
www.amazon.com
www.amnesty.org
www.anz.com
www.apache.org
www.badbreath.com
www.chase.com
www.christmas.com
www.coke.com

www.dingoblue.net.au
www.disneyland.com
www.eb.com
www.ebay.com
www.etrade.com.au
www.excite.co.uk
www.excite.com
www.excite.com.au
www.excite.de
www.ferrari.com
www.greengrocer.com.au
www.ipaustralia.gov.au
www.irs.gov
www.jaycar.com.au
www.kmart.com.au
www.kodak.com
www.lloydstsb.co.uk
www.mp3.com
www.netguide.com
www.nutrition.com
www.olympics.com

www.organic-lifestyle.co.uk
www.peppermints.com
www.pg.com
www.pringles.com
www.rctoys.com
www.reebok.com
www.reel.com
www.slashdot.org
www.smh.com.au
www.sonymusic.com
www.superbowl.com
www.thesims.com
www.thinkgeek.com
www.vicks.com
www.web21.com
www.wildfm.com.au
www.wired.com
www.worldcup.com
www.xe.net/ucc

Newsgroup
News:alt.rec.collecting.stamps.marketplace

part 3

Marketing fundamentals in the interactive age

■ **8**...*The role of product in Internet marketing*   ■ **9**...*Promotion 1: Internet in promotional mix*   ■ **10**...*Promotion 2: The Internet as a promotional medium* ■ **11**...*Pricing strategies*   ■ **12**...*Distribution*

The third section of the book focuses on incorporating the strategic elements of marketing into the application of online marketing. The focus of this section of the book revolves around exploring how each element of the marketing mix can be used in the online world, and what impact the Internet can have on individual elements. Strategic issues of engaging in online activities are examined in the context of setting objectives and developing segmentation and positioning strategies.

Chapter 8 sets out the issues surrounding the types and nature of products that can be sold through the Internet. This chapter works through the conceptual foundations and theories of product and new product development. This is examined to demonstrate how the Internet can facilitate the development of products, or be integrated as part of a digital product.

Chapters 9 and 10 review the interaction between the promotional mix, web sites, and on and offline promotion. **Chapter 9** specifically examines the philosophical foundations of promotion, and how these integrate into the communication of the web site to the user. The emphasis in this chapter is on using the conventional offline promotional mix to engage the user's attention and interest while they are offline, and drive them online to the web site. The chapter also examines the online promotional functions, such as banner advertising, in the role of attracting the online users to a site. **Chapter 10** explores the role of the web site as a promotional tool, and examines how different types and styles of web design, web sites and individual web pages can be integrated into the marketing mix and promotional mix. This chapter continues to examine the philosophy of post-modern consumption web sites, and how this influences site design.

Chapter 11 explores the nature of price online, and pressures on pricing exerted by the Internet. The chapter explores the nature of the total price concept, pricing objectives and pricing strategies in the context of Internet and interactive product delivery.

Chapter 12 rounds out the marketing mix section by discussing the issues and implications of delivery in the Internet arena, including on and offline delivery. It explores the nature of the marketspace–marketplace dichotomy created by the Internet's involvement in physical product ordering and delivery.

The role of product in Internet marketing

'Arthur listened for a short while, but being unable to understand the vast majority of what Ford was saying he began to let his mind wander, trailing his fingers along the edge of an incomprehensible computer bank, he reached out and pressed an invitingly large red button on a nearby panel. The panel lit up with the words "Please do not press this button again"'

Adams, D. 1979, *The HitchHikers Guide to the Galaxy*, Pan Books, London.

LEARNING objectives

After reading this chapter, you should be able to:

- appreciate why a clear understanding of the product is critical to successful marketing

- explain why creating a definition of Internet-related products is so difficult

- know which types of product are most suited to the Internet

- be able to identify the most successful types of Internet-related product

- understand which elements of the traditional new product development process are relevant to the evolution of new online products.

Introduction

The key to a successful marketing plan and strategy is to have a clear understanding of the product and how to communicate its benefits to the consumer. Although this seems obvious, in reality it is very rare for organisations to seriously consider what their 'product' is, does, or represents for the customer. Many take a relatively simplistic approach by focusing on the functions and physical characteristics of their product. In other words, they take an organisational, rather than a customer-focused, view of what it is that they are producing and selling.

For marketing purposes the product is conceptualised as a total bundle of benefits that the seller is offering to potential consumers. These benefits exist on different levels, with the relative value of specific benefits varying considerably between individual consumers. To help understand the product better and for practical purposes of communication, to clarify what the company's 'product' is, a number of models have been developed. Of these, the multilevel product concept is the most common model.

Online products are often difficult to clearly articulate to the potential consumer, whereas the relative benefits of purchasing an existing product that simply uses the Internet as a distribution channel can be easily understood. The challenge for online marketers is to get the broader population online. Once online they can use the Internet for e-commerce, to supplement or replace their existing offline transactions.

The relative importance of the online component of the total product needs to be clarified in light of the strategic direction and needs of the overall organisation. Technological capacity and the ability of online companies to deliver mass customisation has a significant impact on the way in which new products and services are being developed and delivered. Ad hoc product variations and redesigns, which may appear best suited to designing for the Internet, are potentially damaging to the overall brand and image of the organisation. Although formalised, sequential approaches to new product development may not necessarily appear to be the most appropriate means of new, online, product development, they still have a valuable role to play in maintaining a consistent planned approach to product development.

The purpose of this chapter is to investigate what is involved in the definition of online product and the importance of spending time on this activity. Product definition and formalised development processes are critical in the creation of new physical products. This is due to the flow-on effect in terms of new equipment and production facilities. In the case of services and online activities, however, where incremental change is possible, many organisations have taken an informal trial and error approach to new product development. After examining which products and product types are most suited to online marketing activities (and also have successful results), the chapter concludes with a discussion on the value of adapting established, new product development processes in the online environment.

What is the product?

The product is arguably the central component of any marketing strategy. While manipulation of the full marketing mix is essential to a coherent marketing plan, without the product there is nothing to promote, distribute or price. Defining the product accurately, and from a consumer rather than an organisational perspective, is critical to the marketing communication process. If the marketer or salesperson is unclear as to precisely what the product is and what it does, it becomes difficult, if not impossible, to communicate the benefits of the product and persuade consumers to trial it.

With origins in the selling of physical goods, marketers often take a simplistic approach to the issue of product definition. They rely primarily on tangible or measurable features to explain and differentiate their organisation's offering. For example, cars are sold on style, pizzas on the number and variations of topping, and computers on relative speed and processing capacity. Even in the intangible sphere of services, products are sold primarily on externally observable criteria such as time (delivered overnight), place (the neighbourhood store) or price (best value).

The problem with an approach such as this is that consumers do not buy the physical features, they buy the benefits that will accrue from these features. Ownership of the product which goes faster, quieter or for longer gives the customer a range of benefits which may or may not have been considered by the marketer. The notion of product as a collection of benefits rather than features is not new to marketing literature (Levitt 1960; Kotler & Armstrong 1994). '**Product**' is variously defined in the literature but all definitions include the following key points:

- first, the product is the total bundle of benefits that the seller offers the consumer (McColl-Kennedy & Kiel 2000). This includes the visible product, any intangible benefits such as the status and prestige, lifestyle benefits such as convenience, and ancillary services such as warranties and help lines.

- second, the consumer buys the function that they believe the product will perform, rather than the product per se (Fojt 1996). Products are purchased as solutions to problems, or to fulfil needs or wants. A Pokemon doll is bought for the enjoyment it will bring, not for the fact it is a yellow, extruded plastic shell with red and black painted patterns.

Despite this intellectual acceptance of product as a set of benefits, there remains a residual tendency of managers to focus more attention on features rather than benefits in both the development process and promotional aspects. Nowhere is this more apparent than with complex and technological products, which are pushed to market on the basis of faster computer chips, more megahertz and gigabytes and less explanation as to why these new elements are of any value to the customer. Customers purchase products based on the degree to which they satisfy a need, meet a want or deliver satisfaction. Good marketing is based on developing a product which meets these perceived needs rather than adding superfluous features in the production process to satisfy the producer's aesthetic whims.

Multilevel product concept

Conceptualising the full dimensions of the product being offered is made simpler by applying a **multilevel product concept**. This concept regards a product as consisting of three distinct layers or levels. These are the:

- **core product** — the benefits that the product will provide
- **actual product** — the tangible product including style and accessories
- **augmented product** — any additional benefits or services attached to the purchase of the actual product, such as social prestige or service warranty.

For example, in the case of a car, the core product is convenient transportation. The actual product is the make, model, colour and style of the car. The augmented product is the free follow-up service, the status of the make and the repayment system. The breakdown of the multilevel product concept is illustrated in figure 8.1.

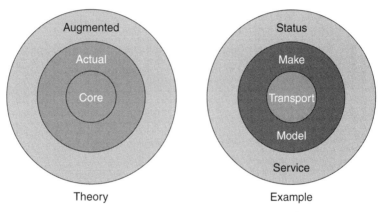

Theory   Example

Figure 8.1 Multilevel product concepts: theory and example illustration

While the multilevel product concept is intuitively appealing and conceptually simple, its application is extremely difficult. The core product for any particular item or type of product may vary significantly from individual to individual or between target groups. The underlying benefit of some products is easy to define and is consistent across consumers; for example, the underlying function of food is to satisfy hunger. The motivation to own or use other products, particularly new, complex, technologically or socially visible ones, is more complex. For example, what is the core product that is sought by purchasers of music CDs? Is it entertainment, identification with a particular social group or image building?

Understanding and acknowledging that the marketplace may perceive a range of core benefits for the same physical product or identical service allows marketers to better position themselves relative to their competitors. As a strategic tool the total product concept is invaluable to the development and implementation of any marketing plan.

Spending the time to clarify the nature of the core product is not simply an intellectual exercise of limited practical value. A clear definition of the core benefit is fundamental to effective marketing communication. A consistent core product provides consumers with continuity across minor product variations and reduces the risk of adoption associated with new products. Many truly innovative new products, such as birth control pills and personal computers, failed in their initial market release due to poor core product definition (Valentin 1994). In each case marketers failed to explain how the underpinning benefits of the new technology would enhance consumers' lifestyles.

The online product

The nature of the Internet complicates the process of defining the boundaries of the online product. The value of being online and what that can offer, in terms of developing, refining and articulating the product concept, is the focus of this chapter. The Internet itself is not considered the 'product' of interest to online marketers. That particular product domain is left in the hands of Internet Service Providers' (ISP) marketing strategies.

Online product concept

In order to apply the multilevel product concept to online products, the company is required to answer the basic question, 'What role does the Internet play in determining overall product benefits?'.

The problem with this question is that the best and most accurate answer is — 'it depends'. The online product can exist predominantly as part of the core, the actual or the augmented product, depending on the goals of the organisation, the needs of its target client group and the nature of the products that are being sold.

Core product offerings will always be defined in terms of the underpinning benefit that the product offers the consumer. Common core offerings of disparate products include concepts such as convenience, security or enjoyment. For example, the core benefit of convenience is equally relevant to all night shopping, ATMs and home delivery. Online products which offer the core benefit of convenience include online banking systems which allow consumers 24 hour access to their accounts (www.anz.com), online payment of bills (www.bpay.com.au) and online enrolment in university courses (www.mscisOnline.org).

The actual product is normally associated with the physical elements of the product offering. The Internet is considered central to the actual product of the organisation, where the focus of the company's overall product is its online presence. For example, the Internet would form part of the actual product of those organisations which exist predominantly, or exclusively, online, or for which the online presence is content dominated. Products that fit this definition include sites such as search engines that exist purely for the purpose of acting as online intermediaries (www.yahoo.co.uk) or online media outlets such as newspapers (www.nytimes.com) and magazines (www.salon.com).

Currently, the most common use of the Internet as part of the overall product offering of an organisation is as part of the augmented product. Augmented products are any additional benefits or services attached to the purchase of the actual product. This describes most commercial, government and not-for-profit web sites. The Internet presence within these traditional manufacturing, retailing and service organisations is designed to supplement existing products or to add value to the firm's overall product offering. This is achieved by giving consumers access to additional services (www.hp.com) or information (www.ford.com) in the online environment.

Inevitably, there will be clusters of industries focusing on each different level of the product. Traditional manufacturers use the Internet primarily as part of the augmented product by providing detailed information about product characteristics (www.hoover.co.uk), distribution networks (www.ptm.com.au) or additional services such as online assistance (www.compaq.com). Classification of the online product is based on the reason why the product is online, and how that contributes to the product's overall value to the end consumer. In addition, it is possible for multiple firms in a single industry to segment the market according to the level of product that it is focused on, as illustrated in figure 8.2.

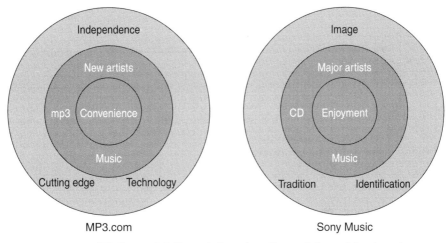

MP3.com   Sony Music

Figure 8.2 Recorded music online and the multilevel product concept

As highlighted in figure 8.2, different organisations in the recorded music industry are focusing their strategies on different levels of their product, according to the target market segment they wish to attract and retain.

Online continuum

Products should be evaluated, in terms of their suitability for online activities, on the basis of a continuum between tangible and intangible. Few products, however, are considered to be purely tangible (physical product) or purely intangible (pure service). Rather, services are conceptualised as existing along a continuum of intangibility with predominantly tangible products such as sugar, timber and coal at one end of the continuum and predominantly intangible products such as education, counselling and entertainment at the other. The vast majority of goods exist somewhere between the extremes. As a result, some product categories, with their mix of tangible and intangible features, are particularly suited to online development and delivery.

Figure 8.3 highlights the typical relevant online content for a variety of product types. From this continuum it can be seen that while all product categories and organisations could potentially benefit from online activity, the relative importance of the online element varies considerably.

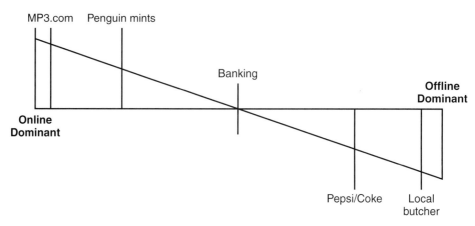

Figure 8.3 The product continuum

Information-based or digital products, for example, are ideally suited to the online environment. Not only do they exist in their entirety online, they can be modified, paid for and delivered to consumers online (www.redhat.com). The Internet, therefore, is central to the definition and articulation of these organisations' products.

Physical products, on the other hand, still need to be transported from a storage area offline, through standard distribution or delivery channels. Penguin Mints (www.peppermints.com) manufacture a caffeinated peppermint candy, which, while sold primarily through the web site, still requires physical distribution and shipping. Consequently, the value of going online for most retailers lies not in direct sales but in providing an alternative for specific classes of customer. For many existing companies, particularly those already well established in the retail or services sector, the Internet is an adjunct to the main product offering. The Internet presence, however, is still important as it is focused on its role in the ancillary function of communication or distribution, rather than as the product.

Finally, there are organisations and products for which the Internet is currently of relatively little value. While this still seems to be a difficult concept to grasp for some Internet consultants, not every company will find immediate value in the Internet. Bayne (2000) cites a discussion with a local house painter in which the painter questions whether he should be online. Bayne's argument for why the painter should be online was based on whether anyone else was online, not whether being online would have any value to the painter. While arguments are being made that the Internet should be integral to the operations of all organisations, since this is the way of the future, most businesses operate in the present. The reality is that there are still many organisations for whom online activities are still largely irrelevant. They are irrelevant either because the Internet is insufficiently advanced, or because their target markets are not online. As discussed previously in chapter 7, organisations should create only an online presence, and incorporate web-based activities into their product offerings, if by doing so they are adding value to their product for their consumers. In the case of many small service-oriented businesses, such as the local dentist or hairdresser, such use of the Internet will add little value to the existing client base.

Where does the web site fit in?

The Internet is the medium, the web site is the interface and, while both contribute to the overall product concept, neither is the firm's 'product'. The importance of the web site and its relative contribution to the definition of the overall product concept depends on its role in the strategic direction of the organisation.

While there will be a close correlation between the relative role of the Internet in the product's definition (as discussed in relation to the multilevel product concept) and the contribution of the web site, the relationship is not perfect. In order to determine what the web site's role in the product is, it is necessary to focus on the primary purpose of the site rather than its content. A single web site can be used for a number of functions. These include:

- dissemination of information
- interactions with both the organisation and other customers
- ordering mechanisms and distribution channels.

Try doing that with a standard instore display or pizza delivery truck.

The notion of a web site as a product severely narrows and limits the overall definition of value that the organisation is trying to communicate, and offer, to the target market. A web site in itself is valuable only if it provides the means to achieve a particular end, that is, the core product.

Web sites may provide access to entertainment (www.warnerbros.com), information (www.bom.gov.au), distribution channels (www.ups.com) or simplify the process of accessing other pertinent sites (www.excite.de). Informationbased web sites can either play a fundamental role in the definition of the core product (www.cnn.com) or provide an additional benefit as part of the augmented product (www.nescafe.com). The content and design of the site may provide the user with a reason to return after the initial visit. The issues relating to the design of these types of sites are covered in chapter 10. The focus here is on the role of the site as a facilitator rather than being the product itself. Companies must keep this in mind so that the Internet presence remains in line with their strategic objectives and marketing mix.

Successful Internet products

Online commercial successes have been inconsistent. Some categories of product appear to flourish (specialist goods), others have met with more limited success (movies on demand). Even within categories such as specialist retailing, Amazon.com has 'succeeded' (despite their apparent aversion to making profit) whereas the DVD reseller, Reel.com (www.reel.com), struggled to maintain operations. In analysing the opportunities for online products to be successful, three broad categories will be examined:

- products that require a traditional distribution system to operate in conjunction with online activities (physical products)
- products that do not require a complementary physical distribution system (services and digitised products)
- products that are Internet-specific (hardware and software).

Physical products: Traditional delivery in the new world

E-commerce retailing has dominated much of the attention surrounding online commercial activity. Virtual stores selling traditional physical goods such as books (www.amazon.com), clothing (www.gucci.com) and sporting equipment (www.sportschalet.com) are competing directly with the traditional, bricks and mortar retail outlets. In response, many established department stores (www.walmart.com) and catalogue retailers (www.innovations .com.au) are moving into the online environment, generating the e-commerce genre of 'clicks and mortar'. The **clicks and mortar** retail concept merges traditional retailing knowledge with online shopping and e-commerce solutions. However, the common point to all of these operations is that the goods they are selling still require storage and transportation to get from the place of order and purchase (online) to the final consumer.

There have been two factors associated with the types of physical products that have been most successful in online sales:

- the classification type of the products sold by the e-commerce presence
- consumer empowerment as a means of generating sales of physical goods.

Products according to classification

Within marketing literature it is common to classify products according to whether they are:

- **convenience products** purchased regularly, with little thought and usually at low cost, such as shampoo (www.pertplus.com)
- **shopping products** purchased less frequently and with a degree of comparison shopping required, such as perfumes or fragrances (www.hugo.com)
- **specialty products** that are highly specialised, sparsely distributed and actively sought after by specific target groups (www.ozemail.com.au/~whips).

From the consumer's point of view, buying online gives access to international outlets and also provides additional product information previously unavailable. This aids customers in making rational purchase decisions. Consequently, the Internet is most suited to those products which either require considerable effort to find information on and to evaluate, or those which are selectively distributed or difficult to access in local communities. The global reach of the Internet, and ease of purchase, has also meant that international impulse purchases can also occur, especially for unique, specialist items with cheap shipping costs. The difference between in store and online impulse shopping is six to eight weeks for delivery.

Products fitting within each of the classifications listed above have been successfully traded on the Internet. However, the value of incorporating online elements to the product mix varies across categories. The category that has benefited the most from the expansion of e-commerce has been that of specialty goods. The Internet has opened up international markets in previously hard to find (or access) goods. Users and collectors of these items have been able to purchase products that were previously unavailable to them. Shopping goods purchasers have also benefited because it is quick, easy and relatively cheap to access a range of information to assist in the decision-making process. This is particularly true in terms of price comparisons for identical goods from alternative suppliers.

Convenience goods tend to be the least successful product when sold individually due to their low per unit value. There have been notable successes for convenience goods when they are delivered as part of a wider service; for example, online grocery shopping (Reedy, Schullo & Zimmerman 2000).

In an alternative classification, Peterson et al. (1997) suggest that products and services can be categorised along three dimensions:

- *cost and frequency of purchase*: the lower the cost and higher the frequency of purchase, the less likely consumers were to use the Internet
- *value of proposition*: the degree to which products are tangible/physical goods or intangible/service-oriented. The more intangible, service-oriented goods are better suited to, and more successful in, online transactions.
- *degree of differentiation*: where highly differentiated goods, such as speciality items, are found to be particularly successful on the Internet. Speciality goods are less prone to high levels of price competition, when compared to less differentiated goods.

The primary weakness when it comes to the consumer-buying experience is that, unlike traditional shopping activities, it engages only two of the five senses (sight and sound) (Phau & Poon 2000). However, research and development is under way to provide the third sense of smell (www.trisenx.com). Retailers recognise that the purchasing experience is more than just a rational, logical process of determining the product that provides the best match between attributes and needs. Rather, it is a full experience based on all five senses, so that when buying fruit, shoppers typically rely not just on sight but also on smell and touch. Similarly, retail outlets attract specific clientele by managing the physical experience through the servicescape and atmospherics. When shopping online these sensual sources of influence on the final purchase decision are severely reduced, which impacts on the types of products suited to online selling. The fresh perfume sample handed out at the point of purchase in a department store cannot yet be downloaded from the Web.

Phau and Poon (2000) looked at the types of products that were selling online. They examined the types of products bought by current Internet users, and those who were intending to buy online. These are listed in table 8.1.

Table 8.1 Products most likely to be purchased online

Product	Internet Buyer (Rank)	Non Internet Buyer (Rank)
Computer software	1	7
Financial information	2	3
Videos/music	3	2
Newspapers	4	5
CDs	5	1
Flowers	6	8
Stock market quotes	7	4
Weather information	8	5
Consultancy services	9	9
Insurances	10	(13)
Wine	(11)	10

Source: Phau, I. and Poon, S. 2000, 'Factors influencing products and services purchased over the Internet', *Internet Research: Electronic Networking Applications and Policy*, vol. 10, no. 2, pp. 102–11.

There is a fairly high degree of consistency between what people are currently buying, and what those who are not currently online purchasers of goods, intend to buy. The difference between the intention to buy and the purchasing was only found in the order of the importance between the products.

Consumer empowerment

One of the outcomes of the growth of technology and communications, for all areas of marketing, not just online activities, has been a stronger perception of consumer empowerment. Empowerment is an important component in the perception of service quality and satisfactory outcomes since, when consumers feel in control, they are likely to perceive the outcome of an experience positively. If they feel that they are at a disadvantage to the seller of the product they tend to feel dissatisfied with the experience even if, in purely objective terms, the outcomes are identical.

This increase in perceived power is due primarily to the fact that consumers now have access to levels and quality of information that have not previously been available. The underlying assumption of rational decision-making models is that individuals will make choices to ensure optimal outcomes based on an evaluation of all the available information. As the amount of information available to the consumer increases, better quality decisions can be made. This is empowering for customers as they can now make clearer comparisons regarding different product and company offerings, thereby maximising their purchasing power.

With the expansion of online commercial activities, consumers are able to engage not only in local but also in global comparative shopping. While most carry out detailed searches alone as part of their personal information-seeking behaviour prior to the purchase of a product, there exists in the online market a range of opportunities for information aggregating services. Shopping services such as Pricescan (www.pricescan.com) and Smartshop (www.smartshop.com) minimise the effort taken by consumers in the comparative process by centralising information about specific product categories. Such web sites contribute significantly to the ongoing perceived empowerment of customers and assist in increasing the competition between online retailers and traditional outlets.

A second source of consumer empowerment has emerged as a result of online trading through online auction houses such as E-bay (www.ebay.com). This empowerment relates to the relative anonymity and time independence nature of the Internet which allows individuals, who would ordinarily be concerned about engaging in second-hand trading activities, to feel relatively secure in conducting these activities online. Auction web sites allow ordinary consumers to invite strangers to inspect goods online, engage in negotiations and bid for items in a safe alternative to more traditional ad hoc retail activities such as the garage sale or flea market stall. In addition, global auction sites and the interest-driven nature of web searches allows auction bidders to access a range of second-hand goods that were not previously accessible.

The removal of social and physical barriers, and the lack of immediacy of communications, means that consumers are able to make more rational, thought out choices than would be possible in a traditional auction environment. Interactions between sellers of goods and potential buyers are relatively safe as both have control over how much or how little personal information is traded along with sale items. A global market in second-hand and collectable items has emerged that, without the empowering technology of the Internet, would remain untapped. Collectable items that would have been traded at swap meets and garage sales can now be made available to the world, rather than just the people in the local neighbourhood.

Despite the many advantages of online auction systems for the sale of physical goods, there is still a need for individualised, ad hoc distribution systems (such as those outlined for sporadic exporters in chapter 6). Informal distribution channels, such as those needed by E-bay sellers, become dependent on international mail and courier systems. Difficulties arise when email can take a matter of minutes to settle an auction transaction, and shipping and payment can take months to finalise.

Services and digitised products

Services and digitised products, specifically information-based products, are in many ways better suited to the online environment than physical products. Unlike the products mentioned above, neither of these categories of product requires an additional offline component (such as an established distribution network) for their success. Although both services and the digitised product may be available in an alternative format offline, the online component is specifically designed and capable of being used and distributed entirely online.

Services

Services are particularly suited to online delivery, given that many of the traditional problems associated with service delivery and the unique characteristics of services are minimised online. A detailed discussion on the selling of services online is undertaken in chapter 13. Again, due to the unique characteristics of the Internet, most online services are available 24 hours a day, 7 days a week, with minimal down time. Further, because services are intangible, many can be directly distributed online. This is particularly true of those services directed at information-oriented activities, such as providing financial or legal advice. Even if a service is directed at a person or possession, for example hair dressing or garden maintenance, the Internet can contribute to greater service quality by:

- allowing for bookings online
- providing additional information or service
- enhancing the communication process between providers and clients.

The four unique characteristics of services marketing which can be applied to the Internet are:

- *intangibility*: the propensity of services not to be associated with physical goods, although service can range from purely intangible (counselling) through to servicing a tangible good (car repairs) or tangible person (masseur)
- *inseparability*: the consumer and the producer must be present for the service to occur, since a hairdresser cannot ship a haircut to a client to install at home, nor can the client leave their teeth at a dentist. Inseparability is also quite heavily associated with the Internet as the consumer must be present at the computer to surf the Web, engage in real-time chat, or read and answer email.
- *inconsistency* in the quality of service delivery. This is a major ongoing issue due primarily to the 'people' element of the services marketing mix. The social separation which occurs due to the online environment, combined with the capacity to standardise key elements of the service process, are significant attractions to services marketers who intend to move into the online environment. However, inconsistency still exists online in that a site may respond differently based on the time of day, level of traffic, the state of the user's computer or what other programs the user is running at the time.
- *perishability*: This relates to the fact that a service cannot be stored, saved, restored or returned. A bad encounter at a web site cannot be returned (with digital receipt) for a better time at the same site. The Internet helps to deal with perishability by having web sites available 24 hours a day, 7 days a week (24–7). This reduces the traditional problems encountered by services marketers of time dependency and excess capacity. The downside is that server access and server traffic cannot be stored, and excess bandwidth cannot be stockpiled for use when demand is higher than expected. Managers of web sites still need to use the same demand management techniques as their services marketing counterparts.

Information as product

The product category for which the Internet is most suited, and for which it was designed, is information. Freiden et al. (1998) argue that information as a product has sufficient unique characteristics to differentiate it from both physical goods and services. They identify the characteristics of the information product as follows:

- information has a mathematical form (mode) regardless of the medium of transmission, or alternatively, information has the capacity to be digitised without any loss of content
- the mode of information refers to whether the information exists symbolically as words, pictures, numbers or sounds
- the medium refers to the physical means by which information is delivered to users (i.e. print, broadcast, digital or visual media)
- information may be uniformly consumed by more than one person at different locations at the same time
- while information is the same for all customers, individuals may choose to use it differently
- there is no theoretical limit to the supply of information from any single producer
- consuming information does not deplete or distort it.

The marketing implications of treating the information product as a separate category help focus on its particular suitability in the online environment. Three elements in particular are important here — the nature of information, the fact it is an inexhaustible resource and the ratio between production and replication costs.

First, the nature of the product is such that direct online delivery is only possible through digitisation. Once in the form of a digital product, all information is capable of customisation and direct delivery online to consumers. This is irrespective of the content of the information product, which can manifest itself as music (www.mp3.com), news (www.skynews.co.uk) or advice (www.askthedrs.com). It may also come in the form of data such as that collected by the government (www.abs.gov.au) or market research companies (www.mediaafrica.co.za). The flexible nature of information, and the ease of its distribution, removes many of the problems of economies of scale. It also removes the need for distribution channels and issues of export regulations inherent in the sale and delivery of physical products via the Internet.

Secondly, information can be replicated indefinitely without distortion and can be consumed simultaneously at multiple locations, making it particularly suited to the demands of online consumers. The Internet is time and place independent and consequently, the demand for online products can occur at any time and from any location. This characteristic of the information product makes it extremely well suited to an environment where the demand for instantaneous replication is high.

The final point is related to the cost-to-replication ratio; that is, information is very expensive to generate but cheap to replicate. Depending on the medium of distribution, the variable unit costs of information products are extremely low. For example, the cost of direct distribution online is very low when compared with more traditional methods, such as printing. Profit maximisation for information providers relies on achieving high volumes of output which, via its global access, the Internet environment is able to easily provide. Given the nature of the information product and the reach of the Internet it is clear that the two are extremely compatible and complementary. This creates almost ideal conditions for commercial success. The downside to information as an online product is that the majority of consumers are still reluctant to part with money for information that they download. Because of the case of transactions for trading and exchanging information between individuals, including swapping music files across networks such as Napster or Gnutella, online consumers are developing a resistance to paying for information. (Napster and Gnutella are file-sharing systems that have predominantly been used for the exchange of mp3 files between Internet users, much to the annoyance of the recorded music industry.)

Developing a successful, quality, information-based product requires marketers to consider each of the following four elements, represented by the acronym FACT. These are:

- *form* — the mode and medium through which the information is to be made available
- *accuracy* — how well the information represents the phenomena it purports to describe
- *completeness* — how much of the target phenomenon the information describes
- *timeliness* — whether the information is up to date or current (Freiden et al. 1998).

Internet marketing INSIGHT
ABC online

The information product is clearly the type of product most suited to the online environment. While many organisations use the Internet to access information, the media is one industry that is solely dependent on information for its continued existence and profitability. The widespread diffusion and adoption of the Internet has had a significant impact on both consumer expectations and the way in which news is delivered.

The Internet is similar to other electronic media, such as radio and television, in that it has the capacity to provide the consumer with easily accessible, regularly updated, information. Unlike other electronic media, however, the Internet shares a number of similarities with the traditional print media. As with print media it has information that is more permanent and accessible and can be repeated as and when desired. Further, the reader not only customises the experience by making the choice as to which stories to follow up (based on headlines), but has the option to delve more deeply into a given topic or subject area (through the use of embedded hyperlinks).

As discussed above, information-based products all share four key characteristics which impact on the way in which they are marketed. In the case of the media information product, these characteristics impact on how it is developed online in the following ways:

■ form. The mode and medium throughout which the information is made available is new. It is concentrated on web pages distributed via the Internet and provides users with a combination of visual, audio and written cues, hence combining the benefits of all traditional media forms. Further, the ability to customise allows the exact nature of the information to vary from user to user.

■ accuracy. In terms of accuracy, online media information is identical to the traditional print mode and superior to electronic modes. In the case of traditional electronic media, information is first written and then read out by people, often in a live situation. This provides a greater margin for error than in alternative forms of written communication which go through multiple checking processes before final consumption by the end user.

■ completeness. It is in the area of completeness that online media information products have their strongest advantage. Unlimited by the time and physical space restrictions of newspapers, magazines, television and radio broadcasts, online media products can be hyperlinked to a range of related web sites, historical stories on the same topic or stories on related people and issues.

■ timeliness. The timeliness of the Internet for media outlets is similar to, although a little slower, than that existing for radio broadcasts. However, it is at least as fast as television 'news flashes' and considerably more timely than standard news broadcasts or print media.

Although there are some Internet specific news services, the majority are off-shoots of existing, large scale media organisations. Adding online services allows traditional media outlets to provide additional, complementary products to their clients while simultaneously adapting to the new demands being generated by Internet-based clients.

ABC Online (www.abc.net.au) is a typical example of how a traditional major media source is working in the new environment. It combines the benefits of being an online information product (as listed above) with the broader benefits which arise out of being part of the Internet (as discussed in chapter 3).

The front page gives key information, such as updated news headlines which include the time of last update, as well as providing users with the opportunity to choose a specific ABC product. For example, the user can select by media type (Radio Australia or ABC TV) or by field of interest (science, youth, rural and/or health care). Facilities exist to consume information in visual, text or audio formats as well as providing ample opportunity to interact both with the ABC and other users on a variety of topic areas. The site adds value for ABC viewers by providing transcripts of stories which have already been broadcast, as well as further information on specific issues which, due to time and space restrictions, would not normally be available.

By taking full advantage of the opportunities offered by delivering the information product online the ABC provides an extensive, stand-alone service for those who wish to consume media information primarily online. In addition, the site provides a valuable, complementary product for those who prefer more traditional methods, but who are interested in delving deeper into specific issues.

Internet-specific product opportunities

This section briefly discusses some of the opportunities that exist for the development of products which are Internet specific and totally reliant on the online economy for their existence and success. Strauss and Frost (1999) classify these products into three broad categories — hardware, software and services. Given that online services will be examined in detail in chapter 13 only the first two categories, as areas of Internet-based product successes, will be discussed here.

Hardware

The diffusion of the Internet into mainstream commercial and communications activities required the development and purchase of a range of physical communications hardware products. These include items such as modems, servers, data lines and personal computers. The boom in Internet-based commerce has resulted in a rapid growth in the demand for the physical infrastructure.

Although most of these facilitating products are common in the marketplace, there is an ongoing demand for improvements to the existing technologies and for the development of new technologies that will fulfil the same functions, but with added benefits.

Infrastructure requirements have substantially increased in line with rising customer expectations and with the increase in user numbers. Most of the activity that occurs in this segment of the market is best described as business to business transactions that are designed to help providers develop services that will ultimately benefit the end user. In relation to infrastructure products it is important to recognise that the end user does not purchase these products directly. Rather they purchase the benefits that accrue from the installation of improved infrastructure products.

From the users' perspective, the main infrastructure costs are in the purchase of modems and PCs to enable home access to the Internet. Recent technological advances, however, are reducing the infrastructure needs of end users through the development of convergent technologies. For example, the development of Web TV (www.webtv.com), which allows access to the Internet via a television set, means that it is no longer necessary for potential Internet users to purchase the earlier enabling technology of a personal computer. This field of hardware development has been a major success for technology-based companies and is set to continue as one of the main beneficiaries of the move online.

Software

Once again software products can be divided into the business to business market and end users. The important distinction is that while end users benefit from the outcomes of the business-oriented software, they are not the intended clients. For example, while end users benefit from the security of encrypted e-commerce software, this benefit is only a part of the seller's overall product package. The development and sale of the software that enables this security benefit to occur is directed not at the final user of the commercial site, but at the owners and operators of the site. Other industrially oriented software products include database authoring and audio/video digitising software.

Within the consumer market the main focus of software development has been in providing products that make sense of the data being disseminated from commercial and other web sites. The main focus on business to consumer software is centred around the decryption and decoding of messages being sent via audio and video serving software, mail servers and web servers. Consequently, the opportunities for software development in the consumer and industrial markets are complementary in that the consumer requires viewer/reader software to make sense of the services delivered by the corporate web sites.

New product development

Sustained competitive advantage for a company relies on it developing products that are perceived by consumers as superior in some way to the competition. As more new products enter the market, consumer expectations, in terms of quality and functionality, rise. A firm's sustainable competitive advantage is dependent upon its ability to generate new products that are valued by the market (Samli & Weber 2000). Most often these 'new products' are simply variations of existing products in response to consumer feedback. There are very few products that are considered breakthrough products that fundamentally change the way in which consumers behave.

The Internet and the World Wide Web were breakthrough products. Their impact was significant and sustained, and required consumers to learn a totally new behaviour. The benefits in the first instance were difficult to define and communicate to the wider population. However, given the length of time access has been commonly available through university sources and commercial providers, neither the Internet nor the World Wide Web can still be considered 'new'. The discussion of new product development in this context will be confined to the new ways in which companies are integrating online activities into the product mix. While there is considerable overlap in the activities of different organisations, and many have developed very similar online products or services, any variation to the firm's total product mix, which incorporates a new use of its online capacity, can be considered new for the purposes of this discussion.

Some of the attractions of online marketing activity are the immediacy of interactions and the ability to mass customise and alter product offerings quickly and simply in light of expressed consumer preferences. As a result many online companies are offering a plethora of increasingly differentiated and complex online products.

Success, and long-term survival, in the online environment is as much dependent on strategic direction and adherence to a strategic approach as it is offline. While the time pressures being exerted by consumers as a result of the rapid advances in technology may render traditional sequential models of new product development obsolete, this does not mean that purposeful, explicit and strategic approaches to online new product development should be abandoned. Even with the time pressures exerted by rapidly advancing technologies and market expectations, this has not rendered all strategic approaches to online new product development obsolete. However, the processes may need modification, and expediting, in light of changing economic and social conditions, and rising customer expectations. There is no substitute for a purposeful, explicit and strategic approach to product development, even if the traditional models may not be the most fashionable or the fastest method available.

Ad hoc additions to the product range are ultimately detrimental to the future of the organisation. Rapid expansion of product lines without due consideration to the impacts on company image, existing product offerings or total implementation costs, will hurt the company in the long run. New products need to be carefully incorporated into the existing product line-up to avoid cannibalising the existing market share. Considerations such as, 'Will the addition of a free news channel take market share from the subscription channel? Will full content online news articles compete with the offline magazine sales? Is a new product really necessary, or is it change because the company has not changed recently?' need to be taken into account. Just because daily changes can be made to the online product does not mean that it should be tinkered with frequently. Consistency is one of the hallmarks of good service, and constant revisions and changes to a web site structure reduce the consistency of the site performance.

New products in online marketing refer to significant changes in the overall value proposition of specific company products. Daily updating of a news web site does not constitute a new product for the organisation despite the content of the site being completely changed each day (www.abc.com). This is because the bundle of benefits and value being offered to the consumer has remained constant. As the core value proposition for the site, abc.com offers access to up-to-date news information from around the world. However, if the site was to add or remove new features or change the site map, this would be considered a product modification and, therefore, a new product for the overall organisation. Similarly, if an online software company changed its ordering and distribution mechanism from a traditional mail-out and delivery approach, to downloading of applications, the fundamental benefits being offered to the consumer would have substantially changed and, therefore, the new system would constitute a new product.

Various models of new product development have evolved over time, most of which have adhered to the sequential phase models where each part of the process follows one step after the other. Conceptualising models in this format may work for dance routines, but the reality of the new product development process is that it is not sequential. The process is iterative, with the flexibility to revisit elements of earlier phases, and to conduct phases concurrently, in order to reduce the time to market and maximise competitive advantage. However, flexibility should not translate into a lack of process or structure, despite the frequent use of the word to describe or justify the actions of the adhocracy. Without an underlying process to guide new product development, the consistency of the brand image of the firm can be seriously compromised as ad hoc additions to the product undermine the benefits of a strategic approach to marketing management. Keeping the process flexible means being able to move backwards and forwards through the steps without regarding each decision made to be irreversibly carved in stone.

Although many models of new product development exist, this chapter cannot do justice to them all. Booz-Allen and Hamilton's (1982) seven step model of new product development will be used to demonstrate how an existing, pre-Internet model of product development is still applicable in the online environment. One of the most important issues to remember is that not everything that works on the Internet was developed after 1993 and Netscape. This model outlines seven elements of the new product development process:

1. *New product strategy* examines the strategic decisions associated with the company's decisions to implement new products.
2. *Exploration and idea generation* are the methods, and madness, of developing new product concepts and defining the product concept.
3. *Screening* is the analysis of the product against the industry, organisational capacity and market demand.
4. *Business analysis* is the rigorous phase of assessing the commercial viability of the products that survived the screening phase.
5. *Development* is the point of initial construction of pilot or beta versions of the product.
6. *Test marketing* is the initial release of a product into a controlled market environment to gauge the potential of the product in the open market.
7. *Commercialisation* is the full scale release of the surviving product into the wider marketplace.

The remainder of this section will explore each of these phases and comment on their relevance to the development of a new online product. Several of these steps, such as business analysis, are common in content and process across different industries and types of product. Others, such as the exploration and test marketing phases, can be further developed or modified to take advantage of the unique capabilities of the Internet. It is the sections which are best suited to the Internet that receive more detailed examination in this chapter.

New product strategy

Sustained, long-term success is based on a sound, consistent strategy. New products should be added to an organisation's product mix only if those products are consistent with the direction that the firm wishes to take and if they provide value of some sort to the organisation's client base. The temptation in both service-based organisations and those with a significant Internet presence is to bypass formal strategic planning for new products in favour of ad hoc incremental changes.

The broad strategic direction of the company sets the framework for the style and extent of new product development. From this broad direction, there are two main issues to be considered for developing new product strategies:

- is the aim of the new product development team to maintain currency with the market simply by making incremental changes to existing products to update their appeal to the target market, or is it to develop entirely new products for the firm? In most cases there will be a balance between existing product modification and new product development. However, the degree of emphasis on each element needs to be made explicit.
- do any financial or non financial constraints need to be clarified? For example, it may be outside the vision of the company to develop products for export markets, or the company may have established a 'me-too' strategy of copying existing market successes.

If the most senior level of the organisation decides that diversification is an appropriate strategy then the limits to exploration will be considerably broader than if senior management decides on a strategy of niche marketing.

Having established that the organisation has a new product orientation, Lawless and Fisher (1990) argue that there are sources of durable competitive advantage. The strongest are:

- the ability to provide a superior product function
- extensive or more relevant distribution
- special characteristics of the producing firm (including reputation).

Less durable are competitive advantages derived from:

- product form, such as styling or aesthetics
- promotional activities
- pricing strategies.

The difference in determining the longevity of the competitive advantage is the degree to which each of the elements of the advantage can be easily copied by competitors. Pricing strategies are easily copied, as are promotional activities such as competitions and giveaways. Netscape's initial decision to release its web browser for free was quickly followed by Microsoft, meaning that any new web browser on the market will not be able to compete on price, and will need to position new products on a more substantial product advantage.

Exploration

Exploration is the phase during which product design teams develop new product concepts that are consistent with the overall strategic direction of the organisation. Within this exploration phase there are two interdependent tasks:

- idea generation during which broad product concepts are derived from a range of sources
- product definition, which occurs when the broad product concept is articulated into a specific potential product format.

Idea generation

Ideas for new products can emerge from a variety of sources, both formal and informal. During this phase the maximum number of new product concepts are developed. Formal sources of new ideas include analysis of competitors' products, research and development activities, and formal market research of customer needs. Although market research is essential to the fine tuning and development of marketing strategies, its value is more limited with respect to the generation of new ideas and breakthrough products. Given the limited information available to consumers, most suggestions emanating from market research prompt minor variations to existing products rather than totally new product concepts (Wilson 1994). In fact, most breakthrough product ideas, particularly those of a technological nature, originated from a push production orientation without the input of consumer needs analysis or market research (Beard & Easingwood 1992; Valentin 1994).

Other common sources of new product ideas include an analysis of customer complaints about existing products, suggestions for improvement made by suppliers and customers, and the personal experiences of employees. Techniques for stimulating discussion of new ideas for products include the use of focus groups and brainstorming sessions. In these discussions individuals freely contribute ideas without constraints placed on them by limited organisational resources. As outlined in chapter 16 (Market research), most of these traditional techniques can be easily adapted for use in the online environment. The advantages of moving online are that the minimisation of social constraints will result in greater freedom of expression and the lack of time and geographic constraints will give access to a larger sample and wider range of opinions.

While these techniques have been successful for some products, the generation of ideas is a difficult process due to the limitations of individuals being able to conceptualise new product concepts. Durgee, O'Connor and Veryzer (1998) give an innovative alternative to the generation of new product ideas by breaking down the notion of product into three distinct elements then cross matching new ideas relating to each element. The three elements are:

- *function*: what the product actually does
- *technology*: how the product functions
- *criteria*: how well it performs.

Table 8.2 demonstrates how products can be broken down into these elements. New product ideas are generated primarily through modifications to the columns in the middle and on the right.

Table 8.2 Distinction between function, technology and criteria

Function	Technology	Criteria
Carry people	Jet engine	More efficient
Keep dry	Umbrella	Inexpensive
Calculate statistics	Computer	Minimal effort
Disseminate information	Internet	Wide coverage
Drive car	Electricity	Cleaner

Source: Durgee, J., O'Connor, G. and Veryzer, R. 1998, 'Using mini-concepts to identify opportunities for really new product functions', *Journal of Consumer Marketing*, vol. 15, no. 6, pp. 525–43.

The function of information dissemination can be carried out via a number of technologies or media. The criteria column, however, helps to determine the best combination of function and technology to achieve a specific outcome.

In a further technique for generating ideas within product categories, Shillito and Demarle (1992) propose that the functional element of the product can be described by subdividing it into a verb and an object. Listerine, for example, is divided into the verb 'clean' and the object 'breath'. Word association of this type, combined with the broader product definition proposed by Durgee, O'Connor and Veryzer (1998), allows a less constrained approach to product idea generation. The unique features of online technology are well established, and, by conducting such word experiments within the overall framework of possibilities, innovative new uses for these features are possible. However, at the conclusion of the idea generation process it is important to take these broad ideas and refine them into a specific product concept through the process of product definition.

Product definition

Although product definition is fundamental to effective product development, in practice it is difficult to implement effectively and is generally considered to be 'tedious, time-consuming and error prone' (Jiao & Tseng 1999). Despite the negativity associated with the process (as discussed earlier in this chapter), it remains essential to effective marketing management. Without a clear understanding and definition of the product, all marketing efforts become confused and difficult to develop into a coherent overall strategy.

Product definition is the outcome of the first phase of the product development process. Before developing a final statement of product definition a number of key strategic activities need to be undertaken. These include analysis and agreement on the prevailing market conditions, what the product is expected to contribute to the firm's strategic direction and a description of the constraints within which the product development team must operate (Wilson 1994).

Various approaches to the task of product definition have been reported in the product development and marketing literature. One approach is to define the product in terms of its purpose or functionality. In other words, the product is what it does (Durgee, O'Connor & Veryzer 1998). Taking the functional approach to product definition, products are considered to be tools through which individuals moderate their relationship with the environment in which they exist. Clothing, for example, provides warmth and protection while the telephone provides a means of instantaneous verbal communication with someone who is not in close proximity. In terms of specific online products the focus of the definition is what the online element of the product does rather than its form (or the appearance or features of the web site). Consequently, the main focus of online product definition (using this perspective) is to view the online element as either a distribution or a communications medium.

Much of the literature on product definition is derived from the manufacturing and engineering sectors. Although both areas emphasise the technical aspects of product definition, there is an increasing awareness that successful new products will be those that are designed to meet the needs or specified requirements of the final consumer, whether that consumer is an individual or an organisation. Jiao and Tseng (1999) highlight the need for a structured, iterative requirement management system to be implemented simultaneously with the product definition process to ensure that the final outcome reflects both organisational and consumer needs. Requirement management refers to the process of creating, disseminating, maintaining, and verifying requirements (Fiskel & Hayes-Roth 1993). This process is based on four key functions:

- *requirement elicitation* — eliciting customer needs and acquiring the voice of the customer
- *requirement analysis* — interpreting customer needs and deriving explicit requirements that can be generally understood
- *requirement tracking* — continuous interchange and negotiation within the project team with respect to conflicting and changing objectives
- *requirement verification* — ensuring that the product design complies with the set of requirements.

Although the process may seem complex, it is entirely consistent with the marketing approach to customer satisfaction. Online capacity can be used to complement, and to a certain extent, automate these functions as the market research capacity of the company web site is explicitly incorporated into the new product development process. For example, requirement elicitation can be facilitated through the use of feedback forums and online communities. The information derived from these sources can be analysed within the organisational structure. In addition, customer feedback regarding the interpretation of their requirements into a proposed new product can be incorporated into the communications function of the site.

Through the interactive capacity of the Internet, customers can become partial employees who assist in the tracking and verification processes. This would provide a consumer perspective that would ensure consistency of product offerings and company image. Internally, this feedback and information can be incorporated into the firm's overall strategic and financial plans to determine which, if any, of the proposed products or services will be developed.

This process of incorporating customers into the design team, by maximising the use of the interactive capacity of the web site, can be used to develop new product specifications for both online and traditional products. Manufacturing companies can incorporate the feedback acquired through this process into the development of new physical products which can then be promoted or distributed via the web site or through traditional channels. For service-oriented firms, or those with digital products, the process can directly contribute to the enhanced development and testing of new, tightly defined, and highly refined, product concepts.

Screening

Screening involves an analysis of the product concept in light of the overall objectives, resources and requirements of the firm. Ideally, screening should be undertaken using a formalised approach, whereby all new product ideas are evaluated against consistent criteria. The reason for doing this is to reduce the number of product ideas generated to a manageable number of high potential projects. Anschuetz (1996) identifies six key categories of judgemental screening criteria which can be used in the initial analysis of new product concepts. These six criteria are:

1. *strategic screens*: is the product concept consistent with achieving the strategic aims of the organisation?
2. *consumer screens*: does the product add value, or is it perceived as being superior from a consumer benefit perspective?
3. *product development screens*: is the proposed product consistent with the technical capacity of the firm?
4. *package development screens*: can the product be packaged within the current capacity of the organisation?
5. *manufacturing screens*: can the product be manufactured given current equipment and access to raw materials?
6. *regulatory and legal screens*: what are the anticipated times and issues involved from a legal and regulatory perspective?

At this stage of the process, filtering out the plausible ideas for further analysis is a largely qualitative process and is based on a certain degree of subjectivity. Product concepts either pass the strategic filter and move on to the next stage or are rejected on one or more grounds. During screening the majority of ideas are eliminated; however, effective new product development processes should allow for a third option of recycling. **Recycling** is an option for those ideas that do not fit the current needs of the organisation or company but which could be retained and reworked for potential re-evaluation at a later date (Rosenau 1996). Although screening should be rigorous, errors can be made. These result in either **go errors**, the decision to pursue an idea which eventually turns out to be a mistake, or **drop errors**, the decision to not pursue an idea which would have been a market success.

In terms of the development of online products, the rigour with which the screening process is undertaken will depend on how important the new product offering or variation is to the overall product mix of the organisation. For example, the addition of a new feature to a pre-existing web site is more likely to pass the screening process than the original decision to go online. What is important in the screening process is that all new product ideas are evaluated using the same criteria, whether that product is predominantly online, physical or a service. Consistency of the product mix is essential to the strategic development of any company.

Business analysis

Those products which survive the initial screening should then be subject to a business analysis in which the product idea is evaluated in terms of its expected sales, costs and capital investment (McColl-Kennedy & Kiel 2000). During this phase estimates are made of key success factors, including the size of the market, demand for the new product and likely profitability. Key financial measures to be estimated at this stage include:

- the cost of development (hours and capital)
- prototype and pilot costs
- manufacturing costs
- marketing costs, including advertising, packaging and promotion
- pricing levels

- anticipated sales (units and revenue)
- payback measures (return on investment, profit contribution, anticipated margins) (Boike & Staley 1996).

Business analysis is more intensive than the initial screening and requires a quantitative approach to determine the financial implications of proceeding with product development.

Development

Once it is established that there is a market need for the new product and that it has a reasonable likelihood of success, the actual product is developed. Additional market research is undertaken, with final users at this stage fine tuning the product concept and ensuring that the potential market understands and values the benefits of the new product. Depending on the type of product involved, this stage can include concept testing. Concept testing involves a detailed description of the product being presented to consumers for opinion and analysis, the development of prototypes, and user-based testing.

Beta test marketing

Beta testing of prototypes is a common technique employed online by software development companies and is becoming more common in technology-orientated firms. Widespread distribution of early versions of programs, usually free, allows the company to receive feedback and further refine the product in light of actual user concerns. This technique has been successfully employed by a range of companies. Most notable has been Netscape, who have a propensity to release beta versions of the web browser (www.netscape.com) and TRG who release beta versions of their handheld computers to members of the test group (www.trgnet.com). The beta concept is not for every commercial product or manufacturing sector — the final version of the car, aircraft or medical drug is usually preferred ahead of a beta test version for human testing. Beta testing is separate from the test marketing phases as the purpose of beta testing is to remove problems from the product, and bring the product to a final release candidate level. Test marketing is the phase that occurs after the product has been deemed suitable for release to the mass market.

Test marketing

Test marketing involves the limited scale launch of the final product, with an associated marketing campaign, to gauge the likelihood of wider scale success. The benefits of using the test marketing include lower costs than a full scale launch and experience in logistical and operational issues associated with the new product deployment. It also allows an assessment of the effectiveness of both the product and the marketing strategies. However, there are a number of drawbacks. These include the fact that it exposes the new product to competitors, often before the company is ready to move into a full production phase. This leaves the product vulnerable to copying, and the test marketing results may be unreliable due to abnormal competitor activity in the market (for example sales promotion activities or price discounting). Further, there are some products that are not suited to the test market scenario, particularly products that are dependent on mass adoption by diverse user groups (Olson 1996). For example, the utility value of email may not have arisen in a controlled test market as the number of users with email accounts, *who knew each other's addresses*, may have been very small. The ultimate value of a service like email is dependent on the number of other people with access to the same service. Undertaking a test market phase is only advisable if the firm has a product suited for trial in a small, controlled environment. Products such as the TRGPro palm pilot models (www.trgnet.com) were test marketed among a small group of volunteers, as the products were self-contained and not dependent on mass market adoption for their value. Consequently, not every company will carry out this step in the process.

Successful test marketing relies on defining an appropriate test market. This market should be representative of the broader market, yet relatively self-contained to avoid contaminating the final market should full commercialisation proceed. The online environment is borderless and, as a result, the notion of a contained test market is difficult, if not impossible, to transpose. Limited releases of products online are difficult and can be achieved only if access to certain areas of a web site is restricted to potential users. This in itself makes the test market atypical. While practical at a management level, it is ultimately self defeating as the idea of test marketing is to see how the product performs under normal market conditions. Instead of relying on a controlled test market, this step is often replaced by limited feature beta test releases of online products. This means that the market reaction can be gauged, while some of the remaining problems with the product can be addressed.

Commercialisation

The final stage for a successful product is its launch into the open market with full marketing campaigns and production runs. Very few product ideas survive the rigorous process (outlined above) to make it to this stage. Of those that do survive to this point, even the most rigorous product development processes may still fail in the open market. However, given the plethora of new products that survive to become old products, the news is quite positive for new products once they reach the open market.

Online new product development

While the staged approach to new product development is not always implemented, it does provide a framework that assists companies in taking an ordered approach to new product investments. While these methods are tried and tested in the offline world, the question remains as to the extent that these processes are relevant in the online environment. How can techniques designed to produce a limited range of products be used in an environment where mass customisation and speed of delivery are increasing customer expectations daily? Is it possible to carry out a rigorous process of new product evaluation and still be in the market in time to capitalise on new product opportunities?

In this increasingly competitive and speed-oriented environment it is tempting to take short cuts to the market. The problem with the short cut approach is that long-term success is still dependent on a systematic approach to new product development. New product development still requires planned thought, whether the product is destined for on or offline consumption.

FOCUS ON
Strategy ◉

Evolution and planned revolution: New product development in the new marketplace

A lot of new product development literature has a strong Darwinian or evolutionary ancestry to it. Traditionally, new products were seen as being cast into the open market, where the market forces provided the primordial soup from which the strong product was to evolve as a survivor. Massey (1999) criticises the appropriateness of taking an evolutionary or Darwinian approach to new product development, pointing out that evolution, as opposed to planning, involves a degree of random generation. The implication of Darwinian new product development theory is that products are randomly developed, released on to the market and then retained or removed depending on the survival of the fittest (the product that best satisfied customer need). Massey (1999) argues, quite reasonably, that most companies do not randomly develop and release a plethora of new products on the off chance that evolution (and luck) will return a profitable dividend. Companies may appear at times to act in a completely random manner, but for the most part (and longevity of the CEO), they all employ some form of planning process.

The criticism of evolutionary new product development makes sense in the traditional industries and markets. However, the nature of the Internet has meant that companies in the online environment appear to be more subject to random changes. There are two major reasons for the development of evolution online.

Firstly, the low, up front cost of experimentation in the development and release of new, online, information-based products means that there is less financial disincentive to take a Darwinian approach to new product testing. Strategically, giving into this temptation is unwise as long-term damage can be done by releasing inconsistent, poor quality or underprepared products direct to the consumer. However, the cost of such activities is only felt in the long term.

Secondly, the increasingly popular practice of pre-releasing prototype products (usually software) online and then allowing potential customers to suggest, or even make modifications, changes the dynamics of product development. It takes the technical aspects of the new product development and modification out of the direct control of the organisation, thus contributing to random product development. The development of a viable gift economy and open source culture on the Internet has led to several Darwinian product developments. Most notably has been the evolution of Linux. Linux typified the evolutionary nature of product design by incorporating the users, as much as the developers, in the design and modification of the product.

However, most companies will still need formal, new product development processes for their online products, at the very least for consistency with the company's strategic development.

Part of the strategic development of online products also involves using new product portfolios instead of taking an idea by idea approach to new product development. A **new product portfolio** is a collection of new product concepts that are within the ability of the organisation to develop. They must also be attractive to customers and deliver both long- and short-term corporate objectives, spreading risk and diversifying investments (Gill, Nelson & Spring 1996). Using this approach, complementary products can be evaluated together as part of a broader portfolio. This reduces the risk of drop errors, as products which may not survive scrutiny alone, may be profitable as part of a larger product bundle. This method is particularly suited to the online environment where interdependence between services, providers, software and hardware makes it difficult to isolate any single product for analysis.

Summary

Despite its centrality to the whole of the organisation's strategic direction, 'product' is an area that tends to be neglected by marketers. Most take a relatively simplistic view of the firm's product offering, primarily defining it in terms of functions and features rather than conceptualising it from a benefit perspective.

In the online environment the notion of product and product definition is particularly complex. Online products are primarily information-based, which means that they require a re-evaluation of marketing strategies. The role of the online element of the product in the product mix needs to be clearly defined within the context of the firm's overall strategic objectives. While in some cases an online presence is central to the organisation's product mix, in others it may be regarded simply as an add-on element of the augmented product. The importance of the Internet, web site and online activities of the organisation is best conceptualised as being part of a continuum.

Successful online organisations understand the importance of clear product definition and the role of the Internet. Online successes are not confined to discrete industry groupings. The range of products appropriate to online commerce vary from physical goods (for which the Internet is a means of one-on-one communication and ordering system) to services and digitised information products which can be directly distributed via the Internet.

The flexibility and speed that is characteristic of the Internet has contributed to a less formalised approach to new product development online. There is little evidence of companies that develop a new online product taking the same rigorous approach as that used for physical goods. Despite the ease with which new products can be developed online, however, ad hoc variations are potentially damaging. Therefore, alternative, but formalised, systems of new product development need to be implemented in the online environment. Maintaining a systematic approach to both product development and definition will help ensure that companies based in the online environment will maximise their chances of long-term relevance to the consumer and, therefore, success.

Discussion questions

8.1 How does the multi-level product concept assist online marketers to better understand their product offering? Give an example of a product or organisation whose online product best fits the category of:

(a) core product

(b) actual product

(c) augmented product.

8.2 Using the example of online banking, define three alternative core products that this service could be providing. Based on this definition of the core product, position the online banking service for three distinct target markets.

8.3 Position the following companies on the online continuum: News Corporation, Amazon, Microsoft, Yahoo!, Disney, Harrods, Sony.

8.4 Explain why speciality goods are one of the more successful categories of products sold online. What are some of the barriers to selling convenience goods online? How can these be overcome?

8.5 What types of products do you believe will be most successful in terms of online purchasing over the next five years? Justify your choice and give examples where appropriate.

8.6 How has the increased availability of technology contributed to the trend towards consumer empowerment? What are the implications of this movement for commercial users of the Internet?

8.7 Services marketing has developed a distinct approach to marketing strategy, based on the unique characteristics of services. How do you think marketing tools and strategies will need to be modified to take account of the newly defined category of the information product?

8.8 What opportunities do you see for the development of new Internet-specific products? What key characteristics will these new products have?

8.9 Why is the process of product definition so important to the development of successful marketing strategies? What are some of the difficulties encountered in trying to define the online product?

8.10 To what extent is the traditional new product development process applicable to organisations operating in the new online environment? What are its limitations and what are the benefits to following such a process?

References

Anschuetz, N. F. 1996, 'Evaluating ideas and concepts for new consumer products'. In M. D. Rosenau, A. Griffin, G. Castellion & N. Anschuetz, *The PDMA Handbook of New Product Development*, John Wiley, New York.

Bayne, K. M. 2000, *The Internet Marketing Plan*, 2nd edn, John Wiley, New York.

Beard, C. & Easingwood, C. 1992, 'Sources of competitive advantage in the marketing of technology-intensive products and processes', *European Journal of Marketing*, vol. 26, no. 12, pp. 5–18.

Boike, D. & Staley, J. 1996, 'Developing a strategy and plan for a new product'. In M. D. Rosenau, A. Griffin, G. Castellion & N. Anschuetz, *The PDMA Handbook of New Product Development*, John Wiley, New York.

Booz-Allen & Hamilton Inc. 1982, *New Product Management for the 1980s*, Booz-Allen & Hamilton Inc., New York.

Durgee, J., O'Connor, G. & Veryzer, R. 1998, 'Using mini-concepts to identify opportunities for really new product functions', *Journal of Consumer Marketing*, vol. 15, no. 6, pp. 525–43.

Fiskel, J. & Hayes-Roth, F. 1993, 'Computer-aided requirements management', *Concurrent Engineering: Research and Applications*, vol. 1, no. 2, pp. 83–92.

Fojt, M. 1996, 'Virtual Frontiers', *Internet Research: Electronic Networking Applications and Policy*, vol. 6, no. 2/3, pp. 82–4.

Freiden, J., Goldsmith, R., Takacs, S. & Hofacker, C. 1998, 'Information as product: Not goods, not services', *Marketing Intelligence and Planning*, vol. 16, no. 3, pp. 210–20.

Gill, B., Nelson, B. & Spring, S. 1996, 'Seven steps to strategic new product development'. In M. D. Rosenau, A. Griffin, G. Castellion & N. Anschuetz, *The PDMA Handbook of New Product Development*, John Wiley, New York.

Jiao, J. & Tseng, M. 1999, 'A requirement management database system for product definition', *Integrated Manufacturing Systems*, vol. 10, no. 3, pp. 146–53.

Kotler, P. & Armstrong, G. 1994, *Principles of Marketing*, 5th edn, Englewood Cliffs, NJ, Prentice-Hall.

Lawless, M. & Fisher, R. 1990, 'Sources of durable competitive advantage in new products', *Journal of Product Innovation Management*, vol. 7, pp. 35–44.

Levitt, T. 1960, 'Marketing myopia', *Harvard Business Review*, vol. 38, no. 4, July/August, pp. 45–56.

Massey, G. 1999, 'Product evolution: A Darwinian or Lamarckian phenomenon?', *Journal of Product and Brand Management*, vol. 8, no. 4, pp. 301–18.

McColl–Kennedy, J. R. & Kiel, G. C. 2000, *Marketing: A Strategic Approach*, Nelson ITP, Melbourne.

Olson, D. 1996, 'Postlaunch evaluation for consumer goods'. In M. D. Rosenau, A. Griffin, G. Castellion & N. Anschuetz, *The PDMA Handbook of New Product Development*, John Wiley, New York.

Peterson, R., Balasubramanian, A & Bronnenberg, B. 1997, 'Exploring the implications of the Internet for consumer marketing', *Journal of the Academy of Marketing Science*, vol. 25, no. 4, pp. 329–46.

Phau, I. & Poon, S. 2000, 'Factors influencing products and services purchased over the Internet', *Internet Research: Electronic Networking Applications and Policy*, vol. 10, no. 2, pp. 102–11.

Reedy, J., Schullo, S. & Zimmerman, K. 2000, *Electronic Marketing: Integrating Electronic Resources into the Marketing Process*, Dryden Press, Fort Worth.

Rosenau, M. D. 1996, 'Choosing a development process that's right for your company'. In M. D. Rosenau, A. Griffin, G. Castellion & N. Anschuetz, *The PDMA Handbook of New Product Development*, John Wiley, New York.

Samli, A. & Weber, J. 2000, 'A theory of successful product breakthrough management: Learning from success', *Journal of Product and Brand Management*, vol. 9, no. 1, pp. 35–55.

Shillito, M. & Demarle, D. 1992, *Value, Its Measurement, Design and Management*, John Wiley, New York.

Strauss, J. & Frost, R. 1999, *Marketing on the Internet: Principles of On-line Marketing*, Prentice-Hall, New Jersey.

Valentin, E. 1994, 'Commentary: Marketing research pitfalls in product development', *Journal of Product and Brand Management*, vol. 3, no. 4, pp. 66–9.

Wilson, E. 1994, 'Improving marketing success rates through better product definition', *World Class Design to Manufacture*, vol.1, no. 4, pp. 13–15.

Web sites

www.abc.com
www.amazon.com
www.anz.com
www.bom.gov.au
www.bpay.com.au
www.cnn.com
www.compaq.com
www.ebay.com
www.excite.de
www.ford.com
www.gucci.com
www.hoover.co.uk
www.hugo.com
www.innovations.com.au
www.mscisOnline.org
www.nescafe.com
www.netscape.com
www.nytimes.com
www.ozemail.com.au/~whips
www.pertplus.com
www.pricescan.com
www.ptm.com.au
www.redhat.com
www.reel.com
www.salon.com
www.smartshop.com
www.sportschalet.com
www.trgnet.com
www.trisenx.com
www.ups.com
www.walmart.com
www.warnerbros.com
www.webtv.com
www.yahoo.co.uk

CHAPTER

9

Promotion 1
Internet in promotional mix

LEARNING *objectives*

After reading this chapter, you should be able to:

- apply the promotional mix to web site promotion on and off the Internet
- outline how promotion can be used to attract potential users to a web site
- understand the philosophy and theoretical foundations of promotion
- recognise the value of integrated marketing communications for the promotion of web sites
- demonstrate how the offline promotional mix can be used to promote the web site
- outline the promotional mix and how it can be used online
- recognise the role of banner advertising in web site promotion
- appreciate the differences between on and offline promotion.

Introduction

There are two ways of approaching the Internet in regard to the promotional mix: viewing the Internet as a promotional tool, and viewing the role of the Internet in the promotional mix. This text examines both approaches, first by reviewing the role of the Internet in the promotional mix and, second, by looking at the web site as a promotional tool. As both this and the following chapter will overview the interrelationship between the Internet and the promotional mix, there will be a degree of crossover between the content of the two chapters.

Promotion and the Internet: Something new, something borrowed and something not-so-new

Promotion is one area of marketing that is so frequently misunderstood that it can feel justifiably annoyed when somebody says, 'advertising' instead of 'promotion'. The promotional mix represents six elemental techniques designed to raise awareness of, and influence attitudes towards, a product, service or organisation, through personal and impersonal media. When the Internet arrived on the scene, it put in a strong bid for the seventh spot in the promotional mix, up until the time it was noticed that the promotional mix could be applied on the Internet just as much as the Internet could be part of the mix. This created a problem for academic judgements regarding the promotional mix and the Internet — the mix can be applied to the Internet, and on the Internet, and the Internet itself could be seen as a new element of the promotional mix.

For the sake of simplicity, the focus of this chapter is on the role of the Internet as it becomes integrated with the existing promotional mix. Chapter 10 will examine the Internet as a promotional medium, focusing on the role of the web site as a new promotional mix element. Having established this basic differentiation between the Internet as a promotional medium and the Internet as an element of the promotional mix, how can promotional activities involving the Internet be integrated into the traditional promotional mix?

Attracting users to the online world: Promoting the web site

The beauty of the Web is that it provides an unlimited supply of paradoxes in that just about every element that would, could or should, be considered a virtue, is every bit as much a vice. The open landscape where anyone with a web account can publish a web page has created a boundless, seamless digital environment of shared voice, where millions of web sites cry out like street hawkers. Of course, the problem with a million voices crying out is that the only way to get sudden silence involves a great disturbance in the force, and in the meantime, the cacophony of noise versus signal just about renders the system useless. Web pages on the Internet are set up with the express purpose of attracting people to the digital marketspace to meet, use and interact with the company's online offerings.

However, the nature of the Internet is so heavily focused on interest-driven transactions, and populated by people engaged in search behaviours, that attracting users to a web site has become a specialist skill in itself. The role of promotion, and the promotional mix, in this context, is not to deliver customers to the site, but to deliver the address of the web site to customers in such a way that they will develop an interest, and seek out the site by themselves.

The ideal scenario for a promotions planner dealing with an Internet site is to develop a level of pre-existing interest in the site, or the company's product offerings, and to be able to translate this interest into a site visit. To this end, Kiani (1998) and Kierzkawski (1996, in Kiani 1998) detailed a five-step model of the movement from awareness to purchase/repurchase, which is outlined in figure 9.1.

Awareness ⟶ Attraction ⟶ Visit/contact ⟶ Purchase ⟶ Repurchase

■ Figure 9.1 Five steps from awareness to repurchase
Source: Kiani, G. 1998, 'Marketing opportunities in the digital world', *Internet Research: Electronic Networking Applications and Policy*, vol. 8, no. 2, pp. 185–94.

The five elements of the model are:

- *Awareness*, which represents the classic starting point of all advertising theory. Awareness is regarded as the cornerstone of a successful promotional campaign as action cannot take place without consumers being aware of the product or service with which they are going to interact. Just as the product needs to exist to be promoted, awareness of the product must exist for the product to be found to be consumed. While a fundamentally basic concept, creating awareness of the product, service or web site is a complex task. In the context of Internet marketing, awareness is necessary for two reasons. First, awareness of the existence of a web site encourages search behaviour for that site if the site is perceived to be able to meet a user's needs or wants. Loosely translated, if the consumer wants to research various types of cars on the Web, they need to know that car comparison sites exist before they start looking for those types of sites. Second, the awareness of the URL of the site can expedite search behaviours by bringing the customer directly to the web presences rather than via search engines or indexes.

- *Attraction* is the level above awareness. Simply being aware of a product or service is no guarantee of any desire to actively use it, find it, buy it, or seek out its home page on the Internet. In order for the awareness to be of value to the marketer, it must also convey a sense of attraction so that the recipient wants to visit the web site, and will take active steps to meet this desire. The principles behind attraction are similar to those associated with the motivations for innovation adoption in that the web site represents a minor, continuous innovation in the life of the consumer, and will be assessed and adopted according to the models laid out in chapter

4. In essence, if consumers have no desire to visit a web site, they will not pursue their level of awareness beyond a simple acknowledgment that it exists.

- *Visit/contact* is the translation of awareness, attraction and motivation into trial adoption by visiting the web site. It is at this point in the exchange that the principles of web site design espoused in the following chapter form the main basis of the success or failure of the web site. The purpose of the web site is not simply for the visit contact, but to facilitate a transaction between customer and company during the visit. A small number of visits to a web site which result in the completion of desired transactions (purchase/download) is preferable to a large number of visits with no follow through or purchase behaviours.

- *Purchase* is the ultimate culmination of the purpose of the web site. Purchase in this context can either relate to use and enjoyment of the web site, or to the actual purchase of goods or services from the site. Promotion plays a lesser role in comparison to price and product at this point in the consumer behaviour.

- *Repurchase* represents the return and reuse of the site, either to reorder products, or to re-experience the web site. Design strategies such as customisation, frequency of update and freshness of content, all of which are covered in the next chapter, outweigh the value of any added offline promotion at this point. However, as with offline promotion, there is a degree of value inherent in the use of post-purchase promotion which is used to reduce cognitive dissonance. Cognitive dissonance occurs where the user feels less satisfied with a purchase decision immediately following the decision, but before fully experiencing the product. This period of doubt can be reduced by affirmative communication strategies that reassure consumers that they made the right purchase decision.

The value of the promotional mix in this five-part performance is most dominant in the opening two elements. Having built the web site, and stocked it with content, products and interactive features, promotion's role is to deliver the awareness and attraction of the site to the user. Much of what the Internet is experiencing in terms of trying to drive customers to a location is very similar to the experiences of tourism marketing and retail marketing. Consequently, a large portion of the standard promotional mix will apply to Internet marketing with little need for adaptation. The methods and techniques used to get a customer to pick up a phone and call 1-800-SOMEBODY for information will differ only in use of the medium of contact to the techniques used for motivating a similar visit to www.1-800-somebody.com.

Philosophy of promotion

One of the most important things to consider with the use of the promotional mix in promoting a web site is that awareness is nothing compared to attraction, and that attraction is meaningless without a supporting action (Aitchison

& French-Blake 1999). Promotional messages must be in a form that delivers a message to intended recipients so that they want to know more, and take active steps to find out more about a product, idea, service or web site that has been promoted to them.

In order to develop promotional messages that can reach out and touch the motivational circuits of people's minds to the extent that they want to load up Netscape to find out more about your site, the promotional message needs to consider some basic philosophical issues. Marketing is now an accepted part of contemporary society, and carries with it both expectations and responsibilities. Unfortunately, many of the expectations associated with promotion are not positive and, for the most part, are in need of an update. Promotional messages have spent a long period of time targeting the lowest common denominator, and rehashing previously successful themes in place of developing new ideas and applications. The arrival of the Internet into the promotional campaign strategy has created a new challenge for marketers — should the promotional message sell the use of the product or sell the use of the web site?

The answer that has started to emerge from the practitioner field is to sell both messages simultaneously. Let the world know of the product and the web site in a combined unified message of the company's offerings to the market. Build awareness of the site through the promotion of the product, and let the site be the reinforcing message for the product. The objective is to create sufficient interest in the product to bring people to the web site. Alternatively, use the web site as the teaser for the introduction of a new product or campaign where only the URL is displayed.

The problem with the offline promotion of the URL is that the offline world is a dead pointer (Dieberger 1997). **Dead pointer** is a charming term which refers to any time a URL is displayed in a medium where it cannot be accessed by clicking, or immediate interfacing with that medium. The dead pointer is the predominant form of media in the real world.

Any web site address seen in an offline context needs to be transferred into the online world. In order to make the jump from billboard to web browser, offline promotion of the Internet addresses needs exceptionally high unaided recall, or some form of supplementary media in terms of print or direct mail. Relying on unaided recall alone can work for only short, quick and easy addresses such as www.mp3.com or www.icq.com. For the most part, outdoors, radio and television URL promotion must be both memorable, and supplemented by print or direct mail campaigns, or listing in the telephone directory. Many services, rather than relying on the customer to recall an address such as www.youreallyoughttobewritingthisdown.com have the web site listed in the telephone directories, beside their contact phone, fax and email address. This service becomes exceptionally valuable where the telephone directory is also available online, so that the URL in the listing can be accessed as a live pointer. The best method of handling URL recall is to make the most of any opportunity to place the address beside traditional points of contact, such as on letterheads, business cards, bills or in the conventional advertising.

Foundations of promotion

Promotion is built on effective communication from producer to consumer, where the messages sent and received are identical, and relay information of value to the consumer. Understandably, this is easier said than done, given the number of places in the communications channel where a message can be misinterpreted, poorly received or simply missed in the clutter. For the purposes of this chapter a familiarity with the basic principles of advertising and promotion is assumed.

Six tenets of promotion

The art of successful promotion is built around the foundation of six key ideals, which were expressed by Aitchison and French-Blake (1999) in a review of the state of cutting edge advertising. These six factors focused on advertising, but are applicable to all elements of the promotional mix. They are built around the understanding that creativity is a subjective experience, that no objective 'truth' exists in a trade that works in the realm of persuasion, and that the role of good promotion is to reach the highest, not lowest, common denominator with the target market. Aitchison and French-Blake's (1999) six core tenets of promotion are:

- *Promotion should be about empowerment*: Positive promotion that offers consumers information on how a product, idea, service or web site will improve their life, will have greater success than the promotion of negative messages. The purpose of persuasive promotion is to encourage the customer to feel positively towards a concept, and to enable customers to see how they can incorporate this idea into their lives. Consequently, web promotion should aim to show how visiting a web site can have a positive impact on the customer's life, from providing enlightenment (www.izs.org) to providing product information (www.transmeta.com) or even a few laughs (www.dilbert.com).

- *Promotion can signpost social change*: the mass media promotion of Internet address, email address and the constant stream of encouraging messages for the general public to experience the online world has helped signpost the movement of the Internet into mainstream life. However, it is indicative of the acceptance and adoption of the Internet that a URL can be found just about anywhere a flat surface can support an address. The successful diffusion of the Internet through society was aided in part by the mass commercialisation of the Web, and the widespread display of positive Internet messages from advertising which went some distance to countering the early negative accounts of life online portrayed in the conventional news media. When a URL can be found on the side of a can of cat food (www.whiskas.com.au), society appears to have accepted the use of the Internet as part of mainstream culture.

- *Promotion can support and encourage*: The most value to be gained from a good promotional campaign is not in the value of the new customer created, but in the value of the reaffirming of the brand loyalty of an existing customer. Relationship marketing-oriented promotional campaigns, from online advertising to sending a thank you email to a recent user of the web site, or through offline promotion thanking users for making a web site popular can go a long way towards the long-term success of a web presence.

■ Figure 9.2 Cat and mouse: Whiskas.com.au and the cat food URL
Source: Whiskas, 2000, 'Mince with Beef & Vegetables', Whiskas, Victoria.

■ *Promotion can send news*: Promotion can be about spreading a message rather than persuading a targeted audience member to perform an action. Promotion occasionally loses sight of the need to simply inform the public without the need to put in a persuasive element. Simply stating the existence of a web address may be enough to meet the needs of the market, particularly when the web site is supporting a popular brand (www.nike.com), series (www.nfl.com) or event (www.olympic.org).

■ *Promotion can be used to share experiences*: Promoting a web site as a shared experience may not seem to be the most obvious method of conveying a URL address message to the masses. However, the use of promotional techniques to explain how accessing a corporation's web presence is a shared experience for people just like the target adopter helps increase the sense of relevance of the site to the adopter. Australian Internet startup D-Store (www.dstore.com.au) emphasises the 'real people, just like you' message of clients and staff of the enterprise. This message strategy is based upon delivering a sense of shared experience to potential and current users of the D-store site. Relevancy and importance of the message to the recipient aids recall, and improves the likelihood of the address breaking through the clutter to reach the targeted recipient.

■ *Promotion can be used to answer a dream*: This is probably the hardest, yet most effective role of promotion. If the promotional messages used by the organisation can tap into the dreams, needs and wants of the target market, then the recall, motivation and desire to access the site will be significantly stronger. Tapping into the dreams of the target adopter requires the promoter and site designers to really understand the needs, wants and motivations of their users so that messages get the appropriate emotional responses. Of course, it takes more than a www.dreamscancometrue.com address for URL and web sites to answer a dream. The access to facilities such as cybercommunities can facilitate that dream-answering capacity by putting people with shared interests, hopes and aspirations in touch with each other (www.vtown.com.au).

The value of the six tenets lies in their individual case-by-case application to a promotional campaign based on the type and nature of the web site and associated company, product or service being promoted. A family-oriented recreational site could start a campaign series with an emphasis on support and encouragement to bring people online and into the entertainment set. Later in the campaign, the message could be informational to announce new features, or shared experience to show how other similar families are engaging in the use of the site.

Integrated marketing communications: This goes with this and this goes with that

Integrated Marketing Communications (IMC) represents a marketing promotions approach that attempts to utilise the value of a comprehensive plan of image and message strategies to present a consistent message across a range of communications methods, to provide consistency and clarity to maximise effectiveness (Belch & Belch 1997). Roughly translated, IMC represents the notion of presenting a unified image in any publicly displayed message from a corporation, organisation or individual. Integration of IMC and the Internet extends beyond the simple neccssity of matching logos and imagery from offline promotion to the web site. The reverse is also true of needing to add the corporate URL to the off-line promotional materials of the organisation so that the web site becomes an integrated part of the promotional mix. It means tightening up the message strategies across the board so that the web site, paid advertising and any public comment by the organisation all portray the same message.

Message consistency

Message consistency comes about in several ways. The first method is by having all aspects of corporate communications conveying the same message. It's not easy for a company that promises 'family friendly content' in advertising and on its web site to maintain a message consistency if the corporate spokesperson is seen as aggressive and unpleasant in a television interview. Similarly, the same web site must be certain that any site to which it links is within the 'family friendly' definition it operates — clicking from a children's cartoon web site into a collection of adult theme animation most likely will not constitute a consistent message strategy.

The second area of message consistency comes about through the integration of design strategies across the promotional mix, including the Internet, to produce a consistent corporate look. This includes using the same logos, slogans and corporate colours across the board, from uniforms, building colours, through to web sites and outdoor advertising. The problem most frequently faced by corporations in maintaining an integrated package is in replicating the colour and design aspects of the company's communication strategy. Selection of a specific type of colour (bright pink) as a key element may lead to difficulties when trying to replicate the colour scheme online (www.eagleboys.com.au) as well as across the promotional mix.

Message clarity

Message clarity is also enhanced through the use of IMC whereby the corporation attempts to deliver a single message to its client market. The danger inherent in all segmentation-based IMC programs is that the image the corporation wishes to portray to one target group may be inconsistent with the messages being sent to other target markets. The problem for large-scale operations such as Coca-Cola is presenting a consistent corporate image across a range of product lines tailored for different markets. To some extent, clashes will arise between the position of different products, as in the case of Sprite and Diet Coke. Both soft drinks are owned by the Coca-Cola corporation, and espouse two divergent viewpoints. Sprite advocates that image is nothing, thirst is everything while Diet Coke pushes a strong imagery component associated with the cola. Compounding the Coca-Cola conundrum is the fact that the web sites for the two products (www.dietcoke.com and www.sprite.com) bear little resemblance to the point-of-sale displays and vending machines. These two examples illustrate that maintaining a consistent image and message between brands, promotional materials and the company is a complex task.

Communicating the URL: Home (page) on the range

For the purposes of this chapter, the examination of the promotional mix is limited to its role in promoting the awareness of a corporate web site. Web site promotion may be conducted as part of the core promotional message, as an incidental element, or as a reference point for further information.

The role of the web site in the promotional mix is dependent on its relationship to the product, and the sale of the product. The web site can play a promotional role in one of four different points in the sales process:

- *Pre-purchase*, where the role of the site is to encourage purchase, either through persuasion or the provision of product information. Pre-purchase web sites have an emphasis on providing product demonstrations, either through downloadable samples of the product (www.downloads.com) or through demonstrating how other customers have used the service, such as the television domain (www.www.tv) or products (www.peppermints.com/testimonials.asp). Product information sites like the online Hoover store (www.hoover.co.uk) offer a range of information on their products through the use of an interactive product selector that narrows the choice of appliances by specific features. These sites are often used as additional sources of information for offline campaigns such as the Australian Commonwealth Bank's stock trading promotion (www.comsec.com.au).
- *Point of purchase*, where the site is facilitating the purchase as a point of purchase display and purchase/distribution channel. Point of purchase sites are the direct purchase catalogue of the Internet, with promotional plans designed to either supplement print media catalogues (www.innovations.com.au) or offering printed catalogue versions of the web site where the focus is primarily on Internet promotion (www.ferretstore.com). Promotion of point-of-purchase sites tends to either be through existing printed

media, or in the case of specialist stores, through online services or product referral from other related sites.

■ *Purchase*, where the web site is the product, as in the case of online service or product delivery. Subscription-based web sites usually operate to specified target markets and tailor their promotional campaigns accordingly — for example, the Sydney Morning Herald offers a free daily news and subscription-based access to the news archives (www.smh.com.au) and promotes this within its own newspaper readership. They are also promoted online through search engines and indexes such as Yahoo! as is the case for the subscription-based Cyberstudy101 education web site (www.cyberstudy101.com).

■ *Post purchase*: where the web site operates as a support site or aids in post-product reinforcement of the purchase decision. This is particularly valuable where the product is prone to generating high levels of cognitive dissonance. The Sims (www.thesims.com) web site provides a combined post-product support system where the users of the game can either access help and support (if the game is proving too difficult) or additional elements and challenges (if the game proved too easy). The web site itself is promoted on the packaging of the game and within the software itself.

The significance of these four different roles is that each has an impact on how the web site is integrated into the promotional mix. Where a product is distributed solely on the Internet, the emphasis of the promotional mix is in providing information about the product web site as much as the product. Amazon.com has to emphasise both the site address and the service it offers in all of its promotional materials so that customers can find the store online.

In contrast, Dietcoke.com simply needs to work as a post-purchase support site where the images and messages of Diet Coke are reinforced in the online environment as Coke has an almost ubiquitous offline distribution presence. There are no hard and fast rules as to the role the web site can, or should, play in the sales process. Web sites can be tailored to work at each stage of the process by providing product information for new purchases, a point-of-sale e-commerce solution, and after-sales service support for existing customers (www.compaq.com). Where the distinction between presale and post-sale web sites becomes important is in determining the positioning of the site address in the promotional message to be delivered across the promotional mix. Pre-sale web sites need to be promoted independently of the product, either to encourage visits to the site to use the product (www.mp3.com) or to create awareness of the pre-purchase product information available online (www.comsec.com.au). Post-product sites can have their promotional messages integrated within the product (www.thesims.com), on the product packaging (www.whiskas.com.au) or as an adjunct service to the online corporate presence (www.hoover.co.uk). The aim of the post-purchase web site is to supplement and add value to the product experience and, consequently, depends on the translation of interest in the product into interest in the web site. In contrast, pre-purchase sites aim to convert interest in the web site to purchase or use of the product by demonstrating the value of the product through the web site.

Elements of the promotional mix

Promotion is one element of the marketing mix that can be expanded out into a complex subset of elements, each with certain advantages and disadvantages for message delivery. The **promotional mix** represents seven different forms of marketing communications techniques which are defined by Belch and Belch (1997) and others as:

- *Advertising*, which is any form of mass communication paid for by an identified, or identifiable sponsor, that is non personal and targeted towards persuading members of a particular market segment. Advertising has the advantage of being able to create images and symbols, making the demonstration of how a web site works, or what the Internet is, particularly well suited to the advertising genre. The disadvantage of advertising is that it is the broad brush of communications and, as such, lacks the interactivity or targeted finesse of personal selling or direct marketing.

- *Direct marketing activities*, by which products and services are offered to market segments in one or more media at a more personalised level. Usually direct marketing is conducted by phone or mail, with the attempt to solicit either immediate response (catalogue buying, phone shopping) or to deliver promotional materials. It has an unsurpassed ability to be used by marketers for narrowly defined targeted marketing in that messages can be custom tailored and mailed directly to the target recipient. The disadvantage of direct mail is a lower market profile in that mail-out campaigns do not get incidental viewing by non-targeted members of the audience. In addition, the propensity of direct mail to be used for unsolicited mail-outs has led to the medium gaining a reputation for being junk mail, rather than as a value-added service. America Online (AOL) had a very well known (to the point of notoriety) policy of mailing out unsolicited copies of their installation disks and CDs. Although the company became known in the Internet community as one of the leading providers of drink mats, the AOL direct mail campaigns did reap the rewards for persistence, and for offering low cost samples of Internet life with increased subscription rates, and high brand recognition.

- *Personal selling*, is the hand-to-hand combat of marketing promotion where personal communications techniques are used to sell a product to an individual in a personalised, face-to-face environment. Personal selling offers an unparalleled level of customisation, interactivity, flexibility and feedback in a very specific and localised transaction. The disadvantage of personal selling is that it is one to one, rather than one to many, and is a very labour-intensive method of promotion. Personal selling is not usually associated with web promotions except where the customer is being offered the web site as a point of after-sales service, or as a post-product reinforcement site.

- *Point of sales/point of purchase* are in-store displays, including a range of promotional elements such as posters, signs, displays and materials designed to influence the consumer's choice at the point of purchase. The advantages to promoting web sites and the Internet is that the consumer gets given the direct relationship between the web site and the product at the point of purchase which can be valuable, particularly to post-purchase web sites. However, the downside to in-store promotions is that the customer leaves the web site address behind as they leave the store, either with or without the product which the web site was designed to promote.

- *Publicity* is any form of non-personal mass promotional activity that is not paid for by the organisation. Most frequently this refers to news articles or editorial comments but can also be seen as incidental placements in films, video or television footage where the product or organisation is an incidental, rather than paid, part of the background. The obvious advantage of this method is the low cost associated with the genuine publicity events that occur through media reviews of the web site, or incidental featuring of the web site in media coverage. The downside to publicity is the lack of control exerted over the use of the URL, and the potential for incomplete or inaccurate reporting of the address and web site. Advertising of URLs at sporting stadiums has the advantage of the incidental news coverage during the sports reports, although it is more common to see only half the address, or have the address obscured by the sporting event it was sponsoring.

- *Sales promotions* are marketing activities conducted to stimulate short term growth in sales through techniques such as coupons, prize promotions and competitions and free samples. The advantage to the sales promotion is that it encourages goodwill among consumers and tends to stimulate immediate sales. Offers such as buy two, get one free encourage brand switching and immediate sales spikes. The major disadvantage of these elements is that the consumer market is becoming exceptionally sensitive to sales promotions, and willing to engage in brand switching to track the promotional offers. This is particularly rampant where switching costs are low, for example, web sites, where the use of sales promotions to encourage visits to a web site will not necessarily guarantee loyalty. It is far more likely a customer will track through the different sales promotions online and collect a range of offers from different web sites.

- *Public relations*, which is the deliberate, planned and sustained effort to institute and maintain an understanding between an organisation and any group with which the company needs to communicate, such as government, citizen groups or the media. Public relations campaigns concerning web sites are usually based around developing a stated corporate position on an issue, and directing further inquiries to the web site where greater depth of information can be made available. The advantage of this approach is that depth and clarity of information on a subject can be more readily accessed by the general public or media than through press conferences or other PR tools. Public relations has traditionally been seen as a subordinate support function, although PR is being used as a corporate positioning tool. In regard to the Internet, many PR battles are being fought out between major corporate players online, such as Netscape and Microsoft, to demonstrate how they are providing the best benefit for the online world. In their PR statements (and battles) the web sites are often promoted as arenas for watching the argument and rebuttal between the rival PR camps. MP3.com (www.mp3.com) and the Recording Industry Association of America (www.riaa.com) spent a large portion of their respective PR web space in conducting an ongoing debate as to which organisation was providing the best outcome for the music industry and the consumer during their court battles over copyright infringement.

The role and value of these elements for the promotion of a web site is examined below. It is accepted that whatever list of suggested uses for on and offline promotion that is committed to paper will become out of date as the development, and creative application, of these techniques will outpace any update to this book. For the most part these illustrations are given as examples of what has been done, and potentially what could be done in the future. The difficulty with predicting the future is that most predictions are done in the present based on past experience. Predicting history is easier, but there is less market demand for it, especially in the area of successful tools and techniques online. The most important factor in the online promotional game is to remember to monitor, evaluate and adjust the techniques based on their success. The number of extraneous factors that influence the viability of a promotional campaign is huge, and the best laid promotional plans of mice and men are often led astray at the last moment. For the most part, the promotion of a web site in the offline world is extremely compatible with the techniques associated with the promotion of services and travel destinations.

Three dimensions of promotion: Message, format and context

The objective of all forms of promotion is to say the right thing to the right person at the right time, and have them receive, perceive and interpret the message in the right way (Kiani 1998). In order to achieve this outcome, there are three main dimensions that a promotional message needs to balance, and these are illustrated in figure 9.3.

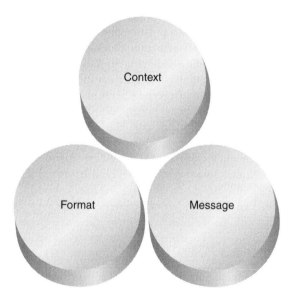

Figure 9.3 Three main dimensions of advertising

Source: Kiani, G. 1998, 'Marketing Opportunities in the Digital World', *Internet Research: Electronic Networking Applications and Policy*, vol. 8, no. 2, pp 185–94.

Kiani (1998) outlined the three point structure as:

- *message*, which was the meaning to be transferred from the advertiser to the audience
- *format*, which are the attributes of the advertisement that attract the audience's attention
- *context*, which is the format or media of the promotional message.

Each context offers the message certain opportunities for audience attraction and message interaction. A good promotional message needs to balance out its strength in each of the dimensions so that the message is supported by an appropriate format and the best use of the opportunities available in that context (figure 9.4).

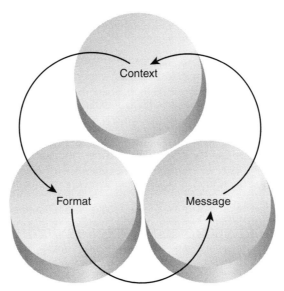

Figure 9.4 The pattern for successful communication

Source: Kiani, G. 1998, 'Marketing Opportunities in the Digital World', *Internet Research: Electronic Networking Applications and Policy*, vol. 8, no. 2, pp 185–94.

For the most part, promotional messages are able to be tailored and adapted to the context and format of the available types of advertising media. Messages for delivery in television commercials are developed with consideration of the opportunities for delivering animation, sound, and slice of life in 15- to 30-second slices. Print media messages are tailored to be longer, more informative and detailed to take advantage of the format's longer reading time compared to poster or billboard print adverts.

The problem facing any campaign for promoting a web site is that no matter how carefully tailored or crafted their message can be, the URL presented in the campaign is still a dead pointer, and this places a greater restriction on the context of the message. Finding a hyperlink online means that a mouse click later the audience can be at the advertiser's web site. Reading a URL on the side of a bus on the drive to work does not have that immediacy of opportunity. Double clicking the side of a bus with a mouse or any other pointing device does little more than draw attention to yourself, and certainly does not bring the web site any closer. In this light, the objectives of the offline advertising campaign for a web site need to be developed to motivate the audience into taking the URL from the dead pointer into a live medium.

As mobile Internet access increases through the advent of **wireless application protocols** (WAP), Internet-equipped mobile phones and hand-held computers, the speed with which the marketplace can go live to a web site from a dead pointer will increase. Until that time, the objectives of the offline promotional campaigns are generally restricted to a focus on awareness and attraction, with the aim of getting a visit/contact outcome when the audience eventually reaches their Internet connection.

Reviving the dead pointer: Mixing it up in the promotion of the URL

As outlined above, the promotional mix has a range of functions designed to influence the audience to act on the advertiser's message. Each of these techniques has a specific role to play in the make-up of a good promotional campaign, and each can be adapted to suit just about any promotional campaign, depending on the message to be delivered and the objectives of the campaign. The following section outlines the way in which some of the elements of the mix can be applied to the creating of awareness and interest in the URL. Whether a visit or contact occurs as a result of the awareness is dependent on more factors than can be described in this section.

Creating awareness: Image is nothing, context is everything

There are four major contexts in which a web site address can be encountered in the offline environment.

1. *Outdoor advertising*, which covers the range of any outdoors-related materials from sky writing (difficult but achievable) through to bus sidings, billboards and the humble student noticeboard.
2. *Indoor advertising*, which deals with the television, cinema, radio, direct mail, magazines and other printed or broadcast advertising materials consumed inside a private home or at a business. Sales promotion and point-of-sales advertising are also covered under the indoor advertising banner.
3. *One to One to Web* covers the personally communicated URL through personal selling, word of mouth and personalised communication on letterheads and business cards.
4. *Product Dot Com* covers the inclusion of the URL on the product, packaging or instructional materials accompanying the product.

Context 1: The great outdoors: The URL in the real world

Advertising is the life blood of the communications plan in that it covers any paid form of mass communication with an identifiable sponsor, and the non-personal targeted message approach can be found stuck to the side of just about any accessible flat surface, moving vehicle or broadcast medium.

The purpose of the outdoor URL is dependent on the context and location of the address compared to the location of the business and/or the product being promoted through the web site. In general, the closer a URL is to the store or product being offered, the more likely it is to be used for the purposes of providing an additional point of contact to the store telephone number. The placement of the URL on a billboard, advertisement or other outdoor promotional object away from the store is designed to generate awareness of the product or company which the web site supports. Figure 9.5 demonstrates the use of the URL as a brand identifier and point of further information for the Storage King services.

■ Figure 9.5 Storage King and the outdoor URL
Source: Storage King, 2000, *Storage King Self Store*, Brisbane, Australia.

The value of the URL on the store front is twofold. First, it advertises the brand name in a distinctive and memorable manner in that remembering the store name (which you would want to do anyway) means you're a dotcom or dotcomau from finding the informational web site. Second, the current fashion associated with having a dotcom presence can be leveraged into branding and IMC mileage as an expression of the innovation of the organisation.

In the second instance, the IMC mileage is further enhanced by a consistent corporate image between the web presence and the physical store location, as demonstrated by figure 9.6 where Sanity music's store front and web front sport matching corporate images.

In this instance, the web site also works to extend the value of the Sanity music chain by providing the shopper with a range of additional music services, such as the Top 40 charts, information and the ability to buy Top 40 albums straight from the chart through the web site or from in-store.

In contrast to proximity URL advertising used by Sanity and Storage King, the placement of web site addresses on billboards, bus sidings and other locations can be used for teaser campaigns, providing access to greater information or for awareness campaigns. Figure 9.7 demonstrates the Commonwealth Bank's use of the billboard URL advertisement in place of the usual contact telephone number associated with seeking further product information.

■ **Figure 9.6** Sanity Music web store and physical store

Source: Sanity Music, 2000, *Sanity Music Store*, Aspley, Brisbane and www.sanity.com.au

■ **Figure 9.7**
Commonwealth Bank
Comsec billboard

Source: Comsec, 2000, 'Trade US Shares Online with Aussie Dollars', roadside billboard, Sandgate Road, Northgate, Queensland (see also, www.comsec.com.au).

The advertising works along the lines of being a both a teaser campaign and an awareness generator. Those members of the audience with an interest in online trading would already have experience in seeking and finding information online so the Comsec campaign (www.comsec.com.au) would simply be a (dead) pointer in the right direction. It also serves to raise awareness of the activities of the Commonwealth Bank's Comsec group for customers (current and potential) who have an interest in online share trading but who were not familiar with the company's activities.

The final category of outdoor offline advertising belongs squarely to the teaser campaign advertisements which are designed to draw attention to the web site's address, and inspire curiosity about the content and nature of the site. Homehunter (www.homehunter.com.au) used a teaser campaign for their web site in a series of bus-shelter advertising placements as illustrated by figure 9.8.

■ **Figure 9.8**
Finding a place in the sun:
Homehunter.com
Source: from Homehunter, 2000, 'Find your place in the sun', Bus shelter, Brisbane, Australia.

The Homehunter campaign uses the outdoor advertisement as a teaser to mention the function of the web site as providing real estate online from a wide geographic catchment area ranging through the Queensland and New South Wales regional areas (although why they were advertising in suburban Brisbane is another question). Web site content was drawn from advertising placed with affiliated newspapers in the APN news network (www.apndigital.com.au). The site was also able to take advantage of ancillary advertising in the affiliated regional newspapers that form the core of the site content. Homehunter is able to tie both outdoors advertising of the URL with secondary support material from the home delivery URL promotion in the regional newspapers.

Context 2: Home delivery: Bring home the dotcom

The second context for the promotion of a web site targets getting the dead pointer URL into the home of the target audience and onto their computer. There are several indoor advertising venues for the enthusiastic (and cashed up) web site promoter. The most obvious point for advertising is to take advantage of the traditional in-house media of television, newspaper and magazine advertisements. Although the great debate of Internet-related advertising is focused around the value of online versus offline, and the role of traditional channels such as television and radio, one of the most obvious methods of attracting attention to a web site is to use printed materials.

Web site addresses can be easily attached to direct mail and direct marketing services to provide high context promotion for the web site. Having received the catalogue or direct mail flyer, and taken the time to read it, the audience has a higher level of inherent interest in the products or services offered by the company. Placing the URL with the direct mail materials allows the user to take immediate action based on the initial interest by accessing the web site, much in the same manner they may have placed a phone order.

Broadcast advertising, based on radio or television, has its respective advantage of tapping into an existing advertising medium that is both understood by the consumer and the advertising agency. A degree of controversy exists around the value of the URL in television advertising with conflicting reports coming from the very few commercial studies to have investigated the area (www.nua.ie/surveys). The problems for television arise from the fact that online users tend to have traded their television watching time for Internet time. In contrast, however, Internet users are more prone to investigate URLs seen on television when they are online, and some studies are beginning to demonstrate the simultaneous use of the television and Internet connection. Overall, this particular aspect of promotion of the URL is best used as an adjunct to the existing television commercial by tagging the address onto the advert with company name and logo, rather than running a specific advert for your web site.

Radio can also be used for the promotion of the URL and, as with television, the reports in from industry and academia are mixed. Radio advertising networks cite only the success stories for their dotcom advertisers, and the academic investigation of this area remains limited to examining media consumption involving Internet users. The industry–academia consensus is that radio is the medium most commonly used in conjunction with web browsing in that many people have the radio playing while working on the computer. On the basis of this, Monster.com.au ran a promotional series of advertisements for their job-finding service, and reported web site activity spikes following the announcement of their URL on one of the national radio networks. Unfortunately for the scientific analysis of this event, the major provider of this information was the radio network who announced the Monster.com.au URL, so the independence of the data cannot be verified. Having a reasonably simple and memorable domain name, coupled with a popular topic area, would also have contributed to the success of dotcom's advertising as well as their selection of the radio as their advertising medium.

The other area of indoor advertising of interest occurs out of the home and inside retail stores with point of sales displays. While these are not strictly 'at home' advertising, point of purchase displays can be used in a variety of ways to promote the corporate web site, particularly if used in conjunction with promotional specials such as competitions, cash backs or other prize giveaways where additional details of the promotion are listed at the web site. Alternatively, the site itself can operate as a complementary service to the product, as is the case with the Personal Trading Post (figure 9.9).

■ **Figure 9.9**
Personal Trading Post
point-of-sale display
Source: Personal Trading Post,
2000, *Point of Sale Display*,
Brisbane, Australia.

The value of the in-store display where it links to a complementary service is that it can still offer the service to the customer even when the physical goods have been exhausted. Finally, the instore display can appear in places not traditionally associated with point-of-sales promotional materials such as the boom gate on a parking lot.

Internet marketing INSIGHT
Wilson Parking: Parking with a domain name

One of the more interesting impacts of the Internet has been the spread of unexpected domain names and web sites. For the most part, car parks have remained relatively anonymous concrete structures tucked away in vaguely convenient locations throughout cities and towns. These formerly anonymous service facilities have found a place for promotion online and, while occasionally baffling, their web sites do provide an insight into just how versatile the Web can be for promotion.

Wilson Parking (www.wilsonparking.com.au) takes the opportunity to introduce their web site to visitors using their car park via the boom gate entrance. Opportunities to publish the URL on the parking ticket are limited insofar as the ticket (and URL) have to be returned to the car park in order to exit. As illustrated by figure 9.10, the advantage of the boom gate domain name is both the visibility, and the few seconds of captured target market — you cannot avoid this particular advert space.

(continued)

••••••••••••••••••••••••••••••••■ **Figure 9.10** The Web address boom: Wilson Parking
Source: Wilson Parking, 2000, 'Boom Gate', Elizabeth Street Car Park, Brisbane, Australia.

The purpose behind the Wilson Parking web site is to espouse the benefit and value of parking with their particular chain of car parks. Car park locations, features and benefits are given, including the hours of operation for the major venues (mentioning the 24–7 availability for a car-parking facility should not require an opening and closing time for each day). In addition, the site displays the address, location and small photograph of the featured car park for ease of identification of that parking venue. It's not quite possible to book a space from the web site yet, nor have the Wilson group taken the opportunity to install webcams for a view of the car park (and number of free spaces) from your computer.

On the specialist end of the car-parking scale comes the Discount Airport Parking (www.airportpark.com.au) who offer an online booking facility for their parking spaces. In addition, they also use their parking web site to link with their affiliated car rental web site (www.alwaysrentacar.com.au). The strategic integration of a service for car storage and car rental through the affiliated web sites allows for a leverage of both the capacity of the web sites to handle booking of parking space and rental car, and for the co-promotion of both services through the two sites.

Of course, not everyone with a car park web address is in the temporary car storage business. Carpark.com.au is a start up company that specialises in the listing of car parks around Australia. This handy reference system will eventually become the metaindex of the dotcom car parks of Australia (and beyond), proving that there's more to business on the web than domain parking, when parking domains are this popular.

Context 3: One-to-one to Web: Up close and personal

The third major element of the promotion of the URL is through personal selling and word of mouth. Personal selling of a web site in this context is closely related to the traditional role of personal communication where the salesperson is directed to emphasise the existence of the web site to the customer. This method was used in part by several banks and building societies to encourage the use of online banking, in addition to the promotion of the telephone bank services. In addition, the ANZ bank, among others, promotes its online banking systems (www.anz.com) through their telephone banking services.

The one area of traditional IMC that is attracting the most attention in the promotion of Internet sites has been the oldest method of marketing — word of mouth. Word-of-mouth advertising has seen a major revamp, being repackaged as 'viral marketing' because the marketing message is spread through the community in a fashion not dissimilar to that of an infectious virus. While a more charming metaphor probably does exist, viral marketing has several elements that make it extremely valuable for the promotion of web sites. Viral marketing and recommendation by reputation as a strategy has been examined in chapter 7. In this context, however, promotion by word of mouth and word of mouse is recommended where the site contains a medium to high level of complexity, engages in services that can be used as a topic of conversation, or for which users would seek the opinions of their friends and family. While viral marketing seems to have virtually everything going for it, there is one major problem that can be faced by a successful online word-of-mouth campaign, and this is commonly referred to online as 'the Slashdot effect'.

FOCUS ON
Strategy 👁

Slashdot effects

The Slashdot effect is cited by Adler (1999) as the 'spontaneous high hit rate upon a web server due to an announcement on a high volume news web [site]'. The effect was named after the propensity of web sites (and their host servers) to suffer massive spikes in server activity as a result of the site being posted to Slashdot as recommended reading. This word of mouse advertising was beneficial in exposing the site to a wide array of readers of similar nature and psychographic profile, but also had a serious downside in the traffic overload caused by the exposure. Many web sites listed at Slashdot often carried single page statements to the effect their servers had overloaded, or their ISP had shut them down, because the outbound traffic experienced from the Slashdot effect had overwhelmed their technical capacity.

In marketing terms, the Slashdot effect is the result of an imbalance between the Weibe's (1951, in Kotler & Roberto 1989) five factors which are:

1. *The force*, which is the degree to which a person is motivated towards a goal (social change) based on the person's predisposition to the idea and the stimulation of the change message. In terms of the Internet, force is a significant element of the success of a web site in that the Internet is interest-driven. In general, the first principle for a successful Internet web site is that the campaign to which it relates must have sufficient externally generated interest to encourage the user to seek out the web site.

2. *The direction*, is the knowledge of how and where to respond positively to a campaign's objectives, namely, the presence and means of carrying out the objectives. For Internet-based marketing this relates to two functions: access to the web site and navigation within the site. Access to the web site relates to the ease with which the site can be found by the casual user, and by people who have not had frequent contact with the site. Navigation within the site relates to the degree to which the user has difficulty in accessing the information that they seek from the web site.

(continued)

---

3. *The mechanism* is traditionally associated with existence of an agency, office or retail outlet that enables an individual to translate motivation into action. In the case of the Internet, this translates into both the existence of the web site, and the existence of the relevant information on the web site.

4. *Adequacy and compatibility* reflect the ability and effectiveness of the agency in performing its task. This element is particularly relevant in designing a web site to match a specific function. Compatibility represents the degree to which the site can be accessed by a variety of web browsers, modem speeds and operating systems. Adequacy also represents the capacity of the web site's server to cope with the traffic to the site, and deliver the necessary information in a timely and effective manner.

5. *Distance* is an individual's assessment of the energy and cost required to change an attitude or behaviour in relation to the expected reward. In terms of the web site, distance represents the amount of effort and time required in finding the web site and accessing the relevant information.

The Slashdot effect represents the disparity between the combined power of force, direction and distance against the capacity of mechanism, adequacy and compatibility. Where force, direction and distance reach an unplanned artificial peak through a viral marketing event such as being referenced at Slashdot, the impact can overwhelm the planned systems associated with mechanisms and adequacy. Every marketer's dream is to have a high level of interest in their advertising, and huge demand for their products and services. Unfortunately for the web-based marketer, this dream can turn into a nightmare when an unplanned viral marketing event overwhelms the organisation's capacity to deliver its web site to the waiting public.

The final avenue of communication that can be used to promote the URL and web site is that of interpersonal communication. Web site addresses can be added to business cards, letterheads, and envelopes in any place that the address or phone number for the organisation can be found.

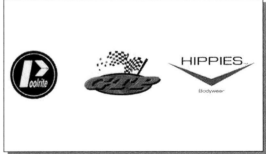

Figure 9.11 The domain of the business card

Source: Palmer, R. 2000, 'Ross Palmer', *Palmergroup Business Cards*, Palmer Group, Australia.

The advantage of the business card is that it is both portable and easy to distribute. The majority of business card exchanges occur to give contact details to an interested party so that further communications can take place. Adding a business card with a web address to a personal sales pitch allows the customer to take a tangible reminder of the sales exchange, and a written copy of the address, back to their computer if they wish to find out more from the web site.

Context 4: Product dot com

The fourth place to promote the URL for the web site is on the product and packaging. This simple method can be used to encourage repurchase, reordering, and to assist in promoting sites that add to the reduction of post-purchase cognitive dissonance. This assumes the value of the site is in the post-purchase follow-up, and is not needed to encourage the initial purchase. These sites can be focused around offering value-added services, such as additional software downloads (www.thesims.com), product updates (www.microsoft.com) additional product use suggestions (www.lego.com) and cybercommunities (www.pepsi.com.au).

Promotional mix online 101: Using the promotional tool kit online

There is a range of Internet-specific promotional tools such as exchanging links, which are unique to the Internet. While cross-promotional ventures and shared venues are common in the offline world, there are no equivalent functions to a link or banner exchange that can take the shopper from one store to the other with minimal effort. Developments in teleportation may lead to a point where inter-store link exchanges are viable, but this is a long way down the public transport track.

Banner advertising: Click here to receive more promotional materials

Banner advertising is the most common, and most accepted, form of paid advertising on the Internet. The purpose behind the banner ad is to create small advertising placements, using the same techniques as offline promotion, which are live pointers to the promotional web site. Unlike offline advertising, the live pointer aspect can take a consumer straight to the web site with only one click of a mouse. The disadvantage to the advertiser is the relatively low rate of click throughs associated with banner advertising with few, if any, advertisements gaining double-figure response rates.

In addition, the banner ad has spawned a range of related genres of interactive advertising, all of which rate below it in terms of popularity.

The culture of the Internet is still predominantly opposed to advertising that:
■   does not create value
■   is not relevant
■   or which creates a nuisance.

These three advertising sins have a disturbingly high tendency to appear in pop-up advertising which are those smaller browser windows containing banner ads. Many pop-up ads, particularly those from web hosting companies such as Geocities (www.geocities.com) or Xoom (www.xoom.com), have spawned a range of free software filters that are designed to prevent the advertisement from displaying (www.analogx.com).

Other methods, such as interrupt pages, where access to the next section of the web site requires the user to click past an advertisement cost the user time and effort as they attempt to find the content they thought they were accessing. Interrupt sites were designed with the assumption that the user would accept the break in content much as they were used to accepting advertising. The problem with the nature of the Internet is that the reader has more than 57 channels of alternative sources of satisfaction for any point where the advertising starts interrupting the content.

The important thing concerning the advertising banner and its kindred promotional spirits is that they are very young advertising media. Much of the early research into banner advertising has focused on the need for copy testing (Hofacker & Murphy 1998) and the impact of multimedia, sound and animation on click through rates (Rae & Brennan, 1998). The problem for researchers in the field is that the motivational factors behind Internet use, web page and preferred web page design have not yet been established. Trying to determine how and why people respond to advertising elements in a web page is a difficult task, especially when most people cannot state how and why they react to the rest of the web page.

The banner advertisement is also fraught with technical problems not found in the majority of other advertising media. First, as illustrated by figure 9.12, the range of available advertising sizes is somewhat more limited than even the classified section of a newspaper.

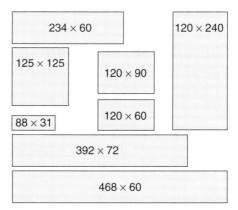

■ **Figure 9.12** Banner advertising shapes and sizes
Source: Adrotator.com (www.adrotator.com), and hand sculpted into blank shapes.

Second, the actual parameters acceptable to most advertising banner networks in terms of file size, and use of animation limit the creative capacity of the banner. As a general guide, the accepted industry standard is between 7k to 10k in size, no animation and no audio. This does not leave a lot of room for promotional messages and, consequently, the advertising relies heavily on clever creative with strong visual appeal, rather than any large amount of text (figure 9.13).

Cat got your mouse?

■ **Figure 9.13** Clever creative in banner advertising
Source: www.adornis.com

Third, banner advertising networks are yet to establish a consistency between the display methods and costs. Link Exchange (www.linkexchange .com) owned by Microsoft offers free banner advertising on the basis of a ratio of approximately 4:1 where, for every four advertisements shown on the advertiser's site, the network will show one of the advertiser's banners. Other exchange networks range from 1:1 banners down to 10:1. The paid rates are also variable, depending on the coverage of the exchange network, and the estimated value of the targeted segment. One banner agency that promotes on MP3.com offers a higher price for exclusively carrying band advertising on MP3.com compared to the rate for the banner advertisements appearing anywhere across their network.

Finally, banner advertising is still very susceptible to poor psychographic placement, as the psychographic profiles of the broadcast web sites and the target users are still subject more to guesswork than market research. However, banner advertising and related online advertising are still the best method for engaging in paid advertising and promotion on the Internet. While the acceptance (or more accurately active rejection) levels of banner advertising has been changing with the evolution of the Internet market, the change has been towards the positive. As the Internet market matures, and segmentation techniques used by web sites and banner placement services become increasingly more sophisticated, the value (and click-through rate) of banner advertising is set to increase. At this stage, it is still an experimental format, particularly when it comes to banner placement by market segment.

Promotional mix online 102: The distinct differences

The promotional mix exists on and offline in relatively equal measures in that the majority of the techniques can be applied to both environments. However, there are two very significant differences between the online promotional mix and the offline mix. First, the user incurs costs to encounter advertising online that are not incurred in the offline world. The average commute to school or work will provide access to a wide range of different advertising messages as an incidental part of the day's travel time. Costs incurred in the incidental encounter of a billboard at a train station are counted in terms of time spent reading the advertisements while waiting for the train. Users of the Internet are usually paying a per-minute charge on their online times and, consequently, are incurring both time and financial costs when viewing online advertising. No sane advertising executive would consider charging fifty cents to a dollar for watching a billboard being put up, and then expect the advertisement to be successful. However, many advertising executives fail to realise that the user incurs costs in encountering advertising online, particularly where the advertising is slow to load on their PC.

Second, email is not a direct mail channel, no matter how nice it would be if the Internet users would accept the same level of digital junk mail as they do paper mail. Again, the major issue concerning junk email is the cost incurred by the user in receiving the mail. Unlike the offline postal service where the costs of a mail-out are borne by the sender, the cost of email is picked up by the receiver, who will feel justifiably annoyed at spending time and money downloading unsolicited junk mail. Direct mail online can exist where it is voluntarily incurred by the user subscribing to an advertising mailing list. No matter how tempting a mass unsolicited mail-out may seem in terms of dollars per customer annoyed, the damage to the branding and image of the company will far outweigh any potential benefit. Similarly, there is no real point to purchasing an email database list from a list reseller, since most users cannot tell the difference between unsolicited spam and resold mailing list spam. The Internet has ushered in an age of relationship-based direct marketing where the consumer has become empowered to invite direct marketers to become part of their lives, and reject those who show up uninvited. The impact of relationship marketing on the Internet (and vice versa) will be examined in chapter 14. The most important promotional message to remember is that there are no advantages to willingly destroying your organisation's online reputation by engaging in spamming activities. Unless your corporate strategy lists alienating potential customers as a promotional objective (as was the case for the Sex Pistols' mission statement), leave the unsolicited direct mail to the real world, and use the rest of the promotional mix online.

 # Summary

The promotional mix operates on and offline with a remarkable degree of similarity of intent, and a widely divergent set of methods. Offline promotion of the web site needs to focus on generating recall of complex addresses so that the dead pointer media can convert product interest into web site visits. The emphasis on trying to create recall and interest simultaneously has created a challenging array of issues for web site promoters. In order for advertisers of new media products to handle these challenges, they need to understand both the basic philosophy of promotion, and how the advanced techniques, such as IMC, can be applied to their needs. Web addresses are appearing anywhere and everywhere they can be fitted, written, packaged or printed. Domain names now grace the sides of cars, blimps, buildings as well as taking pride of place on letterheads and business cards.

On the surface, the promotional mix in the live media of the Web seems to have the easier task of simply needing to generate interest (and a mouse click). To level the playing field, the advertising and promotion methods most commonly found online have more restrictions in shape, size and placement than any offline conditions. Even banner advertising, the most pervasive of online promotion, is limited in size and application. The complexity of the promotion of the web site on and offline is matched only by the complexity of developing the appropriate promotional site, which is examined in the following chapter.

Discussion questions

9.1 Are all of the elements of the promotional mix applicable for online promotions? If no, why not? If yes, which is the hardest to apply to the online environment?

9.2 What are the four points in the sales process? How can a web site's promotion influence each of these stages?

9.3 Why do web sites need integrated marketing communications? Should web sites have the same message for all segments or different messages for different viewers?

9.4 Pick one element of the promotional mix and explain how it can be used on and offline to promote web sites for physical goods and digital services. Is the role of the web site and the emphasis of the promotional message influenced by the type of product being promoted?

9.5 Is there such a thing as too much publicity? What could be some of the negative impacts of being too popular online?

9.6 Collect a series of advertising banner advertisements of the various shapes and sizes outlined by Adrotator. Which of the six tenets of promotion is most usable in banner advertising? Which was the most common tenet used in the banner ads you collected?

9.7 What are the fundamental differences between on and offline advertising?

References

Adam, S. 1996, *The Dilbert Principle*, Harper Business, New York.

Adler, S. 1999, 'The Slashdot Effect', *Linux Gazette*, http://www.linuxgazette.com/issue38/adler1.html

Aitchison, J. & French-Blake, N. 1999, *Cutting Edge Advertising: How to Create the World's Best Print for Brands in the 21st Century*, Prentice-Hall, Sydney.

Belch, G. E. & Belch, M. A. 1997, *Introduction to Advertising and Promotion: An Integrated Marketing Communications Perspective*, 4th edn, Richard D. Irwin Publishers, New York.

Dieberger, A. 1997, 'Supporting social navigation on the world wide web', *International Journal of Human–Computer Studies*, vol. 46, pp. 805–25.

Hofacker, C. F. & Murphy, J. 1998, 'World Wide Web banner copy testing', *European Journal of Marketing*, vol. 32, no. 7/8, 1998, pp. 703–12.

Kiani, G. 1998, 'Marketing Opportunities in the Digital World', *Internet Research: Electronic Networking Applications and Policy*, vol. 8, no. 2, pp. 185–94.

Kotler, P. & Roberto, E. 1989, *Social Marketing: Strategies for Changing Public Behaviour*, Macmillan, New York.

Rae, N. & Brennan, M. 1998, 'The relative effectiveness of sound and animation in Web banner advertisements', *Marketing Bulletin*, vol. 9, pp. 76–82.

Web sites

www.airportpark.com.au
www.alwaysrentacar.com.au
www.anz.com
www.apndigital.com.au
www.carpark.com.au
www.compaq.com
www.comsec.com.au
www.cyberstudy101.com
www.dietcoke.com
www.dilbert.com
www.downloads.com
www.dreamscancometrue.com
www.dstore.com.au
www.eagleboys.com.au
www.ferretstore.com
www.homehunter.com.au
www.hoover.co.uk
www.icq.com
www.innovations.com.au
www.izs.org
www.lego.com
www.microsoft.com
www.monster.com.au
www.mp3.com
www.nfl.com
www.nike.com
www.olympic.org
www.peppermints.com/testimonials.asp
www.pepsi.com.au
www.sanity.com.au
www.smh.com.au
www.sprite.com
www.thesims.com
www.transmeta.com
www.tv
www.whiskas.com.au
www.wilsonparking.com.au
www.vtown.com.au

Promotion 2:
The Internet as a promotional medium

'It's not that there's one way of doing something that's right, and another one that's wrong. It's what's appropriate at the time.'

Aitchison, J. and French-Blake, N. 1999, *Cutting Edge Advertising: How to Create the World's Best Print for Brands in the 21st Century*, Prentice-Hall, Sydney.

LEARNING objectives

After reading this chapter, you should be able to:

- explain the role of the Internet and the Web in the promotional mix

- discuss the theory and philosophies of web site design

- recognise and identify the three schools of web site design

- give an overview of the issues involved in integrating the design philosophies with common types of web sites

- distinguish between different types of web site attractors and home page types

- identify the six 'M's' of web site design.

Introduction

The Internet, and the Web, represent a new environment for promotional techniques and methodologies. Like television, the Internet can provide dynamic content, colour, sound and animation. Unlike television, the Internet is an interactive medium and offers two-way communication opportunities. This doesn't make it the personal salesperson of the broadcast media; rather, it makes it a unique environment where the consumer and the advertiser meet on relatively level terms, and negotiate the exposure to the advertising message. The dual-edged sword of Internet-based promotions means that the consumer has both the power to actively seek and actively avoid promotional information. Consequently, the promoter needs to give consideration as to how and why consumers would want to seek out and engage with their promotional web sites.

The purpose of this chapter is to identify the marketing implications and decisions that need to be considered in the design of a web site. In particular, the chapter looks at the theoretical and philosophical issues of web site design. It also outlines the different types of web site attractors and home page types that are available to be used when designing a customer-oriented web site. Finally, it outlines a six-stage model of web site design that integrates both the philosophical and practical issues of site creation and management.

Elements of the hypertext mark-up language, web site programming and similar microlevel implementation techniques are not covered in this book as the emphasis is on the strategic direction and design theories of the web site. Readers looking for material on the area of technical implementation are advised to investigate online sources. Information may be found on any of the sites listed under Yahoo's World Wide Web directory (dir.yahoo.com/Computers_and_Internet/Internet/World_Wide_Web) or Webmonkey (www.hotwired.lycos.com/webmonkey). Webmonkey offers a range of information — from basic HTML, through to complex site design and advanced e-commerce solutions. However, the emphasis here is on the design philosophies behind the creation of successful web sites.

F O C U S   O N
Strategy ◉

Marketing versus programming: The philosophical divide

The reason for developing a chapter in this text on the subject of web site design philosophy is to recognise that marketing and the web design sector have two different functions to perform. The rapid development of the IT sector and the Internet has brought with it inevitable levels of friction as various groups claim responsibility for managing Internet functions.

The marketing sector believes that it should have the responsibility for site development. Many marketers believe that a web site is a promotional interface with the customer and, therefore, part of their public relations and advertising portfolio. The IT division believes that since the Internet is about computers, it should be their job, since they handle the computing tasks.

In general, the IT and marketing departments need to work together to implement any major web site developments. This usually sits badly with both areas, since a long history of animosity exists between marketing and engineering and IT.

This has arisen from the fact that decisions made concerning product, as part of the marketing mix, have to be implemented by the engineering sections. Engineering and IT often feel that marketing is trying to 'dumb down' engineering's complex product. At the same time marketing feel that they are delivering a more 'user friendly' interface, and that engineering is forever making products too complex for anyone not equipped with a science degree. There are sufficient Dilbert (www.dilbert.com) cartoon strips to demonstrate engineering points of view about the validity and wisdom of marketing driven changes. (Marketing is yet to develop a Dilbert-equivalent corporate icon to express the frustration of dealing with engineers.)

In the development of web sites, marketing needs to be able to put forward ideas, suggestions and the desire for functions they wish to see implemented, and then be willing to accept the engineering/IT verdict. The skills and specialisation of marketing are in understanding the customer and communicating the value of the product to the customer. When marketing proposes an idea that engineering does not believe can be delivered, marketing has to back down and defer to the experience of the engineers. Similarly, when designing a web site, the marketing department needs to focus on the needs of the customers and how they can be met by the technologies available.

Until such time as marketing can interact with engineering and IT to produce a product or web site that is technically sound and meets customer needs, the best laid marketing plans will often go astray. Engineering, IT and marketing are all specialist skills that need to be used in balance. The marketing department's need to make adjustments to the marketing mix must be considered as much as the capacity of IT and engineering to deliver a solution to those needs.

●●●●●●●●●●●●●●●●●●●●●●●●

Value and role of internet in promotion: Marketing on the Web

The value of the Internet in promotion has yet to be comprehensively established to any academic or practitioner's satisfaction. This is hardly surprising since it took television nearly fifty years to develop the slickly packaged rating meters, buy rates and coverage statistics. Now these features are being expected from a medium that has not even made it to being a teenager, let alone become a sophisticated adult of content delivery.

Three major areas of immediate value have been identified for the role of the Internet in promotion. Firstly, the Web offers a low-cost alternative to the standard costs associated with advertising, product placement and other conventional promotional expenditures (O'Connor & O'Keefe 1997). Web sites can be developed for a fraction of the cost of a major media campaign, although web sites themselves can also be scaled upwards in costs as quickly as any other promotional venture.

Secondly, the Web provides a much more level playing field — everyone has equal access opportunities and there is a much greater share of voice (Watson, Akselsen & Pitt 1998). **Share of voice** refers to the ability of all users in the Internet arena to be able to promote themselves, and speak freely without one or more players being able to buy the 'voice', as can occur in restricted broadcast media like television or radio. The inability of the Web to have a central management committee, or to be able to be controlled from a central hub, has created a free open market of voice, where competition is based on message desirability rather than capacity to purchase media time and space.

The third, and most recent value of the Internet for promotion is focused on the notion of the web site as a product, service, place and advertisement all rolled up into a single interactive package. Unlike the split between billboards, retail outlets and television advertising, well-crafted Internet promotional pages can offer a non-intrusive advertising function. This type of advertisement has the potential to handle immediate order fulfilment as the consumer is engaged in the high involvement environment (Ranchhod 1998). When the customer is at the web site, the product they're reading about is available for purchase with only a few mouse-clicks. The web page in this instance is a mixture of salesperson, retail store, product catalogue and billboard advertisement, giving an exceptional coverage of the promotional mix through a single access point.

The Internet: A recap of the good, the bad and the interactive

In chapter 3 the unique features of the Internet were outlined. This chapter will provide a quick recap of the important features of the Web as a medium for promotion. The viable and valuable features of the Internet for the purposes of promotion (identified by Ju–Pak (1999)) are:

- *multimedia capacity.* The Internet can offer the depth of information of a newspaper article while having the visual appeal of television and the audio strength of radio. Although there are still some production constraints, which are raised below, the Internet allows for a mixture of audio, video, text, graphics and animations to be combined in an interactive forum unparalleled in other media.
- *24–7 coverage.* The Internet exists around the clock, readily accessible from the safety and security of the consumer's home, and without the need for 24–7 staffing. While other avenues of conventional promotion also do 24–7 shifts, consumers are more likely to complain about having billboard advertising in their homes than they are about having promotional web pages on their computer screens.
- *audience selectivity and selective audiences.* As an interest-driven medium, the Internet offers a more precise targeting mechanism for selecting the customer, and for the customer to select the advertiser. Advertising can be

placed on selective web sites based on site content, site genre and even in reaction to key words used at a search engine. This degree of flexibility in targeting exceeds even that of direct mail for potential accuracy and value.

- *global exposure.* Although the Internet is a worldwide medium, global does not mean universal. Advertisers need to keep that particular reality check in mind when designing campaigns with global reach, as not everyone in every country will be online.

- *interactivity.* The killer application of online promotion is the ability and capacity of the Internet to be more than a passive medium, while allowing the delivery of push-based media content. **Push-based content** is where the web site sends information to the user in a manner more associated with standard television or radio broadcasting. This means that the content is streamed from the server to the user's computer with limited or no interactive elements for the consumer to adjust. Services such as Infogate (www.infogate.com) offer push-based broadcasting of content over the Internet through specialty screen-saver software. Push-based screen savers also feature a high level of sponsor advertising content. The greater value of Internet push media comes from being able to click on a selected element of the content and access the interactivity of the Internet from within the push broadcast.

- *production quality.* The Web is a place of inconsistent production quality. Sites which rely on graphics and animations are often plagued with download problems that do not occur with television or radio. Advances in streaming audio and video technologies have been steadily improving quality and speed of distribution. However, the problem remains that it still takes time to download the complex introduction sequence of graphics and hypertext which are taken for granted with television. People don't have to wait five minutes for the next advert to load, and the playback of the Sunday night movie doesn't pause every few minutes as the rest of the footage attempts to download. Even though much of the potential of the Internet for production quality is yet to be fully realised, a lot of high quality production can be achieved within the current technical constraints. Designers need to retain an awareness of the technical constraints facing the target customers, and the general conditions of the Internet, when deciding on interactive elements to add to a web site.

Metatheory of web site design

Web site design is a combination of art and science, much like typography, graphic design and interior decorating. The development of a web site brings together the issues of purpose, functionality and decor with concerns of speed, reliability and aesthetic value. Initial developments in web page design focused on functionality and new technology ahead of message and image creation. It was considered more important to see what could be achieved with the technology than to see what message could be sent. The message design element of web sites still existed during the 'technology for the sake of experimentation' period, in that a company which chose to implement a bleeding edge technology site portrayed an image of innovation and daring. Users of early web sites accepted, with varying degrees of grace, that some sites would crash, fail to load, or just not work as experiments with Java, Javascript, Flash animations and other new technologies evolved.

The frontier mentality of early web design gave way to an emphasis on image and message once the responsibility for the web site moved from the domain of IT specialists to the domain of graphic designers and marketers. Concurrently, marketing was also undergoing a process of re-evaluation of its role in society, and its creation of image, message and symbolism.

Post-modern consumption and the Internet

The irony of the Internet is that a medium designed for annotating physics research papers ended up being in the middle of a post-modern debate over the role of marketing in society. **Post-modern consumption** relates to the creation and negotiation of image, social role and social meaning through the use, purchase, consumption, and now creation, of goods and services in the online environment (Patterson 1998). It was previously referred to in the construction of identity in cybercommunities in chapter 5. In this context, post-modern consumption occurs through the appropriation of marketing from 'content that is produced to be consumed' to 'experiential marketing interaction online'. **Experiential marketing** is based on the threefold notion of interactivity, connectivity and creativity creating a marketing dialogue rather than the monologue of traditional one-way media. **Interactivity** is seen as the degree of give and take between the consumer and the producer of the marketing message, and the extent to which the message adapts to the consumer.

Connectivity is the sense of one-to-one communication and the feeling that the marketer is meeting the consumer's needs on an individual basis. In an era of mass customisation, automation and reduced human contact in the consumer service provider environments, a sense of connectivity through a web site can go some distance to replace the connectivity lost from the decline of personal interactions. Connectivity also explores the extent to which the consumer feels a connection with the brand or product, and uses the imagery of the brand, product or corporation as part of their self-identity.

Creativity is the recognition that the market has a wide range of choice for content, ideas and experiences. This requires the marketer to do more than simply recycle existing ideas over and over again. Global competition has created access to an array of new stimuli at the product level and increased exposure to new ideas. Consequently, the market has become increasingly sophisticated in its need for creativity through entertainment, information and site design. The degree of competition in the creative imagery market has expanded so that one size no longer fits anyone, let alone fits all.

Examining post-modern consumption in terms of a market demand for interactivity, connectivity and creativity expands the application for the commercial web site to go beyond being a digital billboard or order form into becoming an experiential consumption event. However, a word of caution — not everybody wants a post-modern experiential event for a web site. Raman and Leckenby (1998) point out that the dominant value sought from web sites is the utility of the exchange. Practical use and value of the web site for pragmatic purposes such as price comparison, product information and ease of purchase, far outweighs the hedonistic pleasure that might be found in interacting with a web site. It is possible to combine modernist utility-functionality with the post-modernist experiential marketing needs by emphasising utility of purpose of the web site with interactivity, connectivity and creativity. Giving the customer the information or service they want in a new, creative way which they can access, interact with or use easily, can answer the needs of the modern and post-modern consumers simultaneously.

Metatheory 101: Styles of web site structures

There are two levels of web site design, node level and site level. **Node level** represents the interaction of elements within a page and includes design components, selection of colours and the use of images and text. **Site level** works on the look and feel as well as the navigation of the site. The difference between node level and site level is illustrated in figure 10.1.

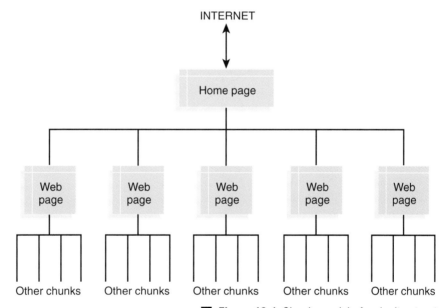

Figure 10.1 Simple model of web site structures

Source: Wan, H. A. and Chung, C. 1998, 'Web page design and network analysis', *Internet Research: Electronic Networking Applications and Policy*, vol. 8, no. 2, pp. 115–22.

Wan and Chung (1998) illustrate a model of a simple web site which makes use of a linear structure based on providing links from a home page through five sub-pages and beyond into the scientifically named 'other chunks' element. Each node in this diagram is represented as the web page and associated other chunks.

Site level design focuses on the overall direction of the site, including the decision to select a linear or non-linear path model. Linear sites are best represented by directory sites, such as Yahoo (www.yahoo.com), where a clear, linear path of directory and subdirectory can be followed. Non-linear sites are those sites where interaction occurs between web pages within the site, as is illustrated in figure 10.2.

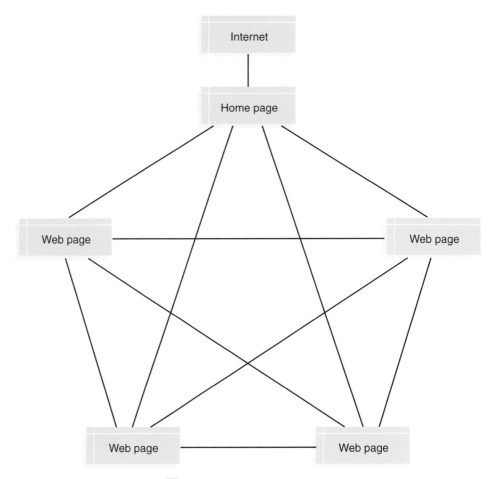

················■ **Figure 10.2** Simple model of a non-linear web site structure

From the point of entry, the user has a direct line of passage to each page within the site, from every other page. A simple five-page site such as that illustrated allows for a multitude of paths and interlinks. (Strictly speaking, a five-factorial model creates 120 potential paths of navigation, even more if multiple relationships exist between subsections of two or more pages.) Even with only five pages interacting, it becomes obvious that the addition of many more pages will result in a complex diagram of paths, and a wide range of user experiences.

Determining which site model to use is dependent on a range of factors, including the interrelationship between the content of the site, the nature of the interaction being designed and the overall complexity and variety of paths through the site. **Search engines** and portals tend towards streamlined linear sites which rely on narrowing content at each level such as about.com (www.about.com). In contrast, database sites like the Internet movie database (IMDB)(www.imdb.com) or online encyclopedia (www.eb.com) rely on creating massive levels of interaction between content pages on the site. For example, IMDB has every actor, movie, director and supporting crew cross-referenced to each other. A site map for an operation as complex as IMDB would resemble a plate of noodles rather than an intelligible diagram such as those illustrated in figures 10.1 and 10.2.

Metatheory 102: Strategic frameworks for web site design

Development of a web site is a strategic decision that needs to be undertaken long before any thoughts of the more mundane issues of page design are even considered. As with a promotional plan, there are several strategic objectives that need to be established, systems of measurement to consider and other strategic questions that need to be answered. Chapter 7 outlined the strategic decisions that needed to be made before a company established an online presence. Having determined that an Internet presence is needed, and that the goods and/or services offered by the company are suited to online delivery and distribution, the corporation needs to establish a planned approach to its web site. Lu and Yeung (1998) developed a conceptual level framework for designing web sites. Conceptual site design takes into consideration the macro-level decisions relating to feasibility and acceptability, including concerns as to the functionality, useability and usefulness of the site. Figure 10.3 illustrates Lu and Yeung's (1998) multiple layer approach to web site design.

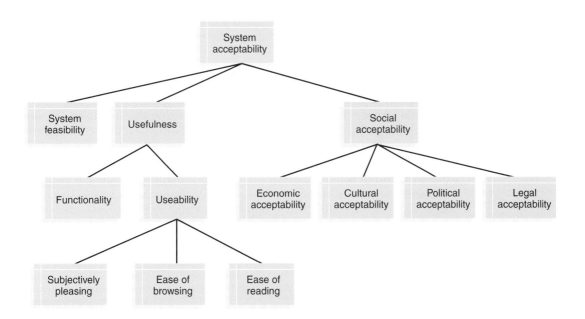

Figure 10.3 Strategic framework for site design

Source: Lu, M. and Yeung, W. 1998, 'A framework for effective commercial Web application development', *Internet Research: Electronic Networking Applications and Policy*, vol. 8, no. 2, pp. 115–22.

The decision tree supports eleven different functions through three layers, which together affect system acceptability. **System acceptability**, a concept borrowed from software design, is whether the software will do what it is supposed to do and whether it does this in a manner acceptable to the end user. The twelve different functions that make up the layers are:

■ *system feasibility*: the ability of the available technology to deliver a web site that has been conceptualised, but not yet fully designed. It consists of four sub-components (not illustrated in the diagram).

1. *economic feasibility*: the balance between the rewards and the costs of establishing a web site and its perceived benefits. Will the gains made in revenue, reduced costs or image outweigh the costs of creating and maintaining the web presence? If the objective of the site is cost reduction, obviously the running costs of the site must not exceed the potential savings from its operation.

2. *technical feasibility*: the capacity of the technology available to the organisation and to the target market. Both the front and back end of the company system need to be considered, particularly if the web site is intended to be integrated into existing database systems. However, making a smoothly integrated and operational web site for the organisation is only half the battle. The web site must consider technical capacities of the target user to ensure that the functionality of the site falls within that range. Setting up the finest online video-on-demand distribution service which is neatly integrated into the organisation's legacy systems is a waste of time and money if the client target groups don't have the capacity to decode the video. This is a particularly important consideration to reiterate at the node level where the content of the site needs to be designed to be as widely compatible as possible. Site design must be a balance between organisational technical capacity and the technology available to the target market.

3. *operational feasibility*: probably the most important question in the feasibility study — will the customer, staff, suppliers, management or other targeted groups actually use the site? If the target group for the organisational web site has little or no intention of using the site, then the site should not go ahead. Too many web sites are being developed on expert-driven production orientation where, effectively, the company tells customers to use the web site, whether they want to or not. Similarly, the introduction of web-based systems designed to improve internal efficiencies will not work if the organisational staff do not want to use them.

4. *organisational feasibility*: the integration of the web site into the company's existing operations. Will the web site become an adjunct to current sales channels or create internal competition? Can the supply lines and distribution channels already in existence be adapted to support the web site? The key to establishing organisational feasibility is to explicitly state where the role and function of the web site integrates into the existing operations of the company, and whether it will replace or augment existing functions, or create a new function.

■ *usefulness*: a combination of functionality and useability to determine if the web site does actually help the target user accomplish the intended outcomes. If the role of the web site is to facilitate a transaction or service, such as online banking, is it secure, easy to use, and does it actually transfer funds and pay bills?

1. *functionality*: the extent to which a site has the information, systems and functions to do what it promises to do. Information such as how to use the functions, what each button does, and details on shipping costs, colours, sizes and similar product detail need to be available, up to date and accessible in a useable format.

2. *useability*: the extent to which a site can be operated easily by the target group. A site may be fully functional, have incredible depth of information, massive arrays of services and be totally unusable because of poor layout, design or colour choice. The useability of a web site is both a node level and structural level issue. At the node level, font selection, page design, colour selection and the use of graphics versus text all contribute to issues of readability, download speed and other useability functions. These issues are examined in three sub-elements of useability:

   - *subjectively pleasing*: the aesthetic value of a web site. Some web sites are akin to artwork in their design values, whereas others may choose to resemble modular kitchen units for the prefabricated component look. All design choices in developing a web site at the node level relate back to the issue of subjectively pleasing — does the site look good, and is it easy on the eye?

   - *ease of browsing*: the structural level issue of intra-site navigation. Has the site been designed to facilitate movement through it, or do the users come across dead ends, blind alleys and other web obstacles? Can a user traverse the length and breadth of the site without recourse to the browser's back button? Are links from one page to another obvious, if they are meant to be obvious or does the user have to search for them each time? Is there a consistency to the design of the site, so that pressing the red button on any given page, for example, will have the same result? Ease of browsing is therefore a cross between the design considerations of architecture and store layout and the information signposting of graphic layout and readability. A hallmark of consistent navigation design principles is the extent to which the navigation is independent of the content of the site. If a user could successfully navigate a site which contained only blank pages, then the site is at least well designed, even if rather boring to read.

   - *ease of reading*: the most challenging of the useability functions in that it represents the extent to which the content of the page is readable to the target user. Readability is one of the most misunderstood functional elements of site design. When the Internet was first freely available, the type and nature of the early adopters and innovators meant that the average reading level of users was exceptionally high. Most users had some connection to a university education, either being academics, university students or university graduates. The Internet itself was primarily text-based due to the download speed of text sites vastly outpacing the graphics sites that were available at the time. The development and spread of faster Internet access, and the improvements in the speed of graphics sites triggered a change in web site design.

When university education was no longer the entry criterion to the Internet, a design movement started to emphasise readability as being a factor of the lowest common denominator. Sites became concerned with the prospect of being too highbrow, wordy or complex for the lowest level user of the Internet, rather than maintaining a focus on the needs of their target market. Readability should be about targeting the highest common denominator in the target market for the product. Highest common denominator targeting allows for the majority of the target population to find a site readable, understandable and culturally appropriate without needing to 'dumb down' any major sections of the content (Aitchison & French-Blake, 1999).

Sites with a global focus are advised to focus on developing multilingual and multicultural versions of their web sites that are region specific for internationally targeted markets. However, regardless of the language or culture being targeted by the web page, the primary focus on readability is to set a level appropriate for the targeted customer group, irrespective of whether this level meets the needs of the lowest denominator for the entire population of the Internet.

■ *social acceptability*: the interaction between the content of the web site and the accepted values of the society in which it is targeted to operate. One of the paradoxes of the global reach of the Internet is that it has allowed content into nations that would not otherwise have been exposed to it. The Internet itself has a range of cultural and social values that are distinct from the common mores of society. The absence of a central controlling authority has led many to believe that the Internet is a value-neutral environment, free from social restraints and legal obligations. This has been expressed in various forms, from the mistaken belief that laws of copyright and defamation do not apply, through to the belief that governments have no right of censorship over Internet publications. The reality of the Internet is that it is subject to local legislation, and even though the publication of materials on a global server may be legal, the viewing of these materials may be illegal under local law.

Several attempts have been made to have the Internet declared a legal nation for the purposes of taxation, citizenship and, most recently, for point of origin of manufactured goods and services. However, few governments support the idea of developing such a global digital nation considering the potential for conflict between physical governments and the new digital 'country'. In any case, social acceptability operates at two levels, the Internet acceptability, and the local acceptability. Internet acceptability represents the degree to which the site contravenes established Internet social customs, such as sites promoting mass unsolicited mail.

Social acceptability breaks down into four elements of legal, political, economic and cultural acceptability:

1. *legal acceptability*: the legality of the product, service or ideas being sold, promoted or displayed by the web site. As mentioned elsewhere, export restrictions apply to all products sold over the Internet, including intangible elements such as software. The licence agreement for most software originating from the United States includes the list of countries

against which America has active trade embargos, and citizens of these nations are asked politely not to install the software. Netscape Navigator was required to have two versions of its product, one for the American domestic market and one for international release because America had export restrictions on the encryption software used in the program.

2. *political acceptability*: the degree to which the product, service, good or idea is acceptable to the government or political parties of the target market's home country. Legal products, such as information on abortion, may be politically sensitive issues, and the promotion of politically insensitive ideas, such as prejudicial sales policies, may cause loss of sales (product boycotts and bans) or negative publicity for the corporation. The inappropriate portrayal of various ethnic cultures, social groups and gender roles may also lead to political backlash. The Internet may not have a central government, but the majority of countries attached to the Internet have forms of government controls that can be brought to bear against any web site owner who breaches accepted national or international standards. Of course, the whole role and purpose of the web site can be to breach political acceptability by publishing ideas contrary to government-held views (www.freetibet.org).

3. *economic acceptability*: directly related to economic feasibility in that it considers economies of scale, and whether the product will reach enough users who have sufficient disposable income to purchase the product

4. *cultural acceptability*: the degree to which the web site integrates with the cultural beliefs of the target adopters. However, it need not be acceptable to every culture in existence that may be online. The designers must be sensitive to the cultural beliefs, religious views and way of life of the target market when adding content and links to the site. Web sites that specifically target messages aimed at subgroups of the population who have either controversial cultural standards, or standards that conflict with established religious viewpoints must be prepared to receive criticism for their content. However, if the content is appropriate for the target market, this criticism must be counted as simply a price of doing business in an environment where virtually everyone has access to every web site.

The purpose of the Lu and Yeung (1998) model is to establish a range of checkpoints in the development of the web site, and to ensure that goals and objectives of a web site are set with functionality, acceptability and feasibility in mind. Having established the strategic direction by working through a process outlined by the model, the next phase of planning is to determine the design philosophy for the web site.

Design philosophy: The art of the Web

The design philosophies of the web site are based on the collision between the capacity of the Internet to deliver the vision of the designer, and the desire of the organisation to be bleeding edge, cutting edge or conservative in their use of Internet technologies. One of the most important criteria influencing the design of a web site is the need to understand the end user and to maintain the integrity of the corporate image.

Unlike conventional or real-world advertising, there is vast potential for technical problems, conflicts and catastrophes that designers need to second guess. The television broadcast signal is a standard format no matter what brand of television is on the receiving end. Internet Explorer and Netscape Navigator still have conflicting specifications in terms of what content they can accept without risk of crashing, freezing or simply not displaying the page. The more a site relies on cutting- or bleeding-edge technology, the greater the risk of incompatibility. At the same time, the web site must be a reflection of the corporation it was established to serve, and often a cutting-edge, high-risk site is as much a part of the corporate image as aggressive television advertising.

The second major design consideration is where the web site will be housed and supported within the corporate structure. Is it the responsibility of the IT department, marketing, PR, sales, or nephew of the CEO? Is the design going to be maintained in-house or by external consulting? All of these issues are part of the strategic development of the Internet presence overviewed in chapter 7.

The three design schools

The **design school concept** represents the notion that a series of recurring techniques, ideas and philosophies can be grouped together as a distinctive 'school' of thought. The development of the Internet from text-based media in the early 1990s to the graphics and multimedia orientation towards the latter half of the decade has created a range of schools of thought concerning Internet design. However, the rapidly evolving nature and youth of the Internet have combined to create a concept which has both a shelf life and half-life.

First, the shelf life of the design school idea relates to the fact that as dedicated web-oriented production services mature through the product lifecycle, the adaptation of existing print, visual and audio design procedures will make way for theories, philosophies and methods of design derived solely from web construction experience. Television first adapted stage, theatre and live performance concepts to the broadcast media, and later worked up to the use of prerecorded, tightly edited and produced packages. As the Internet evolves into something that resembles the stability associated with television and radio, more design philosophies will emerge.

The second notion of the design school is that it is an idea with a half-life, in that a design school theory will not go away overnight. The half-life concept is taken from the physical breakdown of nuclear materials where the amount of a material left after a period of the half-life will be approximately half of the material at the start of the time period. A dominant idea will not fade instantly to nothing and vanish without a trace. Rather, it will gradually break down in dominance over a period of time, but most likely will not disappear entirely. As the development of the Internet progresses, and more Internet-specific theories are created, the dominance of any of the design schools will dissipate, but not disappear.

Abels, White and Hahn (1997) defined three distinct approaches to web site design theory based on the adaptation of experience, research into human computer interface design, or design philosophies from the printed media.

Design school 1: Rampant ad hocery, voodoo programming and personal experience

The first and most prevalent form of Internet design school is based on a hybridisation of personal experience, voodoo programming and web design and rampant ad hocery in implementation. Without descending too far into the depths of programming subculture terms, much of this first design school owes its ancestry to the dominance of the IT sector in the development of the Internet and Web. Initially, web sites were seen as the domain of the IT department, who may or may not have welcomed input from other sections such as marketing or PR. Most likely they welcomed content, but for the most part, web sites were driven by technical understanding rather than marketing objectives. The production orientation of the IT side of web design is not necessarily any more or less appropriate than a customer focus, as it does represent a prevalent design concept.

The advantage of this school is that the implementation and design protocols are shaped from experiential development that has come from doing first and learning later. When the web was first established, even conceptualising it to explain in a market research survey was hard enough. Actually getting useful data from a survey that asked people who had possibly never heard of Netscape what they wanted from a web site in appearance and feel was impossible. Sites which had webmasters who could adapt to, and stay abreast of the rapid development of new technologies, flourished and survived. Personal experience and instinct proved valuable tools in the accelerated Darwinian world of early web site programming.

The problem with Darwinian development is that survival of the fittest depends on the fittest retaining their adaptive abilities that got them through the last cull. The downside to the approach came quite quickly from two related areas: rampant ad hocery, and voodoo programming.

- *rampant ad hocery*: the reliance on an unstructured approach based on implementing incremental changes, updates and features. The flaw in this design is that it leaves no room for planned change, as it tends to be a reactionary rather than pro-active approach to design. Usually, rampant ad hocery is closely associated with tight deadlines and a production attitude that emphasises having 'something out there' at the expense of detailed planning and consideration of the web site.
- *voodoo programming*: programming using guesswork of any system, feature, or code that the programmer does not truly understand (Raymond 1996; Raymond 2000). By implication, whether it works or fails, the programmer will never really know why or how it happened. The term was coined in reference to the 'voodoo economics' expression used by George Bush in 1979 to describe apparently random actions that led to changes in the economy. The randomness and guesswork nature of voodoo programming has spawned a similar approach of voodoo design, where the success of the site design occurred from a combination of forces not fully understood by the people responsible for creating it. In combination, rampant ad hocery and voodoo design led to a wave of highly successful sites that were difficult to replicate because nobody knew how or why they worked, or had the faintest

idea of how to document the processes that led to their development. The problem with this is that it makes planning a web site very difficult if the concepts that led to the last success cannot be identified or explained. Absence of forward planning and reliance on ad hocery and voodoo design leaves the site open to problems associated with feature creep.

Internet marketing INSIGHT
The precautionary tale: Feeping creaturism

A precautionary note is taken from *The New Hacker's Dictionary*, a tome which outlines the development of the IT culture that ultimately spawned much of the intellectual infrastructure behind the Internet. 'Creeping featurism' has two definitions, one rather heavily intertwined with hacker culture and difficult to translate into common terms, and the second:

> 'the tendency for anything complicated to become even more complicated because people keep saying "Gee, it would be even better if it had this feature too"...The result is usually a patchwork because it grew one ad-hoc step at a time, rather than being planned' (Raymond 2000)

The danger inherent in web site design and the Internet is that it is very easy to simply implement another page, or link, or function which was not originally designed into the infrastructure of the site. One of the frequent and justified criticisms of the Internet as an advertising medium is that the ease of correction of web sites has led to a culture of 'near enough is uploaded, good enough will be implemented next week'. Deadlines are met by uploading incomplete work that is progressively updated, repaired or subjected to intentional feature creep.

From the marketing point of view, it is important to maintain a close eye on the needs and wants of the target consumer compared with the functions being implemented into the software, web site or feature list. Marketing has been as guilty as programming for randomly adding elements that are portrayed as 'features' that do little more than annoy the user, or overly complicate simple existing tasks. Constant web site redesigns, and the inclusion of larger graphics, more sound and animations at the expense of download times and ease of navigation are all major causes of promotion-led feature creep. The worst offender of all, however, is any site that switches from having an accessible front page index to having a 30 second or longer introductory animation. The aim of a good web site is to deliver the content to the customer as cleanly and quickly as possible, so as to encourage the customer further into the site. The aim is not to make them stand at the door of the store for five minutes before deciding to show them a 30 second advertisement on the glory of the company, and then let them into the store. By the time the digital song and dance routine is over, the customer, along with Elvis, has left the building. Good site content tailored to the needs of the customer will beat bells and whistles displays in the contest for the customer's attention online.

Source: Raymond, E. S. 1996, *The New Hacker's Dictionary* (3rd edn), MIT Press; Raymond, E. S. 2000, 'The Jargon Manual', Version 4.2.0 http://www.tuxedo.org/~esr/jargon/

The true value of the individual experience design school is in the fact that these are the philosophies and applications most likely to form the basis of the development of web-oriented design theories. However, in the context of strategic Internet marketing, the value of a web site is defined more by the integration of the functions and features into the organisation's operations than by the degree to which it contributes to the understanding of web design. Consequently, a more structured and formalised approach to site design is needed for the integration of the Internet and offline functions.

Design school 2: Human factors research

The second school of thought takes its theoretical design principles from the research and development in the human computer interaction. This wide-ranging spectrum of research covers everything from colour selection through to eyeball tracking in reading a computer screen. It represents a systematic and scientific orientation to web site design, relying heavily on the use of design testing in relation to specific tasks (Abels, White & Hahn 1997). As a web site design philosophy, it is closely associated with the standard pretesting and copytesting techniques commonly associated with advertising campaigns, and draws much of the same praise and criticism. The disadvantage of this approach is the heavy emphasis on task-specific design testing which can lead the site to designing itself around task production, which may not be consistent with the role or purpose of the site.

Design school 3: Written rules and printed protocol

The third style of web site design is summed up fairly succinctly by the jargon phrase '**webify**' meaning to put a piece of (possibly already existing) material on the web (Raymond 2000). '**Webification**' could best describe the adaptation of the rules and protocols of printed media into web site design strategies. The textual nature of the early Internet and the limited array of graphic capacity fostered an environment where desktop publishing skills from the mid 1980s found a new application in the early 1990s. Node level design issues of colour, image placement, and the use of fonts became increasingly important issues in page design as hypertext code became more sophisticated, and allowed a greater range of creative expression. Given that the early code standards allowed for about two types of fonts (Times New Roman and Courier) and the exotic array of **bold** and *italics* (underline was usually reserved for hyper-links), the development of hypertext code allowing specific fonts and sizes was adopted with much enthusiasm. Consequently, as the sophistication of the Web interface increased, so did the capacity of the Internet to reflect traditional print media. Newspaper web sites have quite often attempted to replicate the column, sub-column and side-bar design of the printed copy on their web pages, with varying degrees of success.

None of the three design schools mentioned are exclusive applications. A successful web site will revolve around the appropriate selection and application of varying elements from each approach. Nor is any one particular methodology superior to another as a classically designed, pre-tested and planned web site may be every bit as good or bad as a site designed on the fly, with little planning and copious improvising. The important focus should remain on emphasising the need for the final product to meet the needs of the customer, rather than slavishly obeying a set of design principles or philosophies.

Strategic integration: Putting the site together

The value of an integrated web site is that it taps into all aspects of the marketing mix, and not just the promotional arm. Web site design should be determined by examining the nature of the product being offered to the consumer, since a site supporting an information-rich technology will differ quite noticeably from a site designed to supplement a tangible product (Palmer & Griffith 1998). Palmer and Griffith (1998) also note that the impact of the Internet and the new technologies of web-based marketing will not be universally felt, and will differ by core product offering. Companies distributing pure information products, such as software or music, will be able to conduct business solely in an online environment. Distributors of tangible goods will still require back-end channel systems to support their web sites, and will need to face some of the complexities of sporadic exporting. Determining the appropriate site style and design is based on the combination of type and nature of the product being promoted. Web sites are viewed as the overall site style and design, whereas the home page is treated as the individual page. The difference is most notable when dealing with an organisation with a range of products and services, such as Nike, (www.nike.com) who have a specific web site style (club) and a range of home page types depending on the nature of the product (retail sale for shoes, advocacy for health and fitness, brand image for the corporate logos).

Attractors on the Web: Types of web sites

Watson, Akselsen and Pitt (1998) outlined a principle of Internet presence design that emphasised creating an 'attractor' on the Web rather than web site. They saw the ideal scenario as a corporation that took the same consideration in designing and developing a web site that it would take in setting up a store, theme park or major public attraction. **Attractors** were specifically intended to be sites that had the most potential to interact with the greatest number of visitors in the target market. At the same time, these sites were designed to offer interaction that was specific to the objectives of the firm, and difficult for competitors to replicate (Watson et al. 1998). However, these are exactly the same processes required for the design of a good service. One of the things that has been learned from the services industry is that superficial features and attractors are quickly and easily imitated, for no real gain across the board for either the originator or replicator. Differentiation, on and offline, is based on providing a hard-to-replicate core function that meets the needs of the target market, and is integral to the service or product experience offered by the company.

In the development of Internet attractors, Watson et al. (1998) identified eight styles of web sites:

- *entertainment parks*: sites designed primarily to entertain customers and users with high levels of interactivity, contests and prizes. These types of sites rely heavily on creating a sense of telepresence or attempting to bring the user into a flow state, and make heavy use of interactive elements. The purpose of the site is to encourage repeat visits, either to win recurring prizes, or to continue playing with the digital toys on display. These are the digital Disneyland of the Internet where fun and play have priority over information and sales pitches. Of course, having moved the visitor into a positive mind-set, the web site may also try to sell a product or two on the way to recoup the cost of investment, but this is not the main aim of the design.

  Site level design features include the use of easy-to-follow paths and pre-determined event areas such as games, puzzles and contests. Node level interactions feature a large number of interactive elements, most of which will take a certain period of time (up to five minutes) to load. The waiting time is frequently used to explain either the rules or instructions of the game. Games can either be based on Java (www.freefungames.com) or Macro-media Shockwave (www.cartoonnetwork.com/games) programming.

- *archive sites*: these focus on providing historical information about the company, or a service allowing access to historical exhibitions. These are the online equivalents of museums in that they contain large amounts of special interest information around select topics such as the historical development of the company. Alternatively, they may provide a historical service such as the Microsoft Museum (www.microsoft.com/mscorp/museum/home.asp) or Dejanews (www.deja.com) which archives a range of posts from USENET. Site design emphasises a logical structure, normally based on a hierarchy or topic or time line. Node level design places a strong focus on interlinking related topics and information, forming a giant interactive database (www.imdb.com).

- *exclusive sponsorships*: sites dedicated to the promotion of an exclusive sponsorship event, such as a charity sports event (www.charitychampionship.com), concert series (www.mp3.com) or movie (www.apple.com/quicktime). Apple sponsors several movie promotion web sites as examples of the power and capacity of the QuickTime media software (www.lordoftherings.net). The purpose of these sites is to showcase corporate involvement in the event as per a standard sponsorship arrangement. In addition, they are used to generate a large amount of traffic and interest with the idea of redirecting some of the traffic to the sponsor's web site. Both node and site level designs emphasise the strengths and abilities of the organisation sponsoring the event.

- *town hall sites*: a public forum for debate, discussion and online public speaking. These are often hosted and moderated forums where invited guests are available for semi-public debate on topical issues, or where regular hosts interview guests in a digital talk show environment (www.macshowlive.com). Town hall structures have a split function of live action areas and an archive of previous events. There is a strong degree of crossover between the node design of the archive and the site level interactivity orientation of the entertainment park in Town Hall designs.

- *club*: sites dedicated to supporting and hosting cybercommunities, discussed in depth in chapter 5. Cybercommunity structures either exist as the focus for the site (www.slashdot.org) or as an integrated element of an entertainment park (www.channelv.com.au) or promotional web site (www.pepsimax.com). The distinguishing factor of the club site is the strong emphasis on either room-based environments, with a site level designed to allow passage between related rooms, and node level structures that facilitate chat and communication.

- *gift shops*: sites that focus on providing giveaways, free offers and downloadable software such as screen savers (www.screensavers.com), songs (www.mp3.com) or demonstration versions of games (www.happypuppy.com). This style of site also includes the metarewards sites such as Beenz (www.beenz.com). **Metarewards** sites offer loyalty incentive schemes such as frequent flyer miles or equivalent for registering demographic details at various member sites. Site level considerations for gift shops relate to the capacity of the server system to support the download traffic, including the need to have multiple download mirrors during times of peak traffic, and a design that allows quick access to the 'gifts'. One of the best designed gift shop sites is Palmgear (www.palmgear.com) which has the look and feel of a content index (node design), with the most popular software listed on the front page for swift download, and linked to further information (site design).

- *freeway intersections*: the crossroads of the Internet which operate as portals (www.zdnet.com), search engines (www.google.com) or content indexes (www.yahoo.com). **Portal sites** are designed to offer gateways into specific content, such as news (www.abc.com), related services (www.bigpond.com) or the rest of the Internet (www.excite.co.uk). Portals usually include a range of customisable information services such as news reports, weather forecasts and horoscopes. These sites borrow most heavily from the printed media design school by deliberately trying to replicate the look and feel of newspapers.

  Search engine sites operate in one of three ways: diet portal (www.go.com), search-only (www.google.com), or metasearch (www.dogpile.com). **Diet portals** are web search engines that have added progressively more layers of portal style content, without becoming fully committed to the portal concept. **Search-only** sites have gone in the opposite direction by offering sparse looking pages that are simply designed to accept a search term and output a search result. **Metasearch engines** are web sites which access and search multiple web search engines simultaneously and return a compiled report of likely sites matching the search criteria. Content indexes provide a hierarchical structure with multiple layers of directories and subdirectories of sites grouped by content.

- *customer service centre sites*: established for the purpose of providing after-sales support for customers, and updates or product use information. These sites are usually part and parcel of retail sites which offer product information and sales. Kodak (www.kodak.com) offer a sophisticated after-sales service web site which offers retail support such as specialist films, advice on photography, and downloadable upgrades to digital camera software. The design of a customer service site tends to resemble a catalogue of either products, or common concerns. Node level functionality looks at issues of searchable content, frequently asked question lists, and constant updates where problems or issues may be subject to change.

These styles are not mutually exclusive in so far as it is possible to have a site with dominant elements and several other attractor types integrated — Disneyland is primarily an entertainment park, but operates gift shop functions and archival functions. Thus a web site should be designed to integrate the features of the attractors which are appropriate to the strategic intent of the Web presence.

Categories of design: Types of home pages

At the node level of web site design, there are several choices to be made concerning the type and nature of the web page, or cluster of web pages. Dholakia and Rego (1998) established a typology of web pages to illustrate the different purposes for which an element of a web site could be used. Their nine types of web pages are:

- *advocacy pages*: tailored to promote the corporation's position on an issue, such as Reebok's statement on human rights (www.reebok.com/humanrights/home.html)
- *brand image pages*: classic promotion advertisement pages that are the online equivalent of advertising or endorsement pages (www.wine.com)
- *comparative pages*: provide head to head comparisons between products or brands, much like a consumer choice guide, or a direct comparison advertising series (www.zdnet.com/techlife)
- *corporate pages*: promote the organisation, organisational goals and objectives. Frankly these should be as far to the back of the site as technically possible in an interactive medium (www.royal-doulton.com/company .html). Unless your core business is into big-noting your mission statement, leave the corporate propaganda to the annual reports.
- *direct response pages*: interactive pages seeking immediate user feedback, from surveys (www.greenfieldonline.com) through to customisable music selections (www.peoplesound.com)
- *index pages*: the front-end pages of the site design that allow users a wide range of choices to navigate further into the web site (www.zdnet.com)
- *political pages*: dedicated to the pursuit of support for votes, causes, candidates and campaigns. Consistent with the nature of election campaigning, these pages tend to have short life spans in the lead-up to an election, and either disappear because the candidate was successful or unsuccessful. Either way, most election pages disappear shortly after the election date.
- *public service pages*: differ from advocacy pages in that these pages are set up to support worthy causes or social campaigns, rather than encourage the reader to support the corporation's point of view. Depending on your degree of cynicism, Reebok's human rights page could also be a public

service announcement for Amnesty International, or a statement of the corporation's belief that its use of third world labour is acceptable. For a less controversial public service page, McDonald's offers information on the Ronald McDonald House Charities (www.rmhc.com).

■ *retail sales pages*: the home shopping channel of the Internet with dedicated content systems and functions all unashamedly trying to sell a product. Pure and obvious commercialism is appreciated in an environment where the line between supplied content and advertorial is becoming increasingly blurred. Internet users prefer to be told that you are selling them a product rather than having to guess as is the case with sites like Shop.com (www.shop.com) and subsections of sites like CDNow (www.cdnow.com) and Amazon (www.amazon.com).

The 6M of web site design

Pope and Forrest (1997) established a six-step plan for establishing and maintaining sports marketing web sites, which integrate strategic marketing considerations with implementation issues of a web site to create the six 'M' of web site design.

1. *Mission.* Define the role and purpose of the web site within the organisational structure. The mission outlines the two most important functions of the web site — what purpose it has in the organisational structure, and who are its target markets. Through this chapter the selection of web site style, page type and site design has been based on target market selection. Without this initial decision as to whom the web site will serve, the company will be unable to produce a viable or valuable web site by anything less than voodoo design. At the very least, the web site designers should be informed as to the strategy behind the decision to develop a web presence so that they can tailor a site that works for, rather than against, the corporate strategy.

2. *Margin.* Allocation of budget lines and resources to the Internet presence should be done in the same manner as allocations to any other business activity. The site needs to be subjected to cost benefit analysis, with benefits specified in a measurable context, or as clearly stated as possible. If a web site is being developed as a cost-cutting measure, the areas from which the costs are to be reduced must be examined to see if the web site is achieving its purpose. If the purpose of the web site is for a more nebulous objective to improve the corporate image, it is important to allocate it the same criteria as would be expected of any other promotional tool.

3. *Mechanics.* Mechanics relate to the technical aspects of the design and the production of the web site. Work through the Lu and Yeung (1998) design framework models, investigate the type and nature of the Internet attractor you want to build to achieve the goals set by your mission, and determine whether to outsource or develop inhouse talent.

4. *Marketing mix.* The fundamental premise of this whole section of the text is to integrate the marketing mix into the web site and the web site into the mix. The web presence should be promoted in the conventional elements

of the mix as even the very basic function of attaching the URL of the site to every piece of company material, from packaging to post-it notes, gives the web presence the same respect as the corporate name.

5. *Maintenance.* Define your scheduled servicing protocol as every 100 000 hits, or every six months, or as required. As mentioned in chapter 8, the frequency of updating of the web site is dependent on the nature of the product that it is serving. A news-oriented web site should be updated every few minutes during a crisis situation, as soon as fresh information comes to hand. Scheduled servicing of the web site should be built into the mechanics of the site design so that high turnover content is dynamically derived as part of a database-driven web site, enabling faster access and updating. Maintenance can also include updates and incremental improve- ments, although these improvements should be conducted in a systematic and planned manner rather than incremental ad hocery, or the site risks a serious case of feature creep.

6. *Metrics.* Metrics are the array of measurements available to determine the traffic around, through and into a web site. The problem with the Internet as far as market research, ratings data and similar metrics is concerned, is that nobody has had a chance to develop a decent measurement for the interactive online world. Examination of web site metrics involves the careful analysis of all available data, from server logs through to qualitative feedback from visitors.

 Summary

Like any element of the marketing mix, the development of a comprehensive web site design strategy is a complex planning task. Understanding the inter- action between the objectives of the marketing plans and the capacities of the web site is vital to ensure that the site achieves its potential. Being able to inte- grate the needs of the customer with elements of the site design, and the capacities of the Internet brings marketing one step closer to achieving the dream of maximising the potential of the web site. But each step along the path to that goal must be a planned move.

Even with the rapid development of technologies, tools and strategies for web sites, and the outbreak of the Internet into wider and more diverse equip- ment from computers to mobile phones to hand-held devices, the fun- damental philosophy of design remains constant. A web site offered as part of a marketing mix must meet the needs of the customer while delivering mes- sages set by the organisation's promotional and marketing goals. To this end, many and varied methods can be employed, but all of them return to a common core philosophy. Successful online marketing is not just about having a good web site — it is about having a good web site which is an integrated part of the marketing mix. Each of the design element techniques, from the approaches of three design schools through to the application of the 6M of site design need to be considered in the context of the role of the web site in the marketing strategy of the organisation.

Discussion questions

10.1 What are the three elements of experiential marketing? How do these three elements relate to web site design?

10.2 Outline the difference between node level and site level design. How do site level design and node level design interact when it comes to the development of a web site?

10.3 Outline the elements of Lu and Yeung's (1998) framework. How well does this framework cover the strategic issues of web site design?

10.4 Compare and contrast the three design schools. Find a web site that represents an example of each of the design schools.

10.5 Is there a role for ad-hoc design in the development of web sites? Can web sites be planned out in advance or is creeping featurism a natural element of web site development?

10.6 How does the web design interact with the marketing mix? Give examples of how each element of the mix interacts with the site design.

10.7 What is the purpose of an attractor web site? Identify the eight attractor types and give examples of sites which match these attractors. Can a site use more than one attractor? If so, how many different types of attractors can be used before the site loses its focus?

10.8 What is the relationship between attractor sites and home page types? Which is more important to tailor to the target market — an attractor site or a home page type?

10.9 Outline the 6M of web site design. Is one element more important than the others when designing a web site?

10.10 Can a web site be everything to everyone? Can market segmentation and interactivity be used to create a web site with universal appeal, or should web sites target only individual market segments?

References

Abels, E. G., White, M. D. & Hahn, K. 1997, 'A user-based design process for web sites', *Internet Research: Electronic Networking Applications and Policy*, vol. 8, no. 1, pp. 39–48.

Aitchison, J. & French-Blake, N. 1999, 'Cutting edge advertising: How to create the world's best print for brands in the 21st century', Prentice-Hall, Sydney.

Dholakia, U. M. & Rego, L. L. 1998, 'What makes commercial web pages popular? An empirical investigation of web page effectiveness', *European Journal of Marketing*, vol. 32, no. 7/8, pp. 724–36.

Ju-Pak, K. 1999, 'Content dimensions of web advertising: A cross-national comparison', *International Journal of Advertising*, vol. 18, pp. 207–31.

Lu, M. & Yeung, W. 1998, 'A framework for effective commercial Web application development', *Internet Research: Electronic Networking Applications and Policy*, vol. 8, no. 2, pp. 115–22.

O'Connor, G. C. & O'Keefe, B. 1997, 'Viewing the Web as a market-place: The case of small companies', *Decision Support Systems*, vol. 21, no. 3, pp. 171–83.

Palmer, J. W. & Griffith, D. A. 1998, 'An emerging model of web site design for marketing', *Communications of the ACM*, vol. 41, no. 3, pp. 44–52.

Patterson, M. 1998, 'Direct marketing in post-modernity: Neo-tribes and direct communications', *Marketing Intelligence and Planning*, vol. 16, no. 1, pp. 68–74.

Pope, N. & Forrest, E. 1997, 'A Proposed Format for The Management of Sport Marketing Web Sites', *Cyberjournal of Sports Marketing*, vol. 1, no. 1, http://www.cjsm.com/Vol1/Pope&Forrest.htm

Raman, N. V. & Leckenby, J. D. 1998, 'Factors affecting consumers' "Webad" visits', *European Journal of Marketing*, vol. 32, no. 7/8, pp. 737–48.

Ranchhod, A. 1998, 'Advertising into the next millennium', *International Journal of Advertising*, November, vol. 1, pp. 427–38.

Raymond, E. S. 1996, *The New Hacker's Dictionary* (3rd edn), MIT Press, Massachusetts.

Raymond, E. S. 2000, 'The Jargon Manual', Version 4.2.0 http://www.tuxedo.org/~esr/jargon/

Wan, H. A. & Chung, C. 1998, Web page design and network analysis, *Internet Research: Electronic Networking Applications and Policy*, vol. 8, no. 2, pp 115–22.

Watson, R. T., Akselsen, S. & Pitt, L. F. 1998, 'Attractors: Building mountains in the flat landscape of the Internet', *California Management Review*, vol. 40, no. 2, pp. 36–56.

Web sites

dir.yahoo.com/Computers_and_Internet/Internet/World_Wide_Web
www.abc.com
www.amazon.com
www.beenz.com
www.bigpond.com
www.cartoonnetwork.com/games
www.cdnow.com
www.channelv.com.au
www.charitychampionship.com
www.deja.com
www.dilbert.com
www.dogpile.com
www.eb.com
www.excite.co.uk
www.freefungames.com
www.freetibet.org
www.go.com
www.google.com
www.greenfieldonline.com
www.happypuppy.com
www.imdb.com
www.kodak.com
www.lordoftherings.net
www.macshowlive.com
www.microsoft.com/mscorp/museum/home.asp
www.mp3.com
www.nike.com
www.peoplesound.com
www.pepsimax.com
www.palmgear.com
www.infogate.com
www.apple.com/quicktime
www.reebok.com/humanrights/home.html
www.rmhc.com
www.royal-doulton.com/company.html
www.screensavers.com
www.shop.com
www.slashdot.org
www.tuxedo.org/~esr/jargon/
www.hotwired.lycos.com/webmonkey
www.wine.com
www.yahoo.com
www.zdnet.com

CHAPTER

11

Pricing
strategies

*'Internet access —
$29.99 a month.
Computer — $2499.
Finding useful
information quickly on
the Web — priceless.
There are some things
money can't buy. For
everything else, there's
MasterCard.'*

Derived from MasterCard's
1999 'Priceless' advertising
series.

LEARNING
objectives

After reading this chapter, you should be able to:

explain the role of total price concept in determining price setting in electronic marketing

understand the pressures exerted on pricing by online and offline factors associated with the Internet

outline the three pricing objectives and how these objectives are influenced by other elements of the marketing mix

overview different types of pricing strategy

recognise the role of product in pricing online activities

explain the impact of total cost to the consumer including international currency transactions on Internet price setting.

Introduction

One of the ongoing debates in e-commerce revolves around the issue of price. What is an appropriate price for an online product or service? How can it be determined? Will consumers actually pay it? In marketing, price refers to what people are prepared to give up, or sacrifice, in order to own a particular product or use a service. The price that consumers are willing to pay for a product represents what are they prepared to exchange for it and, given that the medium of exchange in developed economies is money, most pricing discussions focus exclusively on financial components. This chapter, however, takes a broader view and begins with a discussion of the total price concept. The **total price concept** recognises that money is only one component of the perceived cost of purchase from the consumer's perspective. In addition it takes into consideration all other costs, such as the **social and psychological costs**, associated with a purchase. This model is particularly useful when looking at what consumers are prepared to pay for products online and for online services, given the level of perceived risk and the uncertainty involved in online purchases.

While the same basic principles of pricing apply both online and offline, competitive pressures arc exercising a strong downward pressure on prices charged by Internet-based organisations. Comparative shopping has been simplified and this has led to a stronger emphasis by consumers on price minimisation. Although some costs to the company are reduced in the online environment, many companies are struggling to make a profit via Internet sales. After an examination of the pressures being exerted on Internet-based companies, specific pricing strategies, tactics and issues are discussed including the perceived link between price and quality, methods of payments and the total cost of online purchases.

It is important to note that this chapter is concerned with the strategic issues surrounding the pricing element of the marketing mix in the online environment. Its role is not to review basic economic approaches to pricing or provide computational guides to setting explicit prices. Rather it discusses strategies and tactics for pricing activities that support and complement the organisation's strategic marketing position.

Total price concept

Price has been variously defined by economists and marketers but, in its simplest terms, price is 'something of value that is exchanged for something else' (McColl-Kennedy & Kiel 2000). What is valued by the consumer and organisations in modern economies is most commonly money. However, to confine this discussion of pricing strategies to purely financial terms is to take an overly simplistic view of this element of the marketing mix.

Price has two key components. First is the financial element which is represented by the amount of money an individual will pay to use a service or own a physical good. The monetary element of price is the easiest element of a competitor's marketing mix to analyse, track and copy. The second component of price consists of all other 'costs' that the consumer perceives to be involved in the transaction. These costs are intangible, difficult to replicate and must be managed in conjunction with the financial components to develop an overall pricing mix. Without an understanding of the total price concept, firms become too reliant on the purely financial aspects of the exchange and open themselves up to price-based competition commonly referred to as 'price wars'. Early in the days of subscriber-based content on the Internet, too many of the start-up companies based their price as equal to or higher than the offline equivalent product. These pricing strategies failed because they were priced on the basis of the value they believed they were offering (convenience, speed) and not the costs that the consumer felt they were paying (uncertainty, poor reception, inadequate coverage of specific areas of local content) above the monetary price.

Total price concept: A consumer perspective

Different writers identify different components of the total price concept, and occasionally will agree with each other to form a common set of elements. What is important for marketing professionals to remember is that price involves more than just financial components as total price concept represents both financial amount paid plus the sum of all other 'social' prices. Fine (1990, p. 331) represented the total price with the following formula, known as the Compensatory Price Formulation:

$$P = p_m + \sum_{i=1}^{n} p_i$$

where P is the total price, p_m is the monetary or financial component and p_i represents the set of social prices associated with the transaction.

By broadening the concept of price to include these additional elements, marketers are able to develop suitable pricing mixes to attract different target markets. A major criticism of this particular formula is its assumption of additivity, an assumption that can only hold if each of the subcategories of price are independent. In reality this is rarely the case. The value of the model is not how it describes reality, but how it helps expand the thinking of marketers when it comes to setting prices in the real world. Money is not the sole element of price, and this model brings the different non-financial components into focus so that they can be addressed in pricing strategies.

Fine (1990) identifies four key categories of these **intrinsic social prices**: time, effort, lifestyle and psyche.

Time

Time expended in a particular consumption activity represents benefits or opportunities forgone. For example, if purchasing a product online means that the consumer has to wait two weeks for delivery rather than acquiring the product immediately, they have lost the benefit of owning that particular item during that waiting period. The great challenge between online and offline shopping has always been based around the offline shopper being able to take the product home, while the online shopper waits for the product to come around to their house. In contrast, intangible goods purchased online can often be made available instantly, such as subscription web sites (www.thewell.com), domain name registration (www.npsis.com) or product downloads from a site (www.pilotgear.com). Delays associated with shipping products ordered online will usually be minimal, although the time delay needs to be factored to prevent the organisation from running out of stock in the period between ordering and delivery. Where this becomes particularly perverse is where an intangible good is ordered over the Internet (software) and is delivered in a tangible format (CD). Many major league business to business software packages can be bought online, registered online but not downloaded or delivered through that medium. For some products, such as Microsoft Office which takes up four CDs, this makes some form of sense. It may well take just as long to download three gigabytes of data as it would for the CDs to arrive in the mail.

Effort

Downloading three gigabytes of data is more than just a time cost, given the effort that would be required to ensure all of the data were downloaded correctly, checked and then installed. Personal effort or input into the exchange in effect represents a bartering of individual services for the final product. This effort can take many forms. In the case of online marketing it usually involves activities such as searching for information or taking on the role of 'partial employee' as you fill in your own order forms, pass on financial and personal information or engage in extended comparative shopping tactics. The greater the effort (and usually this will also involve increased time costs as part of the transaction) the greater the total price of the item will be. Considering the difference in effort costs between simply selecting goods off a shelf and paying in cash against trawling through dozens of pages of an online catalogue, entering credit card details, shipping addresses and filling out a registration form, plus confirming the purchase by email, it is a wonder online retailing took off at all. The amount of effort required for online transactions needs to be traded off against, oddly enough, convenience and time. The sale can be made if the effort price is right; for example, if the convenience of late night electronic banking outweighs the complications of establishing the account.

Lifestyle

Where purchasing a product involves a significant change in some aspect of the individual's personal habits or lifestyle, the perceived costs involved in that exchange increase. This is particularly relevant for online transactions. While many people welcome the opportunity to do banking online, for others the change in lifestyle that the loss of personal interactions with individual tellers represents is significant. The perceived costs of losing those personal relationships is, for many people, a cost greater than the benefits of 24–7 access to banking services. As more and more online customers become used to depending on the Internet for sales and banking transactions, Internet marketing is becoming a more mainstream part of people's lifestyles. Shopping online for clothing (www.katies.com.au) will remove the social aspect of the shopping activity and, consequently, the benefits received from the social interaction must be compensated by the total price of the online shopping.

Psyche

This element of the total price concept relates to the idea of perceived social risk and represents the potential loss of self-esteem, privacy or pride or any aspect of the product purchase which could adversely impact on the individual's self-esteem. Translated into the online environment such **psychic costs** include the fear that the transaction will not be secure and that credit card details may be stolen. Other psychic costs include:

- the loss of privacy which occurs as a result of online transactions and which could lead to unwanted emails and tracking of purchasing behaviour
- the fear of ridicule from friends or associates who themselves have adverse opinions about purchasing online
- the fear that transactions may be fraudulent and that the paid for items may not arrive.

Any of these social costs may be great enough, either alone or in combination, to deter the potential consumer from purchasing online regardless of the financial cost.

Consumer-oriented research will assist in determining what other non-financial aspects are important in different purchasing situations and it then becomes the role of the marketer to understand how all these forces interact and to develop strategies to minimise these non-financial costs in the eyes of the consumer. Ultimately, what consumers are looking for is value and it is the value perception of the overall product that will determine the price that the buyer is willing to pay and the seller willing to accept.

Total price concept in electronic markets

As more businesses and industries move into the online environment, it is interesting to compare the perceived costs of doing business in each environment from both the buyer and seller perspective. Buyers typically try to minimise the price of any given product so that their overall purchasing power increases without them needing to create additional wealth. Sellers try to exert upward pressures on price to ensure that they are able to operate profitably and survive in the longer term and maximise return on each item sold. The ultimate aim of all marketing activity is to create mutually beneficial exchanges between marketers and consumers where the price is right for both parties. The relative importance of each of the elements of price will influence whether individual buyers will head to the Internet in search of better purchasing power, or stay offline and confirm their decision to remain active primarily in the traditional environment.

If the perceived costs of purchasing a particular product online outweigh those of purchasing in a traditional retail environment then it would not be strategic for the suppliers to move the bulk of their retail activities online. The popularity of the Internet and e-commerce in the street press has led many organisations to work to their weakness by shifting a focus to the online world that is high cost to both them and their customers. Over time the relative perceived costs and benefits of purchasing in the different environments will vary and need to be monitored so that firms can optimise the relative mix of products available online and offline. Audio distribution over the

Internet was originally too high in time and effort costs when the Web was first opened to the general public. With the rapid advances in audio compression, and the popularity of the mp3 file type, audio can be successfully retailed online as a pure digital product (www.mp3.com). In contrast, video has not developed at a similar pace, and is still not within the appropriate total price range for the marketplace. It is expected that with the continued development of better video software, and more consumer access to fast Internet connections, the online video market will also evolve into a viable online business area.

Strader and Shaw (1997, 1999) compare how perceptions of price differ for consumers between traditional and electronic markets across the following price components:

- *product price* (P_C) — the sum of the production costs, coordination costs and profits of the value chain that provides the product or service
- *search costs* (SC_C) — the time, effort and money involved in searching for a seller who has the product required at an acceptable price with acceptable features and quality
- *risk costs* (RC_C) — the costs involved in minimising transaction risk as well as the costs associated with losing value in a transaction
- *distribution costs* (DC_C) — the costs associated with physically moving the product from the seller to the buyer
- *sales tax* (T_C) — self-explanatory, but can include import tariffs, local, state and national taxes
- *market costs* (MC_C) — the costs associated with participating in a market.

A comparison of their findings of relative costs between markets is given in table 11.1.

Table 11.1 Comparison of costs to the consumer

Cost	Traditional market	Electronic market
Product cost	Higher	Lower
Search cost	Higher	Lower
Risk cost	Lower	Higher
Distribution cost	Lower	Higher
Sales tax	Higher	Lower
Market cost	Lower	Higher

Source: Strader, T. J. and Shaw, M. J. 1999, 'Consumer cost differences for traditional and Internet markets', *Internet Research: Electronic Networking Applications and Policy*, vol. 9, no. 2, p. 83.

Consumers perceive the online products to be cheaper in social price terms with regards to time and effort costs but more expensive in psychic costs. Strader and Shaw (1999) see two key marketing strategy implications. First, current online purchasers may be considered as a 'psychographically' distinct segment that is prepared to take risks and which should, therefore, be treated differently to the traditional market. Second, if the organisation wishes to either broaden the base of its online market, or persuade existing clients to do business via the organisation's web pages, the main focus of their combined pricing and promotional strategy should be directed at reducing perceived risk, not necessarily at reducing the financial cost of the transaction.

Shopping online may not necessarily be primarily concerned with cost, therefore the mad rush displayed by organisations to offer products at cost or below cost are actually unnecessary. Some online companies may even be able to turn a profit if they offered convenience and risk reduction to their customers rather than slashing their prices.

Pressures on Internet pricing

The perceived, and in some cases, actual lower costs of service provision in the online environment are creating a general downward pressure on prices. Part of the problems faced by the '**clicks and order**' regime of online trading stores like Amazon.com and CDNow.com is that they are perceived as being lower-overhead operations due to their lack of physical locations. The minor glitch in this view of reality is that these organisations ship tangible goods, which means they need extremely tangible warehousing and logistics chains. Amazon.com needs to stockpile popular selling books in the same manner as any other book store and consequently faces the same physical costs as other stores, without the safety valve release of having several hundred chain store shops to use for storing the books. All the average consumer can see of Amazon.com is their web site and consequently do not perceive them as a physical wholesaler.

However, customer perceptions alone are not moving the market price downwards; there are several reasons for this pressure to reduce prices in the online environment.

Lower costs to the seller

Despite the perception that online delivery is cheaper and that online store fronts by their virtual nature will result in lower costs to the company, the savings for Internet-based companies are not uniform. Strader and Shaw (1999) examined the seller costs in both traditional and online markets with the following results.

As can be seen from table 11.2, while being an Internet-based organisation may result in lower prices for some products due to the actual lower costs of production and distribution, these savings vary across industries. Product type has a significant impact on whether or not the move online will result in actual financial savings or in savings of the intangible components of prices such as time and effort. The only product types with consistently lower costs are those that are information-based products or those that can be digitised, as discussed in chapter 8.

Table 11.2 Comparison of costs to the seller

Cost	Traditional market	Electronic market	Electronic market (digital products)
Advertising cost	Higher	Lower	Lower
Overhead cost	Higher	Lower	Lower
Inventory cost	Higher	Higher	Lower
Production cost	Higher	Higher	Lower
Distribution cost	Lower	Higher	Lower

Source: Strader, T. J. and Shaw, M. J. 1999, 'Consumer cost differences for traditional and Internet markets', *Internet Research: Electronic Networking Applications and Policy*, vol. 9, no. 2, p. 83.

Cost savings for online companies can be realised through a range of alternative business practices, including the following:

- *Reductions in overhead costs.* Overhead costs can be reduced not only because online stores do not have to rent or construct an actual building for customers (www.thinkgeek.com). In addition, costs can be reduced by not holding inventory (www.ebay.com), having lower staffing needs, being able to choose locations that are cheap and convenient to the organisation rather than convenient to the customer (www.auran.com) and strategic partnerships with geographically dispersed suppliers (www.gnu.org) (Strauss & Frost 1999).

- *Increasing the role of the customer.* Getting customers to do their own transaction administration online as 'partial employees' can save the business time and money (Hofacker 2000). The Australian Taxation Office (www.ato.gov.au), as well as other tax collection agencies such as the US Internal Revenue Services (www.irs.gov), offers an electronic tax return submission system. Mougayar (1997) estimates that the cost of producing and processing an invoice electronically is approximately 10 per cent of the cost of traditional methods and, similarly, the cost of customer service requests can be reduced by approximately 75 per cent by directing inquiries online. Interactive help functions (support.microsoft.com) can reduce the need for customer support lines and call centres.

- *Producing and distributing promotional material online.* The production and distribution of catalogues and other promotional materials is demonstrably cheaper online. Once the initial brochure has been designed and placed online, the cost of accessing and sending the information contained in it is negligible. Similarly, minor changes to content can be adjusted at costs far below those incurred for the hard copy equivalent (Strauss & Frost 1999).

Environmental turbulence

The speed of technological advance and the ever-changing nature of the technological environment adds to the downward pressure on prices, given that what was cutting-edge technology on Tuesday seems to be obsolete by

Friday. Moore's Law of Computing which, in general terms, equates to computers doubling in speed and capacity every year (there are several variations, some slow down in the equation and numerous other technicalities are involved as well) which means that anything that is current today is in the process of becoming obsolete for tomorrow. Given that the Internet exists solely in computer-based environments, the progressive gains in processing power, storage space and decrease in cost indicate that the Internet itself is rapidly developing in a very unstable manner. Unlike most environments, as the 'size' of the Internet expands, it can actually begin to take up less space because storage technologies fit more into less space. In other words, it can become bigger, more complex, more intense and develop more features in the next 12 months than it has in the last six months.

Traditionally, in more stable environments, manufacturers sought to recover their research and development costs in the early stages of the product life cycle by using a **price skimming** strategy. This approach allowed a high initial price to be charged until the top end of the market was saturated before gradually reducing the price over time. Computers have displayed a perverse tendency to remain constant in price while their capacity, power and usefulness increased at a dramatic rate. With retail prices holding steady, resale values of computers plummet rapidly as the next generation of computer is released with the same market price and a significant increase in capacity.

Contemporary high technology markets are characterised by an unusually large degree of environmental turbulence. Specifically, product life cycles in such industries are becoming shorter and product performance capabilities are increasing, both in absolute and relative terms compared to price (Smith, Sinha, Lancioni & Forman 1999). Consequently it is difficult for organisations operating in these markets to develop or pursue stable long-term pricing policies.

Product variations, or new versions of existing products such as software, appear regularly thus making prior versions obsolete, usually within months of the initial launch. Consumer resistance to paying high prices for the first iteration of a product has been exacerbated by this trend, leading to the belief that the current technology has too limited a lifespan to be regarded as a worthwhile investment. The fact that these new versions of the product do, in fact, offer better value in that they represent enhanced performance means that consumers are less likely to pay top prices in the first instance but wait instead for the perceived, inevitable fall following the newest release. Even in the distribution of low-cost, no-cost software such as Linux (www.linux.org), users may prefer to delay the adoption of the cutting-edge software (greater capacity, higher effort cost and higher perceived risk of crash) for the lower social cost older versions (lower perceived risk, lower effort).

Taxation issues

Currently, Internet-based product sales and services are mostly tax exempt due to the fact that the medium reaches across national and international borders. There are currently no universal sales or other tax laws which can cover such transactions, although some individual states (notably California) and countries have found a way to introduce taxation mechanisms. Consequently, there

It must be noted here that neither culture believes in intellectual theft, even if some people mistakenly tout the banner of gift culture when they engage in intellectual theft. At the very core of the gift movement is the right to choose to sell or give away the idea. Giving away someone else's intellectual property is not a part of the gift culture, nor will it ever be part. This illegal activity gives no value to the community because the giver is not delivering their efforts. Instead, they are trading the stolen efforts of others and are not producing anything new or valuable in the eyes of the gift culture.

The gift economy and the tradition of routing around damage often mean that providers of pay-for-use services face stiff competition from their free counterparts. In order to survive in this environment, the pay-per-use systems must provide greater value than the free competitor, either in effort, utility, reward or outcome, as they cannot compete on the financial price. If the service, product or good is of sufficient value, the consumer will be willing to pay a financial price for it.

Universal pricing knowledge

Better access to pricing information means that potential customers are able to engage in local, national and international comparison shopping at a minimal financial cost. Whereas in the past pricing information was difficult and expensive to obtain, the existence of shopping agents such as PriceScan (www.pricescan.com) and FIDO: the Shopping Doggie (www.shopfido.com) allow consumers to access price-based information about a range of products with ease. In this sort of environment the lowest price operator usually gets the sale (Peattie & Peters 1997; Strauss & Frost 1999; Reedy, Schullo & Zimmerman 2000).

From a marketing management perspective the global nature of the Internet exacerbates the downward pressure of pricing. Consumers no longer confine their information search to local suppliers who have borne the cost of transportation, taxes and other duties on items. Consequently, differential international pricing strategies are undermined as world's lowest cost becomes the standard by which local prices are measured. However, lowest price alone is not enough to guarantee success online — given the international nature of the market, low-priced competitors may be priced out of the market by their distribution costs so that more expensive local competitors still end up with the sale.

While the existence of this sort of information and service is empowering for consumers, it must be constantly borne in mind that the same information is equally available to competitors. Traditional approaches to pricing need to be re-thought in light of this almost perfect access to information. (Reedy, Schullo & Zimmerman 2000). More than ever, competitive advantage needs to be based on more than low prices. Clear product differentiation and quality information to supplement the product or service appear to be two effective means of assisting in the reduction of price sensitivity among online consumers in this increasingly transparent and competitive environment (Alba et al. 1997).

Setting pricing objectives

Pricing objectives refer to what the marketer wants to achieve strategically through the setting of a specific price level. Successful marketing practice dictates that these objectives should be consistent with the overall strategic, financial and positioning objectives of the organisation as a whole. In other words, setting prices and price objectives is not undertaken in isolation from the management of the rest of the organisation. Rather, prices should support the overall positioning and other strategic activities of the firm.

The key principles driving pricing objectives remain constant whether the organisation is operating primarily online, in a traditional marketing environment or uses a combination of both. Consequently, this section will provide a review of key underpinning principles rather than focus on the formulae for setting price levels to achieve these objectives. For details on turning these principles into specific price-setting techniques, consult any good basic marketing text.

There are three key categories of pricing objectives:

- financial objectives — monetary considerations for price setting
- market-based objectives — strategic and long-term tactical decisions as to how price will be used for gaining and defending market share
- psychological objectives — relate to the message sent to the consumer by the price.

Financial objectives

Financial objectives can further be subdivided into cost-based objectives versus profit-oriented objectives. In the context of the move into online commerce, an additional consideration in the setting of final prices to the consumer based on financial objectives is whether these objectives are short or long term in nature. As outlined above, many investors in Internet-based businesses are looking for long-term returns on their investments and, consequently, are prepared to wear short-term losses in the hope of generating long-term profits.

Cost-based objectives

The most common, and conceptually simple, financial objective of pricing is to cover the costs of production. Cost-plus pricing, where costs are covered and a percentage or dollar amount is added to each unit of output to contribute to profit, is the most common form of pricing used by new and small businesses (Carson et al. 1998). This is particularly relevant in the online environment. With relatively low barriers to entry, the Internet provides an ideal environment for small and start-up businesses.

Despite the conceptual simplicity, implementing a cost-plus objective has a number of limitations of particular relevance for companies operating in the online environment. The most problematic issues facing the cost price marketer are the accurate determination of the final cost of individual items in advance, given the flexibility of costs of individual components, combined with the difficulty in attributing joint costs to specific items (Baker, Graham, Harker & Harker 1998). Even where it is possible to accurately determine and allocate costs, further limitations of this approach include the fact that it ignores consumer demand, the influence of competitors, economies of scale as production increases and does not distinguish between variable and sunk costs (Winker 1991).

Attributing specific costs to intangible products is more difficult than attributing such costs to tangible products (Lovelock, Patterson & Walker 1998). Given that a large proportion of Internet-based products are services or information products, this limitation is of particular relevance. The ease with which services and information can be delivered online frequently leads to an underestimation of the true costs associated with the development and delivery of such services. The cost of intellectual property invested into online services and products is frequently overlooked in that an idea can be seen as low cost to produce, although in reality, it may have taken hundreds of person hours to develop into a workable application.

Profit-oriented objectives

Profit-oriented pricing objectives take one of two key forms. Either the intention of the organisation is to achieve a specific target return on investment or it is to maximise overall profits from the product to the organisation. Both of these approaches require marketers to be confident about the assumptions they make regarding both consumer and competitor behaviour.

Return on investment objectives require the price setters to decide on how long it should take to recoup investment costs before generating a clear profit. The skill lies in balancing the short-term needs of the organisation and the long-term strategic benefits of bearing a loss for a longer period in anticipation of a greater profit later (Brassington & Pettitt 1997). Profit maximisation differs in that rather than seeking a set return or profit it aims to make the most money possible. Despite popular perception, this does not necessarily involve setting a high price. The final price set will depend on a combination of elasticity of demand for the product, availability of substitutes and consumer preferences (McCarthy, Perrault & Quester 1997).

Given the volatility of the e-commerce environment, the success of profit-oriented approaches to date have been limited. However, one area where cost recovery has worked is in the domain of software pricing, where low-cost, high-volume sales have returned significant rewards for shareware software creators.

Downward pressures on pricing have extended the likely period of non-profit-making marketing activity. Even well-known firms and established online businesses such as Amazon.com continue to operate under loss-making conditions with the expectation that eventually the return on investment will be realised and profits will start to accrue. The zone of tolerance for investors is being tested and pressure for profits is becoming more intense.

Market-based objectives

While clearly the long-term survival of organisations does depend on their ability to perform financially, the objectives underpinning the pricing strategies of specific products or product lines do not necessarily have to be grounded in either cost or profit objectives. Prices determined according to market-based objectives can be based either on a desire to achieve a certain market share or alternatively can be driven by consumer expectations.

Market share objectives

Market share objectives are aimed at either penetrating a new market to gain significant market share in a relatively short time period or maintaining market share in a competitive environment and pricing products to minimise the adverse impact of new entrants. Loosely translated, keeping the prices low tends to lock out competitors and encourages brand loyalty to the first mover in the market.

Market share objectives normally apply when the market is highly competitive and consists of a relatively large number of similar offerings. When market share objectives are used as a defensive mechanism in oligopolistic environments consisting of a few large competitors, it is important to ensure that the resultant pricing practices do not arise as a result of collusion or any other illegal practice. The difficulty faced in oligarchy scenarios is that the movement of price by one of only three companies is usually matched quickly by the other two to defend their market share, creating a situation of unintended collusion. Microsoft (www.microsoft.com) was forced to give away its browser software for free when the other competitor groups such as Netscape (www.netscape.com) and Lynx (www.browser.org) continued to release their browser software for free.

While new industries and companies tend to rely on cost-based pricing policies, players in more mature markets tend to align themselves more often with market share objectives. The original Internet service providers, for example, based their pricing strategies primarily on financial objectives and cost-based issues. In the current environment, building and maintaining market share is a higher priority with pricing packages costing less and new entrants emphasising a combination of low cost and high service. One of the main problems with market share objectives is that they have a tendency to lead to price wars. In such cases, it is the bigger and more established providers who win as they usually have the cash reserves to back short-term loss.

Consumer expectations and reference pricing

Taking a true marketing orientation requires firms to balance their pricing objectives (organisation-oriented objectives) with the needs of their consumers. Frequently consumers will have a '**reference price**' in their mind as to what they believe a product or service to be worth and will use this as the basis of determining whether or not to go ahead with a trial purchase. Adaptation level theory explains how individuals apply past prices to new situations to form cognitive reference points against which future prices can be judged (Betts & Goldrick 1996).

The reference price serves as a central point of consumer decision making and evaluation activities (Monger & Feinberg 1997). If a consumer develops a reference price of $10 for an item and is charged $15, they will be dissatisfied with the purchase. If, on the other hand, they are able to purchase the same product for $7, they will be extremely satisfied. Reference prices are determined on the basis of consumer experience with identical or at least similar products. Where there are a number of close substitutes, it is relatively easy for consumers to develop appropriate reference prices and, in highly competitive situations, it is common for organisations to simply meet market price. Consumers are becoming increasingly sophisticated in their determination of appropriate reference prices in the online environment as competitive pressures increase.

Consumer price knowledge is based on a combination of consumer characteristics and product category. Despite the popularity of segmenting the market on demographic variables, literature in this area is inconclusive. Estelami (1998) found no significant differences in consumer price knowledge on the basis of demographic factors including age, race and gender, a finding which is supported by Krishna et al. (1991) and Wakefield and Inman (1993). Other authors such as Calantone and Sawyer (1978), Kotler (1997) and Uncles and Ehrenberg (1990), however, have found links between demographic variables and pricing knowledge.

In terms of product categories, clear trends have emerged with consumers showing greater accuracy in price estimation for more familiar products and essential household appliances such as televisions and refrigerators than for less familiar categories such as recreational and luxury items (Estelami 1998). This finding has significant implications for online marketers in that if a consumer already has a set reference price for an item, it is difficult to vary too much from this. It would be expected that online reference prices for specific products would vary from those expected in traditional environments and also, given the downwards pressures previously discussed, be lower than average. As consumers become more familiar with online purchasing, a new set of reference prices may emerge. Reference pricing could therefore be seen as an additional pressure contributing to price competition online.

An important point to remember about reference pricing is that what constitutes an appropriate price varies considerably between individuals, particularly for intangible services. While there are similar clusters across the market, there is no single reference price for any particular product or service. Similarly reference prices have been found to vary considerably according to the mode of payment used (Monger & Feinberg 1997). This point is of particular relevance to online marketers and will be discussed in greater detail in a later section. A further issue in relation to reference pricing is that, given that reference prices are developed on the basis of consumer experience, it is possible to significantly change consumer reference prices over time. These varying levels can work to the detriment of the organisation if pricing is considered as an isolated function rather than as a support for the total marketing strategy. This is particularly evident when retailers engage in regular sales or price reductions. By regularly offering products at lower prices, consumers change their point of reference to the extent that 'normal' prices seem excessive in comparison (Betts & Goldrick 1996).

With all the variables involved, a marketer requires detailed primary market research to fully understand what constitutes an appropriate reference price within a specific target market. Simply putting a $2.99 on a service and hoping for the best is not the optimum pricing strategy for the new frontier.

Psychological objectives

Each of the categories of pricing objectives discussed has a strong objective base. Even reference prices which can be more flexible are grounded in prior consumer experiences and expectations have been developed on objective grounds. In this section we will look at the influence of subjective, psychological objectives as a contributing factor in determining overall pricing strategies and levels.

Positioning and the price–quality relationship

Where consumers are unfamiliar with a product or if they believe that they lack the personal expertise to objectively judge its quality, many will rely on price as a guide. For many people a high price is indicative of a high quality product. This phenomenon has been used in marketing in the positioning and pricing strategies of prestige goods for centuries. It is a pricing technique that is particularly suited to products where the core benefit being sought is highly intangible. For example, it is common in the cosmetics industry and for image-oriented products such as luxury clothes and cars. Prestige pricing differs from other high-price strategies such as price skimming in that its ultimate success depends on its continuity. It is a long-term strategy designed to support a position in the market of quality and scarcity.

Prestige-oriented pricing is effective only when direct comparisons between the qualities of one firm's offering with another are difficult. This is particularly true of expert services and image-oriented luxury products. Within the context of Internet-based marketing, the use of high prices to support a prestige positioning strategy is fairly limited. It occurs primarily in relation to Internet support services, such as web page designers or consultants who rely on intangible benefits and have a pool of expertise that it is difficult for non-experts to accurately rate.

In terms of companies which are selling online, the prestige pricing approach can be maintained if this is integral to the general positioning strategy of the firm. Porsche or Louis Vuitton (www.vuitton.com), for example, would compromise their traditional market position if they were to use an alternative pricing approach in the online environment and start to compete with other manufacturers of similar products on the basis of price. Agents of these companies, however, may find it beneficial to compete on some aspects of price relative to other dealers of identical products to the extent that such competition complies with their distribution agreements.

Minimisation and exploitation of non-financial price components

Explicitly acknowledging that the total cost to the consumer in any transaction consists of more than just the financial component gives marketers greater freedom in developing their pricing mix. If, after research into the target market, it is found that there are specific psychological costs which are preventing the potential consumer from purchasing online, then part of the pricing mix needs to include a strategy designed to minimise these costs. Alternatively it may be determined that consumers are prepared to pay a premium online to avoid the perceived additional non-financial costs of conducting identical transactions in a traditional environment. Understanding the needs of the different segments of the market may lead to a multi-segment pricing strategy for the organisation.

Online retailing is one area which has had mixed success overall. Taking grocery shopping as an example (www.greengrocer.com.au), the non-financial costs of loss of control and choice and the fear that systems may not be secure are sufficient deterrents. Even if the financial cost is identical to shopping at a local supermarket, not being able to see and touch the produce in advance outweighs the other benefits for certain target markets. At the same time there is a distinct market segment which values time and perceives the additional costs of time lost and inconvenience as being sufficient deterrents to traditional shopping activities that they are prepared to pay a premium to shop online.

To appeal to the first group, online retailers must reassure potential customers that systems are secure and offer some sort of guarantee as far as security and quality of produce are concerned. It may also be necessary to offer lower financial prices as an incentive to move online. For the second segment which is positively predisposed towards the concept no special incentives are required — only that the organisation deliver on its promises and provide a realistic alternative to traditional shopping activities.

This example also serves to reinforce the point that there is no generic market for firms moving online. Determining what aspects of price are most important to different market segments requires detailed market research and the determination of specific pricing strategies to meet the unique needs of each group.

Pricing strategies

Pricing strategies have two main functions:

■ to support the overall marketing mix and positioning strategy of the organisation

■ to assist in achieving the organisation's objectives, both financial and non-financial.

Overall, companies have three main options in pricing strategies. They may choose to enter the market:

■ below the average price charged for similar products or services

■ around the average price charged for similar products or services

■ above the average price charged for similar products or services.

In deciding on the 'correct' pricing strategy it is important to remember that, as is the case with all strategic decisions, there is no clear formula that will decide what the 'best' approach is. It is this strategic aspect of marketing management that requires flexibility and judgement based on the information available. Within the context of a book such as this it is possible only to discuss alternatives for pricing options — it is not possible to be prescriptive. As long as the final pricing strategy and pricing mix used achieve the two functions highlighted above, it can be seen as appropriate.

The determination of final price levels is influenced by the cost of producing the actual product or service in question. Once basic costs have been covered, the price charged to consumers will be a reflection of a combination of the firm's positioning strategy and the other elements of the marketing mix. While the role of the marketing mix is to support the positioning strategy, each element adds to the overall costs that must be covered by the price.

The role of price as a mechanism for supporting the overall position and its integration into the overall marketing strategy is best illustrated by example. For a luxury item like Chanel perfumes (www.chanel.com) a high price will not only cover the cost of the manufacture of a superior quality product but also ensures that any loss of economies of scale experienced due to selective distribution policies and the cost of targeted promotional activities are covered. At the same time, the image of quality and exclusivity is maintained for both the target market and aspirational markets. Similarly, highly accessible brands such as Bonds (www.bonds.com.au) charge a price commensurate with their image as a family brand which simultaneously ensures that all costs of production, distribution and promotion are covered.

Regardless of whether an organisation is primarily profit-oriented or not for profit, all have financial goals which must be met. Pricing of specific products and services helps to meet these financial objectives. As previously discussed, in commercial organisations these goals relate to profit. In many not-for-profit organisations the function of price is to assist in the partial or full cost recovery of activities. The Scouting movement (www.scouts.co.uk), for example, charges a participation fee to cover ongoing costs plus additional fees for special activities such as camps.

When incorporating a web site into the overall marketing activities of the organisation, the explicit cost of developing and maintaining that site becomes a further element in the determination of the final price. The existence of a web site may add to overall costs or help reduce them depending on the role of the site in relation to the overall operations of the company and the willingness of clients to use it. For example, a web site that is primarily a source of information and an additional promotional element will add to overall costs (www.comsec.com.au). If, however, the web site is designed so that customers can take an active role in service delivery by processing orders (www.wal mart.com) or undertaking specific transactions (www.lloydstsb.co.uk) then it is likely that the web site will ultimately deliver both cost savings and a reduction in prices. Regardless of whether the site adds to costs or helps reduce them, a full understanding of the cost of development and maintenance is needed so that it can be incorporated into the overall pricing strategy of the company.

Issues in pricing for online activities

There are three key issues in pricing that the online marketer must take into consideration which may vary in importance from those of concern to traditional marketers. These are:

- the nature of the product being priced
- the total cost of the product to the consumer (explicit versus hidden costs)
- international currency transactions and the impact of different payment systems.

Nature of the product

As discussed in chapter 8, the exact nature of the online element of the product mix is often difficult to define. However, effective pricing strategies, particularly if the expectation is for online products to contribute to cost recovery, are dependent on a clear understanding of what the firm's online product is. To make a difficult situation even more complex, the bundle of promotion, distribution and product for intangible online goods and services is often inseparable to the point that the company has to ask if people are paying money to access an advertisement, read a catalogue or receive a service.

The simplest case is where the online product is a tangible good and the Internet is being used primarily as an alternative distribution channel such as the case of Compaq Online (www.compaq.com). In such cases the price of the product can be based on the normal retail price, with variations according to the aim of the online presence. If the aim is to move consumers from traditional shopping activities to online activities, then lowering the entrance price for shopping online is the appropriate strategy as an incentive to change behaviour. Southwest Airlines (www.southwest.com) offers all of its discount tickets for sale only through the web site to encourage passengers to use the online booking service. Similarly, lower costs can be used as a risk reducer to encourage use of the online distribution channel for those who are concerned about security or other aspects of online retailing (Van den Poel & Leunis 1999; see also chapter 12). If, however, the site simply exists as a convenience factor and as an adjunct to the main business of the firm, then the same pricing levels should be used to reinforce the image of the company in both environments (www.colesonline.com.au).

The situation becomes more complex where the nature of the product is not clearly defined. Information products, while particularly suited to the online environment, need to be priced in such a way that consumers believe that information acquired this way is good value for money. Newspapers, for example, cost around $1 to purchase in hard copy. The main benefits of a hard copy newspaper are as follows. It can be read in sections, skimmed for an overview of key issues, taken on a bus to read, is available at different times of the day as required and can be used afterwards for a variety of other things such as packing and wrapping. Online news information on the other hand is able to be updated throughout the day, does not require disposal and is searchable for key terms and stories. Competition among media outlets, however, dictate that most news information available online is free. Despite earlier attempts to charge for online use, most newspapers are available without cost to the consumer (and are a lot harder to use for wrapping fragile email!). What this demonstrates is that despite a number of demonstrable key benefits for online newspapers, these are not valued sufficiently by the public for them to part with a dollar a day to use them. Offline prices cannot always be used as a guide for online services, particularly when the two goods appear similar on the surface, but offer fundamentally different value to the consumer.

Similarly purely online services are difficult to price. The expectation of free information and service makes it difficult for purely online services to make money online. Prices are low and there is strong consumer resistance to paying for information so that a large amount of activity must be available free. It is really only when the service or information becomes highly customised to meet individual client needs that traditional cost recovery pricing methods can be employed.

FOCUS ON
Strategy

Shareware pricing and the gift economy

One of the many apparent paradoxes of the Internet is how free software can be profitable for the individual or organisation who gave it away for free. Part of the software distribution models in existence are the shareware licence agreements where the author of the program makes the software freely available for no cost, but instead asks for a donation of around $5 to $10 if the software proves useful.

The pricing system is based on the idea that high volume sales at low prices can reap higher returns than pricing at the market expectation for software around the $50 to $100 price tag.

The shareware principle operates in two distinct forms. First, shareware software positions itself in the gift economy as a display of programming skill and prowess which can be recognised with payments of social price in terms of recognition and intrinsic psychic rewards. Second, it offers specific valued digital goods, with little or no physical product, for a very low margin. By providing tailored goods that meet a market niche, the program offers high value for low financial costs.

Related to, but slightly more extreme, is the freeware licence system where the software is financially free, but requires a token action (e.g. people who download postcardware send a postcard to the author of the software) or support of a cause favoured by the author (e.g. Shonenware at www.proxomitron.cjb.net). These pricing systems are heavily influenced by the gift culture and place a significant value on social costs as a pricing mechanism.

In addition to the shareware model of pricing, MP3.com (www.mp3.com) offers an alternative view of the sponsored gift economy. Artists wishing to use the MP3.com distribution mechanisms are required to make a minimum of one of their tracks available for free download before the band is accepted on the site. In addition, the organisation encourages the bands to sell low cost CDs and provide tracks for subscriber-based music channels, and runs 'payback for playback' promotions where artists receive money based on the extent to which their free materials were played by the general public. Again, the gift economy of the Internet is respected by the freely available product, and underwritten by the MP3.com decision to financially back their artists who distribute free music.

Given the purely information-based nature of online music, MP3.com have exploited the consumer's desire for low-cost/no-cost products, while offering mechanisms of payment (subscription channels, CDs) and tailoring the price to match the value-to-cost ratio demanded by the market.

When dealing with both information products and services online, marketers need to develop internal policies as to how charges will be made. For example, should the cost relate to the time taken to perform the service or access the information or should it be done on a size of final outcome basis? To simplify the process many organisations choose to use a price lining approach where distinct levels of price are set to reflect approximate levels of effort, time and outcomes rather than try to determine exact costs. For example, instead of charging a dollar per byte of memory for an information product, set amounts of $20, $30 or $50 may be set within which upper limits of memory are set. This is a popular approach to use when it comes to the pricing of Internet access where individuals can buy packages of time and web space.

Total cost to the consumer

Related to the previous point is the need to consider not just what the online price is, but what the total cost to the consumer will be. Comparison shopping tends to reflect only the online cash price offered, and none of the supporting costs. Where the product is not based on information, the total cost of the product to the consumer will also include a handling and postage charge, plus costs incurred by shipping times. What may be seen on the surface as being a bargain for the consumer could end up costing substantially more than it would from a trip to the local retail outlet. From the marketer's perspective this raises an interesting pricing issue which also, to a certain extent, has ethical implications for the company's marketing practice. Should retailers advertise the price of their product as an 'item alone' online to which packaging and delivery are added? Alternatively, should they give a single price which covers the total cost? Is it possible to anticipate all potential cost factors on shipping to establish an anticipated price?

Advertising the cost of the product without on-costs will almost always give the impression that it is cheaper to purchase online. The problem for the retailer is if the reality is very different, the consumer usually has strong cognitive dissonance, and often generates feelings of being 'ripped off' or cheated by the web site. Online marketers should consider taking a total cost approach and bundling the distribution costs in with the product cost as a way of improving customer relations and avoiding dissatisfaction among users. Distribution options and their importance in online marketing are covered in depth in chapter 12.

International currency transactions and the impact of different payment systems

One of the ongoing issues for Internet-based transactions is the continuing concern about security issues due to different payment systems. In addition, there are problems associated with pricing and conducting transactions in a global trading environment of fluctuating currency prices. Taking the international aspect first, the easy solution that many (particularly US-based traders) have taken is to limit the geographic area which they will service, either by law or by choice. These restricted transactions cancel out the global benefits of the Internet and, particularly for large organisations, cost a substantial level of international goodwill. The prime offender of internationally focused web sites with US-only policies was Geocities.com, which frequently offered special bonus deals, price discounts and competitions to its subscribers which applied only if the reader lived in America. Suffice to say, any email address holder with a non-US domain name felt left out of the promotion, particularly when country of origin was a requested part of the demographics given over when signing into the service.

The main issues which prevent new and established organisations from engaging in international transactions are related to distribution networks (to be covered in chapter 12) and developing appropriate pricing and financial transaction systems. Converting from one currency to another usually attracts a substantial banking fee which must be ultimately borne by the consumer, whether this is covered by handling charges, within the price or explicitly as the consumer converts currency. International credit cards can be valuable in this context for large traders but for the small trader or individual using auction systems such as E-bay this is not an option. E-bay does offer a credit card service to the sellers of products through the international site (www.ebay.com) but, surprisingly enough, this offer is valid to only American citizens. Similarly, MP3.com (www.mp3.com) offers a bank account service for payments which, again, is available only to residents of the US and its territories. It appears that a rough linguistic code is emerging from the Internet where international means Canada and worldwide means Canada and other nations without a shared border to America. However, until the international currency issue is resolved, the full potential of the Internet will be restricted, and even more restricted as long as major financial groups believe that America is the Internet, and that the Internet is an American territory.

For major corporations the problems of international trade can be minimised through the use of credit cards and other financial transaction systems. What is important from a marketing perspective, however, is how these different forms of transaction and payment systems impact on the overall perception of price on the part of the potential consumer. There are several mechanisms for online payments that can be used by businesses online. These are:

- *Credit cards*. The most common forms of transaction tool for online trading. Most e-commerce web systems are calibrated to accept credit card orders for a set fee. The problem emerges for the wholesaler/retailer at how high that set fee becomes, and what impact that has on the total cost of the product. This becomes more of problem for high-volume, low-cost goods where multiple transactions of a small amount of currency generate a higher fee than few larger transactions of the same value.
- *Offline transfers*. The conventional non-Internet-dependent methods of payment, including direct debit, online banking, cheques and payment services systems like Bpay (www.bpay.com.au). Although not officially sanctioned as

a respected mechanism of payment for security reasons, cash in an envelope is still a major part of small-business and person-level transactions, which are negotiated online and settled in the post.

- *Electronic cash.* Predates the Internet through the use of non-credit smart cards, Cybercash (www.cybercash.com) and digital tokens. All of these systems depend on the creation of a centrally respected authentication system to verify the cash is real, the transaction is secure and the payment is received by the supplier. Cybercash has a surprisingly high level of social risk cost associated with it when compared to credit card usage. For the most part, Cybercash has not received the widespread support it requires to be fully established as a legitimate payment mechanism. This has been due to the battle over standards, concerns on encryption and verification, and the success of credit card payment mechanisms for the bulk of online trans-actions. Digital money still seems to be in the process of reinventing (and patenting) the wheel, although developments in portable computing and mobile Internet access may increase the viability of the system as it moves off the Internet and into the real world.

- *Barter, Beenz and other things.* These represent the developments of non-cash methods of exchange on the Internet. Bartercard (www.bartercard.com) has been able to transfer its non-monetary exchange system into the online world. Similarly, Beenz (www.beenz.co.uk) offers a token-based system where users of the Beenz site can gain credits for purchasing goods and services by being part of the Beenz loyalty system. Other organisations have arranged internal currencies based on loyalty incentive schemes similar to frequent flyer points that can be cashed in for goods, or upgrades of the services available at the site such as the GeoRewards program from Geocities (www.geocities.com)

Overall, mechanisms of payment need to have the basic criteria of security, authenticity and respectability. Security is necessary to ensure that the value received from the buyer becomes legitimately held by the seller and cannot be intercepted or interfered with by a third party. Authenticity relates to the value exchange operating as it would in the offline environment so that the digital economy retains the appropriate levels of economic scarcity to secure the value of the digital unit of currency. Respectability in this aspect refers to the endorsement of the system of digital payment by offline and online financial and trade agencies. One of the major impediments on the road to digital cash has been the lack of support for a single system by competing suppliers who want proprietary ownership over the currency. If paper currency had been subjected to a similar patenting war, it is likely barter would have remained the dominant trade force.

Summary

Pricing is a major aspect in determining how people will gain value from the Internet, both as providers and consumers of services, goods and ideas online. Total price concept stands out as a method of assisting the marketer in determining how to set their price in the Internet environment. In particular, by understanding that pricing is more than just dollars for transaction, and includes psychic costs and social costs, marketers can adjust their pricing accordingly to match the needs of their target segment.

In addition, prices on the Internet are under pressure from a range of factors from both online and offline in the attitudes of the market, the type and nature of the product and the belief that prices online should be lower than offline, even where there are no reasonable financial grounds for this to be the case. To counter the problems faced by the increased downward pressure on prices, online marketing needs to move away from pricing based on reactions to the market and towards more strategic decisions. Decisions should be based on market, psychological or financial objectives which are integrated into the overall strategic direction of the company's web presence. By careful use of an integrated marketing approach, pricing can be used to assist the whole of the mix, and the overall business outcomes for the organisation.

The final value of a strategic approach to pricing is the recognition that the whole of the mix is affected by the choice of price. A holistic approach to pricing strategy, which takes the total cost to the consumer into account, given that currency exchanges and international shipping affect the price perception, will lead to greater online commercial success than price set by costing considerations alone.

Discussion questions

11.1 Define the total price concept. How does this impact on price setting in the Internet marketplace?

11.2 What are the elements of social price? How can a web site be tailored to reduce social costs associated with online shopping?

11.3 Where a company has an online and offline retail presence, should the online prices be higher, lower or the same as the retail store price?

11.4 How significant is the role of referent pricing when setting prices for online services such as subscriber-based information services? Does the type and nature of the product influence the referent price?

11.5 What are the three major pricing objectives? Pick one of these and give an example of how a web site can be tailored to support this objective. What role do the other elements of the mix play in designing the site to support this objective?

11.6 What are the three main options in pricing strategies for companies entering the online market? Find web sites which give examples of each of these strategies.

11.7 What are some of the costs borne by the consumer engaged in online purchasing which are outside of the control of the company? How do they impact on the consumer's purchase intention and price perceptions? What can organisations do to assist the consumers in reducing these costs?

References

Alba, J., Lynch, J., Weitz, B., Janiszewski, R., Saywer, A. & Wood, S. 1997, 'Interactive home shopping: Consumer, retailer and manufacturer incentives to participate in electronic marketplaces', *Journal of Marketing*, vol. 61, July, pp. 38–54.

Baker, M. J., Graham, P. G., Harker, D. & Harker, M. 1998, *Marketing: Managerial Foundations*, MacMillan Education, Melbourne.

Betts, E. J. & Goldrick, P. J. 1996, 'Consumer behaviours and the retail sales: Modelling the development of an "attitude problem"', *European Journal of Marketing*, vol. 30, no. 8, pp. 40–58.

Brassington, F. & Pettitt, S. 1997, *Principles of Marketing*, Pitman Publishing, Melbourne.

Calantone, R. & Sawyer, A. G. 1978, 'The stability of benefit segment', *Journal of Marketing Research*, vol. 15, no. 3, pp. 395–404.

Carson, D., Gilmore, A., Cummins, D., O'Donnell, A. & Grant, K. 1998, 'Price setting in SMEs: Some empirical findings', *Journal of Product and Brand Management*, vol. 7, no. 1, pp. 74–86.

Estelami, H. 1998, 'The Price is Right . . . or is it? Demographic and category effects on consumer price knowledge', *Journal of Product and Brand Management*, vol. 7, no. 3, pp. 254–66.

Fine, S. H. 1990, *Social Marketing: Promoting the Causes of Public and Non-profit Agencies*, Allyn and Bacon, Boston.

Hofacker, C. F. 2000, *Internet Marketing 3rd Edition*, John Wiley & Sons, New York.

Kotler, P. 1997, *Marketing Management: Analysis, Planning, Implementation and Control*, Prentice-Hall, Englewood Cliffs.

Krishna, A., Currim, I. S. & Shoemaker, R. W. 1991, 'Consumer perceptions of promotional activity', *Journal of Marketing*, vol. 55, no. 2, pp. 4–16.

Lovelock, C., Patterson, P. & Walker, R. 1998, *Services Marketing: Australia and New Zealand*, Prentice-Hall, Sydney.

McCarthy, E. J., Perrault, W. D. & Quester, P. G. 1997, *Basic Marketing: A Managerial Approach*, Irwin, Sydney.

McColl-Kennedy, J. R. & Kiel, G. C. 2000, *Marketing: A Strategic Approach*, Nelson ITP, Melbourne.

Monger, J. E. & Feinberg. R. A. 1997 'Mode of payment and formation of reference prices', *Pricing Strategy and Practice*, vol. 5, no. 4, pp. 142–7.

Mougayar, W. 1997, *Opening Digital Markets*, McGraw-Hill, New York.

Ovans, A. 1999, 'Taxing the Web', *Harvard Business Review*, July–August, pp. 18–19.

Peattie, K. & Peters, L. 1997, 'The marketing mix in the third age of computing', *Marketing Intelligence and Planning*, vol. 15, no. 3, pp. 142–50.

Raymond, E. S. 1999, *The Cathedral and the Bazaar*, O'Reilly, Sebastopol.

Reedy, J., Schullo, S. & Zimmerman, K. 2000, *Electronic Marketing: Integrating Electronic Resources into the Marketing Process*, Dryden Press, Fort Worth.

Smith, M. F., Sinha, I., Lancioni, R. & Forman, H. 1999, 'Role of market turbulence in shaping pricing', *Industrial Marketing Management*, vol. 28, pp. 637–49.

Strader, T. J. & Shaw, M. J. 1997, 'Characteristics of electronic markets', *Decision Support Systems*, vol. 21, pp. 185–98.

Strader, T. J. & Shaw, M. J. 1999, 'Consumer cost differences for traditional and Internet markets', *Internet Research: Electronic Networking Applications and Policy*, vol. 9, no. 2 pp. 82–92.

Strauss, J. & Frost, R. 1999, *Marketing on the Internet: Principles of Online Marketing*, Prentice-Hall, New Jersey.

Uncles, M. D. & Ehrenberg, A. S. 1990, 'Brand choice among older consumers', *Journal of Advertising Research*, vol. 30, no. 4, pp.19–22.

Van den Poel, D. & Leunis, J. 1999, 'Consumer acceptance of the Internet as a channel of distribution', *Journal of Business Research*, vol. 45, pp. 249–56.

Wakefield, K. L. & Inman, J. J. 1993, 'Who are the price vigilantes? An investigation of differentiating characteristics influencing price information processing', *Journal of Retailing*, vol. 69, no. 2, pp. 216–33.

Winker, J. 1991, 'Pricing'. In M. J. Baker (Ed.), *The Marketing Book* (2nd edn), Butterworth-Heinemann, Oxford.

Web sites

support.microsoft.com
www.amazon.com
www.ato.gov.au
www.auran.com
www.bartercard.com
www.beenz.co.uk
www.bonds.com.au
www.bpay.com.au
www.browser.org
www.chanel.com
www.colesonline.com.au
www.compaq.com
www.comsec.com.au
www.cybercash.com
www.ebay.com
www.geocities.com
www.gnu.org
www.greengrocer.com.au
www.irs.gov
www.katies.com.au
www.linux.org
www.lloydstsb.co.uk
www.microsoft.com
www.mp3.com
www.netscape.com
www.npsis.com
www.pilotgear.com
www.pricescan.com
www.proxomitron.cjb.net
www.scouts.co.uk
www.shopfido.com
www.smh.com.au
www.southwest.com
www.taxfreeinternet.org
www.the-times.co.uk
www.thewell.com
www.thinkgeek.com
www.vuitton.com
www.walmart.com

CHAPTER

12

Distribution

'Parallel to this traditional delivery of education, education was also delivered via the postal service, as training by correspondence, a century-old concept... Thus, receiving formal education, without being face-to-face with the instructor, is an old and accepted concept...

Kostopoulos, G. K. 1998, 'Global delivery of education via the Internet', *Internet Research: Electronic Networking Applications and Policy*, vol. 8, no. 3, pp. 257–65.

LEARNING objectives

After reading this chapter, you should be able to:

- explain how the Internet has impacted on the distribution of products, services and ideas
- outline a three-step method for determining distribution channels
- identify the differences between transactions based in marketspace and marketplace
- recognise the mechanisms for creating value in the marketspace, and how online businesses can make use of these value chains
- identify the major issues that have arisen from using the Internet as a distribution medium
- outline the factors which influence perceptions of the Internet as a viable non-store distribution mechanism
- recognise the technical and personnel considerations involved in using the Internet for distribution
- appreciate the interaction of the four elements of the marketing mix in designing products for delivery and distribution online.

Introduction

The art of distribution is as old as the art of war itself. Careful management of supply lines between secured territories and advance portions of armies made the difference between success and failure for many military campaigns. In the battle for the consumer dollar, the management of supply lines is every bit as vital. The advent of the Internet as a legitimate and popular distribution channel for ideas and services has meant that marketers need to be able to address the new needs of this channel — and the need crises and problems these create.

This chapter sets out to overview the impact of the Internet on the fourth element of the promotional mix — distribution. It examines the methods and means of distributing online, and how to set up offline support structures to aid online sales. In addition, it examines the nature of transactions that remain solely within the domain of the Internet, where product, payment and distribution are all contained within computer-mediated environments.

The Internet and distribution: You can get there from here

The Internet is a big place. The advantage of the Internet is that it can be accessed from just about anywhere, without needing to physically relocate to it, through it or around it, as is the case with interactions with places and spaces in the offline world. The disadvantage of the Internet is that the real world still exists along with the Internet in a linear, analogue and eminently physical format. Consequently, when it comes time for the results of Internet activity to arrive courtesy of the offline world, all the lessons learnt over hundreds of years of shipping goods in the physical world can be applied. Distribution, often seen as the less glamorous cousin of the marketing mix, has finally come into its own in the online world.

Of course, distribution, which is the management of the logistics of taking the product to the market, and from the market to the consumer, still has to deal with changes in marketing environments. Upgrades to technologies have improved supply line management, supply chain controls and created entirely new genres of physical goods management, such as just-in-time supply lines. Increases in the speed and access of data exchanges are creating environments where the customer practically interacts with the manufacturer through the mediated environment of the retail store. The customer never notices that the scanner data taken from their grocery shopping heads back through the logistics channel to order a replacement tin of beans for the one just purchased. All they notice is whether the beans are available on the shelf.

With Internet retailing and shopping, the consumer may not even notice whether or not the shelf is there — the assumption made when ordering from a web site is that the seller has a full stockpile of goods for sale, and it will be a quick step from click to ship.

In services marketing, distribution of the service is inherently bound up with the customer who is being serviced, since a haircut needs both hairdresser and hair to be co-located for the service to take effect. With the Internet, co-location of service and Internet user can be achieved through telepresence, online systems and automation. Banking, shopping and other information-dependent services are increasingly shifting to location-independent distribution systems, through their corporate web sites. The assumption made is that the customer also seeks location-independent services, or at least, will seek them once shown the right direction and closed bank branches. Closing down physical locations has been seen as a faster track method of moving people online than showing them the benefits of digital distribution.

Determining the right distribution

There are no golden rules in marketing beyond the simple understanding that a customer orientation means being directed by the needs of the market (within reason) and not orientating the market in your direction. Distribution channels have tended to suffer from the assumption that the customer will tolerate any form of distribution if the price is cheap enough and the product good enough. This has not always been the fast track to success hoped for by marketing managers. Mols (1998) outlined a three-step model of the ideal method of determining distribution channels.

Step 1: Ask first

Mols (1998) proposes the idea of asking the customer about the distribution channels that would suit them. The ideal scenario allows the customer to determine what types of channel delivery services would suit them and which would best meet their needs and maximise their likelihood of purchase. Included in this market-oriented approach were the instructions to examine distribution price sensitivity and any existing reference prices for distribution. Logistic planners needed to consider both the demand for services, and the willingness of the customer to pay for the services. Stratified levels of pricing involved charging a range — from premium prices for maximum services, through to a minimum cost for minimum service standard. Having a range of delivery prices available tends to provide the most value for logistic management. Many of the major e-commerce sites specify delivery by levels of speed, where a premium is paid for overnight express shipping for next day delivery, down to a low cost for longer shipping times. Amazon.com offers three levels of international shipping speed, ranging from almost overnight courier services through the standard international mail, down to the potluck (in terms of speed) of shipping by sea. Clients choose their delivery channel services and service standards by the price they are willing to pay.

In addition, Mols (1998) emphasises the need to know the market, and the distribution needs of each segment carefully. In particular, caution was advised where the movement into digital distribution offered great benefit to the supplier (e.g. banks) but inflicted a range of costs on the customer (loss of face-to-face contact, increased complexity of transaction, increased social cost of trusting online transactions). Shifting to digital distribution of services because of the perceived cost savings may become a false economy if the company ends up losing the customer base because it did not want to enter online exchange. Some services, and sales of goods, need to be conducted offline as consumers may still want to touch, taste, feel and see the product, or experience the face-to-face aspects of the service.

Step 2: How can the services be provided?

Having determined what the market wants in a distribution channel, and how much it will pay for that service, the next step is finding out how to implement these ideas (Mols 1998). Practicality and pragmatism need to be the dominant considerations for a marketing manager when arranging distribution channels based on market demand. It is also critical to involve the other elements of the company that will be affected by the channel selection — for example, if the market wants 24–7 digital distribution of products, it may be wise to include the engineering and IT divisions of the organisation in the decision-making process. If the channel cannot be feasibly constructed within the resources of the organisation, then modifications to the channel concept need to take priority over meeting the exact needs of the market. Even pizza delivery services set limits on where, when and how they can deliver a pizza, rather than offering a blanket (and impossible) distribution promise of delivering anywhere in 15 minutes or less. The single most important facet in delivery is reliability. If the service is delivered once at an unreasonable time frame, the consumer will expect it always to be delivered at that speed. It is better to set the reference social price on speed of distribution as higher than the actual social cost, so as to be able to impress, rather than frequently disappoint.

Step 3: What are the costs of the alternative channels?

Having determined the best available option, set prices on the second, third and fourth alternative strategies of distribution. Give the customer options, based on speed and price, so that they feel a greater sense of control over their distribution channel. This is particularly valuable in the distribution of information where the end user knows their capacities (personal and technical) to handle the product. Subscriptions to information services should be available in a range of options of timeliness, quantity and frequency.

In addition, know the market segments most likely to be needing your distribution mechanisms, tailor information to those needs, and specify that the distribution is set to those levels. The Smithsonian Institute (2k.si.edu) offers a virtual tourism function that is unashamedly set for distribution to those members of the population who can handle high-bandwidth, graphics-intensive sites. The costs for establishing an alternative low-bandwidth mechanism include financial considerations (replicated effort) and the loss of the creative freedom available in the high bandwidth version. It also involves loss of the types of interactive media that could be used and the social costs of presenting a potentially below-standard exhibit. Consequently, and understanding the balance between corporate reputation and market tolerance, the Smithsonian elected to have an exclusive web site ahead of lowering its standard.

Saying it in delivery: IMC and distribution mechanisms

The selection of a distribution mechanism must also be consistent with the integrated marketing communications message being put out by the company and the web site. Establishing an elitist corporate message with the look and feel of the web site, coupled with the organisation offline method (www. harrods.co.uk) can be ruined by the selection of a low-cost distribution mechanism. Similarly, budget-oriented sites which aim to sell more for less (or less for less) than their competitors, need to consider the total price implications of their shipping alternatives. Being the discount king of DVDs on the Internet works up until the point the client is faced with premium priced shipping charges.

Distribution mechanisms can also be used to portray marketing messages, particularly where the company wants to portray itself as having local distribution networks, such as D-Store (www.dstore.com.au). Alternatively, small localised organisations may wish to make use of internationally known distribution systems such as UPS (www.ups.com) or FedEx (www.fedex.com) to mask the size and nature of their business.

The worldwide place: Distribution over the wire

The Internet exists at two distinct levels. The first level is the physical representation of the network through computers, wires, cables and the human users of the system. Computers that use the Internet independently of human users are mostly employed by search engine companies, and tend not to be engaged in online commerce. For the most part, computers have not yet been given authority to approve their own purchases over the Internet due to security considerations (and the general lack of enthusiasm towards letting computers buy parts for themselves).

The second level of the Internet exists within the computers, and has various labels to designate it, such as cyberspace (Gibson 1984) or the marketspace (Weiber & Kollman 1998). **Cyberspace**, as a concept, predates the mass availability of the Internet and is an inexact, albeit more romantic, vision of the global computer network environment. In this environment, distribution is primarily concerned with locating ideas (occasionally liberating them) and moving bits rather than atoms (Negroponte 1995).

F O C U S   O N
Strategy ⦿

Cyberspace: It's not what you think, it's where you think

William Gibson probably never considered his view of a dark cyberpunk future to be the ideal word to describe the Internet. The cyberspace of Gibson's mind was a less-than-pleasant digital environment populated with less-than-pleasant people intent on less-than-legal activities in a less-than-real environment. The term cyberspace has since become co-opted to mean anything from the entirety of linked networked computers everywhere, through to a defintion of the Internet. Worse yet, it is being used to describe the Web. The problem with the adaptation of the word to describe just about everything digital is that it has lost sight of the initial meaning. Cyberspace was the shared consensual hallucination between millions of users who defined their world, based in physical objects, through mental constructs.

(continued)

The implications of this in marketing are many, and not least of them is a consideration of the movement of 'place' from the physical (controllable) world to the consumer's (uncontrollable) mind. Marketing in cyberspace has encountered a new delivery conundrum to add to the list of problems already faced when shifting from physical to digital worlds. In the new environment of the Internet, the delivery of information goes straight from the originator to the consumer's mind, without much more than the distribution channel in between. In comparison, services and physical goods move through a range of intermediary stages, as illustrated in figure 12.1.

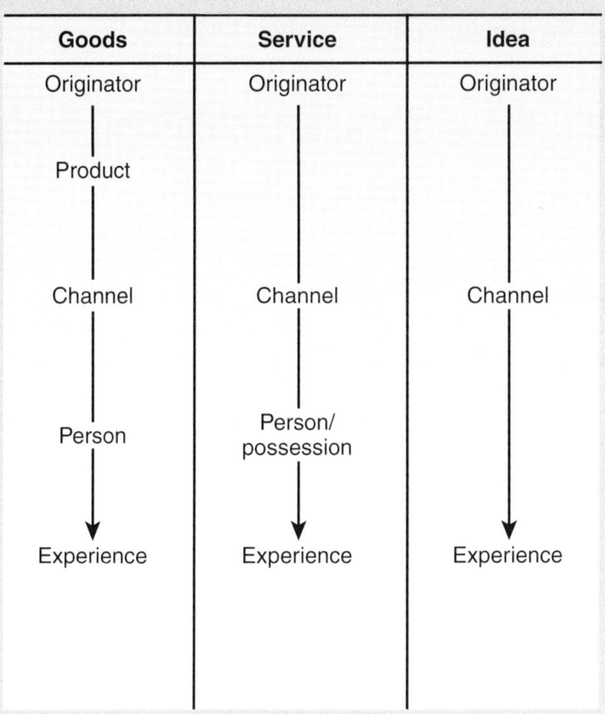

Goods	Service	Idea
Originator	Originator	Originator
Product		
Channel	Channel	Channel
Person	Person/ possession	
Experience	Experience	Experience

Figure 12.1 Origin to experience: Movement of goods, services and ideas

Source: Author's ergosphere

Delivery of the idea product in this phase goes from originator to experience without the intermediary physical phases of delivery found in other products or services.

Cyberspace exists as the channel of delivery of the experience, which occurs in the mind of the receiver, either in Raymond's (1999) 'noosphere' or 'ergosphere'. The **noosphere** exists as the territory of ideas which encompasses the space of all thoughts, and exists in a purely conceptual form. Below it exists the '**ergosphere**' as the space of work, or the application of ideas that emerge from the noosphere.

The marketing implications of this have a significant impact on the delivery of ideas across the Internet. None of these three environments exist in a physical location, yet the online marketer is expected to deliver information across cyberspace into the noosphere or ergosphere (see figure 12.2).

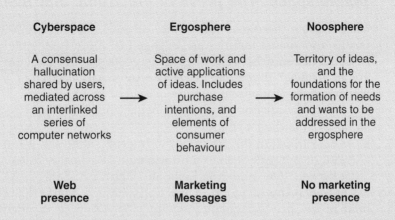

Cyberspace	Ergosphere	Noosphere
A consensual hallucination shared by users, mediated across an interlinked series of computer networks	Space of work and active applications of ideas. Includes purchase intentions, and elements of consumer behaviour	Territory of ideas, and the foundations for the formation of needs and wants to be addressed in the ergosphere
Web presence	**Marketing Messages**	**No marketing presence**

Figure 12.2 From cyberspace to noosphere

Source: Adapted from Raymond, E. S. 1999, *The Cathedral and the Bazaar*, O'Reilly, Sebastopol.

As the target destination of the product moves away from the cyberspace channel and into the mind of the consumer, it heads further away from established marketing ground and into new frontiers. What must be appreciated is that the new delivery address is in the mind of the receiver directly. Idea products are designed to elicit emotional, psychological or psychic reactions within the mine of the consumer. As a result, idea products do not engage with the consumer in a physical context, meaning that delivery occurs directly within the mind of the consumer, rather than the physical world. Even services are becoming increasingly based in the ergosphere and noosphere where they offer 'peace of mind' rather than '35 repairs to a car', as part of the service encounter. In the delivery of ideas, the more abstract a product becomes (given that intangibility is an abstract starting point) the more likely it is to be targeted to be delivered into the noosphere.

At the lower level, the ergosphere is engaged with promotional messages, service outcomes, non-marketing related ideas and other intangible products that compete for delivery in the least controllable environment of all — the customer's mind. Services marketing has long recognised that the state of mind of the customer determines, in part, how well the service is received, performed and evaluated. Now information products need to also consider that delivering into the noosphere makes their products every bit as vulnerable to the vagaries of the customer's mind. Distribution is no longer solely the domain of those moving atoms in a physical environment. Now it is possible to take an idea from the originator's mind to receiver's mind through the channel of cyberspace without the real world getting in the way.

Marketspace operates as a parallel to the physical world marketplace. It is the conjunction between ideas and exchange, where goods, services, ideas and money can be exchanged as items of value. The marketspace–marketplace continuum addresses how the value chains of product services, procurement, distribution and production can be developed and used in both the on and offline environments.

Marketspace: The place of electronic distribution

Marketspace is the digital twin of the physical marketplace, where virtual value chains and virtual logistics are engaged to move intangible goods and ideas across data networks, with little or no recourse to physical environments. They are an artificial, intangible market for information (Weiber & Kollman 1998). A marketspace is defined by three parameters:

- *content*: the idea or information being traded
- *context*: the digital channel
- *infrastructure*: in this instance the Internet, although it can be any data network or network of shared information (Rayport & Sviokla 1994; Pattinson & Brown 1996; Weiber & Kollman 1998).

Content is the lifeblood of the transaction in marketspace, and was examined in the product chapter (chapter 8). Context, the digital channel, has been examined among the unique features of cyberspace in chapter 3 and, in part, in the study of cybercommunities (chapter 4). The context of the marketspace is the location in cyberspace where exchanges take place. This can be either in a cybercommunity, in an established online market (www.carpoint.com.au) or on an ad hoc basis in newsgroups (news:alt.ads.forsale). Infrastructure is the technology that supports the marketspace, and is not limited to the Internet, in that non-Internet-based information networks can also support marketspaces. For the purposes of this chapter, the main focus of attention will remain on Internet-based marketspaces such as Deja.com. Deja.com is an information exchange, bounded by:

- content: as a market specialising in the exchange and referral of product information, and the archiving of USENET discussions
- context: in that it occurs only within the digital confines of the Deja.com web site
- infrastructure: mostly the Internet, although Deja.com can be available through mobile phones and wireless hand-held computers. While these later technologies are technically part of the Internet, they also represent a new area of Internet infrastructure.

The role and value of the Internet as a mediator of marketspace is based on the nature of the information product, and the ability of the Internet to facilitate fast and effective movements of data. Information as a product is not subject to the lead times and shipping problems of physical goods. Multiple replication does not reduce or extinguish the original source and it can be instantly transported to any point in the production value chain (Mason–Jones & Towill 1997; Jones & Vijayasarthy 1998).

Marketspaces: Three outcomes of information exchange

Weiber and Kollman (1998) examined the division of marketplace and marketspace, and identified three outcomes:

- *performance improvements in the marketplace*: where information is exchanged to improve the efficiency of the offer of the physical products. These exchanges are usually focused around using the distribution channel as a data collection source to determine more information about the consumer.

This is particularly prevalent when consumer profiles can be established and tracked easily, and in conjunction with data use activities, such as downloads for **patches** of registered software from a web site (www.adobe.com).

■ *freestanding output in marketspace*: where information becomes a product to be traded, such as in cybercommunities where knowledge is traded (www.control-escape.com), data are exchanged (www.h2g2.com) or created and experienced online (www.click2send.com). The Internet creates the capacity for individuals to trade a range of information, from additional elements for software (www.poserworld.com) to their own music (www.mp3.com), through collective marketspaces. While individuals can also establish these elements on their own web sites (erther.qgl.org), placing the information at the relevant marketspace (www.mp3.com/erther/) increases the propensity of the information to be found, and the likelihood of social or financial reward.

■ *additional consumer value in marketspace*: through the development of overlaps between marketspace and marketplace, information can be used to add value to tangible goods. This is where web sites can be used to demonstrate additional product uses and recipes (www.masterfoods.com). Alternatively, the combined value of a tangible product, such as an MP3 player, is dependent on accessing information (mp3 sound files) from an online source.

With the acceptance of the existence of the twin spheres of trading of tangible and intangible goods, companies need to be able to review how they operate in standard value creation, and how virtual value can be developed, enhanced or created.

Value in the marketspace: Virtual channels and chains

The existence of a marketspace does not create a virtual channel or virtual value chain for an organisation with information to trade. Creation and management of the supply lines of information remain the responsibility of the organisation seeking to trade in the marketspace. **Value chains** divide a company into an array of strategically relevant elements which can be identified physically and technologically, and for which the customer is willing to pay money (Porter 1985, in Weiber & Kollman, 1998). **Virtual value chains** are those elements of the value chains that are based on information. They were previously identified as supporting elements and exist as items of value in their own right in the marketspace. Value in the marketspace is derived from one of two avenues, as identified by Weiber and Kollman (1998). Firstly, traditional value chains can be examined for relevant information resources to be developed into virtual value chains. Secondly, value chain creation can be performed by the collection, systemisation, selection, combination, and distribution of information through specific virtual value creation exercises (Weiber & Kollman 1998). In this context, the virtual value chain is developed within the context of the marketspace, and is not derived from the physical values chain. Figure 12.3 illustrates how the virtual value and physical value chains interact to create the 'marketplace and marketspace' and 'marketplace or marketspace' environment of modern business.

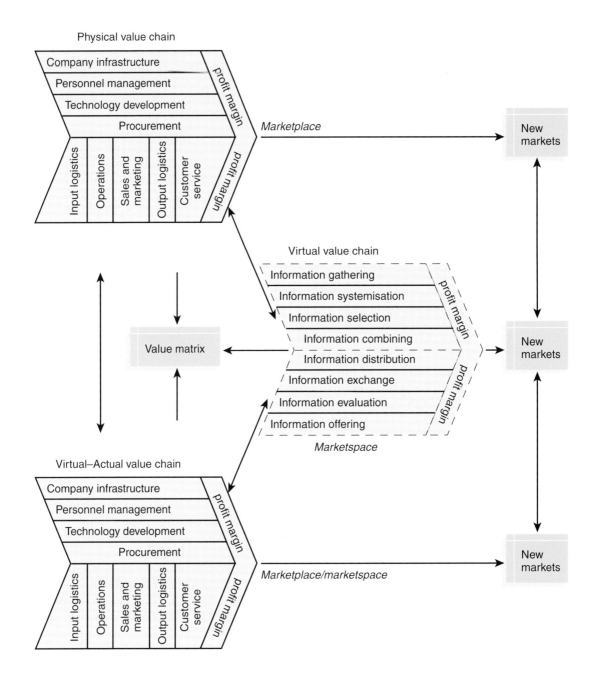

Physical value chain

| Company infrastructure |
| Personnel management |
| Technology development |
| Procurement |

Input logistics | Operations | Sales and marketing | Output logistics | Customer service

profit margin

profit margin

Marketplace → New markets

Virtual value chain

| Information gathering |
| Information systemisation |
| Information selection |
| Information combining |
| Information distribution |
| Information exchange |
| Information evaluation |
| Information offering |

profit margin

profit margin

Marketspace

Value matrix ←

→ New markets

Virtual–Actual value chain

| Company infrastructure |
| Personnel management |
| Technology development |
| Procurement |

Input logistics | Operations | Sales and marketing | Output logistics | Customer service

profit margin

profit margin

Marketplace/marketspace → New markets

Figure 12.3 Marketspace, marketplace and the value chain

Source: Weiber, R. and Kollman, T. 1998, 'Competitive advantages in virtual markets — perspectives of information-based marketing in cyberspace', *European Journal of Marketing*, vol. 32, no. 7/8, pp. 603–15.

The figure illustrates how the three value chains co-exist and interact in the marketplace/marketspace environments. In particular, the figure illustrates how new markets can be created by the development and refinement of virtual and virtual–actual value chains, just as physical value chains can be used to create new markets in the marketplace. However, refinement of the value chains and the development of the new markets is not without potential problems. One of the most overlooked aspects of Internet distribution is that the creation of wholesaler direct markets (which match all of the criteria of the Weiber and Kollman (1998) **virtual–actual value chains**) can cannibalise existing markets held by other members of the physical distribution channels.

The big issues in Internet distribution

The most significant problem created by the Internet has been the removal of geographic barriers between supplier, wholesaler and customer. Geographic barriers have often been used to the advantage of the supply chain planners who have broken down distribution mechanisms by territories or geographic holdings (Palumbo & Herbig 1998). Given the Internet's capacity to shrink the distribution channels, and create instant distribution, channel conflicts have arisen where wholesalers have sold directly in competition with their conventional retail outlets. In addition, non-store retailing, which describes the bulk of business to consumer transactions online, has had a long history of problems with security and perceived risk. These predate the Internet and have been carried over into the electronic commerce environment.

Channel conflicts

Palumbo and Herbig (1998) illustrated the three key problems created by use of the Internet as a distribution mechanism. The Internet is global, has 24–7 access and reduces the distance between manufacturer and end user. The downside to this is threefold:

- *channel conflict*: arises when the manufacturer is competing for the same customers as the retailers and distributors. Even small production operations such as iFive, who manufacture Penguin Mints (www.peppermints .com) and sell direct to the market, are competing against online retailers such as Thinkgeek (www.thinkgeek.com), approximately four USA national retail outlets, and nearly 20 other USA-based retail outlets. This raises the question: whose customer is it anyway? Is iFive the retailer or wholesaler, and which regional areas are they entitled to compete in against their on and offline supply channels? The problem is exacerbated when the manufacturer has a longer set of supply lines and an established market distribution system, and provides product information through their central web site. Even if the manufacturer does not sell direct to the consumer, they will still need to provide a link or referral to a local supplier and, in many cases, it will be one of many regional suppliers.
- *territory*: formerly the easiest way to distribute sales representatives and retail franchises was by allocating geographic regions and coverage zones. With the development of Internet-based retailing, the question is one of whether the Internet is a territory, or whether it negates the need for territory-based distribution. Conflict in the channel can arise when one of

the territory-based distributors uses the Internet to retail to the global market in an attempt to take sales from other regions.

- *international distribution*: the third problem faced by online distribution. As noted in Applications for business and non-business (chapter 6), selling through the Internet can create situations where companies can become sporadic exporters. The danger of sporadic exporting is that the logistical considerations, in regards to shipping, packaging, insurance and other export issues, are often considered only after the decision to ship globally is announced publicly. As mentioned above, it is more important to design a supply channel by asking what the customer wants, and how the organisation can deliver, than by agreeing to deliver without knowing what this will entail for the organisation. (Planned international marketing through the Internet is examined in chapter 15.)

Non-store distribution mechanism

The problems of convincing customers to buy from a non-store environment are not unique to the Internet, nor are they a new phenomenon caused by electronic commerce. The specific issue of credit card security in the computer-mediated environment is localised to the Internet, but the sixteenth century principles of safely sending a cargo load of gold to pay for a range of products purchased by catalogue is just as risky. Issues of security, encryption and secure transaction mechanisms have their historical roots in international (and intercommunity) trade since humans first started trading over distances greater than the local village square.

Non-store buying research in marketing was primarily concerned with the use of catalogue sales and similar direct response marketing mechanisms, including home shopping channels and telemarketing. Van den Poel and Leunis (1999) examined the perceptions of consumers towards a range of non-store buying mechanisms, including the Internet, and found that in general terms it was perceived as a riskier method than store-based buying, irrespective of the channel of purchase. They also uncovered three '**risk relievers**' that could be used to mediate perceived risks of non-store purchasing. These are:

- *money-back guarantee*: negates the financial risks associated with non-store buying. The difficulty for web retailers of online services and idea-based products is how to establish when to use the money-back guarantee — can a consumer claim a refund because they did not enjoy the song or because they did not understand the point of the digital story they just bought?
- *offering well-known brands*: seen as a social price control mechanism in that the consumer was more comfortable with known brands as they had some degree of offline or traditional store experience with the products or brands. This is not a terribly useful or reassuring finding for newcomers to the Internet retail market and for new brands trying to leverage the advantages of the Internet. It does indicate, however, that social price (chapter 11) influences choice of distribution. Where a brand is unknown in a non-store mechanism, it is also an innovation adoption experience (chapter 3) that does not have the in-store opportunities of vicarious adoption (seeing

it in use) or in-store trial. This is particularly significant for high social cost objects, such as fashion clothing, or complex technologies which need either demonstration or explanation. Offering a well-known brand mediates these problems as the consumers have a pre-existing understanding of the brand reputation, even if the product is unknown to them.

- *selling at a reduced price*: helps the consumer feel that the social price experience is mediated by the financial gain (chapter 11). Of course, selling at a discount works only if the distribution channel costs do not exceed the perceived or actual savings made by purchasing online. The consumer will not see value in a 20 per cent discount for a product if the shipping costs are such that the total price is greater than that they would pay in-store — and they have to wait four to six weeks to receive the product.

However, when all three risk relievers are present for an Internet site, Van den Poel and Leunis (1999) found that the web site was seen as a superior channel of distribution and purchase than even the in-store retail outlets. Offering risk relievers, combined with the advantages of home shopping on the Internet, was regarded as having a greater value to the consumer than the traditional store environment. In addition, when the consumer needs to ask questions, Van den Poel and Leunis (1999) found that the speed and interactivity of email led to greater consumer satisfaction than that experienced through traditional mail order products or in-store experiences.

Making it so: Technical implications of Internet distributions

This book has specifically tried to avoid heading into the technical discussions of the limits and restrictions of marketing online that are imposed by the physical hardware and software constraints of the Internet. Under the principles of **Moore's Law**, since the writing of this book began, computers have doubled in speed and capacity again. As well, Netscape and Internet Explorer have released two or more new versions of their browser client. What is presented here are the technical constraints that need to be considered when approaching the design and development of an Internet distribution mechanism, because no matter how fast a computer becomes, or how much bandwidth is available, somebody will write a program or design a site that needs more resources than are available.

It is also noted that the technical considerations of distribution on the Internet are affected by the type of product and the nature of the distribution channel. Van den Poel and Leunis (1999) outlined three types of distribution function:

- non-store information channel
- non-store reservation channel (offline shipping)
- non-store purchase and distribution channel.

In very general terms, the capacity required for each of the three types of channels listed above should increase from 'non-store information channel' to 'purchase and delivery channel'. However, this is a broad generalisation, given that free music samples (distributed as information concerning an upcoming album release (www.kylie.com)) can take up greater network capacity than the purchase and delivery of an entire digital book (www.stephenking.com). For the most part, the technical considerations listed below stand as advice to consider for any aspect of Internet delivery. They are developed at a conceptual and managerial level rather than being hardware or site specific, taking into account the rapid developments in computing and technology.

Technical considerations 101: Keeping it real

The real world has a very strong role to play in the practice of marketing in digital environments. While much of the thinking about online marketing revolves around the conceptual space in which the Internet exists, the physical equipment of cyberspace will often determine the success and failure of an online marketing venture. Video on demand ventures, which require high-bandwidth data streams being delivered to fast servers and played through specialist software packages will fail if any of these elements are missing. In order to deliver services online, Kostopoulos (1998) outlined the three key technical factors that need to be considered:

- *network access*: the capacity to access the Internet, or the associated wireless Internet services. It should not need to be said that the value of a web site to a customer is only as good as the customer's ability to access the site, but it has to be said. Too many companies are moving to digital delivery of goods, services and sales ideas without considering whether the customer base is online, or even wants to be online. Online distribution of software has become increasingly common, even if it leads to the problem of having the software required for getting online in the first place only being available from a web site. Network access also refers to the capacity to access secured systems and environments which are regulated by passwords or other security mechanisms. Digital delivery of services, such as online libraries and searchable databases, are often restricted to the IP domain of the subscriber institution. This means that unless the IP address matches part of the recognised group, the individual user cannot access the network, even if they are a member of the subscriber organisation.

- *server capacity*: the ability of the technology to deliver the web presence and web delivery channel to the end user. This is most dramatically illustrated by the Slashdot effect described in chapter 9, although it can also be found in less extreme examples of slow download times and an inability to fully load web pages. Digital distribution is extremely vulnerable to server problems, just as physical distribution is vulnerable to transportation problems. Multiple redundancy is required to ensure that the capacity exists to service normal and predicted demand. An excess capacity should also be available in case of extraordinary demand. One of the difficulties faced by organisations using the Web as their distribution channel is balancing capacity against excess. It is better to have an excess capacity on the server or bandwidth that is held in reserve, than to have customers unable to access the site. This advice appears to run contrary to the purpose of examining the value chain to reduce waste and inefficiency. In contrast to the physical world of the marketplace, excess demand over capacity results in people looking for an alternative method of satisfying their needs, rather than queuing up earlier next time. You can turn fans away from a sporting event and have them queue up again next time. Turn people away from your web site, and they will find another site to meet their needs.

- *compatibility*: originally defined by Kostopoulos (1998) as browser compatibility, but has moved into the need to be compatible with the appropriate format for the end user. Compatibility issues also extend into how the digital information will be presented to the user (in terms of control, choice and how dependent the distribution channel is on proprietary software). One area where the proprietary format has been locked into place to a large extent is in the distribution of QuickTime movies (www.quicktime.com) which is a proprietary format from Apple Computing (www.apple.com). The advantage to this approach is the relative guarantee of consistency of playback through the QuickTime client. The downside is that the user has no control or choice over the client type, and is forced into acquiring the third party software to view or use the distribution site. Similarly, although Adobe Acrobat **Portable Document Format (PDF)** (www.adobe.com) is presented as a universal file format across a range of systems, it remains primarily a proprietary system, viewed through the Acrobat Reader platform. An alternative viewing software 'Ghostscript' is available, although PDF tends to be mostly associated with Adobe Acrobat (www.cs.wisc.edu/~ghost/index.html). In contrast, the MP3 file format can be read through a wide range of players, both hardware and software, giving a wider range of choices for the end user. There are five general rules for establishing compatibility to the widest market:
- use the widest accepted protocol. Security is through obscurity, compatibility is through open and widespread acceptance.
- remember that Macintosh, Linux and Unix users may also like to see your products as much as the Windows client base.
- accept that the **bleeding edge/cutting edge** is the narrowest part of the user base. The widest part of the user base is still using the older version of the software you intend to use to distribute your product.
- use Mol's (1998) guidelines for establishing a distribution format if there is no readily visible market standard. If a standard exists for distribution of the product, use the standard protocols to save time and money on developing a new method.
- if you have to establish your own protocol, provide free versions of the reader/viewer software as widely as possible and as quickly as possible. Costs of creating a new data viewing protocol can be recovered from the encoding software, or by licensing the software to other organisations. Adobe's success with the PDF format resides largely in the mass acceptance of the free Acrobat viewer software.

There are other considerations for creating distribution channels that are compatible with the target market of the product. Most important of all is to understand that while technology is a major facet in making a successful digital delivery, it is the people behind the technology that determine the success or failure of the product.

Technical considerations 102: People make the process

Kostopoulos (1998) reviewed the challenges faced by distance education after moving from the century-old postal and paper distribution mechanism into the digital delivery format. Among the concerns of technical problems, management of change and conversion of analogue material to digital distribution, the consistent element of the challenge was related to the role of people. The three major challenges facing digital distribution of higher education are also consistent with challenges faced at a broader level of the digital market. These are:

- *technology mastering*: the ability of people in an organisation to master the available technology and increase their skills to a level where they can adapt to changes and new technologies. Kostopoulos (1998) pointed out that the rapid speed of development and wide range of technologies involved in digital distribution made it nearly impossible for a single person to master the totality of channel technologies.

- *staff training*: is broken down into two problems for digital distribution. Firstly, the time must be found to train existing staff in the methods required for distribution of services and ideas over the digital network, while servicing the on and offline channels. Secondly, staff must be motivated to move into new networks and distribution channels and out of their areas of comfort and expertise. These two factors are important for marketing distribution channels. This is because the staff of an organisation will undergo the same type of innovation adoption process to use the new technologies for production and distribution as they would to use them to receive the content. Consequently, organisations need to address the innovation adoption needs of their staff by reducing the social costs of adoption of the new production and distribution techniques. Entwined with this issue is the fact that new technologies will require training, and training will take time, effort and money away from some other facet of the organisation's operations. These costs need to be carefully balanced with a view to the longer term operation of the organisation. It may be worth reducing the initial product offering in the digital delivery modes to enable the staff to gain experience in the new environments and new channels so as to have the long-term benefit of a confident and skilled workforce.

- *content restructuring*: the challenge of reformatting the product into the marketspace and making it suitable for online delivery. Information products which have traditionally been delivered into the marketplace through face-to-face presentations may require completely new techniques for delivery to the marketspace. Modification to products (chapter 8) may also create other ramifications for promotion (chapter 9) and pricing (chapter 11). A service that was previously delivered in a single session may now be able to be purchased in sub-units through the marketspace. For instance, a training certificate course may have previously been available only as a single 12-week program in the marketplace. Content restructuring for digital delivery may break it down into three modular units which can be packaged as a single course, or as individual elements.

Technical and human constraints operate to influence the value chains and worth of the marketspace for delivering products and services across the Internet. The people and technology of distribution channels also influence how this element of the marketing mix impacts on the whole of the mix. Similarly, the other elements of the mix have a significant impact on the selection of marketing channels.

Putting the pieces together: Distributing the mix

Each part of the marketing mix does not operate in isolation. Each element interacts and affects the other three components in a variety of ways. Price determines part of the perception of the product, a factor which is usually the domain of promotion. The quality of the production of the product helps determine the price, as well as impacting on the IMC message by appearance of the product. Promotion (and IMC) help establish referent prices and in the case of idea product, advertising is often part of the product itself. Among this, methods of distribution influence the mix in the on and offline markets. The impact of the rest of the mix on the distribution channel must be considered in order to successfully establish the appropriate distribution of a product.

Distribution and product

The first and most notable aspect of the impact of distribution is that it determines, in part, the product that can be offered through that channel. While products are usually produced without consideration to channels, the advent of the marketspace has led to companies attempting to develop products to maximise their share of the distribution channel. Weiber and Kollman (1998) pointed out that information-based marketing consists of three elements:

- **digital transmission of information**: the direct broadcast or narrowcast of streaming content in a digital format to the end receiver. This includes the headline news service Pointcast (www.pointcast.com) which transmits news and weather information to subscribers.
- **interactive transmission of information**: where the receiver can interact with the information being received, and can be used as the basis for determining other elements of the information received. For example, players involved in an online game of Quake 3 interact with the game information received. Similarly, though less violently, individuals involved in conversations in cyber-communities are also engaged in interactive transmissions of information.
- **individualised transmission**: based on user-customised behaviours that occur without the interaction of the user. This includes direct mail, subscriber-based referral systems such as Firefly (outlined in chapter 10), and sites which use cookies to remember the user's previous preference for information or services.

All three elements of information-based marketing are dependent on their distribution channels. Transmission itself is determined by the nature of the channel (broadcast, narrowcast, Internet). Interactivity is heavily channel dependent as information channels need to be developed to ensure ease of two-way communication. Finally, only a select array of channels can provide one-to-many-to-one transmission at a scalable and economically viable level.

In order to access the functionality of the Internet as a distribution medium, it becomes necessary to tailor the product to be information dependent. No matter how hard a company tries to force physical goods into the online arena, certain goods, such as food and drink cannot yet be digitised and distributed as information. The Star Trek world of food replicators which can turn digital recipes into real food is a long way into the future. Companies wanting to access Internet opportunities need to tailor their products to the channel, rather than attempt to alter the channel to suit their products.

Distribution and price

The total price concept was raised in chapter 11 as a major influence on pricing decisions on the Internet. This is due to the impact distribution can have on the final price of an online purchase. Distribution channels create their own set of costs, both financial and social, which are normally absorbed into the supply lines between manufacturer and retailer. In the standard retail environment, the customer is rarely privy to the channels and supply lines that support the stocks of goods at the local supermarket. When transacting directly with the wholesaler/manufacturer in the marketspace, the consumer has to bear these end costs themselves, and usually for the first time. White (1997) examined the attitudes towards international trade on the Internet and found that financial and social cost implications directly related to the distribution of goods. Firstly, consumers often had problems with the cost of shipping of goods ordered from a web site. Consumers believed that the absence of a physical store should have reduced the total price. Secondly, the social cost of the uncertainty of shipping played an important part in contributing to the total price of a product. A major element of the uncertainty was the lack of knowledge concerning shipping information with regard to:

- *shipping speed*: how quickly could the goods be received?
- *viability of shipping fragile or perishable goods*: would the shipping mechanism be effective in delivering the goods safely or quickly enough to avoid perishing in transit?
- *local alternatives for face-to-face pick-up*: consumers feel more comfortable in being able to access high involvement products for themselves at a traditional store rather than take the psychological risks associated with shipping fragile goods or perishable goods.

Each of these three elements demonstrates that the selection of a distribution channel can impact on the overall total price of a product, even before the actual financial cost of distribution is factored into the equation.

Distribution and promotion

The distribution of an idea can also be the promotion of an idea, depending on where the idea is distributed and which arm of the mix claims the credit. Social marketing writers have long recognised that separating the distribution and promotion of an idea is largely arbitrary, given that both tend to occur in parallel (Fine 1990; Kotler & Roberto 1989). Marketing information products that are dependent on the acceptance, use and sale of ideas also creates a similar problem in determining where the online promotion of an idea ends and where the distribution begins. Is the web site that is devoted to the principles of open source computing (www.opensource.org) a promotional site for the idea or the idea itself? To what extent does the movement of an idea from the mind of the originator into the mind of the recipient owe the journey to promotional techniques or idea distribution tools? For the most part these questions are academic in nature, until they reach the point where a practitioner wishes to take greater control over the movement and diffusion of their ideas. Determining the dividing line between promotional technique and marketspace distribution technique will become an increasingly difficult problem as more ideas are promoted and distributed across the Internet.

Internet marketing INSIGHT

mp3.com — the music of the marketspace

Music is the ultimate product for distribution across the Internet. Millions of users of legal, quasi-legal and downright illegal MP3 files represent the acceptance, by the consumers, of the Internet as a legitimate marketspace of music information products that can be moved from creator to consumer (or consumer to consumer). One web site that stands out as one of the more comprehensive marketspaces for the transaction of music files (in a legitimate marketing forum) is MP3.com. It is noted that there are many other music marketspaces besides MP3.com on the Internet. However, MP3.com offers a way in which, by creating a strong distribution channel, a marketspace can be tailored to capture all elements of the marketing mix.

The MP3.com system works on the basis that musical artists can subscribe to the site for free. They are offered a mechanism by which Mp3.com will host their music files, plus additional information, and make these files available to the general public through the MP3.com marketspace. Within the marketspace, the artists are able to control their pricing for individual songs (free, purchase only), and ancillary service goods such as CDs and subscription channels (figure 12.5).

The marketspace on Mp3.com operates by facilitating an environment in which the artists control their marketing messages of price, product and promotion while using the provided distribution channels. Even within the context of the distribution channel, choice exists for the artist to select from three different methods of distribution for their music (**streaming only, free download, paid channel**). The marketspace provides additional value-added services such as ticket sales and booking offered by mp3.com. Other related artist services include

▪ a custom built HTML editor designed to integrate with the Mp3.com web page, and

(continued)

- access to a range of collaborative ventures with related companies, such as Cafepress (www.cafepress.com)
- and additional promotional services.

At the corporate level, mp3.com is also creating a range of virtual value chains through the use of download tracking. This requires users to log their email addresses with mp3.com before the music will play. The stated purpose of the system is to create a traceable database of musical preferences, as well as providing a mechanism for following market trends. These data are used to assist the sale of on-site advertising space.

For the customer, value chains are created with the use of the My.MP3.com service which allows registered users to create their own online music stations, receive product recommendations, and to use the interactive systems of My.MP3.com to tailor the music product received. This is as recommended by Weiber and Kollman (1998) in their three elements of information-based marketing.

The final element in the MP3.com operational strategy is to provide a product that the market wants (music in Mp3 format) at a price desired by the market (free/low cost) through a range of channels (streaming, download, subscription) sought after by the customer.

Summary

Distribution has seen both radical change and a renewal of purpose with the advent of the Internet. Products and services once considered solely in terms of their atoms and component parts can now be seen as both parts of the marketspace and marketplace. Information associated with a product can be traded in the marketspace as product, and services can be performed to ideas and information, creating a range of new value chains within the online world.

To cope with the marketspace and marketplace, several methods of channel design, such as Mols' (1998) three-step process, have been developed to assist distribution managers. Even then, the Internet's global reach and borderless marketspace can create conflict, as traditional markets and distribution channels find themselves in competition with Internet-based supply lines. Marketers also need to be mindful of technical and human limitations when developing digital distribution channels both at the corporate and consumer level. Although it may be technically possible for the company to deliver through the marketspace this does not guarantee that the consumer will want to receive the information in electronic format. Finally, distribution, both digital and physical, does not operate in isolation. Decisions made regarding the exploitation of marketspace value chains can influence the pricing and promotion of the company's product. Likewise, product selection determines whether the Internet can be used as a primary distribution channel, a virtual value chain or not at all.

Discussion questions

12.1 Has the widespread adoption of the Internet had a significant impact on the distribution mix? How does the Internet differ from other non-store retailing channels?

12.2 What are the three steps to determine the right distribution channel?

12.3 Define marketspace. Give an example of a set of marketspaces that do not have a physical world marketplace counterpart. Can a marketplace exist without having a marketspace associated with it?

12.4 What are virtual value chains? Can they exist outside of the marketspace? What are some of the value chains and virtual channels that can be created in the marketspace?

12.5 Does the Internet create more distribution problems than it solves? Discuss with reference to channel conflicts.

12.6 What are the three risk relievers for non-store distribution mechanisms? What impact does the use of these three risk relievers have on the other elements of the marketing mix?

12.7 What are some of the technical considerations to keep in mind when determining the value of the Internet as a distribution medium? Does the type of product on offer or the type of web site used for delivery, impact on these considerations?

12.8 How do the four elements of the mix interact with regards to digital distribution of idea products? What are some of the considerations of the product, price and promotion of ideas being distributed through cyberspace?

References

Fine, S. H. 1990, *Social Marketing: Promoting the Causes of Public and Non-profit Agencies*, Allyn and Bacon, Boston.

Gibson, W. 1984, *Neuromancer*, Ace Books, New York.

Jones, J. M. & Vijayasarthy, L. R. 1998, 'Internet consumer catalogue shopping: Findings from an exploratory study and directions for future research', *Internet Research: Electronic Networking Applications and Policy*, vol. 8, no. 4, pp. 322–30.

Kostopoulos, G. K. 1998, 'Global delivery of education via the Internet', *Internet Research: Electronic Networking Applications and Policy*, vol. 8, no. 3, pp. 257–65.

Kotler, P. & Roberto, E. 1989, *Social Marketing: Strategies for Changing Public Behaviour*, Macmillan, New York.

Mason–Jones, R. & Towill, D. R. 1997, 'Information enrichment: Designing the supply chain for competitive advantage', *Supply Chain Management*, vol. 2, no. 4, pp. 137–48.

Mols, N. P. 1998, 'The Internet and the banks' strategic distribution channel decisions', *Internet Research: Electronic Networking Applications and Policy*, vol. 8, no. 4, pp. 331–37.

Negroponte, N. 1995, 'Bits and Atoms', *Wired 3.01* (http://www.wired.com/wired/archive/3.01/negroponte.html)

Palumbo, F. & Herbig, P. 1998, 'International marketing tool: The Internet', *Industrial Management and Data Systems*, vol. 6, pp. 253–61.

Pattinson, H. & Brown, L. 1996, 'Chameleons in marketspace: Industry transformation in the new electronic marketing environment', *Internet Research: Electronic Networking Applications and Policy*, vol. 6, no. 2/3, pp. 31–40.

Porter, 1985. In Weiber & Kollman, 1998, 'Competitive advantages in virtual markets — perspectives of "information-based marketing" in cyberspace', *European Journal of Marketing*, vol. 32, no. 7/8, pp. 603–15.

Raymond, E. S. 1999, *The Cathedral and the Bazaar*, O'Reilly, Sebastopol.

Rayport, J. F. & Sviokla, J. J. 1994, 'Managing in the marketspace', *Harvard Business Review*, vol. 72, no. 6, pp. 141–50.

Van den Poel, D. & Leunis, J. 1999, 'Consumer Acceptance of the Internet as a Channel of Distribution', *Journal of Business Research*, vol. 45, pp. 249–56.

Weiber & Kollman 1998, 'Competitive advantages in virtual markets — perspectives of "information-based marketing" in cyberspace', *European Journal of Marketing*, vol. 32, no. 7/8, pp. 603–15.

White, G. K. 1997, 'International on-line marketing of foods to US consumers', *International Marketing Review*, vol. 14, no. 5, pp. 376–84.

Web sites

2k.si.edu
erther.qgl.org
my.mp3.com
www.adobe.com
www.amazon.com
www.apple.com
www.cafepress.com
www.carpoint.com.au
www.click2send.com
www.control-escape.com
www.cs.wisc.edu/~ghost/index.html
www.deja.com
www.dstore.com.au
www.fedex.com
www.h2g2.com
www.harrods.co.uk
www.kylie.com
www.masterfoods.com
www.mp3.com
www.mp3.com/erther
www.mp3.com/skylab17
www.opensource.org
www.peppermints.com
www.pointcast.com
www.poserworld.com
www.quicktime.com
www.stephenking.com
www.thinkgeek.com
www.ups.com

Newsgroup

news:alt.ads.forsale

part 4

Strategic marketing applications for the Internet

■ **13**...*Services marketing online* ■ **14**...*Relationship marketing in a 'one-to-many-to-one' environment* ■ **15**...*International marketing* ■ **16**...*Marketing research*

The fourth section of the book examines the application of the Internet in specific marketing contexts. These four chapters build upon the basic principles of marketing explored in part 3, and the new aspects of marketing and consumer behaviour on the Internet outlined in part 2. **Chapter 13** explores how services can be delivered across the Internet, and the changing nature of service delivery as a result of the influence of the Internet in product definition and delivery. **Chapter 14** reviews the development of relationships between consumers and business online, and how the Internet can be used to facilitate stronger business to business relationship links. **Chapter 15** examines the issues of international marketing, including the impact of the Internet as an export medium, country of origin effects and an environmental analysis of the global Internet marketspace. The final chapter of the section, **Chapter 16** overviews the types and nature of market research that can be conducted on the Internet. It focuses on both the adaptation of existing offline method, and the creation of Internet specific research techniques, along with exploring the impact of market research on online privacy and anonymity.

CHAPTER 13

Services marketing online

'Speculating about the future of technology in international services marketing is intriguing and dangerous. It is intriguing because "what if" thinking is inherently fun, but it is dangerous because even relatively safe predictions can sometimes be wrong.'

Fisk, R. 1999, 'Wiring and growing the technology of international services marketing', *Journal of Services Marketing*, vol. 13, no. 4/5, pp. 311–18.

LEARNING *objectives*

After reading this chapter, you should be able to:

- recognise the differences between services and goods product and what impact this has on the online delivery of services

- define and classify online and offline service products

- outline the types of consumer search behaviour, and associated service products, that occur in online service delivery

- overview the issues of training customers to be co-producers of services

- explain the difference between using technology for the sake of technology and using technology to enhance service delivery.

Introduction

In many ways, all Internet-based marketing can be considered part of the broader services marketing industry. The nature of data transmission is inherently intangible and the perceived benefits of operating online such as increased convenience, empowerment and time saving are all also intangible. This chapter focuses on service products which are distributed online. These can include stand-alone service products such as educational services as well as service components of bundled products such as software with an online help function.

The marketing of services online is, in some respects, less complex than services marketing in the traditional environment. Several of the main problems associated with services marketing, such as time dependency and the necessary one-on-one interactions between service staff and customers, are reduced, if not eliminated in the online environment. However, to fully understand the benefits of shifting some components of service delivery online, it is necessary to have a detailed understanding of the traditional service product, issues surrounding its effective delivery and marketing, and an appreciation as to how the relative importance of these issues varies according to service product classifications.

This understanding of the service product then allows for a more in-depth understanding, not only of observable consumer behaviour in relation to services marketing, but also an appreciation of the motivations which underlie these behaviours.

The service product

As is the case for the development of any marketing strategy, clear and concise service product definition is essential (Reedy, Schullo & Zimmerman 2000). The specific service products under consideration here are services that are sold and/or distributed via the Internet. It does not include the provision of the Internet service per se. The reason for this is that ISPs operate as traditional service providers in the economy — their link with the Internet is based on the specific product they are selling.

Although service products, like physical products, can be described as the core product and the bundle of benefits they deliver to the consumer (see chapter 8), services are harder to both define and explain. When discussing service products, it is important to note that there are very few products which could be considered 'pure' services. All products exist on a continuum with the majority combining elements of the physical (for example, a computer) with the service product (for example, help lines and repair warranties). The focus of this chapter is on the service component of the total product package that can be delivered in the online environment.

On the Internet, it is harder to distinguish between goods and services, given the intangible nature of the Internet. Most of e-commerce is related to the provision of a service, or retailing event, rather than a physical good. However, Langford and Cosenza (1998) proposed that a service/good analysis should focus on determining the extent to which each element of a service process can be seen as being more like a tangible or intangible product. Their method was to consider a holistic approach to the examination of the product and associated strategies, to determine whether services theory or tangible goods theory was best suited to each step. This is illustrated in figure 13.1.

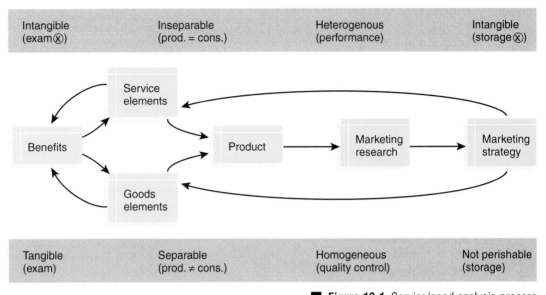

Figure 13.1 Service/good analysis process

Source: Langford, B. E. and Cosenza, R. M. 1998, 'What is Service/Good Analysis?', *Journal of Marketing Theory and Practice*, Winter, pp. 16–26.

The analysis process begins by establishing the product benefits that the customer buys and how these product benefits are perceived (chapter 8). These benefits are then divided by using the four traditional points of differentiation between goods and services to distinguish those which are primarily service elements and those which are goods elements. For example, conventional wisdom would see online ordering and using a remote hosting service as being a pure service, which has the product benefits of:

- hosting on a remote computer rather than the customer's own computer
- 24–7 access to the web site for the general public (rather than access relying on the owner of the site being online)
- economies of scale whereby a series of sites can share a larger and more powerful single computer and connection than each could afford separately (Reedy, Schullo & Zimmerman 2000).

Using the Langford and Cosenza (1998) model to examine an Internet hosting company, it can be seen that although the core service (web hosting) is intangible, the consumption of the service (hosting of the web site) is separable and occurs without the customer needing to be either physically present at the computer, or telepresent at the server. Performance of the server is more homogenous (standardised equipment) than heterogeneous (traffic demands,

Slashdot effects) although it remains predominantly perishable (bandwidth not used cannot be stockpiled for later use). In effect, the separability aspect of the service makes this product benefit element more akin to goods than services, which should be reflected in the marketing strategy decisions.

Traditional points of differentiation

Much has been written about how precisely services differ from physical goods and, although there are some variations to be found in the literature, the four defining factors are:

- **intangibility**: service products are performances which have none of the physical characteristics of goods in that they cannot be touched, tasted, seen, heard or observed before performance occurs (Langford & Cosenza 1998). Intangibility is a key element of the Internet itself and, consequently, much of the work of services marketing that can be used to address or exploit this issue is useful in e-commerce.
- **inseparability**: the simultaneous consumption and production of the services that require the consumer/recipient and the service delivery mechanism to be in close proximity during the service (Bateson 1996). For the most part, inseparability has been a strong element of the Internet given that the average user will be present at the computer as the Internet service they are using is taking place (circumstances such as automated downloading, or similar advanced systems allow the user to leave for food or sleep while the computer handles the transaction. Of course, the computer is then inseparable from the automated service transaction).
- **inconsistency**: relates the fact that no two services encounters will be identical due to the human influence of the service, and the high level of variability between consumer, service provider and service environment (Woodruffe 1995). A common criticism of both service and the Internet has been the tacit acceptance of inconsistency as an excuse for poor standards. Inconsistency is a factor that needs to be addressed, either through service roles or through service design, rather than an excuse for poor delivery. On the Internet, inconsistency occurs in a range of areas, including web site design, changes in site navigation, variable access speeds to popular sites and the change of addresses of popular sites.
- **perishability**: services can not be stored, stockpiled, or used once the service opportunity has passed (McGuire 1999). It is not possible to send a client back to last Thursday to use the spare seat on an airplane or take advantage of the empty hotel room. Resolving service perishability will be one of the first major commercial applications of time travel. Until such time services marketing needs to address the issues of load sharing, management of demand and levelling out peaks and troughs in demand.

To fully appreciate the relative costs and benefits of taking services online, an understanding of problems and limitations facing services marketers in a more traditional marketing environment is needed. Without this understanding, the appropriate mix of online versus traditional service delivery for any given organisation will be difficult to determine with any degree of accuracy or success.

Intangibility

Services differ from physical goods in that they are intangible; that is, they cannot be directly evaluated using any of the physical senses. For most authors, intangibility is the fundamental point of differentiation for service products. However, this is not as clear cut as it could be, given that there is no clear dichotomy between the tangible and intangible as tangibility exists along a continuum. At one end of the continuum are products which are dominated by their tangible characteristics such as salt or coal while at the other are products which are dominated by the intangible such as education and counselling services. Most products exist somewhere between these extremes. Products such as fast food meals are placed at an almost central point of tangible (the meal) and intangible (cooking of the meal, service and so on). Figure 13.2 illustrates the intangibility continuum.

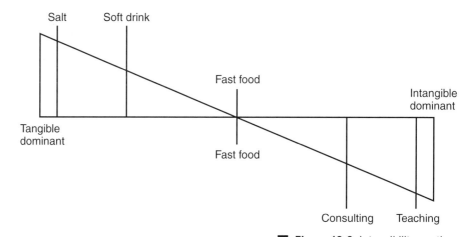

■ **Figure 13.2** Intangibility continuum

Source: Derived from Shostack, G. L. 1977, 'Breaking Free from Product Marketing', *Journal of Marketing*, April. In S. Baron & K. Harris 1998, *Services marketing: Text and cases*, Macmillan Press, London.

From a consumer perspective, intangibility means that it is difficult to objectively evaluate one service relative to another. Unlike physical goods which can be compared on the basis of size, colour, material, durability and so on, services have no clear, externally observable points of comparison. The consequence for consumers is that services represent a relatively high-risk purchase (Lovelock, Patterson & Walker 1998). For marketers, the problems associated with intangibility include added difficulties in defining and communicating the service product, particularly in terms of quality. To overcome this issue, services marketers rely heavily on tangible cues associated with the positioning of the service and its delivery. This includes the design of premises commensurate with the service firm's positioning strategy, selection of uniforms for staff, and the use of logos, gifts and warranties associated with the service purchase. Adding to this problem for services on the Internet is the absence of the **servicescape** or physical service location where these physical images can be used. (Chapter 10 examined the use of the web site for an alternative delivery of tangible cues.)

Operationalising the concept of intangibility is also extremely difficult. Similarly, identifying the intangible elements of the total product offering is complicated as processes and outcomes may both be intangible.

Bebko (2000) developed a two-by-four matrix of tangibility to assist in the understanding and classification of the service product. Under this schema, a process is judged as intangible where no 'evidence' exists for the consumer to experience, whereas a tangible process is one where some amount of evidence is available for the consumer to evaluate. Four levels of tangibility outcomes exist:

- purely intangible service outcomes, where no residual physical evidence exists to 'prove' a service has taken place (This could also be known as the Internet, as there are no physical traces of the Internet to be found in the real world.)
- an intangible service outcome which is bundled with a product
- a tangible service outcome
- a tangible service outcome bundled with a product.

Table 13.1 outlines a range of common products which combine tangible and/or intangible processes with tangible and/or intangible outcomes.

Table 13.1 Service intangibility classification

	Intangible process	Tangible process
Tangible service outcome/ product bundle	Film developing	Carpet installation
Tangible service outcome	Dog grooming	Pizza shop
Intangible service outcome/ product bundle	Online order of clothing	Retail book store
Intangible service outcome/ product bundle	Internet services	Medical services

Of most interest to Internet marketing and service delivery on the Internet is how to deal with intangible services that deliver intangible outcomes, given that these are both the hardest to market, and the most common to be found online.

Inseparability

A second key feature of services is the fact that for all personal and many other services, production and consumption occur simultaneously. For example, a haircut cannot take place if both the client and hairdresser are not in the same place at the same time. The higher the level of inseparability between the person and the good, the less likely it is that the service can be delivered across the Internet. This means that the method of service production is as important to the consumer as its delivery because the producer is present when the service is used (McGuire 1999). Most consumers have little interest in the personality of the factory worker that produced their car, their working conditions or how they look.

In contrast, the personal characteristics of the service provider and the cleanliness and comfort of the surroundings in which they work is of vital interest to the consumer who is present as the service is produced. The inseparability criterion derives from the importance of people in the services marketing mix (McColl-Kennedy & Kiel 2000). The people performing the service are, to the consumer, an integral part of the product. In many cases they are the product or, at least, the human face of the organisation they represent. In e-commerce, the web site replaces the person as the first impression. Most people are not concerned about the EDI systems that support the transfer of their money from their account to the store's account during an EFTPOS transaction, but in an online banking transaction, the look and feel of the site become an important aspect of the transaction.

Inseparability also adds to the perceived risk experienced by consumers. Instead of the usual evaluate–purchase–consume sequence of consumer buying behaviour, services require a purchase–consume–evaluate approach. It is not possible to evaluate a service until after it has been both purchased and consumed (Lovelock, Patterson & Walker 1998). Consequently, the purchase decision is made on the basis of little, if any, objective information. In addition, many services are difficult to assess. The selection of a web site designer is a complex task in that the customer may view other sites created by the designer, but these are not necessarily indicative of the success of the sites or the suitability of the designer to the task at hand. A well-designed site may fail to achieve the sales or promotional objectives because of poor selection of a web-hosting service, or online promotion service.

Inconsistency (heterogeneity)

Due in part to the problem of inseparability and the person-to-person interactions characteristic of services, it is difficult to guarantee consistent service from one delivery to the next. This can be due either to variations in the performance of the service provider or changed expectations or mood of the client. No two service interactions are identical (Zeithaml & Bitner 1996). Online service delivery is subject to the vagaries of the Internet, including Internet-wide congestion (sometimes referred to as 'Internet weather' — www.mids.org/weather), or site-specific traffic loads (Slashdot effects) or the congestion at the local ISP. As a result, Internet services can be inconsistent due to factors well beyond the control of the Internet marketer, just as extraneous factors impact on real-world service delivery.

Perceived service quality is largely based on service providers consistently meeting the expectations of customers rather than any specific objective measures. Over time, organisations, such as McDonald's, have gained a reputation for quality service provision by scripting customer to provider interactions and providing a consistent service product across time and location. In the quest to minimise inconsistency, many service providers have become increasingly scripted, production line-oriented and automated in delivery.

Internet-based services offer the opportunity to provide heavily scripted features and functions while giving the illusion of variability and interaction. Intelligent systems which are programmed to respond to if–then statements concerning consumer questions will consistently produce the same path if the same answers are given. This can increase consistency (though occasionally at the expense of accuracy — the site can consistently offer the wrong answer). While this may be appropriate for mass consumption services such as fast food, certain types of retailing and routine financial transactions, the variability or inconsistency of service delivery between customers is one of the major strengths of key service industries.

Customisation is both expected and demanded for services such as legal advice, psychological counselling and complex financial advice (Woodruffe 1995). Inconsistency in the services' marketing strategy is both its greatest strength and potentially its greatest weakness. Achieving the optimal balance between customisation and consistent service quality is one of the major challenges facing service managers. Cybercommunity structures offer the greatest opportunity to develop inconsistency as a saleable point for services which require a large amount of human interaction. The important factor to remember in determining the extent to use the Internet to attempt to eliminate inconsistency is the extent to which this inconsistency is a part of the benefits sought by the consumer in terms of personal service, customisation and human interaction.

Perishability (storage capacity)

Unlike physical goods which can be manufactured and then stored off site until required, services are perishable or time dependent. This is particularly true of personal services and entertainment. Once the opportunity to experience a show, football game or other event has passed, it is lost forever (Fisk et al. 2000). Similarly, it is not possible to store all the spare rooms a hotel may have on a quiet night for use at a later date when bookings exceed the number of rooms available. Internet sites which suffer from fluctuating demand cannot transfer the demand curve backwards in time to use the stockpiled bandwidth from last week.

From a managerial perspective, the major implication of this time dependency is the need to manage demand, primarily through pricing and promotional activities, to ensure the effective use of resources within the organisation. If demand is not managed adequately, two problems arise. First, lowered costs in terms of equipment, staffing and facilities become disproportionately large in relation to overall costs with the result that total capacity is underutilised. Second, customers who are either unable to experience the service during peak times or are given substandard service due to resource constraints are likely to become dissatisfied with the service provider and switch to an alternative supplier (Lovelock, Patterson & Walker 1998).

While the differences between physical goods and services impact significantly on the way in which services-oriented marketers develop and implement strategies, it is important to recognise that most products combine elements of both of them. An effective goods–service analysis in which similarities and differences are explicitly identified is essential if optimal strategies are to be developed (Langford & Cosenza 1998).

Impact of online delivery for traditional service concepts

How then does the move to online delivery affect the issues associated with the marketing and delivery of services? The online environment is well suited to the delivery of quality service. As a product which is essentially intangible and information based, services can be delivered directly online and do not necessarily need to be supplemented with traditional service delivery outlets.

In many ways technology, and specifically the Internet, have minimised, if not eliminated, the problems stemming from the unique characteristics of the service product. Specific areas where online services can be perceived as 'superior' to traditional delivery include the following:

- *reduced time dependence* — 24–7 access to web sites reduces the dependency on the service provider needing to have extended opening hours, and allows the consumer to make first contact (web/email) at their leisure, rather than within a set time frame (9–5) for phone or direct contact (Anon. 1996; Brindley 1999).
- *consistent service delivery* — uses web sites and automated systems for service delivery can provide a consistency of performance in the transaction. Registration of domain names through online forms allows for a fast, consistent transaction service compared to either calling a salesperson or delivering a handwritten form over a counter (www.npsis.com).
- *consistent imagery and branding* — careful selection of site design (chapter 10) to develop a consistent branding mechanism. It can operate as the equivalent of a servicescape for delivering tangible service cues (www.pizzahut.com.au).
- *customer lead customisation* — the consumer can arrange elements of a web site to select those with most value and significance to their own interests. Customised search portals (www.yahoo.com), newspapers (www.afr.com.au), music selections (www.mp3.com) and information filters (www.infobeat.com) all offer the customer a series of components to arrange into a customised package.
- *consumer empowerment* — arose from the range of choice for service delivery across the Internet and, in effect, across the world. Access to services which have traditionally been regionally based, such as radio stations, are available to a global audience, such as All India Radio (air.kode.net) or Bayerischer Rundfunk station (www.br-on-line.de) which offers streaming audio and video. Globalisation of services has empowered the consumer with wider choice, and with the ability to access specialist needs from practically any supplier in the world.
- *effective separation of production and consumption* — the producer of the service is able to upload a divisible information product or service (see chapter 8 and chapter 12) that can be consumed in their absence.

The three most significant benefits for services marketers moving online are improved consistency, greater consumer empowerment and the move away from time and place dependency. The following insight outlines how services can be delivered across the Internet, so as to take advantage of these benefits.

One of the major areas of service provision on the Internet is the delivery of Internet services such as web hosting, domain registration or email server hosting. The provision of services for the new medium in the new medium poses some interesting applications for service marketing. In the early days of the Internet, the service provision of Internet hosting tended to be a local industry as the host was usually the same provider for the company's Internet access and web site. Commercial ISPs provide a varying range of server space with their monthly accounts (usually 5 to 10 meg.). Gradually, as the Internet user base expanded, more companies offered dedicated web site hosting as a core service, instead of a supplementary service to their Internet access provision.

Phpwebhosting.com is a US-based company which provides a unique approach to online service delivery of web site hosting by offering a no-frills, flat-rate service to anyone in the world, thus removing the initial issue of separability. What makes the Phpwebhosting strategy interesting is the fact that they have used the Internet to negate the need for either service provider or consumer to be near to point of production. The client base of the company, which operates out of Indianapolis, has grown tremendously, and now covers every continent with the exception of Antarctica — all accessing the **server farm** which is located in Fort Lauderdale, Florida.

■ **Figure 13.3** phpwebhosting.com

Source: www.phpwebhosting.com

(*continued*)

The service has a very clearly defined market that targets experienced Internet users and web developers with clear and explicit statements to the effect that technical support will be deliberately limited. It is possible to sign up for the service, and operate effectively without ever engaging in any form of communication with the company, as the sign-on process is automated and, barring password problems, all interaction is between the user and the server farm. Inseparability has been conveniently addressed by the use of a single product sold through an automated system which leads into a user-controlled interface, all of which operates with a reasonable degree of consistency. Problems occasionally arise as with any web site, but for the most part, each log-in is through the same method, and greeted by the same interface.

Consistency, as stated previously, is the key criterion consumers use in the evaluation of service quality (Lovelock, Patterson & Walker 1998). Online services can be easily programmed to deliver the same consistent service to individual consumers over time and between consumers. For example, if you need a telephone number and choose to log into the White Pages (www.whitepages.com.au) you will encounter an identical interface each time, the same interface as millions of others encounter in their transactions. There is no room for misinterpretation, confused instructions or misunderstandings due to accents; errors in reading out numbers or variability in the mood, personality or quality of the staff member involved in the interaction. Similarly, ATMs offer a consistent, non-judgemental service to all clients. One of the surprising findings of Citibank (www.citibank.com) when introducing ATMs in the 1980s was that the early adopters of the new technology were not, as expected, the young and well-educated, but non-English speakers and those with poor education or communication skills.

The impersonal technological interface gives consumers the freedom to make mistakes without being judged or to get advice without feeling self-conscious or embarrassed. Health advice and information on what are often perceived as socially embarrassing issues such as domestic violence (www.famvi.com) or contraception (www.contraception.net) can be accessed through anonymous online services. No-one need ever know the personal concerns of the individuals involved. In addition, the information given via such services will not change over time. If a consumer forgets how to conduct a transaction or what specific actions to take in a given situation, accessing the same site with the same request will result in consistent outcomes. This is rarely achievable in traditional service delivery, as providers often forget the details given in the previous encounter.

A second major benefit for consumers in using online equivalents of traditional services is the shift in the power base to being more customer oriented (Anon. 1996). The process of service delivery can be seen as a constant struggle for control between the organisation, service workers and the customer. Ideally, this triangle of control should be balanced and each participant should feel that they have a significant element of control in the situation (Bateson 1996). Often, however, one or more players feels disempowered and out of control. A customer may have a special request or need that does not fall neatly within the standard practices or policies of the organisation. For example, at a function a customer may request that a meal be prepared in a certain way such as salad without dressing. If the standardised service does not allow for variations like this, the customer loses face in asking and the serving staff feel out of control because they are unable to comply with the request and, as a result, management is perceived to have a disproportionately high level of control. Similarly, in some face-to-face interactions, particularly where staff are paid commission, customers may feel pressured into purchasing services they do not necessarily need, thus taking the focus of control away from the client and towards the contact staff (Zeithaml & Bitner 1996).

Moving services into the online environment helps to shift the balance of power in favour of the consumer. The nature of the Internet is such that services must be sought at the discretion of the individual consumer and not pushed at them. Pressure to purchase is minimised due to the anonymous interface between service provider and user. This allows consumers to have the power to terminate the service encounter without any of the social restrictions that usually arise during a face-to-face encounter. Consumers are further empowered by their ability to customise the services they use according to their needs. Also, the search capacities of the Internet make comparisons of different service offerings, prices and so on, significantly easier.

Customers are empowered to trade valuable, but financially cost-free information, for services (see chapter 16, Market Research) more effectively in the online environment. The choice to participate lies with the consumer. Unlike many face-to-face encounters, customers have the luxury of being able to spend time considering the implications of such a transaction prior to involvement and can terminate the transaction at any time with relative ease.

A third major benefit of online service delivery is that it represents a move away from time and place dependency. This in turn helps to overcome many of the problems associated with inseparability and perishability. Given the remote delivery inherent in the production of online services there is no need for direct real-time interaction to take place. The process and method of service production becomes less important as the consumer is no longer required to be physically present in the **service factory** at the time of production (Bateson 1996). Consequently, it is possible for service providers to be located anywhere in the world and not necessarily within close proximity of the client base thus removing place dependency. In addition, online banking, and loan applications, remove the need for the initial contact between staff and customer during the application process (www.ewizard.com.au).

Similarly, the separation of production and consumption in online services means that they can be available at any time. Service providers can either automate responses to allow for 24–7 service delivery or for complex customised services work in joint ventures with partners across time zones to allow for 24–7 access to expertise or production. Automated services and the information they provide can be stored online unlike traditional services which cannot be stored. The difficulties of managing demand and excess capacity are less of a problem for online services marketers, although some difficulties still arise when the technology is incapable of supporting surges in demand during a Slashdot effect, power outage, or server downtime. As technology improves and the bandwidth problem is solved, the issue of excess demand for capacity should be fully resolved for online service delivery.

Defining the service product

As stated before, services are difficult to define and communicate not only because of their intangibility, but because most service products form part of a larger product package.

Classifications of service products

Various classification systems for services have been developed over time and although none is perfect, all help determine where a particular service sits relative to others. The value for managers in taking the time to evaluate their service offerings in terms of various classification systems is that not all service types are equally appropriate for on-line delivery. Although the following classifications are not exhaustive, they do provide a guide as to the types of criteria by which services can be classified and the compatibility between service type and online delivery.

People-directed versus thing-directed services

Service products take form only when they are directed at an outcome which means a service must occur to a person or product (or place). People-directed services are any services which are applied directly to the consumer, for example, haircuts (www.hairpolice.com), massages (www.massage.com) or counselling (www.gnfc.org.uk) and so on. Thing-directed services focus on the possessions of the consumer. Thing-directed services include lawn mowing (www.lawngents.com), house painting (www.pugetpainters.com), veterinary services (www.petpro.com.au) and car repairs (www.pitstop.co.nz) (Lovelock, Patterson & Walker 1998).

In traditional service delivery, one of the limitations of people-directed services is that the individual has to be present while the service is delivered (McColl-Kennedy & Fetter 1999). Due to the time and place independent nature of the Internet, however, people-directed services aimed at people's minds, rather than bodies, are particularly suited to delivery over the Internet. These include correspondence courses (www.acs.edu.au), accounting (www.kennedy.com.au), proofreading (www.englishexpert.com/proof) and web site design (www.realm.ca) all of which focus on the service of information and ideas. Information product services are the ideal product for online delivery, whereas services directed at possessions or things are less suited to online delivery. However, supplementary services, such as additional information on ongoing care for the object (servicing, cleaning or maintenance) can be delivered effectively via the Internet and can be used to form part of a broader service product package.

Customisation vs standardisation

Not all services are inconsistent in form and delivery as many can be customised to satisfy the majority of consumers (Wright 1995). Traditional examples of effective customised services include organisations such as McDonald's who offer a standard product range in familiar surroundings and with strict service standards over a wide range of outlets (www.mcdonalds.com). Online examples of effective standardisation include any information services delivered via the medium of FAQs (www.faqs.org) or those that rely on mass circulation of newsletters to which consumers can subscribe (www.drudgereport .com). Standardised, information-based services are the areas where the move to online delivery results in the greatest convenience and savings for the organisation.

Despite the heavy focus on the Internet as the delivery channel most suited to customisation, in the case of service delivery this conventional wisdom needs to be questioned. The interpretation of customisation for the Internet relates to the fact that for many information-based services customers are able to pick and choose from a range of standardised information packages to create their own 'unique' product. Central to the customisable service product are a variety of standardised products. While this does result in a degree of customisation, the full ability to customise relies on providing capacity for person-to-person interactions or access to data manipulation. In most cases, the costs involved in a fully customised online service (for example, www.gov.au) are prohibitively expensive for the average consumer. Customised online services are often more illusion than reality.

Discrete vs continuous service

A third useful classification is to determine whether the service act is continuous or discrete. Continuous services are those for which the consumer has an ongoing demand and builds a relationship with the service provider through regular contact. Examples include banks (www.anz.com), insurance companies (www.fai.com.au) and telecommunications services (www.ericsson .se). Discrete services are those where customers are less familiar with the service provider and may be in contact with them for the first time. Alternatively, the relationship may involve discrete services provided intermittently, for example, a hospital visit (www.mater.ie) (McGuire 1999).

The Internet is particularly suited to maintaining information flow in established relationships between providers and clients engaged in continuous service provision. Such communications can strengthen loyalty and trust and provide customers with additional services and information to augment the core service offering. Discrete services are less dependent on the development of ongoing relationships; however, in these cases the value of the Internet is again focused on information provision. By providing clear and useful information on a service firm's web site, it becomes easier for consumers to compare service offerings on key criteria, thereby reducing the risks inherent in the transaction.

Using the above classifications it can be argued that a standardised, person-oriented, information-based service product is the type of service most suited to online delivery. This does not mean, however, that other types of service are unsuited to the medium. Rather, their design and implementation need to be carefully planned to complement existing offerings. At the same time a close eye must be kept on budgets to ensure that the service created is in fact delivering value for money for both customer and provider.

Customer support

One of the major areas of growth in online service product development has been in the field of customer support. Few corporations these days are without a web site to support their sales functions and provide after-sales service through help lines (support.microsoft.com), downloadable updates of software (home.netscape.com/smartupdate/), support advice (www.quake.com/support) or automated software systems (www.glsetup.com). When considering the role that the web site plays in the overall definition of the firm's service product, it is important to determine the extent to which online service is the core service product or if it simply forms part of the augmented service product. In this evaluation, only the service elements of the firm's overall product offering are considered. For example, the fully defined product of a computer purchase may include a range of services as part of the augmented product, with processing power being the core and the machine itself being the actual product.

Online service as core product

Online activity as the core of the service product occurs in situations where the organisation does not offer an alternative method of service delivery but focuses its service activities purely online. The types of organisations that fulfil this description include search engines (www.google.com), retail outlets that exist entirely online (www.amazon.com) and Internet-based information aggregators (www.freshmeat.net) or service brokers (b2b.yahoo.com). Organisations for which online activities form the core product tend to be new firms that have developed and evolved specifically to take advantage of the opportunities available in delivering an Internet service, such as banner advertising (www.bcentral.com) or digital product distribution (www.tucows.com) (Strauss and Frost 1999; Reedy, Schullo & Zimmerman 2000).

Online service as augmented product

More commonly, established organisations such as department stores (www.myers.com.au), major accountancy firms (www.hrblock.com) or suppliers of common goods such as groceries (www.woolworths.com.au), use the Internet and the services it provides as a means of augmenting their existing service products. In such cases, the web site and services offered through it are based on the assumption of an existing relationship with the consumer. A firm may offer online product assistance (www.kelloggs.com/recipes) or regular updates on product development for those who are registered with the organisation as potential or current clients (www.hoover.co.uk). Other uses of online services as part of the augmented service product are to provide:

- a venue for entertainment in a bid to create and sustain brand loyalty (www.pepsimax.com.au)
- reinforcement of the decision to purchase from the organisation in an attempt to reduce post-purchase cognitive dissonance
- additional services which complement existing products (www.hp.co.nz). For example, the use of search facilities for online versions for back issues of magazines or journals (www.brw.com.au).

In addition, service products can also be categorised by their capacity to be translated into international services, which is examined in the Focus on Strategy vignette.

FOCUS ON
Strategy

International services: Wiring and exporting services

The globalisation of the Internet has led to many services becoming international exporters of services without initially intending to reach a global market. Clark and Rajaratnam (1999) classified international services as one of four possible types:

- *contact-based* — services where people cross borders to perform services, such as consultancy, teaching or other skills-based delivery of service
- *vehicle-based* — services relayed across a communications channel such as television, radio, or the Internet
- *asset-based* — services which require establishing a head office and/or production facility in a new country
- *object-based* — services that can be impregnated onto a physical object (CD, video cassette), or where the service is applied to an object (repairs to machinery).

For Internet-based services, vehicle-based and object-based exporting is the most common form of international trade that these organisations can, and will, conduct by being online. The majority of Internet-based services are engaged in delivering their core service product using the Internet, with the emphasis on delivering within the confines of the PC. Clark and Rajaratnam (1999) observed four factors which impact on the delivery of vehicle-based services:

- the medium must have the capacity to carry the service — for example, MP3.com streaming audio is viable only on modem speeds of 56k or higher
- access limitations such as licences, contracts, exclusivity arrangements with offline providers and territorial limitations that can apply to restrict Internet-based international services. Many of the competition web sites (particularly ones requiring you to punch a monkey in banner adverts to enter) are limited to being able to provide prizes only to US residents. As yet, there are no international laws to prohibit the punching of monkeys in banner adverts, so these sites continue to offer rewards to people who are not eligible to receive them.
- the need for specialised equipment or software — restricts access to the delivery vehicle. Consumers need to have an Internet connection, plus the relevant software to access the service delivery on the site. Constant upgrading and development of display software such as Macromedia Flash (www.flash.com) or Shockwave (www.shockwave.com) often require users to upgrade their viewing software before the service can be accessed. Of greater concern (and frustration) has been the propensity of technologies such as DVD to become regionalised. Regional codes for software products limit the ability to export vehicle- and object-based services which are dependent on these technologies.

(continued)

■ the development and diffusion patterns of the existing technologies which relate to the spread of the channel of delivery of the service (examined in chapter 4 under diffusion of innovations). International compatibility issues between channels such as the PAL-NTSC incompatibility for video and television distribution, and the increasing problems with regional coding on other delivery channels is limiting the spread of technology-based services.

The development and spread of service delivery over the Internet create the ability for information-oriented services to become internationally available without having to develop networks or franchises.

One of the larger impacts of 'location joining' whereby services can operate across borders without crossing the national boundaries is to start to break down the sovereignty of a nation. Problems arising from the difficulties in determining jurisdiction for service liability, taxation, consumer protection agencies and regulation of 'vice' services such as online gambling have led some governments to attempt to impose limitations on the access to the services. However, for the most part, the strongest advocate of the increased range of choice has been the average consumer who is faced with a greater range of service choice from cross-national and international providers.

Consumer behaviour and the online service product

Traditionally, services have been regarded as an experience and so the main focus of services marketing has been to get clients to try the service and then evaluate and compare it with similar offerings. The intangibility of the service offering has meant that both marketers and consumers have accepted relatively vague pre-purchase explanations of service benefits as the norm for this style of product. Quality, outcomes and service benefits are often implied through visual cues such as the environment in which the service is conducted and pricing schedules, rather than being explicitly stated. Consequently, comparisons between service offerings have traditionally been extremely difficult.

From the consumer's perspective, the service product can be defined not only in terms of the benefits accrued from using it, but also as a function of the behaviours involved that lead to the decision to purchase. Using a consumer behaviour-oriented approach to service product definition, services can be more effectively marketed if strategies are designed around a fuller understanding of the consumer's pre-purchase behaviours. In other words, knowing what the customer wants, and how they go about finding something to meet that want is the key to good services marketing.

Search behaviours and service type

One of the consumer benefits of shopping for, and using services online is that the nature of Internet interactions is still fundamentally text-based. The move to online service delivery, however, has forced a change in the marketing and definition of service products and benefits from implication to explicit statement. In other words, an online services marketer needs to clearly, verbally state the nature of the service offering and the benefits to the consumer. This in turn makes it easier for direct comparisons between the products of various service firms to be made. As the nature and complexity of the service product varies considerably across industries, so too does the consumer behaviour associated with pre-purchase information gathering (Venkatraman & Dholakia 1997). One useful classification system is based on the service product attributes. The way in which consumers seek information, choose services and evaluate their effectiveness depends on the characteristics of the service-product combination in question. The following attributes are important in determining the style of consumer behaviour followed.

- **search attributes** — those that have some clearly defined criteria based on which different offerings can easily be compared across a range of service providers. Online services, such as search engines (www.google.com or www.metacrawler.com), can be easily compared based on accuracy and usefulness of the results each return for the same keyword search.
- **experience attributes** — those services that can be evaluated only after experiencing the service, given that the quality and outcomes may be specific to the transaction or event. The involvement in a cybercommunity, or online service involving a range of human participants is an experience attribute service given that the performance of the other participants cannot be evaluated prior to purchase or experience of the service.
- **credence attributes** — experience-oriented services that are difficult to assess even post-purchase, due to the limited expertise and knowledge of the consumer, and the complexity of the service. Most commonly, these involve the activities of a highly skilled or highly trained practitioner in a complex area, such as law or medicine, or involving complex service events that cannot be easily judged against other experiences (Hofacker 2000).

Search attribute product

Products high in search attributes are those that have some clearly defined criteria based on which different offerings can be easily compared. Traditionally, physical goods have been described as high in search attributes, given the ease with which two brands of washing machine or car can be compared. In terms of consumer behaviour, search attribute products:

- have relatively low levels of perceived risk
- can be evaluated prior to purchase
- involve relatively low search times
- have decisions made on them strongly influenced by mass media such as advertising.

The increasing degree of tangibility of the service product in the online environment has moved many Internet-based services into the category of search attribute product, as various web-based service provisions can be assessed simultaneously, or through comparative shopper web sites (www. getconnected.com).

Experience attribute product

Services have been traditionally described as experience-based products, as a full evaluation of the quality and outcomes of the service cannot be made prior to purchase. Rather, the service must be first experienced and then evaluated and compared with similar services experienced in the past. Much of the content of the Internet is experience based, from information services such as CNN (www.cnn.com) through to entertainment sites (www.virtualworld .com.au), chat sites (www.InsideTheWeb.com), or music sites (www.mp3.com). One of the major difficulties facing high bandwidth products such as streaming audio (www.abc.net.au), video (movies.go.com/trailers), or downloadable services such as Mp3 files (www.napster.com) is the need to commit time (and download quota) to the acquisition of a product before being able to experience a trial version of it.

Credence product

Credence products, like experience attribute products, cannot be effectively evaluated and compared prior to purchase. Where credence products differ, however, is that, due to the limited expertise and knowledge of the consumer, it is difficult to evaluate service quality even after consumption. Products falling within this range are any high level professional services such as surgery (www.surgery.com) and health advice (www.surgerydoor.co.uk), financial planning (www.mmfm.co.uk) or legal advice (www.legalaccess.com.au).

Risk reduction strategies

In the marketing and consumer behaviour literature, it is generally accepted that services are perceived by consumers to be a high-risk purchase. Chapter 12 discussed different methods of risk reduction, and strategies for lowering consumer barriers to online purchasing. Different levels of risk are associated with different service types with credence-based services products regarded as significantly higher in risk when compared with search- or experience-based services (Hofacker 2000; Mitra, Reiss & Capella 1999). Accordingly, consumers aim to minimise risk prior to purchase, primarily through the collection and evaluation of quality pre-purchase information about the service and service provider (Knowles-Mathur, Mathur & Gleason 1998). Service providers of perceived high-risk services are referred to established in-depth sites which can step the user through the processes of the service, and the likely outcomes. This is accomplished by informing the potential client and reducing the psychic costs associated with high-risk products.

Training the customer to be a co-producer

The only consistent new element in the expanded services marketing mix developed across the literature is the inclusion of 'people' in addition to product, price, promotion and place. People, both employees and customers, are vital to the overall service experience. Due to the inseparability factor, the behaviour of customers is integral to the success and quality of the service experience. This factor presents considerable problems for the service marketer in ensuring consistency and quality in the service offering.

Consumers are constantly trained and rewarded by service organisations for their part in the service interaction using both visible (financial rewards for assessing services) and invisible methods (removal of service alternatives by closing bank branches). The effectiveness and perceived quality of a service interaction is directly related to the extent to which the consumer is familiar with the organisation's expectations of their behaviour, and the way in which they interact both with the service providers and the environment in which the service is offered (Brindley 1999). McDonald's, for example, has implicitly trained its customers to queue appropriately, order from a set menu and even clean up after themselves. Any customer who varies from this strict script will have a sub-optimal service experience. This acceptance that the customer's actions at the time of service production will impact on service quality and outcomes is **co-production**. In other words, customers are seen as co-producers of the service and partial employees of the organisation (Wikstrom 1996). In the context of the Internet, most users are not required to clean up the web site when they leave, although they are increasingly being expected to use self-service systems to construct their own entertainment, educational or informational experience. Customisation-oriented news web sites effectively end up making the consumer the editor, forcing them to develop their own look, feel and content preferences. Thus far, most sites have not required the consumer to write their own news stories. However, cybercommunities-oriented news sites such as Slashdot (www.slashdot.org) do rely heavily on the submission of articles, stories and links to the editorial team, and place an emphasis on the customer-driven interactive discussion forums. In other words, customers of the Slashdot service are writing their own content, picking their own content, and cleaning up the site as they leave.

Many consumers have resisted making online purchases because of the perceived risk of feeling exposed when they are faced with a new learning situation. For those who are not computer literate, the stress involved in learning these new tasks can represent a social and psychological cost great enough to prevent use of online services, regardless of the potential benefits. Using current technologies, Internet-based services are available only to those who feel confident in the use of computers, have a reasonable degree of literacy and are able to effectively use search engines. All of these must be learnt just in order to access online services, let alone actually use them.

While computer-literate and Internet-savvy consumers may have learnt the general approach for using sites, the specific actions needed to get maximum benefit from a particular service site will vary considerably between organisations.

Technology as the means not the end

Ultimately, the success of online services will depend on marketers remembering that technology is a tool. It should be recognised for what it is — a means to the end, not the end in itself. With increasingly complex software available at affordable prices, it is tempting to focus on competitor sites and try to outdo them in creativity and interactivity. In the end, however, web site effectiveness and the value of online services will be determined according to the extent to which the organisation meets the needs of its customers and meets or exceeds their expectations of service delivery. Exceeding expectation of service delivery does not mean exceeding needed service capacity, nor does it give site designers a licence to engage in **creeping featurism**.

The constant over-evolution of web search systems is becoming the running battleground between the needs of the consumer, and the desire of the search sites to become one-stop Internet shops. Yahoo.com has expanded the initial directory service into providing everything from a shopping mall, through to free email, web sites, and a customisable news service. Several other search sites have chosen to pursue the Yahoo.com model, and have increasingly moved away from the search functionality into providing portal services. The problem for the consumer is that those users who relied on the search-only function of a site (such as www.infoseek.com) which has 'evolved' into a portal (www.go.com) often find themselves swamped with 'features' that they neither need nor want. Technological developments are outstripping market needs, and the finite limit of how many people actually need horoscopes, weather and stockmarket reports along with a filtered news wire service, free email, web site recommendations and 'Coffee Recipe of the Day' service in a search engine will have to be reached. Even sites which rebadged to become search-only systems (www.google.com) have begun the steady slide towards developing portal interfaces (or integration and merger with existing interfaces such as Yahoo.com).

Fisk et al. (2000) identify six weak links in the customer–technology interface which can seriously undermine the quality of the organisation's online service outputs. These are:

1. *automated idiocy* — in the rush to automate and standardise services, many organisations use systems which lead to illogical outcomes. It must always be borne in mind that online services which are automated can respond in only limited ways — the true interaction of the person-to-person service experience is easily lost in the move to online service delivery.

2. *time sink* — this occurs when the time involved in conducting a service transaction using the new technology is in fact greater than that involved in using existing technologies. It is still often quicker and easier to ring up and ask for information than navigate the web in search of it.

3. *'law of the hammer'* — based on the idea that a child with a hammer sees every other object as a nail. Applied to Internet-based services, this law serves to remind creators of the technological interface that design should focus on customer needs, not the needs of the designer. What is appealing from a technological perspective may simply confuse and put off a client.

4. *technology lock* — one of the biggest problems in the customer–technology interface is the fact that designs often persist long after their functional value is gone. The most notable example of technology lock in recent times was the Y2K bug — a situation which arose because the practice of saving space on computer memories by using only the last two digits of the year persisted long after it was no longer necessary.

5. *the last inch* — most problems for service delivery online occur at the point of customer–Internet contact. Often in the 'last inch' of service delivery breakdowns occur due to the lack of training on the part of customers, design faults or incompatible systems.

6. *high tech versus high touch* — sometimes a problem cannot be solved simply by accessing information and databases online. Many problems are complex and require person-to-person interaction. High-tech solutions are often not the most effective and may ultimately present an image of an uncaring organisation to clients.

To ensure that the move to delivering Internet-based services is smooth and effective the following steps are recommended (Fisk et al. 2000):

- provide marketer input into the technology of customer interface design
- stay customer focused, not machine focused
- make services technology invisible to the customer — customers are interested only in the service outcomes, not how they got there, what they did on the way, or how fundamentally clever the programmer was for developing the process
- insist on a design that delivers service flexibility that adequately meets the needs of the consumer without excessive complexity.

Summary

The Internet opens up a whole new world of opportunities for services marketers, not only to create new, online service products, but to enhance their current service product mixes. As in all areas of marketing, however, the key to successful service product development and delivery is to fully understand the complexity of the product involved and then listen to the needs of the consumer before responding with a specific service offering. The flexibility of the Internet, and the relatively low marginal costs involved in new service product development online, provide a range of temptations for services marketers to become technologically rather than consumer driven. Successful services firms, however, are those that recognise the technology as being the means to the end (customer satisfaction) rather than the end in itself.

This chapter has examined the nature of the service product in detail, both as it exists traditionally and as it is being adapted in the online environment. In doing so, it has shown how some of the traditional difficulties facing services marketing, such as the normal lack of service consistency, are easier to overcome via Internet delivery. It also examined classifications of service products, the nature of the online service product and its relationship to the total service offering of the organisation. Finally, the chapter concludes with a reminder of the importance of staying customer, rather than technology focused, in the design and delivery of online services.

Discussion questions

13.1 Outline the traditional points of differentiation between goods and services. Which of these differences has the greatest impact for online service delivery?

13.2 How has online delivery altered offline service delivery? Give examples of how web-based services can impact on offline services.

13.3 Do online services have to have an offline presence? Can a service exist purely in the online medium or does it still require some offline capacities? Discuss with examples.

13.4 Outline the classifications of service product. Find online examples of each type of service product.

(continued)

13.5 Discuss the value of online customer support. Should it be used as a core product or augment product?

13.6 Do online international services face similar problems to online goods exporters? How can service exporters deal with the problems of being sporadic exporters?

13.7 What are the three types of service attribute? How do these differ from each other?

13.8 What risk reduction strategies can online services marketers use to encourage adoption of their services?

13.9 What are the ethical considerations inherent in co-production? Should the company charge a premium price for allowing product customisation or should the customer be entitled to a lower price for the services products that they co-produce?

13.10 Is technology a means to an end or the end in itself? Should services adopt technologies that might be beneficial in the future or use only proven technologies for service delivery?

References

Anon. 1996, 'Banking on the Internet', *Internet Research: Electronic Networking Applications and Policy*, vol. 6, no. 1, pp. 31–2.

Bateson, J. 1996, *Managing Services Marketing Text and Readings*, 3rd edition, Dryden, Fort Worth.

Bebko, C. 2000, 'Service intangibility and its impact on consumer expectations of service quality', *The Journal of Services Marketing*, vol. 14, no. 1, pp. 9–26.

Brindley, C. 1999, 'The marketing of gambling on the Internet', *Internet Research: Electronic Networking Applications and Policy*, vol. 9, no. 4, pp. 281–6.

Clark, T. & Rajaratnam, D. 1999, 'International services: Perspectives at century's end', *Journal of Services Marketing*, vol. 13, no. 4/5, pp. 298–310.

Fisk, R. 1999, 'Wiring and growing the technology of international services marketing', *Journal of Services Marketing*, vol. 13, no. 4/5, pp. 311–18.

Fisk, R., Grove, S. & John. J. 2000, *Interactive Services Marketing*, Houghton Mifflin, Boston.

Hofacker, C. 2000, *Internet Marketing,* 3rd edition, Wiley, New York.

Knowles-Mathur, L., Mathur, I. & Gleason, K. 1998, 'Service advertising and providing services on the Internet', *The Journal of Services Marketing*, vol. 12, no. 5, pp. 334–47.

Langford, B. & Cosenza, R. 1998, 'What is service/good analysis?', *Journal of Marketing Theory and Practice*, Winter, pp. 16–26.

Lovelock, C., Patterson, P. & Walker, R. 1998, *Services Marketing*, Prentice-Hall, Sydney.

McColl-Kennedy, J. R. & Kiel, G. C. 2000, *Marketing: A Strategic Approach*, Nelson ITP, Melbourne.

McColl-Kennedy, J. & Fetter, R. 1999, 'Dimensions of consumer search behaviour in services', *Journal of Services Marketing*, vol. 13, no. 3, pp. 242–65.

McGuire, L. 1999, *Australian Services: Marketing and Management*, MacMillan, Melbourne.

Mitra, K., Reiss, M. & Capella, L. 1999, 'An examination of perceived risk, information search and behavioural intentions in search, experience and credence services', *Journal of Services Marketing*, vol. 13, no. 3, pp. 208–28.

Reedy, J., Schullo, S. & Zimmerman, K. 2000, *Electronic Marketing: Integrating Electronic Resources into the Marketing Process*, Dryden Press, Fort Worth.

Shostack, G. 1977, 'Breaking free from product marketing', *Journal of Marketing*, vol. 41, pp. 73–80.

Strauss, J. & Frost, R. 1999, *Marketing on the Internet: Principles of On-line Marketing*, Prentice-Hall, New Jersey.

Venkatraman, M. & Dholakia, R. 1997, 'Searching for information in marketspace: Does the form — product or service — matter?', *Journal of Services Marketing*, vol. 11, no. 5, pp. 301–16.

Wikstrom, S. 1996, 'The customer as co-producer', *European Journal of Marketing*, vol. 30, no. 4, pp. 6–13.

Woodruffe, H. 1995, *Services Marketing*, Pitman, London.

Wright, L. 1995, 'Avoiding services marketing myopia'. In W. Glynn & J. Barnes (Eds), *Understanding Services Management*, Wiley, Chichester.

Zeithaml, V. & Bitner, M. 1996, *Services Marketing*, McGraw Hill, New York.

Web sites

www.abs.gov.au
air.kode.net
b2b.yahoo.com
home.netscape.com/smartupdate/
movies.go.com/trailers
support.microsoft.com
www.abc.net.au
www.acs.edu.au
www.afr.com.au
www.amazon.com
www.anz.com
www.bcentral.com
www.br-on-line.de
www.brw.com.au
www.citibank.com
www.cnn.com
www.contraception.net
www.drudgereport.com
www.englishexpert.com/proof
www.ericsson.se

www.ewizard.com.au
www.fai.com.au
www.famvi.com
www.faqs.org
www.flash.com
www.freshmeat.net
www.getconnected.com
www.glsetup.com
www.gnfc.org.uk
www.go.com
www.google.com
www.hairpolice.com
www.hoover.co.uk
www.hp.co.nz
www.hrblock.com
www.infobeat.com
www.infoseek.com
www.InsideTheWeb.com
www.kelloggs.com/recipes
www.kennedy.com.au
www.lawngents.com
www.legalaccess.com.au
www.massage.com
www.mater.ie
www.mcdonalds.com
www.metacrawler.com
www.mids.org/weather
www.mmfm.co.uk
www.mp3.com
www.myers.com.au
www.napster.com
www.npsis.com
www.pepsimax.com.au
www.petpro.com.au
www.phpwebhosting.com
www.pitstop.co.nz
www.pizzahut.com.au
www.pugetpainters.com
www.quake.com/support
www.realm.ca
www.shockwave.com
www.slashdot.org
www.surgery.com
www.surgerydoor.co.uk
www.tucows.com
www.virtualworld.com
www.whitepages.com.au
www.woolworths.com.au
www.yahoo.com

CHAPTER 14

Relationship marketing in a 'one-to-many-to-one' environment

'Trust, especially among the trading partners in electronic commerce, reinforces the prospect of continuity in a relationship and a commitment to extend an inter-organisational relationship.'

Ratnasingham, P. 1998, 'The importance of trust in electronic commerce', *Internet Research*, vol. 8, no. 4, pp. 313–21.

LEARNING objectives

After reading this chapter, you should be able to:

- understand the domain of relationship marketing, including the core philosophies and definitions

- outline the three levels of relationship marketing online

- recognise the opportunities for value of building relationships over the Internet

- apply marketing theory and practice to create commercial relationships online

- recognise the barriers to the creation of online relationships

- overview the role and value of cybercommunities in relationship marketing

- understand the role and importance of trust in e-commerce

- appreciate the application of business to business marketing on the Internet.

Introduction

Since the mid-1980s, the focus in marketing theory and practice has shifted from the transactional to the relationship-based approach. Basically this means that consumers are now perceived as the sum total of their potential lifetime value rather than a collection of individual sales opportunities.

This chapter overviews the issues concerning the definition and domain of relationship marketing, including the core philosophies and definitions that apply to both on and offline relationships. It examines the three operational levels, from tactics to strategy to philosophy, and how these can be applied to improve the value of building relationships over the Internet, for both consumer and producer. In addition, the chapter overviews the impact of the unique features of the Internet and how this serves to help or hinder the creation of online relationships, and what practical steps can be used to resolve difficulties and enhance the positives, including the use of cybercommunities and the methods of creating trust online. Finally, the chapter briefly overviews the value of the Internet to business to business marketing, and the types of applications best suited to online delivery.

Domain of relationship marketing

Relationship marketing requires the organisation to get to know its customers, their needs and their motivations. Based on this knowledge, the organisation then develops customised programs which are designed to increase the value of the customer to the organisation. These programs often include actions such as setting up loyalty schemes, pro-actively contacting customers to ensure satisfaction or developing special offers available to only certain categories of customers, all of which are focused on increasing the value of the customer to the organisation.

Defining relationship marketing is almost as difficult as trying to nail down a working definition of post-modernism. Unlike post-modernism, relationship marketing has no modernism equivalent to provide a convenient excuse to avoid setting the parameters. The problem with defining relationship marketing is that there are nearly 50 published definitions of the subject, and at least three 'definitive' statements on the topic. Grönross's (1994) definition of relationship marketing is as follows:

Relationship marketing is to identify and establish, maintain and enhance and, when necessary, also to terminate relationships with customers and other stakeholders, at a profit, so that the objectives of all parties are met, and that this is done by a mutual exchange and fulfilment of promises.

At this point asking two relationship marketers for a definition of relationship marketing and its core principles will result in at least four definitions and five 'must have' variables (plus two LISREL models and decent sized headache). Morgan and Hunt (1994), along with Sheth (1994 in Harker, 1999) and many others have differing views on the 'true' definition of relationship marketing. For those interested in exploring the range of definitions available, Harker (1999) reviews 26 of the available definitions in search of a common thread between them (and the chance to be definition number 27).

The decision to select Grönross's definition is based on the compatibility of the work with the marketing concept used in this text. This particular definition recognises that the needs of the consumer and the organisation must be met, at a profit, for the relationship marketing to continue. Many interpretations of relationship marketing focus too heavily on being consumer dominated in the pursuit of long-term loyalty. In addition, Grönross recognises the need of the organisation to be able to terminate the relationship where necessary, which supports this text's established principle of targeted marketing, and the underpinning notion that not every customer is the right customer. Of course, other followers of relationship marketing will have their preferred definition, and it is accepted that disagreements will arise over the choice of definition. In a complex, and sometimes volatile new sub-discipline of marketing, there will always be points of contention over the selection of definitions and implied favouritism towards one school of thought over the others.

Core concepts of relationship marketing

Relationship marketing is about developing an ongoing product relationship that places emphasis on retaining and improving business relations with the customer. The idea operates in contrast to the traditional approach of marketing which emphasises gaining new customers and larger market share as the key determinants to successful business. Rather than pursuing each customer and transaction as a new event, the relationship marketer will attempt to develop an ongoing series of transactions with the consumer, to increase customer loyalty and reduce the need to acquire new customers.

The emphasis on relationship marketing is based on a pair of key assumptions:

- *the lifetime value of the customer*: the total value of the customer to the organisation. Ideally, as customers stay with the relationship, they will increase their value to the organisation, increase their rate of purchase and spread positive word of mouth to encourage new customers to join. The flaw in this idea is the possibility that the customer will become increasingly more expensive over time, as loyalty schemes, reward programs and other arrangements cut into the value margin between retaining a customer and gaining a new one. For example, a loyalty incentive scheme from a computer manufacturer may involve offering a lifetime guarantee for free labour on repairs to their computers. As the loyal consumer base ages, their products will reach the end of their useful operational life around the same time, and the manufacturer may find the repair costs exceeding the total value of the customers.
- *customer loyalty*: the cornerstone of relationship marketing, as the theory assumes that the development of trust, commitment and responsiveness will result in the customer feeling a reciprocal loyalty to the organisation, and will not simply encourage the consumer to play one company off against another to maximise their personal gain.

Loyal customers are those individuals who exhibit both behavioural and psychological commitment to the organisation. Behavioural commitment is exhibited through:

- repeatedly buying from the one supplier when alternatives exist. Online, this can occur through repeat visits to a web site, or preferred use of a single search engine or index.
- increasing the amount of transactions with that supplier, either by purchasing more, or more frequent visits to the web site; or
- providing constructive feedback and suggestions, which is the provision of unsolicited materials, suggestions or advice. Taken to the logical extension, many loyal customers of software products will produce materials, patches and other associated materials for the company (see chapter 17 and porting). The enthusiasm and loyalty that can be exhibited online is occasionally unsettling for companies who are not used to the response to popular software packages. If, as was the case with ID Software (www.idsoftware.com), the company can capitalise on the loyal customer base by working with them, they can build incredibly strong loyalty to the organisation.

Psychological commitment to the organisation is based around the mental processes associated with the development of a successful relationship. Consumers have established psychological commitment when they:

- would not consider terminating the relationship, or using an alternative supplier
- engage in positive word of mouth referral
- hold a positive attitude towards the supplier, relationship, and are experiencing beneficial outcomes from the exchange.

Although these are the strongest indicators, the development of strong relationships between consumer and supplier can be exhibited through alternative methods. One interesting problem that can arise from a strong consumer relationship with an organisation is a very negative reaction to a corporate takeover that merges the preferred brand into the new venture. Disney's takeover of the Infoseek brand was not the success it expected, as the relationship and loyalty that had been built with the Infoseek brand was not immediately transferable to the Go.com branding. In fact, many individuals who had previously been loyal to the Infoseek brand switched providers when Go.com removed the Infoseek branding from the service. Purchasing an organisation with strong customer relationships requires the purchaser to maintain the elements that have formed the strong bond, rather than assume the relationship loyalty can be transferred to the new group identity.

Suitability for relationship marketing

Gilbert, Powell-Perry and Widijoso (1999) established six points to determine when the relationship marketing paradigm was most suited for application. These are:

- *There is an ongoing or periodic desire for the service on the part of the customer.* Where customers know that they require a service over a recurring period of time (e.g. hairdressing) they are more likely to engage in a business relationship than for one-off events (e.g. wedding catering).

- *The service customer controls the selection of the service supplier.* The targeted customer for a relationship marketing campaign must be the person who ultimately makes the purchase decision, for example, Dell Computer (www.dell.com) would need to target their relationship marketing focus at the IT purchaser, rather than the end user in a firm.
- *There exists an alternative choice of suppliers.* There is no real need for relationship marketing in a monopoly environment, or where the service customer is restricted in their choice of providers. In contrast, highly competitive environments such as the Internet create the need to develop ongoing relationships with repeat visitors.
- *Brand switching is a common phenomenon.* In a competitive market of multiple alternative means of satisfaction, relationship marketing is a strategic alternative to price-based competition or cyclical sales promotions. One of the major factors for encouraging the development of relationship marketing online is the range of providers of similar services and the ease of brand switching. Developing ongoing relationships and brand loyalty will become the key to longevity for Internet services as the market gradually matures, and brand-loyal customers become the key to financial viability.
- *Word of mouth (WOM) is an especially potent form of communication about a product.* Personal referrals, web site recommendations and other methods of word of mouth were overviewed in chapter 9. The Internet is a medium that is almost tailor-made for word of mouth (even having a sub-genre of 'word of mouse') with the ease of passing web site addresses through email, IRC or messenger services such as ICQ (www.icq.com).
- *There is an ability to cross-sell products.* The Internet provides an organisation with the capacity to develop a web site with multiple layers of service options, product alternatives and content which can be cross-sold to enhance the user's experience. Yahoo–Geocities (www.yahoo.com, www.geocities.com) offers nearly a dozen product alternatives that can be cross-sold with their initial relationship marketing offering of free email (Yahoo) or free web pages (Geocities).

Web sites also have the opportunity to collect the requisite data for the development of personalised services and the formation of web-based relationship marketing (see chapters 10 and 16).

Philosophical principles of relationship marketing

Having established the visible indicators of successful relationship marketing, and the conditions under which it is most suitable, the priority for online marketers is to determine how to aid, abet and develop online relationships. In order to do this successfully, it is necessary to explore the principles behind successful relationship marketing. The three core principles which are most consistently recognised as having the greatest impact are:
- **trust**, which is the willingness to rely on an exchange partner in whom one has confidence, and this includes a belief in the trustworthiness of the partner, and the reliance on the other partner to perform (Moorman et al. 1993; Grönross 1994).

- **commitment**, which is the perceived need to maintain the relationship, either because of the inherent value of staying, or because of the costs associated with leaving the exchange (Geyskens et al. 1996 in Wetzels, de Ruyter & van Birgelen 1998).
- **reciprocity**, which is basically the notion of equality, mutual obligation and Bagozzi's (1975) exchange theory.

As with the definition of relationship marketing, a really fast way to start a fight in a relationship marketing bar is simply to ask for the three most important variables in determining how a relationship can be formed and modified. For the purposes of this book, only the three keys of trust, commitment and reciprocity will be examined in regard to developing and assisting online relationships.

Trust

Developing trust is a major issue facing the online marketer. This is due to the relatively new nature of the Internet, the residual impact of many earlier sensational stories in the media regarding the potential power of the Internet to invade privacy, and the unethical behaviours of a small number of providers on the Web, trust is particularly difficult to develop in this new environment.

Doney and Cannon (1997, in Jevons & Gabbott 2000) outline five processes by which trust can be formed in business relationships. These are:
- *calculative processes*, which try to second guess the value of cheating or defrauding the relationship. This theory is derived from economics and comes complete with a set of complex mathematical equations (and the assumption of perfectly rational behaviour) that indicates that if the benefits of cheating do not outweigh the costs of being caught, then the parties to the transaction will be honest.
- *prediction of future intent on past behaviour*, which uses the past actions of a party to determine the likelihood of acting in a fraudulent manner in the future. This method is difficult to achieve in some areas of the Internet where no transaction history exists, but can be a very positive method where transaction histories can be accessed. E-bay (www.ebay.com) offers access to transaction histories of bidders/sellers through ratings systems, and offers the opportunity to contact participants of past transactions. Other systems, such as archived newsgroups or bulletin boards can provide history to transactions, and can be searched for examples of where fraudulent transactions have been encountered and reported to the community (Arunkundram & Sundararajan 1998).
- *credibility*, which is where trust is derived from the capability and capacity of the other party to deliver on their promises. Web sites which offer sample downloads, trial products, peer reviews and user ratings all provide indications of the credibility of the organisation to deliver on their promise.
- *motive assessment*, which is based on interpreting the motives of the transaction partner. This assumes that the exploitative party will be obviously exploitative, look like trouble and be recognised for not having the transaction partner's interest at heart. This is a difficult method of trust, since the operation of any commercial exchange should have an equal split

between offering the customer what they want (consumer's interest) and gaining the best deal for the company (self-interest).

- *transference process*, which works on the principle of word of mouth, third party referral and trust by recommendation. The Internet has provided a range of systems and services for the ranking and rating of third party groups, such as Epinions (www.epinions.com) which offer reviews on products and services written by users of the products. Newsgroups tailored towards specific product categories will contain commentary regarding the trustworthiness (or otherwise) of companies that are involved in their specific area.

Trust in the online environment is particularly important before an initial transaction occurs, let alone as a part of developing an ongoing relationship. Although trust alone does not gain the sale (more mundane issues of the marketing mix such as price covers that avenue), it is a major factor in getting to the point of consideration for purchase. If the price is right, but the person does not trust the company, then the sale will not go ahead (Jevons & Gabbott 2000). (Developing trust online is covered in detail below.)

Commitment

Commitment is almost the end game state in relationship marketing. Trust is a key element to the formation and continuity of the relationship, whereas commitment is more towards the operationalisation of the contractual obligations. Once a relationship is formed, commitment is dependent on a range of factors, such as:

- *service and product quality*, which influences the purchaser's desire to stay within the relationship. Poor quality and inadequate delivery of the goods and services will reduce the desire of the consumers to continue with the relationship. Several popular community interaction-based web sites, including Slashdot, discovered the problem of maintaining product quality over an extended period of time, particularly where the product was dependent on cybercommunities and/or co-production by the consumers (see chapters 5 and 13). A major factor of any ongoing relationship formed between Slashdot and their customers concerns the quality of the information and discussion. Similarly, we find cybercommunities are dependent on maintaining relationships that are based on the quality of the community interaction.
- *satisfaction*, which is the degree to which the relationship continues to meet the needs of the organisations involved. It differs from service quality in that a high quality service can still provide an unsatisfactory experience, and still be the grounds for departing the relationship. Online search engines that begin as search functions (www.google.com) that evolve into either complex portals (www.go.com) or large hierarchical structures (www.yahoo.com) can all provide exceptionally high quality services that may not satisfy the needs of the customer.

As with the rest of relationship marketing, commitment has multiple conflicting definitions. Morgan and Hunt (1994) suggest commitment is an **affective event** based on liking, emotional attachment and a sense of bonding with the other party. The less romantic view is the **calculative approach** (spawned from economics) which takes commitment as being a balance sheet of costs, benefits, gains, losses, rewards and punishments that is constantly tallied, and all the time the ledger remains in the positive, commitment will be maintained. Somewhere in between these two extremes of romance and maths lies the middle ground of actual application of relationship management. The two types of commitment have an impact on the following areas:

- intentions to stay in the relationship
- desire to stay in the relationship
- performance of the relationship
- willingness to invest in the relationship
- developments of alternatives
- opportunistic behaviour (Wetzels, de Ruyter & van Birgelen 1998).

Affective commitment has a positive impact on the first four influences and a negative impact on the last two, as the more the individual is committed to the relationship, the less desire they have to engage in opportunism or to seek alternative arrangements. Calculative commitment is more likely to be prone to seeking alternatives and looking for opportunistic outcomes to alter the balance sheet. There is an evident bias in the literature towards preferring the affective side of commitment for long-term relationships. In reality, performance of the relationship is every bit as influenced by the profit and loss calculations of calculative commitment as it is by the sensitive 'touchy-feely' approach of affective commitment.

For online marketers, the lesson to learn from commitment is to not only continue to balance the profit and loss sheets of the relationship, but to also trust instinctive desires to maintain commitment. Online relationship marketers need to have a longer term focus, rather than simply using Internet relationships as short-term opportunistic events.

Reciprocity

Reciprocity is the basic function of exchange in that it simply represents 'the mutual exchange and fulfilment of promise' (Grönross 1994). If this looks familiar, it is because Bagozzi (1975) proposed the ideal generic law of marketing in exchange theory (see any decent introduction to a marketing text for details). The key to reciprocity is that the totality of the exchanges must balance over the course of the relationship, which means that individual exchanges can favour one partner or the other providing that the overall outcomes remain equal. In addition, the basis for reciprocity can move beyond simple financial exchange to include such functions as:

- increasing stability by reducing risk and uncertainty
- establishing legitimacy
- increasing effective and efficient resource usage
- accessing resources not currently available to the organisation.

In addition to the three core principles outlined above, there is a range of influencing factors that help form (or dissolve) relationships in both business to business and consumer markets. However, for the purposes of this book, we have restricted the review of relationship marketing concepts to just these three elements.

Relationship marketing online

Having established an overview of some of the key elements of relationship marketing theory, this section sets out to outline the application of these ideas to the Internet. The development of trust, and issues associated with the creation and reinforcement of the perceptions of credibility and trustworthiness is of most interest to Internet marketers trying to establish successful short- and long-term e-commerce relationships.

Three levels of relationship marketing

The application of relationship marketing is based around one of three functions, either as a tactic, strategic direction or corporate philosophy. Tactics operate from the ground level straight to the end client and are usually short term in focus and nature. Strategic directions aim to provide a more cohesive medium term approach to engaging consumers and locking them into longer term relationships. Finally, relationship marketing philosophy is applied as the core focus and direction of the corporation, and underpins key functions such as strategic direction and planning processes.

Tactics

Tactical level application of relationship marketing is aimed at the initial recruitment and development of the relationship whereby incentives are offered to the consumer for their initial involvement with the company. Many portal-based web sites, such as Yahoo (www.yahoo.com), Excite (www.excite.com), or Go.com (www.go.com) offer short-term bonuses and benefits for signing up with the service provider. These typically include teaser deals of 30 days' free access to a subscription function, or discounts for members at allied corporate stores. Similarly, MP3.com uses the My.mp3.com service to develop a relationship with new listeners, either by offering free music, or free compilation CDs. For the most part, these are not designed to develop trust nor enhance credibility, and they are not presented as tools of commitment and reciprocity. They are incentive schemes which are designed to get the user from pre-purchase to purchase, or to shift from their current relationship to the new provider. Effectively, these are little more than sales promotion tools that linger after the initial transaction has been finalised. Tactical application also covers the actual implementation of the strategic and philosophical directions.

Strategic direction

Strategic direction provides the organisation with a series of medium- to long-term objectives involving the recruitment, selection and development of business to consumer or business to business relationships. The distinguishing point between strategic and tactical direction is that the strategic direction of a business to business relationship would be to develop mutually dependent, **just-in-time** supply systems, whereas the tactical direction is the implementation of the supply systems. Strategic relationship marketing decisions for web site owners include the outsourcing of key content areas, such as newsfeeds (www.aap.com.au) for portal web sites (www.excite.com.au). Similarly, review-based web sites such as Epinions (www.epinions.com) depend heavily for their existence on the formation of strong relationships with key content-providing customers.

Relationship marketing philosophy

The relationship marketing triangle is the relationship marketing philosophy, which is basically the marketing concept aimed at long-term relationships rather than one-off transactions. Developing a focus on relationship marketing requires the organisation to adopt a philosophy of seeing the customer as a partial employee of the organisation, and including the needs of this employee–customer in the long-term development of the organisation.

Value of relationship building in new media

Given the relatively brief period of involvement of commerce in the Internet, development of long-term relationships between businesses and consumers has unfortunately been left to the wayside in the frantic rush to be online. Many of the success stories of online marketing have come from those companies which have decided to forgo quick returns to focus on long-term development of a selective customer base for relationship networks. In an environment best known for rapid change, long-term investment and focus has delivered a higher rate of success, since it has been less prone to chasing short-term trends (and its own tail). Instead, by focusing on moving into the new environment in conjunction with business partners and consumers, this has fostered an emphasis on delivering value to all parties. Of course, there have been some people in the Internet commerce business who have asked how they can quickly attain long-term strategies and the rewards of long-term investment. For the most part, even with the legendary speed of 'Internet time', long-term investing still takes time, commitment and effort (Yoffie & Cusumano 1999).

The value of creating relationships online lies not only in the development of viable commercial exchanges (which should be the number one priority of the relationship), but also in augmenting existing relationships through new channels. Business to business users who would be dependent on developing proprietary **electronic data interchange (EDI)** systems can make use of intranets, secured web sites and email. Small to medium providers of business to business services can also develop ongoing relationships with organisations through the Internet as they can deliver services in the same manner as their larger rivals. Even retail outlets can make use of the Internet's interactive functions to establish ongoing relationships with clients, including repeat orders (www.thinkgeek.com) that can be modified online.

Additional value can be derived by the business or consumer engaged in an offline relationship by moving the relationship online because it provides an opportunity for a lower risk entry into the market. Issues of trust, commitment and reciprocity within the existing relationship can be confirmed and maintained in the relationship with the movement to online delivery. Positive experiences within an existing relationship can be used to reinforce other business to business relationships with online providers.

Creating relationships online

Gilbert, Powell-Perry and Widijoso (1999) examined the value of the Internet to the hotel industry, particularly in regard to models and methods of improving relationships. They outlined five sequential steps to develop long-term customer retention and their associated strategic and operational guidelines which are illustrated in table 14.1.

Table 14.1 Approaches to long-term retention of customers

Stage	Strategic guidelines	Operational objective	Web mechanism
1. Identify	Start with customers Exploit unique properties of Internet technology	Compile information on what an individual purchases or may want Create a profile of the customer	Incentivised online questionnaire
2. Improve	Exploit unique properties of Internet technology Build relationships with customers	Improve aspects of the service that are not meeting or exceeding the expectation of customers	Customised online questionnaire Emails
3. Inform	Exploit unique properties of Internet technology Build relationships with customers Leverage existing business	Increase the knowledge of customers about the hotels and the loyalty scheme to enhance brand loyalty	Direct emailing Electronic newsletters Online noticeboards and updates Online information centre
4. Tempt	Exploit unique properties of Internet technology Build relationships with customers Leverage existing business Build a service, not a web site	Persuade customers to try new service, product or sector Persuade customers to purchase more through personalised contact	Direct emailing Special electronic promotion leaflets Automated cross-selling
5. Retain	Exploit unique properties of Internet technology Build relationships with customers Leverage existing business Build a service, not a web site Think radically	Develop new loyalty-building schemes aimed at retaining and reinforcing the link with customers	Exclusive web site and services for loyalty scheme members Online members' magazines Online members-only customer services

Source: Gilbert, D. C., Powell-Perry, J. and Widijoso, S. 1999, Approaches by hotels to the use of the Internet as a relationship marketing tool', *Journal of Marketing Practice: Applied Marketing Science*, vol. 5, no. 1, pp. 21–38.

The five-step approach incorporates the Butler Group's web strategies, which are outlined as:

- treat the Internet as a new medium and exploit the unique properties (chapter 3)
- start with the customers by defining who they are and what they want to know (chapters 7 and 16)
- build relationships with customers by getting to know them (chapter 16), customising content for them (chapter 10) and ensuring relevance to them
- build a service (chapter 13) not a web site (chapter 10) by giving customers value (chapter 11) for time and money, through providing options not available elsewhere (chapter 8)
- leverage existing business by building on assets such as branding (chapter 7), operational infrastructure, information and customer relationships (this chapter)
- think radically to achieve the best chance of obtaining the benefits offered by the technology (this book).

These six strategic ideas are layered as a series of steps to undertake, so that the use of the unique features of the Internet is the first phase, and remains part of the final phase, with the other five tasks making incremental contributions along the way.

Identify more about the customer through database analysis

Understanding the customer is the core to identifying the needs of the customer, and to being able to match those needs with the company's product offerings. While customer profiling technology exists both online and offline, the Internet offers a range of interactive options that can provide immediate feedback to the organisation. Web sites can be monitored for increased traffic flow, and movements through the site can be tracked, following the release of offline advertising. Similarly, online bookings and online registrations allow for the creation of a customer database which can be matched against an incentive-based questionnaire. In return for providing demographic, psychographic and miscellaneous purchasing pattern data, users can receive special offers (www.preferredguest.com) or access to premium services (www.flybuys .com.au) in exchange for the time and value provided to the company.

Improve and make the product or service more attractive

This relationship marketing function is more valuable as a post-transaction or pre-customisation function to enable a better understanding of the client's needs. Once the user has experienced the service or product, they can use the web site to either suggest improvements to the service, or additional features that would be valuable to their particular needs. In addition, **loyalty schemes** that have a unique user identifier, in conjunction with structured feedback programs, can be used to turn regular customers into **mystery shoppers**. Yahoo's e-commerce division (store.yahoo.com) automatically emails the purchaser with a link to a feedback system to rate their e-commerce system, and the merchant vendor, providing the option for the consumer to make suggestions for any improvements to the service. **Permission-based email marketing**, including follow-up emails, are a recommended mechanism for gathering suggestions and feedback. Complex data collection, surveys or product tests are best suited to web-based survey pages, rather than trying to rely on the complexities (and vagaries) of HTML email.

Inform to build the customer's knowledge of the company

Using the web page as a promotional tool, and informing the customer of the latest deals, specials and rewards for being part of the relationship is covered as part of web site design (chapter 10). In addition, direct email messages of a newsletter (www.bravenet.com), and online noticeboards (msg.mp3.com) and information centres can be used to educate the customer as to other functions and features of the service. The creation and maintenance of popular community orientated discussion boards can also be used to develop a cybercommunity (chapter 5).

Tempt customers to purchase more regularly

Once a relationship has been established with the customer through a web site, the next stage is to increase the portfolio of product offerings to the customer, and increase the rate of purchase or amount of purchase. This can be done by persuading the customer to try new services, new features or to upgrade the initial package to a higher price product with more features. For example, Internet host Webcentral (www.webcentral.com) offers an entry level package and the opportunity to move through up to 10 levels of expansions (with approximately 25 additional services which can customise the hosting product). As the users' needs exceed the current level of service, they are automatically contacted by Webcentral to be offered an appropriate product to meet their new needs.

In addition to offering expanded services, relationship marketers can offer service bundles, such as the holiday packages offered to frequent flyers (www.qantas.com.au). Web sites can also be used as part of a chain of special offers between allied relationship marketers, as is the case with the Starwood Preferred Guest (www.preferredguest.com) site which links together a series of hotel chains to offer benefits to loyal customers across a range of locations and services.

Retain the customer by developing different forms of loyalty schemes

Variety is the spice of relationship marketing in that each customer has differing needs and wants during the relationship, so the creation of a range of loyalty incentives is useful for maintaining value. Again, research into meeting the needs and wants of the customer is needed; however, common functions such as the ability to access FlyBuys point totals online (www.flybuys.com.au), access special services, for example, trip planners (www.star-alliance.com), or self-customisation of the web site (www.epinions.com) can be used to develop a basic range of alternatives. Relationship marketers will need to customise their offerings in light of what is technically possible (chapter 10) and what the partners in the relationship need or want. The different services must add value to the relationship for them to work as loyalty incentives. The emphasis at this point in the relationship is adjusting product offerings to meet the needs of current clients and customers with whom the relationship has proved to be valuable, and worth defending against competitors.

Limitations, distractions and problems: Barrier to online relationship marketing

The Internet is not the perfect environment for relationship marketing. Many of the traditional facets of relationship marketing are heavily dependent on face-to-face transactions, with more than enough LISREL models indicating how the physical appearance of the salesperson influences the desire to build the relationship beyond the transaction level. Similarly, the literature on trust contains a substantial bias towards the development of trust based on personal interactions in face-to-face settings. Very few of the ideal trust-building mechanisms have been portrayed as being a computer, email or a text document.

The other major concern with the Internet as a medium for relationship marketing is the heavy dependence on the credibility of the Internet, computers and consumer comfort with Internet transactions as a factor in dealing with online partners.

FOCUS ON
Strategy 👁

The credibility of computers

Relationship marketing is one aspect of marketing that lives and dies on the basis of trust between two parties. While contractual obligations can be legally enforced to ensure completion of a transaction, there are no mechanisms to force trust onto a person or company. Consequently, reputable firms spend a considerable amount of time and resources in defending their brands, corporate reputations and perceived image in the community, particularly as it relates to being a fair trading partner.

When a company moves into dealing with online customers, branding, reputation (online and offline) and corporate image become a major consideration in the effectiveness of e-commerce. However, one aspect of online dealing is often overlooked by companies seeking to expand, or move their services online, and that is the credibility of the Internet as a transaction medium. Gilbert, Powell-Perry and Widijoso (1999) point out that social acceptance of the Internet is a key to the development of e-commerce.

Social acceptance of the Internet is dependent on a wide variety of factors, including government attitudes towards freedom of information, concerns over privacy, and the sensationalistic fashion of the conventional media running horror stories of the evils of the Internet (and promoting their web site as a place to find out more information on these stories). However, one of the major keys to Internet credibility is the perceived credibility of the computer. Tseng and Fogg (1999) outlined the issues associated with credibility and computing technology. For their research, credibility was composed of expertise and trustworthiness. Expertise is the perception of knowledge, ability, skill and capacity to perform a function accurately. Trustworthiness is a hybrid compound of good intentions, truthfulness and being unbiased (but not necessarily objective) as a representation of the 'morality' of the source.

(continued)

While it is difficult to conceive of computers as having a particular 'morality', the influence of popular culture has influenced perceptions of computers as having moral trends (good and bad). Cinematic icons such as 'HAL9000' (from the movie and book *2001: A Space Odyssey*) and the actions of 'SkyNet' in the 'Terminator' movie franchises have given a darker edge to the broader public perception of computers. Balancing the Hollywood computer villains against their 'good' counterparts of 'R2D2' (*Star Wars*), the 'T-800' (*Terminator 2*) and any movie where the computer has to save the day by performing impossible feats (*Independence Day*, any given James Bond film), has led to a popular culture acceptance of computers as having morality. Increased anthropomorphism of computing technology is also lending credence to the implied morality of computers (if the machine crashes, it is usually perceived as a 'bad computer' much in the same way the family pet would be scolded for misbehaviour).

The potential problem with the increasing acceptance of computers as innately credible objects is the credibility that is conferred to information displayed by the computer (Tseng & Fogg 1999). However, not all instances of computer use invoked credibility, as it is not an apparent issue where the users are:

- unaware of the computer in systems such as an automobile's fuel injection system, or 'smart chips' in household appliances (few people have ever felt that they cannot trust their toasters)
- unlikely to expect bias or incompetence, such as the use of a pocket calculator, or digital timer mechanism
- unlikely to have an investment in the transaction, such as idle web surfing, recreational computing use or gaming
- using the computer as a transmitter for video or audio.

These are regarded as credibility neutral situations as they do not invoke the two elements of credibility.

However, for the considerations of marketing, the areas of computer credibility that directly affect relationship marketing are when computers:

- *act as knowledge repositories*, which arises when the computer is used to access information, either online or through prerecorded media of CD-ROMs. The credibility of the computer as an unbiased arbiter of facts is affected if the content of the material delivered is frequently discredited by being out of date, innaccurate, or contradicted by an alternative, more credible source. This can have the dual impact of reducing the credibility of the source, such as the Web, while also reducing the computer's own credibility.
- *tutor or instruct users*, which can occur through self-paced tutorials, online help systems or computer-based education programs. Loss of credibility, either by not meeting client training needs, or giving the wrong instructions, have an impact on relationship marketing web sites which seek to offer additional knowledge, education or advanced training to registered users.
- *report measurement*: which can be as simple as performing calculations in a spreadsheet, or as complex as reporting **GPS (Global Positioning System)** locations. Computers have a higher perceived accuracy in reporting maths results, and errors in calculation, when they occur, have a greater negative impact on computing credibility.

- *help render virtual environment*: which is where the computer is used to assist in the development of a telepresence, or virtual presence in an online world. This also occurs where the computer is used to render virtual shopping environments, such as catalogue web sites. Different colour calibrations between the computers of the shopper and the web site developer may lead to the reduction in the credibility of the computer if the image on screen does not match the actual product. In addition, virtual worlds are subject to the capacity and ability of the computer to deliver the environment in near real time. Cybercommunities used for relationship marketing that depend on real time interaction, timeliness and service interactions are dependent on the user's computer to deliver accurate information. Loss of data during a voice instruction, or the delay caused by lag during time sensitive activities will reduce the credibility of the computer and the cybercommunity.

For many readers of this text, their level of experience with computers is such that they can tell when to attribute credibility problems to the computer, and when the loss of credibility is incurred elsewhere (e.g. poor content of a web site is not the fault of the user's desktop computer). However, inexperienced users of computers and the Internet may be unable to determine where the responsibility for the fault should lie (a new user of the Internet may blame their computer for problems that are occurring on a web site). Similarly, perceptions of credibility of the medium and the message may be bundled together in that computers can be blamed for problems with content on the Internet.

For relationship marketers it is important to understand how the other parties to the relationship perceive computers and the Internet. If the intended parties to the relationship have a very poor perception of technology, the Internet or online transactions, then these perceptions will have a negative influence on their desire to participate in online relationships. If they perceive computers not to be credible, then they are not going to use them for engaging in a relationship based on trust.

Value of cybercommunities for building relationships

Cybercommunities are unique in that they can both benefit from, and be a part of an online portfolio of relationship marketing. As the purpose of the relationship is to create value, a community constructed around shared involvement in the relationship with a company (either by post-purchase relationship, or registration) can be used to create a community of value to the user. These communities offer an exclusive 'club' of support for users of the product, and can decrease **cognitive dissonance** with the formation of the relationship.

A key feature of the relationship-building aspect of the cybercommunity is that active involvement in the community increases **switching costs**, as users will not only need to find a new provider, but will also lose the social support mechanism associated with the current community. Community users can also share product or service experiences and collaborate in the design and refinement of products with suggestions, so that a single customisation meets the needs of multiple members of the community. In word-of-mouth communities such as Epinions (www.epinions.com), the fundamental strength of the group is drawn from the community structure, and the relationships (commercial and social) that form between the users of the community.

Internet marketing INSIGHT
Epinions and the 'Web of Trust'

Epinions is a system that depends heavily on honesty, integrity, peer review and the kindness of strangers. The system is based on peer review of products by 'ordinary people' who register to become providers of reviews. In return, the reviewers receive a pro rata cash payment schedule based on the number of hits to their reviews, and the success of their reviews in assisting online shoppers. Apart from being one of the world's largest collections of **market mavens**, Epinions also uses a slightly unusual method of **collaborative filtering** by setting up a 'web of trust' mechanism.

The 'web of trust' is designed to artificially reproduce the word of mouth and market mavenism by concentrating on areas of shared interest, and reviewers with good track records for reviews. Working on the assumption that the user will select reviewers they perceive to be credible, and who have a similar interest (e.g. Internet marketing), the Epinions system will filter subsequent opinions based on the match between the trusted Epinions member (an Epinionater?), and linked systems. Figure 14.1 illustrates the 'Web of Trust'.

The Epinions.com 'Web of Trust'

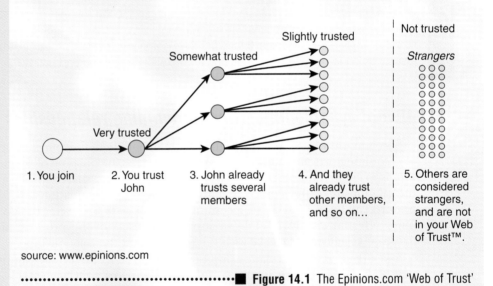

source: www.epinions.com

••■ **Figure 14.1** The Epinions.com 'Web of Trust'
Source: www.epinions.com

The use of a trust-based collaborative filtering system for registered users also enhances the relationship marketing between the user and Epinions. By adopting this method, they can track the relationship paths between users, find and highlight successful users (and reap the rewards of their popularity), and gain useful network data for targeting group emails for special offers.

Role of trust in e-commerce

In effect, trust has no greater role in e-commerce than it does in the offline world. All commercial transactions are based on trust, either in the opposite party to deliver, or in the laws of the land to enforce delivery. What does differ is the extent to which trust must be based on a more limited set of information than most people are used to dealing with in offline transactions. Trust, credibility and apparent ability to deliver on the promises made are mediated in the offline world by numerous visual cues such as servicescape, branding and overall impressions derived from the face-to-face encounters with the organisation. The **lean media** environment of the Internet strips away most of these cues, leaving only the web site as the physical representation of the company (chapter 10). Even then, the nature of the Internet is such that the visual cues provided by a web site may be no indication of the size or quality of the firm that owns and operates it.

Operational conditions: Where does trust need to occur?

It may be a shorter list to define where trust is not needed in online commerce. For the most part, wherever an offline merchant exchange would incur the need for trust (i.e. every time), then it can be reasonably expected that trust will be an issue online. However, Ratnasingham (1998) outlined the following list as a selection of the more common areas of where trust is a heightened issue in online commercial exchanges:

- a sending/seller/merchant trading partner to a receiving/buyer/customer trading partner (which describes most commercial transactions), specifically those trading for the first time with each other
- a customer and a bank, where trust is derived from faith in the bank's systems performing the tasks in a secure manner, and that transactions such as bill payment conducted online will be validated appropriately
- a bank and a merchant, such as the relationship of trust between credit card verification systems and banks, so that the merchant can fulfil an order with the confidence that the credit card has been validated
- a merchant and a customer, which is the conviction that all parties are operating in good faith, so the merchant may assume the customer is of good credit, and the customer may believe the merchant will deliver the goods or services as promised
- a trusted third party or other trading parties such as E-bay (www.ebay.com), or other auction houses, where the seller and buyer place trust in the third party auction systems to deliver the promised service and to validate the appropriate bids.

Barriers to trust

It is necessary to note that developing trust in this new environment remains problematic for a number of reasons. Beyond the financial risk component of ensuring secure transactions, trust development is inhibited by a number of factors which are exacerbated by the unique features of the Internet. Trust, under normal circumstances, is enhanced by face-to-face interactions, social activity and shared experience. The lean media environment of the Internet neatly removes these enhancements, and creates its own set of barriers to make the process of trust formation more difficult. The specific barriers inhibiting trust development between Internet-based partners include the lack of:

- *co-presence in time and space*: a feature that is a benefit for e-commerce in allowing 24–7 global access also makes it a problem for customers to experience the same direct face-to-face (or one-to-one) transaction that they can receive in a real world store.
- *the entire human bandwidth (sight, hearing, smell, touch and taste)*, which is comprehensively eliminated by transactions conducted in lean media. Trust has to be placed in substitute features such as sound files, images, and virtual environments — all of which lack the external validation by the recipient.
- *capacity for interruption, feedback and learning*. which is also known as interactivity. Despite the interactive nature of the Internet, immediacy of interruption and communication is limited to voice transmissions only.
- *prior familiarity with one another*, which began life as anonymity, post-modern consumption and the capacity to be a dog on the Internet (*New Yorker* 1993) has turned into a disadvantage for building trust. What if your client is a dog? Without the prior familiarity or external third party verification, there are few methods of reaching any reasonable level of confidence in the identity of the opposite party (Ratnasingham 1998).

Despite the existence of these barriers, however, an alternative viewpoint sees the Internet and associated technologies as being a positive, rather than negative, influence on the development of long-term relationships. This viewpoint is based on the idea that information about a consumer leads to better service which in turn leads to loyalty, trust and commitment.

Improving trust online

Improved communications are at the core of this approach. Undoubtedly the Internet has increased the capacity of organisations to communicate and interact with their customers on an individual level. The interactivity and customisation possible through Internet transactions means that a greater level of information transfer is possible and in many cases is occurring. Whether this translates into a corresponding increase in trust which, in turn, leads to better relationship development remains to be seen. In the meantime, Ratnasingham (1998) provides three mechanisms for developing 'web trust' which are:

- *business practices disclosure*, which is where the ISO9000 standards of the world are applied to web pages as the company discloses how it conducts its business practice. Of course, the company then has to abide by the practices it has disclosed, or it will lose all credibility.
- *transaction integrity*, which is where the business ensures that the transactions are completed, billed and acted upon as per agreement
- *information protection*, which is the agreement of privacy, and the undertaking to use the customer's information only in an agreed manner (i.e. not on-sell it to mailing list brokers).

However, as Ratnasingham (1998) points out, the business must be able to demonstrate continuity of practice and adherence to its own policies to increase the sense of trust in the organisation. In addition, the organisation is well-advised to investigate the perceived risk-reduction strategies outlined in chapters 11 and 12.

Business to business

While this text focuses almost exclusively on consumer marketing, a large proportion of marketing activity undertaken in the new economy occurs in the business to business sector. (This tendency to focus strongly on the consumer market is also a feature of the emerging literature in online marketing.) Business to business transactions have as much, if not more, from which to benefit in the new online environment. This section focuses on how business relationships are changing and being improved by the new technology.

Business to business marketing online

Business to business e-marketing activities cover a broad range of applications ranging from simple information dissemination about product specifications, pricing and so on through to the integrated supply chain relationships designed to optimise the distribution process. Supply chain management involves the full coordination of order generation, order taking and distribution. Effective use of new technologies in business to business marketing can lead to lower purchase costs, reduced inventory, enhanced logistics efficiency, increased sales and lower marketing costs. Turban et al. (2000) identify the following entities involved in the online business to business marketing transactions in table 14.2.

Table 14.2 Online business to business activities

Entity	Concern
Selling company	Marketing management
Buying company	Procurement management
Electronic intermediary	Third party electronic service provider
Deliverer	Party who delivers the actual product
Network platform	Internet, intranet, extranet
Protocols and communication	EDI, comparison shopping, software agents
Back-end info system	Intranet and enterprise resource planning systems

Source: Derived from Turban, E., Lee, J., King, D. and Chung, H. M. 2000, *Electronic Commerce: A Managerial Perspective*, Prentice-Hall, New Jersey.

In designing a web site aimed at developing the business to business market, the same key issues that apply to consumer-based retail marketing apply, except in this case, the customer is the corporation. Further, in the business to business market, product customisation has always been the rule which makes the online environment particularly suited to this form of activity.

The key attractions of Internet-based business to business marketing are first, the improved capacity to build better supplier–purchaser relationships and second, the improved efficiency with which transactions can be undertaken. By integrating the systems of buying and selling the company's product, inventories are reduced, down time is minimised and both parties are able to provide better service by learning more about each other through their integrated transactions.

New roles and new opportunities: Market makers

One of the new features of business to business marketing to emerge from the spread of the Internet is the development of new electronic market makers. **Market makers** bring together buyers and sellers on a single site by offering an unbiased service of content and advice. The dominant prediction of the role of market makers in the business to business environment is that they will act as a focus for commodity transactions where issues of price and availability are critical for the buyer (see chapter 12 and marketspaces).

Overall, the use of the Internet in the business to business sector is still in its infancy. As existing technologies that have been designed to facilitate the relationships between businesses are modified or superseded by Internet-friendly versions, the area is likely to grow exponentially. For the most part, business to business transactions online still end up with a single person being responsible for the decision to purchase and, consequently, much of the consumer behaviour literature concerning online purchasing intentions still applies in this arena.

 ## Summary

The discipline of relationship marketing remains an evolving and dynamic area of marketing research where new theories, models and understandings are constantly being developed and tested. The dynamic nature of the sub-discipline makes it ideally suited to the rapid development of Internet marketing, as both areas are finding new ground and developing new understandings of how and why consumers seek relationships online and offline. Online, relationship marketing can contribute an understanding of the factors that lead individuals and businesses to place their trust in a web-based merchant to provide their goods and services, despite the limited available external validation measures. As relationship marketing establishes itself both academically and in the commercial marketplace, it increasingly finds itself ideally suited to guide the future directions of Internet marketing.

Discussion questions

14.1 Does the lack of a single established definition for relationship marketing hamper its application to Internet marketing? How can Internet marketers overcome the confusion surrounding the definition and domain of Internet marketing?

14.2 What are the conditions best suited to relationship marketing? Are these conditions universally applicable to all markets on the Internet, or are there specific markets that best reflect these conditions?

14.3 Outline the three principles of relationship marketing, and how they are affected by the manner in which companies conduct e-commerce.

14.4 Can an e-commerce site apply the tactical level of relationship marketing without adopting the strategic and philosophical direction? Collect examples of web sites that support your argument.

14.5 What are the steps to take to create an online relationship for the long-term retention of a customer? Choose an e-commerce provider and demonstrate how that provider can use these steps to enhance business, or, what steps are currently used by the provider.

14.6 Outline the barriers to online relationship marketing. What practical methods can organisations use to reduce the impact of these barriers?

14.7 Is the value of cybercommunities their capacity to build relationships, or is it to derive market research information? Discuss.

14.8 Is trust a necessary component of e-commerce? Can price be used in place of trust to entice purchasing?

14.9 Collect examples of each of the types of online business to business marketing sites. Which of these areas has the greatest dependency on trust and relationship marketing? Which has the least? Discuss with examples.

References

Arunkundram, R. & Sundararajan, A. 1998, 'An economic analysis of electronic secondary markets: Installed base, technology, durability and firm profitability', *Decision Support Systems*, vol. 24, pp. 3–16.

Bagozzi, R. 1975, 'Marketing as exchange', *Journal of Marketing*, vol. 39, October, pp. 32–9.

Gilbert, D. C., Powell-Perry, J. & Widijoso, S. 1999, 'Approaches by hotels to the use of the Internet as a relationship marketing tool', *Journal of Marketing Practice: Applied Marketing Science*, vol. 5, no. 1, 1999, pp. 21–38.

Grönross, C. 1994, 'From marketing mix to relationship marketing: Towards a paradigm shift in marketing', *Management Decision*, vol. 32, no. 2, pp. 4–20.

Harker, M. J. 1999, 'Relationship marketing defined? An examination of current relationship marketing definitions', *Marketing Intelligence and Planning*, vol. 17, no. 1, pp. 13–20.

Jevons, C. & Gabbott, M. 2000, 'Trust, brand equity and brand reality in Internet business relationships: An interdisciplinary approach', *Journal of Marketing Management*, vol. 16, pp. 619–34.

Moorman, C., Deshpande, R. & Zaltman, G. 1993, 'Factors affecting trust in market research relationship', *Journal of Marketing*, vol. 57, January, pp. 81–101.

Morgan, R. M. & Hunt, S. D. 1994, 'The commitment–trust theory of relationship marketing', *Journal of Marketing*, vol. 58, July, pp. 20–38.

New Yorker, 1993, 'On the Internet, nobody knows you're a dog' [Editorial cartoon], *New Yorker*, 5 July 1993.

Ratnasingham, P. 1998, 'The importance of trust in electronic commerce', *Internet Research*, vol. 8, no. 4, pp. 313–21.

Tseng, S. & Fogg, B. J. 1999, 'Credibility and computing technology', *Communications of the ACM*, vol. 42, no. 5, pp. 39–46.

Turban, E., Lee, J., King, D. & Chung, H. M. 2000, *Electronic commerce: A managerial perspective*, Prentice-Hall, New Jersey.

Wetzels, M., de Ruyter, K. & van Birgelen, M. 1998, 'Marketing service relationships: The role of commitment', *Journal of Business and Industrial Marketing*, vol. 13, no. 4/5, pp. 406–23.

Yoffie, D. & Cusumano, M. A. 1999, 'Building a company on Internet time: Lessons from Netscape', *California Management Review*, vol. 41, no. 3, pp. 8–28.

Web sites

msg.mp3.com
My.mp3.com
store.yahoo.com
www.aap.com.au
www.bravenet.com
www.dell.com
www.ebay.com
www.epinions.com
www.excite.com
www.flybuys.com.au
www.geocities.com
www.go.com
www.google.com
www.icq.com
ww.idsoftware.com
www.preferredguest.com
www.qantas.com.au
www.star-alliance.com
www.thinkgeek.com
www.webcentral.com
www.yahoo.com

International marketing

> *'Luckily there are two differences between global marketing in the digital age and exploration in the 15th century ... with a few clicks of your mouse, you can sail around the world in a matter of seconds. You don't have to worry about getting scurvy or being stuck in the doldrums.'*
>
> Bishop, B. 1999, *Global Marketing for the Digital Age*, NTC Business Books, Chicago.

LEARNING *objectives*

After reading this chapter, you should be able to:

- appreciate whether all Internet marketing is international marketing by default, or whether distinctions can be made between local and global online marketing

- recognise the impact of entry mode on online international marketing

- outline the types of export industries involved in international marketing

- explain how the Internet has impacted barriers to exporting

- recognise the framework for examining the conceptual issues associated with international export marketing and the Internet

- outline the major issues of analysing potential international markets

- describe the steps involved in implementing an international web presence.

Introduction

In some ways a chapter on international marketing, in a text on Internet marketing, may seem redundant. After all, one of the key features of the medium is that the Internet is inherently international and global in its reach. Therefore, logically, it would appear that any marketing undertaken on the Internet is, by default, international. In practice, however, this logic does not hold up. For various reasons, such as product type, distribution issues and ability to supply a global market, many online marketers and sellers choose to deliberately limit their reach.

This chapter explores the deliberate integration of the Internet into a planned international marketing strategy. Although some international Internet successes have happened as a natural outgrowth of the global reach of the medium, the focus here is on examining the issues and techniques of maximising success for internationally oriented firms.

Some of the big winners in the international marketing stakes have been small- to medium-size enterprises, particularly those with a highly specialised focus that would, under 'normal' circumstances, be unable to enter the world of international commerce. For these firms, traditional issues of obtaining export and import licences, negotiating a place in the international distribution chain and finding an appropriate promotional medium, are circumvented by the individual control and global reach of the Internet.

However, although things may be easier now for smaller firms, the Internet is not a level playing field when it comes to international marketing campaigns. Larger firms still have greater resources and, although everyone can access a web site, it does not necessarily follow that everyone can obtain the goods. The physical products still need to be delivered, which requires the issue of international distribution to be overcome. Worldwide alliances also still remain a key to widespread international success.

As with all marketing, some target markets are more attractive than others. Just because mass communications on a global scale are possible, it does not necessarily mean that marketing to all countries is necessarily the most effective and suitable approach for organisations to take. The principles of market segmentation are as valid in international online marketing as they are in traditional marketing.

Although some potentially profitable niche markets may exist at a worldwide level, the attractiveness of most markets is determined by national characteristics such as access to technology, economic power, political stability, digital capabilities and freedom of expression. All of these characteristics need to be evaluated before a specific market can be considered sufficiently attractive to invest in through an Internet-based approach to international marketing.

Despite the many benefits of going online for international marketing purposes, there remain many obstacles and limitations. Overall, the full effects of the Internet on the conduct of international trade remain to be seen. While some commentators see the impact of the Internet as a revolution for international marketing, others see it as simply another tool, with the core issues, such as import restrictions, tariffs and cultural barriers, remaining constant.

Is all Internet marketing, international marketing?

Despite the global reach of the Internet, not all web-based marketing can realistically be classified as international. While anyone, anywhere, can access the promotional and informational materials on a given web site, actually accessing the full range of services and products offered by the company running the web site may be limited by geographical or other constraints. As is the case with all aspects of the Internet, some companies choose to take full advantage of the range of benefits offered by the medium while others choose a more limited role.

Web sites can be classified in terms of their commitment to internationalisation and globalisation. The different classifications are:

domestic: web sites that offer only goods and/or services to those within the local area. Examples of such web sites would include small businesses or local service businesses, such as pizza delivery (www.pizzahut.com.au), medical services (www.tmvc.com.au), home care agencies (www. helpagency.com.au), regional associations (www.nzart.org.nz) and local councils (www. brisbane.qld.gov.au).

■ *international by default*: web sites that do not actively seek international clients but which will provide goods and services to anyone within the capabilities of the organisation. Companies that fall into this category are usually involved in some sort of specialist product aimed at a niche market; for example, hobby suppliers (www.ehobbies.com), collectables (www.whim .com.au) or innovative toys (www.rctoys.com).

■ *international by design*: companies with a full international orientation, which actively seek external markets for their goods and services. Such companies include some of the newly created dot com style organisations which have developed as a result of the Internet's potential to enhance the internationalisation process. Examples include Amazon.com and MP3.com, both of which were designed to service global markets over the Internet. Alternatively, these web sites can belong to large, well-established, internationally oriented companies such as McDonald's (www.mcdonalds .com), BHP (www.bhp.com.au) or Pepsi (www.pepsi.com, www.pepsi.co.uk, www.pepsi.com.nz, www.pepsi.com.au, www.pepsi.de). In this case the web site often operates as an adjunct to existing global or international campaigns.

Characteristics of these sites are given in table 15.1.

Traditional issues to be addressed for international marketing are no less important if firms choose to use the Internet as part of their communication or distribution strategy. Key decisions still need to be made regarding the overall strategy to be employed by the organisation, specifically whether to take a global perspective or localised approach, as well as determining the appropriate method of market entry.

Table 15.1 Key characteristics of different international orientations

Characteristic	Domestic	International by default	International by design
Language	Local only	Local only	English, plus others
Payment	Online payment systems not normally in place, or restricted to local currency	Some online options, but cheque or other methods more common	Fully integrated online payment options
Currency	Local	Local or $US	Various — includes currency conversion
Ordering/booking systems	Phone, fax, in person Rarely online	Some online, but tend not to be automated (fax, email, phone)	Predominantly online, fully integrated systems
Distribution	Local only	One-off for international orders; heavy use of post office and couriers; expensive per order	Networks of distributors in different countries; economies of scale

Globalisation vs localisation

The fundamental strategic decision for any organisation seeking to expand its activities beyond its national boundaries is whether to take a global or local approach. Global marketing strategies work with the common aspects of different markets and attempt to develop single campaigns of equal relevance worldwide. Localisation, also referred to as the international approach, emphasises the unique nature of different markets and develops a unique marketing mix for each. (Localisation, however, emphasises the unique nature of different markets and develops a unique marketing mix for each. The 'localisation' approach may also have an international scope, however it markets specifically, or locally, to a particular market.) In reality, many organisations that engage in international marketing, particularly those from highly developed nations, are not 'marketing' at all. Rather, they are simply broadening the base of their existing selling operations (Jevons 2000). While such an approach can be successful, particularly in times where there are shortages of the firms' product in these new markets, sustained success requires a more strategic approach.

Most organisations that choose to 'go international' have developed a successful domestic strategy that they use as the foundation for their expansion (Simmonds 1999). The choice is whether to base the strategies for all markets on this winning formula or to modify and adapt to the local conditions of the new market. Levitt (1983) is one of the major proponents of the global approach, which he defines in terms of constancy, or of treating the world as a single entity in which the same products are sold in the same way everywhere. Support for globalisation has come not only from highlighting successful examples, such as Coca-Cola, but also from economic principles, such as the positive economies of scale when selling on a global basis. However, even the major global players such as Pepsi (www.pepsi.com) and Coke (www.coke.com) have regional variations in their products, either to comply with local laws or to customise their offering to local tastes. Global marketing focuses on similarities between markets and has arisen, in part, as a result of the improvements in communications technology. Improved access to technology and quality of communication in turn have led to increased cross-cultural interactions resulting in a worldwide homogenisation of customer desires (Ramparapu, Timmerman & Ramparapu 1999). Chapter 2 overviewed the impact of global homogenisation of the market in post-modern marketing.

When considering the globalisation approach in the online environment, the path of least resistance is simply to deliver a product to a homogenous global audience. Given that web sites are accessible in their local format regardless of the point of access, and the Internet is fundamentally interest driven, providers may have no reason to tailor the offering for any market beyond their local sphere. Further, there is the issue to consider — what exactly is the 'local' market in the online environment? Is it the physical and geographical place of the physical location of the web site operator or does it exist less tangibly in a sub-sector of cyberspace? Can a medium that is inherently free from time and geographic constraints ever really exist using any method other than globalisation? (Some of these conceptual issues are addressed in chapter 12 (Distribution), in particular, the concepts of **marketspace** and the **noosphere/ ergosphere**.)

While the inherent nature of the Internet raises some interesting questions regarding export and other forms of international marketing, in reality most organisations do not exist only as online entities. Instead they are country-specific organisations that are taking advantage of a development in technology that will help consolidate their local position. The Internet would do this by offering the additional benefits of convenience, added value in terms of information dissemination and time independence for service. Most consciously international operators using the Internet are not global, but rather international in their orientation. This excludes, of course, those firms that become international by default, or who go online purely to better service a very restricted and constrained geographic market.

The localised (or international) approach presumes that markets and consumers vary considerably from one culture to another and from one country to another. Firms that take this orientation develop new and different marketing mixes for each environment in which they operate. In some cases, the changes may be relatively minor and apply to only one element of the marketing mix. For example, although McDonalds is often cited as an example of international standardisation and global marketing, in reality, there are subtle differences, not only in pricing, but also in the actual product offerings between countries (Simmonds 1999). Even apparently similar countries such as Australia and England will vary in terms of the specific variations on product offerings (the inexplicable addition of sausages to the breakfast pancakes in the UK, and the equally odd addition of beetroot to the McOz burger). However, the core benefits of a clean and safe environment, core menu offerings and similar service standards are retained. While some authors see globalisation as being the future of all international marketing, they admit that at this stage there are still major difficulties in the effective implementation of such an approach (Jain 1989).

Two tiers of trading: Globalisation with localisation

In many ways, the future of international trade (with respect to the Internet) will be two tiered. While there is a certain appeal to the globalisation approach, in that it represents a low-risk, familiar option, the basic human need for variety is not met by such approaches. Many consumers seek differentiation and, consequently, a well-designed and focused localisation strategy may in fact be a better option for serving the needs of particular behavioural and niche markets.

Localising in the global village helps to offer the point of differentiation that many consumers seek. Competitive success in the global environment is based on three key components — unique perceived value, cultural resources and targeting, and positioning on the basis of 'localness' (Ger 1999). Unique perceived value is the tradable aspect of a local culture which is specific to that group, such as an indigenous heritage or specific cultural iconography. Of these, cultural resources are the least tangible and hardest to replicate. While Ger (1999) accepts that the global products that represent the 'good life' such as Levi–Strauss jeans (www.levi.com) or Mercedes cars (www.mercedes.com) are desirable in all societies, he also acknowledges the symbolic value of uniqueness. This is where it is possible for a local producer of a specialised product to achieve international success as they market and sell the flavour of a particular culture or perceived lifestyle. **Cultural goods**, with universal appeal, can form the basis of an international marketing campaign based on the Internet. Certain cultural capital resources are associated with all societies; for example, the Irish and the Welsh nations are associated with Celtic symbolism and cultural heritage. A firm that capitalises on this heritage can achieve an international following.

It is important to remember that each target market being pursued comes with a certain amount of cultural, societal and economic history. Consequently, it is often more appropriate to design separate marketing mixes for different target markets. Each marketing mix should create a common base of cultural heritage between buyer and seller. This must also be combined with a realistic assessment of economic value (Ger 1999). The most obvious common heritage symbol is language and, to date, the Internet has been dominated by English due to its cultural heritage as a predominantly US-based medium (Palumbo & Herbig 1998). Further, English is increasingly becoming not only the language of commerce, but is also spreading as the most common language spoken worldwide. Despite this, however, as the Internet extends its reach, it is becoming more common for local pages in languages other than English to appear. Firms that operate online, and which choose a conscious international strategy, rather than simply serving the domestic market or becoming international by default, are most likely to either develop their pages in English, as the language of international trade (regardless of the firm's country of origin) or, alternatively, to develop web sites with multi language pages to cater for different target markets (Samiee 1998). By adopting this strategy, customised communications emphasising different product benefits to different target markets can be achieved with minimal cross-target contamination.

Internet marketing INSIGHT

G'daymate.com: Selling the 'ocker' Australian online

Even before the Crocodile Dundee movie series indelibly branded the 'Ocker Aussie' image onto the global market, Australians have been able to export the cultural goods of the Outback lifestyle. In addition to the export of cultural goods being conducted by the Australian cinema movement (and the 10 000 or so backpackers deployed into the UK and Europe each year), two other uniquely Australian companies are making use of 'localness' as part of their global strategy.

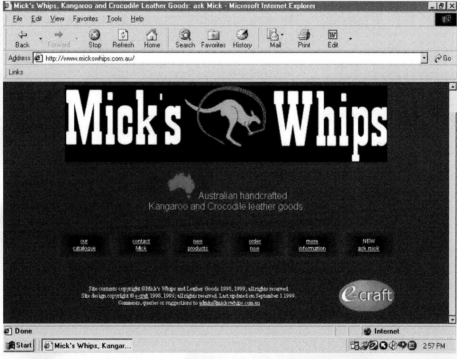

■ **Figure 15.1** Mick's Whips web site

Source: www.mickswhips.com.au

Mick's Whips (www.mickswhips.com.au) sells a range of Australian handcraft made from native kangaroo and crocodile leather goods. As well as the inherent product advantage of using native animal products, the online store sells the autobiography of the whip-maker, and an instructional video on whipcracking (which is apparently an Australian national sport). Within a global market of specialist goods, Mick's Whips uses the localisation strategy of being unashamedly Australian and using native materials for the international products. The only concession to the global market has been the conversion of the prices into US dollars, rather than the local currency (this could also relate to the fluctuating nature of the Australian dollar when compared to the stability of the US dollar).

(continued)

The second Australian company to offer a global focus using the local Australian cultural goods is R. M. Williams, which operates stores in both Australia and around the world.

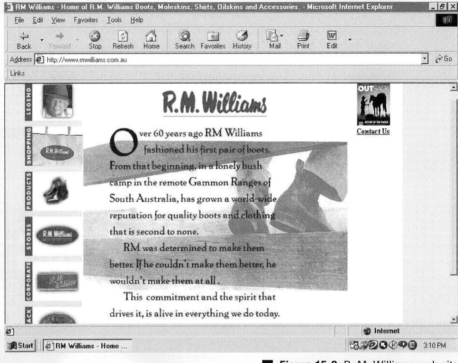

Source: www.rmwilliams.com.au

The web site offers an online store, as well as listing 'local' stockists for Australia and the selected range of countries with stores or distributors. The site also emphasises the Australian aspect of the organisation, with a prominent section of the site dedicated to the legends associated with R. M. Williams (the man and the company). In particular, the emphasis is placed on selling a core product (chapter 8) of a quality, Australian, tangible good, bundled with the cultural goods associated with the outback lifestyle. R. M. Williams emphasises the fact that the products are made to be part of the Australian outback way of life by indicating that key decisions for product selection are made on the basis of, 'Will it wear along the Birdsville track?'. However, this is not to say that the R. M. Williams web site has a local focus. Given that the online store requests that the customer specifies their region from a range of over 200 countries, the site indicates that the firm has an intentional global distribution orientation for their store.

Simmonds (1999) warns that consumers in different international markets will often have different motivations to buy the same product. The customised regional web page is one way of addressing these different needs. He highlights that a further trap that international marketers often fall into is setting the wrong entry price. Tied in with consumer motivations, it may be that what is commonplace in one country may become a status symbol in another. This means that demand for the product will allow relatively higher prices to be charged due to its perceived prestige. The ability to set higher prices internationally than domestically due to this scarcity factor is particularly valuable for those engaging in online export from relatively weak economies to strong economies such as the US. Cultural products that bring with them a certain differentiation or status for the purchaser can be sold at a higher price internationally than could be afforded in the local economy. Conversely, products that are exported from relatively strong economies to weaker economies may need to be sold at lower prices in the export market due to local economic conditions.

When modifying the marketing mix to suit different national target markets there is always a risk of contamination, as potential clients from different regions can browse the information for other regions. Given the ease of price comparisons over the Internet and price sensitivity of many Internet shoppers, for example, the customised international strategy of different mixes for different markets may actually damage the overall image of the organisation (Palumbo & Herbig 1998).

FOCUS ON
Strategy ◉

Regionalising a global web presence

Developing localised web pages has been a reasonably common aspect of Internet commerce for a large portion of the globally focused e-commerce companies, for example, providers of service portals, such as Excite, and their chain of regional sites. Excite provides a portal-style search engine, with an interface that can be customised, that offers a range of headline news articles, infotainment pieces, and other services such as email accounts. The 'franchise' is offered in a range of regional sites in the United States, Australia, the United Kingdom, France and Germany.

Despite being a global company, Excite offers a range of regional customisations, from the relatively spartan (and uncluttered) interface for the Excite Australia, through to the language translations for the UK, French, and German web sites. The most interesting aspect of the European chain of Excite sites is the relatively homogenous design between the three pages. With the exception of the localised content, such as the news, the navigation of the site remains consistent between the languages.

In contrast, Excite Australia (which is accessible through excite.com.au and excite.co.nz, a fact sure to annoy the New Zealand reader) bears only passing resemblance to the European designs. Oddly enough, it is also the only site to specify a regionalised brand, although this could in part be a position strategy (which would also annoy the New Zealand user). Routing a New Zealand web surfer to a .co.nz site to be welcomed to 'Australia' is poor form, considering the infotainment coverage on the site is predominantly Australian (although the user can restrict their web search to NZ sites only).

It seems ironic that an organisation which offers multilingual sites, regionalised URLs and a range of internationally focused services can mistakenly combine two distinctly independent countries into the one regional site.

Entry mode — is it still an issue?

The second big issue that has traditionally faced international marketers is the mode of entry. What is the most effective way of getting the product to the final consumer in the new market? Options include:

- *exporting*: selling some of what the company produces to overseas markets (www.peppermints.com)
- *licensing*: selling the right to use the company's process, trademark or patent to another firm for a fee or royalty (www.starbucks.com)
- *contract manufacturing*: handing control of the manufacturing of the goods over to a local entity while retaining control of the marketing function (www.mcdonalds.com and www.mcdonalds.com.au)
- *management contracting*: the seller provides management skills while others own the production and distribution facilities (www.accenture.com and www.dentalsales.com)
- *joint venturing*: an international marketing arrangement whereby a domestic and overseas company enter into a long-term relationship (www.optus.com.au)
- *wholly owned subsidiary*: a separate business operation is set up by the original company in the international market of choice (www.newscorp.com.au and www.webmd.ca)
- *multinational corporations*: companies with a direct investment in several countries. They tend to operate their businesses depending on the opportunities that present themselves anywhere in the world (www.bhp.com.au) (Quester, McGuiggan, Perrault & McCarthy 2001).

While the Internet does allow businesses to deal directly with the final consumer, the individualised approach does not offer the same economies of scale and other benefits associated with more traditional structures of international marketing. For most firms, one-to-one transactions with consumers do not represent the most cost effective or realistic option. The value of the Internet to international marketing is often not so much in the direct communication with consumers but in the development of relationships with international partners. Business-to-business international transactions are becoming simpler and more integrated as a result of the expansion and development of Internet technologies (Samli, Wills & Herbig 1997). Regardless of which option is being used to enter the market, Internet technologies can help facilitate the development of relationships with suppliers, channel members, local agents and the full range of other organisations and individuals involved in the development of an international marketing strategy.

In the digital age the decision as to how to enter the market is still important, particularly for larger firms and firms that already have an international marketing focus. Where the Internet is being seen as having the most impact in changing international marketing behaviour, however, is in the opening up of export opportunities to small and niche businesses which ordinarily would not have had the resources or inclination to develop a world wide presence.

Export industries

The decision to export a proportion of the firm's product used to be made largely on the basis of a surplus in the domestic market, combined with recognition of an opportunity in an external market. The export company was often a local success that sought to replicate its achievements in a new market once the major opportunities in the domestic market had been exhausted. The Internet, with its global reach, has since allowed firms to slip into an export orientation without necessarily planning to become an international firm.

Types of exporting

Not all Internet-based organisations have the same commitment to internationalisation, even among those that decide to expand their activities beyond the local market. Basically there are two types of online exporters, regular and sporadic.

Regular exporting

Regular online exporters fit the mould of the more traditional, offline exporter in that they have a clear commitment to developing an international orientation and are prepared to put the resources in to develop an international marketing program. For these organisations, export activity is the core to their business, not just an add on. To take a clear international orientation requires the firm to develop safe, secure, online ordering and payment systems. There must also be, for all physical goods, an adequate and appropriate method of delivery. Such systems require significant investments of financial and human resources and, in many cases, will also involve the development of strategic alliances with local partners. This would not only ensure delivery of goods, but would also assist in complying with local regulations.

Sporadic exporting

Sporadic exporters have benefited the most from the online environment. These are the companies that tend to be reactive rather than proactive in the development of an international marketing orientation. Often small or niche businesses, these organisations respond to international inquiries and, where possible, orders, but do not have the same investment in export infrastructure that is apparent with regular exporters. Their international activities tend to be opportunistic rather than part of an integrated strategy. Although sporadic exporters are not always as planned as regular exporters, sporadic export activity can be very profitable. Further, it is not uncommon for sporadic export to be a precursor to the development of an integrated, regular export orientation.

For many firms, the commitment and risk of developing a regular export orientation in the first instance is too great. Sporadic export activity provides an opportunity to develop an international orientation with relatively low risk. This is consistent with traditional stage-based or evolutionary views of the development of international marketing activities (Andersen 1993). One of the key benefits of the gradual development of international markets is the experiential learning that occurs within the organisation prior to a major investment in export or other international marketing activities. This evolutionary approach allows the organisation to develop a sound foundation of skills on which to base their future development (Bennett 1997).

The widespread adoption of the Internet has caused some Internet commentators to fundamentally question the premises on which contemporary models of export and international marketing are based, particularly as they relate to small or medium size enterprises. The opportunities that are offered to firms, in relation to international activities, by going online may fundamentally change the evolutionary or stage-based models of international marketing development (Hamill 1997). Companies may be able to effectively leapfrog the sporadic and early export stages and move directly into a full export orientation without the need for local success or a strong domestic base. This would be entirely due to the capabilities of the new technologies.

Impact of the Internet on barriers to export

Of particular interest when looking at the impact of the Internet is the role it can play in breaking down many of the traditional export barriers. Hamill and Gregory (1997) group these barriers into the following categories:

- *psychological barriers* include perceptions of high costs, excessive risk, issues of ethnocentrism and the problems associated with 'psychic distance'
- *operational barriers* include day-to-day issues such as excessive paperwork, delays in payment, transportation problems and distribution difficulties
- *organisational barriers* arise due to the lack of resources, human and financial, within the organisation to deal with the extra demands of international marketing activity. They also arise due to the lack of knowledge about, and experience in, foreign markets.
- *product/market barriers* refer to the specific issues of product modification, export restrictions, etc. that impede international trade.

While the first and most obvious effect of the Internet on international marketing is the potential for direct export to individual consumers, its main impact is in the access to information that it provides to potential exporters. As a medium, the Internet is best designed to both seek and send information. In the early stages of deciding whether to broaden the company's base to include the international market, relevant information is invaluable. Many of the problems which traditionally face new firms seeking to export, in terms of finding out about suppliers, local regulations and so on, have been minimised with the wider diffusion of the Internet (Bennett 1997). This access to information, combined with a common international Internet protocol and culture, also assists in reducing the psychic distance often felt between countries. The overarching Internet culture transcends traditional cultural blockages and, therefore, facilitates the development of international relationships. This was felt particularly by early users of the Internet.

Hamill (1997) has related specific Internet applications (or advantages) to each category of international marketing barriers. These are shown in table 15.2 opposite.

Table 15.2 Internet applications that assist in overcoming barriers to internationalisation

Barrier	Application/Advantage
Psychological	• Increase in international awareness, confidence and commitment through access to global information sources • Participation in global network communities • Enquiries and feedback to www site from potential global consumers
Operational	• Simplified export documentation through electronic data transfers • Electronic payments • Online export assistance
Organisational	• Access to low cost export market research resources • Improved knowledge of international markets and culture • Reduced dependence on traditional agents and distributors through direct marketing • Establishment of virtual network of partners
Product/market	• Country/market selection decision made easier by online export market research • Consumer/market orientation through customer, agent etc. feedback and comment • Cost savings through electronic market research and lower costs of communication • Adoption of global niche rather than country-centred strategies

Source: Hamill, J. 1997, 'The Internet and international marketing', *International Marketing Review*, vol. 14, no. 5, pp. 300–23.

In addition to these modifications and changes to specific applications, Quelch and Klein (1996) identify new business models in the field of international marketing as a result of the expansion of the Internet. Two models of specific interest are the online global information support/service-based organisations and the global transactional model.

Online global information support/service-based organisations

In the first of these models, the primary motivation of the firm is to either provide information or additional service via the web site. This is a strategy often used by established multinational or international firms that already have a presence across several nations. In many cases the reason for taking this approach is that, despite the set-up and running costs, it is often cheaper to provide an automated (or semi-automated) international service and information system than it is to provide the same service either face-to-face or via the telephone. An example of such a service is the Federal Express (www.fedex.com) tracking system which allows customers to track exactly where their parcel is at any given time.

Global transactional models

Companies without an existing international presence more commonly employ the global transactional model. However, it is also becoming more popular among established, multinational firms as a means of adding greater value to the overall product and service package. Under this model companies expand the capabilities of the web site to include online transactions. This is particularly suited to firms with information-based products or those which act as online intermediaries. Examples of this type of international business model include software companies (www.bpftp.com), music retailers (www.mp3.com) and information brokers (www.b4bfilmtv.com.au).

Conceptual framework for exporting and the Internet

As is the case with all aspects of marketing on the Internet, it is possible to adapt existing frameworks to explain activity in the new environment or, alternatively, to develop new models. Samiee (1998) is one author who has developed an alternative conceptual framework designed to explore the potential roles of the Internet in export marketing.

Six axioms, or fundamental guiding principles, underpin the framework which is presented in figure 15.3. These are:

- that sustainable competitive advantage cannot be solely derived from access to the Internet, or by developing a web page, although absence from the Internet may constitute a disadvantage
- non-exporting companies cannot expect to become exporters overnight by virtue of having a web site that can enable international transactions
- the level of overall consumer spending is not affected by Internet penetration and use
- security of communications and data is of paramount importance in the development of Internet-based export firms
- the Internet can assist in the minimisation or removal of certain structural impediments to export
- although the Internet can apply to all firms, export companies on the Internet can be broadly classified according to whether their primary target market is the end user or other channel members or manufacturers.

Within this broad framework or environment, the actual use and benefits derived from the Internet by export firms will depend on the type of exporter (i.e. regular or sporadic exporters), Internet applications and transaction types, and existing structural constraints such as import restrictions.

Sporadic exporters tend to be fairly limited in their conscious use of the Internet to generate international business, relying primarily on the occasional unsolicited order. By contrast, regular exporters use the Internet for a variety of purposes including:

- marketing research into relevant markets and on competitors
- promotional activities, such as banner advertising
- email campaigns
- linked web sites
- order taking.

In terms of applications, the Internet can be used to either enhance business processes or to generate revenue. The use of the Internet to improve the process of conducting export business occurs through the facilitation or automation of specific functions. These include inventory management, purchasing and shipment tracking. However, online business processes tend to be firm specific, expensive to develop and difficult to access.

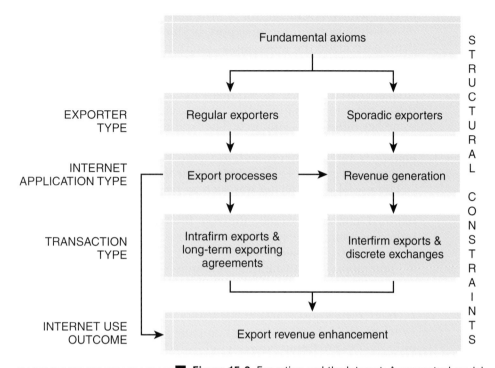

Figure 15.3 Exporting and the Internet: A conceptual model

Source: Samiee, S. 1998, 'Exporting and the Internet: A conceptual perspective', *International Marketing Review*, vol. 15, no. 5, pp. 413–26.

Alternatively, the focus of the company's Internet application can be more strongly placed on revenue generation. Developing a system for revenue generation depends on making it widely accessible. Such systems differ from business processes in that they must be accessible by clients. This means that they cannot rely on proprietary software. The main methods of revenue generation via the Internet involve order generation or inventory management for intermediaries.

The final consideration in this framework is the transaction type, specifically whether it is an intra- or inter-firm transaction. Intra-firm transactions are common in large, multi-site, multinational firms. Such transactions need to be highly coordinated and tend to be pre-negotiated and policy driven. In contrast, inter-firm transactions are more difficult to predict as they are individually driven and negotiated.

The final value of the Internet as a tool for enhancing export business will be a function of all of these variables and the costs, both direct and indirect, involved in setting up the system. To establish the value of the Internet to the export activities of the organisation, the management needs to determine what incremental revenue is directly attributable to the move online.

Differences between traditional and online exporters

Although, as Samiee (1998) points out, being online is not necessarily a source of competitive advantage for a firm and going online does not transform a domestic business into an export business, large numbers of international firms have made the move. In an interesting study, Bennett (1997) compared the characteristics, attitudes and behaviours of traditional export firms that had not moved their operations in whole or in part to the Internet, and Internet-based exporters. Although many concerns about exporting, such as fluctuations in exchange rates, were consistent for both types of exporters, some key differences emerged. The typical number of years that online organisations had been exporting was significantly lower, fewer online businesses employed foreign agents and, as would be expected, online exporters had a far higher degree of confidence in their technological expertise.

The use of the Internet was seen as particularly beneficial by smaller companies which perceived that it significantly lowered the cost of entry into international markets. Overall, the top five perceived benefits of adopting an online presence for export activities were:

- creation of new sales leads
- generation of international awareness of the firm
- penetration of unfamiliar markets
- avoidance of setting up foreign branches
- help with export marketing research.

In terms of the barriers facing companies that exported, only four significant differences were found between web-based exporters and traditional exporters. Online exporters saw the need to obtain foreign representation as being significantly more of a barrier than traditional exporters. Traditional exporters, on the other hand, perceived a lack of knowledge about foreign markets, the financial costs of exporting to new markets and the competition for the firm's available resources to be more significant barriers than online exporters.

Overall, this study is interesting in that it shows that there are more similarities than differences between online and traditional exporters. Consequently, it may not be necessary to introduce new models and theories for online exporting; rather, it may be more appropriate to simply modify the existing theory.

 ## SMEs, internationalisation and the Internet

The perceived big winners in the move to online export activity are small to medium size businesses. Many of the barriers to export which previously faced such organisations are minimised, if not entirely removed, when operating in the online environment. In the past, any move into overseas markets was accompanied by a multitude of expensive and time-consuming procedures to ensure that import requirements were met, distribution outlets secured and local agents employed. The advent of online export marketing does not eliminate these barriers and processes. However, for the individual trader, small business or sporadic exporter, the Internet offers opportunities to expand beyond the local market and experiment with the possibilities of international marketing.

The main focus of small business interactions on the Internet has been on retailing and direct sales activities online. This is due to the popular perception that, because all web pages have a global reach, the online environment represents a level playing field for all users. Where many of the benefits of being online are realised for small business, from a global as well as local perspective, is in the supply chain. The supply chain provides many cost savings as a result of being able to deal directly with suppliers, particularly those who are based overseas, rather than the costly alternative of having to rely on agents or other intermediaries.

Although, in theory (from a retailing perspective) anyone can sell items internationally simply by putting up a web page advertising their products or services, in reality, success is more likely for small businesses if they operate as part of a broader strategic network rather than as an individual. Strategic networks can provide a variety of functions, from improving economies of scale by centralising key functions (such as collating market intelligence), through to cross-promotion of firms and products. Golden and Dollanger (1993) identified four major types of inter-organisational relationships to describe the interactions between small businesses. These are:

- *confederation*: firms which compete with one another but maintain some functional activities in common. These activities are coordinated by central management. (www.fox.com, www.foxkids.com, www.foxfamily.com)
- *conjugate collectives*: firms which have contractual arrangements for symbiotic purposes (www.dell.com and www.microsoft.com)
- *agglomerate collectives*: firms which compete within the same industry but have no contractual business arrangements, but act conjointly to develop and expand the overall user base for the competitive products. For example, distributors of Linux (www.redhat.com and www.debian.com) attempt to increase the overall market size for Linux products while trying to expand their own market
- *organic collectives*: firms which engage in traditional networking in an indirect and non-contractual form (www.thinkgeek.com, www.slashdot.org, www.freshmeat.net)

Cooperation in these relationships varies from horizontal (confederation) to vertical (conjugate collective) and contractual (conjugate) to non-contractual (agglomerate collectives, organic collectives) (Hamill 1997).

As with many other marketing models, the benefits of traditional networks can be transferred into the new online environment. Poon and Jevons (1997) apply Golden and Dallanger's network classification to the online activities of small businesses. They do this as an attempt to demonstrate the ways in which the Internet can be used to improve inter-organisational relationships and link these with Internet marketing strategies. A summary of their findings is given in table 15.3 on page 386.

The extent to which these options are pursued depends on the nature of the business and the objective of the relationship. For example, organic collectives most commonly emerge in the social sector where the common goal is not profit-oriented, but rather a more intangible outcome of education, improvement of social relations, promotion of an ideal and so on. On the other hand, small operators or individual operators are more likely to become involved in confederations, where the firm can take advantage of the combined resources of the group to achieve economies of scale and maximum reach.

Table 15.3 Improving inter-organisational relationships through the Internet

Interorganisational relationship	Definition	Suggested marketing strategies
Confederation	Firms which compete with one another but maintain some functional activities in common that are co-ordinated by central management	• Central management provides resources for members to market their products and services online • Reciprocal linking as part of the membership agreement • Cross promotional ventures • Horizontal networks between confederation websites
Conjugate collectives	Firms which have contractual arrangements for symbiotic purposes	• Allows for reciprocal linking • Pooled market intelligence on an intranet system • Shared market intelligence to improve supplier-buyer relationships • Relationship marketing • EDI
Agglomerate collectives	Firms which compete within the same industry but have no contractual business arrangements	• Trade associations provide market intelligence data on its home site for member use • Mutual agreements to between trade associations to market products and services • Push based marketing to increase demand for the product, and increase the size of the market
Organic collectives	Firms which engage in traditional networking in an indirect and non contractual form	• Reciprocal links, and web rings • Advertise products and provide low-cost/free services for charity members of community networks on the Internet • Link community calendar of events to homepages

Source: Poon, S. and Jevons, C. 1997, 'Internet-enabled international marketing: A small business network approach', *Journal of Marketing Management*, vol. 13, pp. 29–41.

A further consideration for small businesses entering international commerce via the Internet (as opposed to traditional channels) is whether the resources of the firm are strong enough to support such a move. Although it is simpler to engage in limited export opportunities through one-on-one interaction via web pages, anything beyond this individualised approach should be undertaken only after a thorough analysis of the firm's strategic aims and internal capabilities.

Analysing potential markets

Not all countries are as equally attractive to the online international marketer. As is the case with any export or internationally oriented business, key economic and social indicators must be taken into consideration prior to a move into a particular country. Although the Internet has global reach and provides the capacity to interact with individuals and firms worldwide, it does not mean that firms are obliged to engage in international commerce. Traditional indicators of whether a firm should enter a market include determining the new market's average income, distribution of wealth, political stability and regulatory frameworks. These remain important for companies engaging in an Internet-based international marketing strategy. The additional effort and cost required to develop a full international orientation for a web-based company, particularly when this activity is directed at targeted markets, must be recovered in sales for the strategy to remain viable.

Bishop (1999) developed a detailed rating system to assist in determining which markets are most attractive to the online entrepreneur. The Global Digital Marketing Index is based on an evaluation of 10 categories, each of which is rated out of five (at 0.5 increments) before being converted into a score out of 100. The 10 categories are:

- **economic power**: based on a calculation of per capita GDP with high scores indicating higher relative economic power
- **economic growth**: based on published growth rates from international economic forums and then divided by two to give a score out of five. The higher the growth rate, the more opportunities are likely to be present for digital entrepreneurs.
- **economic stability**: based on the inflation rate, with lower levels of inflation indicating higher economic stability
- **trading level**: determined by the ratio between the country's GDP and its total level of trade, with a high rating indicating that the country is open to trade and likely to welcome digital marketers
- **political environment**: a qualitative measure based on indicators such as the type of government (democracy vs military dictatorship), judicial system, the stability of the government etc.
- **freedom of expression**: a qualitative measure based on the willingness of the society to accept divergent opinion and the extent to which it encourages debate via the media and other outlets
- **bureaucratic index**: based on the level and number of regulations and procedures that must be navigated by the exporter/international marketer to enter that country's market
- **telco infrastructure**: the number of telephone lines per 100 citizens. The higher the number of lines, the greater the capacity of the citizens of that country to conduct business over the Internet.
- **digital capabilities**: the number of computers owned per 100 people in the country. The greater the number of computers, the higher the rating and the more likely that the population will be engaged in online activity.

- **online resources**: the level of online activity within the country, based on statistics such as the number of domain names registered.

Bishop has listed the top 10 most attractive markets for online entrepreneurs (based on the calculations made from the index above) as follows:

Table 15.4 The top 10 international online markets

Rank	Country	Rating	Country domain
1	Netherlands	90	.nl
2	Luxembourg	88	.lu
2	Norway	88	.no
4	Canada	87	.ca
4	Finland	87	.fi
4	United States	87	.us
7	Denmark	85	.dk
7	Switzerland	85	.ch
9	Australia	84	.au
10	New Zealand	83	.nz

Source: Derived from Bishop, B. 1999, *Global Marketing for the Digital Age*, NTC Business Books, Chicago.

The lowest ranking countries using this index were the Russian Federation (29), Egypt (27) and China (21). A detailed discussion of the relative merits of 50 different markets for online export and other commercial activity is given in Bishop's book, *Global Marketing for the Digital Age* (1999).

Although this index is quite detailed and provides a ready guide for those interested in entering into international commerce via the Internet, it does not take into consideration all relevant points. For example, many of the objective measures used are relative rather than absolute measures. While there may be more computers per capita in Luxembourg than in Canada, the actual size of the market in Canada will be larger and, therefore, more attractive to many exporters. Also it does not take logistical infrastructure into consideration. Transport considerations are of particular importance when dealing with physical goods online and may limit the attractiveness of certain markets. For example, the geographic distance involved in transporting fresh products to Australia and New Zealand may preclude them from being a viable market despite the fact that, using this index, they rate higher than the UK and Singapore. Other problems with the index include the assumption that each criterion is of equal importance in the decision to develop an export market, and that the criteria are summative.

Despite these shortcomings, the Global Digital Marketing Index provides a useful model for developing an objective measure of market suitability, prior to engaging in an online international marketing strategy.

Another point to keep in mind is that any index of this type represents the state of play at a given point in time. Regular updates, at least annually, are necessary to review not only the application of criteria, but the criteria themselves. For example, while the state of current technology means that the number of phone lines per 100 is a useful indicator of potential Internet reach, new technologies which allow Internet access without the need for phone lines will make this criterion redundant.

Implementing the international web presence

Although the specific steps involved in implementing a global marketing strategy may vary between companies and industries, Bishop (1999) has identified eight global marketing imperatives which apply across the board. These are outlined in the sections following.

Overcome personal boundaries

Overcoming personal boundaries refers to the need to seriously evaluate, and re-evaluate, the business that the company is in. Are there any unnecessary restrictions being placed on activities due to traditional perceptions of appropriateness? Artificial barriers that are specific to the Internet as an international marketing medium include both psychological and perceived cost elements. It is far more comfortable to remain within the same market and rely on increased penetration for growth than to develop new markets.

Convert atoms into bytes

As discussed in chapter 8 (Product), the ideal product to sell and distribute online is the information product. Further, as also discussed, the firm's total product offering is more than just the physical good — it includes all the additional intangible features which augment the actual product. In making the move online, particularly when entering international markets, the extent to which the firm's traditional product can be augmented or supplemented by digital product variations will enhance the internationalisation process. For example, while the main domestic clients of the company may purchase the tangible good, international clients may be more interested in purchasing the firm's local knowledge and expertise in the industry. Thus, the key international product of the organisation may be information about local industry processes and conditions, not the tangible good. The relative mix of tangible and intangible elements of the offering may vary considerably between markets.

This point relates to the previous one in that it requires companies to re-evaluate what it is that they can offer the international market rather than simply trying to replicate domestic activities in a global environment.

Do not compete, be unique

The worldwide availability of cheap, comparative information (as previously discussed) puts the consumer into a powerful position relative to the seller.

The importance of developing a unique selling proposition is greater in such an environment where competitors and consumers alike have unprecedented access to information about the company and its operations. Without additional, difficult to replicate appeal, consumers will rely on price (chapter 11) as the major influence in a purchase decision.

Be a specialist not a generalist

Access to global niche markets puts the specialist in a stronger position than the generalist. As was pointed out in terms of uniqueness in the previous section, it is the differentiation of product and service offerings that will be the basis of success in this highly competitive and open environment.

Serve a specialised market

In addition to developing a specialised or highly differentiated product, successful global online marketers need to serve specialised markets. In other words, given the reach of the Internet, it is not only possible, but desirable, to limit the firm's appeal to a highly specialised and clearly defined market niche. The more focused the target market is, the easier it is to define members, contact them and modify and develop products to suit their needs. Also, for smaller operations moving into international online marketing, a highly specialised niche strategy allows for controlled growth within the resource capacity of the organisation.

Operate in advanced digital markets

As outlined previously in relation to the Global Digital Marketing Index, some countries are more ready to market over the Internet than others. In the initial stages of international online marketing it is most appropriate to focus on those countries which are most advanced in terms of digital trading. Pioneering work in underdeveloped digital economies is a high cost, high risk strategy.

Develop indigenous digital partnerships

As discussed in chapter 12 (Distribution), when it comes to the sale of physical or tangible goods, logistics remain as important for online businesses as for traditional businesses. Consequently, successful international marketers need to develop sound relationships and partnerships with local agents, distributors and other businesspeople if they are to develop a systematic export strategy. As previously discussed, small businesses with the occasional overseas sale may rely on the standard postal service for delivery of small items; however, anything beyond this requires a formal distribution network as would be necessary for any international business. Indigenous agents have the advantage of knowing the local environment and culture and can facilitate the movement of goods from the Internet-based company's orders through to the final consumer.

Use technology to foster global relationships

Finally, Bishop emphasises the point that while the new technologies available to international marketers are creating unprecedented opportunities, at the end of the day relationships are more important (chapter 14). As long as technology remains in its place as an enabler, the benefits for international business are potentially limitless. However, if it becomes the main focus of the firm's activity, there is a danger of the firm becoming too remote, and losing touch with customers and suppliers. This is particularly evident when firms continually upgrade their technological capacities and, by doing so, outstrip the ability of their clients to access information or take full advantage of the services that are offered.

When dealing in formal international business, Internet-based marketers need also to be aware of the traps which limit the effectiveness of traditional exporters and international marketers. Simmonds (1999) has identified seven common traps which firms may fall into when moving from a relatively safe domestic strategy to pursuing international objectives. These are:

- ranking markets on the basis of the size or growth of demand for the firm's product, rather than on the basis of potential penetration that the firm's strategy will bring. For example, if the United States is judged on its size and growth it represents a highly attractive market for most products. However, if the strategy of the firm does not allow for easy payment through United States facilities, does not list prices in US dollars and does not allow for additional offline promotion in the United States environment, then the company is likely to fail in this market, despite its apparent attractiveness.

- underestimating foreign competitors. This is an issue for online as well as traditional sellers. Although there may be some apparent cost advantages for consumers in buying via the Internet, the benefits of this are often outweighed by the inconvenience of waiting for delivery and potential additional charges, such as postage and customs. Local suppliers of the same or similar goods remain a significant threat.

- variable customer motivations. Customer attitudes vary across cultures and so a single strategy or web page, based on the motivations of the domestic consumer, may fail to interest overseas customers. Good market research into the wants and needs of potential consumers in each target country is needed to maximise the effectiveness of international marketing.

- incorrect or inappropriate pricing. Although it is easy for the traditional exporter to charge substantially different prices to different markets because of the lack of comparative market information, it is not so easy when selling online due to the transparency of the medium. Consequently, different pricing may not be possible and a viable international price must be settled upon prior to export.

- a lack of understanding of the stage of each different market's development (in relation to the product category and the specific firm's brand awareness). A generic strategy assuming equal development is likely to fail as the product awareness of some markets may be low. Therefore, a strategy which stimulates primary demand would be required in some markets, whereas in more advanced markets which have progressed to selective, there would be a need for brand-building strategies.

■ inappropriate choice of partners. This is another risk faced by international marketers of all descriptions, including those that are Internet-based. As previously discussed, unless the product on sale is information-based, there is still a need for quality relationships to be developed with agents and distributors in the local area. This creates the link between final user and Internet marketer.

■ failure to provide adequate protection to a brand as it moves into the international arena. Brand image and positioning must remain consistent throughout the world if the brand is to retain its value. While inconsistent positioning in traditional international marketing activities may not have been a significant problem (due to the lack of communications between markets), in the global Internet environment, consistency is essential (due to the transparency of the medium).

 # Summary

Despite the fact that the Internet is inherently an international medium, not all online commerce can be classified as having an international orientation. Many businesses choose to use the Internet simply to enhance the services they provide for their existing local customers and markets. However, others use the Internet, with varying degrees of success and complexity, to move out of their local environment and into international commerce.

The main type of organisation to benefit from the Internet is the established, small-to medium-size enterprise. In the past, such companies were prevented, largely due to cost issues, from entering international markets. However, with the expansion of e-commerce, a variety of new opportunities were created for these firms. While some took a relatively low key approach to international marketing, and became sporadic exporters that traded on a one-on-one basis with individual clients, others have significantly redeveloped their business systems and order-taking abilities to allow for full-scale international trade in goods and services.

Although the Internet has broken down many traditional barriers to international trade and marketing, it has not removed all risks. The same issues of cultural variations between countries, the need to customise specific aspects of the marketing mix and the need to carefully evaluate countries for potential profitability are consistent whether the international marketer is primarily Internet focused or not. Major benefits for international marketers in the online environment include a reduction of psychic space, improved access to information and lower cost communication. However, without a systematic and strategic approach to international market selection and servicing, these benefits cannot outweigh the risks of leaving the security of the domestic market in favour of internationalisation.

Discussion questions

15.1 Is all Internet-based marketing inherently international? Explain your answer with reference to the different styles of marketing which can be undertaken online.

15.2 Can an environment, such as the Internet, which is based in the ergosphere and the marketspace, be an international marketing arena? Or is it a new place in its own right? Discuss with reference to the implications for online international marketing.

15.3 Given the global reach of the Internet, is entry mode still a key issue for contemporary international marketers? Why?

15.4 Outline and give original examples of the different types of export industries involved in international marketing.

15.5 To what extent has the widespread adoption of the Internet impacted on traditional export barriers?

15.6 Outline the potential roles that the Internet can play in export marketing as outlined in Samiee's (1998) framework.

15.7 Explain the key elements of the Global Digital Marketing Index and demonstrate, with examples, how it can be used to assist in the development of an international online strategy.

15.8 What are the key benefits and limitations of the Global Digital Marketing Index?

15.9 Discuss the main issues involved in the implementation of an international online marketing strategy.

15.10 What are the key traps that international marketers regularly fall into when moving out of the domestic environment? Show, with examples, how these can be minimised in the online environment.

References

Andersen, O. 1993, 'On the internationalisation process of firms: A critical analysis', *Journal of International Business Studies*, vol. 24, no. 2, pp. 209–31.

Bennett, R. 1997, 'Export marketing and the Internet: Experiences of web site use and perceptions of export barriers among UK businesses', *International Marketing Review*, vol. 14, no. 5, pp. 324–44.

Bishop, B. 1999, *Global Marketing for the Digital Age*, NTC Business Books, Chicago.

Ger, G. 1999, 'Localising in the global village: Local firms competing in global markets', *California Management Review*, vol. 14, no. 4, pp. 64–83.

Golden, P. A. & Dollinger, M. 1993, 'Cooperative alliances and competitive strategies in small manufacturing firms', *Entrepreneurship Theory and Practice*, Summer, pp. 43–56.

Hamill, J. 1997, 'The Internet and international marketing', *International Marketing Review*, vol. 14, no. 5, pp. 300–23.

Hamill, J. & Gregory, K. 1997, 'Internet marketing in the internationalisation of UK SMEs', *Journal of Marketing Management*. In J. Hamill (ed.), Special Edition on Internationalisation, vol. 13, no. 1–3, January–April.

Jain, S. 1989, 'Reducing the risks of globalisation', *Long Range Planning*, vol. 53, February, pp. 80–8.

Jevons, C. 2000, 'Misplaced marketing', *Journal of Consumer Marketing*, vol. 17, no. 1, pp. 7–8.

Levitt, T. 1983, 'The globalisation of markets', *Harvard Business Review*, vol. 61, May–June, pp. 92–102.

Palumbo, F. & Herbig, P. 1998, 'International marketing tool: The Internet', *Industrial Management and Data Systems*, vol. 6, pp. 253–61.

Poon, S. & Jevons, C. 1997, 'Internet-enabled international marketing: A small business network approach', *Journal of Marketing Management*, vol. 13, pp. 29–41.

Quelch, J. & Klein, L. 1996, 'The Internet and international marketing', *Sloan Management Review*, vol. 37 (Spring), pp. 60–75.

Quester, P., McGuiggan, R., Perrault, E. J. & McCarthy, W. 2001, *Basic Marketing: A Managerial Approach* (3rd Australasian Edition), McGraw–Hill, Sydney.

Ramarapu, S., Timmerman, J. & Ramarapu, N. 1999, 'Choosing between globalisation and localisation as a strategic thrust for your international marketing effort', *Journal of Marketing Theory and Practice*, Spring, pp. 97–105.

Samiee, S. 1998, 'Exporting and the Internet: A conceptual perspective', *International Marketing Review*, vol. 15, no. 5, pp. 413–26.

Samli, A., Wills, J. & Herbig, P. 1997, 'The information superhighway goes international: Implications for industrial sales transactions', *Industrial Marketing Management*, vol. 26, pp. 51–8.

Simmonds, K. 1999, 'International marketing — avoiding the seven deadly traps', *Journal of International Marketing*, vol. 7, no. 2, pp. 51–62.

Web sites

www.amazon.com
www.b4bfilmtv.com.au
www.bhp.com.au
www.bpftp.com
www.brisbane.qld.gov.au.
www.coke.com
www.debian.com
www.dell.com
www.ehobbies.com
www.excite.co.nz
www.excite.co.uk
www.excite.com
www.excite.com.au
www.excite.de
www.excite.fr
www.fedex.com
www.fox.com
www.foxfamily.com
www.foxkids.com
www.freshmeat.net
www.helpagency.com.au
www.levi.com
www.mcdonalds.com
www.mcdonalds.com.au
www.mercedes.com
www.mickswhips.com.au
www.microsoft.com
www.mp3.com
www.newscorp.com.au
www.nzart.org.nz
www.optus.com.au
www.peppermints.com
www.pepsi.co.nz
www.pepsi.co.uk
www.pepsi.com
www.pepsi.com.au
www.pepsi.de.
www.pizzahut.com.au
www.rctoys.com
www.redhat.com
www.rmwilliams.com.au
www.slashdot.org
www.starbucks.com
www.thinkgeek.com
www.tmvc.com.au
www.webmd.ca
www.whim.com.au

CHAPTER 16

Marketing research

'Small firms are taking advantage of new media in marketing more and more as a means of levelling the playing field of their larger competitors. By using the Internet for global advertising and market research, low-cost electronic mail to communicate with customers, and mobile technologies such as cellular telephones and laptop computers for order-taking and field sales, small firms have been able to establish a local presence with a global reach on a shoestring budget.'

Lynn, G. S., Maltz, A. C., Jurkat, P. M. and Hammer, M. D. 1999, 'New media in marketing redefine competitive advantage: A comparison of small and large firms', *The Journal Of Services Marketing*, vol. 13, no. 1, pp. 9–20.

LEARNING *objectives*

After reading this chapter, you should be able to:

- understand the principles of online market research
- recognise the advantages and disadvantages of using the Internet for data collection
- identify the different types of market research that can be used online
- appreciate the difference between on and offline market research and data collection
- know how to conduct environmental scanning used in Internet market research
- understand how to collect market intelligence data using the Internet
- outline the process and methods of conducting online market research
- appreciate the issues concerning anonymity, privacy and ethics in online research
- understand the limitations of online market research
- overview the process of conducting online market segmentation.

Introduction

Market research is the lifeblood of informed marketing. Without the support of reliable market data, and carefully selected competitor and customer information, marketing becomes a patchwork of guesses, hunches and product failures. This chapter sets out to overview the old and the new of market research on the Internet. It outlines the principles of online market research, including the areas of strength and weakness of the Internet as a tool for data collection.

Emphasis is placed on exploring the different types of market research that can be used online, and how, and where, these different mechanisms are most appropriately applied. This includes an examination of the process and methods of conducting online market research, including environment scanning, and the collection of market intelligence data using the Internet.

This chapter also overviews the value of online market segmentation, both at the population level and the site-specific level, and reviews a method of conducting segmentation. Finally, the chapter explores several of the issues concerning privacy, ethics and anonymity that are raised because of the prevalence of online market research

Foundations of market research: How and why of finding out who and what

The widespread use of the Internet has significantly changed the way in which marketers conduct research. The Internet offers marketers access to both the largest and most significant storehouse of information ever collated and to a level and quality of data never before available.

The online advantage

Using the Internet for marketing-related research involves both the adoption, and adaptation, of traditional market research techniques. Access to global secondary data sources means that all marketers, not only those who are attempting to develop an online presence, can change the quality, quantity and type of resources investigated for marketing purposes. Online information warehouses such as NUA Surveys (www.nua.ie/surveys) bring together a global collation of market research data and statistics that can be used by any marketer with Internet access.

The Internet also provides a wide range of information regarding competitor and consumer intelligence. From a practical perspective, access to online annual reports, consolidated industry reports and trends analyses, either free or on a pay-per-use basis, means that the marketers of today have better and more up-to-date information on the competitive environment than ever before.

From a consumer intelligence perspective, Internet-based research can take the form of either primary or secondary sources. Collection of primary data via the Internet has become a relatively cheap, accessible alternative medium through which to conduct surveys, focus groups and ethnographic research.

The other side of the coin: Disadvantages of the Internet

Despite the many advantages of Internet-based market research, it also has a range of limitations, particularly in the collection of primary data. Due to the limited and skewed sample that the demographics of Internet users present, it is difficult to generalise beyond the sample when conducting Internet-based research. As mentioned in chapter 4, when the Internet was still a new medium, much of the early Internet market research data were skewed towards the analysis of varying degrees of innovators. Given the innovator adopter category comprises less than 2.5 per cent of a population, the data taken from these initial studies cannot be generalised to the offline world. Even with the widespread adoption of the Internet, the online population is still skewed towards innovative, intelligent and financially secure people, just simply by the access requirements of a computer, modem, and monthly account subscription.

The anonymity that the Internet provides allows for easier misrepresentation of research participants while the nature of the text-based medium limits the quality of data obtainable through those activities, usually undertaken on a face-to-face basis such as focus groups and personal interviews. Finally, the findings of market research undertaken on the Internet are often difficult to validate due to the interest-driven nature of the medium. Online surveys tend to be hampered by self-selection biases that are more pronounced on the Internet than even in shopping mall intercepts or telephone surveys.

Review of the market research process

Market research is an essential element of the marketing management process. Without systematic marketing information systems in place, it is impossible for marketers to fully understand either the environment in which they operate, or the consumers for whom they are developing products and services. In chapter 7, many of the strategic decisions that needed to be made were underpinned by the need for reliable market research. Similarly, pricing decisions (chapter 11), market segmentation (chapter 7, chapter 16), and new product development (chapter 9) were also influenced by the outcomes of market research.

Given the heavy dependence on market research within the recommendations in this book, and the marketing industry in general, a brief overview of the process of market research is provided. Typically, marketers will go through the following process in collecting and collating information about the market. Figure 16.1 on the following page illustrates the steps in the market research process.

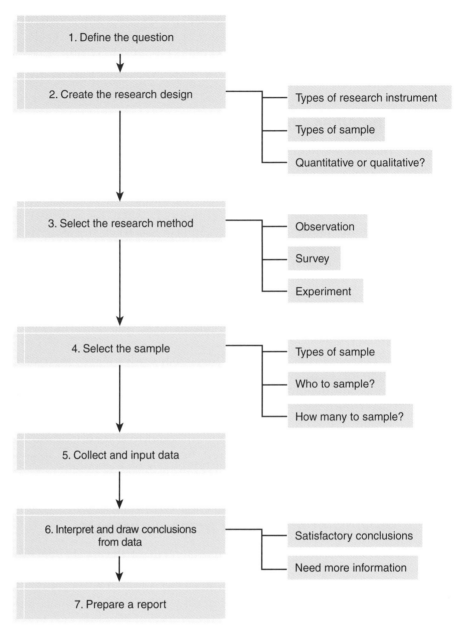

Figure 16.1 Steps in the market research process

Source: Derived from Forrest, E. 1999, *Internet Marketing Research: Resources and Techniques*, McGraw-Hill, Sydney.

It is important to note that at any stage during this process it is possible for the marketer to determine the solution to the problem faced and exit from the process. Similarly, although the steps are presented as sequential, it is often necessary to backtrack during the process for clarification purposes or to collect further information. Forrest (1999) laid out a systematic approach for conducting market research, consisting of eight steps:

1. Define the question/problem

   This first step is critical to the collection of timely, relevant and useful information. If marketers do not take the time to carefully define the question or problem facing them, they can waste many thousands of dollars, and months of time, collecting information which brings them no closer to understanding the consumer or the marketing environment than they were to start with.

   In this stage it is important to differentiate between the problem itself and the symptoms of the problem. Typically it is the symptoms of the problem, for example, a drop in hits to a web site, that alerts the marketer to the fact that there is a problem in the first place. What the marketer needs to do is to find out why hits are dropping, not just how far they are dropping. Discovering that traffic to your web site has increased or decreased is as easy as reading the server logs each day. All this information tells you is that people have (or have not) been visiting. The research question of value is to determine why visits have (or have not) occurred, and what the user did once they arrived at the site.

2. Create the research design

   Once the problem has been identified, the first decision the marketer needs to make is what general approach should be employed to collect the data needed to answer the question. Should the data collected be quantitative or qualitative? What type of research instruments should be used and what type of sample employed? Answering these general questions leads to the next step in the process. The initial temptation for online marketing research is to put up an interactive survey on the front page of the web site and hope that this will capture the needed data. For basic research questions, this may be the appropriate design. However, if the research question is complex, and seeks to determine what value the user wants from the web site, a more complex research design of focus groups, ethnographic studies of the site's cybercommunities and bulletin boards and a series of quantitative surveys may be the best tactic.

3. Select the research method

   Research methods vary according to what type of data is needed and what question needs to be answered. Generally the research method selected will be based on observation, surveys or experiments.

   Observation studies on the Internet tend to be focused around locations of human interaction, such as cybercommunities, USENET or discussion lists. Surveys are primarily based on web sites, although carefully constructed email surveys to an established list of volunteer participants can be equally valuable. Experimental studies, such as those conducted by Hofacker and Murphy (1998) into banner advertisements, rely on the increasing sophistication and complexity of the web page. Experimental designs on the Internet can be facilitated through interactive web pages which are custom tailored to recognise individual users, or to serve different experimental stimuli based on selected or random patterns. For instance, an experiment into the influence of colour on web site popularity could be based on the web server determining the country of origin of the user (based on the IP address), and serving a specific coloured page to them. Alternatively, as demonstrated by Hofacker and Murphy (1998), and outlined in detail below, the computer could be set to randomly choose an experiment stimulus from a pool of options.

4. Select the sample population

Asking the right questions is important. However, it is equally as important to be asking them of the right people. A well-designed survey will provide no useful information to the marketer if it is administered to people who are outside of the population of interest to the organisation. Consequently, appropriate sample selection is critical to the validity of the overall research outcomes.

Questions to be answered within the context of choosing the relevant sample include:

- *who should be sampled?* Do you want current, potential or past users of the web site? Research attempting to discover what people use the web site for will require current users, whereas studies into what people could and would want from a web site should focus on current and potential users. Sites suffering from a sudden drop in traffic should be attempting to contact subscribers who have chosen to leave the service to determine their reasons for departure.
- *how many people should be approached?* Is a minimum quota of people needed for the research design and chosen statistical method to work? Some statistical packages require a minimum number of responses before they will be able to process a useable outcome. The design of an experimental data collection will also require a greater number of respondents than a straightforward single survey type.
- *how should they be chosen?* Should the users of the web site be allowed to self select themselves for the survey, or should an external market research company obtain a data set from offline, or different web sites?

Online research companies such as Greenfields (www.greenfieldonline .com) offer incentives to respondents to join their survey pool. From this pool of volunteers, they run a series of qualification surveys to determine whether the recipient is eligible for the upcoming major studies and, where a recipient qualifies for a survey, they are notified by email that the survey is running, and what incentives are available for completion of the survey.

5. Collect and input data

One of the key advantages to the advancement of technology for market researchers has been the development of instant data input through interactive surveys. The collection of data in a useable form involves the coding of responses, inputting of these responses into a relevant statistical program and editing the data to remove any irregularities. Automation of these functions has accelerated the market response time as well, where certain surveys can provide real time response data to the recipient, thus encouraging them to complete further surveys. Many one-off polls conducted on web sites such as Slashdot (www.slashdot.org) are used to determine the demand for a new feature, or responses to a topical issue. The real-time data collection and processing of the information allows for basic displays of percentages or bar graphs of results, giving the user of the survey an insight into how others responded to the survey. The exchange of user's time is paid for by the revelation of the results of the survey.

6. Interpret and draw conclusions about the data
   The data on their own are of no real relevance unless they have been analysed and interpreted in light of the research questions being asked. Various statistical techniques have been developed over time which highlight issues of significance, the relationships between different types of information and so on. This is a universal step in the market research process, whether the research is examining use of a web site or preference for brands of toothpaste.
7. Prepare a report
   The final report arising from the research process should effectively communicate the results of the process to the appropriate sponsors. Most market research is generated by management who seek to understand the reasons behind trends and the likely outcomes of environmental change. Such reports should focus attention on important decision-making information.
8. Follow up the research
   In the dynamic environment of the Internet, any research conducted is merely a snapshot of a point in time that has already passed, and may already be out of date. The investment of time and money in the initial research should not be wasted by failing to conduct follow-up studies in the mistaken belief that these studies are an unnecessary cost. Monitoring of traffic to a web site needs to be conducted over a long period to determine if cyclical patterns appear, before an understanding of peaks and troughs in activity can be established. Similarly, studies into demand for web site services may be dependent on the availability of current technologies, for example, streaming video may be seen as unnecessary for a news site because of the current poor quality. Should a major change in the technology environment occur (fast streaming video is developed) then the research needs to be conducted again, in light of the change in the environment.

Types of market research

Market research can be classified along a number of different lines. In this instance two categorisations will be used. The first classifies the research according to what it is trying to achieve, that is, its objectives, while the second classifies according to the method employed.

Objective of collection

In defining the scope of the problem, the researcher is also determining the objective of the research to be undertaken. Research objectives can typically be classified as falling into one of the categories described here (Forrest 1999).

Descriptive
Descriptive research does not try to explain why something is happening, instead it simply collects the facts about a situation or environment and collates them. Typically descriptive research is an input into the overall marketing information system where certain variables of general interest to the organisation are tracked over time. This information is often analysed later in light

of specific issues identified within the organisation and its environments. Web site server logs, hit counters and other passive tracking software which describes usage patterns are descriptive data collection tools (figure 16.2).

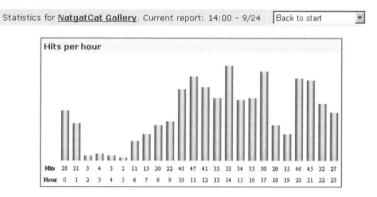

■ **Figure 16.2** Site statistics

Source: www.sitestatz.com/check.cgi?id=natgatcat, courtesy of the author's personal web site counter.

Diagnostic

Diagnostic research not only reports what is happening but tries to explain why it is happening. It attempts to find linkages between different events or, in the case of much consumer research, tries to understand the motivations behind why people do what they do. Diagnostic studies involving web sites may attempt to correlate rises and falls in web site traffic based on placement of advertisements in various media. For example, figure 16.3 demonstrates an upswing in activity in a web site (www.mp3.com/aquataine) following an advertisement for the site on 14/09 and follow-up advertisement on the 21/09.

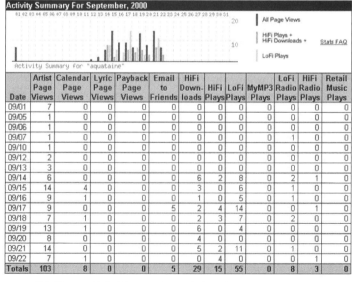

Date	Artist Page Views	Calendar Page Views	Lyric Page Views	Payback Page Views	Email to Friends	HiFi Down-loads	HiFi Plays	LoFi Plays	MyMP3 Plays	LoFi Radio Plays	HiFi Radio Plays	Retail Music Plays
09/01	7	0	0	0	0	0	0	0	0	0	0	0
09/05	1	0	0	0	0	0	0	0	0	0	0	0
09/06	1	0	0	0	0	0	0	0	0	0	0	0
09/07	1	0	0	0	0	0	0	0	0	1	0	0
09/10	1	0	0	0	0	0	0	0	0	0	0	0
09/12	2	0	0	0	0	0	0	0	0	0	0	0
09/13	3	0	0	0	0	0	0	0	0	0	0	0
09/14	6	0	0	0	0	6	2	8	0	2	1	0
09/15	14	4	0	0	0	3	0	6	0	1	0	0
09/16	9	1	0	0	0	1	0	5	0	1	0	0
09/17	9	0	0	0	5	2	4	14	0	0	1	0
09/18	7	1	0	0	0	2	3	7	0	2	0	0
09/19	13	1	0	0	0	6	0	4	0	0	0	0
09/20	8	0	0	0	0	4	0	0	0	0	0	0
09/21	14	0	0	0	0	5	2	11	0	1	0	0
09/22	7	1	0	0	0	0	4	0	0	0	1	0
Totals	103	8	0	0	5	29	15	55	0	8	3	0

■ **Figure 16.3** Diagnostic statistics: Site traffic spikes following advertising

Source: www.mp3.com through the author's band Aquataine.

This most basic of diagnostic research demonstrates the impact of advertising when comparing traffic for the fortnight prior to the advert (16 hits) and following the initial advert (six hits on the day of release, 14 hits the day following). The site received more traffic in the two days following the advertising than in the preceding fortnight. More complex diagnostic research would examine the motivation of the users for visiting the site after having seen or heard the advertising.

Predictive

Predictive research, as the name implies, attempts to predict what will happen in the future based on past experience, trends and events. It takes diagnostic research one step further and applies an understanding of the past in an attempt to determine the likely outcomes of specific changes in an environment, as well as the outcomes of specific marketing activities. This type of research usually involves complex data collection and statistical analysis, often over a long period. Although popular with marketers, it is difficult to do effectively due to the volatility of the marketing and business environments in which marketers operate.

This form of research is used for determining the expected loads on servers hosting popular sites, or sites which will attract **Slashdot effect** sized traffic surges. Dotcom advertising placed during the half break at the US Superbowl or the British FA Cup would be subject to countless predictive efforts to determine the expected traffic loads so as to determine the number of servers required to cope with the demand. Predictive research can also assist an existing web site in determining likely loads on server equipment, either over periods of hours or weeks, in order to schedule down times, server upgrades or other maintenance work.

Method of collection

An alternative classification of market research can be made according to the method employed in collecting the primary data. Again there are three broad categories to consider:

Observational

Observational research involves simply observing what the sample is doing and not directly intervening to determine why they are behaving in a certain way. It does not involve direct questioning of subjects and most would be unaware that they were part of a research project. This type of research is increasing in popularity as increasingly more complex databases become available to track individual purchasing behaviours over time. Observational data in e-commerce occurs as a natural phenomenon where e-commerce sites maintain purchasing histories for their customers. This can occur either for shipping purposes or to develop recommendation systems such as the CFS systems used by Amazon.com (www.amazon.com) covered in chapter three.

Survey

Survey research involves the direct questioning of subjects on a topic of interest to the marketer. Such questioning can be undertaken by mail, over the telephone, via email, web-based questionnaires or through personal interviews. The advantages of surveys are that they are structured, consistent across applications and easy to replicate. In the case of written surveys, it is possible to approach large numbers of geographically dispersed subjects at a relatively low cost. Surveys can generate **quantifiable** data which is both their greatest advantage and disadvantage. While they are able to provide detailed measurable data to which objective analyses can be applied, they are less able to understand motivations behind actions. Greenfields On-line (www.greenfield online.com) conducts most of their market research through online surveys. Online survey systems are also easily available through free providers such as Bravenet (www.bravenet.com) Pollit (www.pollit.com), or Survey Monkey (www.surveymonkey.com).

Experimental

Experimental research involves the manipulation of one or more variables in the environment to determine what their effect is on an overall phenomenon. Typically, for marketers this type of research will involve minor variations to a specific element of the marketing mix to determine what the outcome on consumer behaviour is on a limited sample before committing to widespread change. In the past, most experimental research was conducted in controlled environments such as universities or market research offices. The disadvantage to this situation was that the consumer was acting in an unnatural environment and consequently not influenced by the full range of distracting activities which would occur within the context of day to day behaviour. More recently there has been a trend to conduct such experiments in a more natural environment, for example, in the retailing environment, to better understand consumer reactions.

Internet marketing INSIGHT
Copy testing for online banners

Hofacker and Murphy (1998) conducted an experimental investigation into the copy testing of banner advertisements. Unlike traditional offline copy testing which is conducted in the 'paper and pencil' mode, the experiment was conducted online in a live situation.

Traditional (and offline) copy testing tends to rely on the theories associated with attention, interest, desire, action (AIDA), innovation adoption or hierarchy of effects, all of which work on the principle that the consumer sees the advertisement, thinks about it, and acts on it later. Hofacker and Murphy (1998) noted that these traditional approaches to **copy testing** did not suit banner advertising since the consumer encountered and reacted to the banner in the same context. Direct marketing concepts of direct order, lead generation and traffic generation were found to be more closely aligned with reactions to banner advertising. The interactive nature of the Internet that created the problems for copy testing also created a design advantage of being able to copy test in a live format.

Working on the assumption that clicking on banner advertising equated to an information seeking behaviour, Hofacker and Murphy (1998) set up a copy test experiment that took advantage of the interactivity of the Internet, and the nature of how HTML pages are served to end users. They designed a set of four advertising banners which were placed on a relatively high traffic site, for the duration of 18 days. The selection of the banner advertisement was done at random by the programming of the web site, which ensured that the banners were randomly spread through the study. In addition, the web site recorded a log file of which banner was served, whether it was clicked on, and crude identification details of **IP addresses**, which served as identifiers for the study. The IP addresses provided country of origin details, and domain (.com or .edu) details to determine if the user was from a government, education or commercial Internet access point.

The advantage to conducting the study online was to capture real life data in an unobtrusive manner, capturing actual behaviour in an experimental format. While several factors were unable to be captured (demographic/psychographic details of respondents), the online examination was able to conduct an experimental format at a low cost for a high response rate (2272 useable responses in 18 days).

While the study focused on the analysis of four types of advertising copy, it indirectly highlighted some of the key advantages of online marketing research, including the relatively low cost per high response rate and how non-intrusively such research can be conducted online.

Source: Hofacker, C. and Murphy, J. 1998, 'World Wide Web banner advertisement copy testing', *European Journal of Marketing*, vol. 32, no. 7/8, pp. 713–23.

New paradigm or new routines? Internet-based market research

Market research, like many other areas of marketing, is undergoing a significant change in both approach and practice as a result of the expansion of the new technology of the Internet. Whether or not an organisation has chosen to go online with its retailing or service activities, the existence of the Internet and associated technologies has fundamentally changed expectations regarding market research outcomes.

Changing environments

In the changing technological environment, one of the most significant impacts on market research is the fact that it is now possible to reach a far larger population of individuals for research purposes than it has been in the past. The global reach of the Internet means that it is now economically feasible to have cross-cultural research in a range of areas from tracking consumer spending patterns to probing motivations for purchase.

Inclusivity

Similarly, within a single country, it is cheaper and faster to collect and collate information from a geographically dispersed population base online. The interactivity of the Internet makes it possible to conduct interviews and focus groups with people who have similar problems or needs regardless of their physical location. It also means that those who may previously have been neglected by market researchers have a voice in the process. For example, those who are housebound due to age or disability typically would not have been involved in **mall-intercept** based market research. In the new environment of the Internet, however, they have the same options to contribute as anyone else.

Consumer empowerment

Leading on from this inclusiveness is the fact that the Internet can serve as a tool for consumer empowerment. The anonymity and convenience of web-based interactions means that consumers are better able to contact the relevant people within organisations to give feedback and are more likely to be frank in their opinions while doing so. Rather than having to ask their way through to the complaints department, an email to feedback@company.com or complaints@company.co.nz gets straight to the relevant person.

This also impacts on segmentation research, as examined in chapter 5, in that consumers define themselves by their self interests while engaged in dealing in an online environment. Consequently, research conducted online is prone to receiving more psychographic-orientated data; for example, males who are visibly male/masculine but self identify as female/feminine would be able to respond on the basis of their feminine nature, rather than on an interviewer's perception of them as male.

In addition, the consumer online is inherently proactive rather than reactive, meaning that those involved in marketing-based research online will have different motivations and characteristics from those who are subject to surveys and interviews by virtue of simply being in the right place at the right time. In addition, the use of cybercommunity structures to gather together and host communities of like interests allow consumers to contribute market research information when and where it suits them, rather than having to find a feedback form, interviewer or survey. Relic Entertainment, manufacturer of the Homeworld series of games, has established a section on their web site dedicated to research and development of forthcoming games, where members of the Homeworld gaming community can provide wish lists of features, recommendations, criticisms and suggested solutions to common game problems (www.homeworld.org).

Potential for real-time data

From the marketer's perspective, the revolution in market research which is taking place as a result of new technology is based on the following factors. To start with, information is no longer dated. Rather, it is collected and collated in real time ensuring that minor changes are able to be identified and tracked immediately and that decisions are made on timely and relevant data. Survey Monkey (www.surveymonkey.com) offers the capacity to receive data in real time, or to have it formatted as a traditional SPSS file for conventional offline analysis.

Competitor information

Competitor information is increasingly easy to find as a result of the changing technology. The Internet is employed as a source of information dissemination and promotion of organisational activities and achievements. While this has significant benefits in terms of communicating with potential clients, the same information is accessible to competitors. Thus it is easier than ever before to monitor what is happening in the competitive environment. Movie data concerning ticket sales, cinema screenings and revenue earned which were previously inaccessible box office secrets are available through sites such as Urban Cinefile (www.urbancinefile.com.au) or Dark Horizons (www.darkhorizons.com). Similarly, other business profiles and portfolio information can be accessed online through services such as Ozdaq (www.ozdaq.com) which is an Australian high technologies brokerage site.

Global access

Finally, the Internet with its global access provides individual researchers with greater opportunities for direct interaction with other researchers. In the past it was less likely that ongoing research relationships could be developed between researchers in different parts of the world. Now it is not uncommon for an initial email to lead to an ongoing partnership which extends the boundaries of marketing research.

From a consumer research perspective, this soliciting of information and advice can be undertaken through newsgroups and chat rooms. Involvement in such activities provides researchers with a quick and easy approach to finding out what consumers, and potential consumers, think about issues and topics relevant to the organisation's marketing campaign.

Information storehouse

The Internet is already the largest repository of information and knowledge available. As the Internet continues to expand, the amount and quality of information available to the general public and marketers will continue to grow.

Unrestricted publication

The freedom to publish worldwide through the Internet, however, has significant implications for marketers in terms of the validity and quality of information. The lack of traditional publishing controls means that researchers must take care when using web-based information and verify the authenticity of sources wherever possible. From a marketing management perspective, the key is ensuring that the Internet is used in a way that is most effective and relevant to the needs of the organisation.

Browsing, buying and spying: Using the information storehouse

From a marketing research perspective it is interesting to note how the information on the Internet is being accessed and used. According to Forrest (1999) the main types of information being sought from the Internet for marketing purposes are:

- competitive intelligence (information about competitors) (82 per cent)
- conducting research such as online surveys and focus groups (81 per cent)
- determining broad market trends (72 per cent)
- information about new production techniques and technology (46 per cent)
- information about international markets (36 per cent).

Scanning the environments in Internet market research

The first step in any strategic management process is to scan the environments in which the organisation operates to determine what changes, if any, are occurring before attempting to understand the impact they will have on the operations of the organisation.

This is one area where the Internet can make a major contribution to the ongoing updating of the marketing information system. Selecting key web sites relevant to each of the organisation's key external environments, political-legal (www.politicsonline.com), socio-cultural (www.abs.gov.au), economic (www.nber.org), technological (www.freshmeat.net) and physical (www. environment-agency.gov.uk) and accessing them on a daily or weekly basis can alert marketers to potential changes of significance. Similarly, many information houses will add marketers to an email list to keep them updated on key issues (www.infobeat.com). These services significantly cut down on the time taken for traditional marketing research activities and result in higher quality decision making at all levels of the organisation.

Environmental scanning is integral to effective decision making. The extent to which it is formally incorporated into day-to-day activities varies according to organisation; however, it is possible to discern four key styles of scanning typically employed when using the Internet for this purpose:

- *undirected viewing*: browsing with no clear underlying purpose, this is the online equivalent of flicking through a magazine. While some organisations may perceive such activity as time wasting, given the complex and changing environment of the Internet it is essential to have an overview of what is new in the environment.
- *conditioned viewing*: still without a clear underlying purpose, conditioned viewing is the scanning of general areas of interest with the intention of following up if something of specific interest catches the viewer's eye. This is the online equivalent of perusing the financial pages and headlines.
- *informal search*: relatively unstructured approach to finding out information about a specific topic or for a specific purpose. It is more directed and actively seeks out information about a topic or issue without engaging in an intensive, directed search.
- *formal search*: this refers to a deliberate effort to seek out specific information, usually as part of a formal research plan or design. The search is systematic and the information gathered subjected to critical evaluation and incorporation into the solving of a particular problem.

Market intelligence through Internet-based market research

In addition to general environmental trends, there are two key types of 'intelligence' that market researchers typically seek and which can be easily accessed through effective use of the Internet. These are consumer intelligence and competitive intelligence.

Consumer intelligence

Consumer intelligence refers to the information and knowledge required to fully understand the target consumer behaviours and motivations. The advantage of the Internet to businesses in undertaking research to understand the consumer is that, in many ways, it has removed one of the biggest barriers to small business success in that the information available is accessible by all. In the past, big business had a significant advantage over small business in terms of the quality of information available to it for decision-making purposes. The availability of information through the Internet has significantly closed this gap, particularly in relation to consumer intelligence.

The move from a mass marketing approach to the more individualised approaches, possible as a result of Internet-based marketing, means that there has to be a corresponding shift in the way in which data are collected and collated as they relate to consumer behaviour. As the focus becomes more individual and customised, the ability of the marketer to track the customer becomes more important. Based on the division between relevant primary and secondary data approaches, the following techniques are most commonly used in understanding consumers in the new online environment.

Primary consumer intelligence data

Interactions with consumers online are either text-based, through tools such as interactive surveys or navigation-based, through the tracking of consumer movements and usage patterns online (also referred to as cookie technology).

Electronic surveys and databases are discussed elsewhere in this chapter; however, at this point it is important to note only their main benefits. These are first, that the record is instantaneous and permanent and, second, that it can be used to generate feedback and customise products to individual needs.

Of specific concern here is the navigation-based tracking devices that allow undetected observation of users as they move through web sites of interest. This technology, referred to as **cookie technology**, allows information to be stored on individual web-surfing patterns. These patterns allow organisations to better understand consumers' overall interests and needs so that they can develop customised services to better service the market.

Cookies are of particular value in determining the psychographic make-up of the market but their use is fraught with ethical concerns. It is possible to set up a browser to warn users of the existence of cookies and automatically accept or reject them. Many consumers find the cookies to be a useful tool in ensuring better quality service, such as remembering site preferences or customised settings (my.yahoo.com.au). This is an issue which needs further debate in a wider audience so that standards for behaviour can be developed.

Secondary consumer intelligence data

Much of the information that marketers need to develop segmentation strategies is based on secondary rather than primary data. Much of this relevant information can be accessed via government web sites and consumer survey sites. Although private companies often charge a fee for specific information, broad-based information about key population and economic trends likely to impact on consumer behaviour is available at no cost. The Australian Bureau of Statistics (www.abs.gov.au) provides a wide range of relevant market oriented information for free with the option of paying for more detailed information if needed. Similarly, accessing the Market Research Society of Australia (www.mrsa.com.au) provides details of a range of general consumer survey sites and characteristics which can be invaluable to marketers in understanding key consumer intelligence trends. NUA Surveys (www.nua.ie/surveys) offers links to a range of national and international secondary consumer data web sites.

Competitive intelligence

Competitive intelligence involves the systematic collection of information about competitors to assist in strategic decision making. It helps the organisation to better position its products, to understand what else consumers have access to in a related area and helps to put the organisation in a better position to exploit opportunities and alleviate threats.

As mentioned previously, the promotional materials available from competitors online not only provide potential consumers with relevant information about the company, but also provide competitors with key information. One of the skills of effective web-based marketing from a strategic perspective is to allow customers access to the maximum amount of information that they require while trying to minimise the amount of strategically valuable information available to the competitors.

There is a wide range of sources of competitive intelligence that market researchers can access via the Internet. Key among these are:

- search engines web sites (www.google.com)
- competitive information-based web sites (www.fuld.com)
- trade associations (www.gambica.org.uk)
- personal web pages (www.xoom.com or www.fortunecity.com)
- survey competitors customers online (survey.hotlink.com.au)
- search newsgroups and mailing lists (www.deja.com)
- specialist company information sites (www.3com.com)
- news items (www.abcnews.com)
- outsource to specialist researchers (www.aoir.org)
- discussion groups (news:biz.marketplace).

The key to successful collection of competitive intelligence is differentiating between the useful information contained on these sites, and the general information which does not add to the quality of strategic decision making.

Conducting online market research: New paradigm or new routines?

As with other aspects of the marketing management process, online market research involves the same basic tools and techniques as traditional research but with modifications to take advantage of the unique environment in which it is now operating.

For the purposes of this discussion three key methods will be discussed. These are the most commonly used at present and give examples of both qualitative and quantitative approaches.

Online focus groups

A **focus group** is a small group of people with some key defining characteristic who are brought together to discuss an issue or topic with the assistance of a trained moderator. Due to the interactivity aspect of the Internet it is possible to conduct focus groups among geographically dispersed individuals using the same basic approach for offline groups (www.itracks.com). The new environment overcomes some of the key problems for market researchers, including finding suitable times, places and venues for focus group discussions.

Internet marketing INSIGHT
Online focus groups: Conceptual issues and a research tool

Online focus groups offer a new avenue of many-to-many research without the need for physical proximity that constrains the classical focus group model. Montoya-Weiss, Massey and Clapper (1998) examined the role and value of the **Internet Focus Group (IFG)**. In their study they created a new IFG interface for data collection, which performed the same tasks as many of the existing multi-point chat software such as mIRC (www.mirc.co.uk), ICQ (www.icq.com) or iChat (www.ichat.com). An Internet focus group can occur when and wherever a many-to-many, real-time communications channel can be established, and can be facilitated, logged (and moderated) by a focus group leader.

The impact of technology on the focus group method is seen as having the greatest impact on the dynamics of the focus group environment. Using the advantages of real-time communications across the Internet, the IFG can provide an anonymous discussion environment which can facilitate the discussion of sensitive, controversial or highly charged topics. Montoya-Weiss et al. (1998) discovered a strange advantage of the lean media nature of the Internet in that the absence of social cues forced the participants to work with the ideas presented, rather than judge the participants on physical features. **Lean media** are communications mediums which tend to strip away non-verbal cues and information otherwise available in a face-to-face environment. Even telephone interviews can convey senses of emotion in the intonation of the voice, whereas the IFG presents the words and ideas only as raw text. An experienced Internet user can intone feeling and emotion into their writing through the use of specific writing techniques, such as placing *emphasis* on a word. However, for the most part, the IFG is an environment which does not have the media richness of the face-to-face environment, giving the advantage of forcing attention to the ideas at the cost of the non-verbal information.

Source: Montoya-Weiss, M., Massey, A and Clapper, D. 1998, 'Online focus groups: Conceptual issues and a research tool', *European Journal of Marketing*, vol. 32, no. 7/8, pp. 713–23.

Other advantages to conducting focus groups online rather than offline include the following:

- cheaper and more efficient to conduct
- allows for a greater diversity of participants
- automatic recording of comments leading to higher quality outputs
- the anonymity allows for more frank discussion.

In terms of disadvantages, the main problems that arise relate to:

- technical limitations including the fact that non-verbal cues are missing in most online environments
- biased and potentially misleading samples
- the difficulties inherent in relying on concept descriptions and pictures to get an accurate feel for new products online.

Online surveys

Online surveys as a research tool offer the marketer a number of key advantages. In terms of the data collected, they tend to be more accurate as inputting errors transcribing from written to electronic forms are reduced. Also, the novelty of the experience and ease of use means that fewer surveys are left incomplete. Financially, online surveys are cheaper to produce and are more physically attractive and easier to complete, and can be programmed to prompt for missing or incomplete information. Exploiting the generic benefits of the online environment, it is possible to customise surveys, instantaneously reach large widely dispersed population bases and conduct cross-cultural and international research simultaneously.

Despite these many advantages, online surveys are still less accepted as representative and valuable in the broader research context because of the following limitations. The main issue with online research is that because the Internet is interest-driven, the sample is self-selected; consequently, samples will be inherently biased regardless of any of the usual research safeguards. Similarly, the skewed population of Internet users means that they are not representative of the general population and so any results will need to be qualified with this in mind. Finally, the perceived anonymity of the Internet may encourage responses which are less truthful and which cannot be verified.

When constructing online surveys, the same issues of clarity, simplicity and format apply as they do to traditional surveys. However, in the online environment several other considerations apply. In light of the different expectations of online behaviour, it is important to ensure that surveys are non-intrusive, respect privacy and employ correct 'netiquette'. While it is possible to customise, surveys should be suitable in terms of file size, length and format. Time limits on return should be set as once a file is out it is difficult to control where it will go and who will send it to whom. To overcome problems of bias, suitable and justified sampling methods need to be employed. These can include **unrestricted samples** (everyone who comes into contact with the survey is eligible to fill it in), **screened samples** (only those who fit certain criteria can continue with the survey) or **recruited samples** (email or approach in other ways those specific individuals who are of interest).

Ethnography

Ethnographic research is an area which has been traditionally neglected by marketing researchers. It involves the researcher living with, and becoming part of a community while recording their views, opinions, activities and behaviours. More commonly used in fields such as anthropology and sociology, this technique is rarely used by business researchers for a number of reasons, one of the key ones being the time factor. Becoming an accepted member of a community takes considerable time and effort.

Despite its traditional neglect, ethnographic research is potentially very beneficial in giving marketers a true, deep understanding of the market and their potential clients. The new online environment, however, gives marketers the opportunity to use ethnographic research techniques to better understand the motivations and values of the target market. Specifically, the techniques developed by ethnographers can be translated into the online community environment to help target communications strategies and products to the needs of specific microsegments of which the market researcher may or may not be a part.

Online acceptance into a community is simpler than offline acceptance because of the lack of visual and social cues which discriminate against acceptance in face-to-face relationships. Consequently, the key disadvantage, time, is overcome in this new environment.

New routines

The Internet offers a set of new possibilities for market research, ranging from the integration of new features into existing methods through to the creation of Internet-specific (and unique) data-collection methods. Parackal and Brennan (1999) observed that the online survey can be adapted and upgraded away from the conventional 10 questions with five types of response model of pen and paper to include multimedia, virtual reality and interactivity. Respondents can be asked to manipulate product mix settings, examine and interact with virtual reality models of the product and test-drive virtual features as part of a survey response system (Parackal & Brennan 1999).

Three new forms of Internet-based market research data collection have emerged since the widespread adoption of the Internet as a market research tool. It is expected that as the sophistication of the Internet increases, and more features and functions emerge, more varied and Internet-specific forms of market research will develop over time. In the meantime, this chapter focuses on these existing three forms of market research: unobtrusive observation, click tracking and automated data gathering.

Unobtrusive observation

Unobtrusive observation is the study of USENET groups, web discussion boards and online discussion groups without the need to join or participate in the social group. Unlike ethnography, which involves the researcher living with, and becoming part of a community while recording their views, opinions, activities and behaviours, the unobtrusive observational techniques are performed with no interaction with the society. One of the accepted cultures of the USENET environment is the notion of **lurking**, which is the practice of observing a USENET group for a period of time before entering the fray. This well-established cultural norm assumes that there is usually a greater number of people lurking on a newsgroup than actively participating. The lurkers may simply not be interested in participation or may be acclimatising themselves to the cultural norms of the group. Unobtrusive observation is acceptable in this environment, where it assumed and accepted that reader/observers are not required to participate.

In contrast, unobtrusive observation is not suited to Internet environments which create a sense of telepresence during the interaction. **Telepresence** is the perception of physicality inside a cyberspace environment (Steuer 1992; Shih 1998; Novak, Hoffman & Yung 1998). Within environments that either generate telepresence, such as MUDs or IRC channels where the observer is visible to the participants, ethnography techniques of integration and interaction are required. Where the observer remains invisible to the parties in the interaction, unobtrusive observation can be used as the observational method for data collection.

Click tracking

Click tracking is a web site-specific, data-collection method that tracks the paths and movements of users through a web site (Montoya-Weiss et al. 1998). Click tracking can take one of three forms:

- *Intrasite tracking*: the conventional method of analysing server logs to determine the most frequently accessed web pages and the paths traversed through web sites. Figure 16.4 represents site tracking information regarding the most and least popular pages on a web site.

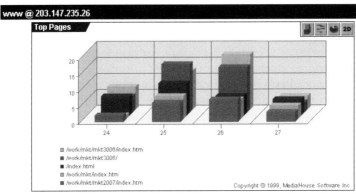

Pages viewed the most	Total for Period	Average for Period	% of Total
/work/mkt/mkt3006/index.htm	40	10.00	7.60
/work/mkt/mkt3006/	37	9.25	7.03
/index.html	27	6.75	5.13
/work/mkt/index.htm	18	4.50	3.42
/work/mkt/mkt2007/index.htm	18	4.50	3.42
/ngc/gallery99/index.html	14	3.50	2.66
/work/index.htm	13	3.25	2.47
/work/mkt/mkt2007/admin/marks.htm	12	3.00	2.28
/spudmonkey/index.htm	11	2.75	2.09
/work/mkt/mkt3006/assessment/literaturereview.htm	11	2.75	2.09

•••••■ **Figure 16.4**
Site tracking: Most popular pages
Source: from statistics from www.stephendann.com

■ *Visitor tracking*: the process of following user movement through a web site to attempt to find a relationship between individually identifiable users and their selected paths through a web site (Parackal & Brennan 1999). These systems are still in their infancy and are the subject of numerous concerns over privacy and anonymity. Figure 16.5 demonstrates the basic information that can be collected about a user visiting a web site, which pages were visited and the type of browser and operating system used.

Session Details	
IP Address	61.12.73.169
Reverse DNS	n/a
From / Via	n/a
Origin Location	Not Available
Time Spent	12 min
Hits / Kilobytes	17 / 93.39Kb
Browser Tag	Mozilla/4.51 [en] (Win98; I)
Referring URL	http://203.147.235.26/ngc/gallery99/index.html

Date and Time	URL
2000-09-27 12:36:00	- user created
2000-09-27 12:36:00	/images/sashpen.jpg
2000-09-27 12:36:03	/ngc/gallery99/index.html
2000-09-27 12:36:03	/moneylogo2.gif
2000-09-27 12:36:08	/ngc/gallery2k/welcometomyego.gif
2000-09-27 12:36:13	/images/footerdotcom.jpg
2000-09-27 12:36:16	/images/natgatcat_watermark2.jpg
2000-09-27 12:36:19	/music/index.htm
2000-09-27 12:36:23	/music/skylab17/skylab17labeltag.gif
2000-09-27 12:36:26	/music/subpop/subpopicon.jpg
2000-09-27 12:46:38	/work/index.htm
2000-09-27 12:46:42	/work/mkt/mkt3006/mkt3006logo.jpg
2000-09-27 12:46:46	/work/mkt/mkt3007/mkt3007logosmall.jpg
2000-09-27 12:46:46	/work/mkt/mkt2007/mkt2007slide.jpg
2000-09-27 12:46:56	/music/subpop/explosion1.gif
2000-09-27 12:48:01	/ngc/index.htm
2000-09-27 12:48:03	/ngc/library/librarylogosmall.gif
2000-09-27 12:48:04	/images/bert02.jpg

················■ **Figure 16.5**
User data
Source: from statistics from
www.stephendann.com

The value to the marketer is where the web site offers an opt-in system, such as a user registration, so that the individual's user preferences can be stored, retrieved and mapped against provided demographic data as they move through a web site. Mp3.com (www.mp3.com) requires that the users log their email addresses for the first few times they download music files to develop a tracking system to monitor downloads. Sites which combine the visitor tracking, user registration and the CFS recommendation systems will be able to give users a value-added service (and reason to subscribe) of site or product recommendations in exchange for the visitor tracking information. By creating an informed participant group, who are willing to exchange their market research data for information and recommendations, many of the concerns of invasion of privacy online can be alleviated. The more informed the consumer is concerning the data that are collected at the web site, the more likely the consumer is to be comfortable with their conscious choice to donate this information to the web site. Problems concerning invasion of privacy and loss of anonymity tend to be focused around sites which mislead the user or misrepresent the data being collected.

■ *Surf tracking* is a system which uses external site collection and collation programs to map the user's surfing behaviours. Software such as Internet

Cartographer (www.inventix.com) create graphical representations of the user's surfing behaviours, and can be used to classify types of web sites into categories and genres. These information sets can later be interrogated to demonstrate the relationship between the various sites visited, or to find an individual site. Figure 16.6 represents a sample of the Internet Cartographer's visual output of a surf tracking map.

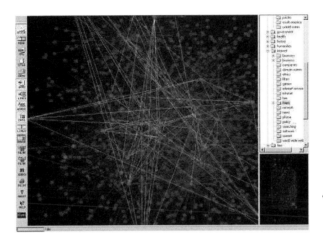

•••••■ **Figure 16.6** Surf maps
Source:
www.inventix.com/images/icart6.gif/

Surfing tracking programs can be used as part of panel surveys whereby the users are given the software, a unique identifier number and either an automated submission system or return mail address. Automated systems can be established to return a data set to a prespecified server after a given period, without the need for the user to remember to submit the information. (Automated upload systems are already implemented for non-market research programs such as the SETI@Home project (www.setiathome.com) whereby processed data are automatically returned to a central collation server.) Alternatively, the user can be given an email address to send surf maps to after a set period of time. This is fraught with the usual problems of mail response rates, and users forgetting to submit their maps. Once submitted, these surf maps can then be analysed as part of web behaviour and usage studies for market segmentation, or other data-gathering exercises.

Automated data gathering

The final advantage of the Internet for market research is the involvement of computers in the initial data-collection process. Many of the problems of data entry, data cleaning and other data entry aspects that are prone to human error can be automated with online quantitative market research. Even basic factors such as requiring survey forms to be fully completed, ensuring that numbered preference lists do not feature the same number twice, and that percentage scores total to 100 per cent can be automated. Users cannot progress to the submission of the page of data until the errors are corrected, a method not available in offline surveys.

In addition, automation of data collection allows for real-time processing of survey data to provide instant basic statistical feedback to the respondent (vr.harrispollonline.com). Ultrafeedback (www.ultrafeedback.com) offers real time processing of surveys, so that users see the immediate feedback, including their response selection highlighted in the final data. Automated data collection of web site responses has also been used in high-pressure, time-dependent market research gathering — a live broadcast of World Championship Wrestling (www.wcw.com) took a live survey poll, announced at the start of the broadcast, to determine which two wrestlers would contest the title belt two hours into the show. The ability to take the data straight into a statistical output enabled WCW to produce a real-time outcome to the data collection without needing the time to conduct manual data entry.

Issues concerning online research

Despite its many advantages, online market research suffers from a number of key limitations. The major concerns of market research online are:

Anonymity

One of the key values sought from the Internet is the anonymity and opportunity to engage in post-modern consumption, creation of identity and detachment from the physical self. Market research has the potential to endanger and destroy the anonymity of the user, and take the opportunity for post-modern consumption away from the Internet. As tracking systems become increasingly more sophisticated and integrated, the capacity to become anonymous within the online world is diminished. While Orwellian concerns of government control and monitoring are not yet reality, the new focus of concern is not 'Big Brother'. Market research and database marketing are often referred to as 'Little Brother', given their greater capacity (and desire) to profile and track individual behaviours, purchases and actions. For the most part, no sinister aims or Orwellian ideals are implied into the market researcher's desire for individual-level market niches and complex integrated profiling databases.

However, developments of tracking software online lead to the concern that the anonymity which encourages freedom to explore sensitive and controversial materials will be removed with the fear that accessing this information could be tracked back to the user. Combining this information with market segmentation data, or using it as a basis for market segmentation can create very narrowly defined market niches that may or may not be used for the wrong purposes. It is easy to imagine that pro- and anti-abortion web sites would be keen to keep their user bases anonymous, and hidden from each other. Similarly, combining web-surfing patterns with existing direct marketing databases of magazine subscriptions, scanner data, financial histories, medical histories, taxation databases and the user's permanent IP address creates just about the ultimate market segmentation technology — and completely strips the individual of any anonymity they might have wanted to have online.

Privacy

Related to the areas of tracking and market research is the issue of online privacy, which exists in the context of being able to conduct secure non-financial transactions without the observation of a third party. The nature of the Internet is such that it contains three levels of public–private spaces. The top level of public spaces are the personally published web sites and the open forums of USENET. The second level of public space is the telepresence-determined spaces of the IRC, MUD and mailing lists where public discussion occurs between members in the digital equivalent of a room. The third level is the private spaces of the Internet which occur when individuals engage in person-to-person or point-to-point conversations and transactions.

Private conversation online can be logged by the users, and by third parties. All operators of IRC servers have the capacity to log and view private channel conversations between users, just as all mail system administrators can view, filter, log and store all mail traffic originating from their server. For the most part, logging of these events does not occur, in part for the technical capacity and hideously large storage spaces required, and in part for the respect for privacy. Certain areas of the Internet need to be left alone, away from the prying eyes of market segmentation tools and market research data collection. While participants in the public forum of USENET accept the presence of lurkers, there is the same unspoken, unwritten law of privacy between two users of a private chat channel on a public IRC server. The data that could be collected are no more or less valuable than the data that could be collected by tapping private phone calls or bugging private homes.

Market research online should, by self-regulation, stay within the boundaries of opt-in services and public domains. Privacy and anonymity are features of the Internet that need to be guarded, protected and secured as natural resources of the digital domain. Once gone, the feelings of anonymity, security, privacy and implicit trust in the Internet environment will not be able to be replaced. If this occurs, then part of the core value of the Internet will be lost, and the Internet itself may lose many of the people who sought these values.

 # Limitations of online research

The Internet is far from perfect, both as a medium of market research and as an institution. Rapid developments in technology, incremental ad-hoc changes and varying international adoption rates make the flawed beauty of the Internet both attractive and deadly for market research. Global markets can be accessed, but the representative nature of the sample is subject to suspicions and limited application offline. Information is there for the taking, if it just can be found, or limited to the point that the flood of information becomes a manageable flow.

Information overload

First, the massive expansion in information available to researchers has led, in many cases, to information overload. Despite the availability of more and better information, many researchers are retreating to one or two traditional sources rather than spending the time and effort trying to break through the clutter and find new sources.

Information quality

Second, the lack of regulation means that the Internet is full of information of varying quality. Whereas traditional publication methods ensure that certain processes and quality measures are followed, online publication of information does not carry these safeguards. A major challenge for researchers is sifting good quality from poor quality research.

Speed

Despite the advances in technology, the speed of the Internet as an information source is still a problem for many. Speed considerations have an impact on both primary and secondary data collection. For example, downloading complex files or poorly designed web sites can take a long time, the consequence of which is many researchers will avoid such sites and the information they contain regardless of quality.

Security

Online security issues mean that for some consumers, the lack of total anonymity provided by a mail survey is not available to online subjects. This in turn leads to a reluctance on the part of subjects to be totally honest in their opinions or in divulging information. In part this is because of the practice of marketers of using such information for unsolicited direct marketing campaigns which many consumers find intrusive and time consuming.

Skewed demography

Although Internet usage continues to grow, not everyone has access to the Internet. Consequently the population is still skewed significantly towards certain demographic and psychographic groups making the validity of any online research questionable in terms of its generalisability.

Ease of access

Finally, related to the last point is ease of access to the Internet. As convergent technologies emerge and are commercialised this will become less of a problem; however, at present the problem of access is still relevant. Not all homes have the equipment to access the Internet and so use for many consumers is still very restricted and intermittent.

Putting the pieces together: Online market segmentation

There are two methods of online market segmentation — studies focused at the macro level segmentation of the Internet population, and those which are focused on the micro level development of target markets for individual web sites.

iVALS, and Internet user types

The division of the online world into various categories, genres and user types was discussed in chapter 4. The value of large-scale segmentation of user types is that it studies the Internet as a population group. Studies such as iVALS (future.sri.com/VALS/VALSindex.shtml) have proven useful for the macro level studies of the Internet and the development and diffusion of the Internet. However, for individual companies, market segmentation is best conducted with the view to tailoring their site to their market, rather than an iVALS or equivalent user category.

Segmentation method

The second method of market segmentation is a two-part approach for researching segmentation, and implementing these segments as strategy. Sarabia (1996) established a basic scheme for the creation of target segments, which is illustrated in figure 16.7.

The focus of this section of the book is on the use of market research to satisfy the needs of the segmentation research level. (Marketing strategy has been the focus of the entire book, and chapter 7 specifically.) Consequently, the focus of this section is on examining the segmentation research level, which consists of the following four steps:

- *Search for and selection of information*, which is influenced by the needs of management, and forms the core purpose of the market research data collection exercise. (Issues of research design, type and nature of data to be collected are discussed above in the market research steps.)
- *Creation of segments* are where the data are analysed using quantitative methods and a series of clusters of homogenous individuals are collated into groups and segments. At this point, the data are simply a cluster of numbers and related responses to key criteria, such as intention to purchase online, combined with geographic region and preferred Internet browser.
- *Description of segments* is where the collective units are labelled and given detailed descriptions, such as Active Browser, for someone who scores highly on Internet use, web site use, preference for online browsing, but does not buy online. Segment descriptions form the basis for the eventual evaluation and selection of the target market.
- *Evaluation and selection* are where the market segments are reviewed against the firm's requirements, and the segment based on the best match is selected. The Active Browser segment may be best suited for site designers to target for brand image pages or comparison pages (chapter 10). However, if the firm conducting the survey is seeking actual purchasing from the online site, the Active Browser is not the best match for the company.

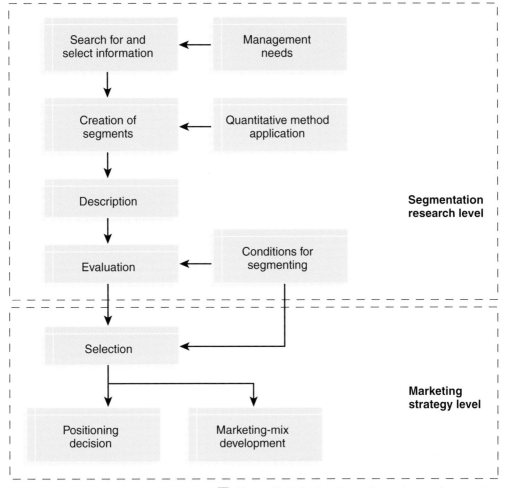

Search for and select information ← Management needs

Creation of segments ← Quantitative method application

Description

Evaluation ← Conditions for segmenting

Segmentation research level

Selection

Marketing strategy level

Positioning decision

Marketing-mix development

Figure 16.7 Basic scheme to create target segments

Source: Sarabia, F. J. 1996, 'Model for markets segments evaluation and selection', *European Journal of Marketing*, vol. 30, no. 4, pp. 58–74.

Sarabia (1996) focused on the selection of the individual segments, which was overviewed briefly in chapter 7, and is examined again in figure 16.8 (see p. 422).

Stages one to four lead to the construction of the evaluation matrix, which is based on determining both short- and long-term values, and dividing the segments into four quadrants of value. The types of variables used are illustrated in figure 16.9 (see p. 423).

Sarabia (1996) uses this list of variables, along with a small platoon of Greek characters, to generate two sets of indexes — short-term variables (Is) and medium- to long-term variables (Im). For the purpose of this section, the emphasis is on what to do with the outcomes of the Greek alphabet soup, not the generation of the formula itself. (Those readers interested in the science and maths of the article are recommended to acquire a copy of it for themselves.) The short-term and medium- to long-term variables are used as indices for the selection matrix (illustrated in figure 16.10, see p. 423).

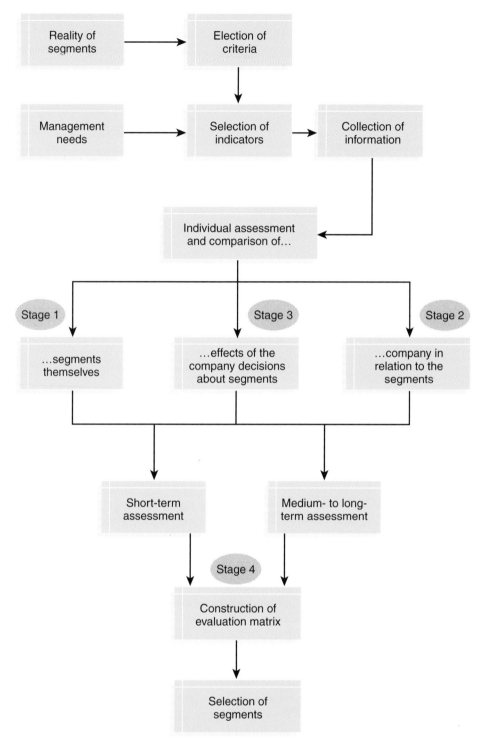

Figure 16.8 General plan for segment evaluation and selection

Source: Sarabia, F. J. 1996, 'Model for markets segments evaluation and selection', *European Journal of Marketing*, vol. 30, no. 4, pp. 58–74.

Variable/indicator		Global variables valuation through short-term		Global variables valuation through medium- to long-term	
01	Accessibility at acceptable cost	02	Sales potential	02	Sales potential
		03	Profitability	03	Profitability
02	Sales potential	05	Level of risk	05	Level of risk
03	Profitability	06	Stability	06	Stability
04	Environment situation sensibility	07	Strategic relevance	07	Strategic relevance
		10	Sustainability against competitors	10	Sustainability against competitors
05	Level of risk	11	Level of adequacy	11	Level of adequacy
07	Strategic relevance	12	Grade of adequate permanence	12	Grade of adequate permanence
08	Level of interest	13	Effect and sign on variable results	13	Effect and sign on variable results
09	Necessity for action	14	Effect and sign on commercial variables	14	Effect and sign on commercial variables
11	Level of adequacy	15	Type of differentiated answer	15	Type of differentiated answer

Figure 16.9 Variables for use in the evaluation matrix

Source: Sarabia, F. J. 1996, 'Model for markets segments evaluation and selection', *European Journal of Marketing*, vol. 30, no. 4, pp. 58–74.

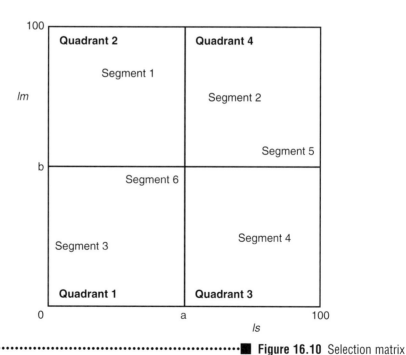

Figure 16.10 Selection matrix

Source: Sarabia, F. J. 1996, 'Model for markets segments evaluation and selection', *European Journal of Marketing*, vol. 30, no. 4, pp. 58–74.

The selection matrix consists of four quadrants, where (a) is short-term value and (b) is medium- to long-term value; (Im) are medium- to long-term variables and (Is) are the short-term variables. In among this statistical and mathematical construct lies the heart of all good management systems — a 2×2 matrix of market segments. These four segments are:

- *Quadrant 1*: represents those segments which have no short-term or medium- to long-term value to the company. These are the segments which are discarded first, and which should not have an influence on the company. Segmentation for Internet users and users' web sites would place people without Internet access in this quadrant.
- *Quadrant 2*: represents those segments with no short-term value, but medium- to long-term value. This could be said to describe the early strategies of e-commerce providers who believed that the initial losses and lack of profitability would be recovered in the long term. Targeting Quadrant 2 segments requires a company to bear initial losses and costs in pursuit of the longer-term value of marketshare, and potentially gaining first mover advantages. Amazon.com (www.amazon.com) gives the strongest indication of having adopted this segmentation strategy.
- *Quadrant 3*: encompasses a segment in which a short-term profit can be taken, but for which there is no medium- to long-term sustainability. Segments such as these may reap quick dividends but will eventually disappear, leaving the company with a product and no market. These segments can occur in rapidly evolving markets, such as the Internet, where a market need springs up overnight, is serviced and disappears equally as quickly. Software and software support often have high-profit, short-term segments appearing around the release of a major operating system (Windows 95, 98 or Windows ME) and disappearing once the initial rush of problems have been solved.
- *Quadrant 4*: is the goldmine sector of the selection matrix. This section contains those segments rated highly for their short- and long-term value. These are the core customers upon which the majority of the company's strategies, web site designs and IMC messaging should be based. For example, Apple Macintosh support web sites such as MacInTouch (www.macintouch.com) would find their Quadrant 4 customers in existing Apple Macintosh owners and Quadrant 3 segments when a new version of the Macintosh OS is released. In contrast, Windows users converting to Macintosh would be Quadrant 2 and existing Windows users with no desire to switch would be Quadrant 1.

Managers of web sites need to compare their web site segmentation selection matrix against those of their company, and the products or services to be delivered through the web site. Ideally, a match of Web Segment 4 to Corporate Segment 4 will see the best result for the organisation and its web site. The worst case scenario for a web site manager is to match Web Segment 1 (no profit now or later) with corporate segment 4 (short- and long-term profit) or the reverse, where the most profitable online segment available has no profitability in the offline services and products. In the first scenario, the web manager will most likely need to delay the deployment and development of a web site until the offline target segment enters the online market. In the second scenario, this may be used as the basis for the development of a new product and/or service (chapter 8).

Summary

This chapter has given an overview of how the spread of the Internet has contributed to a change in the way in which market research is being conducted internationally. The quality and depth of secondary data sources now available has an impact on both competitor- and consumer-related research. With greater information, companies are better able to develop their marketing plans strategically to take advantage of the volatile environments in which they operate.

On a primary data collection level, the Internet offers the advantages of relatively cheap, accessible data through the use of online surveys and focus groups. The major disadvantage which emerges from the adaptation of existing market research tools into this new environment, however, is the fact that the Internet population is still skewed towards the better-educated, wealthier segment of society and, therefore, in many cases the findings of such research cannot be generalised outside of the specific study in question.

Discussion questions

16.1 The Internet has a range of advantages and disadvantages for Internet market research. Outline the pros and cons of using data collected from online sources. Do the advantages outweigh the disadvantages?

16.2 What are differences between descriptive, diagnostic and predictive online market research?

16.3 Which method of data collection is most appropriate for testing new web site designs — observational, survey or experimental? Justify your answers with an explanation of how to use the chosen method for conducting market research on the site.

16.4 What impact does the Internet have on market research? What changes to the market research environments have occurred and what is their impact on data collection?

16.5 Pick a web site or online company, and outline which online methods of scanning key environments could be used by this company.

16.6 Outline the types of market intelligence that can be collected online.

16.7 Using Forrest's (1999) seven-step approach to market research, outline the steps to understand to conduct a market research study into use of cyber-communities. Which of the online market research routines is best suited to this study?

16.8 What are the major limitations of online marketing research? How can these limitations be addressed by market researchers?

16.9 Are anonymity and privacy for sale online? Discuss how market research can be conducted in an online environment that respects anonymity and privacy.

16.10 Discuss the value of the market segmentation for small businesses who are new to the Web.

References

Forrest, E. 1999, *Internet Marketing Research: Resources and Techniques*, McGraw-Hill, Sydney.

Hofacker, C. & Murphy, J. 1998, 'World Wide Web banner advertisement copy testing', *European Journal of Marketing*, vol. 32, no. 7/8, pp. 713–23.

Lynn, G. S., Maltz, A. C., Jurkat, P. M. & Hammer, M. D. 1999, 'New media in marketing redefine competitive advantage: A comparison of small and large firms', *The Journal Of Services Marketing*, vol. 13, no. 1, pp. 9–20.

Montoya-Weiss, M., Massey, A. & Clapper, D. 1998, 'Online focus groups: Conceptual issues and a research tool', *European Journal of Marketing*, vol. 32, no. 7/8, pp. 713–23.

Novak, T., Hoffman, D. & Yung, Y. F. 1998, 'Measuring the flow construct in online environments: A structural modelling approach', http://www2000.ogsm.vanderbilt.edu/papers/flow_construct/measuring_flow_construct.html

Parackal, M. & Brennan, M. 1999, 'Obtaining Purchase Probabilities via a Web-Based Survey: Some Corrections!', *Marketing Bulletin*, 10, pp. 93–101.

Sarabia, F. J. 1996, 'Model for markets segments evaluation and selection', *European Journal of Marketing*, vol. 30, no. 4, pp. 58–74.

Shih, C.-f. 1998, 'Conceptualising consumer experience in cyberspace', *European Journal of Marketing*, vol. 32 no. 7/8, pp. 655–63.

Steuer, J. 1992, 'Defining virtual reality: Dimensions determining telepresence', *Journal of Communication*, 42 (4), pp. 73–93.

Web sites

future.sri.com/VALS/VALSindex.shtml
survey.hotlink.com.au
vr.harrispollonline.com
www.3com.com

www.abcnews.com
www.abs.gov.au
www.amazon.com
www.aoir.org
www.bravenet.com
www.darkhorizons.com
www.deja.com
www.environment-agency.gov.uk
www.fortunecity.com
www.freshmeat.net
www.fuld.com
www.gambica.org.uk
www.google.com
www.greenfieldonline.com
www.homeworld.org
www.ichat.com
www.icq.com
www.infobeat.com
www.inventix.com
www.itracks.com
www.macintouch.com
www.mirc.co.uk
www.mp3.com
www.mp3.com/aquataine
www.mrsa.com.au
www.my.yahoo.com.au
www.nber.org
www.nua.ie/surveys
www.ozdaq.com
www.politicsonline.com
www.pollit.com
www.setiathome.com
www.sitestatz.com/check.cgi?id=natgatcat
www.slashdot.org
www.stephendann.com
www.survey.hotlink.com.au
www.surveymonkey.com
www.ultrafeedback.com
www.urbancinefile.com.au
www.ur.harrispollonline.com
www.wcw.com
www.xoom.com

Newsgroup

news:biz.marketplace

part 5

The future

- **17**...*Future directions*

The final section of the book tackles the hardest issue of all in terms of Internet marketing as it looks at where the Internet is heading, and what sort of issues and implication may unfold. **Chapter 17** also tackles the ethical issues of strategic Internet marketing by examining how the actions of marketers can shape the future of the Internet by affecting online privacy, Internet security and becoming involved in the online lives of the consumers.

Future
directions

'Today our concern must be with that future. For the world is changing. The old era is ending. The old ways will not do ... But I tell you the New Frontier is here, whether we seek it or not. Beyond that frontier are the uncharted areas of science and space, unsolved problems of peace and war, unconquered pockets of ignorance and prejudice, unanswered questions of poverty and surplus ... But I believe the times demand new invention, innovation, imagination, decision. I am asking each of you to be pioneers on that New Frontier'.

Address of Senator John F. Kennedy accepting the Democratic Party nomination for the presidency of the United States, Memorial Coliseum, Los Angeles, 15 July 1960, John Fitzgerald Kennedy Library, www.cs.umb.edu/ jfklibrary/j071560.htm

After reading this chapter, you should be able to:

▪ view future directions for the Internet

▪ outline possible scenarios for the role of marketing in the future

▪ examine the ethical considerations of online marketing

▪ recognise the value of freedom, anonymity, privacy and security for Internet marketing

▪ explore the ethical considerations of strategic Internet marketing, including the issues of privacy, security and intrusive marketing

▪ understand the value of allying marketing to existing forces, social groups and entities that occupy the Internet

▪ outline coping strategies for dealing with the future of the Internet

▪ recognise the value of historical precedent in determining future directions.

Introduction

It seems strange that JFK can have a quote that so aptly describes the challenges faced by marketing when his involvement in the foundation of the Internet, the creation of the space race and the events of the Cold War ultimately contributed to the Internet as we know it today. In part, Kennedy's call to arms rings true to the Internet of today as much as it did to America in the 1960s. The future of the Internet depends on the people shaping its direction and functionality and the actions of the people who use it. Privacy and anonymity are issues of concern that need to be addressed. However, marketing needs to look beyond the narrow walls of e-commerce to aid in the defence of key issues of Internet freedoms, defend open speech and protect the freedom of publication and access to the Internet. Without these freedoms, e-commerce will wither and die as the diversity of the market succumbs to the monopolies and oligarchies that control the print, television and radio media.

This chapter overviews issues of ethics, privacy and security, as well as discussing the value of Internet freedoms to marketing. In addition, it recommends that marketing learns to live with its digital neighbours insofar as the Internet culture and commercial interest can coexist. Finally, it offers a set of strategies for dealing with the rapid changes and upheavals caused by the introduction of the Internet into mainstream society.

What will the Internet be?

Anybody who tries to tell you what the future will be is either trying to sell you something, or is Faith Popcorn. Admittedly, Faith Popcorn does also sell products (The Popcorn Report), but as a general rule, the people most likely to predict the future are selling a product or service that is supposed to protect you from that very same future.

Anyone who can accurately predict the future normally never does it in a popular culture format. Those with that level of insight can be found discussing the outcome of horse races, usually with the punters who just lost their money. Publicly predicting the future is also fraught with an obvious problem — if we know what will happen next, we can change the script.

Anyone involved in the Internet spends a portion of their life predicting the future and another portion tinkering with that future to suit their desired outcomes. The purpose of this book is to report on the present, use a framework of existing marketing theory and enhance the future by learning from the outcomes of past and present.

The final chapter presented in this text contains the inevitable forward thinking, future gazing sections on how the future of the Internet might be, where it might go, and who it will have lunch with when it gets there. Most of the predictions are based on observations of historical cycles and emergent trends. However, some are guesswork with a touch of personal opinion. You must decide which predictions will benefit your marketing career.

When this book was started, Infoseek (www.infoseek.com) existed as an independently branded search engine Web site, Netscape (www.netscape.com) was still version 5.0 and Windows 2000 (www.microsoft.com) was the latest operating system. No-one in the mainstream press had really heard of Napster (www.napster.com) and dotcom stocks were worth buying despite Amazon (www.amazon.com) having not turned a profit.

In the 12 months that followed, Disney's digital operations arm Go.com purchased Infoseek and absorbed it into the Go.com portal. Infoseek, the brand, slowly died out for English-reading Web users (Infoseek still existed for some European languages — see www.infoseek.de). Netscape released the sixth version of their Web browser, only to find it seeking to outbid their open source cousin Mozilla (www.mozilla.org) for marketshare. Microsoft rolled out Windows Millennium Edition (WinMe) and came a distinct second in a court case against the United States government (www.fed.gov) because of the perceived monopoly power of the software giant. At the same time, the Time-Warner/AOL (www.aol.com) merger promised to offer the United States government another monopoly to break up when the Microsoft case was finally over.

Point-to-point (P2P) file sharing became the hot issue as Napster rose to infamy for providing a mechanism for diversely situated computers to share music files (MP3s) directly without routing through a central server. Distributed networking and **wireless application protocols (WAP)** started becoming the flavour of the moment as the Internet was able to be beamed to mobile phones. Nobody could explain why downloading a web site to a telephone was a good idea, but the technology rolled out into handheld devices any way.

Dotcom shares plummeted as increasing numbers of big name ventures closed their online operations, or reappeared with scaled back business plans. After spending large amounts on advertising, many dotcoms wished they had kept their advertising budget for more useful functions such as bill payments and employee salaries. Corporate nay-sayers predicted the death of the book, the compact disk, the Internet and Bill Gates and proclaimed the Y2K bug to be a fraud (nobody has mentioned the Armistice Day Bug on 11 November 2011 — 11/11/11 — yet). All of the predictions of the death of existing media (and Bill Gates) failed to come true, although the portable digital eight-track recorders are becoming more scarce (and Bill Gates did step down as CEO of Microsoft). In the year where the constant was change, one thing did stay the same — Amazon.com failed to turn a profit.

The role of marketing in the future

The future is what it used to be. Contrary to popular opinion, the future has always been this fast-paced, scary and subject to rapid change and development. Plotting the development of 'the future' over time indicates an incredibly steep curve from the discovery of fire through to the registration of fire.com. Taken incrementally, the rate of change, and the major social upheaval caused by fire is remarkably similar to that of the widespread diffusion of information technology. The capacity of the individual to cope with change has, if anything, been improved by the exposure to change. Since first forming consciousness as an individual, the average human still had to learn about fire (less the discovery, more the application) and from there learn about the Internet, and what to do with a computer, keyboard and mouse. It took early humans a long time to come to grips with fire, yet many small children can operate a mouse more easily than their parents (both parent and child have also mastered fire on the way).

So, knowing that the world will continue to change, evolve and generally not be like the good old days (which, in hindsight, were no more the good old days than today is — remember, one day society will look back fondly on the simplicity of the 1990s), what is the role of marketing in all of this? Since the industry only recognises a past that stretches back to the mid 1950s, marketing has been around through some of the more saleable social upheavals in society. Potential scenarios that could govern the future of marketing on the Internet are presented on the following pages.

Scenario one: Getting it right

The most optimistic scenario regarding marketing and the Internet is the notion that the industry 'gets it right', and becomes a useful part of society. To do this, marketing may have to accept some of the responsibilities it prefers to avoid. Marketing, and post-modern consumption, will combine to bring marketing to the forefront as a creator and arbiter of society. It is not as if the marketing industry has a choice in this matter. In effect, being so good at creating imagery and associations between brands, logos and lifestyles has made marketing a natural successor to art and literature as the arbiter of social imagery. It is also the opportunity of a lifetime for marketing to give value to society by consciously choosing to create art and meaning. Budweiser may never become Shakespeare, although more people can respond eloquently to the inquiry 'Wassup?' than will be able to 'compare thee to a summer's day'. Pepsi Max has tapped into a lifestyle culture of extreme sports, which have risen to prominence as society accepts a cola manufacturer's view of acceptable things to do on a weekend including those that involve a human, rollerblades and a very steep drop.

In the role of arbiters of truth, online marketers can use materials from social marketing, cause marketing and similar techniques to help shape the online world. Marketing that supports the ideology behind the open source movement (www.opensource.org), which advocates freedom of choice ahead of monopolistic mono-branded environments and which recognises the value of free speech (even if it is criticising the marketer), will build a valued role in both online and offline society. Most importantly, marketing needs to create a strong alliance with the defenders of the freedom of the Internet.

FOCUS ON
Strategy 👁

Information (and markets) want to be free

The most valuable element of the Internet for any marketer is the share of voice that cannot be dominated by one player. This is the feature that so many marketers have craved for decades as their campaigns languished outside of the price range of big media events, popular television shows and overpriced peak timeslots. Now that freedom of voice has come to the marketers, many of them fear the very thing they have craved for so long.

The fragmentation of the marketplace that occurred with the introduction of the Internet means that marketers need to find places to voice their message where it can meet their markets. Freedom of speech on the Internet is vital to the development of e-commerce, as regulation and control of content on the Internet will mean regulation of the marketing message. If the Internet is placed under more strict controls than television, as was proposed under the now defunct American Communications Decency Act (CDA) (1995), many marketing sites would be forced to shut down to comply with the law. The Act proposed to enforce regulation to limit the content that could be published on the Internet by banning R-rated material, nudity and material regarded as 'patently offensive' (no definition of patently offensive was ever provided, so it would have been decided on a case law basis). As a result of this proposed Act, sites that sold adult-oriented products, sexual goods and services, or health materials concerning breast cancer, prostate cancer and sexually transmitted diseases, were directly banned under the Act. Prohibition of nudity online also prohibited the display of classical Greek art and architecture. In addition, the use of risque advertising messages that are relatively common in magazines and billboards was also restricted for being 'patently offensive'.

Further controls over Internet content, particularly in regard to enforced morality, will limit the promotion of movies, music, art and culture, all of which are freely available offline, but restricted online. Using an image of Michelangelo's statue of David (probably the most famous carved rock in existence) could be prohibited under some of the morality censorship laws promoted to 'save' the Internet from the evils of the world, such as the CDA, since all forms of nudity (including artistic) are potentially banned. The evils of the world, for the most part, are not recruiting and certainly are every bit as interested in keeping innocent minds, under-age viewers and non-users of their products out of their Web sites. Like any other legitimate business, all they want is their own target market of customers arriving at their Web site and using their products.

In order to prosper in the digital economy, marketing needs to ensure that the freedoms it requires to operate effectively are preserved. This will mean that, occasionally, marketing will have to make some sacrifices for the greater good of society, including easing up on copyright protection and trademark suppression. The fight between 2600 Magazine and the Motion Picture Association America (MPAA) demonstrates that marketing needs at times to side with the 'enemy' to protect its own operational freedom. The gist of this court case is that the MPAA is suing the counter-culture organisation 2600 (www.2600.com) for distribution of the DeCSS code which allows DVDs to be played on the Linux platform (Goldstein 2000). The DeCSS system can be used to override regional codes, so the MPAA wish to suppress the DeCSS code in order to maintain strict control over the distribution of DVD. Why is this an issue for marketing? If the DeCSS encryption system spreads widely, marketing may find itself locked out of the new digital media unless it agrees to pay for production licences. The freedom to create and produce advertising for distribution anywhere in the world is at stake, as much as the right to view a DVD on the equipment of the owner's choosing.

Marketing already bears the cost of buying advertising space on television, radio and any other paid placement. Imagine being forced to pay royalties to a central authority for the privilege of producing a piece of content that you still have to pay to have broadcast. Proprietary standards that lock the user into a limited set of choices controlled by the equipment manufacturers can endanger the freedom of the marketer. Any system that can potentially limit competition and reduce channels for the distribution of dissenting ideas (such as advertising for rival systems) will have a negative impact on marketing.

While groups like 2600 seem on the surface to be the enemy of marketing (and frankly, even if they have less than positive views of marketing), the freedoms that they are fighting for are the same freedoms marketing requires to maintain its existence. Marketing needs the Internet to be as free as possible so that it can never be squeezed out of the game by proprietary standards that reduce competition and create monopolies. Share of voice and freedom of expression are the reasons why the Internet has such low entry barriers and is so valuable to small and medium-sized enterprises.

●●●●●●●●●●●●●●●●●●●●●●●●●●

Scenario two: Getting it wrong

It is technically possible for marketing to be kicked off the Internet and politely asked to leave the medium. Prior to the widespread adoption of the Internet by the public in the early 1990s, there was no commercial traffic online, e-commerce was not an option and nobody would tolerate an email advertising campaign. Discussions have already begun to establish second generation Internet systems such as USENET2 (www.usenet2.org) and even a second Internet (www.internet2.com). Should these procedures succeed, it is possible that marketing, and commercial behaviours, may not be invited to play in the new information environment. In order to get kicked out of the Internet (not that this is a recommended strategy), marketers would have to exhibit an unacceptable standard of behaviour, such as constantly and permanently abusing privacy, eliminating anonymity with overly accurate databases and permanently intruding into aspects of Internet life such as email, USENET, IRC and MUDs so as to make the advertising **noise-to-signal ratio** unacceptably high. Given that an average Hotmail account (www.hot mail.com) can accumulate 40 unsolicited spam messages in a fortnight of inactivity, the noise-to-signal ratio is rising steadily. While rogue operators will continue to abuse the system with spam, commercial operators need to remember that access to the Internet is a privilege, not a right, and that the Internet can exist without marketing.

Scenario three: Just not getting it

The third scenario for marketing is the nightmare scenario for online business as marketing simply fails to be relevant to the needs of the digital marketplace. Already many businesses are questioning the effectiveness of marketing, on and offline, and as click-through rates for online advertising drop into fractions of percentage points, questions have to be asked about whether marketing is actually adding value to the medium. Banner advertising that draws four to five per cent click-through rates is praised as remarkable. In contrast, a single link of a relevant site on a medium such as Slashdot (www.slashdot.org) can deliver more people for free in one hour than the most successful banner advertisement can in months. Many Web banner advertisements have click-through rates in the 0.5 to one per cent rate (Rae & Brennan 1998), whereas a Slashdot effect can generate a click-through rate from Slashdot in the vicinity of 10 per cent (Adler 1999).

The discipline of marketing also needs to adapt to the new market and the new consumers emerging from the Internet. Empowered consumers who are educated, literate and interested in their world will make different demands on the marketer than the marketer will be used to addressing. The consumer raised on the Internet will be less willing to tolerate the 'take it or leave it' attitude of marketers used to pushing advertising through a one-way medium such as radio or television. These consumers will simply leave it, and head off to sites that meet their needs and that they have discovered through their own exploration. In this nightmare scenario, marketing will exist online, but will find itself increasingly outmoded and unable to address the consumer. In contrast, the consumer will be far more likely to be able to access the information they need and want faster than the marketer can provide it, simply by knowing how to navigate the Web to seek solutions to their own needs. The obvious solution is to hire the consumer to be the marketer, as used by viral marketing and the idea virus (www.ideavirus.com), but even this approach further disempowers the marketer.

 Ethical considerations of strategic Internet marketing

Strategic Internet Marketing does not occur in a vacuum. The basic marketing considerations of the ethics of promotional materials, persuasive advertising and similar issues still apply to the Internet as much as they apply to the offline world. In addition, online marketing presents its own set of ethical considerations that need to be addressed. Some of these considerations are ones of our own creation, such as the collection and collation of massive amounts of data on individuals in society. How we choose to use this information determines whether we give benefit by customising the product to exactly meet a need, or exploit the consumer's weakness for profit and gain.

Online privacy

Privacy is a major concern and one of the biggest areas where the Internet marketer can make a positive (or negative) contribution to society. One-to-one marketing in the online environment marks the start of an unprecedented opportunity to gain in-depth information about the individual customer (Hoffman & Novak 1996). As database marketing increases the range of data available on the individual, it is possible to build profiles of a consumer based on their purchase patterns that can be cross-referenced with taxation, medical and legal databases. In all likelihood, given the database marketer probably knows the individual better than they know themselves, it is imperative that this information is protected by ethical standards.

Online marketing has the potential to go one step further and collate the browsing activities of the user and add this to existing information. The ethical consideration for marketing is to decide where to draw the line and what information it is necessary or unnecessary for the marketer to gain about the customer. A hotel chain could reasonably want to know the food and beverage preferences of the individual, but should they be entitled to know of any medical considerations, such as infectious diseases, and be permitted to deny the booking on that basis? At what point does a direct marketing firm need to draw the line and say 'We do not need to know this information' ahead of saying 'This information can be saleable'? The potential crisis to be faced by online privacy will arise from consumers seeking to avoid the Internet because of the loss of anonymity and the perceived intrusion of marketing into the private areas of the home via electronic means (see chapter 16 for discussions of the importance of preserving anonymity).

Internet security

Wilson (1999) established five parameters for the operationalisation of online security:
1. *authenticity*: the degree to which the individual can prove that they are who they represent themselves to be and have the authority to conduct the transaction
2. *integrity*: the degree to which the document can be believed to be the genuine article and remain unchanged from the time it was written. Most forms of digital media can be edited after the point of origin.
3. *non-repudiation*: the extent to which the originator of a document can deny responsibility for it and the terms and conditions stated on it
4. *confidentiality*: the extent to which the document can be secured against a third party viewing it without the permission of the signing parties
5. *availability*: the capacity of the document to be delivered and the archive document to be accessed in the future. Electronic contracts, while holding the same legal weight as paper documents, are more easily disposed of and prone to accidental loss through computer failures or deletion.

All forms of data security rely on the protection of the information through technical and organisational structures, rather than post-hoc enforcement measures (Genieva 1997). Highly sensitive transactions should be conducted on secure channels, either through dedicated non-Internet EDI mechanisms, face-to-face transactions or secured courier systems. While online security through encryption is possible, it is preferable to avoid dependence on these mechanisms where alternative channels are available.

In e-commerce solutions, most of the emphasis has been placed on securing the transaction between purchaser client and e-commerce server, to give the customer the illusion of security. However, for the most part, e-commerce solutions are more secure than they are given credit for in the mainstream media and fraudulent card use is more prevalent offline, where you can walk away with the goods rather than wait six weeks for them (and the police) to arrive at the door.

Due to a range of technical issues, the systems are still not fully secure (Swift 2000). Then again, faxing a purchase form with a name, credit card number, address, telephone number and signature is no more secure than using the Internet. The precautionary message here is to continue to develop and enhance security, but not to believe that all systems are secured simply by the use of encryption.

Marketing by intrusion and observation

Throughout this text there have been suggestions of where and when marketing should become involved in aspects of community life on the Internet. Several of these suggestions have involved using the Internet as a giant market research data collection experiment where the day-to-day activities of Internet users can be distilled, bottled and sold as data. This raises the question of privacy insofar as where can marketing acceptably continue to collect data, and when should it draw the line? More importantly, are marketers under any obligation to declare their data collection activities in non-obtrusive marketing research? The Hawthorne effect is enough to make a marketer shy away from wanting to declare their intentions to observe a society, or cybercommunity, but can marketing justify what amounts to cyberstalking in the name of market research?

These questions have no straight answers to ease the conscience of the online marketing researcher. Ethical considerations needed to be judged on a case-by-case basis, since a web site discussion forum hosted at a product web site will produce a different set of expectations among users about the outcomes of their posts than would be expected from a private email list.

Marketing by intrusion is not only limited to the collection and organisation of marketing research data. Intrusive marketing is occurring where promotional materials are interrupting web sites, cybercommunities and other online activities. Most people are gradually coming to accept the pop-up banner as the price of visiting a free hosting web site. However, other experimental marketing techniques such as using **interrupt pages**, which interfere with access to the desired content, are less acceptable than the pop-up banner. The concern for intrusive marketing is the negative reaction to the product, brand and the marketing industry. Maintaining and defending the value of the marketing industry is a vital aspect of enhancing e-commerce online, since the loss of credibility for the industry will have major financial repercussions. Ethical behaviour is a key to developing trust, which is a crucial commodity required to ensure e-commerce continues to expand and thrive.

The ethics of selling the consumer to the consumer

Beyond intrusive marketing also lies the grey areas of selling the consumer to other consumers. Discussions in chapter 5 raised the idea of selling the value of the cybercommunity as being the other members of the community. When this is taken to the logical and financial conclusion of charging entrance fees for fee-paying customers to talk to other fee-paying customers, what product and service is being sold? Are the marketers actually producing anything of value for sale, or are they selling the consumer to other consumers? If we continue to harvest and sell the consumers as tradeable commodities, we will need to either make the consumer a partial employee, or compensate them for their value which we exchanged in the transaction. In similar offline transactions, the provision of a venue, sporting event or other physical world location can be seen as a part trade for the sale of the value of the consumer. Pursuing the current trend towards selling the value of one group of paying clients to another group, without adding some value by the company, is heading into murky waters of customer exploitation.

When (and where) marketing should leave the Internet alone

There are some places in society that marketing should be leaving alone. In the offline world, marketing should stay out of education, history and the development of art. These are areas of society where objective (or subjective) standards beyond the demands of the market should dictate the content of the education taught, the history that is remembered, or the art that is produced. Market researched history to determine what people would prefer to remember the past as being should not replace production orientation historical work that produces a historical account based upon the events that transpired. Online, marketing would be well advised to line up sections of the Internet and declare them no-go areas for promotional activities. Suggested marketing-free zones are:

- *IRC*: leave people alone and let them have their conversations in peace. Nobody would like an unsolicited personal sales pitch to suddenly appear, mid-conversation, during a dinner party. Similarly, showing up unannounced in a chat room and selling your goods is equally impolite and just as much a waste of time and effort as gatecrashing a dinner party.
- *e-mail*: spam is already dividing the online marketing community into those who spam (or would if they thought everyone else was) and those who do not (and would not). Unsolicited e-mail is the online equivalent of interrupting a personal telephone call to tell the two callers how great your product is and then charging them for the telephone call you made to interrupt their conversation. Solicited e-mail is a welcome event and an acceptable form of public relations, advertising and word of mouse.
- *social spheres*: marketing should leave those sections of the Internet that depend on person-to-person social interaction for their existence. We have

sporting events (www.olympics.org), sporting personalities (www.stevewaugh.com.au), reading materials, physical mailboxes and most of the large flat surfaces in the offline world for advertising. Television and radio are saturated with advertising messages and product placements. The Internet is a place where people can get a break from advertising, escape the clutter and take time out from the constant barrage of persuasive messages the marketing industry hammers at them each and every day.

■ *mobile phones*: this is a controversial call to make at the dawning of WAP systems. However, the most important determinant of the success of WAP systems is the degree to which it can add value to the user's life. Constantly having to clear unsolicited advertising messages from the mobile phone screen will reduce the value of the system to the point that it will not be adopted. The collapse of the WAP function will set back the development of point-to-point wireless communications whereby billboards can transmit their contact details on the request of the user. Let the user come to the advertising and promotional message and they will do so willingly and with the intention of spending money. Force the user to constantly delete your message and you are wasting their time, your money and everyone's opportunities for the future.

Putting up with the neighbours

One of the most crucial survivals skills for the new economy is the ability to live with (if not necessarily love) your digital neighbour. Marketing is the interloper into the Internet. As such, marketers are the ones who need to put up with the neighbourhood, learn the rules and generally be on their best behaviour. The Internet was not built for commerce and should not be expected to change to suit the needs and whims of marketers. There are several areas where marketing just needs to shut up and put up with the online world, including the following.

Hackers

Hackers are those individuals who tinker with the digital world to see what makes it tick, and if it can be made to tick in a different platform, different style or more effectively. Hackers are defined as people who enjoy exploring the details of programmable systems and how to stretch their capacities and/or people who enjoy the intellectual challenge of creatively overcoming or circumventing limitations (Raymond, 1996; Raymond, 2000). The term is not to be confused with **cracker** who is a person who breaks the security on a system. Crackers are the antithesis of hackers, and are people who are to be dealt with and ignored as appropriate. In contrast, hackers are the allies and friends of e-commerce, even if both parties have been slow to notice the relationship. True hackers (extenders of systems) will find new ways to use (and break) software products and most likely figure out how to fix these problems, or augment them into features.

One of the most successful games of all time, Quake (www.idsoftware.com), depended heavily on hackers who were able to find, fix and release patches for errors in the original software faster than the manufacturing company.

Skilled hackers are also likely to release their patches to the public (including the manufacturer of the software or hardware) as part of their contribution to the gift economy. If this happens to a product you are developing, the appropriate response is to say 'thank you'. Additional responses include linking to the hacker's Web site and crediting their work. It also indicates you have a product that is worth enough value to somebody's life for them to donate their time to rectify your mistake for free. That is brand loyalty taken to the ultimate extension.

Porting

In a similar vein to hacking, **porting** is also a tribute to the product, rather than a hostile threat to the organisation. Porting is the process of adapting a software package from one platform to another, often unofficially, or vaguely sanctioned. Many of the systems being produced for the Internet by commercial organisations have concentrated on developing software for the dominant Windows platform. While this is a sane, logical decision for a corporation to make, it frustrates non-Windows users who wish to access the benefits and features of the system. Some of these non-Windows users may take it upon themselves to port (translate) the software to their native systems such as Linux, Macintosh, Unix or O/S2 and post the amended software online. These hackers and their ported software perform two functions for e-commerce — first, they open the software service to a new market and second, they demonstrate the inherent value of the Windows native software to other communities.

Many organisations react badly to their software being ported, claiming breaches of intellectual property, financial losses and other damages. Before declaring war on an individual or group that has ported your software to a new platform (or language), consider the following.

- Did your organisation intend to address this market? If so, then contact the group who ported the software, hire them and buy the software, since you had to spend the money on development anyway. If not, consider how you could have lost money from a market you had no intention of entering. Use the ported software as a test of market demand and if the software is a valued product, consider entering that market.
- Do you sell the software or the service mediated by the software? If your core business is selling software then buy out the port and get into the market if it is financially viable. If your business sells its services through the software, yet distributes the software without cost, what on Earth are you complaining about? If the port works with your services, be grateful that the customers are so keen to use your service that they beat their own path to your door (you may just have invented the better mouse trap).
- Are you concerned with legal liability? One of the issues with software porting is the question of liability if something goes wrong. The easiest solution is to disclaim the unofficial software, label it as unofficial and put the appropriate warning stickers on the Web site. Numerous companies advocate caution over the use of third-party parts, software or services which means that precedents exist in the market.

CueCats (www.getcat.com) are small, hand-held scanners designed to scan barcodes from printed catalogues into a computer to link with associated advertising material. The software was designed to be linked with television commercials (containing the CueCats logo) and the hand-held scanner, all of which were designed to increase the speed with which a user of the system could access advertising material. The downside to the software is that it existed solely for the Win95/Win98 market, thereby excluding users of Macintosh computers, Linux, Unix, Windows NT and Windows 2000. CRQ (www.crq.com) provides the software, hardware (CueCats) and services for free to the end user and makes money from advertisers and retailers.

On the hardware side CueCats were freely distributed, either from associated retailers such as Radioshack (www.radioshack.com) or mailed out to selected target markets. CueCats proved to be a source of fascination in the hacking community, with an array of web sites springing up, detailing the dissection of the CueCats and details of how they operated (which made a welcome change from Furby and topsy sites). Several hackers reverse-engineered the software and hardware combination to provide ports to make the CueCats software available to the Linux community.

The reaction of CRQ has been stunningly poor. Rather than welcoming the development of the Linux ports as a sign of market acceptance, the CRQ company sued the developers for breach of intellectual property, several patent infringements and a host of other civil complaints. Sites advocating the reverse engineering procedure had also discovered two hidden 'features' of the CueCats — the unique identification code built into each CueCat and the line in the licence agreement that indicated that the end user did not own the CueCat (despite receiving the device either through cash purchase or unsolicited mail). These sites have also been actively pursued by the lawyers for CRQ.

One of the possible reasons for an aggressive legal response was the discovery of the unique identifier code (and the subsequent 'declawing' web sites to disable that feature). While we do not advocate reverse engineering or tampering with equipment, CRQ's failure to disclose this 'feature' and subsequent hostility to the discovery may indicate that they were not prepared to disclose this information. Conducting unethical business practices, and being discovered to have done so, is more of an issue at stake than initially observed.

All corporations have a right to their intellectual property and reasonable defence of that property. However, if an unethical or questionable activity is discovered by someone engaging in a port of the software or hardware to a new system, the legality of the means of discovery should not and does not take away from the original unethical business practice. Part of the antipathy towards the hackers and the porting of the system was the discovery of this 'feature' that would not have been noticed during normal use. Rather than being open about the unique identifier code, the CueCat manufacturers appeared to have attempted to avoid any questions about the identifier and its impact on privacy and anonymity.

What CRQ failed to do was capitalise on a market opportunity by making an alliance with the hackers and incorporating them into the official sphere of operations. By encouraging individuals to port the Linux software, CRQ could have expanded the service into these markets at a reduced cost to the company. At the time of writing, the official Macintosh port of the software had yet to be released, whereas an unofficial Linux port had already been on the market for several months. Rather than lose the Macintosh customers, it would have been ultimately more productive for CRQ to allow enthusiastic consumers to engage in porting the software so that the Macintosh community had access to the software, and CRQ gained the market. In addition, the strong word of mouse generated by brand-loyal hackers who developed the ported software would also have increased the goodwill towards CRQ. Instead, CRQ misread the intentions of the market (who wanted to gain access to the service) and saw the development of unofficial systems as a threat, rather than a benefit, to the operation of the company.

Parody site

Get a sense of humour. The Internet was spawned from a group mind that reveres the humour of Monty Python and has a long history of producing parodies and poking fun at itself and others. If someone uses a huge chunk of their life to develop a site that parodies your site, take the compliment gracefully, and confuse the life out of the developer by linking to it. If the site is a malicious parody designed to criticise some action or activity your organisation has undertaken, review the reasons why your action has sparked such a degree of effort and outrage. You may find that your organisation is losing goodwill from the action that is being parodied, rather than the parody itself. Address the root cause, not the symptoms, and the damage can be brought under control. Attacking the symptoms (parody sites) and ignoring the cause could cost more goodwill, reputation and public image than ignoring the site.

Fan sites

Remember your fans are those people who set out to support your cause, product, television show or other enterprise by dedicating their time and server space to your materials. One of the concerns that many of the major networks have had regarding **fan sites** is the use of copyrighted materials and the breaking down of their ownership of protected materials if they do not continue to vigorously defend their intellectual property rights. The consideration here is which is more important — hunting down web sites that offer full copies of the television show for downloading, or alienating fan sites that borrow graphics and materials for developing supportive sites. The key is to determine whether the fan site represents a gain or loss of value to the core business of the organisation. If a fan-developed site is actively promoting interest in the product, then consider this to be part of the promotional mix of word-of-mouth and publicity. Lucas Films, one of the more vigorous defenders of copyright materials, has developed a series of mechanisms to engage fans who want to develop pro-Star Wars web sites and still maintain copyright controls.

Lucas Films owns one of the most popular science fiction franchises in history. The Star Wars empire (www.starwars.com) covers just about every conceivable merchandise base with novels, films, television, video games, figures and supporting goods that feed a massive market. With the incredible popularity of the series came the problem of protecting the intellectual properties of the Star Wars universe from being damaged by enthusiastic fans who wanted to show their devotion and dedication to the cause. Over the years, Lucas Films unofficially sanctioned a range of Star Wars events, including parody films, simply by looking in the opposite direction.

With the release of Episode I, Lucas Films took a different angle to bolster their multimillion dollar promotional budget. Instead of persecuting, prosecuting and alienating their fan base, they offered the fans a range of compromises and opportunities, based around a set of key online strategies. These are:

- *build community.* Offering a starwars.com e-mail address and server space for fan web sites, in conjunction with a range of prizes for the best sites, reduced competition to the official site from the unofficial fan sites.
- *gift economy.* While not a strict application of the gift economy, Lucas Films gave away free official images for use on fan sites. This also created a sense of a licensing arrangement that could be used to defend the Lucas Films copyright against commercial infringement, as they could demonstrate the fan sites were authorised delegates of the company, since they had agreed to a licensing arrangement.
- *develop a sense of humour.* The expansion of the community project has seen the Star Wars franchise officially adopt several of the more famous unofficial parodies (Troops, Tie-Tanic) as part of their Internet strategy. Showing a willingness to be parodied and good humour about good humour has increased the support for the company among their loyal customers.

For the cost of reining in their lawyers and accepting a relaxed level of control over the Star Wars franchise, Lucas Films has gained the support of the brand-loyal fan community. In turn, this group of customers is adding considerable value to the Star Wars brand by extending beyond the official product range and using active word-of-mouth and publicity strategies, all of which end up rewarding Lucas Films with a strong brand.

Putting up with the neighbours does not mean tolerating illegal activities. Crackers who attempt to or succeed in distributing pirated software should be pursued in the same manner as any other thief. Similarly, defamation, inaccurate reporting and sites promoting deliberately false information should also be dealt with in the same manner as if the incident had occurred offline. The key is to ensure recognition of online allies, such as the hackers and fans, and to aid them in spreading the positive word about your product while defending against the 'bad guys'. Taking advantage of the support of allied programmers who are willing to do your job for you also requires you to support them, either through recognition or at the very least by not attacking them for wanting to help you expand your markets.

Future proofing a strategic internet marketing text

Future proofing anything is not substantially dissimilar to fool proofing an activity. Somebody will develop a better, faster fool that can override your fool proofing (although if we can find this developer of fools and put them to a better project, the world will be a much enhanced place). Every attempt to develop a 'future proof' technology or system is met by the fact that somebody else develops a better future. This text is designed to have a half life rather than a shelf life, the evolution of ideas, systems, web sites and practices will see half of the new ideas in this book expire. Similarly, with more than 400 web sites cited in this text, several of them will go out of business, change hands, or simply cease to exist. Given the conventional wisdom that nine out of 10 small businesses go broke within their first year, anything greater than a 10 per cent survival rate of the web sites is well ahead of the curve (though 360 failed websites is worrying).

Surviving the future

Given that the world has survived as far as it has, everyone on board has a capacity to adapt to the future. Everyone has a capacity to adapt to the future. Change is a constant that has to be factored into the equation of business life, just as it gets factored into the day-to-day life of the consumer. At some point in any marketer's life they have had to change brands, switch stores, use an alternative product, or accept that a preferred product choice is no longer available. Then, just as now, you had to adjust to the change that occurred and you did this either willingly, reluctantly, or without much consideration. In the development of the future of the Internet, changes will be greeted in much the same way — willingly, reluctantly, or without anyone really noticing the difference.

Predicting (and adjusting to) the future

Randall (1997) proposes five steps for developing strategies for adjusting to the future.
1. *Follow the people*: Consumer behaviour will drive the Internet and determine the outcomes of many of the current issues. Security and privacy will be resolved by market demand as the market either requests (and receives) improved security, or just does not care enough for it to affect their behaviour. Controls on the Internet that annoy consumers will be repealed by populist governments seeking social approval and re-election. Even at the business to business level, the individual is ultimately responsible for the decision of yes or no in the transaction.

2. *The old Internet is not the new Internet*: The current Internet is an evolving medium which will change, adjust, develop and gradually form into something different from the Internet of today. The best analogy is to look at the evolution of television and television content from the first broadcasts to the current products. However, the permanence of Internet culture will continue to flavour the development of the medium as the systems mature and develop over time.

3. *Be radical*: Take Apple Corporation's advice and think different (www.apple.com). Be prepared to try new methods and techniques on the Internet and be prepared for success and failure as it comes, whichever way it comes. The greatest danger facing the novice Internet marketer is not being willing to back their new ideas in the new medium for fear they might fail. Take heart from the fact they probably will fail, but at no greater or lesser extent than they would have failed in the offline world. However, being radical does not mean discarding past lessons, or ignoring existing theory and practice. Radical marketing is about applying best practice that suits your products, your markets and the combined needs of your company and consumer, irrespective of whether it is new or old. Doing what fits best, rather than what has always been done, is the radical approach advocated by the Internet.

4. *Be robust*: Take the hits on the chin, get back up and keep going. The Internet is about long-term focus with short-term adaptability to rapid change. Many businesses that have succeeded in online marketing did so by being aware of the causes of their success and adapting to support those features, while being willing to take the setbacks as they occurred on the way to establishing their long-term success. A surprisingly large number of organisations have sold their method of e-commerce success, as was the case with Digital (www.compaq.com), who first produced the search engine Alta Vista (www.altavista.com) to showcase their server hardware. As the search engine became increasingly successful, they discovered a market for selling the search engine to other companies, who may or may not have also bought the Digital server equipment. Similarly, the more successful search engine systems have been able to on-sell their technology for smaller local area applications within intranets, or intra-site searching, as has been the case with Google (www.google.com). Adapting to where the markets are and what products are in demand is a necessary survival trait. However, despite the success of Alta Vista, Digital still sells the server hardware that drives the search engine.

5. *Focus on the niches*: This advice should be redrafted simply as 'focus on the markets'. The Internet offers unprecedented access to niche markets by allowing the interested consumer to find the interesting producer. However, the current mind set of the marketing discipline is hung up on believing that this can only be used for niche products when it clearly indicates that the consumer can find the marketer, if the consumer wants what the marketer has to offer. Study the needs, wants and desires of the market and see where your product can match up with what the consumer wants, within the constraints of what the company wants to produce. Focus on the markets, find out where they are, what they want and offer it to them

online and the customers will be able to find you every bit as much as you can find the customers.

A sixth and final point does not derive from Randall's examination of survival strategies for the future, but rather from the observation of the best methods of dealing with the changing future.

6. *Have fun*: The world is an inherently interesting place, the Internet is an unstable climate of chaotic change and the ever-shifting sands of the consumer marketplace makes for the rollercoaster ride of a lifetime. Has any period of marketing ever been this much fun? This is one of the most exciting times in the history of civilisation, with more on offer for the individual, company and marketer. Take the opportunities as opportunities, not threats, take the threats as challenges and take the risks as necessary. Enjoy the Internet as a wildly chaotic landscape while it lasts, before it becomes as staid and sober a medium as television or radio. We are living in interesting times and marketing has the opportunity to have the time of its life by being part of the creation of the future.

Learning from history

One of the major problems with the Internet is that while the technology is new, the reactions to the technology have not been unique. When radio was first invented the audio superhighway was developed. When ham radio equipment was readily available, just about anybody could be a broadcaster in a one-to-many-to-one environment. If Breaker-Breaker-Good-Buddy.com is bringing back visions of the late 1970s, CB radio and Smokey and the Bandit, then one-to-many-to-one communications technology has already occupied a place in society. The advent of television had similar problems to that of the Internet in that early television was crude, primitive, expensive and contained woeful content when compared to contemporary television.

By far and away the most surprising reaction to the Internet has been the opportunity to abandon the social constraints imposed by the Industrial Revolution. Prior to industrialism (the manufactured goods superhighway), cottage industries dominated the production landscape as small producers serviced local markets and niche markets. With the development of factory systems and the high demand for manual labour, society recalibrated to cluster workers around their employment sources (factories) in order to expedite the production processes by getting employees to work as fast as possible. Cities, suburbs and whole towns were based around geographies that suited the physical locations of factories, shipyards and other industrial activities.

As the Internet has gradually moved information production into the forefront of contemporary employment, a 'revolution' has taken place. Malone and Laubacher (1998) comment on the 'e-lance' economy with the 'business of one' model, which, oddly enough, looks a lot like cottage industries. Separation of employees from the production location is touted as new and revolutionary, despite having been the dominant industrial model several centuries prior to the Internet.

The development of temporary businesses, loose coalitions of individuals who cluster together for the duration of a project then spread out into their next projects, sounds just like the sort of thing the Internet was designed to support.

But this model of 'temporary companies' is the operational model of Hollywood and the film industries, where the break-up of the big studios was driven by the 'company of strangers' model, some 50 years prior to the development of the Internet.

The lesson from the Internet is to accept that the use or development of a new technology does not negate the lessons of history. Anyone sold on the idea of the Internet as a 'revolution' should be reminded that revolution does mean 360° rotation and going around in circles as much as it means the overthrow of established order.

 # Summary

Like any future, the future of the Internet cannot be predicted with an accuracy. All that we can do is highlight the issues, develop scenarios and adapt to change. Whether online marketers 'get it right' and become an integral, pro-active and productive contributor to sodiety, 'get it wrong' and find themselves in the Internet wilderness or just 'not get it' and fail to capitalise on the advantages that online marketing has to offer is yet to be seen.

Getting it right involves more than technical expertise. It also means developing an understanding of the needs of the online consumer and not only recognising, but addressing ethical concerns relating to issues such as privacy, security, obtrusive market research and the on selling of information about consumers. It also means acknowledging the limits of acceptable marketing behaviour online, respecting co-users and knowing where to draw the line. Although it is impossible to know the future, it is possible to prepare for it by learning from history, taking a few risks, responding to the consumers and most importantly, by having fun and using this evolving technology for its best possible outcomes.

George Bernard Shaw once said of his work that he did not so much finish a book for lack of anything further to say, but lack of anywhere further to say it (Bernard Shaw 1944). Any text on strategic Internet marketing is never going to be finished so much as it will be put on hold to await a further updated release, a bug patch and the correction of the errors of the first edition. Most of these errors will hopefully come from the negative predictions of the Internet, and the darker visions of how it can go wrong. Then again, many of the updates will be corrections to the many hundred web sites that have been referenced throughout the text, as the ever shifting sands of the Internet decide to bury another famous URL into the depths of time. At least those cited here will have their place in history as this text stands as a snapshot of the Internet, past, present and predicted future. From here, the next step for us as marketers, active participants in the Internet and users of the medium, is to set about using, shaping, co-opting and developing the medium into whatever shape it takes, so we have something new to write about in the next edition.

Discussion questions

17.1 Is the future overrated? Discuss whether the future warrants the level of predictive effort that is being put into determining the direction of the Internet.

17.2 Outline your vision of what the Internet will be in five years. How much of this change will result from technological developments and how much will change as a result of human behaviours?

17.3 Review the changes that have occurred on the Internet since you read the first chapter of this book. What impacts have these changes had on your use of the Internet?

17.4 What is the role of marketing in the future of the Internet? Which, if any, of the three models represents the most likely version of the future for marketing online?

17.5 Does marketing have an ethical responsibility to partake in movements to protect Internet freedoms? Should e-commerce incorporate the defence of Internet freedoms as part of a cause marketing strategy?

17.6 How big an impact does privacy have on Internet behaviour? Would the loss of privacy alter consumer behaviour on the Internet?

17.7 Collect a range of web sites that examine the issues of Internet security. What is the most commonly recommended method of securing sensitive data?

17.8 Given the historical precedents of sporting crowds and social clubs selling their members to other members, is this action an ethical consideration for cyber-communities?

17.9 Do you agree with the identified areas that marketing should leave alone (see pages 437–38)? Justify your stance with examples (for or against) keeping marketing out of these areas.

17.10 Should the Internet adapt to meet the needs of marketers, or should marketers adapt to the Internet? Where should the middle ground of compromise be met?

17.11 Compare the cases of CueCats and Star Wars. Which method of dealing with unofficial use of brands and products do you believe will have the best long-term impact for an organisation.

17.12 Which is more important — prediction or the predictive process?

References

Adler, S. 1999, 'The Slashdot Effect', *Linux Gazette*, http://www.linuxgazette.com/issue38/adler1.html

Genieva, E. 1997, 'Legal aspects of the Internet', *International Information and Library Review*, vol. 29, pp. 381–92.

Goldstein, E. 2000, 'A summer of trials', *2600: The Hacker Quarterly*, vol 17, no. 3, pp. 4–5, 47.

Hoffman, D. & Novak, T. 1996, 'Marketing in hypermedia computer-mediated environments: Conceptual foundations', *Journal of Marketing*, vol. 60, July, pp. 50–68.

Malone, T. W. & Laubacher, R. J. 1998, 'The dawn of the e-lance economy', *Harvard Business Review*, September–October, pp. 145–52.

Rae, N & Brennan, M. 1998. 'The relative effectiveness of sound and animation in Web banner advertisements', *Marketing Bulletin*, vol. 9, pp. 76–82.

Randall, D. 1997, 'Consumer strategies for the Internet: Four scenarios', *Long Range Planning*, vol. 30, no. 2, pp. 157–68.

Raymond, E. S. 1996, ' The New Hacker's Dictionary' (3rd Edition), MIT Press, Massachusetts.

Raymond, E. S. 2000, *The Jargon Manual Version 4.2.0*, http://www.tuxedo.org/~esr/jargon/

Shaw, G. B. 1944, *Everybody's Political What's What*, Dodd, Mead & Company, New York.

Swift, D. 2000, 'Flaws in outsourced e-commerce systems', *2600: The Hacker Quarterly*, vol. 17, no. 3, pp. 26–9.

Wilson, S. 1999, 'Digital signatures and the future of documentation' *Information Management and Computer Security*, vol. 7, no. 2, pp. 83–7.

Web sites

www.2600.com
www.altavista.com
www.amazon.com
www.aol.com
www.apple.com
www.crq.com
www.cs.umb.edu/jfklibrary/j071560.htm
www.digital.com
www.fed.gov
www.getcat.com
www.google.com
www.hotmail.com
www.ideavirus.com
www.infoseek.com
www.infoseek.de
www.internet2.com
www.microsoft.com
www.mozilla.org
www.napster.com
www.netscape.com
www.olympics.org
www.opensource.org
www.radioshack.com
www.slashdot.org
www.starwars.com
www.stevewaugh.com.au
www.usenet2.org

Academic references

CHAPTER 1 ■ *The* technological revolution

Dann, S. & Dann, S. 1999, 'Cybercommuning: Global village halls', *Advances in Consumer Research*, vol. 70.

Federal Networking Council 1995, *Resolution: Definition of 'Internet'*, www.fnc.gov/Internet_res.html

Gibson, W. 1984, *Neuromancer*, Ace Books, New York.

CHAPTER 2 ■ *Concepts* and terminology

Berners-Lee, T. 1989, 'Information Management: A Proposal', (www.w3.org/History/1989/proposal.html)

Dann, S. & Dann, S. 1998, 'Cybercommuning: Global village halls', *Advances in Consumer Research*, vol. 70.

Gibson, W. 1984, *Neuromancer*, Ace Books, New York.

Hoffman, D. L. & Novak, T. P. 1996, 'Marketing in hypermedia computer-mediated environments: Conceptual foundations', *Journal of Marketing*, vol. 60, no. 3, July, pp. 50–68.

Kaye, A. 1991, 'Learning together apart'. In A. Kaye (Ed.), *Collaborative Learning Through Computer Conferencing: The Najaden Papers* (pp. 1–24), Springer-Verlag, Berlin.

Montoya-Weiss, M., Massey, A. & Clapper, D. 1998, 'Online focus groups: Conceptual issues and a research tool', *European Journal of Marketing*, vol. 32, no. 7/8, pp. 713–23.

Munzer, T. 1997, 'H3: Laying out large directed graphs in 3D hyperbolic space', 1997 IEEE Symposium on Information Visualisation, October 20–21, Phoenix, AZ, pp. 2–10 (http://www-graphics.stanford.edu/papers/h3/)

Novak, T., Hoffman, D. & Yung, Y. F. 1998, 'Measuring the flow construct in online environments: A structural modelling approach', (http://www2000.ogsm.vanderbilt.edu/papers/flow_construct/measuring_flow_construct.html)

Raymond, E. S. 1999, *The Cathedral and the Bazaar*, O'Reilly, Sebastopol.

Rowley, J. 1996, 'Retailing and shopping on the Internet', *Internet Research: Electronic Networking Applications and Policy*, vol. 6, no. 1, pp. 81–91.

Shih, C.-f. 1998, 'Conceptualising consumer experience in cyberspace', *European Journal of Marketing*, vol. 32, no. 7/8, pp. 655–63.

Spalter, M. 1996, 'Maintaining a customer focus in an interactive age?'. In E. Forrest & R. Mizerski (Eds), *Interactive Marketing: The Future Present*, NTC Business Books, Lincolnwood, IL.

Steuer, J. 1992, 'Defining virtual reality: Dimensions determining telepresence', *Journal of Communication*, vol. 42, no. 4, pp. 73–93.

Varey, R. J. 1999, 'Marketing, media and McLuhan: Rereading the prophet at century's end', *Journal of Marketing*, vol. 63, no. 3, pp. 148–54.

Watson, R. T., Akselsen, S. & Pitt, L. F. 1998, 'Attractors: Building mountains in the flat landscape of the Internet',

California Management Review, vol. 40, no. 2, pp. 36–56.

Weiber & Kollman 1998, 'Competitive advantages in virtual markets — perspectives of "information-based marketing" in cyberspace', *European Journal of Marketing*, vol. 32, no. 7/8, pp. 603–15.

CHAPTER 3 ■ *Unique features of Internet-based marketing*

Arunkundram, R. & Sundararajan, A. 1998, 'An economic analysis of electronic secondary markets: Installed base, technology, durability and firm profitability', *Decision Support Systems*, vol. 24, pp. 3–16.

Bagozzi, R. 1975, 'Marketing as exchange', *Journal of Marketing*, vol. 39, October, pp. 32–9.

Breitenbach, C. S. & van Doren, D. C. 1998, 'Value-added marketing in the digital domain: Enhancing the utility of the Internet', *Journal of Consumer Marketing*, vol. 15, no. 6, pp. 558–75.

Ghose, S. & Dou, W. 1998, 'Interactive functions and their impacts on the appeal of Internet presence sites', *Journal of Advertising Research*, March, p. 28.

Gibson, W. 1984, *Neuromancer*, Ace Books, New York.

Hoffman, D. L. & Novak, T. P. 1996, 'Marketing in hypermedia computer-mediated environments: Conceptual foundations', *Journal of Marketing*, vol. 60, no. 3, July, pp. 50–68.

Holloway, M. 1997, 'Pattie', *Wired*, 5, 12 December.

Leong, E. K. F., Huang, X. & Stanners, P. J. 1998, 'Comparing the effectiveness of the web site with traditional media', *Journal of Advertising Research*.

Merlyn, P. R. & Välikangas, L. 1998, 'From information technology to knowledge technology: Taking the user into consideration' *Journal of Knowledge*

Management, vol. 2, no. 2, December, pp. 28–35.

Murphy, R. 1998, 'Case study: Schuh — Clothing for feet on the Web', *International Journal of Retail and Distribution Management*, vol. 26, no. 8, pp. 336–9.

O'Connor, G. C. & O'Keefe, B. 1997, 'Viewing the Web as a marketplace: The case of small companies' *Decision Support Systems*, vol. 21, no. 3, pp. 171–83.

Ovans, A. 1999, 'Is your web site socially savvy?', *Harvard Business Review*, May–June, pp. 20–1.

Paul, P. 1996, 'Marketing on the Internet', *Journal of Consumer Marketing*, vol. 13, no. 4, pp. 27–39.

Raman, N. V. & Leckenby, J. D. 1998, 'Factors affecting consumers' "Webad" visits', *European Journal of Marketing*, vol. 32, no. 7/8, pp. 737–48.

Ranchhod, A. 1998, 'Advertising into the next millennium', *International Journal of Advertising*, November, pp. 427–38.

Venkatesh, A. 1998, 'Cybermarketscapes and consumer freedoms and identities', *European Journal of Marketing*, vol. 32, no. 7/8, pp. 664–76.

www.wired.com/wired/archive/5.12/maes_pr.html

Winzar, H. 1999, 'Internet Editorial', *Journal of Marketing Practice: Applied Marketing Science*, vol. 5, no. 3, pp. 1–3.

Aggarwal, P., Cha, T. & Wilemon, D. 1998, 'Barriers to the adoption of really-new products and the role of surrogate buyers', *Journal of Consumer Marketing*, vol. 15, no. 4, pp. 358–71.

Alpert, F. 1994, 'Innovator buying behaviour over time: The innovator buying cycle and the cumulative effects of innovations', *Journal of Product and Brand Management*, vol. 3, no. 2, pp. 50–62.

Applebee, A. C., Clayton, P. & Pascoe, C. 1997, 'Australian academic use of the Internet', *Internet Research: Electronic Networking Applications and Policy*, vol. 7, no. 2, pp. 85–94.

Bass, F. M. 1969, 'A new product growth model for consumer durables', *Management Science*, vol. 15, pp. 215–27.

Bellman, S., Lohse, G. L. & Johnson, E. J. 1999, 'Predictors of on-line buying behaviour', *Communications of the ACM*, December, vol. 42, issue 12, p. 32.

Breitenbach, C. S. & van Doren, D. C. 1998, 'Value added marketing in the digital domain: Enhancing the utility of the Internet', *Journal of Consumer Marketing*, vol. 15, no. 6, pp. 558–75.

Browning, J. 1993, 'World Wide Web', *Wired* 1.03, July/August (online at www.wired.com/wired/archive/1.03/eword.html?pg=5).

Csikzentmihalyi, M. 1975, *Beyond Boredom and Anxiety*, Jossey-Bass, San Francisco.

Gregor, S. & Jones, K. 1999, 'Beef producers online: Diffusion theory applied', *Information Technology and People*, vol. 12, no. 1, pp. 71–85.

Hoffman, D. & Novak, T. 1996, 'Marketing in hypermedia computer-mediated environments: Conceptual foundations', *Journal of Marketing*, vol. 60, July, pp. 50–68.

Katz, J. & Aspden, P. 1997, 'Motivations for and barriers to Internet usage: Results of a national public opinion survey', *Internet Research: Electronic Networking Applications and Policy*, vol. 7, no. 3, pp. 170–88.

Kingsley, P. & Anderson, T. 1998, 'Facing life without the Internet', *Internet Research: Electronic Networking Applications and Policy*, vol. 8, no. 4, pp. 303–12.

Mahajan, V. & Peterson, R. A. 1985, *Models for Innovation Diffusion*, Sage Publications, London.

Marsden, P. 1998, 'Memetics: A new paradigm for understanding customer behaviour and influence', *Marketing Intelligence and Planning*, vol. 16, no. 6, pp. 363–68.

Nel, D., van Niekerk, R., Berthon, J. & Davies, T. 1999, 'Going with the flow: Web sites and customer involvement', *Internet Research: Electronic Networking Applications and Policy*, vol. 9, no. 2, pp. 109–16.

New Yorker, 1993, 'On the Internet, nobody knows you're a dog' [Editorial cartoon], *New Yorker*, 5 July 1993.

Parthasarathy, M., Jun, S. & Mittelstaedt, R. A. 1997, 'Multiple diffusion and multicultural aggregate social systems', *International Marketing Review*, vol. 14, no. 4, pp. 233–47.

Reisenwitz, T. H. & Cutler, B. D. 1998, 'Dogmatism and Internet usage by university students: Are dogmatics late adopters?', *Journal of Marketing Theory and Practice*, Summer, pp. 43–50.

Rogers, M. R. 1983, *Diffusion of Innovations*, 3rd edn, Macmillan, London.

Rogers, M. R. 1995, *Diffusion of Innovations*, 4th edn, Macmillan, London.

Venkatesh, A. 1998, 'Cybermarketscapes and consumer freedoms and identities', *European Journal of Marketing*, vol. 32, no. 7/8, pp. 664–76.

CHAPTER 5 ▪ *Creating* cybercommunities

Barnatt, C. 1998, 'Virtual communities and financial services — online business potential and strategic choice', *International Journal of Bank Marketing*, vol. 16, no. 4, pp. 161–9.

Buhalis, D. 2000, 'Marketing the competitive destination of the future', *Tourism Management*, vol. 21, pp. 97–116.

Cothrel, J. & Williams, R. L. 1999, 'Online communities: "Helping them form and grow"', *Journal of Knowledge Management*, vol. 3, no. 1, pp. 54–60.

Coyne, R. 1998, 'Cyberspace and Heidegger's pragmatics', *Information Technology and People*, vol. 11, no. 4, pp. 338–50.

Dann, S. & Dann, S. 1999, 'Cybercommuning: Global Village Halls', *Advances in Consumer Research*, vol. 70.

Figallo, C. 1998, *Hosting Web Communities: Building relationships, increasing customer loyalty and maintaining a competitive edge*, John Wiley, Brisbane.

Flores, F. 1998, 'Information technology and the institutions of identity: Reflections since "Understanding Computers and Cognition"', *Information Technology and People*, vol. 11, no. 4, pp. 351–72.

Gibson, W. 1984, *Neuromancer*, Ace Books, New York.

Hoffman, D. L. and Novak, T. P. 1996, 'Marketing in hypermedia computer-mediated environments: Conceptual foundations', *Journal of Marketing*, vol. 60, no. 3, July, pp. 50–68.

Horn, S. 1998, *Cyberville: Clicks, Culture, and the Creation of an Online Town*, Warner Books, New York.

Kaye, A. 1991, 'Learning together apart'. In A. Kaye (Ed.), *Collaborative Learning Through Computer Conferencing: The Najaden Papers* (pp. 1–24). Springer-Verlag, Berlin.

Kinsella, W. P. 1999, *Shoeless Joe*, Mariner Books, Chicago.

Powers, M. 1997, *How to program a virtual community*, Ziff-Davis Publishers, Seattle.

Rheingold, H. 1993, *The Virtual Community: Homesteading on the Electronic Frontier*, Harper-Collins, New York, p. 5.

Towell, J. F. & Towell, E. R. 1995, 'Internet conferencing with networked virtual environments', *Internet Research: Electronic Networking Applications and Policy*, vol. 5, no. 3, pp. 15–22.

Turkle, S. 1995, 'Life on the screen: Identity in the age of the Internet', Weidenfeld and Nicolson, London.

Whitly 1997, 'In cyberspace all they see is your words: A review of the relationship between body, behaviour and identity drawn from the sociology of knowledge', *Information Technology and People*, vol. 10, no. 2. pp. 147–63.

CHAPTER 6 ▪ *Applications* for business and non-business

Anon. 2000, 'Matt Handbury defends key homemaker turf', *B&T Weekly*, 4 February 2000, vol. 50, no. 2269, p. 1.

Bellman, S., Lohse, G. L. & Johnson, E. J. 1999, 'Predictors of online buying behaviour', *Communications of the ACM*, December, vol. 42, issue 12, p. 32.

Breitenbach, C. S. & van Doren, D. C. 1998, 'Value added marketing in the digital domain: Enhancing the utility of the Internet', *Journal of Consumer Marketing*, vol. 15, no. 6, pp. 558–75.

Buhalis, D. 2000, 'Marketing the competitive destination of the future', *Tourism Management*, vol. 21, pp. 97–116.

Cano, V. & Prentice, R. 1998, 'Opportunities for endearment to places through electronic "visiting": WWW home pages and the tourism promotion of Scotland', *Tourism Management*, vol. 19, no. 1, pp. 67–73.

Doherty, N. F., Ellis-Chadwick, F. & Hart, C. A. 1999, 'Cyberretailing in the UK: The potential of the Internet as a retail channel', *International Journal of Retail and Distribution Management*, vol. 27, no. 1, pp. 22–36.

Griffith, D. A. & Krampf, R. F. 1998, 'An examination of the web-based strategies of the top 100 US retailers', *Journal of Marketing Theory and Practice*, Summer, pp. 12–23.

Hoffman, D. & Novak, T. 1996, 'Marketing in hypermedia computer-mediated environments: Conceptual foundations', *Journal of Marketing*, vol. 60, July, pp. 50–68.

Honeycutt, E. D., Flaherty, T. B. & Benassi, K. 1998, 'Marketing Industrial Products on the Internet', *Industrial Marketing Management*, vol. 27, pp. 63–72.

Landry, T. 1998, 'Electronic Commerce: A New Take on Web Shopping', *Harvard Business Review*, July–August, pp. 16–17.

O'Keefe, R. M., O'Connor, G. & Kung H. J. 1998, 'Early adopters of the Web as a retail medium: Small company winners and losers', *European Journal of Marketing*, vol. 32, no. 7/8, pp. 629–43.

Raman, N. V. & Leckenby, J. D. 1998, 'Factors affecting consumers' "Webad" visits', *European Journal of Marketing*, vol. 32, no. 7/8, pp. 737–48.

Samiee, S. 1998, 'Exporting and the Internet: A conceptual perspective', *International Marketing Review*, vol. 15, no. 5, pp. 413–26.

CHAPTER 7 ■ *Internet* in marketing strategy

Arunkundram, R. & Sundararajan, A. 1998, 'An economic analysis of electronic secondary markets: Installed base, technology, durability and firm profitability, *Decision Support Systems*, vol. 24, pp. 3–16.

Bayne, K. M. 2000, *The Internet Marketing Plan*, 2nd edn, Wiley, New York.

Belch, G. E. & Belch, M. A. 1997, *Introduction to Advertising and Promotion: An Integrated Marketing Communications Perspective*, 4th edn, Richard D. Irwin Publishers, Sydney.

Brassington, F. & Pettitt, S. 1997, *Principles of Marketing*, Pitman Publishing, Melbourne.

Gilbert, D. C., Powell-Perry, J. & Widijoso, S. 1999, 'Approaches by hotels to the use of the Internet as a relationship marketing tool', *Journal of Marketing Practice: Applied Marketing Science*, vol. 5, no. 1, pp. 21–38.

Griffith, D. A. & Krampf, R. F. 1998, 'An examination of the web based strategies of the top 100 US retailers', *Journal of Marketing Theory and Practice*, Summer, pp. 12–23.

Honeycutt, E. D., Flaherty, T. B. & Benassi, K. 1998, 'Marketing Industrial Products on the Internet', *Industrial Marketing Management*, vol. 27, pp. 63–72.

Kalakota, R. & Robinson, M. 1999, *e-Business: Roadmap for Success*, Addison-Wesley, Sydney.

Leong, E. K. F., Huang, X. & Stanners, P. J. 1998, 'Comparing the Effectiveness of the Web Site with Traditional Media', *Journal of Advertising Research*, vol. 38, no. 4, pp. 44–57.

O'Connor, G. C. & O'Keefe, B. 1997. 'Viewing the Web as a marketplace: The case of small companies'. *Decision Support Systems*, vol. 21, no. 3, pp. 171–83.

Pavitt, D. 1997, 'Retailing and the super high street: The future of the electronic home shopping industry', *International Journal of Retail and Distribution Management*, vol. 25, no. 1, pp. 38–46.

Porter. M. E. 1980, *Competitive Strategy*, The Free Press, New York.

Raymond, E. S. 1996, *The New Hacker's Dictionary*, 3rd edn, MIT Press, Boston.

Raymond, E. S. 1999, *The Cathedral and the Bazaar*, O'Reilly, Sebastopol.

Raymond, E. S. 2000, 'The Jargon Manual', Version 4.2.0.

http://www.tuxedo.org/~esr/jargon/

Sarabia, F. J. 1996, 'Model for markets segments evaluation and selection', *European Journal of Marketing*, vol. 30, no. 4, pp. 58–74.

Schlegelmich, B. B. & Sinkovics, R. 1998, 'Viewpoint: Marketing in the information age — can we plan for an unpredictable future?' *International Marketing Review*, vol. 15, no. 3, pp 162–70.

Sen, S., Padmanabhan, B, Tuzhilin, A., While N. H. & Stein, R. 1998, 'The identification and satisfaction of consumer analysis-driven information needs of marketers on the WWW', *European Journal of Marketing*, vol. 32, no. 7/8, pp. 688–702.

Simeon, R. 1999, 'Evaluating Domestic and International Web site strategies', *Internet Research: Electronic Networking Applications and Policy*, vol. 9, no. 4, pp. 297–308.

Viljoen, J. & Dann, S. 2000, *Strategic Management: Planning and Implementing Successful Corporate Strategies*, Addison-Wesley Longman, Sydney.

CHAPTER 8 ■ *The role of product in Internet marketing*

Anschuetz, N. F. 1996, 'Evaluating ideas and concepts for new consumer products'. In Rosenau, M. D., Griffin, A., Castellion, G. & Anschuetz, N., *The PDMA Handbook of New Product Development*, John Wiley. New York.

Bayne, K. M. 2000, *The Internet Marketing Plan*, 2nd edition, John Wiley, New York.

Beard, C. & Easingwood, C. 1999, 'Sources of competitive advantage in the marketing of technology-intensive products and processes', *European Journal of Marketing*, vol. 26, no. 12, pp. 5–18.

Boike, D. & Staley, J. 1996, 'Developing a strategy and plan for a new product. In Rosenau, M. D., Griffin, A., Castellion, G. & Anschuetz, N., *The PDMA Handbook of New Product Development*, John Wiley, New York.

Booz-Allen & Hamilton Inc. 1982, *New Product Management for the 1980s*, Booz-Allen & Hamilton Inc., New York.

Durgee, J., O'Connor, G. & Veryzer, R. 1998, 'Using mini-concepts to identify opportunities for really new product functions', *Journal of Consumer Marketing*, vol. 15, no.6, pp. 525–43.

Fiskel, J. & Hayes-Roth, F. 1993, 'Computer-aided requirements management', *Concurrent Engineering: Research and Applications*, vol. 1, no. 2, pp. 83–92.

Freiden, J., Goldsmith, R., Takacs, S. & Hofacker, C. 1998, 'Information as product: not goods, not services', *Marketing Intelligence and Planning*, vol. 16, no. 3, pp. 210–20.

Fojt, M. 1996, 'Virtual Frontiers', *Internet Research: Electronic Networking Applications and Policy*, vol. 6, no. 2/3, pp. 82–4.

Gill, B., Nelson, B. & Spring, S. 1996, 'Seven steps to strategic new product development'. In Rosenau, M. D., Griffin, A., Castellion, G. & Anschuetz, N., *The PDMA Handbook of New Product Development*, John Wiley, New York.

Jiao, J. & Tseng, M. 1999, 'A requirement management database system for product definition', *Integrated Manufacturing Systems*, vol. 10, no. 3, pp.146–53.

Kotler, P. & Armstrong, G. 1994, *Principles of Marketing*, 5th edition, Englewood Cliffs, NJ, Prentice-Hall.

Lawless, M. & Fisher, R. 1990, 'Sources of durable competitive advantage in new products', *Journal of Product Innovation Management*, vol. 7, pp. 35–44.

Levitt, T. 1960, 'Marketing myopia', *Harvard Business Review*, vol. 38, no. 4, July/August, pp. 45–56

Massey, G. 1999, 'Product evolution: A Darwinian or Lamarckian phenomenon?', *Journal of Product and Brand Management*, vol. 8, no. 4, pp. 301–18.

McColl-Kennedy, J. R. & Kiel, G. C. 2000, *Marketing: A Strategic Approach*, Nelson ITP, Melbourne.

Olson, D. 1996, 'Postlaunch evaluation for consumer goods', Rosenau, M. D., Griffin, A., Castellion, G. & Anschuetz, N., *The PDMA Handbook of New Product Development*, John Wiley, New York.

Peterson, R., Balasubramanian, A & Bronnenberg, B. 1997, 'Exploring the implications of the Internet for consumer marketing', *Journal of the Academy of Marketing Science*, vol. 25, no. 4, pp. 329–46.

Phau, I. & Poon, S. 2000, 'Factors influencing products and services purchased over the Internet', *Internet Research: Electronic Networking Applications and Policy*, vol. 10, no. 2, pp. 102–11.

Reedy, J., Schullo, S. & Zimmerman, K. 2000, *Electronic Marketing: Integrating Electronic Resources into the Marketing Process*, Dryden Press, Fort Worth.

Rosenau, M. D 1996, 'Choosing a development process that's right for your company'. In Rosenau, M. D., Griffin, A., Castellion, G. & Anschuetz, N., *The PDMA Handbook of New Product Development*, John Wiley, New York.

Samli, A. & Weber, J. 2000, 'A theory of successful product breakthrough management: Learning from success', *Journal of Product & Brand Management*, vol. 9, no. 1, pp. 35–55.

Shillito, M. & Demarle, D. 199), *Value, Its Measurement, Design and Management*, John Wiley, New York.

Strauss, J. & Frost, R. 1999, *Marketing on the Internet: Principles of On-line Marketing*, Prentice-Hall, New Jersey.

Valentin, E. 1994, 'Commentary: Marketing research pitfalls in product development', *Journal of Product & Brand Management*, vol. 3, no. 4, pp. 66–9.

Wilson, E. 1994, 'Improving marketing success rates through better product definition', *World Class Design to Manufacture*, vol.1, no.4, pp. 13–15.

CHAPTER 9 ■ *Promotion 1:* Internet in promotional mix

Adam, S. 1996 , *The Dilbert Principle*, Harper Business, New York.

Adler, S. 1999, 'The Slashdot Effect', *Linux Gazette*, http://www.linuxgazette.com/issue38/adler1.html.

Aitchison, J. & French-Blake, N. 1999, *Cutting Edge Advertising: How to Create the World's Best Print for Brands in the 21st Century*, Prentice-Hall, Sydney.

Belch, G. E. & Belch, M. A. 1997, *Introduction to Advertising and Promotion: An Integrated Marketing Communications Perspective*, 4th edition, Richard D. Irwin Publishers, New York.

Dieberger, A. 1997, 'Supporting social navigation on the world wide web', *International Journal of Human–Computer Studies*, vol. 46, pp. 805–25.

Hofacker, C. F. & Murphy, J. 1998, 'World Wide Web banner copy testing', *European Journal of Marketing*, vol. 32, no. 7/8, 1998, pp. 703–12.

Kiani, G. 1998, 'Marketing Opportunities in the Digital World', *Internet Research: Electronic Networking Applications and Policy*, vol. 8, no. 2, pp. 185–94.

Kotler, P. & Roberto, E. 1989, *Social Marketing: Strategies for Changing Public Behaviour*, Macmillan, New York.

Rae, N., & Brennan, M. 1998, 'The relative effectiveness of sound and animation in Web banner advertisements'. *Marketing Bulletin*, vol. 9, pp. 76–82.

CHAPTER 10 ■ *Promotion 2:* The Internet as a promotional medium

Abels, E. G., White, M. D. & Hahn, K. 1997, A user based design process for Web Sites, *Internet Research: Electronic Networking Applications and Policy*, vol. 8, no. 1, 39–48.

Aitchison, J. & French-Blake, N., 1999, *Cutting Edge Advertising: How to Create the World's Best Print for Brands in the 21st Century*, Prentice-Hall, Sydney.

Dholakia, U. M. & Rego, L. L. 1998, What makes commercial web pages popular? An empirical investigation of Web page effectiveness, *European Journal of Marketing*, vol. 32, no. 7/8, pp. 724–36.

Ju-Pak, K. 1999, Content dimensions of web advertising: a cross-national comparison, *International Journal of Advertising*, vol. 18, pp. 207–31.

Lu, M. & Yeung, W. 1998, *A framework for effective, Internet Research: Electronic Networking Applications and Policy.* vol. 8, no. 2, pp. 115–22.

O'Connor, G. C. & O'Keefe, B. 1997, Viewing the Web as a market-place: the case of small companies, *Decision Support Systems*, vol. 21, no. 3, pp. 171–83.

Palmer, J. W. & Griffith, D.A. 1998, An emerging model of web site design for marketing, *Communications of the ACM*, vol. 41, no. 3, p. 44–52.

Patterson, M. 1998, Direct marketing in postmodernity: Neo-tribes and direct communications, *Marketing Intelligence and Planning*, vol. 16, no. 1, pp. 68–74.

Pope, N. & Forrest, E. 1997, A Proposed Format For The Management Of Sport Marketing Web Sites, *Cyberjournal of Sports Marketing*, vol. 1, no. 1, http://www.cjsm.com/Vol1/Pope&Forrest.htm

Raman, N. V. & Leckenby, J. D. 1998, 'Factors affecting consumers' "Webad" visits', *European Journal of Marketing*, vol. 32, no. 7/8, pp. 737–48.

Ranchhod, A. 1998, 'Advertising into the next millennium', *International Journal of Advertising*, November, vol. 1, pp. 427–38.

Raymond, E. S. 1996, *The New Hacker's Dictionary* (3rd edition), MIT Press, Massachusetts.

Raymond, E. S. 2000, 'The Jargon Manual' Version 4.2.0 http://www.tuxedo.org/~esr/jargon/

Wan, H. A. & Chung, C. 1998, 'Web page design and network analysis', *Internet Research: Electronic Networking Applications and Policy*, vol. 8, no. 2, pp. 115–22.

Watson, R. T., Akselsen, S. & Pitt, L. F. 1998, 'Attractors: Building mountains in the flat landscape of the Internet', *California Management Review*, vol. 40, no. 2, pp. 36–56.

CHAPTER 11 ■ *Pricing* strategies

Alba, J., Lynch, J., Weitz, B., Janiszewski, R., Saywer, A. and Wood, S. 1997, 'Interactive home shopping: consumer, retailer, and manufacturer incentives to participate in electronic marketplaces', *Journal of Marketing*, vol. 61, July, pp. 38–54.

Baker, M. J., Graham, P. G., Harker, D. & Harker, M. 1998, *Marketing: Managerial Foundations*, MacMillan Education, Melbourne.

Betts, E. J. and Goldrick, P. J. 1996, 'Consumer behaviours and the retail sales: modelling the development of an "attitude problem"', *European Journal of Marketing*, vol. 30, no. 8, pp. 40–58.

Brassington, F. & Pettitt, S. 1997, *Principles of Marketing*, Pitman Publishing, Melbourne.

Calantone, R. & Sawyer, A. G. 1978, 'The stability of benefit segment', *Journal of Marketing Research*, vol. 15, no. 3, pp. 395–404.

Carson, D., Gilmore, A., Cummins, D., O'Donnell, A. & Grant, K. 1998, 'Price setting in SMEs: some empirical findings', *Journal of Product and Brand Management*, vol. 7, no. 1, pp. 74–86.

Estelami, H., 1998 '*The Price is Right . . . or is it?* Demographic and category effects on consumer price knowledge', *Journal of Product and Brand Management*, vol. 7, no. 3, pp. 254–66.

Fine, S. H. 1990, *Social Marketing: Promoting the Causes of Public and Non-profit Agencies*, Allyn and Bacon, Boston.

Hofacker, C. F. 2000, *Internet Marketing 3rd Edition*, John Wiley & Sons, New York.

Kotler, P. 1997, *Marketing Management: Analysis, Planning, Implementation and Control*, Prentice Hall, Englewood Cliffs.

Krishna, A., Currim, I. S. & Shoemaker, R. W. 1991, 'Consumer perceptions of promotional activity', *Journal of Marketing*, vol. 55, no. 2, pp.4–16.

Lovelock, C., Patterson, P. & Walker, R. 1998, *Services Marketing: Australia and New Zealand*, Prentice-Hall, Sydney.

McCarthy, E. J., Perrault, W. D. & Quester, P. G. 1997, *Basic Marketing: A Managerial Approach*, Irwin, Sydney.

McColl-Kennedy, J. R. & Kiel, G. C. 2000, *Marketing: A Strategic Approach*, Nelson ITP, Melbourne.

Monger, J. E. & Feinberg. R. A. 1997 'Mode of payment and formation of reference prices', *Pricing Strategy and Practice*, vol. 5, no. 4, pp. 142–7.

Mougayar, W. 1997, *Opening Digital Markets*, McGraw-Hill, New York.

Ovans, A.1999, 'Taxing the Web', *Harvard Business Review*, July–August, pp. 18–19.

Peattie, K. & Peters, L. 1997, 'The marketing mix in the third age of computing', *Marketing Intelligence and Planning*, vol. 15, no.3, pp. 142–50.

Raymond, E. S. 1999, *The Cathedral and the Bazaar*, O'Reilly, Sebastopol.

Reedy, J., Schullo, S. & Zimmerman, K. 2000, *Electronic Marketing: Integrating Electronic Resources into the Marketing Process*, Dryden Press, Fort Worth.

Smith, M. F., Sinha, I., Lancioni, R. & Forman, H. 1999, 'Role of market turbulence in shaping pricing', *Industrial Marketing Management*, vol. 28, pp. 637–49.

Strader, T. J. & Shaw, M. J. 1997, 'Characteristics of electronic markets', *Decision Support Systems*, vol. 21, pp.185–98.

Strader, T. J. & Shaw, M. J. 1999, 'Consumer cost differences for traditional and Internet markets', *Internet Research: Electronic Networking Applications and Policy*, vol. 9, no. 2 pp. 82–92.

Strauss, J. & Frost, R. 1999, *Marketing on the Internet: Principles of Online Marketing*, Prentice-Hall, New Jersey.

Uncles, M. D. & Ehrenberg, A. S. 1990, 'Brand choice among older consumers', *Journal of Advertising Research*, vol. 30, no. 4, pp.19–22.

Van den Poel, D., & Leunis, J. 1999, 'Consumer acceptance of the Internet as a channel of distribution', *Journal of Business Research*, vol. 45, pp. 249–56.

Wakefield, K. L. & Inman, J. J. 1993,
'Who are the price vigilantes? An
investigation of differentiating
characteristics influencing price
information processing', *Journal of
Retailing*, vol. 69, no. 2, pp. 216–33.

Winker, J. 1991, 'Pricing'. In M. J. Baker
(ed.), *The Marketing Book 2nd edition*,
Butterworth-Heinemann, Oxford.

CHAPTER 12 *Distribution*

Fine, S. H. 1990, *Social Marketing:
Promoting the Causes of Public and
Non-profit Agencies*, Allyn and Bacon,
Boston.

Gibson, W. 1989, *Neuromancer*, Ace
Books, New York.

Jones, J. M. & Vijayasarthy, L. R. 1998,
'Internet consumer catalogue shopping:
findings from an exploratory study and
directions for future research', *Internet
Research: Electronic Networking
Applications and Policy*, vol. 8, no. 4,
pp. 322–30.

Kostopoulos, G. K. (1998), 'Global delivery
of education via the Internet', *Internet
Research: Electronic Networking
Applications and Policy*, vol. 8, no. 3,
pp. 257–65.

Kotler, P. & Roberto, E. 1989, *Social
Marketing: Strategies for Changing
Public Behaviour*, Macmillan, New York.

Mason–Jones, R. & Towill, D. R. 1997,
'Information enrichment: designing the
supply chain for competitive advantage',
Supply Chain Management, vol. 2, no. 4,
pp. 137–48.

Mols, N. P. 1998, 'The Internet and the
banks' strategic distribution channel
decisions', *Internet Research: Electronic
Networking Applications and Policy*,
vol. 8, no. 4, 331–37.

Negroponte, N. 1995, 'Bits and Atoms',
Wired 3.01 (http://www.wired.com/wired/
archive/3.01/negroponte.html)

Palumbo, F, & Herbig, P. 1998, 'International
marketing tool: the Internet', *Industrial
Management and Data Systems*, vol. 6,
pp. 253–61.

Pattinson, H., & Brown, L. 1996, '
Chameleons in marketspace: industry
transformation in the new electronic
marketing environment', *Internet
Research: Electronic Networking
Applications and Policy*, vol. 6, no. 2/3,
pp. 31–40.

Porter 1985 in Weiber & Kollman 1998,
'Competitive advantages in virtual
markets — perspective of "information-
based marketing" in cyberspace',
European Journal of Marketing, vol. 32,
no. 7/8, pp. 603–15.

Raymond, E. S. 1999, *The Cathedral and
the Bazaar*. O'Reilly, Sebastopol.

Rayport, J. F. & Sviokla, J. J. 1994, 'Managing
in the marketspace', *Harvard Business
Review*, vol. 72, no. 6, pp. 141–50.

Van den Poel, D. & Leunis, J. 1999,
'Consumer Acceptance of the Internet
as a Channel of Distribution', *Journal of
Business Research*, vol. 45, pp. 249–56.

Weiber & Kollman 1998, 'Competitive
advantages in virtual markets —
perspectives of "information-based
marketing" in cyberspace', *European
Journal of Marketing*, vol. 32, no. 7/8,
p. 603–15.

White, G. K. 1997, 'International on-line
marketing of foods to US consumers',
International Marketing Review, vol. 14,
no. 5, pp. 376–84.

CHAPTER 13 *Services marketing online*

Anon. 1996, 'Banking on the Internet',
Internet Research: Electronic

Networking Applications and Policy,
vol. 6, no. 1, pp. 31–2.

Bateson, J. 1996, *Managing Services Marketing Text and Readings (3rd edition)*, Dryden, Fort Worth.

Bebko, C. 2000, 'Service intangibility and its impact on consumer expectations of service quality', *The Journal of Services Marketing*, vol. 14, no. 1, pp. 9–26.

Brindley, C. 1999, 'The marketing of gambling on the Internet', *Internet Research: Electronic Networking Applications and Policy*, vol. 9, no. 4, pp. 281–6.

Clark, T. & Rajaratnam, D. 1999, 'International services: Perspectives at century's end', *Journal of Services Marketing*, vol. 13, no. 4/5, pp. 298–310.

Fisk, R. 1999, 'Wiring and growing the technology of international services marketing', *Journal of Services Marketing*, vol. 13, no. 4/5, pp. 311–18.

Fisk, R., Grove, S. & John. J. 2000, *Interactive Services Marketing*, Houghton Mifflin, Boston.

Hofacker, C. 2000, *Internet Marketing*, 3rd edition, Wiley, New York.

Knowles-Mathur, L., Mathur, I. & Gleason, K. 1998, 'Service advertising and providing services on the Internet', *The Journal of Services Marketing*, vol. 12, no. 5, pp. 334–47.

Langford, B. & Cosenza, R. 1998, 'What is service/good analysis?', *Journal of Marketing Theory and Practice*, Winter, pp. 16–26.

Lovelock, C., Patterson, P. & Walker, R. 1998, *Services Marketing*, Prentice-Hall, Sydney.

McColl-Kennedy, J. R. & Kiel, G. C. 2000, *Marketing: A Strategic Approach*, Nelson ITP, Melbourne.

McColl-Kennedy, J. & Fetter, R. 1999, 'Dimensions of consumer search behaviour in services', *Journal of Services Marketing*, vol. 13, no. 3, pp. 242–65.

McGuire, L. 1999, *Australian Services: Marketing and Management*, MacMillan, Melbourne.

Mitra, K., Reiss, M. & Capella, L. 1999, 'An examination of perceived risk, information search and behavioural intentions in search, experience and credence services', *Journal of Services Marketing*, vol. 13, no. 3, pp. 208–28.

Reedy, J., Schullo, S. & Zimmerman, K. 2000, *Electronic Marketing: Integrating Electronic Resources into the Marketing Process*, Dryden Press, Fort Worth.

Shostack, G. 1977, 'Breaking free from product marketing', *Journal of Marketing*, vol. 41, pp. 73–80.

Strauss, J. & Frost, R. 1999, *Marketing on the Internet: Principles of Online Marketing*, Prentice-Hall, New Jersey.

Venkatraman, M. & Dholakia, R. 1997, 'Searching for information in marketspace: Does the form — product or service — matter?', *Journal of Services Marketing*, vol. 11, no. 5, pp. 301–16.

Wikstrom, S. 1996, 'The customer as co-producer', *European Journal of Marketing*, vol. 30, no. 4, pp. 6–13.

Woodruffe, H. 1995, *Services Marketing*, Pitman, London.

Wright, L. 1995, 'Avoiding services marketing myopia'. In W. Glynn & J. Barnes (eds), *Understanding Services Management*, Wiley, Chichester.

Zeithaml, V. & Bitner, M. 1996, *Services Marketing*, McGraw Hill, New York.

CHAPTER 14 ■ ***Relationship*** *marketing in a 'one-to-many-to-one' environment*

Arunkundram, R. & Sundararajan, A. 1998, 'An economic analysis of electronic secondary markets: Installed base, technology, durability and firm profitability', *Decision Support Systems*, vol. 24, pp. 3–16.

Bagozzi, R. 1975, 'Marketing as exchange', *Journal of Marketing*, vol. 39, October, pp. 32–9.

Gilbert, D. C., Powell-Perry, J. & Widijoso, S. 1999, 'Approaches by hotels to the use of the Internet as a relationship marketing tool', *Journal of Marketing Practice: Applied Marketing Science*, vol. 5, no. 1, 1999, pp. 21–38.

Grönross, C. 1994, 'From marketing mix to relationship marketing: Towards a paradigm shift in marketing', *Management Decision*, vol. 32, no. 2, pp. 4–20.

Harker, M. J. 1999, 'Relationship marketing defined? An examination of current relationship marketing definitions', *Marketing Intelligence and Planning*, vol. 17, no. 1, pp. 13–20.

Jevons, C. & Gabbott, M. 2000, 'Trust, brand equity and brand reality in Internet business relationships: An interdisciplinary approach', *Journal of Marketing Management*, vol. 16, pp. 619–34.

Moorman, C., Deshpande, R. & Zaltman, G. 1993, 'Factors affecting trust in market research relationship', *Journal of Marketing*, vol. 57, January, pp. 81–101.

Morgan, R. M. & Hunt, S. D. 1994, 'The commitment–trust theory of relationship marketing', *Journal of Marketing*, vol. 58, July, pp. 20–38.

New Yorker, 1993, 'On the Internet, nobody knows you're a dog' [Editorial cartoon], *New Yorker*, 5 July 1993.

Ratnasingham, P. 1998, 'The importance of trust in electronic commerce', *Internet Research*, vol. 8, no. 4, pp. 313–21.

Tseng, S. & Fogg, B. J. 1999, 'Credibility and computing technology', *Communications of the ACM*, vol. 42, no. 5, pp. 39–46.

Turban, E., Lee, J., King, D. & Chung, H. M. 2000, *Electronic commerce: A managerial perspective*, Prentice-Hall, New Jersey.

Wetzels, M., de Ruyter, K. & van Birgelen, M. 1998, 'Marketing service relationships: The role of commitment', *Journal of Business and Industrial Marketing*, vol. 13, no. 4/5, pp. 406–23.

Yoffie, D. & Cusumano, M. A. 1999, 'Building a company on Internet time: Lessons from Netscape', *California Management Review*, vol. 41, no. 3, pp. 8–28.

CHAPTER 15 ■ *International* marketing

Andersen, O. 1993, 'On the internationalisation process of firms: A critical analysis', *Journal of International Business Studies*, vol. 24, no. 2, pp. 209–31.

Bennett, R. 1997, 'Export marketing and the Internet: Experiences of web site use and perceptions of export barriers among UK businesses', *International Marketing Review*, vol. 14, no. 5, pp. 324–44.

Bishop, B. 1999, *Global Marketing for the Digital Age*, NTC Business Books, Chicago.

Ger, G. 1999, 'Localising in the global village: Local firms competing in global markets', *California Management Review*, vol. 14, no. 4, pp. 64–83.

Golden, P. A. & Dollinger, M. 1993, 'Cooperative alliances and competitive strategies in small manufacturing firms', *Entrepreneurship Theory and Practice*, Summer, pp. 43–56.

Hamill, J. 1997, 'The Internet and international marketing', *International Marketing Review*, vol. 14, no. 5, pp. 300–23.

Hamill, J. & Gregory, K. 1997, 'Internet marketing in the internationalization of UK SMEs', *Journal of Marketing Management*. In J. Hamill (ed.), Special Edition on Internationalisation, vol. 13, no. 1–3, January–April.

Jain, S. 1989, 'Reducing the risks of globalization', *Long Range Planning*, vol. 53, February, pp. 80–8.

Jevons, C. 2000, 'Misplaced marketing', *Journal of Consumer Marketing*, vol. 17, no. 1, pp. 7–8.

Levitt, T. 1983, 'The globalisation of markets', *Harvard Business Review*, vol. 61, May–June, pp. 92–102.

Palumbo, F. & Herbig, P. 1998, 'International marketing tool: The Internet', *Industrial Management and Data Systems*, vol. 6, pp. 253–61.

Poon, S. & Jevons, C. 1997, 'Internet-enabled international marketing: A small business network approach', *Journal of Marketing Management*, vol. 13, pp. 29–41.

Quelch, J. & Klein, L. 1996, 'The Internet and international marketing', *Sloan Management Review*, vol. 37 (Spring), pp. 60–75.

Quester, P., McGuiggan, R., Perrault, E. J. & McCarthy, W. 2001, *Basic Marketing: A Managerial Approach (3rd Australasian Edition)*, McGraw–Hill, Sydney.

Ramarapu, S., Timmerman, J. & Ramarapu, N. 1999, 'Choosing between globalisation and localisation as a strategic thrust for your international marketing effort', *Journal of Marketing Theory and Practice*, Spring, pp. 97–105.

Samiee, S. 1998, 'Exporting and the Internet: A conceptual perspective', *International Marketing Review*, vol. 15, no. 5, pp. 413–26.

Samli, A., Wills, J. & Herbig, P. 1997, 'The information superhighway goes international: Implications for industrial sales transactions', *Industrial Marketing Management*, vol. 26, pp. 51–8.

Simmonds, K. 1999, 'International marketing — avoiding the seven deadly traps', *Journal of International Marketing*, vol. 7, no. 2, pp. 51–62.

CHAPTER 16 ■ *Marketing* research

Forrest, E. 1999, *Internet Marketing Research: Resources and Techniques*, McGraw-Hill, Sydney.

Hofacker, C. & Murphy, J. 1998, 'World Wide Web banner advertisement copy testing', *European Journal of Marketing*, vol. 32, no. 7/8, pp. 713–23.

Lynn, G. S., Maltz, A. C., Jurkat, P. M. & Hammer, M. D. 1999, 'New media in marketing redefine competitive advantage: A comparison of small and large firms', *The Journal Of Services Marketing*, vol. 13, no. 1, pp. 9–20.

Montoya-Weiss, M., Massey, A. & Clapper, D. 1998, 'Online focus groups: Conceptual issues and a research tool', *European Journal of Marketing*, vol. 32, no. 7/8, pp. 713–23.

Novak, T., Hoffman, D. & Yung, Y. F. 1998, 'Measuring the flow construct in online environments: A structural modelling approach',

http://www2000.ogsm.vanderbilt.edu/papers/flow_construct/measuring_flow_construct.html

Parackal, M. & Brennan, M. 1999, 'Obtaining Purchase Probabilities via a Web-Based Survey: Some Corrections!' *Marketing Bulletin*, 10, pp. 93–101.

Sarabia, F. J. 1996, 'Model for markets segments evaluation and selection', *European Journal of Marketing*, vol. 30, no. 4, pp. 58–74.

Shih, C.-f. 1998, 'Conceptualising consumer experience in cyberspace', *European Journal of Marketing*, vol. 32 no. 7/8, pp. 655–63.

Steuer, J. 1992, 'Defining virtual reality: Dimensions determining telepresence', *Journal of Communication*, 42 (4), pp. 73–93.

Adler, S. 1999, 'The Slashdot Effect', *Linux Gazette*, http://www.linuxgazette.com/issue38/adler1.html

Genieva, E. 1997, 'Legal aspects of the Internet', *International Information and Library Review*, vol. 29, pp. 381–92.

Goldstein, E. 2000, 'A summer of trials', *2600: The Hacker Quarterly*, vol 17, no. 3, pp. 4–5, 47.

Hoffman, D. & Novak, T. 1996, 'Marketing in hypermedia computer-mediated environments: Conceptual foundations', *Journal of Marketing*, vol. 60, July, pp. 50–68.

Malone, T. W. & Laubacher, R. J. 1998, 'The dawn of the e-lance economy', *Harvard Business Review*, September–October, pp. 145–52.

Rae, N & Brennan, M. 1998. 'The relative effectiveness of sound and animation in Web banner advertisements', *Marketing Bulletin*, vol. 9, pp. 76–82.

Randall, D. 1997, 'Consumer strategies for the Internet: Four scenarios', *Long Range Planning*, vol. 30, no. 2, pp. 157–68.

Raymond, E. S. 1996, ' The New Hacker's Dictionary' (*3rd edition*), MIT Press, Massachusetts.

Raymond, E. S. 2000, *The Jargon Manual Version 4.2.0*, http://www.tuxedo.org/~esr/jargon/

Shaw, G. B. 1944, *Everybody's Political What's What*, Dodd, Mead & Company, New York.

Swift, D. 2000, 'Flaws in outsourced e-commerce systems', *2600: The Hacker Quarterly*, vol. 17, no. 3, pp. 26–9.

Wilson, S. 1999, 'Digital signatures and the future of documentation' *Information Management and Computer Security*, vol. 7, no. 2, pp. 83–7.

Appendix: useful web sites

CHAPTER 1 ■ *The* technological revolution

http://chatcity.com.au	*Ozemail*
http://lynx.browser.org	*Lynx*
www.bpftp.com	*BulletProof Software*
www.eudora.com	*Eudora Software*
www.fnc.gov	*The Federal Networking Council*
www.fnc.gov/Internet_res.html	*Federal Networking Council*
www.gnutelliums.com	*Gnutelliums*
www.go.com	*Disney Enterprises*
www.hotmail.com	*Microsoft Corporation*
www.ichat.com	*Ichat Inc.*
www.icq.com	*ICQ*
www.insidetheweb.com	*LookSmart Ltd.*
www.ircle.com	*MacResponse*
www.isoc.org	*Internet Society*
www.isoc.org/internet/history/	*Internet Society*
www.jpilot.com	*JPilot IRC*
www.livinginternet.com	*The Living Internet*
www.microsoft.com	*Microsoft Corporation*
www.mirc.co.uk	*mIRC Co. Ltd*
www.mudconnector.com	*The Mud Connector*
www.napster.com	*Napster*
www.ncsa.uiuc.edu/SDG/Software/Mosaic/	*National Center for Supercomputing Applications*
www.netscape.com	*Netscape*
www.stormwrestling.com/comments/	*Lance Storm*
www.tucows.com	*Tucows Inc.*

▪	www.usenet.org	*WebMagic Inc.*
▪	www.w3.org	*World Wide Web Consortium*
▪	www.washington.edu/pine/	*Pine Information Centre*

CHAPTER 2 ▪ *Concepts* and terminology

▪	cospace.research.att.com	*Cospace*
▪	geocities.yahoo.com	*Yahoo!*
▪	www.airwalk.com	*Airwalk*
▪	www.casio.com/audio	*Casio Inc.*
▪	www.chatcity.com	*Chat City*
▪	www.cybergeography.com	*Martin Dodge*
▪	www.gloriajeans.com	*Gloria Jean's Gourmet Coffees Corporation*
▪	www.heat.net	*Sega.com, Inc.*
▪	www.heretherebemonsters.com	*Apathy International*
▪	www.hotmail.com	*Microsoft Corporation*
▪	www.hungryjacks.com.au	*Burger King Corporation*
▪	www.hwg.org	*HTML Writers Guild, Inc.*
▪	www.idsoftware.com	*id Software, Inc.*
▪	www.itl.nist.gov/iaui/vvrg/index.html	*National Institute of Standards and Technology*
▪	www.mozilla.org	*The Mozilla Organisation*
▪	www.nike.com	*Nike*
▪	www.petersharpe.com	*Peter Sharpe*
▪	www.pizzahut.com.au	*Pizza Hut*
▪	www.software-that-works.co.uk	*International Learning Systems*
▪	www.starwars.com	*Lucasfilm*
▪	www.w3.org/History/1989/proposal.html	*World Wide Web Consortium*
▪	nz.yahoo.com	*Yahoo! Australia and New Zealand*
▪	uk.yahoo.com	*Yahoo! United Kingdom and Ireland*

CHAPTER 3 ▪ *Unique* features of Internet-based marketing

▪	www.auction.go.com	*Disney Enterprises, Inc.*
▪	www.auctions.yahoo.com	*Yahoo!*
▪	www.b2b.com	*Dell Computers*

www.ednow.com	Sagebrush Corporation
www.excite.com.au	Excite Australia Pty Ltd
www.geocities.yahoo.com/Heartland	Yahoo!
www.go.com	Disney Enterprises Inc.
www.lcweb.loc.gov	Library of Congress
www.mypage.go.com	Disney Enterprises Inc.
www.store.yahoo.com	Yahoo!
www.support.microsoft.com	Microsoft Corporation
www.131shop.com.au	131 Shop
www.amazon.com	Amazon.com, Inc.
www.andromedia.com/products/ likeminds/index.html	Macromedia Inc.
www.andronicos.com	Andronico's Market
www.anz.com	ANZ Banking Group
www.barclays-stockbrokers.co.uk	Barclays Stockbrokers Ltd
www.bbc.co.uk	BBC
www.cdnow.com	CDNow Online Inc.
www.centrebet.com.au	Centrebet Pty Ltd
www.citytv.com	CHUM Ltd
www.cnn.com	Cable News Network
www.coke.com	The Coca-Cola Company
www.coke.com/cgi-bin/survey/survey.cgi	The Coca-Cola Company
www.compaq.com	Compaq
www.cpo.cn.net	People's Republic of China
www.cs.umn.edu/Research/GroupLens/	Department of Computer Science, University of Minnesota
www.csh.rit.edu/projects/drink.shtml	Computer Science House of RIT
www.cybermall.com	Cheli Media Group
www.dell.com	Dell Computers
www.dinersclub.com	Diners Club international Ltd
www.discjockey.com	DiscJockey.com, Inc.
www.dymocks.com	Dymocks Booksellers
www.eb.com	Encyclopaedia Brittanica
www.ebay.com	eBay Inc.

www.emerald-library.com	MCB University Press Ltd
www.harrods.co.uk	Harrods Ltd
www.homeworld.org	Relicnews
www.incredibledvd.com/coupons.html	Incredible DVD
www.InsideTheWeb.com	LookSmart Ltd
www.ipaustralia.gov.au	IP Australia
www.library.uq.edu.au	University of Queensland
www.linuxmall.com	EBIZ Enterprises
www.live365.com	Live365.com
www.mp3.com	MP3.com, Inc.
www.orientalcasino.com	CyberCroupier Ltd
www.peppermints.com	ifive Brands
www.pizzahut.com	Pizza Hut
http://www.porsche.com	Porsche
www.shockwave.com	MP3.com, Inc.
www.siteyahoo.com/site	Yahoo!
www.sold.com.au	Sold.com.au
www.thinkgeek.com	Open Source Development Network
www.toysrus.com	Amazon.com, Inc.
www.triplej.com.au	TripleJ Imports
www.webcentral.com.au	WebCentral Pty Ltd
www.whatisthematrix.com	Warner Bros
www.wireplay.co.uk	Wireplay
www.woolworths.com.au	Woolworth's Ltd

CHAPTER 4 ■ *Consumer behaviour*

www.acmecity.com/thematrix/	Warner Bros
www.badmovies.org/	Andrew Barntreger
www.cnn.com	Cable News Network
www.drudgereport.com	WebSideStory, Inc.
www.geocities.com	Yahoo!
www.heat.net	Sega.com, Inc.
www.mtv.com	MTVi Group
www.wilsonweb.com/wmt	Ralph F. Wilson
www.xoom.com	NBC Internet, Inc.

CHAPTER 5 ■ *Creating* cybercommunities

■ bioinfo.weizmann.ac.il/BioMOO/	*Virtual School of Natural Sciences*
■ www.deja.com	*Google*
■ www.geocities.com	*Yahoo!*
■ www.sluggy.com	*Sluggy Freelance*
■ www.userfriendly.org	*User Friendly Media, Inc.*
■ www.vtown.com.au.	*Virtual Communities Ltd*
■ www.well.com	*The Well*

CHAPTER 6 ■ *Applications* for business and non-business

■ 2k.si.edu	*Smithsonian Institute*
■ mydomain.register.com	*Register.com*
■ support.microsoft.com	*Microsoft Corporation*
■ www.louvre.fr	*Musee du Louvre*
■ www.aintitcoolnews.com	*Ain't it Cool*
■ www.bartercard.com	*Bartercard International Ltd*
■ www.BlairWitch.com	*Artisan*
■ www.blairwitch.com	*Artisan*
■ www.centrebet.com.au	*Centrebet Pty Ltd*
■ www.clangregor.com	*The International Clan Gregor Web Community*
■ www.cybermall.com	*Cheli Media Group*
■ www.darkhorizons.com	*Garth Franklin*
■ www.dell.com	*Dell Computers*
■ www.discountwine.com	*Cuvee 19 Wine & Liquor Corporation*
■ www.efa.org.au	*Electronic Frontiers Australia*
■ www.eff.org	*Electronic Frontier Foundation*
■ www.foxmovies.com	*Fox*
■ www.iconocast.com	*Inconocast Inc.*
■ www.jif.com	*JIF*
■ www.marfan.org	*National Marfan Foundation*
■ www.movies.warnerbros.com	*Warner Bros*
■ www.mp3.com	*MP3.com, Inc*
■ www.nameprotect.com	*Nameprotect.com*

www.nike.co.jp	*Nike*
www.pressreleasenetwork.com	*Press Release Network*
www.real.com	*RealNetworks, Inc.*
www.sonicfoundry.com	*Sonic Foundry, Inc.*
www.starwars.com	*Lucasfilm*
www.swd.net.au/geos/	*Synchronicity Web Design*
www.towd.com	*Tourism Offices Worldwide Directory*
www.ups.com	*United Parcel service of America*
www.weeklyspecials.com.au	*Weekly Specials Ltd*
www.whatisthematrix.com	*Warner Bros*
www2.earthcam.com/jfk/	*Earthcam Inc.*

CHAPTER 7 ■ *Internet in marketing strategy*

b2b.yahoo.com	*Yahoo!*
ninemsn.com.au	*Ninemsn Pty Ltd*
stores.yahoo.com	*Yahoo!*
windowsupdate.microsoft.com	*Microsoft Corporation*
www.alp.org.au	*Australian Labor Party*
www.amnesty.org	*Amnesty International*
www.apache.org	*The Apache Software Foundation*
www.badbreath.com	*Proctor & Gamble*
www.chase.com	*J P Morgan Chase & Co*
www.christmas.com	*Christmas.com, Inc.*
www.coke.com	*The Coca-Cola Company*
www.dingoblue.net.au	*dingoblue Pty Ltd*
www.disneyland.com	*Disney Enterprises*
www.eb.com	*Encyclopaedia Brittanica*
www.ebay.com	*eBay, Inc.*
www.etrade.com.au	*Etrade Australia*
www.excite.co.uk	*Excite United Kingdom and Ireland*
www.excite.com	*Excite*
www.excite.com.au	*Excite Australia*
www.excite.de	*Excite Germany*
www.ferrari.com	*Ferrari*

www.greengrocer.com.au	Greengrocer.com.au Pty Ltd
www.ipaustralia.gov.au	IP Australia
www.irs.gov	Internal Revenue Service
www.jaycar.com.au	Jaycar Electronics
www.kmart.com.au	Kmart Australia Ltd
www.kodak.com	Kodak
www.lloydstsb.co.uk	Lloyds TSB
www.mp3.com	MP3.com, Ltd
www.olympics.com	International Olympic Committee
www.organic-lifestyle.co.uk	Organic-Lifestyle.co.uk
www.peppermints.com	ifive Brands
www.pg.com	Proctor & Gamble
www.pringles.com	Proctor & Gamble
www.rctoys.com	DraganFly Innovations, Inc.
www.reebok.com	Reebok International, Ltd
www.reel.com	Hollywood Entertainment Corporation
www.slashdot.org	Slashdot
www.smh.com.au	Sydney Morning Herald
www.sonymusic.com	Sony Music Entertainment Inc.
www.superbowl.com	NFL Enterprises
www.thesims.com	Electronic Arts Inc.
www.thinkgeek.com	Open Source Development Network
www.vicks.com	Proctor & Gamble
www.web21.com	Infospace Inc.
www.wildfm.com.au	Wild FM
www.wired.com	Wired Digital Inc.
www.worldcup.com	FIFA
www.xe.net/ucc	The Universal Currency Converter

CHAPTER 8 *The role of product in Internet marketing*

www.abc.com	ABC Inc.
www.bom.gov.au	Bureau of Meteorology
www.bpay.com.au	Bpay Pty Ltd
www.cnn.com	Cable News Network

www.compaq.com	Compaq
www.excite.de	Excite Germany
www.ford.com	Ford Motors
www.gucci.com	Gucci
www.hoover.co.uk	Hoover
www.hugo.com	Hugo
www.innovations.com.au	Innovations
www.mscisonline.org	Master of Science Degree Online, Regis University
www.nescafe.com	Nestle
www.netscape.com	Netscape
www.nytimes.com	New York Times
www.ozemail.com.au/~whips	Ozemail
www.pertplus.com	Proctor & Gamble
www.pricescan.com	PriceSCAN.com, Inc.
www.ptm.com.au	Palmer Tube Mills
www.redhat.com	Red Hat, Inc.
www.salon.com	Salon.com
www.smartshop.com	Smartshop.com, Inc.
www.sportschalet.com	Sports Chalet
www.trgnet.com	TRG Products
www.trisenx.com	Trisenx, Inc
www.ups.com	United Parcel Service of America
www.walmart.com	Wal-Mart Stores, Inc.
www.warnerbros.com	Warner Bros
www.webtv.com	Web TV Networks, Inc.
www.yahoo.co.uk	Yahoo! United Kingdom and Ireland

CHAPTER 9 ■ *Promotion 1:* Internet in promotional mix

www.airportpark.com.au	Discount Airport Parking
www.alwaysrentacar.com.au	Airport Car Rental Australia
www.apndigital.com.au	APN Digital Pty Ltd
www.carpark.com.au	Carpark Australia Pty Ltd
www.compaq.com	Compaq
www.comsec.com.au	Commonwealth Securities Ltd

www.cyberstudy101.com	*CyberStudy 101, Inc.*
www.dietcoke.com	*The Coca-Cola Company*
www.dilbert.com	*United Feature Syndicate, Inc.*
www.downloads.com	*CNET networks, Inc.*
www.dreamscancometrue.com	*NameDirectNow.com*
www.dstore.com.au	*dstore Ltd*
www.eagleboys.com.au	*Eagle Boys Pizza*
www.ferretstore.com	*NEEPS Inc.*
www.homehunter.com.au	*APN Digital Pty Ltd*
www.hoover.co.uk	*Hoover*
www.icq.com	*ICQ*
www.innovations.com.au	*Innovations Direct Pty Ltd*
www.lego.com	*Lego*
www.microsoft.com	*Microsoft Corporation*
www.monster.com.au	*Monster.com*
www.mp3.com	*MP3.com, Inc.*
www.nfl.com	*National Football League*
www.nike.com	*Nike*
www.olympic.org	*International Olympic Committee*
www.peppermints.com/testimonials.asp	*ifive Brands*
www.pepsi.com.au	*Pepsi Cola Bottlers, Australia*
www.sanity.com.au	*Sanity*
www.smh.com.au	*Sydney Morning Herald*
www.sprite.com	*The Coca-Cola Company*
www.thesims.com	*Electronic Arts Inc.*
www.transmeta.com	*Transmeta Corporation*
www.tv	*The .tv Corporation*
www.whiskas.com.au	*Petcat*
www.wilsonparking.com.au	*Wilson Parking*
www.vtown.com.au	*Virtual Communities Ltd*

CHAPTER 10 **Promotion 2:** *The Internet as a promotional medium*

dir.yahoo.com/Computers_and_Internet/ Internet/World_Wide_Web	*Yahoo!*
www.abc.com	*ABC Inc.*

www.beenz.com	*beenz.com, Inc.*
www.bigpond.com	*Telstra*
www.cartoonnetwork.com/games	*Cartoon Network*
www.cdnow.com	*CDNow Online Inc.*
www.channelv.com.au	*Channel(v)*
www.charitychampionship.com	*LPGA*
www.deja.com	*google*
www.dilbert.com	*United Feature Syndicate, Inc.*
www.dogpile.com	*Infospace Inc.*
www.eb.com	*Encyclopaedia Brittanica*
www.excite.co.uk	*Excite United Kingdom & Ireland*
www.freefungames.com	*Freefungames*
www.freetibet.org	*Free Tibet Campaign*
www.go.com	*Disney Enterprises*
www.google.com	*Google*
www.greenfieldonline.com	*Greenfield Online*
www.happypuppy.com	*Attitude Network Ltd*
www.imdb.com	*The Internet Movie Database Ltd*
www.kodak.com	*Kodak*
www.lordoftherings.net	*New Line Productions Inc.*
www.macshowlive.com	*Mac Show Productions*
www.microsoft.com/mscorp/ museum/home.asp	*Microsoft Corporation*
www.mp3.com	*MP3.com, Inc.*
www.nike.com	*Nike*
www.peoplesound.com	*Peoplesound*
www.palmgear.com	*Palm Inc.*
www.infogate.com	*Infogate*
www.apple.com/quicktime	*Apple Computer Inc.*
www.reebok.com/humanrights/home.html	*Reebok*
www.rmhc.com	*Ronald McDonald House Charities*
www.royal-doulton.com/company.html	*Royal Doulton*
www.screensavers.com	*Screensavers.com, Inc.*
www.shop.com	*Shop.com, Inc.*

www.slashdot.org	*Slashdot*
www.tuxedo.org/~esr/jargon/	*Eric Steven Raymond*
www.hotwired.lycos.com/webmonkey.com	*Wired Digital Inc.*
www.wine.com	*Wine.com*
www.yahoo.com	*Yahoo!*
www.zdnet.com/techlife	*ZD Inc.*

CHAPTER 11 ■ *Pricing* strategies

support.microsoft.com	*Microsoft Corporation*
www.ato.gov.au	*Australian Tax Office*
www.auran.com	*Auran*
www.bartercard.com	*Bartercard International Ltd*
www.beenz.co.uk	*beenz.com, Inc.*
www.bonds.com.au	*Pacific Dunlop*
www.bpay.com.au	*Bpay Pty Ltd*
www.browser.org	*Browser.org*
www.chanel.com	*Chanel*
www.colesonline.com.au	*Coles Supermarkets Australia Ltd*
www.compaq.com	*Compaq*
www.comsec.com.au	*Commonwealth Securities Ltd*
www.cybercash.com	*CyberCash Inc.*
www.geocities.com	*Yahoo!*
www.gnu.org	*Free Software Foundation, Inc.*
www.greengrocer.com.au	*Greengrocer.com.au Pty Ltd*
www.irs.gov	*Internal Revenue Service*
www.katies.com.au	*Millers Retail Ltd*
www.linux.org	*Linux Online Inc.*
www.lloydtsb.co.uk	*Lloyds TSB Bank Plc*
www.microsoft.com	*Microsoft Corporation*
www.mp3.com	*MP3.com, Inc.*
www.netscape.com	*Netscape*
www.npsis.com	*NPS Internet Solutions LLC*
www.pilotgear.com	*Palm Inc.*
www.pricescan.com	*PriceSCAN.com Inc.*

www.proxomitron.cjb.net	*Scott R. Lemmon*
www.scouts.co.uk	*Greater Manchester East Scouts*
www.shopfido.com	*Links260, Inc.*
www.smh.com.au	*Sydney Morning Herald*
www.southwest.com	*Southwest Airlines co*
www.taxfreeinternet.org	*Association of Concerned Taxpayers*
www.the-times.co.uk	*Times Newspapers Ltd*
www.thewell.com	*The Well LLC*
www.vuitton.com	*Louis Vuitton Malletie*
www.walmart.com	*Wal-Mart Stores Inc.*

CHAPTER 12 *Distribution*

2k.si.edu	*Smithsonian Institute*
erther.qgl.org	*erther Music*
my.mp3.com	*MP3.com, Inc.*
www.adobe.com	*Adobe Systems Incorporated*
www.apple.com	*Apple Computer Inc.*
www.cafepress.com	*CafePress.com*
www.carpoint.com.au	*Ninemsn Pty Ltd*
www.control-escape.com	*Vince Veselosky*
www.cs.wisc.edu/~ghost/index.html	*Russell Lang*
www.deja.com	*Google*
www.dstore.com.au	*dstore Ltd*
www.fedex.com	*FedEx*
www.h2g2.com	*BBC MMI*
www.harrods.co.uk	*Harrods Ltd*
www.kylie.com	*Emirecords Ltd*
www.masterfoods.com	*Mars, Inc.*
www.mp3.com	*MP3.com, Inc.*
www.mp3.com/erther	*MP3.com, Inc.*
www.mp3.com/skylab17	*MP3.com, Inc.*
www.opensource.org	*Open Source Initiative*
www.peppermints.com	*ifive Brands*
www.pointcast.com	*Infogate*

www.poserworld.com	GMP Services Inc.
www.quicktime.com	Apple Computer Inc.
www.stephenking.com	Stephen King
www.ups.com	United Parcel Service Of America

CHAPTER 13 ■ *Services* marketing online

www.gov.au	Commonwealth of Australia
air.kode.net	All India Radio
b2b.yahoo.com	Yahoo!
home.netscape.com/smartupdate/	Netscape
movies.go.com/trailers	Disney Enterprises, Inc.
support.microsoft.com	Microsoft Corporation
www.abc.net.au	Australian Broadcasting Commission
www.acs.edu.au	The Australian Correspondence Schools
www.afr.com.au	Financial Review
www.bcentral.com	Microsoft Corporation
www.brw.com.au	Business Review Weekly
www.citibank.com	Citibank Financial Services
www.cnn.com	Cable News Network
www.contraception.net	N.V. Organon
www.drudgereport.com	Drudge Report
www.englishexpert.com/proof	English Experts
www.ericsson.se	Ericsson
www.ewizard.com.au	Wizard Financial Services
www.fai.com.au	FAI General Insurance Company
www.famvi.com	Family Violence
www.faqs.org	Internet FAQs Archives
www.flash.com	Macromedia Flash
www.freshmeat.net	Fresh Meat Software Packages
www.getconnected.com	Getconnected Technology
www.glsetup.com	GLSetup — 3D Graphics
www.gnfc.org.uk	Good News Family Care
www.go.com	Disney Enterprises
www.google.com	Google

▪ www.hairpolice.com	*Hairpolice*
▪ www.hoover.co.uk	*Hoover*
▪ www.hp.co.nz	*Hewlett Packard New Zealand*
▪ www.hrblock.com	*H & R Block Financial Services*
▪ www.infobeat.com	*Infobeat Services*
▪ www.infoseek.com	*Infoseek*
▪ www.InsideTheWeb.com	*LookSmart Ltd*
▪ www.kelloggs.com/recipes	*Kelloggs Company*
▪ www.kennedy.com.au	*Kennedy & Co Chartered Accountants*
▪ www.lawngents.com	*Lawn Gents*
▪ www.legalaccess.com.au	*Legal Access Services*
▪ www.massage.com	*Massage.com*
▪ www.mater.ie	*Mater Misericordiae Hospital*
▪ www.mcdonalds.com	*McDonalds*
▪ www.metacrawler.com	*Metacrawler*
▪ www.mids.org/weather	*Matrix Net*
▪ www.mmfm.co.uk	*MM Financial Management*
▪ www.mp3.com	*MP3.com, Inc.*
▪ www.myers.com.au	*Myer*
▪ www.napster.com	*Napster*
▪ www.npsis.com	*NPS Internet Solutions*
▪ www.pepsimax.com.au	*PepsiMax*
▪ www.petpro.com.au	*The Petpro Group*
▪ www.phpwebhosting.com	*Php Webhosting*
▪ www.pitstop.co.nz	*Pit Stop*
▪ www.pizzahut.com.au	*Pizza Hut*
▪ www.pugetpainters.com	*Puget Painters*
▪ www.quake.com/support	*Quake – id Software*
▪ www.realm.ca	*Realm Communications*
▪ www.shockwave.com	*Shockwave*
▪ www.surgery.com	*iEnhance, Inc.*
▪ www.surgerydoor.co.uk	*SurgeryDoor*
▪ www.tucows.com	*Tucows*
▪ www.virtualworld.com	*Virtual World*

www.whitepages.com.au	White Pages
www.woolworths.com.au	Woolworths
www.yahoo.com	Yahoo!

CHAPTER 14 ■ *Relationship* marketing in a 'one-to-many-to-one' environment

msg.mp3.com	MP3.com, Inc.
My.mp3.com	MP3.com, Inc.
store.yahoo.com	Yahoo!
www.aap.com.au	Australian Associated Press
www.bravenet.com	Bravenet Web Services Inc.
www.dell.com	Dell Computers
www.epinions.com	Epinions Inc.
www.flybuys.com.au	Fly Buys
www.geocities.com	Yahoo!
www.go.com	Disney Enterprises Inc.
www.icq.com	ICQ
ww.idsoftware.com	id Software
www.preferredguest.com	Starwood Hotels & Resorts Worldwide, Inc.
www.qantas.com.au	QANTAS Airways Ltd
www.star-alliance.com	Star Alliance
www.webcentral.com	WebCentral Pty Ltd
www.yahoo.com	Yahoo!

CHAPTER 15 ■ *International* marketing

www.b4bfilmtv.com.au	B4B Co.
www.bhp.com.au	BHP Ltd
www.bpftp.com	Bullet Proof Software
www.brisbane.qld.gov.au.	Brisbane City Council
www.debian.com	SPI
www.dell.com	Dell Computers
www.ehobbies.com	eHobbies.com, Inc.
www.excite.co.nz	Excite New Zealand
www.excite.co.uk	Excite United Kingdom and Ireland

www.excite.com	*Excite*
www.excite.com.au	*Excite Australia*
www.excite.de	*Excite Germany*
www.excite.fr	*Excite France*
www.fox.com	*Fox*
www.foxfamily.com	*Foxfamily.com*
www.foxkids.com	*Fox/FoxKids*
www.freshmeat.net	*Open Source Development Network*
www.helpagency.com.au	*Help Nursing Service Pty Ltd*
www.levi.com	*Levi Strauss & Co.*
www.mcdonalds.com	*McDonald's Corporation*
www.mcdonalds.com.au	*McDonald's Australia*
www.mercedes.com	*DaimlerChrysler*
www.mickswhips.com.au	*Mick's Whips and Leather Goods*
www.microsoft.com	*Microsoft Corporation*
www.mp3.com	*MP3.com, Inc.*
www.newscorp.com.au	*The News Corporation Ltd*
www.nzart.org.nz	*The New Zealand Association of Radio Transmitters Inc.*
www.optus.com.au	*Optus Administration Pty Ltd*
www.pepsi.co.uk	*PepsiCo Inc.*
www.pepsi.com	*PepsiCo Inc.*
www.pepsi.com.au	*Pepsi Cola Bottlers, Australia*
www.pepsi.de.	*PepsiCo Inc.*
www.pizzahut.com.au	*Pizza Hut*
www.rctoys.com	*DraganFly Innovations Inc.*
www.redhat.com	*Red Hat, Inc.*
www.rmwilliams.com.au	*R. M. Williams Pty Ltd*
www.starbucks.com	*Starbucks Corporation*
www.webmd.ca	*WebMD Canada Ventures, Inc.*
www.whim.com.au	*Whimsicalities*

CHAPTER 16 ■ *Marketing* research

future.sri.com/VALS/VALSindex.shtml	*SRI Consulting Business Intelligence*
survey.hotlink.com.au	*WWW.Consult*

vr.harrispollonline.com	*Harris Interactive Inc.*
www.3com.com	*3com Corporation*
www.abcnews.com	*ABC News Internet Ventures*
www.abs.gov.au	*Australian Bureau of Statistics*
www.bravenet.com	*Bravenet Web Services, Inc.*
www.darkhorizons.com	*Garth Franklin*
www.deja.com	*Google*
www.environment-agency.gov.uk	*Environment Agency*
www.fortunecity.com	*FortuneCity.com, Inc.*
www.freshmeat.net	*Open Source Development Network*
www.fuld.com	*Fuld & Company Ltd*
www.gambica.org.uk	*Gambica Association Ltd*
www.greenfieldonline.com	*Greenfield Online*
www.homeworld.org	*Relicnews*
www.ichat.com	*Ichat, Inc.*
www.icq.com	*ICQ*
www.infobeat.com	*Infobeat Services*
www.inventix.com	*Inventix Software*
www.itracks.com	*Interactive Tracking Systems Inc.*
www.macintouch.com	*MacInTouch,Inc.*
www.mirc.co.uk	*mIRC Co. Ltd*
www.mp3.com	*MP3.com, Inc.*
www.mp3.com/aquataine	*MP3.com, Inc.*
www.mrsa.com.au	*Market Research Society of Australia*
www.my.yahoo.com.au	*Yahoo! Australia and New Zealand*
www.nber.org	*National Bureau of Economic Research, Inc.*
www.nua.ie/surveys	*Nua Ltd*
www.ozdaq.com	*Ozdaq*
www.politicsonline.com	*PoliticsOnline, Inc.*
www.pollit.com	*Pollit.com*
www.sitestatz.com/check.cgi?id=natgatcat	*SiteStatz*
www.stephendann.com	*Stephen Dann*
www.survey.hotlink.com.au	*WWW.Consult*

www.surveymonkey.com	SurveyMonkey.com, LLC
www.ultrafeedback.com	Ultra Feedback
www.urbancinefile.com.au	Urban Cinefile
www.ur.harrispollonline.com	Harris Interactive Inc.
www.wcw.com	World Championship Wrestling
www.xoom.com	NBC Internet, Inc.

CHAPTER 17 ■ *Future* directions

www.2600.com	2600 Enterprises
www.altavista.com	Altavista Company
www.aol.com	America Online, Inc.
www.apple.com	Apple Computer, Inc.
www.crq.com	Digital: Convergence Corporation
www.cs.umb.edu/jfklibrary/j071560.htm	Department of Mathematics & Computer Science, University of Massachusetts
www.digital.com	Compaq
www.fed.gov	Federal Government of the United States
www.getcat.com	Digital: Convergence Corporation
www.hotmail.com	Microsoft Corporation
www.ideavirus.com	Do You Zoom, Inc.
www.infoseek.com	Infoseek
www.infoseek.de	Infoseek
www.internet2.com	Internet Corporation
www.napster.com	Napster
www.netscape.com	Netscape
www.olympics.org	International Olympic Committee
www.opensource.org	Open Source Initiative
www.radioshack.com	RadioShack Corporation
www.starwars.com	Lucasfilm
www.stevewaugh.com.au	Steve Waugh
www.usenet2.org	Usenet II

Glossary

24–7 (24 hour 7 day a week) access: the accessibility of the Internet irrespective of time of day or day of the week

3D cyberspace: a graphical representation of the Internet, usually in the form of a first person perspective

actual product: the tangible product including style and accessories

advocates: a member of a cybercommunity who leads by example in the use of the community, and often is a most prolific member of the group

affective commitment: a form of relationship commitment where the more the individual is committed to the relationship, the less desire that individual has to engage in opportunism or to seek alternative arrangements

affective event: a commitment based on liking, emotional attachment and a sense of bonding with the other party

alpha geek: the most technically accomplished or skilful person in some implied context

Archie and Veronica: Archie and Veronica are historical elements of the Internet. Archie is the name given to the Internet FTP search server, and VERONICA (Very Easy Rodent-Oriented Netwide Index to Computerized Archives) was (in her hey day) the best search mechanism for searching **gopher systems.** Both were named after characters from the Archie comics series.

asynchronously: the method by which communications can be conducted in **delayed time**, or without the need for both parties to be present at the exchange

attraction: the level above awareness that conveys a sense of attraction to recipients so that they will want to visit a web site and will take active steps to meet this desire

attractor: a type of web site that is specifically intended to have the most potential to interact with the greatest number of visitors in a select target market

attributes and benefits: the salient attributes considered important to a consumer, and believed to be the basis for making a purchase decision

augmented product: the additional benefits or services attached to the purchase of the actual product such as social prestige or service warranty

avatar: a representation of the user, normally found in social interaction mediums like MUDs, IRC, USENET and email

awareness: the knowledge of the existence of a product, web site or idea

bandwidth: the volume of information per unit time that a computer, person, or transmission medium can handle

bargain hunter: a type of online web user who seeks the free, the trial samples and the giveaways that are available on the Web

bleeding edge/cutting edge: cutting edge is defined as the most recent version of any technology, product or idea. The bleeding edge is the next version of the cutting edge, long before it is sufficiently stable to be released into the marketplace. Bleeding edge is commonly used to refer to new technologies with small, but dedicated, user bases who are willing to put up with flaws, glitches and unfinished goods in order to test the new systems.

blueprint: (also blueprinting): the tool that helps bring together the organisation's requirements for online and offline marketing activities and integrating the two into the overall strategic direction of the company

bureaucratic index: an assessment score based on level and number of regulations and procedures which must be navigated by the exporter/international marketer in entering that country's market

calculative approach: a method of determining commitment to a relationship seen as a balance sheet of costs, benefits, gains, losses, rewards and punishments that is constantly tallied, and all the time the ledger remains in the positive, commitment will be maintained

catalogues: a type of web site designed to offer the facility to order products directly from the web site without needing to access an intermediary or local dealership

click tracking: a web site specific data collection method that tracks the paths and movements of users through a web site

clicks and mortar: online retailing stores which mirror their offline parent companies in both range of products and market positioning

clicks and order: online retailers who do not have a physical retail presence, but still ship physical goods, and require all of the logistics infrastructure of traditional bricks and mortar or clicks and mortar stores

cognitive dissonance: a situation where purchasers feel less satisfied with their purchase decision immediately following the purchase, but before fully experiencing the product

collaborative filtering systems (CFS): a database-driven mechanism for product recommendation which matches the user's profile against similar profiles of other users

commitment: the perceived need to maintain the relationship, either because of the inherent value of staying, or because of the costs associated with leaving the exchange

compatibility (1): the degree to which a site can be accessed by a variety of web browsers, modem speeds and operating systems; (2): the degree to which the Internet relates to the adopter's experience

competitive intelligence: the systematic collection of information about competitors used to assist in strategic decision making

competitor positioning: a positioning strategy based on focusing on a specific competitor and outlining the differences between your product and the competitor's product

complexity: the relative difficulty of using and understanding an innovation

computer-mediated communication (CMC): the use of computers and computer networks as communication tools by people who are collaborating with each other to achieve a shared goal, which does not require the physical presence or co-location of participants and which can provide a forum for continuous communication free of time constraints.

connectivity: the sense of one-to-one communication and feeling that the marketer is meeting the consumers' needs on an individual basis

consumer intelligence (1): the information and knowledge required to fully understand the target consumer, their behaviours and motivations; (2) an oxymoron

convenience product: the type of goods which are purchased regularly, with little thought and usually at low cost

cookie technology: a handle, transaction ID, or other token of agreement between cooperating programs, currently in the context of web browser cookies

co-production: the customers actions at the time of service production that have an impact on service quality and outcomes which makes them co-producers of the service and partial employees of the organisation

copy testing: the methods of testing the effectiveness of an advertisement that measure the reported change in recall, recognition or attitude towards a product

core product: the benefits that the product will provide

core product offering: the underpinning benefit that the product offers the consumer

cost leadership: a strategy direction which orientates the organisation to be the cost leader within the industry by providing the lowest priced goods

cracker: a person who breaks security on a system (not to be confused with hacker)

creativity: a recognition that the market has a wide range of choice for content, ideas and experiences so the marketer needs to do more than simply recycle existing ideas

credence attributes: the experience-oriented services which are difficult to assess even in post-purchase due to the limited expertise and knowledge of the consumer, and the complexity of the service

creeping featurism: the tendency for anything complicated to become even more complicated because people keep saying, 'Gee, it would be even better if it had this feature too'.

cultural goods: the salient, and saleable, aspects of a society's culture which can be used to form the basis of an international marketing campaign based on the ethnic origin of the cultural goods

cultural symbol positioning: a positioning strategy that uses images or icons which incorporate cultural images or icons as part of the product positioning strategy

cybercommuning: the seamless integration of communications technology with social interaction between members of a cybercommunity

cybercommunity: a virtual place where a group of individuals engaged in computer-mediated communication moves beyond basic exchange of information into the formation of a community structure based on the exchange of shared goods of value

cyberdestination marketing: the amalgamation of the cyberenvironment, the services, community, community members, and experiences which are offered under the banner of the cybercommunity name, location or brand as part of **destination marketing**

cyberspace: the shared consensual hallucination between millions of users who define their world, based on physical objects, through mental constructions

database consuming: a consumption pattern whereby the consumer uses database technology to target products in the same way as marketers used it to target customers

dead pointer: the display of a URL in a medium where the web site cannot be accessed by clicking, or immediate interfacing with the URL in that media

delayed time: a message or similar content that can be left in a public forum to be accessed at a later date, without the need for the original poster of the message to be present

design school concept: the notion that a series of recurring techniques, ideals and philosophies can be grouped together as a distinctive 'school' of thought

destination marketing: the amalgamation of tourism products offering an integrated experience to consumers under the brand name of the location

diet portals: a type of web search engines that has added progressively more layers of portal style content, without becoming fully committed to the portal concept

digital capabilities: the number of computers owned per 100 people in the country

digital transmission of information: the direct broadcast or **narrowcast** of streaming content in a digital format to an end receiver

directed buyers: the hard core shoppers of the online world who are online to find the product they want to buy, rather than to research it, play with it or take home a sample version of it

directed information seekers: the type of people who search the Internet for timely, relevant and accurate information on a specific topic or set of topics

disintermediation: a situation where the traditional supply chain breaks down as the manufacturer sells directly to the end consumer, and competes against the retailer for the same customer base

drop errors: the decision to not pursue an idea which would have been a market success

early adopters: the stately and refined members of the adoption cycle compared to the rebellious, devil-may-care risk takers of the innovator category

early majority: the leading edge of the maturity of the market in an adoption cycle

economic growth: a measurement based on published growth rates from international economic forums

economic power: a measurement based on a calculation of per capita GDP

economic stability: a measurement based on the inflation rate with lower levels of inflation indicating higher economic stability

electronic billboards: the basic entry level web sites which consist mostly of static content describing who the company is and what it is they sell for a living

electronic data interchange (EDI): the transmission of standardised data representing business documents, such as purchase orders, invoices and shipping notices, between organisations

electronic market/auction: a web site that is an interaction–transaction web site that acts as a host for the forums of exchange

entertainment seekers: a category of web browser who seeks out the world of online entertainment, from playing Java and shockwave games at web sites through to experiencing the worlds of online gaming, streaming audio or downloaded music

environmental scanning: a method of overviewing and observing the environments in which the organisation operates to determine what changes, if any, are occurring before attempting to understand the impact they will have on the operations of the organisation

ergosphere: the space of work, or the application of ideas that emerge from the **noosphere**

ethnographic research: a data collection method that involves the researcher living with, and becoming part of a community while recording their views, opinions, activities and behaviours

experience attributes: a range of services which can only be evaluated after experiencing the service, given that the quality and outcomes may be specific to the transaction or event

experiential marketing: a method of marketing which is based on the threefold notion of **interactivity**, **connectivity** and **creativity** creating a marketing dialogue rather than the monologue of traditional one-way media

fan site: an unofficial web site set up to support a cause, product, television show or other enterprise

feature creep: the result of **creeping featurism**

file transfer protocol (FTP): the software used for transferring files to or from one computer to another across the Internet

flow: the state of mind where interaction with the Internet becomes a unified movement from one site or event to the next with little or no awareness of distraction, outside influences, or irrelevant thoughts

focus group: a small group of people with some key defining characteristic who are brought together to discuss an issue or topic with the assistance of a trained moderator

free download (1): any file that is available for no cost on the Internet. (2): One of three distribution methods at MP3.com. Free downloads offer the browser the opportunity to download and save a full MP3 file of the song to their local drive. (see **streaming only** and **paid channel**).

freedom of expression: a qualitative measure based on the willingness of a society to accept divergent opinions and the extent to which it encourages debate via the media and other outlets

gift culture: a form of society where status and reputation is ascribed not on how much you have, but on how much value you give to the society by giving things away

global access: the international nature of the medium, and how local web sites have a global presence

global positioning system (GPS): a system of position satellites that can feed geographic coordinates to GPS receivers, thereby letting the users know the exact latitudinal and longitudinal location (and just how lost they really are)

global: a business approach that focuses on intentionally creating an export orientation to deliver product (good, service, idea) to purchasers anywhere within the target market, within the Internet connected world (contrast with **international**)

go errors: the decision to pursue an idea which eventually turns out to be a mistake

gopher: a type of Internet service first floated around 1991, and obsolescent by 1995, by the World Wide Web. Gopher presents a menuing interface to a tree or graph of links; the links can be to documents, runnable programs, or other gopher menus arbitrarily far across the net.

hackers: individuals who tinker with the digital world to see what makes it tick and whether it can be made to tick on a different platform, in a different style, or more effectively. They enjoy exploring the details of programmable systems and how to stretch their capacities, as well as the intellectual challenge of creatively overcoming or circumventing limitations.

hardware infrastructure: the computers, cables, power lines and power supplies that provide the actual backbone through which the Internet is housed and accessed

HTTP (HyperText Transfer Protocol): the software protocol that handles the distribution of web page data

hypermediated communications (HMC): the communications transactions that are conducted via the medium of the Web

inconsistency: the fact that no two services encounters will be identical due to the human influence of the service, and the high level of variability between consumer, service provider and service environment

individualised transmission: the customised or targeted direct information such as direct email, which is based on user behaviours, usually recorded by cookies or other market research data

information publishing: a web site at its most basic, where the content is the experience, and the emphasis is on the provision of information

innovation fascinations: the immediate reaction to an innovation experience by the consumer felt in one of four ways — emotionally, intellectually, social acceptance and practicality

innovators: those people in society who are first to try an innovation

inseparability: the simultaneous consumption and production of the services that requires the consumer/recipient and the service delivery mechanism to be in close proximity during the service

instigators: a member of a cybercommunity who usually is responsible for engaging debates, asking questions and starting topics of conversation

intangibility: the fact that service products are performances which have none of the physical characteristics of goods in that they cannot be touched, tasted, seen, heard or observed before performance occurs

integrated marketing communications (IMC): a marketing promotions approach that attempts to utilise the value of a comprehensive plan of image and message strategies that present a consistent message across a range of communications methods to provide consistency and clarity to maximise the effectiveness

intellectual infrastructure: the content of the Internet created by users of the Internet

interactive transmission of information: a transmission mechanism where a receiver can interact with the information being received, and that interaction can be used as a basis for determining other elements of the information received

interactivity (1): the degree to which a user can interact with a web site in a meaningful manner beyond following internal hyperlinks. (2): the ability to address an individual, gather and receive a response, remember that response, and tailor the next response on the basis of the received information. (3) the degree of give and take between the consumer and the producer of the marketing message, and the extent to which the message adapts to the consumer. (4) the ability of the consumer to engage in a time-and-place independent dialogue with members of the firm.

interest driven: the extent to which the Internet is a pull medium where online experiences are based on the active seeking out of items of interest rather than the passive acceptance of whatever push media delivers to the screen

international: a distribution orientation which is focusing on delivering a product (good, service, idea) primarily to internal markets, but also to a limited range of purchasers who reside outside of the home country of the producer (compare **global**)

internet focus group (IFG): a focus group can occur when and wherever a many-to-many real time communications channel can be established, and can be facilitated, logged (and moderated) by a focus group leader

internet relay chat (IRC): a system of real time text communication which is divided into 'channels' (digital equivalents of rooms) to chat in groups or privately

interrupt pages: online advertising where access to the next section of the web site requires the user to click past an advertisement to find the content they thought they were accessing

intrinsic social prices: the non-financial costs of time, effort, lifestyle and psyche associated with engaging in any behaviour

inverted catalogue: a web site which offers a range of free information on a given subject then has the materials available for sale at the end of the product information

IP address: (Internet Protocol address) the identifier number for everything on the Internet

just in time: the concept of delivering only the exact amount of a product needed for a particular point in the production line just before or just as needed by the production process

lag: the time period between sending the message, and the message being received by the computer or user

laggards: the collective category of non adopters of an innovation deemed to be universal

late majority: the group of later adopters of an innovation which represents over one third of any given market, and is the last major social group to adopt an idea, product or service

leaders: the more senior, experienced or knowledgeable members of a cybercommunity or group who tend to guide the general direction of the group, and handle dispute resolution

lean media: a communications medium that strips away non-verbal cues and information otherwise available in a face-to-face environment

loyalty scheme: a rewards program designed to increase product, brand or corporate loyalty through the use of incentives, prices, frequent flyer points or similar rewards

lurking: the practice of observing an USENET group for a period of time before actively participating in the discussions.

mall-intercept: a method of data collection for surveys or interviews which involves stopping people in shopping centres or other public places to ask them to participate in the survey

market maker: an online service which bring together buyers and sellers at a single site by offering an unbiased service of content and advice, or transaction systems such as auctions

market maven: a person who has a wide range of knowledge concerning markets, pricing, and the best places to buy certain products, services or goods and who will share this information with their friends and peers

marketplace: the conceptual space where value chains and physical logistics are engaged to move tangible goods from producer to consumer in a physical environment

marketspace: the conceptual space where virtual value chains and virtual logistics are engaged to move intangible goods and ideas across data networks, with little or no recourse to physical environments

mass customisation: a category of web site where the content and experience is tailored to the individual user based on their established usage histories, demographics and other provided information

memes: a social unit of imitation indicating that an idea that can be transmitted by adoption or replication of the meme behaviour

metareward: a category of web site that offer loyalty incentive schemes such as frequent flyer points or equivalent for registering demographic details at various member sites

metasearch engine: a web sites which accesses and searches multiple web search engines simultaneously and returns a compiled report of likely sites matching the search criteria

Moore's law: (1) The observation that the logic density of silicon integrated circuits has closely followed the curve (bits per square inch) = $2^{(t - 1962)}$ where t is time in years; that is, the amount of information storable on a given amount of silicon has roughly doubled every year since the technology was invented

MP3: the MPEG (Motion Picture Engineering Group) Layer 3 compression format, designed to turn WAV files (audio) into much smaller audio files for minimal loss in sound quality

multi-user dungeons (MUD): the structured artificial worlds that make use of the real time communications systems to create virtual worlds for communications and interaction

multilevel product concept: a conceptual understanding that regards any product as consisting of three distinct layers of **core**, **actual** and **augmented** products

mystery shoppers: an experiential research method whereby a researcher anonymously engages in a service transaction to determine if the service is up to the expected standard

narrowcasting: the ability to stream specialised content or custom content, has a marginal cost per user lower than that of the revenue per new user

new product portfolio: a collection of new product concepts that are within the ability of the organisation to develop, are most attractive to customers and deliver short and long term corporate objectives, spreading risk and diversifying investments

newsgroups: a topic group or forum housed on **USENET**

niche marketing: a positioning strategy and strategic approach to business where an organisation finds a specialist niche in the market and focuses on this segment with the hope of dominating it

node level: the interaction of elements within a page and includes design components, selection of colours and the use of images and text

noise-to-signal ratio: a ratio used to determine whether a medium is worth using, or a site is worth reading, as a high level of noise renders the medium practically useless. Signal refers to the useful information conveyed by some communications medium; 'noise' is anything else on that medium.

non-optimal solution: an astoundingly stupid way to do something (see also **sub-optimal outcome**)

noosphere: the territory of ideas which encompasses the space of all thoughts, and exists in a purely conceptual form

observability: the level of visibility of the product to other members of the adopter's social group

observational research: a method of research by simply observing what the sample population is doing and not directly intervening to determine why they are behaving in a certain way

one-to-many-to-one communications: the computer-mediated communications that are published by an individual in a public sphere, such as a newsgroup, and read and responded to either directly to the individual, or indirectly to the newsgroup by other readers

online resources: the level of online activity within the country based on statistics such as the number of domain names registered

open source: a type of software distributed in source under licences guaranteeing anybody rights to freely use, modify, and redistribute, the code

opt-in functions/opt-in mailing lists: the systems whereby the user chooses to become involved in the mailing list, or to receive announcements, information and updates as a result of subscribing to the list

packet routing: (aka packet switching): a method of delivering data across a network by breaking the data into small packets at the point of transmission, and having those packets reassembled by the receiver's computer

paging services: a messaging software system that can send short text messages across the Internet

paid channel: (see **streaming only** and **free download**): a method of music delivery through MP3.com which requires the user to pay a monthly subscription fee for permanent access to the audio channel

parody site: a type of web site that either parodies the structure or content of an existing site, for satirical or political purposes

patches: a temporary addition to a piece of code to repair a fault, bug or failure in the software

perishability: the fact that services cannot be stored, stockpiled, or used once the service opportunity has passed

permission based email marketing: (see opt in systems) a method of email marketing where the user chooses to receive advertising mail from companies associated with the controller of the **opt-in system**

permission marketing: a method of recruiting customers who voluntarily agree to receive marketing materials

point-to-point (P2P): a method of file and data sharing between distributed computer networks that uses a central point to coordinate or organise the sharing

political environment: a qualitative measure based on indicators such as the type of government, judicial system and the stability of the government

porting: the process of adapting a software package from one platform to another, often unofficially, or vaguely sanctioned

portable document format (PDF): a universal file format across a range of systems, it remains primarily a proprietary system, viewed through the Acrobat Reader platform

portal site: a type of web site designed to act as gateway into specific content, such as customisable information services such as news reports, weather forecasts and horoscopes and the rest of the Internet

post-modern consumption: the creation and negotiation of image, social role and social meaning through the use, purchase, consumption, and now creation of goods and services in the online environment

price quality: a positioning strategy whereby the product is positioned by price so that high quality prices attract a high price tag to indicate their value, and low end products use discounting techniques

price skimming: a pricing strategy whereby the company charges a high initial price until the top end of the market is saturated before gradually reducing the price over time

price (1): a conceptual statement referring to what people are prepared to give up, or sacrifice, in order to own a particular product or use a service (see **psychic cost**). (2): a measure of what a consumer is prepared to exchange for a product

pricing objective: an objective that outlines what the marketer wants to achieve strategically through the setting of a specific price level for a product

product class: a positioning strategy where the product is positioned against products and/or services outside of the product category

product differentiation: a competitive strategy where the company differentiates its product or service on some specific basis that is valued in the eyes of the consumer

product user: a positioning strategy based on associating a group of users with a product

product: the total bundle of benefits that the seller is offering to potential consumers

promotional mix: the seven different forms of marketing communications techniques

psychic cost: the element of the total price concept which relates to the idea of perceived social risk and represents the potential loss of self esteem, privacy or pride, or any aspect of the product purchase which could adversely impact on the individual's self esteem

purchase: the use and enjoyment of a web site, or to the actual purchase of goods or services from a site

push-based content: a method of Internet-based broadcasting where a web site 'pushes' information to the user in a manner more associated with standard television or radio broadcasting

quantifiable: a form of data that is measurable in numbers and able to be processed in statistical packages

rampant ad hocery: the reliance on an unstructured approach based on implementing incremental changes, updates and features

real community: communities that are time and geography dependent as they are formed around a geographic region, feature or social clustering

real time communications: the person to person Internet communications that are transmitted and received instantly or with a lag of only a few seconds

really new product (RNP): a term to describe the sort of innovation that is ground shaking, revolutionary and extremely likely to fail to be adopted

reciprocity: the notion of equality, mutual obligation and Bagozzi's (1975) exchange theory

recruited samples: a method of sampling which is dependent on approaching specific individuals who are of interest for data collection

recycling: an option for those ideas that do not fit the current needs of the organisation or company but which could be retained and reworked for potential re-evaluation at a later date

reference price: a price established in the mind of a consumer as to what they believe a product or service is worth

relationship marketing: a marketing philosophy that is operationally defined as 'to identify and establish, maintain and enhance and when necessary also to terminate relationships with customers and other stakeholders, at a profit, so that the objectives of all parties are met, and that this is done by a mutual exchange and fulfilment of promises'

relative advantage: the inherent superiority of an innovation over any competing product, service or idea, which was initially difficult to establish given the lack of comparable products associated with the innovation

remote hosting: the process by which a user in one geographic location hosts a web site, files or other information on a computer in another geographic location

repurchase: the return and reuse of a site, either to reorder products, or to re-experience the web site

risk relievers: the elements of sales arrangements that can be used to mediate perceived risks of non-store purchasing

screened samples: a sampling technique that selects only those who fit predetermined criteria

search attributes: attributes that have some clearly defined criteria based on which different offerings can be easily compared across a range of service providers

search engine: a type of web site designed to search the content of the Internet based on the user's input of key words

search-only: a type of search engine web site offering sparse looking pages that are simply designed to accept a search term and output a search result

server farm: a collection of computer equipment assembled for the sole purpose of being servers for web sites, email, IRC or similar systems

service factory: the term used to describe to the physical location at which a service occurs, whether the recipient of the service is present or not

servicescape: the physical location of the service environment

share of voice: the ability of all users in the Internet arena to be able to promote themselves, and speak freely without one or more players being able to buy up the 'voice' of the medium

shopping products: the type of products purchased less frequently and which involve a degree of comparison shopping

site level: the look and feel as well as the navigation of the site (see also **node level**)

slashdot effect (1): a spontaneous high hit rate upon a web server due to an announcement on a high volume news web site. (2): a term to describe what is said to have happened when a web site is virtually unreachable because too many people are hitting it after the site was mentioned in an interesting article on the popular Slashdot news service.

smoot: a unit of length equal to five feet seven inches used as an MIT measurement for surveying geographic locations such as the length of the Harvard Bridge (364.4 smoots)

SMTP: (Simple/Standard Mail Transport Protocol) a software function that handles the protocol for moving mail across a network

social and psychological cost: (see also **psychic cost**): the non-financial costs of a transaction

social infrastructure: the level of the human to human relationships conducted across the medium of the Internet

social network capital: the experience and collective history of a social group

software infrastructure: the domain where the computers of the Internet exchange information

spam: (1) the generic term used to describe any commercial email distribution of a message across email lists, **newsgroups** or IRC channels. (2) a spiced processed ham product (www.spam.com/ci/ci_in.htm).

spamming: the act of broadcasting spam

specialty products: the type of products that are highly specialised, sparsely distributed and actively sought after by specific target groups

streaming only: (see **free download** and **paid channel**) a method of MP3 music file distribution whereby the audio signal is broadcast over the Internet to the recipient computer, but does not result in a copy of the music being saved to the receiver's computer

structured artificial world: a digital representation of the real world, with varying degrees of accuracy

sub-optimal outcome: a resolution to a problem that brings about a less than ideal solution, or which will result in a failure to achieve the best option available (see also **non-optimal solution**)

survey research: the direct questioning of subjects on a topic of interest to the marketer

switching costs: the costs associated with moving from one service provider to a new service provider

system acceptability: an assessment of whether the software will do what it is supposed to do, and whether it does this in a manner acceptable to the end user

TCP/IP (Transmission Control Protocol/Internet Protocol) protocols: a wide area networking protocol that provides the lifeblood of the Internet by being functional, freely available, standard and not subject to control by a central authority

telco infrastructure: the number of telephone lines per 100 citizens. The higher the number of lines the greater the capacity of the citizens of that country to conduct business over the Internet

telepresence: the perception of physicality inside a cyberspace environment that is perceived to be unsolicited, or which has made use of an untargeted bulk

time independence: the ability of many features of the Internet to be accessed around the clock, seven days a week without the need for a physical or personal presence staffing the web site

TLA: a three letter acronym

total price concept: a conceptualisation of pricing that represents both the financial amount paid plus the sum of all other 'social' prices

tourism telepresence: the attempt to give a sense of physical location, or being at a destination, through online or virtual means, usually as a trial experience of a tourist destination

trading level: a measurement determined by the ratio between the country's GDP and its total level of trade with a high rating indicating that the country is open to trade and likely to welcome digital marketers

transactional sites: a category of web site that exist for the purpose of facilitating an exchange of any form, usually buying, but more recently for selling as well

trialability: the degree to which an innovation can be experienced separately from total adoption

trust: the willingness to rely on an exchange partner in whom one has confidence, and this includes a belief in the trustworthiness of the partner, and the reliance on the other partner to perform

undirected information seekers: the classic 'web surfer' model of the users who follow a random interest driven path through the Web, clicking on links of interest and information that looks new, interesting or different

unobtrusive observation: the study of USENET groups, web discussion boards and online discussion groups without the need to join or participate in the social group

unrestricted samples: a sampling technique that regards everyone who comes into contact with the data collection as being eligible to participate

use or application: a positioning strategy where the product is positioned specifically to be associated with a specific task or application

USENET: (originally from Users Network) a large decentralised system of **newsgroups** which cover just about every imaginable (and imaginative) topic available

value chains: a method of dividing a company into an array of strategically relevant elements which can be identified physically and technologically, and for which the customer is willing to pay money

variety and customisation: the levels of change, interaction and customised content that can occur on a web site

virtual bazaars: the business to business focal points where businesses can gather to exchange information, services and buy and sell goods, either through cash, barter or trade arrangements

virtual branding: a promotional method where a web site establishes a presence in the mind of the consumers, independently of the product or service it promotes

virtual communities (1): a group who share a common bond that is not dependent on physical interaction or common geography. (2): the social aggregations that emerge from the Net where enough people carry on those public discussions long enough, with sufficient human feeling, to form webs of personal relationships in cyberspace.

virtual malls: a type of web store hosted on an e-commerce server, with a dedicated linking marketplace web site, joining the diverse store systems together

virtual value chains: the elements of the **value chains** that are based on information, which were previously identified as supporting elements, and which exist as items of value in their own right in the marketspace

virtual–actual value chains: the value chains which combine marketspace value chains with virtual value chains to produce a value chain based on a hybrid information–tangible good product

visit/contact: the translation of awareness, attraction and motivation into trial adoption by visiting the web site

web chat systems: a web based mechanism (similar to the **IRC**) for real time communication

webification: the adaptation of the rules and protocols of printed media into web site design strategies

webify: the action of putting a piece of (possibly already existing) material on the Web

wireless application protocols (WAP): a method for transmitting text data to mobile phones and other handheld wireless devices

Index

ABC online   200–1
accessibility   128, 139
activities   129
actual product   189, 190
additivity   274
advanced digital markets   390
advertising   228
   message, format and context   230–1
advocacy pages   267
advocates   114
aesthetic value of web site   257
affective commitment   352, 353
AIPD model   175, 176
amenities   128–9
ancillary services   129
anonymity of the user   90, 417
Ansoff's strategic growth matrix   168–70
applications of the Internet for business and
      non-business   132–54
archive sites   265
ARPANET   4
attraction (promotion planning)   220–1
attraction of online   57–60
attractions   128
attractors on the Web   57, 264–7
attributes and benefits (positioning)   174
auction houses   62
audience selectivity   250–1
augmented product   189
Australian cultural goods   375–6
automated data gathering   416–17
available packages   129
avatars   93–4
awareness   220
   creating awareness of web sites   232–41

bandwidth   24
banner advertising   241–3, 404–5
bargain hunters   87
Bartercard   295
Bass' contagion-like diffusion model   75–7
Beenz' token-based system   295
behavioural change objectives   163
Berners-Lee, Tim   4, 20, 21
beta test marketing   211
blueprinting   137, 177–8
brand image pages   267
brand selling   310–11
brand switching   350
broadcast model   109–10

budgeting   178
bulletin boards   8
business, value of cybercommunities to
      118–22
business analysis   210–11
business applications of the Internet   132–55
   applications and implemented solutions
      137–54
macro-level strategic decisions   133–7
business to business (B2B) transactions   32
business to business marketing online   365–6
   new roles and opportunities   366

calculative commitment   353
cartoon strips   119–21
catalogues   46
channel conflict   309
click tracking   414–16
clicks and mortar retail concept   138, 194
clicks and order regime   278
client-centred approach   28
closing the deal   30
club sites   266
cognitive dissonance   361
collaborative filtering systems   49–50, 362
collective goods of value   113–14
commitment (relationship marketing)   351,
      352–3
communication (via Internet)   90
communications models   106–12
community
   defintions   112–16
   see also cybercommunities
community concepts
   cybercommuning   114
   cybercommunity, digital village living   114
   nature and structure of cybercommunity
      115–16
   shared goods of value   113–14
comparative pages   267
compatability (innovation)   78–9
compatability (online distribution)   313
competition   140
competitive advantage   143
competitive intelligence   410
competitive strategies (Porter)   165–8
competitor information   406–7
competitor positioning   174
complexity (innovation)   79

computer-mediated communication (CMC) 17, 107, 109, 110
computer-mediated one-to-many-to-one 17, 51, 111–12
computer-mediated one-to-one 110
computers, credibility of 359–61
conceptualising cyberspace 19–20
connectivity 252
consistency (service delivery) 330, 332
consumer behaviour 32, 71–102
  and online service product 338–40
consumer demand 66
consumer empowerment 196–7, 330, 333, 406
consumer expectations
  and reference pricing 286–7
  and the expectation gap 99, 100
  changing 65–6
consumer exploitation 437
consumer intelligence 409–10
consumer knowledge of the company 358
consumer loyalty 348–9
consumer revolution 64–6
consumer service centre sites 266–7
consumer–technology interface, weaknesses in 342
consumers, training as co-producers 340–1
contagion-like diffusion model (Bass) 75–7
content restructuring 314
context (advertising) 231
convenience (of Internet) 90
convenience products 194, 195
copy testing 404–5
core product 189
core product offerings 190
corporate pages 267
Cospace 24, 25
cost 96–7
cost-based objectives 284–5
cost leadership 166–7
cost-oriented objectives 162
cost savings 139
crackers 438, 442
creating awareness of web sites 232–41
creativity 252
credence attribute products 339, 340
credibility of computers 359–61
credit cards 294
creeping featurism 262, 341
cross-selling of products 350
CueCats 440–1
cultural acceptability 259
cultural considerations 36–8
cultural goods 374–6
cultural symbol positioning 174
customer see consumer
customisation 53, 330
  versus standardisation (online services) 334–5
cybercash 295
cybercommuning 94, 114
cybercommunities 4, 17, 91, 105–30, 112, 114
  as reflections of reality 122
  construction of identity in 116–18
  creation 122–9

destination marketing 127–9, 153–4
dichotomous structures 105–6
factors for success 126–7
location of 124–5, 128–9
nature and structure of 115–16
sense of community 125–6
theoretical foundations 106–18
value of for relationship marketing 361–2
value of to business 118–22
cyberculture 36–8, 281–3
cyberdestination marketing 128–9
cybermalls 61
cyberspace 303–5
  conceptualising 19–20
  mapping 20–5
  value of conceptual geography 25–6

DARPA 4
data exchanging 8
dead pointer 222, 232–41
delayed-time communications 7, 17
demographics 419
department stores 62
descriptive research 401–2
design see web site design
design school concept 260
  human factors research 263
  rampant ad hocery, voodoo programming and personal experience 261–3
  written rules and printed protocols 263–4
destination marketing 127–8, 153–4
  factors bringing people to a location 128–9
diagnostic research 402–3
dichotomous structures 105–6
diet portals 266
diffusion of innovations
  need, want, use and show-off approach to adoption 77–8
  personality, predisposition and psychographics 80–1
  Rogers' five features of innovations 78–80
digital corner stores 62
digital money 295
digital neighbours 438–43
digital showcase 58–9
digital transmission of information 315
digitised products 197
direct communication 139
direct marketing activities 228
direct response pages 267
directed buyers 88
directed information seekers 87
discount selling 311
discrete versus continuous online service 335
disintermediation 140
distribution 300–1
  determining the right distribution 301–2
  mechanisms 302–3
  online 303–19
distribution channels, model 301–2
diversification 169–70, 171
domestic web sites 371, 372
drop errors 210

early adopters   83
early majority   83–4
ease of access (to Internet)   419
ease of browsing (web sites)   257
ease of reading (web sites)   257–8
economic acceptability   259
economic feasibility   256
efficiency argument (of moving online)   58
effort costs   275
electronic billboards   46
electronic cash   295
electronic data interchange (EDI)   32, 355
electronic marketing blueprint   137
electronic markets/auctions   47
electronic social sphere   114, 437–8
email   6
email-based marketing   179
email spam   5, 179, 437
entertainment online   63, 147–9
entertainment-oriented objectives   164
entertainment parks   265
entertainment seekers   87–8
environmental scanning   408
Epinions and 'Web of Trust'   362
ergosphere   304, 373
ethical considerations   434–43
ethnographic research   413
exclusive sponsorship sites   265
expectation gap   99, 100–1
experience attribute products   339–40
experiential marketing   252
experimental research   404–5
exploration (product design)   206–9
export industries
    differences between traditional and online
        exporters   384
    online   143–4, 380–3, 384–6
    types of exporting   379–80

factory direct   62–3
fan sites   441–2
fear of the Internet   97–8
file transfer protocol (FTP)   8
financial justification (of online)   57
financial objectives   284–5
flow   17, 94–6
focus groups   411–12
format (advertising)   231
four Ps of marketing   26–7
freeway intersections   266
frequently asked questions (FAQ)   180
fulfilment   30
full interactivity   51–2
functionality (of web site)   257
future directions   429–46

gambling   149–50
generic competitive strategies (Porter)   165–8
generic positioning types (Belch and Belch)   174
gift culture   282
gift economy   292
gift shop sites   266

global access   54, 91, 407
Global Digital Marketing Index   387–8
global exposure   251
global marketing   33
    implementing   389–92
    see also online export industries
global transactional models   381–2
global web presence, regionalisation   377
globalisation versus localisation   372–4
globalisation with localisation   374–7
glossary   481–90
go errors   201
going online see online environment
group level-mediated communication
    computer-mediated one-to-many-to-one   17, 51,
        111–12
    computer-mediated one-to-one   110
    mass media (one-to-many)   109–10

hackers   438–9
hardware infrastructure   3, 202
Hawthorne effect   436
HTML (hypertext markup language)   6
human factors research   263
hypermediated communications (HMC)   107–9

ICQ   95–6
idea generation   206–8
identifying the customers   357
identity, construction of in cybercommunities   116–18
iFive Brands   168
implementation   177–81
inclusivity (online market research)   405–6
inconsistency (service products)   325, 328–9
index pages   267
indigenous digital partnerships   390
individual level-mediated communications   107–9
individualised transmission   315
individualism   31
indoor advertising (of URLs)   236–8
information   31
information access (mediated services)   64
information as product   199–201
information-based marketing   315–16
information dissemination objectives   163
information overload   418
information publishing   44–5
information quality   419
information search   63
information seeking   90–1
information storehouse   407
infrastructure requirements   136
inherent merit (of Internet)   92
inhibitors to going online   60–1
innovation adoption
    and the really new product   71–2
    implication for Internet marketing   85–6
    models   73–7
    overview   81–5
    see also diffusion of innovations
innovation characteristics   78–80
innovation fascinations   77–8

innovators   82–3
inseparability (service products)   325, 327–8
instigators   113
intangibility (service products)   325, 326–7
integrated marketing communications (IMC)   225–6, 302–3, 315
integration   175–6
integrity   31
intellectual infrastructure   4
interactive transmission of information   315
interactivity   30, 49–52, 142, 251, 252
interconnection   30
interest driven   55–6
interface   30
international by default web sites   371, 372
international by design web sites   371, 372
international currency transactions   293–4
international distribution   310
international marketing
    and Internet marketing   371–8
    entry mode   378
    globalisation vs localisation   372–7
international marketing online   33, 370–1
international services   337–8
internationalisation   33
Internet
    as promotional medium   248–69
    credibility of   359–60
    factors preventing full use of   96–9
    future directions   429–46
    history   4–5
    in promotional mix   219–45
    marketing involvement   18–19
    unique features   49–56
    what is it?   3–4
    why people use it   90–2
    see also online headings
Internet adopters
    implications for Internet marketing   85–6
    overview   81–5
Internet culture see cyberculture
Internet literacy   97
Internet marketing see online marketing
Internet Protocol (IP)   3
Internet relay chat (IRC)   7, 124, 125, 437
Internet-specific product opportunities   202–3
Internet user behaviour   89–90
    factors preventing full use of Internet   96–9
    marketing implications   99–101
    specific behaviours   92–6
    why people use the Internet   90–2
Internet users
    categories   87–9
    innovation adoption overview   81–5
interrupt pages   436
intrasite tracking   414
intrinsic social prices   274–6
inverted catalogues   46
investment philosophy   281
involvement   31
iVALS measures   87, 420

lack of desire (to use the Internet)   98–9
laggards   85
late majority   84–5
leaders   113
lean media   17
legal acceptability   258–9
leisure   92
lifestyle costs   275
lifetime value of the customer   348
localisation versus globalisation   371–7
location of cybercommunities   124–5, 128–9
logistics and supply chains   140
The Louvre online   151–2
loyalty schemes   357, 358
lurking   414

macro-level strategic decisions   133–7
maintenance (web sites)   269
mapping cyberspace   20–5
margin (web site design)   268
market-based objectives   285–7
market development   169, 170
market intelligence   408–10
market makers   366
market mavens   362
market penetration   169
market research   396
    method of collection   403–5
    objective of collection   401–3
    online   405–19
    types of   401–5
market research process   397–401
market segmentation   139, 419–24
market share objectives   286
marketing
    alternative readings and the Internet   29–31
    by intrusion and observation   436–8
    three levels of   27–9
    see also online marketing
marketing-focused tactics   29
marketing-free zones   437–8
marketing mix   26–7
    web site design   268–9
marketing philosophy   27–8
marketing strategy   28–9
    Internet in   158–82
marketspace   17, 305, 306–7, 373
    virtual channels and chains   307–9
mass customisation   47–8, 66
mass media   109–10
mechanics (web site design)   268
memes   76–7
message (advertising)   231
message clarity   226
message consistency   225
metarewards sites   266
metasearch engines   266
metatheory
    strategic frameworks for web site design   255–9
    styles of web site structures   253–5
metrics (web sites)   269

mission (web site design)   268
mixed-time systems   7–8
mobile phones   438
money-back guarantee   310
Moore's Law   311
movie promotions   148–9
Mp3.com   317–18
MTV.com   88–9
MUDs (multi-user dungeons)   7, 92, 124–5, 128, 129
multilevel product concept   189–90
multimedia capacity   250
multiple S curves and influence of subcultures   74–5
music   148, 317–18
mystery shoppers   357

narrowcasting   53
network access   312
new market opportunities   139
new product development   203–5
   business analysis   210–11
   commercialisation   212
   exploration   206–9
   new product strategy   205–6
   online   212–14
   product development   211
   screening   209–10
   test marketing   211–12
niche marketing   62, 167–8, 389–90
node level   253
non-financial price components, exploitation of
      288–9
non-linear web site structure   254
non-store distribution mechanisms   310–11
noosphere   304, 373

objectives (online marketing)   159–61
   specific objectives   162–4
observability (innovation)   79
observational research   403, 413–14
'Ocker Aussie' image   375–6
offline
   adaptation to online   61–4
   for promotion of online activities   180
offline fund transfers   294–5
one-to-many broadcast model   109–10
one-to-many-to-one communications   17, 51, 111–12
one-to-one contact   30
one-to-one to Web advertising (of URLs)   238–41
one-way communication   51
online branding   175
online design   181
online distribution   303–9
   and price   316
   and product   315–16
   and promotion   316–18
   channel conflicts   309–10
   non-store distribution mechanisms   310–11
   technical implications   311–15
online environment   56
   adaptation of offline to online   61–4

drivers and attractors   57
   efficiency argument   58
   financial justification   57–8
   open access argument   58
   promotional argument   58–60
factors to consider in going online   56–7
inhibitors   60–1
reasons other businesses are there already   57
online export industries   143
   analysing potential markets   387–9
   axioms   143–4, 382
   breaking down barriers to export   380–2
   conceptual model   145–7, 382–3
   small-to-medium enterprises and
         internationalisation   384–6
online focus groups   411–12
online global information support/service-based
      organisations   381
online market research   405
   advantages/disadvantages   396–7
   changing environments   405–7
   conducting   410–17
   environmental scanning   408
   information storehouse   407
   issues   417–18
   limitations   418–19
   market intelligence   408–10
online market segmentation   419–20
   iVALS and Internet user types   420
   segmentation method   420–4
online marketing   9, 43, 134, 158–82, 430
   advantages for the consumer   65
   and strategic growth options   164–5, 168–71
   as international marketing   371–8
   by intrusion and observation   436–8
   competitive strategies   165–8
   electronic marketing blueprint   137
   ethical considerations   434–43
   evolution   44–8
   future directions   430–4
   how to get and keep users online
      accept rejection as a legitimate choice   101
      lower the barriers to entry   99–100
      lower the expectations   100
      securing the Internet   100–1
   implementation   177–81
   infrastructure requirements   136
   integration   175–6
      of online with existing activities   136–7
   main focus of online activity   135–6
   manage for the long term   181
   objectives   159–61
      specific objectives   162–4
   Rowley's five elements   29–30
   segmentation and positioning   171–5
   what are we trying to achieve by going online?
         134–5, 159–61
online marketing texts, future proofing   443–6
online new product development   212–14
online presence   142, 179
   outcomes of having   142–3

online pricing
  cyberculture 281–3
  environmental turbulence 279–80
  investment philosophy 281
  issues 290–5
  lower costs to the seller 278–9
  nature of the product 291–2
  pressures on 278–83
  taxation issues 280–1
  total cost to the consumer 293
  universal pricing knowledge 283
online products 190
  online continuum 191–3
  online product concept 190–1, 193
  successful 193–203
  total price concept 276–8
  where does the web site fit in? 193
online relationship marketing 354–5
  barriers 359–61
  creating relationships online 356–8
  role of trust 363–5
  value of cybercommunities 361–2
  value of relationship building 355–62
online service
  and consumer behaviour 338–40
  as augmented product 336–7
  as core product 336
  technology as the means not the end 341–2
online service delivery 330–3
  classification 334–6
  customer support 336–8
online surveys 404, 412
open access argument (of online) 58
open source software community 19
operational feasibility 256
operationalising the Internet 18–19
opt-in functions 179
organisational feasibility 256
outdoor advertising (of URLs) 232–6

paging services 7
The Palace 25
parody sites 441
partial interactivity 51
payment systems 294–5
Penguin Mints 168
people-directed versus thing-directed services 334
perishability (service products) 325, 329
permission-based email marketing 357–8
permission marketing 8
personal boundaries, overcoming 389
personal experience 261, 263
personal management services 63
personal selling 228, 238–41, 350
personality traits (innovation adoption) 80
philosophy
  marketing 27–8
  promotion 221–2
  web site design 248–9, 259–64
physical products 192, 194
  consumer empowerment 196–7
  products according to classification 194–6

pleasure 92
point of purchase 226–7
point of sale/point of purchase 228–9
point-to-point (P2P) file sharing 430
political acceptability 259
political pages 267
Porsche.com 59–60
Portable Document Format (PDF) 313
portal sites 61–2, 254, 266
Porter's generic competitive strategies 165–8
porting 439–41
positioning strategies 173–5
  and the price–quality relationship 288
post-modern consumption 34–6, 105, 252–3
post purchase 227
pre-purchase 226
precursors (online retailing) 141–2
predictive research 403
predisposition (innovation adoption) 80
prestige pricing 288
price 273–4
  and online distribution 316
price quality 174, 288
price skimming 280
pricing objectives, setting 284–9
pricing strategies 289–90
primary consumer intelligence data 409
privacy 98, 417–18, 435
product
  and online distribution 315–16
  in Internet marketing 187–214
  multilevel product concept 189–90
  nature of the 291–3
  new product development 203–14
  online product 190–3
  physical 192, 194–7
  services and digitised products 197–201
  what is it? 188
product advertising (of URLs) 241
product class 174
product continuum 192
product definition 208–9
product development 169, 170, 211
product differentiation 166
product dot com 241
product user 174
production quality 251
profit-oriented objectives 285
promotion 29
  and online distribution 316–18
  and the Internet 219
  foundations of 223–5
  integrated marketing communications 225–6
  message, format and context 230–2
  of the web site 219–21, 232–41
  philosophy of 221–2
  value and role of Internet in 249–249–51
promotional argument (of online) 58–60
promotional medium, Internet as 248–69
promotional mix
  elements of 228–30
  web sites in 226–8, 232–41

promotional mix online 241
  banner advertising 241–3
  distinct differences 243–4
promotional objectives 163
psychic costs 276
psychographics 80, 419
psychological objectives 288–9
public relations 229
public service pages 267–8
publicity 229
purchase 221, 227
push-based content 251

radio 148
rampant ad hocery 261
readability (web sites) 257–8
real community 112
real time 17
real-time communications 6–7
real-time data 406
really new product (RNP) 71–2
reciprocity (relationship marketing) 351, 353
recreational services 92, 147–54
recycling 210
reference pricing 286–7
regular exporting 379
relationship marketing 347–8
  core concepts 348–9
  online 354–5
  philosophical principles 350–3, 355
  suitability for 349–50
relative advantage (innovation) 78
remote hosting 17
repurchase 221
repurposing material 180
retail sales pages 268
retailing online 61–3, 138, 194
  advantages and limitations 138–40
  conceptual model 141–3
retaining customers 358
risk reduction strategies 340
risk relievers 310
Rogers'
  five categories of innovators 81–2
  five features of innovations 78–80
Rowley's five elements of online marketing 29–30

S-curve theory of innovation 73–4
sales-oriented objectives 162–3
sales promotions 229
screening (new product concept) 209–10
search attribute products 339
search behaviours and service type 338–40
search engine sites 254, 266, 341–2
search-only sites 266
secondary consumer intelligence data 409–10
security issues 97, 144, 419, 435
segmentation 171–3
  basic tasks 172–3
  methods 420–4
  stages of analysis 173
selective audiences 250–1

self-publishing opportunities 93
selfrepresentation 93–4
selling costs 278–9
separation of production and consumption (online
    services) 330, 333
server capacity 312–13
service/good analysis process 324
service products 197, 198, 323–5
  classification 334–5
  customer support 336–8
  differences from physical goods 325–9
  impact of online delivery 330–3
seven Is for seven Internet brothers (Spalter) 30–1
share of voice 32, 250
shareware pricing, and the gift economy 292
shopping portals 61–2
shopping products 194
site level 253
Slashdot effects 239–40, 403
Sluggy Freelance 119–20, 121
small-to-medium enterprises (SMEs) and
    internationalisation 384–6
SMART objectives 159–60
Smithsonian Institute online 152–3
social acceptability (web sites) 258–9
social infrastructure 4
social network capital 113
social spheres 114, 437–8
software infrastructure 4, 202–3
Spalter's seven Is for seven Internet brothers 30–1
spam see email spam
specialty products 194, 390
speed of the Internet as information source 419
sporadic exporting 379–80
staff training 314
strategic advantage 165–8
strategic decisions 133–4
  guiding the online development 134–7
strategic direction (relationship marketing) 354–5
strategic frameworks for web site design 255–9
strategic growth options 164–5, 168–71
strategic Internet marketing see online marketing
strategic keys to unlocking the potential of the
    Internet 178–81
strategy (marketing) 28–9
structured artificial worlds 114
subjectively pleasing (web sites) 257
successful Internet products 193–203
surf tracking 415–16
survey research 403–4, 412
switching costs 361
system acceptability 256
system feasibility 256

tactics (marketing) 29
tactics (relationship marketing) 354
taxation 280–1
technical feasibility 256
technology
  as the means not the end 341–2
  to foster global relationships 391–2

technology mastering 314
telepresence 17, 414
television 147–8
tempting customers to purchase more regularly 358
terminology 17
territory 309–10
test marketing 211–12
three-dimensional cyberspace 21–5
time costs 274–5
time independence 54–5, 330, 333
time pressures 66
total cost approach 293
total price concept 273–4
   consumer perspective 274–6
   electronic markets 276–8
tourism, destination marketing of 128–9
tourism online 150–4
tourism telepresence 154
town hall sites 265–6
tracking 414–16, 417
transaction 30
transactional sites 45–7
transmission control protocol/Internet protocol
   (TCP/IP) 3
trialability (innovation) 79
trust (relationship marketing) 350, 351–2, 363
   barriers to 363–4
   improving online 364–5
   where does it need to occur? 363
24-7 access 17, 45, 250

undirected information seekers 87
uniqueness 389–90
universal pricing knowledge 283
unobtrusive observation 413–14
unrestricted publication 407
unwanted content 98
use of application (positioning) 174
useability (of web site) 257
usefulness (of web site) 256–8
USENET 5, 7–8, 63, 91
Userfriendly 120, 121
utility-based adoption (of Internet) 91
utility functions 64

VALS measures 87
value chains 307–8
variety 52–3
virtual–actual value chains 309
virtual bazaars 47
virtual branding 175
virtual catalogue sites 62
virtual communities 112
virtual malls 46–7
virtual tourism 152–3
virtual value chains 307
visit/contact (with web site) 221
visitor tracking 415
voodoo programming 261–2
Vtown 123–4

web chat systems 7
web mapping 20–2
web-related software 4–5
web site design 181
   6M of 268–9
   categories of home pages 267–8
   metatheory 251–9
   philosophy 248–9, 259–64
web site structures 253–5
web site visitor classification 87–8
   commercial application 88–9
web sites
   analyse content and use 180
   and online presence 142–3
   creating awareness of 232–41
   in the promotional mix 226–8
   place in online product concept 193
   plan frequent revisions 181
   promotion of 219–21
   providing extra value by visiting 180
   strategic integration 264–9
   types of 264–7
webification 263
webify 263
wholesaling 138
wireless application protocols (WAP) 232, 430, 438
word of mouth referrals 350
World Wide Web 4, 6